200 % TEST
collection dirigée par Achille Pinson

200 % TOEFL iBT

7e édition

- TOEFL iBT (Computer based)
- Préparation complète
- Enrichi par le e-learning

Lara Fenyar
Achille Pinson

prepmyfuture.com

ellipses

ISBN 9782340-071124
©Ellipses Édition Marketing S.A., 2022
8/10 rue la Quintinie 75015 Paris

www.editions-ellipses.fr

TABLE DES MATIÈRES

INTRODUCTION
PRÉPARER LE NOUVEAU TOEFL iBT

Notre approche

Stratégie TOEFL

Comme beaucoup de tests standardisés, le TOEFL n'évalue pas uniquement votre niveau d'anglais mais également votre maîtrise du format de l'examen. Une bonne préparation spécifique au TOEFL améliorera significativement votre score en moins d'un mois. Nous vous proposons d'améliorer votre score TOEFL au travers :

- de méthodes sur toutes les questions types du TOEFL ;
- d'exercices de type TOEFL avec une simulation des conditions d'examen.

Approche innovante avec PrepMyFuture

Depuis 2010, PrepMyFuture développe des solutions innovantes pour faciliter la préparation des examens standardisés. Nous avons développé deux outils :

- la plateforme e-learning ;
- le livre connecté.

Les spécificités de notre approche :
Notre plateforme e-learning permet de mesurer votre progression grâce à la correction automatique des exercices. La plateforme identifie vos forces et vos faiblesses et vous propose des questions adaptées à votre niveau sur les concepts que vous avez besoin de travailler.

Avec les Éditions Ellipses, nous avons créé un livre compatible avec notre plateforme. Vous cumulez donc le confort du papier avec le meilleur de PrepMyFuture :

- suivi de la performance ;
- identification de vos faiblesses ;
- exercices interactifs ;
- entraînement dans les conditions d'examen.

Le livre peut toutefois être utilisé sans la plateforme e-learning (à l'exception des extraits audio qui sont tous en téléchargement libre sur notre site Internet).

Approche complète

Ce livre s'adresse à tous les candidats :

- ceux qui connaissent déjà l'examen comme ceux qui le découvrent.
- pour tous les niveaux d'anglais.

Nous avons porté une attention particulière à la structure du contenu pour que chaque lecteur y trouve son compte. Les différents chapitres sont indépendants et les exercices sont classés par niveau de difficulté. De plus, la plateforme e-learning vous indique les axes d'amélioration. Vous pourrez donc travailler les thématiques sur lesquelles vous perdez le plus de points à l'examen.

Le mode « premium »

Le livre vous donne accès à des fonctionnalités gratuites sur la plateforme PrepMyFuture. Vous pouvez créer un compte gratuit sur http://www.prepmyfuture.com/livre-nouveau-toefl pour accéder aux fonctionnalités suivantes :

- écouter les bandes-son (mode examen et mode entraînement) ;
- reporter ses réponses pour bénéficier de la correction automatique ;
- suivre sa performance et identifier ses forces et faiblesses.

En ligne, vous aurez l'opportunité de basculer en mode « premium ». Le mode premium est payant et optionnel. L'option payante est destinée aux étudiants désirant aller plus loin grâce à deux compléments :

- des contenus additionnels (examens blancs supplémentaires et nouveaux exercices d'entraînement basés sur vos lacunes) ;
- la possibilité d'utiliser la plateforme e-learning sans le livre pour plus de confort : vous avez directement accès aux exercices au format digital et non plus simplement aux grilles pour reporter vos réponses.

Comment organiser sa préparation

1) Découverte du test et de son format

Connaître le format de l'examen est essentiel. Grâce au chapitre d'introduction « Présentation du TOEFL iBT », vous pourrez vous familiariser avec le format et le calcul du score. De plus, ce chapitre vous motivera en vous rappelant les avantages apportés par un bon score TOEFL dans votre parcours professionnel.

Si n'avez pas encore passé le TOEFL, alors commencez par effectuer le MINI TOEFL iBT en conditions d'examen (prévoir un peu plus d'une heure de travail sans aucune distraction). L'objectif est de déterminer votre niveau et de vous familiariser avec le format du test. Il est important d'effectuer ce test en conditions d'examen pour se rendre compte que la difficulté ne réside pas seulement dans les questions mais aussi dans la gestion de son temps, de sa concentration et de sa mémoire.

2) Méthodologie, partie par partie

Consacrez les premières heures de votre préparation à la méthodologie. Chaque partie a ses spécificités, il est donc important de les travailler de manière indépendante avec la lecture de la fiche suivie des exercices d'application liées à la partie. Ce travail vous permettra de :

- connaître les consignes de chaque partie par cœur ;
- gérer votre temps de meilleure façon pour chaque type d'exercice ;
- savoir répondre aux questions types ;
- reconnaître les pièges classiques et les éviter.

3) Entraînements de grammaire et de vocabulaire

Certains points de grammaire sont particulièrement utiles. Par exemple, une bonne connaissance des connecteurs logiques vous permettra de mieux organiser vos productions pour les parties Speaking et Writing. Par ailleurs, une bonne connaissance des pronoms vous permettra d'éliminer des choix de réponse dans les questions de type « référence ». Pour préparer le test de manière efficace, il est donc recommandé de revoir les règles de grammaires utiles pour le TOEFL. Vous les trouverez dans la section « Grammaire ».

De plus, le TOEFL teste des champs lexicaux bien particuliers : la vie universitaire américaine et l'anglais académique. Ces thèmes sont traités dans les sections « Vocabulaire Académique » et « Vocabulaire Vie Universitaire ». Nous avons également compilé des listes de mots « compliqués » apparaissant fréquemment dans le TOEFL, vous les trouverez dans la section « Vocabulaire TOEFL ».

4) Simulations d'examens blancs

Finissez votre préparation par les examens blancs, ils vous permettront de bien gérer votre temps le jour du test.

Utilisation par les professeurs

Plus de 3000 enseignants utilisent nos manuels *200% tests*. Ils jouent un rôle important dans l'évolution de nos livres et de la plateforme e-learning. Nous avons créé pour eux des fonctionnalités gratuites :

- des évaluations gratuites réservées aux enseignants ;
- un tableau de bord pour suivre la performance de leur classe (assiduité des étudiants, estimation du score TOEFL, identification des lacunes à travailler en classe, etc.).

Vous pouvez créer un compte enseignant sur http://www.prepmyfuture.com ou nous contacter par email à cette adresse : enseignants@prepmyfuture.com

Valeur ajoutée pour les directeurs pédagogiques

Le tableau de bord enseignant est utilisé par les responsables des langues pour suivre l'ensemble des étudiants d'un établissement. Il permet également d'attribuer automatiquement des notes de participation grâce à un export au format Excel. L'utilisation de la plateforme e-learning permet alors de libérer du temps de cours pour des activités à forte valeur ajoutée telle que la participation orale tout en préparant efficacement les étudiants au TOEFL.

Vous trouverez plus informations sur http://www.prepmyfuture.com

Nouveautés - 7e édition du livre

Nous mettons à jour chaque année notre méthode *200% TOEFL iBT* pour vous proposer le meilleur support de révision possible. Nous travaillons sur plusieurs volets : la mise à jour des exercices, l'ajout de nouveaux contenus sur les parties les plus utilisées et l'amélioration des explications grâce à vos retours.

Dans cette nouvelle édition, nous avons apporté une attention particulière aux fiches de vocabulaire en y ajoutant des informations culturelles et des exemples. Nous avons également amélioré les explications des expressions écrites afin de vous guider au mieux dans la préparation de cette épreuve.

Présentation du nouveau TOEFL iBT

Présentation du TOEFL iBT

Pour qui, pourquoi ?

Les tests TOEFL (*Test Of English as a Foreign Language*) sont destinés aux étudiants non-anglophones désirant suivre un cursus académique en anglais. Le TOEFL iBT (*Internet Based Test*) est utilisé au niveau universitaire. On le passe généralement pour postuler dans une université américaine (ou un autre programme anglophone) à un niveau licence (*undergraduate*), master (*graduate*, MBA) ou doctorat (*postgraduate*). Il est aussi utilisé pour la gestion des échanges universitaires.

Le TOEFL iBT étant une certification de référence au niveau mondial, il peut être utilisé sur votre CV dans le cadre de votre recherche d'emploi. Il ne s'agit pas d'une certification spécifique au monde du travail comme le TOEIC mais il est tout de même bien reconnu sur le marché du travail.

Enfin, le score TOEFL iBT est valable pendant deux ans. Il est généralement transmis aux écoles directement par ETS, l'organisation éditrice du test. Vous pouvez passer le test autant de fois que vous le désirez mais vous ne pouvez pas le passer plus d'une fois par période de 12 jours.

Comment s'inscrire au test

L'inscription s'effectue auprès des centres d'examen agréés ou sur le site internet d'ETS qui référencie toutes les sessions d'examen publiques (celles d'ETS et celles des partenaires agréés). En France, ETS est représenté par sa filiale ETS GLOBAL qui a un bureau et un centre d'examen à Paris. ETS GLOBAL a son propre site internet, vous devez vous renseigner et vous inscrire directement sur ETS GLOBAL si vous passez l'examen en France.

En France, le passage du test coûte 245 dollars US, le prix diffère selon le pays dans lequel vous passez le test. Une inscription de dernière minute, moins de 4 jours avant la session vous coûtera un supplément de 40 dollars.

Plusieurs sessions sont organisées tous les mois. Il est possible de le passer dans une trentaine de villes en France ainsi que dans plus la plupart des pays.

Les différents types de TOEFL

Il existe 5 variantes du TOEFL, ces tests sont complètement différents et s'adressent à différentes typologies de candidats :

TOEFL iBT (*Internet Based Test*)

Il s'agit du TOEFL le plus courant : si on ne vous précise pas de quel TOEFL on vous parle, alors on sous-entend généralement qu'il s'agit du TOEFL iBT. Ses spécificités : vous le passez sur un ordinateur ou sur papier et il s'adresse aux formations universitaires. C'est la plus difficile des 5 variantes.

TOEFL ITP (*Institution Testing Program*)

Anciennement appelée PBT (*Paper Based Test*), cette variante du TOEFL est exclusivement destinée aux établissements scolaires. Vous ne pouvez pas passer le TOEFL ITP en candidat libre : il est uniquement administré par votre école en format papier. Par ailleurs, le score ITP peut uniquement être utilisé pour les échanges universitaires dans la mesure où l'université partenaire accepte le score ITP, ce qui n'est pas systématiquement le cas.

Le TOEFL ITP est noté sur une autre échelle de score (de 310 à 677 pour le ITP alors que le iBT est noté de 0 à 120). Le TOEFL ITP évalue uniquement la compréhension orale et écrite tandis que le TOEFL iBT évalue aussi l'expression orale et écrite. Enfin, le TOEFL ITP est beaucoup plus facile et plus court que le TOEFL iBT. Il est donc fortement recommandé de se préparer avec un support pédagogique adapté au test que vous allez passer.

PrepMyFuture édite des supports pédagogiques spécifiques au TOEFL ITP qui sont disponibles sur http://www.prepmyfuture.com/toefl-itp

TOEFL Essentials

Comme le TOEFL iBT, le TOEFL Essentials est destiné aux étudiants et évalue les 4 compétences : compréhension orale, compréhension écrite, expression orale et expression écrite. Sa principale différence avec le TOEFL iBT, c'est qu'il ne dure que 1h30, et que son contenu est de 50% anglais académique et 50% d'anglais général.

Les tests TOEFL *Young Students Series*

TOEFL Primary

Cette variante du TOEFL est destinée aux enfants de plus de 8 ans qui apprennent l'anglais au primaire ou qui s'apprêtent à suivre des études en anglais.

TOEFL Junior

Cette variante du TOEFL est destinée aux jeunes de plus de 11 ans qui apprennent l'anglais au collège ou au lycée ou qui s'apprêtent à suivre des études en anglais.

Différences entre le TOEFL et le TOEIC

En France, le TOEIC est la certification la plus répandue avec plus de 200 000 tests passés par an. Il est donc important de saisir les différences entre ces deux tests conçus par le même éditeur américain (ETS).

Le TOEIC et le TOEFL mesurent deux aptitudes différentes. Le TOEIC mesure votre capacité à travailler en anglais tandis que le TOEFL mesure votre capacité à suivre des cours universitaires en anglais.

Si vous avez besoin d'une certification à ajouter à votre CV, alors nous vous recommandons de passer le TOEIC, test plus facile, moins cher et plus connu que le TOEFL sur le marché du travail. Ce conseil n'est valable que si vous travaillez en France, au Japon ou en Corée du Sud, les 3 pays où le TOEIC est très largement répandu.

Le score

Comment est calculé le score

Les tests TOEFL ne sont pas des diplômes avec un niveau à atteindre, il s'agit d'un score. Chaque programme universitaire fixe ainsi le score minimum qui permet de se qualifier pour la formation, le score à atteindre est ainsi différent d'une formation à l'autre. Par exemple, le score minimum demandé par la Harvard Business School est de 109, alors qu'un score de 80 suffit la plupart du temps pour accéder à un échange universitaire aux États-Unis. Par ailleurs, le même établissement n'aura pas les mêmes exigences en fonction du programme choisi, les formations en droit et en littérature seront en général plus exigeantes que les formations scientifiques.

Il faut aussi garder à l'esprit qu'un bon score TOEFL vous permettra de mettre en valeur votre candidature. Il ne s'agit donc pas d'obtenir le score minimum demandé par la formation, mais d'obtenir le meilleur score possible.

Le TOEFL iBT est divisé en 4 sections (*reading, listening, speaking* et *writing*) chacune notée sur 30. Pour obtenir le score total sur 120, il suffit d'additionner le score obtenu à chaque partie.

Comment analyser son score TOEFL iBT

Le score le plus important est le score global sur 120. Certains comités d'admission regardent tout de même le détail des notes. En effet, un score trop faible dans une section peut être considéré comme éliminatoire par certains comités d'admission en particulier dans les programmes les plus sélectifs.

Équivalences score TOEFL :

TOEFL iBT	TOEFL ITP	TOEIC	ref européen
110-120	544-627	945-990	C1
87-109	461-543	786-945	B2
57-86	338-460	551-785	B1

Scores demandés par quelques programmes :

Programme	Score TOEFL iBT minimum
Oxford (tous programmes)	110
Harvard Business School (MBA)	109
Harvard (programmes undergraduate)	100
London School of Economics (standard)	107
London School of Economics (droit)	109
HEC Paris (MBA)	100
Arizona State University	83
Boston University (MBA)	94
Boston University (programmes undergraduate)	84
McGill (école de commerce)	100
McGill (programmes autres que école de commerce)	90
New School (art)	92
Programme CEMS	100

Les changements apportés au TOEFL iBT en août 2019

Le format du TOEFL iBT a évolué en août 2019. Les modifications sont légères et rendent le test moins long. La difficulté et les types de questions n'ont pas changé. Le test dans sa globalité devient moins difficile car il contient moins de questions et vous disposez de plus de temps par question pour certaines parties. C'est une excellente nouvelle pour les candidats car on reprochait régulièrement à l'ancienne version d'être trop longue (une partie de la difficulté du test reposait alors sur l'aspect « course d'endurance » de l'épreuve). Le nouveau test règle ce problème et devient plus accessible. Ne vous réjouissez pas trop vite, le TOEFL iBT reste un test long et difficile.

Voici la liste des principaux changements :

Les épreuves

Section *Reading*

	Ancienne version	MàJ août 2019
Nombre de textes	• 3 (version standard) • 4 (version longue*)	• 3 (version standard) • 4 (version longue*)
Longueurs des textes	900 mots	700 mots
Nombre de questions	• 36 questions (version standard) • 56 questions (version longue*)	• 30 questions (version standard) • 40 questions (version longue*)
Durée du test	• 60 minutes (version standard) • 80 minutes (version longue*)	• 54 minutes (version standard) • 72 minutes (version longue*)

* **Version longue :** Il est possible que votre partie *Reading* comporte 4 passages au lieu de 3. Dans ce cas, vous bénéficierez de 18 minutes supplémentaires. Les concepteurs introduisent en effet des exercices supplémentaires pour tester de nouvelles questions. Dans ce cas, les questions testées ne compteront pas dans le calcul de votre score. Si votre épreuve comporte 4 textes, il ne sera pas possible d'identifier le passage qui ne comptera pas, il faudra donc répondre à toutes les questions avec la même attention aux détails.

Section *Listening*

	Ancienne version	MàJ août 2019
Nombre de bandes audio	• 6 audios (version standard) • 9 audios (version longue*)	• 5 audios (version standard) • 7 audios (version longue*)
Nombre de questions	• 34 questions (version standard) • 51 questions (version longue*)	• 28 questions (version standard) • 39 questions (version longue*)
Durée du test	• 60 minutes (version standard) • 90 minutes (version longue*)	• 41 minutes (version standard) • 57 minutes (version longue*)

* **Version longue :** Il est possible que votre partie *Listening* comporte 7 bandes audio au lieu de 5. Dans ce cas, vous bénéficierez de 16 minutes supplémentaires. Les concepteurs introduisent en effet des exercices supplémentaires pour tester de nouvelles questions. Dans ce cas, les questions testées ne compteront pas dans le calcul de votre score. Si votre épreuve comporte 7 bandes audio, il ne sera pas possible d'identifier le passage qui ne comptera pas, il faudra donc répondre à toutes les questions avec la même attention aux détails.

Section *Speaking*

	Ancienne version	MàJ août 2019
Nombre de tâches	6 tâches : • 2 questions indépendantes • 4 questions *integrated speaking*	4 tâches : • 1 question indépendante • 3 questions *integrated speaking*
Durée du test	20 minutes	17 minutes

Section *Writing*

Cette section n'a pas subi de modifications.

Le calcul des scores

Depuis le 1er août 2019, ETS a mis en place le *MyBest Score* : lorsque vous avez passé le TOEFL iBT plus d'une fois, votre dernier score est calculé à partir de votre meilleure performance sur chaque section.

La préparation PrepMyFuture

Les supports pédagogiques PrepMyFuture (200% TOEFL à partir de sa 5e édition) et la préparation en ligne (prepmyfuture.com/toefl) ont tous été mis à jour sur le nouveau format de l'épreuve.

Livre 200% TOEFL iBT	Année de publication	Version du TOEFL iBT
1re édition	2016	ancienne version
2e édition	2017	
3e édition	2018	
4e édition	2019	
5e édition	2020	version MàJ 2019
6e édition	2021	
7e édition	2022	

MINI TOEFL iBT

Mini TOEFL iBT - READING

READING SECTION DIRECTIONS

The Reading section measures your ability to understand academic passages in English. You will read passages and answer questions about them. Answer all questions based on what is stated or implied in the passage.

There are three passages in a full TOEFL iBT test. You should allow 18 minutes to read each passage and answer the questions about it.

Reportez vos réponses pour analyser votre performance.

Entraînez-vous dans les conditions d'examen.

prepmyfuture.com/book/68/ex/1909

Continental Drift Theory

[P1] Near the beginning of the twentieth century, German meteorologist Alfred Wegener noted that if one were to put the Atlantic coasts of Africa and South America together, they would fit much like a two gigantic jigsaw puzzle pieces; he found similar connections between living organisms found in India, Australia and Antarctica—scientists had been finding nearly identical species of plants and the bones of ancient animals on separate continents, separated only by oceans or other large bodies of water. **These observations led Wegener to propose a startling, new and controversial theory: all the current disparate continents of the world were once one, huge mega-landmass some 200 million years ago.**

[P2] Wegener knew that he would face scepticism, so he did his best to strengthen his theory. He referenced accurate geological maps to demonstrate the uncanny match of geological formations and questioned why coal deposits, commonly associated with tropical climates, would be found near the North Pole and why the plains of Africa would show evidence of glaciers. Wegener also presented examples where fossils of exactly the same prehistoric reptile species were distributed where you would expect them to be if central South America and southern Africa had once been side-by-side. In 1912, he published his theory of "Continental Drift"—where he theorized that continents slowly move around the globe, pulling away from each other and pushing into each other over millions of years—and faced **backlash** from the scientific community.

[P3] "Continental Drift" challenged then-accepted theories and facts in multiple scientific fields. One of Wegener's critics, the geologist R. Thomas Chamberlain, proposed alternative explanations for what Wegener saw. To explain the unusually-similar distribution of fossils, Chamberlain proposed there may once have been a network of land bridges between the different continents, while, to explain the existence of fossils of temperate species being found in arctic regions, he proposed the existence of warm water currents connecting the polar regions to the equatorial zones of the Earth. Modern scientists now look at these explanations as desperate attempts to prevent Wegener's ideas from gaining supporters, but, at the time, reactions by scientists such as Chamberlain did help to **dampen** support for continental drift.

[P4] Wegener's theory did have its rough edges. Wegener did not have a solid explanation for how Continental Drift could have occurred. He proposed that a combination of the centrifugal force caused by the rotation of the Earth and the tidal attraction of the Sun and the Moon may cause the continents to move slowly over time. Unfortunately, Wegener knew these explanations were inadequate. Wegener himself really did not believe that he had the correct explanation for the mechanism, but that this should not stop all discussion of his hypothesis.

[P5] Wegener's theory did gain some support in 1929, when British geologist Arthur Holmes suggested a possible process for continental drift based on the idea that the Earth's mantle* undergoes 'thermal convection'. This is based on the fact that as a substance is heated its density decreases and rises to the surface until it is cooled and sinks again. Holmes believed that this repeated heating and cooling of semisolid rock under the Earth's surface could result in a upward-and-downward current which may be enough to cause continents to move. However, his idea received little attention at the time.

[P6] Not until the 1960's did Holmes' idea—and, therefore, Wegener's original theory—began to be studied by more scientists. Greater understanding of the ocean floor and the discoveries of features like mid-oceanic ridges and geomagnetic phenomena related to these ridges, suggested convection might indeed be at work. These discoveries and more led Harry Hess of Princeton University to publish similar a hypothesis based on thermal convection currents, which he called "sea floor spreading". This idea was basically the same as that proposed by Holmes over 30 years earlier, but now there was much more evidence to further develop and support the idea. The theory of continental drift finally gained the acceptance of the greater scientific community Wegener had sought nearly half a century earlier.

Earth's mantle: a region of hot, dense, semisolid rock in the interior of the Earth between the inner core and the outer surface.

▪ Question 1 Which of the following best expresses the essential information in the highlighted sentence in Paragraph 1? Incorrect choices change the meaning in important ways or leave out essential information.

(A) Because it looked like the various continents could fit together like pieces of a puzzle, Wegener came to believe that they had surprisingly once been a single continent in the distant past.

(B) Wegener felt that his theory better explained how continents had been connected millions of years ago.

(C) Wegener used new and unusual research to support his theory that all the continents of the world had had once been part of a giant, super-continent.

(D) After looking at the shape of the continents, Wegener theorized that all the continents of the world would one day be connected.

▪ Question 2 The word "backlash" in paragraph 2 is closest in meaning to:

(A) acceptance

(B) opposition

(C) review

(D) reversal

▪ Question 3 Why does the author mention "land bridges" in paragraph 3?

(A) to present information supporting Wegener's theory of Continental Drift

(B) to explain how water currents move water to the arctic regions from the equator

(C) to highlight evidence that contradicts Wegener's theory of Continental Drift

(D) to introduce a possible explanation for the spread of animal species across various continents

▪ Question 4 What role did R. Thomas Chamberlain play in the scientific debate over Wegener's theory of Continent Drift?

(A) His theories weren't accepted by many of the scientists at the time, but have since been reconsidered.

(B) He only partly agreed with Wegener.

(C) He proposed alternate hypotheses that could explain Wegener's evidence for Continental Drift.

(D) His contributions opened up interesting questions about continent formation that should be examined.

▪ Question 5 The word "dampen" in paragraph 3 is closest in meaning to:

(A) lessen
(B) move
(C) excite
(D) increase

▪ Question 6 What can be said about Wegener's explanation for the mechanism of Continental Drift?

(A) He believed it was sufficient to explain the movement of continents.
(B) It relied on the motion of the Earth as a cause for the movement of continents.
(C) It could also explain the movement of ocean tides.
(D) He believed the Earth's rotation was enough to cause the movement of continents.

▪ Question 7 According to the passage, all of the following can be said of Arthur Holmes' theory explaining a mechanism for Continental Drift EXCEPT:

(A) It involved the effect of variations in temperature deep under the Earth's surface.
(B) It was greatly supported by later research conducted in the 1960's by other scientists.
(C) Wegener and Holmes worked together to create a hypothesis for the process of Continental Drift.
(D) He believed that thermal convection caused continents to move away from each other.

▪ Question 8 According to Holmes, what could have caused the continental drift?

(A) presence of semisolid rock beneath the continents
(B) the contrasting forces that guide ocean currents
(C) the abrupt drop in the mantle's temperature
(D) the motion of the Earth's mantle

▪ Question 9 Look at the four squares in paragraph 5, **A**, **B**, **C**, and **D**, which indicate where the following sentence could be added to the passage. Where would the sentence best fit?

In fact, they exposed Wegener to ridicule because they clearly could not demonstrate the origin of a force that could have caused the movement of landmasses as large as continents.

Wegener's theory did have its rough edges. **A** Wegener did not have a solid explanation for how continental drift could have occurred. **B** He proposed that a combination of the centrifugal force caused by the rotation of the Earth and the tidal attraction of the Sun and the Moon may cause the continents to move slowly over time. Unfortunately, Wegener knew these explanations were inadequate. **C** Wegener himself really did not believe that he had the explanation for the mechanism, but that this should not stop discussion of a hypothesis. **D**

(A) **A**
(B) **B**
(C) **C**
(D) **D**

▪ Question 10 Directions:

An introductory sentence for a brief summary of the passage is provided below.

Complete the summary by selecting the THREE answer choices that express the most important ideas in the passage. Some sentences do not belong in the summary because they express ideas that are not presented in the passage or are minor ideas in the passage.

This question is worth 2 points.

- "Continental Drift" theorizes that continents are able to move around the globe.
- ________
- ________
- ________

(A) Wegener believed Continental Drift was caused by a process of thermal convection under the Earth's surface.

(B) It attempted to explain how and why similar plants and animals could be found on distant continents.

(C) Wegener discovered the existence of glaciers in Africa and went on to prove that the continent was once closer to the North Pole.

(D) It hypothesized that a land-bridge may once have connected Africa and South America.

(E) Holmes identified in the thermal excursion beneath the Earth's surface a possible explanation for the movement of the continents.

(F) Only after several scientific studies has it been possible to recognize the validity of Wegener's initial hypothesis.

Mini TOEFL iBT - LISTENING (AUDIO)

LISTENING SECTION DIRECTIONS

The Listening section measures your ability to understand conversations and lectures in English. You will hear a conversation or lecture **only one time**, and you will answer some questions about them. The questions typically ask about the main idea and supporting details of the conversation and lecture. Some questions will ask about a speaker's purpose or attitude. Answer the questions based on what the speakers state or imply.

You may take notes while you listen. You may use your notes to help you answer the questions. Your notes will not be scored.

In some question, you will see an audio icon. This means that you will hear, but not see, part of the question.

You should answer each question, even if you must guess the answer.

Reportez vos réponses pour analyser votre performance.

Entraînez-vous dans les conditions d'examen.

Écoutez les fichiers audio.

prepmyfuture.com/book/68/ex/1910

Listen to part of a discussion in an American history class. The professor is talking about President Theodore Roosevelt.

Question 1 What are the main topics of the lecture?

Click on 2 answers.

(A) How Roosevelt was able to pass laws protecting the environment
(B) How Roosevelt became president of the United States
(C) Why Roosevelt wanted to be president of the United States
(D) The kinds of legislation Roosevelt helped pass as president

Question 2 According to the professor, Roosevelt did all of the following EXCEPT:

(A) Write books about his life in the Dakotas
(B) Help increase competition among large companies
(C) Leave a position in government to join a war
(D) Run for political office in the American West

■ Question 3 According to the lecture, what did Roosevelt write about after the death of his wife and mother?

(A) Life in the American West
(B) His career in politics
(C) The conservation of natural resources
(D) His experiences as a Rough Rider

■ Question 4 Listen again to part of the lecture. Then answer the question.

What does the professor mean by this statement?

(A) Roosevelt did not enjoy working with the Republican Party in New York.
(B) Roosevelt did not enjoy being the governor of New York.
(C) After Roosevelt was elected Vice-President, legislators in New York did not have to work with him anymore.
(D) The Republican Party in New York did not expect Roosevelt to become Vice-President.

■ Question 5 What were some of Roosevelt's accomplishments as President?

You can click on more than one answer.

(A) Building a national highway network
(B) Higher standard for food safety
(C) More control of American waterways
(D) Increasing the number and size of national forests

■ Question 6 What can be inferred about Roosevelt's involvement in the Spanish-American War?

(A) It was instrumental in winning the war against Spain.
(B) It made him more famous in the U.S.
(C) He reluctantly became a soldier in the war.
(D) It led to him becoming Secretary of the Navy.

Listen to a conversation between two students regarding a class presentation.

■ Question 7 What is the main purpose of the conversation?

(A) To organize a trip to a museum
(B) To go over material for a test
(C) To prepare for an oral report
(D) To find more material for a presentation

Question 8 According to the conversation, which of the following statements is true?

(A) The two students will meet tonight to finalize their presentation outline.

(B) The two students will likely meet the day before their presentation.

(C) The two students haven't collected all the photos they need for the presentation.

(D) The two students will meet with the professor tomorrow.

Question 9 Listen again to part of the conversation, then answer the question.

(A) She thinks the theory is unrealistic.

(B) She thinks the event happened in another location.

(C) She is unclear what the theory is trying to prove.

(D) She doesn't think he should include the information in the presentation.

Question 10 Listen again to part of the conversation, then answer the question.

(A) Her experience at the museum may be put in a film.

(B) What she was able to do at the museum was uncommon.

(C) She is disappointed she wasn't able to find anything interesting during the excavation.

(D) She didn't know anyone else who was with her at the museum.

Question 11 According to the conversation, what did the woman do at the La Brea Tar Pit Museum last year?

(A) Find the bones of a saber-toothed cat in the tar pits

(B) Meet the scientist who first studied the tar pits

(C) Find paintings of ancient animals found in the tar pits

(D) Search for animal and human remains in the tar pits

Mini TOEFL iBT - LISTENING (SCRIPT)

LISTENING SECTION DIRECTIONS

The Listening section measures your ability to understand conversations and lectures in English. You will hear a conversation or lecture **only one time**, and you will answer some questions about them. The questions typically ask about the main idea and supporting details of the conversation and lecture. Some questions will ask about a speaker's purpose or attitude. Answer the questions based on what the speakers state or imply.

You may take notes while you listen. You may use your notes to help you answer the questions. Your notes will not be scored.

In some question, you will see an audio icon. This means that you will hear, but not see, part of the question.

You should answer each question, even if you must guess the answer.

Reportez vos réponses pour analyser votre performance.

Entraînez-vous dans les conditions d'examen.

Écoutez les fichiers audio.

prepmyfuture.com/book/68/ex/1910

Listen to part of a discussion in an American history class. The professor is talking about President Theodore Roosevelt.

Script non affiché le jour de l'examen :

PROFESSOR: *First as a popular writer, and later as President of the United States, Theodore Roosevelt had a strong influence on the history of the American West. Born in 1858, in New York City, Roosevelt grew up in a wealthy family that was heavily involved in community affairs. Thought he was sickly as a child, suffering several chronic medical conditions, early in life he devoted himself to daily exercise, gaining a physical stamina and love of outdoor sports that became a hallmark of his character.*

Despite an early career as a representative in the New York State government, Roosevelt felt drawn to the American West. He was enamored by the western landscape and the outdoor life of the plains. In 1883, he purchased two ranches in the Dakotas, a remote area of the western part of the United States. These ranches became a refuge for him during difficult times in his life, most notably when his wife and mother both died on the same day in 1884. The isolation and vast landscape of the Dakotas helped him escape the sadness of the loss of his wife and mother, and became a retreat where he could pursue his interest in writing. During his time out West, Roosevelt published books on his experiences ranching and hunting, as well as on other aspects of his life in the Dakotas. Readers of Roosevelt's writings took from his books the perception of western life as having special virtues -- self-reliance, honor, loyalty, determination -- that made it a symbol of the American character.

Returning to politics in 1889, Roosevelt advanced in political office until a decade later he was appointed Assistant Secretary of the Navy and became a leading proponent of war with Spain, which at the time was attempting to reassert control over its colonies in the Caribbean. When war broke out 1898 between the U.S. and Spain, Roosevelt helped organize the "Rough Riders", a volunteer cavalry inside the U.S. army, made up of "cowboys and college students," as he liked to say. In Cuba, Roosevelt and his Rough Riders led a much-publicized horse charge up Kettle Hill in the battle for San Juan Heights. His exploits in the Spanish-American War made him a household name throughout the United States.

Returning home as a war hero, Roosevelt was elected governor of New York in the fall of 1898, but his enthusiasm for reform so annoyed the state's Republican leaders that they arranged for him to run as the national Republican party's vice presidential candidate in 1900. When the Republican ticket won the presidential election, New York's Republican Party breathed a sigh of relief because Roosevelt was now out of their hair.

Less than a year later, however, on September 14, 1901, the assassination of President William McKinley elevated Roosevelt to the nation's highest office. Over the next seven years, he worked tirelessly as the president of the United States to promote social and governmental reform. He passed legislation that broke up some of the country's biggest corporations and brought more competition to the U.S. business sector. Later, he secured passage of federal regulations to control railroad rates and to set quality standards for food and drugs.

For the West, Roosevelt's most important actions as president came in the areas of conservation policy. In 1891, Roosevelt signed a law that to set aside public lands as national forests, and used it to increase federal land reserves from the approximately 40 million acres when he took office to nearly 200 million acres by the end of his time as president. He also ushered in a new era of land management, aimed at sustained and efficient use of natural resources rather than exploitation and development.

Roosevelt initiated similar sweeping change in the western United States through legislation which gave the federal government primary responsibility for dam construction and irrigation projects, bringing scientific expertise and know-how into the planning of canals and reservoirs.

Roosevelt also extended federal control over the scenic wonders of the West, such as setting aside 800,000 acres in Arizona as the Grand Canyon National Monument. By time he left office in 1909, he had created 16 national monuments, 51 wildlife refuges and five new National Parks, including Crater Lake in Oregon and the Anasazi ruins in Colorado. His actions helped Americans recognize these landmarks as "national treasures", not just as a source of natural resources to be consumed, and as such requiring management to sustain them for a growing tourist industry. Without Teddy Roosevelt's dedication to preserving the natural wonders of the United States, the beauty and untouched nature of the American West would be much less than it is today.

▪ Question 1 What are the main topics of the lecture?

Click on 2 answers.

(A) How Roosevelt was able to pass laws protecting the environment
(B) How Roosevelt became president of the United States
(C) Why Roosevelt wanted to be president of the United States
(D) The kinds of legislation Roosevelt helped pass as president

▪ Question 2 According to the professor, Roosevelt did all of the following EXCEPT:

(A) Write books about his life in the Dakotas
(B) Help increase competition among large companies
(C) Leave a position in government to join a war
(D) Run for political office in the American West

▪ Question 3 According to the lecture, what did Roosevelt write about after the death of his wife and mother?

(A) Life in the American West
(B) His career in politics
(C) The conservation of natural resources
(D) His experiences as a Rough Rider

Question 4 Listen again to part of the lecture. Then answer the question.

> **Script non affiché le jour de l'examen :**
> **PROFESSOR**: *Returning home as a war hero, Roosevelt was elected governor of New York in the fall of 1898, but his enthusiasm for reform so annoyed the state's Republican leaders that they arranged for him to run as the party's vice presidential candidate in 1900. When the Republican ticket won the presidential election, New York's Republican Party breathed a sigh of relief because Roosevelt was now out of their hair.*

What does the professor mean by this statement?

> **Script non affiché le jour de l'examen :**
> **PROFESSOR**: *When the Republican ticket won the presidential election, New York's Republican Party breathed a sigh of relief because Roosevelt was now out of their hair.*

(A) Roosevelt did not enjoy working with the Republican Party in New York.
(B) Roosevelt did not enjoy being the governor of New York.
(C) After Roosevelt was elected Vice-President, legislators in New York did not have to work with him anymore.
(D) The Republican Party in New York did not expect Roosevelt to become Vice-President.

Question 5 What were some of Roosevelt's accomplishments as President?

You can click on more than one answer.

(A) Building a national highway network
(B) Higher standard for food safety
(C) More control of American waterways
(D) Increasing the number and size of national forests

Question 6 What can be inferred about Roosevelt's involvement in the Spanish-American War?

(A) It was instrumental in winning the war against Spain.
(B) It made him more famous in the U.S.
(C) He reluctantly became a soldier in the war.
(D) It led to him becoming Secretary of the Navy.

Listen to a conversation between two students regarding a class presentation.

Script non affiché le jour de l'examen :

MAN: *Hi Susan! Sorry to bother you, but I wanted to call and touch base about our La Brea Tar Pits slideshow.*

WOMAN: *No worries. I'm actually between classes right now, so it's no trouble.*

MAN: *Great. I know we still have a few days before we have to do this in front of class, but I think we need to make sure our draft is ready to turn into Professor Johnson tomorrow. He's going to want to see all the data we plan to present this Friday.*

WOMAN: *Sure. Just let me pull out my notes. I've got everything on the computer back in my room, but I've been keeping track of everything we've been talking about here in my notebook.*

MAN: *If I remember correctly, we're going to start off with a series of photos of the tar pits showing what they look like these days. You said you have some photos from your trip last year to Los Angeles.*

WOMAN: *Right. Then you can talk about who first realized the importance of La Brea.*

MAN: *I think I may have even found a picture of him, what was his name?*

WOMAN: *William Orcutt. An oil company scientist, if I remember correctly.*

MAN: *And I've got a photo of the tar pits when he first studied them in 1901. I can explain the popular theory for their origin, along with some evidence that refutes it and one of the alternative theories about how the tar pits were formed. The one I like best is that the oil in the pits came from a comet which exploded over California tens of thousands of years ago and released oil trapped in its core which then fell to Earth.*

WOMAN: *(Disbelieving) Raining oil?! That's so outlandish! No one's going to believe that.*

MAN: *I know, but it sounds so cool. It'll really grab everyone's attention.*

WOMAN: *That's for sure! Then I can talk about my time at the museum last year.*

MAN: *You got to volunteer in an excavation there, didn't you?*

WOMAN: *Yes! I spent two days helping sift through one of the tar pits, looking for bones or human artifacts. I didn't find anything bigger than a tooth or claw, but was able to take photos of some of the large bones and nearly complete skeletons previous excavations discovered. They weren't on display in the museum yet, so my photos show what ancient bones look like before the public gets to see them. It really was a once in a lifetime experience—I don't know anyone who's been able to go behind the scenes like that.*

MAN: *That's going to be your chance to shine! I don't know anyone who has been able to work on a scientific project out in the real world. After you show those pictures of the ancient bones, I can show some of the artistic renderings of some of the extinct species found at La Brea. Which ones do you think I should show?*

WOMAN: *Let's see…I think we need to show a painting of a mammoth, as well as one of those short-faced bears, so that people can see what these animals looked like, since they aren't around anymore.*

MAN: *(Chuckles) Sounds good. I'll definitely show a painting of a saber-toothed cat—after all, it's* *the most famous extinct animal species from California.*

WOMAN: *Hmm…can you send me those photos tonight? I'll need to add them to the slideshow.*

MAN: *Sure. I'll type up the outline for what we want to talk about so I can hand it in tomorrow. Then we should meet on Thursday to go over everything and make sure we're ready for Friday.*

WOMAN: *Perfect! Let me know if Professor Johnson wants us to add anything. I should have time tomorrow evening if we need to do further research.*

MAN: *Sounds like a deal. Bye!*

▪ **Question 7** What is the main purpose of the conversation?

(A) To organize a trip to a museum
(B) To go over material for a test
(C) To prepare for an oral report
(D) To find more material for a presentation

▪ **Question 8** According to the conversation, which of the following statements is true?

(A) The two students will meet tonight to finalize their presentation outline.
(B) The two students will likely meet the day before their presentation.
(C) The two students haven't collected all the photos they need for the presentation.
(D) The two students will meet with the professor tomorrow.

▪ **Question 9** Listen again to part of the conversation, then answer the question.

Script non affiché le jour de l'examen :
MAN: *The one I like best is that the oil in the pits came from a comet which exploded over California tens of thousands of years ago and released oil trapped in its rocky core which then fell to Earth.*

WOMAN: *Raining oil?! That's so outlandish! No one's going to buy that.*

MAN: *I know, but it sounds so cool. It'll really grab everyone's attention.*

WOMAN: *That's for sure!*

NARRATOR: What does the woman mean when she says this ?

WOMAN: *That's so outlandish!*

(A) She thinks the theory is unrealistic.
(B) She thinks the event happened in another location.
(C) She is unclear what the theory is trying to prove.
(D) She doesn't think he should include the information in the presentation.

▪ Question 10 Listen again to part of the conversation, then answer the question.

> **Script non affiché le jour de l'examen :**
> **WOMAN**: *I spent a two days helping sift through one of the tar pits, looking for bones or human artifacts. I didn't find anything bigger than a tooth or claw, but was able to take photos of some of the large bones and nearly complete skeletons previous excavations discovered. They weren't on display in the museum yet, so my photos show what ancient bones look like before the public gets to see them. It really was a once in a lifetime experience—I don't know anyone who's been able to go behind the scenes like that.*
>
> **NARRATOR**: What does the woman mean when she says this :
>
> **WOMAN**: *I don't know anyone who's been able to go behind the scenes like that.*

(A) Her experience at the museum may be put in a film.

(B) What she was able to do at the museum was uncommon.

(C) She is disappointed she wasn't able to find anything interesting during the excavation.

(D) She didn't know anyone else who was with her at the museum.

▪ Question 11 According to the conversation, what did the woman do at the La Brea Tar Pit Museum last year?

(A) Find the bones of a saber-toothed cat in the tar pits

(B) Meet the scientist who first studied the tar pits

(C) Find paintings of ancient animals found in the tar pits

(D) Search for animal and human remains in the tar pits

Mini TOEFL iBT - SPEAKING (AUDIO)

SPEAKING SECTION DIRECTIONS

The Speaking section measures your ability to speak in English about a variety of topics.

In this question, you will listen to a short lecture. You will then be asked to summarize important information from the lecture. You may take notes while you listen to the lecture. You may use your notes to help prepare your response. After you hear the question, you have 20 seconds to prepare your response and 60 seconds to speak.

Reportez vos réponses pour analyser votre performance.

Entraînez-vous dans les conditions d'examen.

Écoutez les fichiers audio.

prepmyfuture.com/book/68/ex/1911

NARRATOR: *Listen to part of a lecture in a biology class. The professor is talking about fungus.*

Question 1 Using points and details from the lecture, explain the various ways in which people use fungi.

Preparation Time: 30 seconds
Response Time: 60 seconds

Mini TOEFL iBT - SPEAKING (SCRIPTS)

SPEAKING SECTION DIRECTIONS

The Speaking section measures your ability to speak in English about a variety of topics.

In this question, you will listen to a short lecture. You will then be asked to summarize important information from the lecture. You may take notes while you listen to the lecture. You may use your notes to help prepare your response. After you hear the question, you have 20 seconds to prepare your response and 60 seconds to speak.

Reportez vos réponses pour analyser votre performance.

Entraînez-vous dans les conditions d'examen.

Écoutez les fichiers audio.

prepmyfuture.com/book/68/ex/1911

NARRATOR: *Listen to part of a lecture in a biology class. The professor is talking about fungus.*

Script non affiché le jour de l'examen :

PROFESSOR: *A Fungus is any member of a large group of plant-like organisms that includes mushrooms, yeasts, and molds. Though they look like plants, Fungi are in fact more closely related to animals than they are to plants because unlike plants, which make their own food, Fungi are like miniature versions of animal stomachs, turned inside-out. Fungi 'eat' by releasing enzymes that break down nutrients into smaller pieces that they can then absorb. Only recently have scientists begun to realize that Fungi includes some of the most important organisms, both in terms of their ecological and economic roles, for the human race, playing an important but often unnoticed role in the cycle of life. By breaking down dead organic material, Fungi release nutrients back into the ecosystem. Most plants rely on Fungi for water and nutrients absorption from the soil.*

For thousands of years, people have been using Fungi for the production of various foods such as bread and some types of cheese, as well as being a catalyst in the fermentation of wine and beer as far back as Ancient Egypt. For several East Asian cultures, Fungi adds a meat-like flavor in the production of rice and soybean products, such as soy sauce. They have also long been used as a direct source of food worldwide in the form of mushrooms and truffles. In fact, Fungi are an important source of dietary fibre and protein, due to their close relation to animals. Fungi also play a central role in some religious ceremonies, where mushrooms are boiled and eaten in order to produce hallucinogenic experiences.

Researchers in the 20th Century began to discover that in addition to being used in the production of food, the unique characteristics of Fungi led to the discovery of one of the most important medical discoveries of all time: antibiotics. In 1928, scientists observed that when bacteria was contaminated by a fungus, a narrow zone formed around the fungus that was free of the bacteria. It was theorized that the fungus was releasing a substance—now known as penicillin--that inhibited the growth of the bacteria. Recently, farmers have begun using Fungi as a natural pesticide to control weeds, plant diseases and insect pests.

▪ **Question 1** Using points and details from the lecture, explain the various ways in which people use fungi.

Preparation Time: 30 seconds
Response Time: 60 seconds

Mini TOEFL iBT - WRITING (AUDIO)

WRITING SECTION DIRECTIONS

The Writing section measures your ability to use writing to communicate in an academic environment.

For this task, you will write a response to a question about a reading passage and a lecture. You may take notes, and you may use your notes to help you write your response. Your response will be scored on the quality of your writing and on how well you connect the points in the lecture with points in the reading.

Reportez vos réponses pour analyser votre performance.

Entraînez-vous dans les conditions d'examen.

Écoutez les fichiers audio.

prepmyfuture.com/book/68/ex/1912

Reading Time – 3 minutes

The Sphinx

Silent and mysterious, the Sphinx of Giza, a 20-meter high, 60-meter long limestone statue with a lion body and human head and set in a deep depression on the edge of the city of Cairo in Egypt, has fascinated people for thousands of years. However, over the last 150 years, researchers have been able to piece together much about its origin and purpose.

The face of the Sphinx

Evidence points to the Sphinx being a statue honoring Haramachis, the "God of the Rising Sun". The orientation of the Sphinx supports this, with the face of the Sphinx facing east. In addition, the face of the Sphinx has been likened to the Pharaoh Khafre, who—like the Sphinx—had jutting ears and square jaw. The remains of a ceremonial beard, one of the most common symbols of kingship in Ancient Egypt, were also found nearby, suggesting the Sphinx had been carved to resemble a pharaoh.

The age of the Sphinx

According to modern Egyptologists, the Sphinx was built on the order of Pharaoh Khafre, a famous, early pharaoh of Egypt. To support this, researchers point to the Sphinx's location and connection to other monuments on the Giza plateau dating to the time of Khafre. Most importantly, the Pyramid of Khafre, one of the large pyramids to the west of the Sphinx, is directly linked to the Sphinx by a giant limestone causeway. This, combined with long-accepted dates for the reign of Khafre, clearly places the building of the Sphinx to around 2500 B.C.

Objects near the Sphinx

Further evidence that Khafre was the inspiration for the Sphinx can be found in two temples directly in front of the Sphinx. Inside one of these temples, which were built using limestone blocks excavated from the Sphinx enclosure, archaeologists found a statue of Khafre. Moreover, between the paws of the Sphinx is a plaque stating that the Sphinx was made for Khafre. Called the "Dream Stele", this plaque was erected by a later pharaoh to commemorate the refurbishing of the Sphinx, which at the time had been almost completely buried by centuries of sand and wind.

NARRATOR: *Now listen to part of a lecture on the topic you just read about.*

▪ **Question 1**

DIRECTIONS: You have 20 minutes to plan and write your response. Your response will be evaluated on the quality of your writing on how well you present the points in the lecture and their relationship to the reading passage. Typically, an effective response will have 150 to 225 words.

Summarize the points made in the lecture, being sure to explain how they contradict specific points made in the reading passage.

Mini TOEFL iBT - WRITING (SCRIPTS)

WRITING SECTION DIRECTIONS

The Writing section measures your ability to use writing to communicate in an academic environment.

For this task, you will write a response to a question about a reading passage and a lecture. You may take notes, and you may use your notes to help you write your response. Your response will be scored on the quality of your writing and on how well you connect the points in the lecture with points in the reading.

Reportez vos réponses pour analyser votre performance.

Entraînez-vous dans les conditions d'examen.

Écoutez les fichiers audio.

prepmyfuture.com/book/68/ex/1912

Reading Time – 3 minutes

The Sphinx

Silent and mysterious, the Sphinx of Giza, a 20-meter high, 60-meter long limestone statue with a lion body and human head and set in a deep depression on the edge of the city of Cairo in Egypt, has fascinated people for thousands of years. However, over the last 150 years, researchers have been able to piece together much about its origin and purpose.

The face of the Sphinx

Evidence points to the Sphinx being a statue honoring Haramachis, the "God of the Rising Sun". The orientation of the Sphinx supports this, with the face of the Sphinx facing east. In addition, the face of the Sphinx has been likened to the Pharaoh Khafre, who—like the Sphinx—had jutting ears and square jaw. The remains of a ceremonial beard, one of the most common symbols of kingship in Ancient Egypt, were also found nearby, suggesting the Sphinx had been carved to resemble a pharaoh.

The age of the Sphinx

According to modern Egyptologists, the Sphinx was built on the order of Pharaoh Khafre, a famous, early pharaoh of Egypt. To support this, researchers point to the Sphinx's location and connection to other monuments on the Giza plateau dating to the time of Khafre. Most importantly, the Pyramid of Khafre, one of the large pyramids to the west of the Sphinx, is directly linked to the Sphinx by a giant limestone causeway. This, combined with long-accepted dates for the reign of Khafre, clearly places the building of the Sphinx to around 2500 B.C.

Objects near the Sphinx

Further evidence that Khafre was the inspiration for the Sphinx can be found in two temples directly in front of the Sphinx. Inside one of these temples, which were built using limestone blocks excavated from the Sphinx enclosure, archaeologists found a statue of Khafre. Moreover, between the paws of the Sphinx is a plaque stating that the Sphinx was made for Khafre. Called the "Dream Stele", this plaque was erected by a later pharaoh to commemorate the refurbishing of the Sphinx, which at the time had been almost completely buried by centuries of sand and wind.

NARRATOR: *Now listen to part of a lecture on the topic you just read about.*

Script non affiché le jour de l'examen :

PROFESSOR: *New data has come to light over the last few decades that call into question much of what we know about the Sphinx. The conventional theory is now, in the view of many, in complete ruins.*

First, in 1993, a police artist made a detailed comparison of the face of the Sphinx with that of Khafre and showed quite clearly that while there are a few minor similarities between the two faces, when looked at from the side, the proflies of the Sphinx and Khafre are radically different. Sphinx's cheeks are very flat, and its jaw juts out strongly from the face. This is unlike statues dedicated to Khafre, which display much sharper cheekbones and a much softer jaw line. Another notable difference is headdress worn by the Sphinx and depictions of Khafre. Researchers showed long ago that the headdress of different pharaohs are quite distinct from one dynasty to another, which is one way Egyptologists often use to date artifacts and carvings they find. While the Sphinx headdress shows very uniform horizontal lines, statues of Khafre show a headdress made of a series of alternating thin lines and broad bands—a clear indication that the Sphinx headdress was not styled after Khafre or any of the pharaohs from his time period.

Second, while there is a causeway connecting the Sphinx to the Pyramid of Khafre, the causeway is built at an angle, which points to a lack of planning on where to build the Pyramid and Sphinx in relation to each other. More troubling are signs of severe erosion on the Sphinx, One would expect to see similar extreme erosion on other monuments at Giza, but archaeologists find that no other monument at Giza has eroded as much as the Sphinx, leading to speculation that the Sphinx is actually much older than other nearby buildings, including the Great Pyramid of Khafre.

Lastly, while most Egyptologists cite the Dream Stele as a direct link between the Sphinx and Khafre, what most do not reveal is that the name "Khafre" does not actually appear on the Dream Stele. What researchers found was a fragment of a pharaoh's name beginning with "Khaf" but the remainder of the name had been broken off centuries ago. More importantly, a different stele was unearthed on Giza which tells how at the grandfather of Khafre found the Sphinx buried in sand. This, if true, would mean that the Sphinx was centuries if not thousands of years older than previously thought.

▪ Question 1

DIRECTIONS: You have 20 minutes to plan and write your response. Your response will be evaluated on the quality of your writing on how well you present the points in the lecture and their relationship to the reading passage. Typically, an effective response will have 150 to 225 words.

Summarize the points made in the lecture, being sure to explain how they contradict specific points made in the reading passage.

MINI TOEFL iBT - SOLUTIONS

Mini TOEFL iBT - READING - Solutions

Reportez vos réponses pour analyser votre performance.

Entraînez-vous dans les conditions d'examen.

prepmyfuture.com/book/68/ex/1909

question 1	A	question 3	D	question 5	A	question 7	C	question 9	C
question 2	B	question 4	C	question 6	B	question 8	D	question 10	B E F

▪ Question 1 - Solution

Which of the following best expresses the essential information in the highlighted sentence in Paragraph 1? Incorrect choices change the meaning in important ways or leave out essential information.

FR : Laquelle de ces propositions exprime le mieux l'information essentielle de la phase surlignée dans le 1er paragraphe ? Les propositions incorrectes changent le sens de manière importante ou omettent des informations essentielles.

(A)	**✓ Because it looked like the various continents could fit together like pieces of a puzzle, Wegener came to believe that they had surprisingly once been a single continent in the distant past.**	**= Comme les différents continents semblaient s'emboîter comme les pièces d'un puzzle, Wegener en est venu à penser qu'ils avaient étonnamment constitué un seul continent dans un passé lointain.** ***« All the current disparate continents of the world were once one, huge mega-landmass some 200 million years ago. » (= « Tous les continents actuellement disparates formaient, il y a environ 200 millions d'années, une seule et même méga masse Terrestre. »)*** ***Cela signifie donc que puisque les continents semblent s'imbriquer parfaitement, comme les pièces d'un puzzle, Wegener formule la théorie selon laquelle les continents ne formaient qu'un il y a très longtemps.***
(B)	Wegener felt that his theory better explained how continents had been connected millions of years ago.	= Wegener pensait que sa théorie expliquait plus efficacement comment les continents avaient été reliés entre eux il y a des millions d'années. *« [it] led Wegener to propose a startling, new, controversial theory » (= « Cela a conduit Wegener à proposer une théorie surprenante, nouvelle et controversée. »)* *C'est un contresens puisque cette proposition de réponse laisse supposer qu'il est communément admis que les continents étaient connectés.*
(C)	Wegener used new and unusual research to support his theory that all the continents of the world had had once been part of a giant, super-continent.	= Wegener a utilisé des recherches novatrices et inhabituelles pour étayer sa théorie selon laquelle tous les continents du monde avaient autrefois fait partie d'un super-continent géant. *« These observations led Wegener to propose a [...] new theory » (= « Ces observations ont poussé Wegener à formuler une nouvelle théorie. »)* *Il n'est donc pas question de recherches mais de simples constats basés sur des observations.*
(D)	After looking at the shape of the continents, Wegener theorized that all the continents of the world would one day be connected.	= Après avoir observé la forme des continents, Wegener a émis l'hypothèse que tous les continents du monde seraient un jour reliés entre eux. *« All the current disparate continents of the world were once one, huge mega-landmass some 200 million years ago. » (= « Tous les continents actuellement disparates formaient, il y a environ 200 millions d'années, une seule et même méga masse Terrestre. »)* *Cette proposition est un contresens : Wegener ne formule pas une théorie selon laquelle les continents seront un jour tous connectés mais qu'ils l'étaient, il y a 200 millions d'années.*

▪ Question 2 - Solution

The word "backlash" in paragraph 2 is closest in meaning to:

FR : Le mot « backlash » dans le paragraphe 2 s'approche le plus du sens de :

(A) acceptance = acceptation

(B) ✓ opposition = opposition

(C) review = vérification

(D) reversal = renversement

⇒ **explication**

FR : *« he published his theory [...] and faced an immediate and harsh backlash from the scientific community. »*
(= Il publia sa théorie [...] et dû faire face à l'opposition à la fois vive et immédiate de la communauté scientifique.)

▪ Question 3 - Solution

Why does the author mention "land bridges" in paragraph 3?

FR : Pourquoi l'auteur mentionne-t-il les « land bridges » dans le paragraphe 3 ?

(A)	to present information supporting Wegener's theory of Continental Drift	= pour présenter des informations soutenant la théorie de Wegener sur la dérive des continents *Contresens : « Thomas Chamberlain proposed alternative explanations for what Wegener saw. […] Chamberlain proposed there may once have been a network of land bridges between the different continents[…] »* *(= « Thomas Chamberlain a proposé des explications alternatives pour expliquer les observations de Wegener. [...] Chamberlain a proposé qu'il y ait pu y avoir autrefois un réseau de ponts terrestres entre les différents continents [...] »)* *Les land bridges (= ponts terrestres) permettent donc de contrer l'un des arguments de Wegener.*
(B)	to explain how water currents move water to the arctic regions from the equator	= pour expliquer comment les courants marins déplacent l'eau de l'équateur vers les régions arctiques *Confusion : « To explain the unusually distribution of fossils, Chamberlain proposed there may once have been a network of land bridges between the different continents[…] »* *(= « Pour expliquer la répartition inhabituelle des fossiles, Chamberlain a émis l'hypothèse qu'il aurait pu exister autrefois un réseau de ponts terrestres entre les différents continents [...]. »)*
(C)	to highlight evidence that contradicts Wegener's theory of Continental Drift	= pour mettre en évidence les preuves qui contredisent la théorie de la dérive des continents de Wegener *« Thomas Chamberlain proposed alternative explanations for what Wegener saw"* *(= « Thomas Chamberlain a proposé des explications alternatives pour expliquer les observations de Wegener. »)* *Ainsi, les land bridges (= ponts terrestres) servent à formuler une hypothèse alternative à celle proposée par Wegener.*
(D)	**✓ to introduce a possible explanation for the spread of animal species across various continents**	**= pour présenter une explication probable de la propagation des espèces animales sur les différents continents** ***« To explain the unusually distribution of fossils, Chamberlain proposed there may once have been a network of land bridges between the different continents while, to explain the existence of fossils of temperate species being found in arctic regions, he proposed the existence of warm water currents connecting the polar region to the equatorial zones of the Earth. »*** ***(= « Pour expliquer la répartition inhabituelle des fossiles, Chamberlain a émis l'hypothèse qu'il ait pu exister autrefois un réseau de ponts terrestres entre les différents continents, tandis que, pour expliquer l'existence de fossiles d'espèces tempérées trouvés dans les régions arctiques, il a proposé l'existence de courants d'eau chaude reliant la région polaire aux zones équatoriales de la Terre. »)***

⇨ **explication**

FR : Chamberlain utilise l'explication des *« land bridges »* (= passages de terre) pour expliquer pourquoi on trouvait des fossiles similaires sur des continents différents.

▪ Question 4 - Solution

What role did R. Thomas Chamberlain play in the scientific debate over Wegener's theory of Continent Drift?

FR : Quel rôle R. Thomas Chamberlain a-t-il joué dans le débat scientifique concernant la théorie de Wegener de la dérive des Continents ?

(A)	His theories weren't accepted by many of the scientists at the time, but have since been reconsidered.	= Ses théories n'étaient pas acceptées par de nombreux scientifiques de l'époque, mais elles ont été reconsidérées depuis. *« At the time, reactions by scientists such as Chamberlain did help to dampen support for Continental drift. » (= « À l'époque, les réactions de scientifiques tels que Chamberlain ont contribué à atténuer le soutien apporté à la théorie de la dérive des continents. »)* *Cela signifie donc que les théories de Chamberlain étaient acceptées à l'époque.*
(B)	He only partly agreed with Wegener.	= Il n'était pas tout à fait d'accord avec Wegener. *« Modern scientists now look at these explanations as desperate attempts to prevent Wegener's ideas from gaining supporters. » (= Aujourd'hui, les scientifiques considèrent ces explications comme des tentatives désespérées d'empêcher les idées de Wegener de gagner des partisans. »)* *On en déduit donc que Chamberlain était en désaccord avec Wegener.*
(C)	**✓ He proposed alternate hypotheses that could explain Wegener's evidence for Continental Drift.**	**= Il a proposé d'autres hypothèses qui pourraient expliquer les conclusions de Wegener sur la dérive des continents.** ***« Chamberlain proposed alternative explanations for what Wegener saw » (= « Chamberlain a proposé des explications alternatives pour expliquer ce que Wegener avait pu observer. »)***
(D)	His contributions opened up interesting questions about continent formation that should be examined.	= Ses contributions ont soulevé des questions intéressantes sur la formation des continents qui mériteraient d'être examinées. *« Modern scientists now look at these explanations as desperate attempts to prevent Wegener's ideas from gaining supporters. » (= « Aujourd'hui, les scientifiques considèrent ces explications comme des tentatives désespérées d'empêcher les idées de Wegener de gagner des partisans. »)* *On peut donc en déduire que Chamberlain n'a pas formulé d'hypothèses suffisamment intéressantes pour relancer le débat sur la formation des continents.*

▪ Question 5 - Solution

The word "dampen" in paragraph 3 is closest in meaning to:

FR : Le mot « dampen » dans le paragraphe 3 s'approche le plus du sens de :

(A) ✓ lessen = abaisser

(B) move = avancer

(C) excite = exciter

(D) increase = augmenter

⟹ **explication**

FR : *« Modern scientists now look at these explanations as desperate attempts to prevent Wegener's ideas from gaining supporters, but at the time they did help to dampen support for continental drift. »*
(= « Les scientifiques considèrent aujourd'hui ces explications comme des tentatives désespérées d'empêcher les idées de Wegener d'obtenir des soutiens, mais à ce moment là, elles contribuèrent à abaisser l'adhésion à la théorie de la dérive des continents. »)

▪ Question 6 - Solution

What can be said about Wegener's explanation for the mechanism of Continental Drift?

FR : Qu'est-ce qui peut être dit à propos de l'explication donnée par Wegener sur le mécanisme de dérive des continents ?

(A)	He believed it was sufficient to explain the movement of continents.	= Il pensait qu'elle suffisait à expliquer le déplacement des continents. *Contresens : « Wegener did not have a solid explanation for how Continental drift could have occurred. […] Wegener himself really did not believe he had the correct explanation for the mechanism. »* *(= « Wegener n'avait pas d'explications solides pour expliquer le fonctionnement de la dérive des continents. Wegener lui-même ne pensait pas avoir l'explication correcte pour expliquer ce mécanisme. »)* *Wegener savait donc que ses explications manquaient de preuves solides pour valider sa théorie de dérive des continents.*
(B)	**✓ It relied on the motion of the Earth as a cause for the movement of continents.**	**= Il se fondait sur le mouvement de la Terre comme cause du déplacement des continents.** ***« He proposed that […] the centrifugal force caused by the rotation of the Earth […] may cause the continents to move slowly over time. »*** ***(= « Il a émis l'hypothèse que [...] la force centrifuge causée par la rotation de la Terre [...] peut faire en sorte que les continents se déplacent lentement au fil du temps. »)***
(C)	It could also explain the movement of ocean tides.	= Elle pouvait également expliquer le mouvement des marées océaniques. *Contresens : « […] the tidal attraction of the Sun and Moon may cause the continents to move slowly »* *(= [...] l'attraction marémotrice du Soleil et de la Lune pourrait ainsi faire bouger lentement les continents. »)* *Cette réponse est donc un contresens : il n'est pas mentionné que la dérive des continents explique le phénomène de marées.*
(D)	He believed the Earth's rotation was enough to cause the movement of continents.	= Il pensait que la rotation de la Terre était suffisante pour provoquer le déplacement des continents. *Proposition incomplète : « He proposed that a combination of the centrifugal force caused by the rotation of the Earth and the tidal attraction of the Sun and Moon may cause the continents to move slowly over time »* *(= « Il a émis l'hypothèse qu'une combinaison de la force centrifuge causée par la rotation de la Terre et de l'attraction marémotrice du Soleil et de la Lune pourrait ainsi faire bouger lentement les continents au fil du temps. »)* *Cette proposition est donc incomplète : la rotation de la Terre ne permet pas à elle seule de justifier la théorie de la dérive des continents.*

⇨ **explication**

FR : Même si Wegener n'était pas certain de cette justification, il pensait que la dérive des continents était en partie liée à la force centrifuge causée par la rotation de la Terre ainsi que les forces d'attraction du Soleil et de la Lune.

■ Question 7 - Solution

According to the passage, all of the following can be said of Arthur Holmes' theory explaining a mechanism for Continental Drift EXCEPT:

FR : D'après le passage, toutes les propositions suivantes à propos de la théorie de Arthur Holmes sur le mécanisme de la dérive des continents sont vraies SAUF :

(A)	It involved the effect of variations in temperature deep under the Earth's surface.	= Il concernait l'effet des variations de température en profondeur sous la surface de la Terre. *« Holmes believed that this repeated heating and cooling of semisolid rock under the Earth's surface [...] may be enough the cause the continents to move. »* *(= « Holmes pensait que ce réchauffement et ce refroidissement répétés de la roche semi-solide sous la surface de la Terre [...] pouvait suffire à provoquer le déplacement des continents. »)*
(B)	It was greatly supported by later research conducted in the 1960's by other scientists.	= Elle a été largement soutenue par des recherches ultérieures menées dans les années 1960 par d'autres scientifiques. *« Not until the 1960s did Holmes' idea [...] begin to be studied by more scientists. [...] The theory finally gained acceptance of the greater scientific community. »* *(= « Ce n'est que dans les années 1960 que l'idée de Holmes [...] a commencé à être étudiée par davantage de scientifiques. [...] La théorie a finalement été acceptée par la communauté scientifique. »)*
(C) ✓	**Wegener and Holmes worked together to create a hypothesis for the process of Continental Drift.**	**= Wegener et Holmes ont travaillé ensemble pour créer une hypothèse sur le processus de dérive des continents.** ***« In 1912 [Wegener] published his theory of Continental Drift. Wegener's theory gained some support in 1929 when Arthur Holmes suggested a possible process for continental drift [...] »*** ***(= « En 1912, [Wegener] a publié sa théorie de la dérive des continents. La théorie de Wegener a été appuyée en 1929 lorsqu'Arthur Holmes a suggéré un processus possible pour la dérive des continents. »)*** ***Si les deux hommes ont travaillé sur la même théorie (Continental drift), il n'est pas mentionné qu'ils aient travaillé ensemble.***
(D)	He believed that thermal convection caused continents to move away from each other.	= Il pensait que la convection thermique provoquait l'éloignement des continents les uns des autres. *« Wegener's theory gained some support in 1929 when Arthur Holmes suggested a possible process for continental drift based on the idea that the Earth's mantle undergoes 'thermal convection.' »* *(= « La théorie de Wegener a été appuyée en 1929 lorsqu'Arthur Holmes a suggéré un processus possible pour la dérive des continents basé sur l'idée que le manteau terrestre subit une convection thermique. »)*

▪ Question 8 - Solution

According to Holmes, what could have caused the continental drift?

FR : Selon Holmes, qu'est-ce-qui a pu causé la dérive des continents ?

(A)	presence of semisolid rock beneath the continents	= la présence de roches semi-solides sous les continents *« Holmes believed that this repeated healing and cooling of semi-solid rock under the Earth's surface could result in an upward-and-downward current which may be enough to cause continents to move. »* *(= « Holmes pensait que ce réchauffement et ce refroidissement répétés de la roche semi-solide sous la surface de la Terre pouvaient entraîner un courant ascendant et descendant qui pourrait suffire à faire bouger les continents. »)* *Ce n'est pas la présence de roche semi-liquide qui explique le mouvement des continents selon la pensée de Holmes. Selon lui, ces changements de températures sont la cause de ce phénomène.*
(B)	the contrasting forces that guide ocean currents	= Les forces opposées qui guident les courants océaniques *« Arthur Holmes suggested a possible process for continental drift based on the idea that the Earth's mantle undergoes 'thermal convection.' »)* *(= Holmes a suggéré un processus possible pour la dérive des continents basé sur l'idée que le manteau terrestre subit une convection thermique. »)* *L'hypothèse de Holmes ne mentionne pas les courants océaniques. Sa théorie se focalise sur les courants causés par la convection thermique qui affecte le manteau terrestre.*
(C)	the abrupt drop in the mantle's temperature	= la chute brutale de la température du manteau *« Holmes believed that this repeated healing and cooling of semi-solid rock under the Earth's surface could result in an upward-and-downward current which may be enough to cause continents to move. »* *(= « Holmes pensait que ce réchauffement et ce refroidissement répétés de la roche semi-solide sous la surface de la Terre pouvaient entraîner un courant ascendant et descendant qui pourrait suffire à faire bouger les continents. »)* *Ce n'est donc pas la baisse de température, mais les changements incessants de cette dernière qui seraient responsables de la dérive des continents.*
(D)	**✓ the motion of the Earth's mantle**	**= le mouvement du manteau terrestre** ***« Arthur Holmes suggested a possible process for continental drift based on the idea that the Earth's mantle undergoes 'thermal convection.' »*** ***(= « Holmes a suggéré un processus possible pour la dérive des continents basé sur l'idée que le manteau terrestre subit une convection thermique. »)***

▪ Question 9 - Solution

Look at the four squares in paragraph 5, **A**, **B**, **C**, and **D**, which indicate where the following sentence could be added to the passage. Where would the sentence best fit?

In fact, they exposed Wegener to ridicule because they clearly could not demonstrate the origin of a force that could have caused the movement of landmasses as large as continents.

Wegener's theory did have its rough edges. **A** Wegener did not have a solid explanation for how continental drift could have occurred. **B** He proposed that a combination of the centrifugal force caused by the rotation of the Earth and the tidal attraction of the Sun and the Moon may cause the continents to move slowly over time. Unfortunately, Wegener knew these explanations were inadequate. **C** Wegener himself really did not believe that he had the explanation for the mechanism, but that this should not stop discussion of a hypothesis. **D**

(A) A

(B) B

(C) ✓ C

(D) D

⇾ **explication**

FR : Cette phrase permet de faire la transition vers la phrase suivante : la théorie de Wegener a été tournée en ridicule. De fait, lui-même n'était pas convaincu par ses propres explications.

■ Question 10 - Solution

Directions:

An introductory sentence for a brief summary of the passage is provided below.

Complete the summary by selecting the THREE answer choices that express the most important ideas in the passage. Some sentences do not belong in the summary because they express ideas that are not presented in the passage or are minor ideas in the passage.

This question is worth 2 points.

- "Continental Drift" theorizes that continents are able to move around the globe.
- ________
- ________
- ________

(A)	Wegener believed Continental Drift was caused by a process of thermal convection under the Earth's surface.	= Wegener pensait que la dérive des continents était causée par un processus de convection thermique sous la surface de la Terre. *C'est ce que Holmes déclare après que Wegener a présenté son hypothèse.*
(B)	**✓ It attempted to explain how and why similar plants and animals could be found on distant continents.**	**= Il a tenté d'expliquer comment et pourquoi des plantes et des animaux analogues pouvaient être trouvés sur des continents éloignés.** ***Cette phrase synthétise correctement les arguments de la première théorie de Wegener.***
(C)	Wegener discovered the existence of glaciers in Africa and went on to prove that the continent was once closer to the North Pole.	= Wegener a découvert l'existence de glaciers en Afrique et a ensuite prouvé que ce continent était autrefois plus proche du pôle Nord. *Wegener n'a pas fait cela. Il s'est reposé sur des cartes qui montrent des traces de glaciers sur le continent africain.*
(D)	It hypothesized that a land-bridge may once have connected Africa and South America.	= Il a émis l'hypothèse qu'un pont terrestre aurait autrefois relié l'Afrique et l'Amérique du Sud. *C'est ce que Holmes déclare dans le but de s'opposer à la théorie de Wegener sur la dérive des continents.*
(E)	**✓ Holmes identified in the thermal excursion beneath the Earth's surface a possible explanation for the movement of the continents.**	**= Holmes a identifié dans le mouvement thermique sous la surface de la Terre une explication possible du déplacement des continents.** ***Holmes a eu un rôle pivot dans le support de la théorie de Wegener.***
(F)	**✓ Only after several scientific studies has it been possible to recognize the validity of Wegener's initial hypothesis.**	**= Ce n'est qu'après plusieurs études scientifiques qu'il a été possible de reconnaître la pertinence de l'hypothèse initiale de Wegener.** ***Comme l'auteur le mentionne, il y a eu des avancées dans le domaine scientifique qui ont mené à une meilleure compréhension du phénomène à l'origine de la dérive des continents.***

Conversion de votre résultat en score TOEFL iBT sur 30

Votre nombre de nombre de points	Estimation score TOEFL iBT
10	30
9	27
8	24
7	21
6	17
5	14
4	11
3	7
2	5
1	3
0	0

Mini TOEFL iBT - LISTENING - Solutions

Reportez vos réponses pour analyser votre performance.

Entraînez-vous dans les conditions d'examen.

Écoutez les fichiers audio.

prepmyfuture.com/book/68/ex/1910

question 1	B D
question 2	D
question 3	A

question 4	C
question 5	B C D

question 6	B
question 7	C

question 8	B
question 9	A

question 10	B
question 11	D

Question 1 - Solution

What are the main topics of the lecture?

Click on 2 answers.

FR : Quels sont les sujets principaux de ce cours ?

Choisissez 2 réponses.

(A)	How Roosevelt was able to pass laws protecting the environment	= La façon dont Roosevelt a fait passer des lois pour la protection de l'environnement *La proposition est en partie vraie mais il s'agit d'un détail du cours.*
(B)	✓ **How Roosevelt became president of the United States**	**= Comment Roosevelt est devenu président des États-Unis** ***L'article évoque longuement l'histoire de Roosevelt avant qu'il devienne président des États-Unis.***
(C)	Why Roosevelt wanted to be president of the United States	= Pourquoi Roosevelt voulait devenir président des États-Unis *Le professeur décrit les principales actions entreprises par Roosevelt mais ne décrit pas ses motivations.*
(D)	✓ **The kinds of legislation Roosevelt helped pass as president**	**= Les lois que Roosevelt a contribué à faire passer quand il était président des États-Unis** ***La deuxième partie du discours est consacrée aux réformes entreprises par Roosevelt sous sa présidence.***

⇝ **explication**

FR : Lorsqu'on vous demande de choisir deux réponses, il faut que vous choisissiez les deux meilleurs choix de réponse. Les autres affirmations peuvent être correctes mais moins pertinentes.

▪ Question 2 - Solution

According to the professor, Roosevelt did all of the following EXCEPT:

FR : D'après le professeur, Roosevelt a effectué toutes les actions ci-dessous EXCEPTÉ :

(A)	Write books about his life in the Dakotas	= Écrire des livres sur sa vie dans les Dakotas *« During his time out West, Roosevelt published books on his experiences ranching and hunting, as well as on other aspects of life his life in the Dakotas »* *(= « Pendant son séjour dans l'Ouest, Roosevelt a publié des livres sur ses expériences d'élevage et de chasse, ainsi que sur d'autres aspects de sa vie dans les Dakotas. »)*
(B)	Help increase competition among large companies	= Aider à accroître la compétitivité des grandes entreprises *« He passed legislation that broke up some of the country's biggest corporations and brought more competition to the U.S. business sector »* *(= « Il a adopté des lois qui ont permis de démanteler certaines des plus grandes entreprises du pays et d'accroître la concurrence dans le secteur commercial américain. »)*
(C)	Leave a position in government to join a war	= Partir du gouvernement pour rejoindre la guerre *« he was appointed Assistant Secretary of the Navy [...] When war broke out 1898 between the U.S. and Spain, [...] Roosevelt and his Rough Riders led a much-publicized horse charge »* *(= « il est nommé secrétaire adjoint à la Marine. [...] Lorsque la guerre éclate entre les États-Unis et l'Espagne [...] Roosevelt et ses Rough Riders mènent une charge à dos de cheval très médiatisée. »)*
(D)	**✓ Run for political office in the American West**	**= Faire campagne dans l'Ouest Américain**

▪ Question 3 - Solution

According to the lecture, what did Roosevelt write about after the death of his wife and mother?

FR : D'après le cours, sur quoi Roosevelt a-t-il écrit après la mort de sa femme et de sa mère ?

(A)	**✓ Life in the American West**	**= La vie dans l'Ouest Américain**
(B)	His career in politics	= Sa carrière en politique
(C)	The conservation of natural resources	= La conservation des ressources naturelles
(D)	His experiences as a Rough Rider	= Son expérience en tant que *Rough Rider*

⇝ **explication**

FR : « *Dakotas helped him escape the sadness of the loss of his wife and mother, and became a retreat where he could pursue his interest in writing. During his time out West, Roosevelt published books on his experiences ranching and hunting, as well as on other aspects of his life in the Dakotas.* »
(= « Les Dakotas l'ont aidé à surmonter la tristesse après la mort de son épouse et de sa mère, et sont devenues un lieu de retraite où il pouvait s'adonner à l'écriture. Pendant son séjour dans l'Ouest, Roosevelt a publié des livres sur ses expériences d'élevage et de chasse, ainsi que sur d'autres aspects de sa vie dans les Dakotas ».)

▪ Question 4 - Solution

Listen again to part of the lecture. Then answer the question.

Script non affiché le jour de l'examen :

PROFESSOR: *Returning home as a war hero, Roosevelt was elected governor of New York in the fall of 1898, but his enthusiasm for reform so annoyed the state's Republican leaders that they arranged for him to run as the party's vice presidential candidate in 1900. When the Republican ticket won the presidential election, New York's Republican Party breathed a sigh of relief because Roosevelt was now out of their hair.*

What does the professor mean by this statement?

Script non affiché le jour de l'examen :

PROFESSOR: *When the Republican ticket won the presidential election, New York's Republican Party breathed a sigh of relief because Roosevelt was now out of their hair.*

FR :

Que veut dire le professeur dans cette phrase ?

« Quand les Républicains gagnèrent les élections présidentielles, le parti Républicain de New York fut soulagé car Roosevelt n'était plus mélé à leurs affaires. »

(A) Roosevelt did not enjoy working with the Republican Party in New York.
= Roosevelt n'a pas apprécié travailler avec le PArti Républicain à New York
C'est probable mais ce n'est pas dit explicitement.

(B) Roosevelt did not enjoy being the governor of New York.
= Roosevelt n'a pas aimé être gouverneur de New York
Ce n'est pas évoqué par le professeur.

(C) ✓ After Roosevelt was elected Vice-President, legislators in New York did not have to work with him anymore.
= Après que Roosevelt a été élu Vice-Président, les législateurs de New York n'avaient plus à travailler avec lui
C'est exactement ce que dit le professeur.

(D) The Republican Party in New York did not expect Roosevelt to become Vice-President.
= Le parti Républicain de New York ne pensait pas Roosevelt deviendrait Vice-Président
Ce n'est pas évoqué par le professeur.

⇒ **explication**
FR : L'expression *« to be out of someone's hair »* signifie « ne plus embêter, causer du tort à quelqu'un, ne plus être dans ses pattes ».
De ce fait, une fois Roosevelt élu, les législateurs de New York n'ont plus eu à travailler avec lui.

▪ Question 5 - Solution

What were some of Roosevelt's accomplishments as President?

You can click on more than one answer.

FR : Parmi les propositions suivantes, lesquelles ont été réalisées par Roosevelt quand il était Président ? Vous pouvez choisir plus d'une réponse.

(A)	Building a national highway network	= La création d'un réseau national d'autoroutes *Roosevelt devient président des Etats-Unis en 1901. Les autoroutes n'existaient pas encore à cette époque.*
(B) ✓	**Higher standard for food safety**	**= La hausse des normes dans l'industrie agro-alimentaire** ***« he secured passage of federal regulations to control railroad rates and to set quality standards for food and drugs. »*** ***(= « il a obtenu l'adoption de réglementations fédérales visant à contrôler les tarifs des chemins de fer et à fixer des normes de qualité pour les aliments et les médicaments. »)***
(C) ✓	**More control of American waterways**	**= Plus de contrôle des cours d'eau américains** ***« gave the federal government primary responsibility for dam construction and irrigation projects »*** ***(= « il a donné au gouvernement fédéral la responsabilité principale de la construction des barrages et des projets d'irrigation »)***
(D) ✓	**Increasing the number and size of national forests**	**= L'augmentation du nombre et de la taille des forêts américaines** ***« Roosevelt signed a law that to set aside public lands as national forests, and used it to increase federal land reserves from the approximately 40 million acres when he took office to nearly 200 million »*** ***(= « Roosevelt a signé une loi qui a fait des terres publiques des forêts nationales, et l'a utilisée pour augmenter les réserves de terres fédérales d'environ 40 millions d'acres lorsqu'il a pris ses fonctions à près de 200 millions. »)***

▪ Question 6 - Solution

What can be inferred about Roosevelt's involvement in the Spanish-American War?

FR : Que peut-on déduire de l'engagement de Roosevelt dans la guerre opposant les États-Unis à l'Espagne ?

(A)	It was instrumental in winning the war against Spain.	= Cela a été décisif dans la victoire contre l'Espagne. *Ce n'est pas mentionné par le professeur.*
(B) ✓	**It made him more famous in the U.S.**	**= Cela l'a rendu plus célèbre aux États-Unis.** ***« His exploits in the Spanish-American War made him a household name throughout the United States. »*** ***(= « Ses exploits dans la guerre hispano-américaine l'ont rendu célèbre dans tous les États-Unis. »)***
(C)	He reluctantly became a soldier in the war.	= Il s'est engagé dans la guerre à contrecœur. *« Roosevelt [...] became a leading proponent of war with Spain »* *(= « Roosevelt [...] est devenu une figure majeure du mouvement pro-guerre contre l'Espagne. »)*
(D)	It led to him becoming Secretary of the Navy.	= Cela lui a permis de devenir ministre de la Marine. *« he was appointed Assistant Secretary of the Navy and became a leading proponent of war with Spain »* *(= Il a été nommé ministre de la Marine et est devenu une figure majeure du mouvement pro-guerre contre l'Espagne. »)*

▪ Question 7 - Solution

What is the main purpose of the conversation?

FR : Quel est le but principal de cette conversation ?

(A)	To organize a trip to a museum	= Organiser un voyage au musée
(B)	To go over material for a test	= Vérifier le matériel nécessaire pour un examen
(C)	**✓ To prepare for an oral report**	**= Préparer un exposé**
(D)	To find more material for a presentation	= Trouver plus d'informations pour une présentation

⇝ **explication**

FR : *« but I wanted to call and touch base about our La Brea Tar Pits slideshow. »* (= mais je voulais t'appeler pour parler de notre diaporama sur *La Brea Tar Pits.*) Ils préparent un exposé sur « La Brea Tar Pits ».

■ Question 8 - Solution

According to the conversation, which of the following statements is true?

FR : D'après les propos rapportés dans la conversation, laquelle de ces propositions est vraie ?

(A)	The two students will meet tonight to finalize their presentation outline.	= Les étudiants vont se voir ce soir pour finaliser le plan de leur présentation *Ils ont discuté du plan (= outline) au cours de leur conversation. Un seul des deux étudiants finalisera la présentation pour la communiquer au professeur le lendemain.*
(B)	**✓ The two students will likely meet the day before their presentation.**	**= Les deux étudiants se retrouveront sans doute la veille de leur présentation** ***À la fin de la conversation, les étudiants se disent « we should meet on Thursday to go over everything and make sure we're ready for Friday ». (= On devrait se retrouver jeudi pour revoir notre présentation et vérifier que tout est prêt pour vendredi.) Ils veulent donc se retrouver pour relire la présentation la veille de l'exposé.***
(C)	The two students haven't collected all the photos they need for the presentation.	= Les deux étudiants n'ont pas encore récupéré toutes les photos nécessaires pour leur présentation *Ils évoquent les photos qu'ils comptent ajouter à la présentation. Ils n'évoquent pas de photo manquante.*
(D)	The two students will meet with the professor tomorrow.	= Les deux étudiants retrouveront le professeur le lendemain *Un seul des étudiants donnera le plan au professeur le lendemain.*

■ Question 9 - Solution

Listen again to part of the conversation, then answer the question.

Script non affiché le jour de l'examen :

MAN: *The one I like best is that the oil in the pits came from a comet which exploded over California tens of thousands of years ago and released oil trapped in its rocky core which then fell to Earth.*

WOMAN: *Raining oil?! That's so outlandish! No one's going to buy that.*

MAN: *I know, but it sounds so cool. It'll really grab everyone's attention.*

WOMAN: *That's for sure!*

NARRATOR: What does the woman mean when she says this ?

WOMAN: That's so outlandish!

FR :

Que veut dire la femme quand elle dit :

« C'est tellement bizarre ! »

(A) ✓	**She thinks the theory is unrealistic.**	**= Elle pense que cette théorie n'est pas réaliste.**
(B)	She thinks the event happened in another location.	= Elle pense que cet événement a eu lieu à un autre endroit.
(C)	She is unclear what the theory is trying to prove.	= Elle n'est pas sûre d'avoir compris ce que cette théorie essaie de démontrer.
(D)	She doesn't think he should include the information in the presentation.	= Elle ne pense pas qu'il devrait inclure cette information dans la présentation. *Elle ne demande pas de retirer cette information. Par la suite, ils sont même d'accord sur le fait que cette théorie marquera les esprits et rendra leur exposé plus « cool ».*

⟹ **explication**

FR : *« Raining oil?! That's so outlandish! No one's going to buy that. »* (= « Une pluie de pétrole ?! C'est tellement bizarre ! Personne n'y croira ! »)

▪ Question 10 - Solution

Listen again to part of the conversation, then answer the question.

> **Script non affiché le jour de l'examen :**
>
> **WOMAN**: *I spent a two days helping sift through one of the tar pits, looking for bones or human artifacts. I didn't find anything bigger than a tooth or claw, but was able to take photos of some of the large bones and nearly complete skeletons previous excavations discovered. They weren't on display in the museum yet, so my photos show what ancient bones look like before the public gets to see them. It really was a once in a lifetime experience—I don't know anyone who's been able to go behind the scenes like that.*
>
> **NARRATOR**: What does the woman mean when she says this :
>
> **WOMAN**: *I don't know anyone who's been able to go behind the scenes like that.*

FR :

Que veut dire la femme quand elle dit :

« Je ne connais personne ayant pu visiter les coulisses de cette façon. »

(A)	Her experience at the museum may be put in a film.	= Son expérience au musée pourrait faire l'objet d'un film. *On parle des « coulisses » au sens figuré, il ne s'agit pas d'un film, il faut le comprendre comme « l'envers du décor ».*
(B)	**✓ What she was able to do at the museum was uncommon.**	**= Ce qu'elle a pu faire au musée n'était pas commun.** ***« It really was a once in a lifetime experience - I don't know anyone who's been able to go behind the scenes like that! »*** ***(= « C'était une expérience qui n'arrive qu'une fois dans une vie ! Je ne connais personne d'autre qui a pu visiter les coulisses de cette façon ! »)*** ***L'étudiante insiste sur le caractère exceptionnel de cette expérience en disant qu'elle ne connait personne d'autre ayant eu une telle opportunité.***
(C)	She is disappointed she wasn't able to find anything interesting during the excavation.	= Elle est deçue de n'avoir rien trouvé d'intéressant durant la fouille *« It really was a once in a lifetime experience » (= « C'était une expérience qui n'arrive qu'une fois dans une vie ! »)* *Elle n'est pas déçue de cette expérience, au contraire !*
(D)	She didn't know anyone else who was with her at the museum.	= Elle ne connaissait pas les personnes qui étaient avec elle au musée. *« I don't know anyone who's been able to go behind the scenes like that! » (= « Je ne connais personne d'autre qui ait pu visiter les coulisses de cette façon ! »)* *Elle ne dit pas qu'elle ne connaissait pas les personnes qui étaient avec elle au musée.*

■ Question 11 - Solution

According to the conversation, what did the woman do at the La Brea Tar Pit Museum last year?

FR : D'après les propos rapportés dans la conversation, qu'a fait la femme au musée La Brea Tar Pit l'année dernière ?

(A)	Find the bones of a saber-toothed cat in the tar pits	= Retrouver les ossements d'un tigre à dents de sabre *Le tigre à dents de sabre est évoqué pour parler des espèces disparues. Il n'est pas associé à la présence de la femme au musée.*
(B)	Meet the scientist who first studied the tar pits	= Rencontrer le premier scientifique à avoir étudié le Tar Pits *Le scientifique qui a étudié en premier le site est évoqué pour dire que l'homme a une photo de lui. Par ailleurs, il est indiqué que le scientifique a commencé ses recherches en 1901. Il n'est donc pas un contemporain des narrateurs.*
(C)	Find paintings of ancient animals found in the tar pits	= Retrouver des peintures d'anciens animaux retrouvés dans le Tar Pits. *Les peintures anciennes sont évoquées par l'homme car il veut inclure des exemples dans l'exposé. Aucun lien n'est fait avec le musée.*
(D)	**✓ Search for animal and human remains in the tar pits**	**= Fouiller pour retrouver des restes humains et animaux dans le Tar Pits** ***« Yes! I spent two days helping sift through one of the tar pits, looking for bones or human artifacts » (= « Oui ! J'ai passé deux jours à aider à passer au crible l'une des fosses de goudron, à la recherche d'ossements ou d'artefacts humains. »)***

Conversion de votre résultat en score TOEFL iBT sur 30

Votre nombre de bonnes réponses	Estimation score TOEFL iBT
11	30
10	27
9	24
8	21
7	18
6	14
5	9
4	6
3	4
2	2
1	1
0	0

Mini-TOEFL iBT - SPEAKING - Solutions

Utilisez la grille ci-dessous pour vous auto-évaluer sur chaque exercice. Additionnez vos scores et multipliez le résultat par 15/2 pour obtenir une note sur 30.

4 points	On retrouve toutes les caractéristiques suivantes : • débit rythmé et fluide, les fautes mineures d'intonation ou prononciation n'empêchent pas la compréhension • vocabulaire varié et maîtrise des structures complexes, les erreurs mineures n'empêchent pas la compréhension • utilisation de l'ensemble du temps imparti, les liens entre les idées sont clairs
3 points	On retrouve au moins 2 des caractéristiques suivantes : • débit assez fluide, les fautes d'intonation ou prononciation rendent plus difficile la compréhension mais le discours reste intelligible • les fautes de vocabulaire et de grammaire ne portent pas atteinte à l'intelligibilité du discours • utilisation de l'essentiel du temps imparti, le développement de la réponse est limité mais la réponse est globalement cohérente
2 points	On retrouve au moins 2 des caractéristiques suivantes : • rythme saccadé, mais le discours reste intelligible mais n'est pas clair par endroit • maîtrise limitée de la grammaire et du vocabulaire, seules les structures simples sont maîtrisées • la réponse correspond à la question mais n'est pas assez développée, le nombre des idées est limité avec des propos vagues et répétitifs
1 point	On retrouve au moins 2 des caractéristiques suivantes : • difficultés de prononciation et hésitations, rythme très saccadé. • les fautes de grammaire et de vocabulaire rendent difficile la compréhension • discours court et répétitions
0 point	Pas de réponse ou réponse hors-sujet

Nous avons pour projet de mettre en ligne un service de correction personnalisée pour les épreuves d'expression orale et écrite. Ce service fera appel à des correcteurs expérimentés qui vous attribueront une note en suivant les critères du TOEFL iBT. La correction détaillée incluera des conseils personnalisés pour vous améliorer. À l'heure où vous lirez ce manuel, le service sera peut-être déjà en ligne sur http://www.prepmyfuture.com/toefl

Réponse type

Reportez vos réponses pour analyser votre performance.

Entraînez-vous dans les conditions d'examen.

prepmyfuture.com/book/68/ex/1911

question 1	q. ouverte

Question 1 - Solution

Using points and details from the lecture, explain the various ways in which people use fungi.

Preparation Time: 30 seconds
Response Time: 60 seconds

FR :

DIRECTIONS: *Donnez-vous 30 secondes pour préparer votre réponse à la question suivante. Puis enregistrez-vous en train de parler pendant 60 secondes.*

En utilisant les points et les détails de la conférence, expliquez les différentes façons dont les gens utilisent les champignons.

Temps de préparation : 30 secondes
Temps de réponse : 60 secondes

→ **explication**

Exemple de réponse

Fungi are full of some very important organisms beneficial to the human race. Today, people use fungi for the production of food such as wine, beer and cheese. Fungi are also an important source of food protein and fiber and contain important digestive proteins. They are also consumed in the form of mushrooms and truffles around the world. Some even boil fungi to use them as hallucinogens in religious ceremonies. However, the most important role of fungi remains its use as an antibiotic which is by far the most important medical discovery of all times.

Évaluation de l'exemple de réponse

Remarques générales / niveau CECRL	Le candidat répond de façon claire et cohérente à la question posée. Il y a quelques fautes mineures, qui ne viennent pas entraver la compréhension de la production orale du candidat. Le niveau de compétence du candidat correspond approximativement au niveau C1 du CECRL et la qualité de la production orale serait égale à un 4/4 dans le système de score du TOEFL iBT.
Respect des consignes	Le candidat répond correctement à la question en se concentrant sur les thèmes introduits et sans répéter plus d'une fois le même concept.
Structure de la réponse	Le candidat commence par une phrase introductive qui pose les bases de son argumentation. Il énumère ensuite chaque argument, qu'il illustre par un exemple, ce qui améliore la compréhension de la production orale. On retrouve les grands axes développés dans la conférence, ce qui démontre la capacité du candidat à comprendre un document audio.
Maîtrise de la langue	Le candidat fait preuve d'une maîtrise avancée de la langue anglaise tout au long de sa production orale. Les phrases sont bien construites et l'utilisation des transitions rend l'oral facile à suivre. Seulement une petite erreur dans la dernière phrase : *the most important role of fungi remains* ***their*** *use as an antibiotic.* Attention, *fungi* est un nom pluriel (le singulier est *fungus*).
Pour aller plus loin	Le débit de parole du candidat doit être naturel, et il est préferable d'éviter de trop nombreuses marques d'hésitation (hum, etc.). Ce dernier ne doit pas être ni trop lent, ni trop rapide.

Mini-TOEFL iBT - WRITING - Solutions

Utilisez la grille ci-dessous pour vous auto-évaluer puis multipliez par 6 pour obtenir une note sur 30.

5 points	On retrouve toutes les caractéristiques suivantes : • réponse efficace à la question • bien organisés et développés, les arguments sont expliqués et soutenus par des détails/exemples • vocabulaire et grammaire variés. Bon niveau d'anglais même si le texte contient quelques erreurs mineures
4 points	On retrouve toutes les caractéristiques suivantes : • réponse efficace à la question même si certains points ne sont pas élaborés. Le texte peut être un peu redondant • bien organisés et développés, les arguments sont expliqués et soutenus par des détails/exemples • vocabulaire et grammaire variés. Le texte contient des erreurs mineures qui n'empèchent pas la compréhension
3 points	On retrouve au moins l'une des caractéristiques suivantes : • réponse à la question avec des explications développées et des détails/exemples • le texte est cohérent et organisé même si certaines idées ne sont pas bien liées entre elles • les mauvaises formations syntaxiques rendent certains passages difficiles à comprendre • la grammaire et le vocabulaire sont corrects mais avec peu de variété
2 points	On retrouve au moins l'une des faiblesses suivantes : • réponse courte et peu développée • texte mal organisé, mauvaises connexions entre les idées • arguments non développés, peu de détails/exemples. Trop de généralisations • vocabulaire inexacte ou inapproprié • nombreuses erreurs de grammaire
1 point	On retrouve au moins l'une des faiblesses suivantes : • texte complétement désorganisé • détails inexistants ou hors-sujets • erreurs grammaticales fréquentes et graves
0 point	• pas de réponse ou réponse hors-sujet • recopiage de quelques mots du sujet • écrit dans une autre langue que l'anglais

Nous avons pour projet de mettre en ligne un service de correction personnalisée pour les épreuves d'expression orale et écrite. Ce service fera appel à des correcteurs expérimentés qui vous attribueront une note en suivant les critères du TOEFL iBT. La correction détaillée incluera des conseils personnalisés pour vous améliorer. À l'heure où vous lirez ce manuel, le service sera peut-être déjà en ligne sur http://www.prepmyfuture.com/toefl

Réponse type

Reportez vos réponses pour analyser votre performance.

Entraînez-vous dans les conditions d'examen.

prepmyfuture.com/book/68/ex/1912

question 1 | q. ouverte

Question 1 - Solution

DIRECTIONS: You have 20 minutes to plan and write your response. Your response will be evaluated on the quality of your writing on how well you present the points in the lecture and their relationship to the reading passage. Typically, an effective response will have 150 to 225 words.

Summarize the points made in the lecture, being sure to explain how they contradict specific points made in the reading passage.

FR :

CONSIGNES : *Donnez-vous 20 minutes pour planifier et rédiger votre réponse. Votre réponse sera jugée sur la qualité de l'écriture et sur la façon dont elle présente les points du cours et leur relation avec le passage lu. En général, une réponse efficace comptera entre 150 et 225 mots. Vous pouvez consulter le passage à lire pendant que vous répondez.*

Temps de réponse : 20 minutes

QUESTION : *Résumez les points soulevés dans la conférence, en veillant à expliquer comment ils remettent en question certains points spécifiques du passage lu.*

⇨ **explication**

Exemple de réponse

The history of the Sphinx has been challenged. First, the Sphinx's features are much stronger than that of Pharaoh Khafre. His ears and jaw are not similar to Pharaoh Khafre's **features** , which are less pronounced. They also have radically different profiles, unlike that of other statues dedicated to Khafre. Furthermore, the headdress worn by the Sphinx does not appear to have been styled after Kahfre. It is thus unclear that the Sphinx was built on the orders of Khafre, as some modern Egyptologists have suggested. While a causeway does connect the Sphinx to the pyramid of Khafre, that causeway is built at an angle which points to a lack of construction planning.

The Sphinx is also the only monument of the Giza **plateau** showing severe **erosions**. Thus, the Sphinx probably belongs to an older time period than other monuments of **the** Giza. Further research demonstrates that the name **k**hafre does not actually appear on the "Dream Stele" plaque. That plaque only shows a portion of a name starting with "Khaf", which could belong to any other Pharaoh. A different plaque was unearthed in Giza, stating that Khafre's grandfather found the Sphinx buried in the sand. With all this data, it is possible that the Sphinx actually had no direct relationship with Kahfre and also dates back thousands of years older.

(219 words)

Évaluation de l'exemple de réponse

Remarques générales / niveau CERCL	Le candidat rédige une analyse cohérente et convaincante des arguments énoncés dans les documents concernant l'origine du Sphinx. En résumant ces points de manière appropriée, le candidat prouve qu'il a une maîtrise adéquate des principales compétences analytiques (lecture et écoute). Le niveau de compétence du candidat correspond approximativement au niveau C1 du CECRL et la qualité du texte écrit serait égale à un 4/5 dans le système de score du TOEFL iBT.
Forme	Le candidat a structuré son essai en deux paragraphes. L'essai aurait pu être mieux structuré, notamment grâce à une phrase d'introduction, qui manque ici. De plus, le candidat aurait pu organiser ses arguments de manière plus claire afin de montrer qu'il est capable non seulement de comprendre des documents, mais également de structurer sa pensée.
Variété et précision du vocabulaire	Le candidat démontre une bonne maîtrise de la langue anglaise. Ses phrases sont bien structurées, quoique parfois un peu courtes. Un éventail plus large de vocabulaire aurait pu être utilisé afin d'éviter les répétitions.
Grammaire, cohésion et cohérence	Aucune faute majeure de conjugaison n'a été faite, ce qui est un bon point. Le candidat a employé des connecteurs pour lier ses phrases entre elles (*Furthermore, while, thus, etc.) ce qui fluidifie son propos. Enfin, le candidat ne formule pas d'arguments contradictoires, preuve de sa bonne compréhension des documents.*
Pour aller plus loin	Le candidat parvient à rapporter objectivement le contenu de la lecture et de l'exposé sans laisser ses opinions personnelles sur le sujet (dans ce cas, l'histoire du Sphinx) influencer la structure ou le contenu de sa production écrite.

Réponse corrigée

The history of the Sphinx has been challenged **over the past few years**. First, the Sphinx's features are much stronger than that of Pharaoh Khafre. His ears and jaw are not similar to Pharaoh Khafre's **physical traits**, which are less pronounced. They also have radically different profiles, unlike that of other statues dedicated to Khafre. Furthermore, the headdress worn by the Sphinx does not appear to have been styled after Khafre. It is thus unclear that the Sphinx was built on the orders of Khafre, as some modern Egyptologists have suggested. While a causeway does connect the Sphinx to the pyramid of Khafre, that causeway **was** built at an angle which points to a lack of construction planning.

The Sphinx is also the only monument of the Giza showing severe **signs of erosion**. Thus, the Sphinx probably belongs to an older time period than other monuments of Giza. Further research demonstrates that the name Khafre does not actually appear on the "Dream Stele" plaque. That plaque only shows a portion of a name starting with "Khaf", which could belong to any other Pharaoh. A different plaque was unearthed in Giza, stating that Khafre's grandfather found the Sphinx buried in the sand. With all this data, it is possible that the Sphinx actually had no direct relationship with Khafre and also dates back thousands of years older than we thought.

Exemple de réponse améliorée

The history of the Sphinx has been a source of ongoing debate for centuries since it is still unsure how old the monument really is, and whom it was ordered by. While Egyptologists used to think the Sphinx was built on the orders of - and to resemble - Pharaoh Khafre, there is now evidence that seems to prove otherwise.

Indeed, when looked at from the side, it becomes clear that the Sphinx and Pharaoh Khafre have different physical features (in particular when paying attention to the Sphinx' ears and jaw). Besides, while the Sphinx was portrayed with a ceremonial beard, thus highlighting the reference to kingship, Egyptologists point out that it could be a reference to any Pharaoh, not just Khafre. Another element which was brought down by modern Egyptologists is the absence of planning as to where the Sphinx and the Pyramids were built, since it appears that, unlike what was thought up until recently, the Pyramids were built much later than the Sphinx.

Indeed, questions also arose as to the age of the Sphinx: the signs of erosion found on the statue, unlike on other monuments on the Giza plateau, are yet another piece of evidence that the Sphinx was actually built long before the reign of Pharaoh Khafre.

In the end, it seems like much of what specialists believed about the Sphinx erodes as time goes, and new theories suggest that the monumental Sphinx was constructed further back in ancient times in Egypt.

Méthodes et Stratégies

SECTION - READING

Méthode

Présentation générale

Durée	• 54 minutes si l'épreuve comporte 3 textes • 72 minutes si l'épreuve comporte 4 textes
Nombre de questions	10 questions par texte, soit : • 30 questions si l'épreuve comporte 3 textes • 40 questions si l'épreuve comporte 4 textes
Nombre de mots par texte	environ 700 mots
Déroulement de l'épreuve	Chaque exercice commence par la lecture du texte. Ensuite les questions s'affichent une à une sur la moitié de la page, vous avez toujours accès au texte sur l'autre moitié de la page. Vous pouvez revenir en arrière et changer vos réponses tout au long de la partie *Reading*.
Consignes officielles	*This section measures your ability to understand academic passages in English. You can skip questions and go back to them later as long as there is time remaining.* *Now begin the Reading section.* *Directions: Read the passage. Then answer the questions.* FR : Cette section mesure votre capacité à comprendre des passages académiques en anglais. Vous pouvez sauter des questions et y revenir plus tard, tant qu'il reste du temps. Commencez maintenant la section Compréhension écrite. Consignes : Lisez le passage. Répondez ensuite aux questions.
Notation	0 à 30 points (25 % de la note finale)

Présentation détaillée

Thèmes des textes

Les textes sont extraits de manuels scolaires de niveau universitaire. Ils traitent de sujets enseignés à l'université : histoire, sciences, sociologie, littérature, etc.

Le thème du texte n'est pas important et n'aura pas d'impact sur votre performance que vous connaissiez le sujet ou non. Sachez que pour figurer dans l'examen officiel, chaque question est testée auprès d'un échantillon représentatif de testeurs. Pour être retenue, une question doit garder la même proportion de bonnes réponses auprès de testeurs d'origines diverses (culturelles, sociologiques, disciplinaires, etc.) Même si vous connaissez bien le sujet du texte, cela ne vous aidera pas beaucoup pour répondre aux questions, le test est conçu de cette manière.

Les questions

Les questions ne testent pas seulement votre compréhension de l'anglais. Le TOEFL est aussi un test d'aptitude qui évalue vos capacités en logique. Il est utilisé par les universités américaines pour sélectionner les meilleurs étudiants que ce soit sur leur niveau d'anglais ou sur leur capacité à comprendre des phrases compliquées. Gardez en tête que les questions de la partie *Reading* du TOEFL sont difficiles même pour un anglophone.

Voici quelques exemples de capacités testées par le TOEFL :

- La capacité à deviner le sens d'un mot à partir de son contexte.
- La capacité à paraphraser l'opinion d'un auteur.
- La capacité à résumer les idées principales d'un texte.
- La rapidité de lecture.
- La mémoire et l'attention au détail.

La quasi-totalité des questions est de type QCM avec 1 seule bonne réponse parmi 4 choix de réponse, ces questions valent le même nombre de points. Certaines questions comptent double (cela est clairement indiqué lorsque c'est le cas).

Dans certains textes, la dernière question est atypique, compte double et nécessite de faire un résumé du texte en sélectionnant 3 phrases parmi 6 propositions (voir la fiche Prose Summary questions).

Stratégies

Conseil n°1 : Bien connaître les questions types

Les concepteurs des questions officielles doivent suivre un cahier des charges précis pour créer les questions. Il y a donc un nombre limité de types de questions. Les questions de même type sont toutes structurées de la même façon. Connaître les différents types de questions et les méthodes qui permettent de les résoudre vous permettra de gagner des points et du temps. Nous analyserons plus loin dans cette partie chaque type de questions.

Pour chaque question, vous devrez rapidement :

1. Identifier le type de question.
2. Appliquer la stratégie de résolution correspondant à ce type de question.

Au cours de votre entraînement, vous allez développer des automatismes qui vous permettront de gagner en efficacité. Au début, ces méthodes vous paraîtront rébarbatives mais, avec l'entraînement, vous les appliquerez rapidement sans même réfléchir.

Conseil n°2 : Savoir gérer son temps et s'entraîner à lire en diagonale

La plupart des questions ne nécessitent pas de comprendre le texte dans son ensemble. De plus, la grande majorité des questions nécessite de relire des détails du texte pour être certain de sa réponse, et cela même si vous avez effectué une bonne première lecture.

Dans ce contexte, la gestion du temps est difficile pour répondre aux 10 questions associées à chaque texte en moins de 18 minutes.

1re méthode : pour les personnes arrivant à finir dans les temps

1. Effectuez une première lecture rapide du texte. N'essayez pas de faire une lecture approfondie du texte lors de la première lecture. Il faut lire en diagonale, retenir les idées principales, identifier le contenu de chaque paragraphe et comprendre le point de vue de l'auteur.
2. Répondez aux questions, vous retournerez vers le texte pour chercher des détails si nécessaire.

2e méthode : pour les personnes ne parvenant pas à finir dans les temps

1. Vous ne réalisez pas de première lecture et allez directement à la première question.
2. Après avoir lu la première question vous commencez la lecture du texte. Il n'est pas nécessaire de lire les choix de réponse, concentrez-vous uniquement sur la question avant d'entamer la lecture du texte.
3. Vous devez lire le texte jusqu'au passage concerné par la question. Une fois le passage du texte identifié, retournez à la question, lisez les choix de réponse et répondez.
4. Dès que vous avez répondu à la question, vous lisez l'énoncé de la deuxième question et reprenez votre lecture jusqu'à ce que vous ayez suffisamment d'éléments pour répondre à la deuxième question.
5. Reproduisez la méthode pour chaque question.

La seconde méthode demande de l'entraînement, mais peut être très efficace si vous manquez de temps en utilisant la première méthode. En effet, la plupart des questions ne nécessitent pas une lecture complète du texte. Ces questions sont faciles à identifier (vocabulaire, référence et paraphrase ainsi que la plupart des questions de détails). Si vous manquez de temps, répondez à ces questions en priorité.

Par ailleurs, vous gagnerez toujours du temps en essayant de prédire la bonne réponse avant de lire les choix de réponses. Ainsi, vous passerez moins de temps à éliminer les choix de réponse un à un, il vous suffit de reconnaître la bonne réponse parmi les choix proposés.

Enfin, n'oubliez pas de répondre à toutes les questions avant la fin du temps imparti, car il n'y a pas de point négatif pour les mauvaises réponses.

N.B. : Il est possible que votre partie *Reading* comporte 4 passages au lieu de 3. Dans ce cas, vous bénéficierez de 18 minutes supplémentaires. Les concepteurs introduisent en effet des exercices supplémentaires dans les parties *Reading* et *Listening* pour tester de nouvelles questions. Dans ce cas, les questions testées ne compteront pas dans le calcul de votre score. Si votre épreuve comporte 4 textes, il ne sera pas possible d'identifier le passage qui ne comptera pas, il faudra donc répondre à toutes les questions avec la même attention aux détails.

Conseil n°3 : Procéder par élimination lorsque nécessaire

Lorsque vous n'êtes pas en mesure de trouver immédiatement la bonne réponse, vous devez procéder par élimination. De plus, si vous êtes à l'aise sur le temps, vérifiez vos réponses au fur à mesure en analysant les choix de réponse un à un.

Certains choix de réponse ne sont pas forcément entièrement faux. Inversement, la bonne réponse peut sembler imparfaite. Il faut garder en tête qu'au TOEFL, il n'y a qu'une seule bonne réponse, vous devez donc choisir celle qui vous paraît meilleure ou « moins mauvaise » que les autres.

La manière la plus efficace d'éliminer des propositions de réponse est de connaître leur structure. Vous pourrez ainsi savoir sur quels arguments éliminer les mauvaises propositions. Il vous suffira de classifier chaque proposition de réponse dans une catégorie. Nous classifions les types de mauvaises réponses dans le paragraphe qui suit.

Conseil n°4 : Connaître la structure des mauvaises réponses

La quasi-totalité des mauvaises propositions de réponse rentre dans l'une des catégories suivantes :

1. **Contresens :** Le concepteur fabrique un choix de réponse en contradiction avec ce qui est écrit dans le passage. Il s'agit souvent d'une inversion entre deux choses ou deux personnes. Ces choix de réponse sont faciles à éliminer si vous avez compris le texte.

2. **Inexact / Exagération :** Le choix de réponse ne correspond pas exactement à ce qui est écrit dans le passage. Ces réponses sont plus difficiles à identifier. Souvent ce type de réponse utilise des adverbes clivants et exagérés comme : *always, any, too much, never,* etc. Dès que vous identifiez ce type de vocabulaire, vous devez vous méfier, il s'agit sans doute d'une mauvaise réponse.

3. **Extrapolation :** C'est le type de réponse le plus courant et le plus facile à traiter si vous avez lu le texte entièrement. Dans ces choix de réponse, le concepteur indique quelque chose qui n'est pas mentionné dans le texte.

4. **Incomplet :** Dans ce type de réponse, l'information est vraie, mais n'est pas représentative de l'idée principale du texte. Il s'agit généralement d'un détail alors que la question vous demande l'idée générale. N'oubliez pas qu'au TOEFL, on vous demande de trouver la meilleure réponse et pas une réponse correcte.

5. **Ne répond pas à la question :** Dans ce type de réponse, l'affirmation est vraie, mais elle est hors sujet. Ainsi il faut vous assurer que le choix de réponse répond bien à la question. Les concepteurs vous tendent des pièges en répétant certaines informations du texte, mais ces informations peuvent être sans lien avec la question posée.

Conseil n°5 : S'entraîner à lire des textes de « type TOEFL »

Les passages du TOEFL iBT sont longs et souvent ennuyeux. L'épreuve étant longue, la gestion de votre concentration est clef pour votre réussite. Il y a deux manières de devenir meilleur dans la gestion de sa concentration :

1. **Appliquer une méthode de manière systématique :** L'application systématique d'une méthode vous permet d'éviter de perdre le fil. En effet, la méthode vous permettra de garder un rythme régulier. Une fois que vous maîtrisez le rythme de l'examen, vous serez capable de savoir si vous êtes dans les temps.

2. **S'entraîner à lire des textes de « type TOEFL » :** Les deux meilleures sources sont les manuels scolaires universitaires américains et la revue *The Economist*.

Conseil n°6 : Maîtriser les mots de liaison

Les mots de liaison (connecteurs logiques) sont essentiels pour la compréhension des textes. Les maîtriser vous permettra d'éviter de nombreux pièges. Il s'agit du seul type de vocabulaire que vous êtes sûr de trouver dans les textes. Connaître les connecteurs logiques sera aussi très utile pour la partie expression écrite pour structurer vos essais.

Vous trouverez la liste des mots de liaison dans la section « Grammaire ».

Exemple

Reportez vos réponses pour analyser votre performance.

Entraînez-vous dans les conditions d'examen.

prepmyfuture.com/book/68/ex/1919

18th Century Travel

[P1] Some people never saw new places, never traveled any distance in their entire lives. People often recalled family members who lived into their eighties or nineties and never traveled very far from their homes. Ten miles was considered far by many and distances such as thirty and forty miles were often the farthest traveled in a lifetime. Even though most people traveled very little, others did voyage a great deal to see friends and family and on business. Transportation was very primitive and the fastest way to go from one place to another was by a galloping horse.

[P2] Most people walked when they needed to go anywhere, usually over considerable distances and in terrible conditions. Even those with horses often walked a great deal. Due to the great distances covered on foot, many people would calculate how far they traveled to take into account physical ailments. Nobody would voyage too far if they had a bad knee or suffered from arthritis. As a result, many people would not travel great distances by foot. Some adventurers of the period, such as Carl Mortiz, did go on long excursions but he was an exception. In addition to the challenges of muddy footpaths, primitive pathways and physical ailments, laws limiting the movement of people were strictly enforced. Throughout England there were pauper laws, which stipulated that paupers could not travel long distances. If a person was found outside of their parish, or district, without sufficient funds, they were arrested and forced to return. Frequently when people arrived at inns without a horse, they were often treated with contempt.

[P3] Traveling by foot was demanding and there were many obstacles along the path. Many people preferred to travel by **well-worn** routes as opposed to remote paths; short-cuts were typically avoided at all cost. Travelers often found that paths contained mantraps. These traps had two strong steel jaws, often with serrated edges, which snapped shut by means of powerful springs when someone stepped on the pressure plate between the jaws. They were typically hidden in the grass and brush and used as deterrents. People were often seriously injured either with broken legs or deep nasty cuts. Other obstacles included spring guns that were wired to a trigger. The gun was fired whenever someone had the misfortune of stepping on the trip wire.

[P4] **When deterrents such as traps and spring guns were laid, being on horseback was no better than walking, but even on the open road, there were always perils on horseback**. Horses demanded a great deal of care. Carts and carriages, like modern vehicles also required maintenance. But horses needed food and water, stabling, grooming, harnesses and veterinary care and most importantly they needed shoes. These were not a problem near home, because there were always familiar blacksmiths, but a cross-country traveler might run into difficulties. Despite the obvious disadvantage of horses, they, along with other pack animals, were often the only option for haulage in some parts of England. Roads and paths were often narrow and winding, making it impossible for carts or carriages to pass. If the roads were better suited, goods were transported in carrier carts and wagons. Long-distance carriers made cross-country trips using large wagons pulled by six or eight horses. Some stagecoaches operated in the same way. Both had to frequently change horses at wayside stops. Stagecoaches did their best to attract passengers by claiming to be the fastest service around. This was false advertising of course, because their speed was usually slower than walking pace.

[P5] A single household might own horses as well as a cart for passenger travel that doubled to transport goods. The cart was often used to move dung, hay, timber, coal and other items. Wealthy gentry and the aristocracy would own at least one carriage that was **solely** for passengers, but their horses might be used for riding and farm work as well. Only the very rich could afford the cost of keeping large, enclosed carriages, along with several horses and servants.

Glossary
wayside: the edge of a road, way, path or highway

▪ Question 1 According to paragraph 1, which of the following is true about traveling in the 18th century?

(A) People traveled the furthest by foot.
(B) Some people never traveled far distances in their entire lives.
(C) The most common means of transport was by horse.
(D) Steam engines were used to transport people.

▪ Question 2 People traveled because:

(A) they wanted to avoid poor weather
(B) they had family, friends and business that were faraway
(C) they liked to ride in stagecoaches
(D) they owned several horses

▪ Question 3 The word "well-worn" (paragraph 3) in the passage is closest in meaning to:

(A) brand-new
(B) close
(C) fashionable
(D) old

▪ Question 4 Which of the following sentences best describes the highlighted sentence in the passage? The other choices change the meaning or leave out information.

(A) Horseback riding was dangerous in remote areas but not on main routes.
(B) Riding a horse in the woods was easy but on a main path it was difficult.
(C) Horseback riding lead to traps and guns.
(D) Walking and horseback riding were equally dangerous.

▪ Question 5 According to paragraph 3, mantraps were dangerous for all of the following reasons EXCEPT:

(A) They were often hidden in the grass and impossible to see.
(B) They possessed powerful, jagged edges and frequently broke legs.
(C) They triggered a gun to scare away the horses.
(D) They usually struck pedestrians when they stepped on them.

▪ Question 6 Why does the author mention the pauper laws in paragraph 2?

(A) to discuss a reason why some people traveled on horseback
(B) to argue that laws were strict in the 18th century compared to modern day
(C) to continue the discussion of the many obstacles people faced while traveling
(D) to contrast the ways in which rich people and poor people traveled

■ Question 7 The word "solely" (paragraph 5) in the passage is closest in meaning to:

(A) partially
(B) only
(C) incomparably
(D) simply

■ Question 8 According to paragraph 4, what can be inferred about haulage options?

(A) Horses, while high maintenance, were sometimes the only option for transporting goods.
(B) Carts and carriers were used to haul goods especially when paths were winding and steep.
(C) Haulage was usually over short distances with horses.
(D) Stagecoaches sometimes helped with transportation of goods.

■ Question 9 Look at the four squares, **A**, **B**, **C**, and **D**, which indicate where the following sentence could be added to paragraph 2. Where would the sentence best fit?

Traveling in general was conspicuous and often only those who could afford a horse even ventured on a journey.

[P2] Most people walked when they needed to go anywhere, usually over considerable distances and in terrible conditions. Even those with horses often walked a great deal. **A** Due to the great distances covered on foot, many people would calculate how far they traveled to take into account physical ailments. Nobody would voyage too far if they had a bad knee or suffered from arthritis. As a result, many people would not travel great distances by foot. Some adventurers of the period, such as Carl Mortiz, did go on long excursions but he was an exception. **B** In addition to the challenges of mud, primitive pathways and physical ailments, laws limiting the movement of people were strictly enforced. **C** Throughout England there were pauper laws, which stipulated that paupers could not travel long distances. If a person was found outside of their parish, or district, without sufficient funds, they were arrested and forced to return. Frequently when people arrived at inns without a horse, they were often treated with contempt. **D**

(A) **A**
(B) **B**
(C) **C**
(D) **D**

■ Question 10 Directions: An introductory sentence for a brief summary of the passage is provided below. Complete the summary by selecting the THREE answer choices that express the most important ideas in the passage. Some sentences do not belong in the summary because they express ideas that are not presented in the passage or are minor ideas in the passage. This question is worth 2 points.

- 18th century people didn't usually travel much, nor did they cover long distances.
-
-
-

(A) Traveling was not easy and people had to possess some wealth and be healthy.

(B) Due to the poor conditions in which people had to travel, most of them suffered from physical ailments.

(C) Mantraps were used in order to prevent people from taking the main roads.

(D) Travelers could encounter several obstacles along the way, some of which were deadly

(E) Poor people could only afford horses, because they needed less maintenance than carriages.

(F) Horses were used to reach those places otherwise inaccessible by carriage and not many people owned both.

Solutions

Reportez vos réponses pour analyser votre performance.

Entraînez-vous dans les conditions d'examen.

prepmyfuture.com/book/68/ex/1919

question 1	B	question 3	D	question 5	C	question 7	B	question 9	B
question 2	B	question 4	D	question 6	C	question 8	A	question 10	A D F

Question 1 - Solution

According to paragraph 1, which of the following is true about traveling in the 18th century?

FR : Laquelle de ces propositions est vraie à propos des voyages au 18e siècle ?

(A) People traveled the furthest by foot.
= Les gens se déplaçaient le plus loin à pied.
piège avec le superlatif (the furthest)

(B) ✓ Some people never traveled far distances in their entire lives.
= Certaines personnes n'ont jamais voyagé sur de longues distances de toute leur vie.
« Some people never saw new places, never traveled any distance in their entire lives ». (= « Certaines personnes n'ont jamais vu de nouveaux espaces, n'ont jamais voyagé de toute leur vie. ») (paragraphe 1, ligne 1)

(C) The most common means of transport was by horse.
= Le moyen de transport le plus courant était le cheval.
« ...the fastest way to go from one place to another was by a galloping horse. » (= « ...le moyen le plus rapide d'aller d'un endroit à un autre était un cheval au galop. »)

(D) Steam engines were used to transport people.
= Les moteurs à vapeur étaient utilisés pour transporter les personnes.
Les machines à vapeur (steam engines) sont évoquées pour parler de la puissance et pas comme un moyen de transport.

Question 2 - Solution

People traveled because:

FR : Les gens voyageaient car :

(A)	they wanted to avoid poor weather	= Ils voulaient éviter le mauvais temps. *Les gens ne voyageaient pas à cause du mauvais temps.* *« When weather was exceptionally bad most middle- and upper- class women avoided going out at all. » (= « Lorsque le temps était exceptionnellement mauvais, la plupart des femmes des classes moyennes et aisées évitaient de sortir »)*
(B) ✓	**they had family, friends and business that were faraway**	**= Ils avaient de la famille, des amis et des affaires loin d'eux.** ***« … most people traveled very little, others did voyage a great deal to see friends and family and on business… » (= « ... la plupart des gens voyageaient très peu, d'autres voyageaient beaucoup pour voir leurs amis et leur famille et pour les affaires. »)***
(C)	they liked to ride in stagecoaches	= Ils aimaient monter dans les diligences. *Bien que les diligences (stagecoaches) étaient utilisées pour le transport de passagers, il n'est pas dit dans le texte que les passagers préféraient ce moyen de transport.*
(D)	they owned several horses	= Ils possédaient plusieurs chevaux. *La possession de chevaux est présentée comme une réalité de la vie au XVIIIe siècle. Ils étaient utilisés pour d'autres buts que le voyage.*

▪ Question 3 - Solution

The word "well-worn" (paragraph 4) in the passage is closest in meaning to:

FR : Le mot « well-worn » dans le passage est plus proche du sens de :

(A)	brand-new	= neuf
(B)	close	= proche
(C)	fashionable	= à la mode
(D) ✓	**old**	**= vieux**

▪ Question 4 - Solution

Which of the following sentences best describes the highlighted sentence in the passage? The other choices change the meaning or leave out information.

FR : Laquelle des phrases suivantes décrit le mieux la phrase surlignée dans le passage ? Les autres choix modifient le sens ou omettent des informations.

(A)	Horseback riding was dangerous in remote areas but not on main routes.	= Monter à cheval était dangereux dans les régions éloignées mais pas sur les routes principales. *Le texte dit l'inverse : « even on the open road » (ici « open road » est un synonyme de « main road »)*
(B)	Riding a horse in the woods was easy but on a main path it was difficult.	= Monter à cheval dans les bois était facile mais sur un chemin principal, c'était difficile. *Le texte dit l'inverse.*
(C)	Horseback riding lead to traps and guns.	= Monter à cheval menait à des pièges. *Le passage évoque les pièges (traps et spring guns) pour dire qu'il sont dangereux soit pour les cavaliers soit pour les piétons mais pas pour établir un lien entre les cavaliers et les pièges.*
(D)	✓ **Walking and horseback riding were equally dangerous.**	**= La marche et le cheval étaient aussi dangereux l'un que l'autre.** ***« being on horseback was no better than walking » (= « être à cheval n'était pas mieux que de marcher »)***

⇝ **explication**

Traduction de la phrase

FR: Quand il y avait quelque chose de dissuasif posé sur la route comme des pièges et des fusils piégés, être à cheval n'était pas mieux que de voyager à pied; mais même sur la grande route, voyager à cheval présentait toujours des dangers

▪ Question 5 - Solution

According to paragraph 3, mantraps were dangerous for all of the following reasons EXCEPT:

FR : Selon le paragraphe 4, les pièges étaient dangereux pour toutes ces raisons À L'EXCEPTION DE :

(A)	They were often hidden in the grass and impossible to see.	= Ils étaient souvent cachés dans l'herbe et impossibles à distinguer. *« [Mantraps] were typically hidden in the grass and brush and used as deterrents. » (= « [Les mantraps] étaient généralement cachés dans l'herbe et les broussailles et utilisés comme moyens de dissuasion. »)*
(B)	They possessed powerful, jagged edges and frequently broke legs.	= Ils possédaient des bords puissants et dentelés et brisaient souvent les jambes. *« These traps had two strong steel jaws, often with serrated edges, which snapped shut by means of powerful springs when someone stepped on the pressure plate between the jaws »; « People were often seriously injured either with broken legs or deep nasty cuts. »* *(= « Ces pièges étaient munis de deux mâchoires en acier solide, souvent dentelées, qui se refermaient grâce à de puissants ressorts lorsque quelqu'un marchait sur la plaque de pression située entre les mâchoires » ; « Les gens étaient souvent gravement blessés, soit par des jambes cassées, soit par des coupures profondes et méchantes. »)*
(C)	**✓ They triggered a gun to scare away the horses.**	**= Ils actionnaient un pistolet pour faire fuir les chevaux.**
(D)	They usually struck pedestrians when they stepped on them.	= Ils heurtaient généralement les piétons en leur marchant dessus. *« [Mantraps] had two strong steel jaws, often with serrated edges, which snapped shut by means of powerful springs when someone stepped on the pressure plate between the jaws. »* *(= « Les mantraps avaient deux solides mâchoires en acier, souvent dentelées, qui se refermaient à l'aide de puissants ressorts lorsque quelqu'un marchait sur la plaque de pression entre les mâchoires »)*

▪ Question 6 - Solution

Why does the author mention the pauper laws in paragraph 2?

FR : Pourquoi l'auteur mentionne-t-il les lois pour les pauvres dans le 2ᵉ paragraphe ?

(A)	to discuss a reason why some people traveled on horseback	= pour expliquer pourquoi certaines personnes voyageaient à cheval *Les gens voyageaient avec et sans les chevaux. Il est vrai qu'un cheval était un symbole de richesse, mais même les gens riches voyageaient à pied.*
(B)	to argue that laws were strict in the 18th century compared to modern day	= pour démontrer que les lois étaient plus strictes au 18e siècle que de nos jours *Le passage précise que les lois étaient strictes mais il ne mentionne pas les lois d'aujourd'hui.*
(C) ✓	**to continue the discussion of the many obstacles people faced while traveling**	**= pour poursuivre la discussion sur les nombreux obstacles que les gens rencontraient lorsqu'ils voyageaient** ***« In addition to the challenges of mud, primitive pathways and physical aliments, laws limiting the movement of people were strictly enforced. »*** ***(= « Plus encore que les défis de la boue, des chemins mal entretenus et des obstacles, il y avait des lois qui limitaient le mouvement des personnes et elles étaient strictement suivies. »)***
(D)	to contrast the ways in which rich people and poor people traveled	= pour comparer la façon dont les riches et les pauvres voyageaient

▪ Question 7 - Solution

The word "solely" (paragraph 5) in the passage is closest in meaning to:

FR : Le mot « solely » dans le 2e paragraphe est plus proche du sens de :

(A)	partially	= partiellement
(B) ✓	**only**	**= seulement**
(C)	incomparably	= incomparablement
(D)	simply	= simplement

▪ Question 8 - Solution

According to paragraph 4, what can be inferred about haulage options?

FR : Selon le paragraphe 4, que peut-on déduire à propos des moyens de transport des marchandises ?

(A)	✓ **Horses, while high maintenance, were sometimes the only option for transporting goods.**	**= Les chevaux, bien que nécessitant beaucoup d'entretien, étaient parfois la seule option pour le transport des marchandises.** ***« Despite the obvious disadvantage of horses, they, along with other pack animals, were often the only option for haulage in some parts of England. »*** ***(= « Malgré les inconvénients manifestes des chevaux, ils étaient souvent, avec d'autres animaux de bât, la seule option pour le transport dans certaines régions d'Angleterre. »)***
(B)	Carts and carriers were used to haul goods especially when paths were winding and steep.	= Les charrettes et les porteurs étaient utilisés pour transporter les marchandises, surtout lorsque les chemins étaient sinueux et escarpés. *Les chariots et les calèches n'étaient pas utilisés quand les chemins étaient escarpés et sinueux.*
(C)	Haulage was usually over short distances with horses.	= Le transport se faisait généralement sur de courtes distances avec des chevaux.
(D)	Stagecoaches sometimes helped with transportation of goods.	= Les diligences aidaient parfois au transport des marchandises. *Le passage ne mentionne pas les diligences et le transport de marchandises ensemble.*

■ **Question 9 - Solution**

Look at the four squares, **A**, **B**, **C**, and **D**, which indicate where the following sentence could be added to paragraph 2. Where would the sentence best fit?

Traveling in general was conspicuous and often only those who could afford a horse even ventured on a journey.

[P2] Most people walked when they needed to go anywhere, usually over considerable distances and in terrible conditions. Even those with horses often walked a great deal. **A** Due to the great distances covered on foot, many people would calculate how far they traveled to take into account physical ailments. Nobody would voyage too far if they had a bad knee or suffered from arthritis. As a result, many people would not travel great distances by foot. Some adventurers of the period, such as Carl Mortiz, did go on long excursions but he was an exception. **B** In addition to the challenges of mud, primitive pathways and physical ailments, laws limiting the movement of people were strictly enforced. **C** Throughout England there were pauper laws, which stipulated that paupers could not travel long distances. If a person was found outside of their parish, or district, without sufficient funds, they were arrested and forced to return. Frequently when people arrived at inns without a horse, they were often treated with contempt. **D**

(A) **A** *La phrase suivante introduit les problèmes liés aux longues distances parcourues à pied et non pas à cheval.*

(B) ✓ **B** ***La phrase justifie parfaitement l'exception mentionnée dans la phrase précédente, clarifiant le fait que malgré les longs voyages de Carl Moritz, les voyageurs rencontraient des obstacles même en étant à cheval.***

(C) **C** *n'a pas de lien avec la phrase qui précède et celle qui suit*

(D) **D** *n'a pas lien avec la phrase qui précède et celle qui suit*

⇒ **explication**

FR : « Les voyages en général étaient ostentatoires et souvent, seuls ceux qui pouvaient s'offrir un cheval s'aventuraient à voyager. »

▪ Question 10 - Solution

Directions: An introductory sentence for a brief summary of the passage is provided below. Complete the summary by selecting the THREE answer choices that express the most important ideas in the passage. Some sentences do not belong in the summary because they express ideas that are not presented in the passage or are minor ideas in the passage. This question is worth 2 points.

- 18th century people didn't usually travel much, nor did they cover long distances.
-
-
-

(A)	✓ **Traveling was not easy and people had to possess some wealth and be healthy.**	**= Voyager n'était pas facile et les gens devaient posséder des richesses et être en bonne santé.** ***Bon résumé du deuxième paragraphe.***
(B)	Due to the poor conditions in which people had to travel, most of them suffered from physical ailments.	= En raison des mauvaises conditions dans lesquelles les gens devaient voyager, la plupart d'entre eux souffraient de problèmes physiques. *L'auteur ne dit pas que les gens souffraient de maux physiques à cause des conditions dans lesquelles ils voyageaient.*
(C)	Mantraps were used in order to prevent people from taking the main roads.	= Des *mantraps* étaient utilisés afin d'empêcher les gens d'emprunter les routes principales. *Cela n'est pas mentionné dans le texte. Les pièges rendaient certains chemins plus dangereux que d'autres et les voyageurs préféraient emprunter des chemins qui avaient déjà été testés par d'autres.*
(D)	✓ **Travelers could encounter several obstacles along the way, some of which were deadly**	**= Les voyageurs pouvaient rencontrer plusieurs obstacles sur leur chemin, dont certains mortels.** ***Bon résumé du 3e paragraphe.***
(E)	Poor people could only afford horses, because they needed less maintenance than carriages.	= Les pauvres ne pouvaient s'offrir que des chevaux, car ils nécessitaient moins d'entretien que les calèches. *L'auteur mentionne que les chevaux, d'une certaine façon, nécessitaient plus de maintenance que les fiacres.*
(F)	✓ **Horses were used to reach those places otherwise inaccessible by carriage and not many people owned both.**	**= Les chevaux étaient utilisés pour atteindre les endroits autrement inaccessibles en calèche et peu de gens possédaient les deux.** ***C'est exactement ce que dit l'auteur dans les deux derniers paragraphes. Les chevaux étaient utilisés pour les chemins étroits dans lesquels les chariots ne passaient pas. De plus, seules les familles riches pouvaient posséder chariots et chevaux.***

Question type : Detail questions

Description

Dans ces questions, on vous demande de rechercher un détail dans le texte. La bonne réponse est une reformulation de ce qui est dit explicitement dans le texte : aussi, elle ne reprendra pas exactement les mêmes mots que le texte, mais exprimera la même idée.

L'intitulé des questions vous indique généralement dans quel paragraphe il faut chercher l'information.

Exemple

Ce type de question est formulé sous la forme :

- *According to the paragraph X … occurs because…*
- *According to the paragraph X, which of the following is true of …?*
- *The author's description of … mentions which of the following?*
- *According to paragraph X, why did … do …?*
- *It is stated in paragraph X that…*

Since the early 1920s, most geologists have favored a "biogenic" theory of oil formation, in which organic matter became buried in ancient sediment where, under a combination of pressure and temperature increases over millions of years, it transformed into oil. However, since 1979, an opposing "abiogenic" theory of oil formation has been promulgated, and has been increasingly debated in academic circles. According to this theory, what is now oil actually began as hydrocarbon compounds that became trapped within the earth's mantle during the formation of the earth. Due to intermittent variations in subsurface pressure over time, some of these hydrocarbons rose from the mantle into the earth's crust, slowly condensing and over millennia forming reservoirs of oil throughout the crust.

According to the paragraph, which of the following is true?
(A) The biogenic theory of oil formation has been proven incorrect.
(B) The abiogenic theory claims that oil formation relies on sub-surface temperature changes.
(C) The abiogenic theory proposes that oil reservoirs are created when oil seeps into the crust from the earth's surface.
(D) The biogenic theory of oil formation is dependent on both temperature and pressure changes.

Solution

(A) Contresens : Les scientifiques ne sont pas d'accord sur la théorie à adopter.
« an opposing "abiogenic" theory of oil formation has been promulgated, and has been increasingly debated in academic circles »

(B) Inexact – Confusion entre pression et température :
« Due to intermittent variations in subsurface pressure overtime »

(C) Contresens : Le pétrole viendrait des profondeurs de la Terre (le manteau), pas de la surface. *« some of these hydrocarbons rose from the mantle into the earth's crust »*

(D) La bonne réponse : *« under a combination of pressure and temperature increases »*

Méthodologie

Il est probable que vous ne vous souveniez pas du détail dont il est question après votre première lecture. Vous devrez donc retourner dans le texte pour aller chercher l'information.

Il y a deux manières de trouver la bonne réponse :

- Chercher la bonne solution et la retrouver parmi les choix proposés.
- Éliminer les mauvais choix de réponse un à un. Sur ce type de question, la méthode de l'élimination est particulièrement efficace si vous ne devinez pas rapidement la bonne réponse.

Il est très important de bien comprendre comment les concepteurs construisent les mauvais choix de réponse (plus de détails dans les stratégies générales). Une bonne connaissance de la méthodologie des concepteurs vous aidera à éliminer efficacement les mauvais choix un à un. Chaque mauvais choix de réponse de type « détail » rentre en effet dans l'une des catégories suivantes :

- contresens
- inexact / exagéré
- extrapolation
- ne répond pas à la question

Méthode à adopter :

1. Identifiez le fait à analyser en lisant la question, ne vous attardez pas sur les choix de réponse. Essayez de déterminer des mots-clefs pour une recherche plus facile dans le texte.
2. Trouvez l'endroit où le fait est abordé dans le texte. Lisez attentivement la phrase contenant le mot-clef.
3. Essayez de deviner la bonne réponse.
4. Retrouvez la bonne réponse parmi les choix de réponse.
5. Si vous n'avez pas réussi à deviner la bonne réponse ou que vous avez un doute, éliminez les mauvais choix de réponse un par un en les classant dans les catégories de mauvaises réponses.

Entraînement - Detail questions

Reportez vos réponses pour analyser votre performance.

Entraînez-vous dans les conditions d'examen.

prepmyfuture.com/book/68/ex/1920

Since the early 1920s, most geologists have favored a "biogenic" theory of oil formation, in which organic matter became buried in ancient sediment where, under a combination of pressure and temperature increases over millions of years, it transformed into oil. However, since 1979, an opposing "abiogenic" theory of oil formation has been promulgated, and has been increasingly debated in academic circles. According to this theory, what is now oil actually began as hydrocarbon compounds that became trapped within the earth's mantle during the formation of the earth. Due to intermittent variations in sub-surface pressure over time, some of these hydrocarbons rose from the mantle into the earth's crust, slowly condensing and over millennia forming reservoirs of oil throughout the crust.

Question 1 According to the paragraph, which of the following is true?

(A) The biogenic theory of oil formation has been proven incorrect.

(B) The abiogenic theory claims that oil formation relies on sub-surface temperature changes.

(C) The abiogenic theory proposes that oil reservoirs are created when oil seeps into the crust from the Earth's surface.

(D) The biogenic theory of oil formation is dependent on both temperature and pressure changes.

Bats make their homes throughout the globe, save only for the very coldest of regions near the poles. Most bats are active at dawn or dusk, or in the dark of night. During the daytime, they usually hide in caves or (should they live in a forest or jungle) under a deep canopy of leaves; for bats that live in urban areas, old abandoned buildings are a common sanctuary for them. As can be seen by the way bats swarm through the sky, they are quite social creatures, mostly living in large groups throughout the year. The females of some species even gather for collective birthing. Despite the folklore surrounding bats, only some species, so-called 'vampire bats', actually drink blood. These species live solely in the tropical or subtropical regions of Central and South America, where they feed on the blood of mammals or birds; they are also often carriers of rabies.

Question 2 According to the paragraph, what is a common misunderstanding about bats?

(A) Bats are less active during daylight hours.

(B) All bat species drink blood.

(C) A majority of bat species live in Central and South America.

(D) Bats gather together for social activities like flight or birthing.

While Bran Stoker's Dracula is its most famous incarnation, vampires—recently dead humans who come back to prey upon the living by drinking their blood—have been a part of different culture's superstitions for thousands of years, and come from every region of the world. While we can safely put aside the idea that vampires are the actual undead, folklorists and historians have over the last century proposed a variety of so far unsatisfying theories to explain the persistence of the vampire across the centuries. One theory held that many vampire stories originated from people's fear of being buried alive, an unsettlingly common experience before the 20th Century. Another supposed that it came from a rare medical condition called porphyria because it can cause a sensitivity to light and is treated with blood extract; however, this was found to be without basis in medical fact. The most likely theory is that people misinterpreted certain natural changes that a dead body goes through, changes that seem to echo descriptions often associated with vampires.

Question 3 According to the paragraph, which of the following is true?

(A) Legends and myths about vampires began with a story by Bram Stoker.

(B) One theory about the origin of the idea of vampirism comes from a newly-discovered medical condition.

(C) Over time, there have been various theories about why stories of vampires have lasted for so long and in so many places.

(D) Being buried alive was the most popular theory before the 20th century for how vampires were created.

Solutions

Reportez vos réponses pour analyser votre performance.

Entraînez-vous dans les conditions d'examen.

prepmyfuture.com/book/68/ex/1920

question 1	D	question 2	B	question 3	C

Question 1 - Solution

According to the paragraph, which of the following is true?

FR : D'après le paragraphe, laquelle de ces propositions est vraie ?

(A)	The biogenic theory of oil formation has been proven incorrect.	= La théorie biogénique de la formation du pétrole a été démentie. *Les scientifiques ne sont pas d'accord sur la théorie à adopter.* *« an opposing "abiogenic" theory of oil formation has been promulgated, and has been increasingly debated in academic circles »* *(= « une théorie opposée, dite "abiogénique", de la formation du pétrole a été promulguée et fait l'objet d'un débat croissant dans les milieux universitaires. »)*
(B)	The abiogenic theory claims that oil formation relies on sub-surface temperature changes.	= La théorie abiogénique affirme que la formation du pétrole repose sur les changements de température sous la surface. *« Due to intermittent variations in sub-surface pressure over time »(= « En raison des variations intermittentes de la pression souterraine au fil du temps »)*
(C)	The abiogenic theory proposes that oil reservoirs are created when oil seeps into the crust from the Earth's surface.	= La théorie abiogénique avance que les réservoirs de pétrole sont créés lorsque le pétrole s'infiltre dans la croûte terrestre depuis la surface de la Terre. *Le pétrole viendrait des profondeurs de la Terre (le manteau), pas de la surface.* *« some of these hydrocarbons rose from the mantle into the Earth's crust » (= « Certains de ces hydrocarbures sont passés du manteau à la croûte terrestre. »)*
(D)	✓ **The biogenic theory of oil formation is dependent on both temperature and pressure changes.**	**= La théorie biogénique de la formation du pétrole dépend à la fois des changements de température et de de pression.** ***« under a combination of pressure and temperature increases » (= « sous une association d'augmentations de pression et de température »)***

▪ Question 2 - Solution

According to the paragraph, what is a common misunderstanding about bats?

FR : D'après le paragraphe, laquelle de ces affirmations est le préjugé le plus répandu concernant les chauves-souris ?

(A)	Bats are less active during daylight hours.	= Les chauves-souris sont moins actives pendant la journée. *Cela est vrai mais il n'est pas précisé qu'il s'agit d'un préjugé courant.*
(B)	**✓ All bat species drink blood.**	**= Toutes les espèces de chauves-souris boivent du sang.** ***« Despite the folklore surrounding bats, only some species, so-called 'vampire bats', actually drink blood. »*** ***(= « Malgré le mythe répandu à propos des chauves-souris, seules certaines espèces, appelées "chauves-souris vampires", boivent réellement du sang. »)***
(C)	A majority of bat species live in Central and South America.	= La majorité des espèces de chauves-souris vivent en Amérique centrale et en Amérique du Sud. *Les chauves-souris vivent presque partout. L'Amérique centrale et l'Amérique du Sud sont mentionnées seulement pour certaines espèces : les chauves-souris « vampires ».* *« Bats make their homes throughout the globe » (= « Les chauves-souris ont élu domicile dans le monde entier. »)*
(D)	Bats gather together for social activities like flight or birthing.	= Les chauves-souris se rassemblent pour des activités collectives comme le vol ou la mise bas. *Cela est vrai mais il n'est pas précisé qu'il s'agit d'un préjugé courant.*

▪ Question 3 - Solution

According to the paragraph, which of the following is true?

FR : D'après le paragraphe, laquelle de ces propositions est vraie ?

(A)	Legends and myths about vampires began with a story by Bram Stoker.	= Les légendes et les mythes sur les vampires ont commencé avec une histoire de Bram Stoker. *Le livre de Stoker est mentionné comme l'histoire de vampire la plus célèbre. Il n'est pas indiqué qu'il s'agit de la première. Il est même suggéré que les légendes sont antérieures au livre.* *« have been a part of different culture's superstitions for thousands of years » (= « font partie des superstitions de différentes cultures depuis des milliers d'années »)*
(B)	One theory about the origin of the idea of vampirism comes from a newly-discovered medical condition.	= Une théorie sur l'origine de l'idée de vampirisme provient d'une maladie récemment découverte. *La maladie n'est pas récente. Il est indiqué que cette maladie n'aurait jamais existé.* *« however, this was found to be without basis in medical fact. » (= « Cependant, il a été constaté que cette affirmation n'était pas fondée sur des éléments médicaux. »)*
(C)	✓ **Over time, there have been various theories about why stories of vampires have lasted for so long and in so many places.**	**= Au fil du temps, diverses théories ont été avancées pour expliquer pourquoi les histoires de vampires ont duré si longtemps et se sont répandues dans autant d'endroits.** ***« a variety of so far unsatisfying theories to explain the persistence of the vampire across the centuries » (= « une série de théories jusqu'ici peu convaincantes pour expliquer la persistance du vampire à travers les siècles »)***
(D)	Being buried alive was the most popular theory before the 20th century for how vampires were created.	Avant le 20e siècle, être enterré vivant était la théorie la plus répandue pour expliquer l'apparition des vampires. *Attention avec les mots trop forts tels que « most ». Il est vrai qu'il s'agit d'une théorie populaire mais il n'est pas précisé qu'il s'agit de la théorie la plus populaire.*

Question type : EXCEPT detail questions

Description

Dans ces questions, on vous demande d'identifier la seule information factuelle fausse. Ce type de question est similaire aux questions de type « information factuelle », mais au lieu de vous demander quelle est la seule information vraie, on vous demande de choisir la seule information fausse parmi des informations vraies.

Tout comme dans les questions de type « information factuelle », les choix de réponse sont des reformulations de ce qui est dit explicitement dans le texte. L'intitulé des questions vous indique généralement dans quel paragraphe il faut chercher l'information.

Exemple

Ce type de question est formulé sous la forme :

In her paintings, Frida Kahlo repeatedly employed pre-Colombian Aztec symbols, such as skeletons or bleeding hearts that were traditionally related to the emanation of life from death and light from darkness. In this way, her art mirrored much of the artwork of her time, with its idealization of Aztec or native Mexican culture. Her works commonly alluded to her country's struggle to emerge as a nation after subjugation by Spain and the United States, usually portrayed in romantic and nationalistic ways. One notable painting, Self-Portrait on the Border between Mexico and the United States, for instance, depicts Kahlo wearing a bone necklace and standing next to an Aztec temple in a jungle under a blood-red sun, while far in the distance behind her in the painting can be seen smokestacks, light bulbs, and robots under an American flag.

The passage mentions each of the following as an Aztec symbol or image found in Kahlo's paintings EXCEPT
(A) skeleton
(B) smokestack
(C) temple
(D) bleeding heart

(A) *"Frida Kahlo repeatedly employed pre-Colombian Aztec symbols, such as skeletons or bleeding hearts"*

(C) *"One notable painting, [...] depicts Kahlo wearing a bone necklace and standing next to an Aztec temple"*

(D) *"Frida Kahlo repeatedly employed pre-Colombian Aztec symbols, such as skeletons or bleeding hearts"*

La bonne réponse est (B).

Méthodologie

Il est probable que vous ne vous souveniez pas des détails dont il est question après votre première lecture. Vous devrez donc retourner dans le texte pour aller chercher l'information.

Même si ce type de question est très proche des questions de type « information factuelle », la méthode de résolution diffère un peu.

Il y deux manières de trouver la bonne réponse :

- Identifier l'information fausse et vérifier dans le texte que l'information est effectivement fausse ou non donnée par l'auteur.
- Éliminer les mauvais choix de réponse un à un en vérifiant si chaque information est vraie ou fausse. Il est très important de bien comprendre comment les concepteurs construisent la bonne réponse. Dans ce type de question, la fausse information rentre dans l'une de ces deux catégories :
  - Contresens ou inexact : Le choix de réponse ressemble à une information du texte, mais ne veut pas dire la même chose. Il peut s'agir d'une exagération par rapport au texte (les mots de type *always*, *never* doivent éveiller vos soupçons) ou même d'un contresens important (inversion cause/conséquence ou inversion de sujets).
  - Extrapolation : Le concepteur ajoute une information qui n'est pas explicite dans le texte. Il utilisera alors le même type de vocabulaire que dans le texte. L'information pourra même être plausible et conforme du point de vue de l'auteur. Dans ce type de question, la règle est simple : si l'information n'est pas explicite dans le passage alors vous pouvez sélectionner le choix de réponse.

Méthode à adopter :

1. Identifiez le fait à analyser en lisant la question ET les choix de réponse. Essayez de déterminer des mots-clefs pour une recherche plus facile dans le texte.
2. Si vous avez deviné quelle était la bonne réponse et que celle-ci entre dans la catégorie « contresens ou inexact », il faut alors que le texte contredise explicitement le choix de réponse. Dès que vous avez trouvé une contradiction, vous n'avez pas besoin d'éliminer les autres choix de réponse.
3. Si la bonne réponse est de type « extrapolation » alors la méthode la plus raisonnable est d'éliminer les choix de réponse un à un. Pour cela, vous devez trouver une reformulation de toutes les informations vraies dans le texte. Cela jusqu'à ce qu'il ne reste plus qu'un choix de réponse.

Stratégies

Conseil n°1 : Se méfier des mots clivants

Les mots clivants tels que *always* ou *never*, de même que toutes les exagérations doivent éveiller vos soupçons. En effet, le concepteur va se servir de ces mots pour invalider une proposition qui paraît vraie. Par exemple, si le texte dit « L'oiseau se nourrit de fruits et de graines », la phrase « l'oiseau mange toujours des graines » sera considérée comme étant en contradiction avec le texte.

Conseil n°2 : Se méfier des choix de réponse ressemblant trop à ce qui est dit dans le texte

Lorsqu'une proposition de réponse reprend exactement les mêmes mots que le texte, méfiez-vous, il peut s'agir d'un piège de type « contresens ». Il faut se méfier des inversions sujet/verbe, des tournures négatives et d'éventuelles voix passives. Ces choix de réponse sont faciles à éliminer, mais demandent d'être attentif aux détails.

Entraînement - EXCEPT detail questions

Reportez vos réponses pour analyser votre performance.

Entraînez-vous dans les conditions d'examen.

prepmyfuture.com/book/68/ex/1921

On July 16, 1994, a small, fragmented comet known as Shoemaker-Levy began crashed into the atmosphere of the planet Jupiter, causing a chain of massive explosions of unimaginable intensity. Despite predictions, the collisions produced scars that were visible from Earth by land-based observatories, orbiting satellites and even small telescopes in people's backyards. One fragment triggered a blast equivalent to 250 million tons of TNT—several times more powerful than all the world's nuclear weapons combined. Another created a hole in the planet's atmosphere the size of the Earth itself. While the full extent of the damage that it inflicted on Jupiter took years to assess, one thing became perfectly clear: The long-held scientific belief that comets are harmless had been dispelled forever.

Question 1 According to the paragraph, each of the following is true EXCEPT:

(A) Shoemaker-Levy broke into smaller pieces before it hit the atmosphere of Jupiter.

(B) Shoemaker-Levy illustrated to many people the danger of comets.

(C) One of the comet fragments caused the largest explosion ever observed.

(D) It was expected that Shoemaker-Levy was not going to be observable from Earth.

For decades, scientists have been attempting to explain why at least 90 percent of the universe seems to be "missing"; that is, the total amount of observable matter—stars, dust, planets and other celestial bodies—does not contain enough mass (and therefore gravity) needed to form galaxies or galaxy clusters. To account for this disparity, scientists have speculated on the existence of what they call "dark matter", an invisible as yet unobserved force which could provide enough gravitational pull for galaxies to form. It is believed that dark matter is created by neutrinos, sub-atomic particles created by nuclear fusion, radioactive decay or the collisions of other more complex particles; they are by far the most common type of particle in the universe, and were long assumed to have no mass. But new evidence has recently come to light which is shattering our understanding of neutrinos.

Question 2 The passage mentions each of the following EXCEPT:

(A) scientists have proven the existence of dark matter

(B) dark matter may partly be a by-product of radioactivity

(C) visible celestial bodies don't have enough gravity to create galaxies

(D) new information about neutrinos is changing scientists' understanding of them

While Bran Stoker's Dracula is its most famous incarnation, vampires—recently dead humans who come back to prey upon the living by drinking their blood—have been a part of different culture's superstitions for thousands of years, and come from every region of the world. While we can safely put aside the idea that vampires are the actual undead, folklorists and historians have over the last century proposed a variety of so far unsatisfying theories to explain the persistence of the vampire across the centuries. One theory held that many vampire stories originated from people's fear of being buried alive, an unsettlingly common experience before the 20th Century. Another supposed that it came from a rare medical condition called porphyria because it can cause a sensitivity to light and is treated with blood extract; however, this was found to be without basis in medical fact. The most likely theory is that people misinterpreted certain natural changes that a dead body goes through, changes that seem to echo descriptions often associated with vampires.

▪ Question 3 According to the paragraph, each of the following has been a theory explaining the origin of the myth of vampires EXCEPT:

(A) popular stories of people who supposedly drank blood

(B) a common fear of accidental burial

(C) a misunderstood medical condition

(D) a lack of information about what happens to a body after death

Solutions

Reportez vos réponses pour analyser votre performance.

Entraînez-vous dans les conditions d'examen.

prepmyfuture.com/book/68/ex/1921

question 1	D	question 2	A	question 3	A

■ Question 1 - Solution

According to the paragraph, each of the following is true EXCEPT:

FR : D'après le paragraphe, toutes ces propositions sont véridiques à l'exception de :

(A) Shoemaker-Levy broke into smaller pieces before it hit the atmosphere of Jupiter.
= Shoemaker-Levy s'est brisé en petits morceaux avant de toucher l'atmosphère de Jupiter.

« fragmented comet » signifie qu'il y a plusieurs morceaux de comète

« the collisions » est au pluriel, il y a donc plusieurs impacts.

(B) Shoemaker-Levy illustrated to many people the danger of comets.
= Shoemaker-Levy a démontré à de nombreuses personnes le danger des comètes.
« The long-held scientific belief that comets are harmless had been dispelled forever. » (= « La croyance scientifique établie de longue date selon laquelle les comètes sont inoffensives a été définitivement écartée. »)

(C) One of the comet fragments caused the largest explosion ever observed.
= L'un des fragments de la comète a provoqué la plus grande explosion jamais observée.

« several times more powerful than all the world's nuclear weapons combined » (= « plusieurs fois plus puissant que toutes les armes nucléaires du monde réunies »)

Même si ce n'est pas dit explicitement, on peut raisonnablement déduire de la comparaison avec les armes nucléaires qu'il s'agit de la plus grande explosion jamais observée.

(D) ✓ It was expected that Shoemaker-Levy was not going to be observable from Earth.
= On s'attendait à ce que Shoemaker-Levy ne soit pas observable depuis la Terre.
La proposition joue sur la confusion entre la comète et les traces d'impact. Les scientifiques ne pensaient pas qu'il serait possible de voir les traces d'impact depuis la Terre mais rien n'est précisé concernant l'observation de la comète elle-même.

■ Question 2 - Solution

The passage mentions each of the following EXCEPT:

FR : Le passage mentionne chacune de ces propositions à l'exception de :

(A)	**✓ scientists have proven the existence of dark matter**	**= les scientifiques ont prouvé l'existence de la matière noire** ***L'existence de la « matière noire » n'est toujours qu'une hypothèse.***
(B)	dark matter may partly be a by-product of radioactivity	= la matière noire pourrait être en partie un sous-produit de la radioactivité *« It is believed that dark matter is created by neutrinos, sub-atomic particles created by nuclear fusion, radioactive decay or [...] »* *(= « On pense que la matière noire est créée par les neutrinos, des particules subatomiques créées par la fusion nucléaire, la désintégration radioactive ou [...]. »)*
(C)	visible celestial bodies don't have enough gravity to create galaxies	= les corps célestes visibles n'ont pas assez de gravité pour créer des galaxies *« celestial bodies—does not contain enough mass (and therefore gravity) needed to form galaxies or galaxy clusters »* *(= « les corps célestes - ne contiennent pas suffisamment de masse (et donc de gravité) pour former des galaxies ou des agrégats de galaxies »)*
(D)	new information about neutrinos is changing scientists' understanding of them	= de nouvelles informations sur les neutrinos modifient la compréhension qu'en ont les scientifiques *« But new evidence has recently come to light which is shattering our understanding of neutrinos. »(= « Mais de nouvelles découvertes sont récemment tombées, qui bouleversent notre compréhension des neutrinos. »)*

▪ Question 3 - Solution

According to the paragraph, each of the following has been a theory explaining the origin of the myth of vampires EXCEPT:

FR : Selon le paragraphe, toutes les propositions suivantes sont des théories expliquant l'origine du mythe des vampires à l'exception de :

(A)	**✓ popular stories of people who supposedly drank blood**	**= des récits populaires de personnes ayant prétendument bu du sang**
(B)	a common fear of accidental burial	= une peur commune de l'enterrement accidentel *« originated from people's fear of being buried alive » (= « est né de la peur des gens d'être enterrés vivants »)*
(C)	a misunderstood medical condition	= une maladie mal comprise *« came from a rare medical condition called porphyria »* *(= « provient d'une maladie rare appelée porphyrie »)*
(D)	a lack of information about what happens to a body after death	= un manque d'information sur ce qui arrive au corps après la mort *« people misinterpreted certain natural changes that a dead body goes through » (= « Les gens ont mal interprété certains changements naturels que subit un corps sans vie »)*

Question type : Vocabulary questions

Description

Dans ces questions, un mot complexe du texte est surligné et vous devez trouver le meilleur substitut du mot parmi les choix proposés.

Les concepteurs partent du principe que vous ne connaissez pas le sens exact du mot surligné. Ils attendent donc de vous que vous deviniez son sens à partir du contexte :

- sens de la phrase complète ;
- sens du paragraphe dans son ensemble.

Ce type de question est moins facile qu'il n'y paraît, car le mot surligné peut avoir plusieurs sens. Il faut dans ce cas déterminer le sens du mot dans le contexte où il est utilisé.

Enfin, la compréhension du contexte et du point de vue de l'auteur est utile pour les questions les plus difficiles. Dans celles-ci il faut choisir entre plusieurs mots aux sens proches. Il faut alors déterminer la connotation (positive ou négative) qui s'approche le plus du point de vue de l'auteur.

Exemple

Ce type de question est formulé sous la forme :

- *The word … in the passage is closest in meaning to…*
- *In stating …, the author means that…*

> *In her paintings, Frida Kahlo repeatedly employed pre-Colombian Aztec symbols, such as skeletons or bleeding hearts that were traditionally related to the* ***emanation*** *of life from death and light from darkness. In this way, her art mirrored much of the artwork of her time, with its idealization of Aztec or native Mexican culture. Her works commonly alluded to her country's struggle to emerge as a nation after subjugation by Spain and the United States, usually portrayed in romantic and nationalistic ways. One notable painting, Self-Portrait on the Border between Mexico and the United States, for instance, depicts Kahlo wearing a bone necklace and standing next to an Aztec temple in a jungle under a blood-red sun, while far in the distance behind her in the painting can be seen smokestacks, light bulbs, and robots under an American flag.*
>
> ***The word emanation is closest in meaning to***
> *(A) decline*
> *(B) hopelessness*
> *(C) creation*
> *(D) strangeness*

Solution

(A) FR : déclin

(B) FR : désespoir
On peut créer un adjectif à partir d'un nom en lui ajoutant le suffixe « -less » (Ex : *hope* → *hope**less*** = sans espoir).

(C) FR : création

(D) FR : étrangeté
On peut créer un nom à partir d'un adjectif en lui ajoutant le suffixe « -ness » (Ex : *strange* → *strange**ness*** = étrange).

La bonne réponse est (C).

Méthodologie

La bonne réponse doit être en adéquation avec :

- le sens de la phrase ;
- le point de vue de l'auteur ;
- les expressions idiomatiques.

Méthode à adopter :

1. Comprendre la phrase.
2. Essayer de deviner le sens du mot.
3. Traduire chacune des propositions.
4. Éliminer les propositions « non idiomatiques ».
5. Éliminer les mots non compatibles avec le sens de la phrase.
6. Choisir parmi les propositions restantes.
7. Confirmer votre réponse en relisant la phrase en remplaçant le mot surligné avec votre réponse. Le sens ne doit pas changer.

Stratégies

Conseil n° 1 : La connotation des mots est importante

Lors de votre lecture du contexte, vous devez identifier si le mot surligné a une connotation positive, négative ou neutre. Servez-vous de votre compréhension générale du texte.

Conseil n° 2 : Utilisez les racines lexicales, les préfixes et suffixes

Même si vous ne connaissez pas le mot, vous connaissez sans doute sa racine lexicale, son préfixe ou son suffixe. Cela vous donne un indice pour deviner le sens du mot.

Entraînement - Vocabulary questions

Reportez vos réponses pour analyser votre performance.

Entraînez-vous dans les conditions d'examen.

prepmyfuture.com/book/68/ex/1922

In her paintings, Frida Kahlo repeatedly employed pre-Colombian Aztec symbols, such as skeletons or bleeding hearts, that were traditionally related to the **emanation** of life from death and light from darkness. In this way, her art mirrored much of the artwork of her time, with its idealization of Aztec or native Mexican culture. Her works commonly alluded to her country's struggle to emerge as a nation after subjugation by Spain and the United States, usually portrayed in romantic and nationalistic ways. One notable painting, Self-Portrait on the Border between Mexico and the United States, for instance, depicts Kahlo wearing a bone necklace and standing next to an Aztec temple in a jungle under a blood-red sun, while far in the distance behind her in the painting can be seen smokestacks, light bulbs, and robots under an American flag.

Question 1 The word "emanation" is closest in meaning to:

(A) decline
(B) hopelessness
(C) creation
(D) strangeness

Since the early 1920s, most geologists have favored a "biogenic" theory of oil formation, in which organic matter became buried in ancient sediment where, under a combination of pressure and temperature increases over millions of years, it transformed into oil. However, since 1979, an opposing "abiogenic" theory of oil formation has been **promulgated**, and has been increasingly debated in academic circles. According to this theory, what is now oil actually began as hydrocarbon compounds that became trapped within the earth's mantle during the formation of the earth. Due to intermittent variations in sub-surface pressure over time, some of these hydrocarbons rose from the mantle into the earth's crust, slowly condensing and over millennia forming reservoirs of oil throughout the crust.

Question 2 The word "promulgated" is closest in meaning to:

(A) spread
(B) debunked
(C) withheld
(D) tested

While Bran Stoker's Dracula is its most famous incarnation, vampires—recently dead humans who come back to prey upon the living by drinking their blood—have been a part of different culture's superstitions for thousands of years, and come from every region of the world. While we can safely put aside the idea that vampires are the actual undead, folklorists and historians have over the last century proposed a variety of so far unsatisfying theories to explain the persistence of the vampire across the centuries. One theory held that many vampire stories originated from people's fear of being buried alive, an **unsettlingly** common experience before the 20th Century. Another supposed that it came from a rare medical condition called porphyria because it can cause a sensitivity to light and is treated with blood extract; however, this was found to be without basis in medical fact. The most likely theory is that people misinterpreted certain natural changes that a dead body goes through, changes that seem to echo descriptions often associated with vampires.

Question 3 The word "unsettlingly" is closest in meaning to:

(A) confusingly
(B) continually
(C) sensibly
(D) disturbingly

Solutions

Reportez vos réponses pour analyser votre performance.

Entraînez-vous dans les conditions d'examen.

prepmyfuture.com/book/68/ex/1922

question 1	C	question 2	A	question 3	D

Question 1 - Solution

The word "emanation" is closest in meaning to:

FR : Le mot « emanation » a un sens proche de :

(A) decline = déclin

(B) hopelessness = désespoir
- *le suffixe -ness est utilisé pour créer un nom à partir de l'adjectif (strange = étrange)*
- *le suffixe -less est utilisé pour créer un adjectif à partir d'un nom (hopeless = sans espoir)*

(C) ✓ creation = création

(D) strangeness = étrangeté
le suffixe -ness est utilisé pour créer un nom à partir de l'adjectif (strange = étrange)

Question 2 - Solution

The word "promulgated" is closest in meaning to:

FR : Le mot « promulgated » a un sens proche de :

(A) ✓ spread = propager

(B) debunked = démystifié

(C) withheld = retenu

(D) tested = testé

⇝ **explication**
FR : *promulgated* = promulgué (au sens propre : publier une loi de manière à ce qu'elle soit applicable)

Question 3 - Solution

The word "unsettlingly" is closest in meaning to:

FR : Le mot « unsettlingly » a un sens proche de :

(A) confusingly = prêter à confusion

(B) continually = continuellement

(C) sensibly = sensiblement

(D) ✓ disturbingly = inquiétant

⇝ **explication**
FR : *unsettlingly* = troublant

Question type : Inference questions

Description

La réponse à ce type de question n'est pas explicitement écrite dans le texte. On vous demande de faire une déduction à partir des informations du texte. Il s'agit de comprendre ce qui est sous-entendu par l'auteur. Ces questions insistent particulièrement sur les relations logiques de type cause/conséquence évoquées dans le texte.

Exemple

Ce type de question est formulé sous la forme :

- *What does the author imply that … ?*
- *In the passage, what can be inferred about … ?*

Il est important de connaître le verbe *to infer* qui signifie « déduire/sous-entendre ».

In her paintings, Frida Kahlo repeatedly employed pre-Colombian Aztec symbols, such as skeletons or bleeding hearts that were traditionally related to the emanation of life from death and light from darkness. In this way, her art mirrored much of the artwork of her time, with its idealization of Aztec or native Mexican culture. Her works commonly alluded to her country's struggle to emerge as a nation after subjugation by Spain and the United States, usually portrayed in romantic and nationalistic ways. One notable painting, Self-Portrait on the Border between Mexico and the United States, for instance, depicts Kahlo wearing a bone necklace and standing next to an Aztec temple in a jungle under a blood-red sun, while far in the distance behind her in the painting can be seen smokestacks, light bulbs, and robots under an American flag.

It can be inferred from the paragraph that

(A) Kahlo felt that the Mexican people had not been treated well by Spain or the United States.
(B) Kahlo visited an Aztec temple near the border of the United States.
(C) Kahlo fought directly for the independence of Mexico from Spain and the United States.
(D) Kahlo preferred pre-Colombian symbols over those from other cultures.

Solution

(A) Kahlo est décrite comme une opposante à l'impérialisme américain et espagnol.

(B) Elle a fait son autoportrait dans cette configuration. Il ne s'agit pas d'une situation réelle, mais d'une métaphore.

(C) Née en 1907 Frida Khalo n'a pas elle-même participé à la guerre d'indépendance du Mexique (19010-19020), elle était trop jeune pour cela.

(D) Kahlo utilisait régulièrement des symboles précolombiens, rien ne laisse sous-entendre qu'elle préférait ces symboles aux autres.

La bonne réponse est (A).

Méthodologie

La bonne réponse respecte les contraintes suivantes :

- Elle est en accord avec le point de vue de l'auteur du texte.
- La bonne réponse n'est pas nécessairement la plus véridique, la meilleure réponse est celle qui est suggérée par le texte. Si vous ne pouvez pas citer un extrait du passage qui permet de déduire la réponse que vous avez choisie, alors vous n'avez pas trouvé la bonne réponse.

La résolution de ces questions est assez proche de la résolution des questions de type « information factuelle ». Au lieu de chercher une reformulation d'une information factuelle du passage, vous cherchez un sous-entendu d'une information factuelle du passage.

Stratégies

Conseil n°1 : *Linking words*

Bien maîtriser les relations de cause, de conséquence et d'opposition. Elles vous permettront de comprendre les liens logiques entre les éléments. Vous trouverez la liste des mots de liaison dans la section « Grammaire ».

Conseil n°2 : Méfiez-vous des mauvaises réponses de type « ce n'est pas mentionné dans le texte »

Comme mentionné ci-dessus, même si un choix de réponse comporte une information véridique comme « le fleuve se déverse dans la mer », il ne s'agit pas de la bonne réponse si l'auteur ne l'a pas sous-entendu dans le texte. De la même manière que pour les questions de type « information factuelle », vous devez être capable de justifier votre réponse à partir de ce qui est écrit dans le texte.

Entraînement - Inference questions

Reportez vos réponses pour analyser votre performance.

Entraînez-vous dans les conditions d'examen.

prepmyfuture.com/book/68/ex/1923

On July 16, 1994, a small, fragmented comet known as Shoemaker-Levy began crashed into the atmosphere of the planet Jupiter, causing a chain of massive explosions of unimaginable intensity. Despite predictions, the collisions produced scars that were visible from Earth by land-based observatories, orbiting satellites and even small telescopes in people's backyards. One fragment triggered a blast equivalent to 250 million tons of TNT—several times more powerful than all the world's nuclear weapons combined. Another created a hole in the planet's atmosphere the size of the Earth itself. While the full extent of the damage that it inflicted on Jupiter took years to assess, one thing became perfectly clear: The long-held scientific belief that comets are harmless had been dispelled forever.

Question 1 It can be inferred from the paragraph that:

(A) Since Shoemaker-Levy, other comets have been observed crashing into planets.

(B) Physical evidence of the Shoemaker-Levy impact was visible for years afterwards.

(C) The Shoemaker-Levy comet was only observable by the most powerful telescopes.

(D) The Shoemaker-Levy comet was the first to be seen to hit a planet.

Bats make their homes throughout the globe, save only for the very coldest of regions near the poles. Most bats are active at dawn or dusk, or in the dark of night. During the daytime, they usually hide in caves or (should they live in a forest or jungle) under a deep canopy of leaves; for bats that live in urban areas, old abandoned buildings are a common sanctuary for them. As can be seen by the way bats swarm through the sky, they are quite social creatures, mostly living in large groups throughout the year. The females of some species even gather for collective birthing. Despite the folklore surrounding bats, only some species, so-called 'vampire bats', actually drink blood. These species live solely in the tropical or subtropical regions of Central and South America, where they feed on the blood of mammals or birds; they are also often carriers of rabies.

Question 2 According to the paragraph, which of the following can be inferred about bats?

(A) Most prefer caves to other locations when resting.

(B) They are not found in urban areas.

(C) They prefer to rest in well-lit places when not flying.

(D) They are not found in certain regions of the planet.

For decades, scientists have been attempting to explain why at least 90 percent of the universe seems to be "missing"; that is, the total amount of observable matter—stars, dust, planets and other celestial bodies—does not contain enough mass (and therefore gravity) needed to form galaxies or galaxy clusters. To account for this disparity, scientists have speculated on the existence of what they call "dark matter", an invisible as yet unobserved force which could provide enough gravitational pull for galaxies to form. It is believed that dark matter is created by neutrinos, sub-atomic particles created by nuclear fusion, radioactive decay or the collisions of other more complex particles; they are by far the most common type of particle in the universe, and were long assumed to have no mass. But new evidence has recently come to light which is shattering our understanding of neutrinos.

▪ **Question 3** According to the paragraph, it can be inferred that:

(A) galaxy formation may require less gravitational force that previously thought

(B) neutrinos may actually have mass

(C) neutrinos are primarily created through collisions with other particles

(D) galaxy formation may require a different force other that gravity

Solutions

Reportez vos réponses pour analyser votre performance.

Entraînez-vous dans les conditions d'examen.

prepmyfuture.com/book/68/ex/1923

question 1	D	question 2	D	question 3	B

Question 1 - Solution

It can be inferred from the paragraph that:

FR : Qu'est-ce qui peut être sous-entendu par le paragraphe ?

(A)	Since Shoemaker-Levy, other comets have been observed crashing into planets.	= Depuis Shoemaker-Levy, d'autres comètes ont été observées s'écrasant sur des planètes. *Il est sous-entendu que les comètes sont dangereuses mais aucune autre collision n'est évoquée.*
(B)	Physical evidence of the Shoemaker-Levy impact was visible for years afterwards.	= les preuves matérielles de l'impact de Shoemaker-Levy ont été visibles pendant des années après l'accident. *Il n'est pas dit que les traces d'impact ont disparues. Les « années » sont mentionnées pour dire que les scientifiques ont pris plusieurs années à mesurer les dégâts engendrés par les impacts.*
(C)	The Shoemaker-Levy comet was only observable by the most powerful telescopes.	= La comète Shoemaker-Levy n'était observable que par les télescopes les plus performants. *Le texte décrit l'observation des traces d'impacts, pas la comète elle-même. De plus, comme la comète était gigantesque, il aurait pu être possible de l'observer à partir d'instruments moins sophistiqués.*
(D)	**✓ The Shoemaker-Levy comet was the first to be seen to hit a planet.**	**= La comète Shoemaker-Levy a été la première à être vue en train de rentrer en collision avec une planète.** ***« the collisions produced scars that were visible from Earth by land-based observatories » (= « les collisions ont laissé des traces visibles depuis la Terre par les observatoires terrestres. »)***

Question 2 - Solution

According to the paragraph, which of the following can be inferred about bats?

FR : D'après le paragraphe, que pouvons-nous déduire concernant les chauves-souris ?

(A)	Most prefer caves to other locations when resting.	= La plupart préfèrent les grottes aux autres emplacements pour se reposer. *Ce n'est pas mentionné dans le texte.*
(B)	They are not found in urban areas.	= On ne les trouve pas dans les zones urbaines. ***Contresens*** *On les trouve dans les zones urbaines.* *« for bats that live in urban areas, old abandoned buildings are a common sanctuary for them « (= « pour les chauves-souris qui vivent dans les zones urbaines, les vieux bâtiments abandonnés sont un sanctuaire habituel »)*
(C)	They prefer to rest in well-lit places when not flying.	= Elles préfèrent se reposer dans des endroits bien éclairés lorsqu'elles ne volent pas. ***Contresens – C'est l'opposé.*** *Well-lit = bien éclairé* *Elles se reposent dans l'ombre.* *« During the daytime, they usually hide in caves » (= « Pendant la journée, elles se cachent généralement dans des grottes »)*
(D)	✓ **They are not found in certain regions of the planet.**	**= On ne les trouve pas dans certaines régions de la planète.** ***« Bats make their homes throughout the globe, save only for the very coldest of regions near the poles. » (= « Les chauves-souris vivent partout dans le monde, sauf dans les régions les plus froides, près des pôles. »)***

▪ Question 3 - Solution

According to the paragraph, it can be inferred that:

FR : D'après le paragraphe, nous pouvons déduire que :

(A)	galaxy formation may require less gravitational force that previously thought	= La formation des galaxies pourrait nécessiter moins de force gravitationnelle qu'on ne le pensait auparavant. *Même si cela est peut-être vrai, le texte promeut seulement l'hypothèse de la « matière noire ».*
(B)	✓ **neutrinos may actually have mass**	**= Les neutrinos pourraient en fait avoir une masse.** ***« were long assumed to have no mass » (= « On a longtemps pensé qu'ils n'avaient pas de masse. »)***
(C)	neutrinos are primarily created through collisions with other particles	= Les neutrinos sont principalement créés par des collisions avec d'autres particules. *Trois types de processus de création sont nommés. le texte ne sous-entend pas que l'un d'entre eux est le plus important.*
(D)	galaxy formation may require a different force other that gravity	= La formation des galaxies peut nécessiter une force différente de la gravité. *Même si cela est peut-être vrai, le texte promeut seulement l'hypothèse de la « matière noire ».*

Question type : Opinion / Purpose questions

Description

Ce type de question vous demande de déterminer l'opinion de l'auteur. Généralement, ces questions se réfèrent à un point particulier du texte. On vous demande, par exemple, pourquoi l'auteur utilise tel ou tel argument.

Exemple

Ce type de question est formulé sous la forme :

- *Why does the professor mention … ?*
- *The professor present … in paragraph 3 in order to …*

Méthodologie

Ces questions ne demandent pas nécessairement d'avoir lu le texte dans son ensemble. Le concepteur des questions se concentre généralement sur un lien logique ou un sous-entendu localisé précisément dans l'intitulé de la question.

Pour répondre correctement à la question, il faut porter son attention sur la manière dont le l'auteur amène son idée. La réponse n'est pas écrite explicitement, mais est sous-entendue.

Stratégies

Conseil n°1 : Connaître les verbes exprimant le but.

Il s'agit des verbes qui seront probablement utilisés dans l'intitulé des questions ou dans les choix de réponse :

- *to emphasize* = mettre l'accent sur
- *to highlight* = souligner
- *to underline* = souligner
- *to discuss* = débattre

Conseil n°2 : Faites attention aux fautes de type « mauvaise logique »

Il faut bien différencier les causes et les conséquences. Les mauvaises propositions de réponse vont vous pousser vers ce type de confusion. Il en va de même pour les confusions entre l'exemple et l'argument défendu par l'exemple.

Entraînement - Opinion / Purpose questions

Reportez vos réponses pour analyser votre performance.

Entraînez-vous dans les conditions d'examen.

prepmyfuture.com/book/68/ex/1924

Seawater is one of the most familiar substances on earth and, at the same time, one of the most mysterious. It has been calculated that there are 1.4 billion cubic kilometers of it all over the world. Seawater is both the **crystal blue liquid of advertisements for tropical islands and the gun-metal grey menace of a storm at sea.** If we are to understand how the ocean works, we need to know some basic facts about the substance that fills the ocean basins.

Question 1 The author of the paragraph mentions the "crystal blue liquid of advertisements for tropical islands and the gun-metal grey menace of a storm at sea", in order to:

(A) explain that metal is one of the elements contained in seawater.
(B) illustrate how the sea can either please or endanger men.
(C) point out that seawater is present in many different contexts.
(D) demonstrate that seawater can have different colors.

ABSENCE OF GREAT SCHOLARS SINCE THE FIRST CENTURY BC

From traditional history we know much about scholars of ancient Greece. **Even too much.** We know all the dialogues of Plato with his pupils. And we know about Archimedes, about Heraclitus, we have some pieces of information about mythical Pythagoras. Look anywhere, there is always some information... We studied thoroughly about Euclid. And all of sudden — a gap! Since about the first century BC there has been a gap.

Question 2 Why does the author of the paragraph write that we have "even too much" information about scholars of ancient Greece?

(A) Because he doesn't see any use in knowing all about Plato, Archimedes and Euclides.
(B) Because there is an imbalance between the abundance of information about Greek scholars and that about scholars of the first century BC.
(C) Because he does not particularly like to study the ancient Greek period.
(D) Because researchers should have focused more on scholars of the first century BC.

Entranced by the scientific discoveries of his day, Benjamin Franklin sometimes regretted having been born too soon. He missed "the Happiness of knowing what will be known 100 Years hence." By then there would be "Discoveries made of which we have at present no Conception." He was right about that. But we may be permitted a **small regret of our own** for having been born too late to enjoy his company.

Question 3 Why does the author suggest the presence of a "small regret of our own"?

(A) Because Benjamin Franklin could not see our future inventions.
(B) To imply that Benjamin Franklin was born too late.
(C) To suggest that, after all, Benjamin Franklin's idea of happiness was wrong.
(D) Because he wishes we could have met Benjamin Franklin.

Solutions

Reportez vos réponses pour analyser votre performance.

Entraînez-vous dans les conditions d'examen.

prepmyfuture.com/book/68/ex/1924

question 1	C

question 2	B

question 3	D

Question 1 - Solution

The author of the paragraph mentions the "crystal blue liquid of advertisements for tropical islands and the gun-metal grey menace of a storm at sea", in order to:

FR : L'auteur du paragraphe mentionne « le liquide bleu cristal des publicités pour les îles tropicales et la menace gris métal d'une tempête en mer », pour :

(A) explain that metal is one of the elements contained in seawater.
= expliquer que le métal est l'un des éléments contenus dans l'eau de mer.
L'adjectif « gun-metal » se réfère à la couleur de l'eau de mer dans certaines situations comme les tempêtes.

(B) illustrate how the sea can either please or endanger men.
= illustrer comment la mer peut aussi bien plaire aux hommes que les mettre en danger
Bien que l'auteur mentionne des exemples sur les bons et mauvais côté aspect de la mer, il parle avant tout de l'eau de mer.

(C) ✓ point out that seawater is present in many different contexts.
= souligner que l'eau de mer est présente dans de nombreux contextes différents
C'est exactement ce que veux dire l'auteur. En effet, il écrit que l'eau de mer est présente partout dans le monde en donnant de nombreux exemples.

(D) demonstrate that seawater can have different colors.
= démontrer que l'eau de mer peut avoir différentes couleurs
Ce n'est pas le but de l'auteur.

Question 2 - Solution

Why does the author of the paragraph write that we have "even too much" information about scholars of ancient Greece?

FR : Pourquoi l'auteur du paragraphe écrit-il que nous avons « même trop » d'informations sur les intellectuels de la Grèce antique ?

(A)	Because he doesn't see any use in knowing all about Plato, Archimedes and Euclides.	= Parce qu'il ne voit pas l'utilité de tout savoir sur Platon, Archimède et Euclide. *Ce n'est pas ce pense l'auteur. Il n'y a rien dans le paragraphe qui puisse justifier cette hypothèse.*
(B)	✓ **Because there is an imbalance between the abundance of information about Greek scholars and that about scholars of the first century BC.**	**= Parce qu'il y a un déséquilibre entre l'abondance d'informations sur les savants grecs et celle sur les savants du premier siècle avant Jésus-Christ.** ***C'est bien ce que communique l'auteur avec exaspération en comparant le surplus d'informations du temps des Grecs avec le vide (« gap ») qui suit.***
(C)	Because he does not particularly like to study the ancient Greek period.	= Parce qu'il n'aime pas particulièrement étudier la période de la Grèce antique. *Ce n'est pas ce que l'auteur sous-entend.*
(D)	Because researchers should have focused more on scholars of the first century BC.	= Parce que les chercheurs auraient dû se concentrer davantage sur les savants du premier siècle avant Jésus-Christ. *L'auteur n'exprime pas de jugement sur les travaux des chercheurs.*

■ Question 3 - Solution

Why does the author suggest the presence of a "small regret of our own"?

FR : Pourquoi l'auteur suggère-t-il la présence d'un « petit regret de notre côté » ?

(A)	Because Benjamin Franklin could not see our future inventions.	= Parce que Benjamin Franklin n'a pas pu voir nos futures inventions. *Franklin n'a pas vécu assez longtemps pour voir nos inventions modernes et l'auteur le sait. Ses regrets ne portent donc pas sur cela.*
(B)	To imply that Benjamin Franklin was born too late.	= Pour laisser entendre que Benjamin Franklin est né trop tard. *Ce n'est pas ce que l'auteur sous-entend.*
(C)	To suggest that, after all, Benjamin Franklin's idea of happiness was wrong.	= Pour suggérer que, finalement, l'idée que Benjamin Franklin se faisait du bonheur était fausse. *L'auteur ne partage pas son opinion sur les idées de Franklin à propos du bonheur.*
(D)	✓ **Because he wishes we could have met Benjamin Franklin.**	**= Parce qu'il souhaite que nous puissions rencontrer Benjamin Franklin.** ***C'est ce que l'auteur essaie de communiquer : la société aurait bénéficié de la presence d'un homme brillant et l'auteur regrette d'être né trop tard pour avoir profité de sa compagnie.***

Question type : Sentence simplification questions

Description

Dans ces questions, on vous demande de reformuler une phrase complexe. Les reformulations simplifient la phrase d'origine. La bonne réponse est celle qui :

1. conserve le sens de la phrase d'origine ;
2. ne retire pas d'informations importantes.

Exemple

Ce type de question est formulé sous la forme :

- *Which of the following best expresses the essential information in the highlighted sentence?*

Since the early 1920s, most geologists have favored a "biogenic" theory of oil formation, in which organic matter became buried in ancient sediment where, under a combination of pressure and temperature increases over millions of years, it transformed into oil. However, since 1979, an opposing "abiogenic" theory of oil formation has been promulgated, and has been increasingly debated in academic circles. According to this theory, what is now oil actually began as hydrocarbon compounds that became trapped within the earth's mantle during the formation of the earth. ***Due to intermittent variations in subsurface pressure over time, some of these hydrocarbons rose from the mantle into the earth's crust, slowly condensing and over millennia forming reservoirs of oil throughout the crust.***

Which of the following best expresses the essential information in the highlighted sentence in the paragraph? Incorrect choices change the meaning in important ways or leave out essential information.

(A) Because of changes in sub-surface conditions, hydrocarbons rose from deep within the earth to transform into pockets of oil underground.

(B) Hydrocarbons have risen through the earth's crust over millions of years to form reservoirs of oil, despite variations in subsurface pressure.

(C) Hydrocarbons originated in the earth's mantle due to sub-surface pressure, slowly rising to the surface over millions of years.

(D) Oil tends to collect into reservoirs in the earth's crust more quickly as the oil comes closer to the earth's surface.

Solution

<u>Traduction de la phrase d'origine :</u> À cause des variations intermittentes de pression sous la surface de la Terre, une partie de ces hydrocarbones s'élève du manteau de la Terre et entre dans la croûte terrestre, se solidifiant lentement en formant, au cours des millénaires, des réservoirs de pétrole dans la croûte terrestre.

(A) Un peu moins précis que la phrase d'origine (pression → conditions, manteau terrestre → profondeurs de la Terre), mais on conserve le sens de la phrase.

(B) Inexact & erreur de logique
"have risen through the earth's crust"
Les poches de pétrole sont formées dans la croûte terrestre. Elles ne la traversent pas.
Erreur de logique, mauvaise utilisation de *despite* (= malgré).
Les variations de pression sont la cause de la montée des hydrocarbones.

(C) Erreur de logique & ce n'est pas mentionné dans la phrase
Erreur de logique, les hydrocarbones ne sont pas créés par la pression sous la surface de la Terre.
Il est dit que ce sont les variations de pression qui sont la cause de la montée des hydrocarbones.
"slowly rising to the surface over millions of years."
Cela n'est pas dit dans la phrase d'origine.

(D) Ce n'est pas mentionné dans la phrase d'origine.

Méthodologie

1. Repérer les idées importantes qui doivent absolument figurer dans la réponse.
2. Éliminer les choix de réponse qui ne contiennent pas ces éléments.
3. Pour chaque proposition restante, recherchez de possibles contresens.

Stratégies

Conseil : Attention aux propositions qui ne reprennent qu'un détail

Pour être correct, le choix de réponse doit reprendre l'ensemble des idées importantes de la phrase d'origine. Si la proposition de réponse ne reprend qu'une partie de la phrase ou seulement un détail alors elle est probablement fausse.

Entraînement - Sentence simplification questions

Reportez vos réponses pour analyser votre performance.

Entraînez-vous dans les conditions d'examen.

prepmyfuture.com/book/68/ex/1925

Bats make their homes throughout the globe, save only for the very coldest of regions near the poles. Most bats are active at dawn or dusk, or in the dark of night. **During the daytime, they usually hide in caves or (should they live in a forest or jungle) under a deep canopy of leaves; for bats that live in urban areas, old abandoned buildings are a common sanctuary for them**. As can be seen by the way bats swarm through the sky, they are quite social creatures, mostly living in large groups throughout the year. The females of some species even gather for collective birthing. Despite the folklore surrounding bats, only some species, so-called 'vampire bats', actually drink blood. These species live solely in the tropical or subtropical regions of Central and South America, where they feed on the blood of mammals or birds; they are also often carriers of rabies.

Question 1 Which of the following best expresses the essential information in the highlighted sentence in the paragraph? Incorrect choices change the meaning in important ways or leave out essential information.

(A) Bats often don't get to choose where they rest when not flying because they may live near urban areas or in the wild.

(B) Bats have been known to abandon buildings they rest in, preferring to live in caves or forests.

(C) When not flying, bats will often rest in a dark locale underground, under heavy foliage, or inside buildings, depending on the environment in which they live.

(D) During daylight hours, bats will leave the forests or jungles they fly in to hide in caves or buildings.

For decades, scientists have been attempting to explain why at least 90 percent of the universe seems to be "missing"; that is, the total amount of observable matter—stars, dust, planets and other celestial bodies—does not contain enough mass (and therefore gravity) needed to form galaxies or galaxy clusters. **To account for this disparity, scientists have speculated on the existence of what they call "dark matter", an invisible as yet unobserved force which could provide enough gravitational pull for galaxies to form**. It is believed that dark matter is created by neutrinos, sub-atomic particles created by nuclear fusion, radioactive decay or the collisions of other more complex particles; they are by far the most common type of particle in the universe, and were long assumed to have no mass. But new evidence has recently come to light which is shattering our understanding of neutrinos.

▪ Question 2 Which of the following best expresses the essential information in the highlighted sentence in the paragraph? Incorrect choices change the meaning in important ways or leave out essential information.

(A) The possible existence of dark matter has created difficulties in the current theory of galaxy creation.

(B) Because known celestial objects do not seem to have enough gravity to create galaxies, scientists are proposing that gravity may not be the primary force in galaxy formation.

(C) Because observed celestial objects did not seem to have enough gravity to shape galaxies or galaxy clusters, people hypothesized that an as-yet undetected force may actually provide the gravity capable of creating them.

(D) Scientists hypothesize that the formation of galaxies and galaxy clusters may be causing the creation of an invisible, so far unseen force called dark matter.

While Bran Stoker's Dracula is its most famous incarnation, vampires—recently dead humans who come back to prey upon the living by drinking their blood—have been a part of different culture's superstitions for thousands of years, and come from every region of the world. While we can safely put aside the idea that vampires are the actual undead, folklorists and historians have over the last century proposed a variety of so far unsatisfying theories to explain the persistence of the vampire across the centuries. One theory held that many vampire stories originated from people's fear of being buried alive, an unsettlingly common experience before the 20th Century. Another supposed that it came from a rare medical condition called porphyria because it can cause a sensitivity to light and is treated with blood extract; however, this was found to be without basis in medical fact. **The most likely theory is that people misinterpreted certain natural changes that a dead body goes through, changes that seem to echo descriptions often associated with vampires.**

▪ Question 3 Which of the following best expresses the essential information in the highlighted sentence in the paragraph? Incorrect choices change the meaning in important ways or leave out essential information.

(A) Because of a lack of accurate knowledge about what a body goes through after death, it is most probable that people misread those changes as signs of vampirism.

(B) Vampirism shared many characteristics with the appearance of a body after death.

(C) It is likely that because people misunderstood descriptions of vampirism they tended to misidentify merely dead bodies as vampires.

(D) People tended to see vampirism as the natural result of a misinterpretation of why certain people die.

Solutions

Reportez vos réponses pour analyser votre performance.

Entraînez-vous dans les conditions d'examen.

prepmyfuture.com/book/68/ex/1925

question 1	C	question 2	C	question 3	A

Question 1 - Solution

Which of the following best expresses the essential information in the highlighted sentence in the paragraph? Incorrect choices change the meaning in important ways or leave out essential information.

FR : Laquelle de ces propositions exprime le mieux les informations essentielles de la phrase surlignée dans le paragraphe ? Les propositions incorrectes changent le sens de manière significative ou omettent des informations essentielles.

(A) Bats often don't get to choose where they rest when not flying because they may live near urban areas or in the wild.

= Les chauves-souris n'ont souvent pas la possibilité de choisir l'endroit où elles se reposent lorsqu'elles ne volent pas, car elles peuvent vivre près de zones urbaines ou dans la nature.
La phrase d'origine se contente de mentionner les habitats des chauves-souris. La phrase ne précise pas si les chauves-souris ont la possibilité de choisir l'endroit où elles vont se reposer.

(B) Bats have been known to abandon buildings they rest in, preferring to live in caves or forests.

= Les chauves-souris sont connues pour abandonner les bâtiments où elles se reposent, préférant vivre dans des grottes ou des forêts.
Les bâtiments abandonnés sont un habitat courant pour les chauves-souris. La phrase ne mentionne pas une baisse d'utilisation de ce type d'habitat.

(C) ✓ When not flying, bats will often rest in a dark locale underground, under heavy foliage, or inside buildings, depending on the environment in which they live.

= Lorsqu'elles ne volent pas, les chauves-souris se reposent souvent dans un endroit sombre, sous terre, sous un feuillage dense ou à l'intérieur de bâtiments, selon l'environnement dans lequel elles vivent.

(D) During daylight hours, bats will leave the forests or jungles they fly in to hide in caves or buildings.

= Pendant la journée, les chauves-souris quittent les forêts ou les jungles où elles volent pour se cacher dans des grottes ou des bâtiments.
Contresens
Si elles vivent dans la jungle, les chauves-souris se reposent sous les arbres. Elles n'ont pas besoin de trouver des grottes ou des bâtiments pour être à l'ombre.

explication

FR : Pendant la journée, elles se cachent généralement dans des grottes ou (si elles vivent dans la forêt ou la jungle) sous une épaisse canopée de feuilles ; pour les chauves-souris qui habitent dans les zones urbaines, les vieux bâtiments abandonnés sont un sanctuaire habituel.

▪ Question 2 - Solution

Which of the following best expresses the essential information in the highlighted sentence in the paragraph? Incorrect choices change the meaning in important ways or leave out essential information.

FR : Laquelle de ces propositions exprime le mieux les informations essentielles de la phrase surlignée dans le paragraphe ? Les propositions incorrectes changent le sens de manière significative ou omettent des informations essentielles.

(A) The possible existence of dark matter has created difficulties in the current theory of galaxy creation.

= L'existence possible de la matière noire a créé des difficultés dans la théorie actuelle de la création des galaxies.
La « matière noire » est évoquée comme une explication à l'anormalité observée, pas comme une source de problèmes.

(B) Because known celestial objects do not seem to have enough gravity to create galaxies, scientists are proposing that gravity may not be the primary force in galaxy formation.

= Comme les objets célestes connus ne semblent pas avoir une gravité suffisante pour créer des galaxies, les scientifiques avancent que la gravité n'est peut-être pas la force principale dans la formation des galaxies.
Les scientifiques ne remettent pas en question le rôle de la gravité dans la création des galaxies.

(C) ✓ Because observed celestial objects did not seem to have enough gravity to shape galaxies or galaxy clusters, people hypothesized that an as-yet undetected force may actually provide the gravity capable of creating them.

= Parce que les objets célestes observés ne semblent pas avoir assez de gravité pour former des galaxies ou des amas de galaxies, les chercheurs ont émis l'hypothèse qu'une force non encore détectée pourrait en fait fournir la gravité capable de les créer.

(D) Scientists hypothesize that the formation of galaxies and galaxy clusters may be causing the creation of an invisible, so far unseen force called dark matter.

= Les scientifiques émettent l'hypothèse que la formation des galaxies et des amas de galaxies pourrait être à l'origine de la création d'une force invisible, jusqu'à présent non détectée, appelée matière noire.
D'après la phrase, la « matière noire » fournit la masse nécessaire à la formation des galaxies.

⇒ **explication**

FR : Pour tenir compte de cette disparité, les scientifiques ont spéculé sur l'existence de la « matière noire », une force invisible et pas encore observée qui pourrait fournir assez de force gravitationnelle pour que les galaxies se forment.

▪ Question 3 - Solution

Which of the following best expresses the essential information in the highlighted sentence in the paragraph? Incorrect choices change the meaning in important ways or leave out essential information.

FR : Laquelle de ces propositions exprime le mieux les informations essentielles de la phrase surlignée dans le paragraphe ? Les propositions incorrectes changent le sens de manière significative ou omettent des informations essentielles.

(A)	**✓ Because of a lack of accurate knowledge about what a body goes through after death, it is most probable that people misread those changes as signs of vampirism.**	**= En raison d'un manque de connaissances précises sur ce que subit un corps après la mort, il est très probable que les gens interprètent à tort ces changements comme des signes de vampirisme.**
(B)	Vampirism shared many characteristics with the appearance of a body after death.	= Le vampirisme partage de nombreuses caractéristiques avec l'apparence d'un corps après la mort. *La logique de la phrase originale est omise. Le lien entre les caractéristiques des cadavres et le mythe du vampirisme est mentionné dans le but de justifier une théorie. Ce n'est pas mentionné dans ce choix de réponse.*
(C)	It is likely that because people misunderstood descriptions of vampirism they tended to misidentify merely dead bodies as vampires.	= Il est probable que, parce que les gens comprenaient mal les descriptions du vampirisme, ils avaient tendance à identifier à tort des corps simplement morts comme des vampires.
(D)	People tended to see vampirism as the natural result of a misinterpretation of why certain people die.	= Les gens avaient tendance à considérer le vampirisme comme le résultat naturel d'une mauvaise interprétation de la raison pour laquelle certaines personnes meurent. *La logique est conservée mais l'explication est trop différente de la phrase originale.*

⇨ **explication**

FR : La théorie la plus probable est que les gens ont mal interprété les altérations naturelles d'un cadavre, des changements qui semblent reprendre les descriptions souvent associées aux vampires.

Le but de la phrase originale est de donner une explication potentielle à l'origine du mythe des vampires.

Question type : Insert text questions

Description

Dans ces questions, on vous demande d'insérer une phrase dans le passage. La question est sous forme de QCM et on vous propose 4 emplacements différents pour insérer la phrase.

La bonne réponse est l'emplacement qui :

1. permet de respecter l'organisation du texte avec un enchaînement logique entre les idées ;
2. respecte les règles de grammaire en portant attention aux mots de liaison.

Exemple

Ce type de question est formulé sous la forme :

Look at the four squares, A, B, C, and D, which indicate where the following sentence could be added to the passage. Where would the sentence best fit?

Travelling in general was conspicuous and often only those who could afford a horse even ventured on a journey.

[P2] Most people walked when they needed to go anywhere, usually over considerable distances and in terrible conditions. Because roads were not paved many travellers had to endure heavy, oppressive mud. This was considered to be the greatest obstacle because it was taxing to walk through and dangerous for both horses and wheeled vehicles, such as carriages. Many women wore patterns, or protective overshoes, so that dresses, hems and stockings wouldn't get damaged in the mud. When weather was exceptionally bad most middle- and upper-class women avoided going out at all. This often resulted in poor church attendance. A

[P3] Even those with horses often walked a great deal. B Due to the great distances covered on foot, many people would calculate how far they travelled to take into account physical aliments. Nobody would voyage too far if they had a bad knee or suffered from arthritis. As a result many people would not travel great distances on foot. Some adventurers of the period, such as Carl Mortiz, did go on long excursions but he was an exception. C In addition to the challenges of mud, primitive pathways and physical ailments, laws limiting the movement of people were strictly enforced. Throughout England there were pauper laws, which stipulated that paupers could not travel long distances. If a person was found outside of their parish, or district, without sufficient funds, they were arrested and forced to return. Frequently when people arrived at inns without a horse, they were often treated with contempt. D

Méthodologie

1. Lisez attentivement la phrase à insérer.
2. Repérez les zones d'insertion dans le texte et analysez l'enchaînement des idées, vous n'avez pas besoin de tout lire attentivement. Éliminez les zones d'insertion qui ne permettent pas un enchaînement logique des idées.
3. S'il vous reste plusieurs choix de réponse possibles, alors vous devez éliminer les choix restants grâce aux règles grammaticales. Pour cela, lisez attentivement les mots qui précèdent et suivent les zones d'insertion.

Stratégies

Conseil n°1 : Les liens logiques entre les idées

La plupart du temps, ce type de question vous donne un argument supplémentaire ou un exemple qui permet de renforcer une idée. Dans ce cas, vous n'avez qu'à trouver l'idée à laquelle est associée la phrase à insérer. Une fois ce travail effectué, il devrait vous rester un maximum de deux propositions de réponse, le choix s'effectue alors grâce aux règles grammaticales.

Conseil n°2 : Les mots de liaison

Les mots de liaison sont importants pour déterminer si l'insertion est grammaticalement correcte. Il faut donc les connaître parfaitement et apporter une attention particulière à ceux-ci. Vous trouverez une liste des mots de liaison dans la section « Grammaire ».

Entraînement - Insert text questions

Reportez vos réponses pour analyser votre performance.

Entraînez-vous dans les conditions d'examen.

prepmyfuture.com/book/68/ex/1926

A The Spanish Civil War began with a military coup. There was a long history of military intervention in Spain's political life. B But the coup of 17–18 July 1936 was an old instrument being used for a new purpose. C In this sense, the military rising against Spain's democratic Second Republic was the equivalent of the fascist takeovers that followed the coming to power of Mussolini in Italy (1922) and Hitler in Germany (1933) and which were also designed to control similar manifestations of social, political, and cultural change. The escalation from military coup to civil war was crucially dependent on factors that were external to the Spanish arena. D

Question 1 Look at the four squares the paragraph, A, B, C, and D, which indicate where the following sentence could be added to the passage. Where would the sentence best fit?

It aimed to halt the mass political democracy set in train by the effects of the First World War and the Russian Revolution, and accelerated by the changes of the 1920s and 1930s.

A The Spanish Civil War began with a military coup. There was a long history of military intervention in Spain's political life. B But the coup of 17–18 July 1936 was an old instrument being used for a new purpose. C In this sense, the military rising against Spain's democratic Second Republic was the equivalent of the fascist takeovers that followed the coming to power of Mussolini in Italy (1922) and Hitler in Germany (1933) and which were also designed to control similar manifestations of social, political, and cultural change. The escalation from military coup to civil war was crucially dependent on factors that were external to the Spanish arena. D

(A) A
(B) B
(C) C
(D) D

At first sight, all adult bees look alike. A The head has two large eyes, one on either side, a mouth underneath, and two feelers in front. B These feelers, present in all insects, reach simply gigantic dimensions in some species, like the longhorn beetles we used to play with when we were children. The chest, or thorax, has two pairs of wings at the sides, and three pairs of legs underneath; it is joined to the ringed abdomen by a slender waist. C Looking at them more closely we shall, however, discover differences between the various individuals forming a colony. D

■ Question 2 Look at the four squares the paragraph, A, B, C, and D, which indicate where the following sentence could be added to the passage. Where would the sentence best fit?

It is true of each of them that the body is divided into three distinct parts: head, chest or thorax, and abdomen.

At first sight, all adult bees look alike. A The head has two large eyes, one on either side, a mouth underneath, and two feelers in front. B These feelers, present in all insects, reach simply gigantic dimensions in some species, like the longhorn beetles we used to play with when we were children. The chest, or thorax, has two pairs of wings at the sides, and three pairs of legs underneath; it is joined to the ringed abdomen by a slender waist. C Looking at them more closely we shall, however, discover differences between the various individuals forming a colony. D

(A) A
(B) B
(C) C
(D) D

A The Mediterranean world has a special beauty to it. The stark light, the soaring mountains, the sparkling sea, and much else contribute to make landscapes that have long attracted people from afar. B Apparently, little has changed since the eighteenth century: today one-third of all international tourism in the world involves Mediterranean countries. But, in fact, a good deal has changed, including the landscapes themselves. C The beauty of the Mediterranean mountains is in a way a sad one. D Skeletal mountains and shell villages dot the upland areas of the Mediterranean world, dominating the physical and social landscape.

■ Question 3 Look at the four squares the paragraph, A, B, C, and D, which indicate where the following sentence could be added to the passage. Where would the sentence best fit?

Dr Johnson once said that the grand object of all travel is to see the shores of the Mediterranean.

A The Mediterranean world has a special beauty to it. The stark light, the soaring mountains, the sparkling sea, and much else contribute to make landscapes that have long attracted people from afar. B Apparently, little has changed since the eighteenth century: today one-third of all international tourism in the world involves Mediterranean countries. But, in fact, a good deal has changed, including the landscapes themselves. C The beauty of the Mediterranean mountains is in a way a sad one. D Skeletal mountains and shell villages dot the upland areas of the Mediterranean world, dominating the physical and social landscape.

(A) A
(B) B
(C) C
(D) D

Solutions

Reportez vos réponses pour analyser votre performance.

Entraînez-vous dans les conditions d'examen.

prepmyfuture.com/book/68/ex/1926

question 1	C	question 2	A	question 3	B

Question 1 - Solution

Look at the four squares the paragraph, A, B, C, and D, which indicate where the following sentence could be added to the passage. Where would the sentence best fit?

It aimed to halt the mass political democracy set in train by the effects of the First World War and the Russian Revolution, and accelerated by the changes of the 1920s and 1930s.

A The Spanish Civil War began with a military coup. There was a long history of military intervention in Spain's political life. B But the coup of 17–18 July 1936 was an old instrument being used for a new purpose. C In this sense, the military rising against Spain's democratic Second Republic was the equivalent of the fascist takeovers that followed the coming to power of Mussolini in Italy (1922) and Hitler in Germany (1933) and which were also designed to control similar manifestations of social, political, and cultural change. The escalation from military coup to civil war was crucially dependent on factors that were external to the Spanish arena. D

(A) A *Le pronom « it », réfère à quelque chose qui a déjà été mentionné dans le texte, il est donc impossible de placer la phrase à cet endroit.*

(B) B *Le pronom « it » ne peut se référer à « history of military intervention ».*

(C) ✓ C ***« it », se réfère alors à « military coup », ce qui est possible.***

(D) D *« escalation from military coup to civil war » n'est pas le sujet de la phrase. « it » se réfère à « coup ». De plus, « escalation » est une réaction, ou la conséquence d'une action passée, cela n'aurait donc pas de sens de le mentionner comme quelque chose qui aurait un but spécifique. (« aimed at »)*

Question 2 - Solution

Look at the four squares the paragraph, A, B, C, and D, which indicate where the following sentence could be added to the passage. Where would the sentence best fit?

It is true of each of them that the body is divided into three distinct parts: head, chest or thorax, and abdomen.

At first sight, all adult bees look alike. A The head has two large eyes, one on either side, a mouth underneath, and two feelers in front. B These feelers, present in all insects, reach simply gigantic dimensions in some species, like the longhorn beetles we used to play with when we were children. The chest, or thorax, has two pairs of wings at the sides, and three pairs of legs underneath; it is joined to the ringed abdomen by a slender waist. C Looking at them more closely we shall, however, discover differences between the various individuals forming a colony. D

(A) ✓ **A** ***La phrase confirme ce qui est écrit juste avant « All adult bees look alike » (= « Toutes les abeilles adultes se ressemblent »). En effet, « it is true of each of them that the body is divided into three distinct parts ».***

(B) B *La phrase parle des abeilles pas de leurs têtes.*

(C) C *Ni la phrase qui précède, ni celle qui suit ne parle du corps des abeilles, la phrase serait hors-sujet.*

(D) D *Il ne serait pas correct de placer une liste de similitudes entre abeilles juste après la phrase qui annonce la présence de différences entre les individus d'une colonie : « differences between the various individuals forming a colony. »*

▪ Question 3 - Solution

Look at the four squares the paragraph, A, B, C, and D, which indicate where the following sentence could be added to the passage. Where would the sentence best fit?

Dr Johnson once said that the grand object of all travel is to see the shores of the Mediterranean.

A The Mediterranean world has a special beauty to it. The stark light, the soaring mountains, the sparkling sea, and much else contribute to make landscapes that have long attracted people from afar. B Apparently, little has changed since the eighteenth century: today one-third of all international tourism in the world involves Mediterranean countries. But, in fact, a good deal has changed, including the landscapes themselves. C The beauty of the Mediterranean mountains is in a way a sad one. D Skeletal mountains and shell villages dot the upland areas of the Mediterranean world, dominating the physical and social landscape.

(A) A *Cela ne respecterait pas la progression logique du texte. L'auteur passe du global à des cas précis. Du monde méditerranéen à ses côtes (= « shores »).*

(B) ✓ **B** ***À cet endroit, la phrase est à la fois une confirmation de ce qui est dit juste avant et une introduction pour ce qui suit.***

(C) C *La phrase viendrait contredire la phrase qui suit.*

(D) D *Il n'y a pas de lien cohérent avec la suite.*

Question type : Prose Summary questions

Description

Dans ces questions, vous devrez choisir 3 propositions parmi 6 qui résument au mieux les idées principales du texte. Ces questions valent deux points.

N.B. : Pour des raisons techniques, nous n'avons pas pu reproduire ces questions à l'identique dans nos supports. Il s'agit d'un inconvénient de notre couplage avec le numérique. Nous avons donc volontairement transformé ces questions en QCM classiques. Sur le plan pédagogique, elles sont pratiquement identiques aux questions que vous rencontrerez le jour de l'épreuve (en moyenne, vous rencontrerez 2 questions de ce type sur l'ensemble de l'épreuve).

Exemple

Ce type de question est formulé sous la forme :

An introductory sentence for a brief summary of the passage is provided below. Complete the summary by selecting THREE answer choices that express the most important ideas in the passage. Some answer choices do not belong in the summary because they express ideas that are not presented or are minor ideas in the passage. This question is worth 2 points.

Drag your answer choices to the spaces where they belong. To remove an answer choice, click it. To review the passage click on View Text.

"Continental Drift" theorizes that continents are able move around the globe.

•

•

•

(A) Wegener believed Continental Drift was caused by a process of thermal convection under the Earth's surface.
(B) It hypothesized that a land-bridge may once have connected Africa and South America.
(C) It attempted to explain how and why similar plants and animals could be found on distant continents.
(D) Many scientists criticized the Wegener's theory because it lacked an adequate explanation for how Continental Drift occurred.
(E) Thermal convection pushes hot, semi-solid rock upwards where it cools near the Earth's surface.

Méthodologie

Il y a 2 types de mauvaises réponses :

1. Contresens ou phrases inexactes.
2. Les propositions reprenant un détail du texte ne pouvant pas être considérées comme une idée générale.

N'oubliez pas qu'il s'agit de sélectionner les idées les plus importantes. Le fait qu'une réponse soit véridique et mentionnée dans le texte n'en fait pas nécessairement une bonne réponse. Le concepteur crée la plupart des mauvaises réponses en reprenant presque mot pour mot un détail insignifiant du texte, c'est comme cela qu'il analyse votre capacité à identifier et résumer un cours universitaire.

Entraînement - Prose Summary questions

Reportez vos réponses pour analyser votre performance.

Entraînez-vous dans les conditions d'examen.

prepmyfuture.com/book/68/ex/1927

Mammalian palaeontological and archaeological work in southern Africa has a history reaching back nearly two centuries, though this initially took the form of what Underhill calls a "Victorian penchant [for] the recognition and collection of artefacts". Probably the first published report of a fossil from South Africa was made in 1839 and it was not until early in the twentieth century that palaeontological work began in earnest published seminal works on the Stone Ages of South Africa. What might be described as the modern era began some 20 years later. South African mammalian palaeontology received a major boost with the report of Australopithecus africanus from Taung, and by the second half of the 1930s Broom had begun to describe material from the extremely rich limestone caves of the then Transvaal, which continue to yield new forms. The palaeontological importance of Namibia (then South West Africa) only began to be appreciated during the 1920s, but the importance of this country for Eocene and Miocene mammalian evolution has since become abundantly clear through the ongoing work of Martin Pickford and colleagues. The systematic study of southern African archaeology has a similar history, beginning with the work of Goodwin and van Riet Lowe. However, archaeologists were not at first concerned with the faunal element, apart from human remains, which received attention from very early on. One of the earliest general faunal reports was that of Brain on material from Bushman Rock Shelter. From these beginnings there has developed exponentially a body of information on around 650 taxa collected from over 600 sites in more than 150 degree-squares dating from the Eocene onwards. With such an ever-growing wealth of data it has become increasingly difficult, especially for non-specialists, to find information on specific taxa*.

*Taxa: In biology, a taxon (plural taxa; back-formation from taxonomy) is a group of one or more populations of an organism or organisms seen by taxonomists to form a unit.

■ **Question 1** An introductory sentence for a brief summary of the passage is provided below. Complete the summary by selecting the THREE answer choices that express the most important ideas in the passage. Some sentences do not belong in the summary because they express ideas that are not presented in the passage or are minor ideas in the passage. This question is worth 2 points.

- Mammal fossils in southern Africa have been an object of studies for about two hundred years.
-
-
-

(A) Archaeological studies in Africa started with Underhill in the Victorian Age.

(B) The modern era of palaeontological work in southern Africa began in the 1920s.

(C) The initial focus of archaeologists working in southern Africa was on faunal remains.

(D) Paleontological and archaeological studies in southern Africa have developed similarly.

(E) A total of 650 taxa have been collected only in Namibia.

(F) Archaeological studies have led to the creation of a database so vast that it is almost confusing for non-experts.

The decision to turn pirate was usually driven by one of two forces: on the one hand, grievances such as abject poverty, unemployment and a generally bleak future; and, on the other, greed or the lure of easy money. Fleeing from justice was another powerful driver: the 'sea had always served as a refuge for the lawless and criminal elements in society'. In the late Middle Ages, the years between 1250 and 1500, there were places that enjoyed economic growth in the Mediterranean which presented many perfectly legal opportunities for enterprising individuals, especially highly skilled artisans. But there were also pockets of stagnation with rising levels of unemployment accelerated by population growth, and spots where endemic poverty was made worse by the incessant raids and counter-raids of various sea powers and their regular navies, who were in turn backed up by privateers – or corsairs – operating with a licence, and pirates operating without one. Not surprisingly, grievance and greed worked together to turn some locations into piracy hot spots – some of which survived into the nineteenth century. Piracy centered, among other places, on the English Channel, a highly important seaway, a rich commercial artery, an essential link in the trade which formed the foundation for the rising economy of the western world. On the other hand, it was also a political frontier between two evolving, ambitious and belligerent monarchies, England and France. Throughout this period those two countries were hostile to each other. While the commercial world needed stability in order to function satisfactorily and to the benefit of nearly everyone, the political world was far from stable. On the grounds of both expense and war-weariness of the troops, it was beyond the means of any monarch to continue declared, open warfare for more than a few years. It was much cheaper, and more effective, to operate unofficially. One means of doing so was to encourage piracy.

Question 2 An introductory sentence for a brief summary of the passage is provided below. Complete the summary by selecting the THREE answer choices that express the most important ideas in the passage. Some sentences do not belong in the summary because they express ideas that are not presented in the passage or are minor ideas in the passage.

- People had specific reasons to become pirates.
-
-
-

(A) In the late Middle Ages, all artisans began to enjoy a period of financial prosperity.

(B) England and France fought over the control of the Channel.

(C) Poor life conditions caused certain areas to have a higher presence of pirates.

(D) Oftentimes, in periods of political and financial crises, rulers would become pirates.

(E) The English Channel became a piracy hot spot for both political and commercial reasons.

(F) Monarchs would use piracy to undermine the enemy powers.

Geoffrey Chaucer (C.1342–1400) was perhaps the most creative spirit ever to write in English. Indeed, it could be argued that he created English as a medium of art. Before him, we had a tongue, spoken and to some degree written. After him, we had a literature. He came, to be sure, at a good time. In his grandfather's day, England still had a hieratic-demotic language structure. Only the plebeians habitually spoke English, in a variety of bewildering regional forms. The ruling class spoke French and wrote in Latin. Edward I and his son Edward II spoke French. They understood some English, though they certainly did not, and probably could not, write it. Edward III, born in 1312—he was a generation older than Chaucer—spoke English fluently. The Hundred Years' War, which he launched five years before Chaucer was born, opened a deep chasm between England and France that made the close interaction and simultaneous development of their culture no longer possible. The use of French in official transactions went into precipitous decline. The rise of English as the language of law and government was formally recognized by the Statute of Pleading (1362), when Chaucer was a young man. It ordered that in all the courts, all cases "shall be pleaded, showed, answered, debated and judged in the English tongue." The following year the lord chancellor, for the first time, opened Parliament with a speech in English. A new era was about to begin.

▪ Question 3

Directions: An introductory sentence for a brief summary of the passage is provided below. Complete the summary by selecting the THREE answer choices that express the most important ideas in the passage. Some sentences do not belong in the summary because they express ideas that are not presented in the passage or are minor ideas in the passage.

- Geoffrey Chaucer used English for artistic purposes.
-
-
-

(A) Chaucer's contribution was fundamental to the development of the English language.

(B) Chaucer is considered to be the most creative person ever lived.

(C) The Hundred Years' War was the reason why the English and the French culture had separate developments.

(D) In Chaucer's time, English was only spoken by the lower class, while nobles would use French and Latin.

(E) The use of English in official institutions represented a milestone in its development as a language.

(F) The Statue of Pleading caused a rapid decrease in the use of French.

Solutions

Reportez vos réponses pour analyser votre performance.

Entraînez-vous dans les conditions d'examen.

prepmyfuture.com/book/68/ex/1927

question 1	B D F

question 2	C E F

question 3	A C E

■ Question 1 - Solution

An introductory sentence for a brief summary of the passage is provided below. Complete the summary by selecting the THREE answer choices that express the most important ideas in the passage. Some sentences do not belong in the summary because they express ideas that are not presented in the passage or are minor ideas in the passage. This question is worth 2 points.

- Mammal fossils in southern Africa have been an object of studies for about two hundred years.
-
-
-

(A) Archaeological studies in Africa started with Underhill in the Victorian Age.

= Les études archéologiques en Afrique ont commencé avec Underhill à l'époque victorienne.
Underhill a seulement utilisé l'adjectif « Victorian » dans sa description. Il n'est pas dit que que les études archéologiques débutèrent pendant la période Victorienne.

(B) ✓ The modern era of palaeontological work in southern Africa began in the 1920s.

= L'ère moderne des travaux paléontologiques en Afrique australe a commencé dans les années 1920.
« Probably the first published report of a fossil from South Africa was made in 1839 and it was not until early in the twentieth century that palaeontological work began in earnest published seminal works on the Stone Ages of South Africa. What might be described as the modern era began some 20 years later. »
(= « Le premier rapport publié sur un fossile d'Afrique du Sud date probablement de 1839 et ce n'est qu'au début du vingtième siècle que les travaux paléontologiques ont commencé sérieusement avec la publication d'ouvrages de référence sur l'âge de pierre en Afrique du Sud. Ce que l'on pourrait décrire comme l'ère moderne a commencé une vingtaine d'années plus tard. »)

(C) The initial focus of archaeologists working in southern Africa was on faunal remains.

= Les archéologues travaillant en Afrique australe se sont d'abord concentrés sur les vestiges de la faune.
« However, archaeologists were not at first concerned with the faunal element » (= « Cependant, les archéologues ne se sont pas tout de suite intéressés à la faune »)

(D)	**✓ Paleontological and archaeological studies in southern Africa have developed similarly.**	**= Les études paléontologiques et archéologiques en Afrique australe se sont développées de manière similaire.** ***« The palaeontological importance of Namibia (then South West Africa) only began to be appreciated during the 1920s, but the importance of this country for Eocene and Miocene mammalian evolution has since become abundantly clear through the ongoing work of Martin Pickford and colleagues. The systematic study of southern African archaeology has a similar history »*** ***(= « L'importance paléontologique de la Namibie (alors Sud-Ouest de l'Afrique) n'a commencé à être reconnue que dans les années 1920, mais l'importance de ce pays pour l'évolution des mammifères de l'Éocène et du Miocène est depuis devenue évidente grâce au travail continu de Martin Pickford et de ses collègues. L'étude systématique de l'archéologie de l'Afrique australe a une histoire similaire »)***
(E)	A total of 650 taxa have been collected only in Namibia.	= Un total de 650 taxons a été collecté uniquement en Namibie. *L'auteur ne spécifie pas si toutes les taxes ont été collectées en Namibie. De plus, l'information n'aurait pas été de première importance compte tenu du thème général du paragraphe.*
(F)	**✓ Archaeological studies have led to the creation of a database so vast that it is almost confusing for non-experts.**	**= Les études archéologiques ont conduit à la création d'une base de données si vaste qu'elle en devient presque confuse pour les non spécialistes.** ***« With such an ever-growing wealth of data It has become increasingly difficult, especially for non-specialists, to find information on specific taxa »*** ***(= « Avec une telle abondance de données, il est devenu de plus en plus difficile, surtout pour les non-spécialistes, de trouver des informations sur des taxons spécifiques. »)***

- **Question 2 - Solution**

An introductory sentence for a brief summary of the passage is provided below. Complete the summary by selecting the THREE answer choices that express the most important ideas in the passage. Some sentences do not belong in the summary because they express ideas that are not presented in the passage or are minor ideas in the passage.

- People had specific reasons to become pirates.
-
-
-

(A)	In the late Middle Ages, all artisans began to enjoy a period of financial prosperity.	= À la fin du Moyen Âge, tous les artisans ont commencé à bénéficier d'une période de prospérité financière. *« many perfectly legal opportunities for enterprising individuals, especially highly skilled artisans ». (= « de nombreuses opportunités parfaitement légales pour les personnes qui entreprennent, en particulier les artisans hautement qualifiés »)* *Le texte ne réfère pas à tous les artisans mais seulement à ceux extrêmement qualifiés. Le texte porte sur le sujet de la piraterie, cette information n'est donc pas de première importance.*
(B)	England and France fought over the control of the Channel.	= L'Angleterre et la France se sont disputées le contrôle de la Manche. *L'auteur dit que l'Angleterre et la France étaient en guerre, il ne dit pas que la cause du conflit est liée au contrôle de la Manche (= English Channel).*

(C)	**✓ Poor life conditions caused certain areas to have a higher presence of pirates.**	**= Les mauvaises conditions de vie ont fait que certaines régions ont connu une présence plus importante de pirates.** ***La phrase résume bien les premières lignes du paragraphe.***
(D)	Oftentimes, in periods of political and financial crises, rulers would become pirates.	= Souvent, en période de crise politique et financière, les dirigeants se transformaient en pirates. *L'auteur dit que, dans certaines conditions, les dirigeants utilisaient la piraterie comme un moyen d'affaiblir leurs ennemis. Il ne dit pas qu'ils devenaient eux-même pirate.*
(E)	**✓ The English Channel became a piracy hot spot for both political and commercial reasons.**	**= La Manche est devenue un point stratégique de la piraterie pour des raisons politiques et commerciales.** ***« Piracy centered, among other places, on the English Channel, a highly important seaway, a rich commercial artery, an essential link in the trade which formed the foundation for the rising economy of the western world. On the other hand, it was also a political frontier. »*** ***(= « La piraterie se concentrait, entre autres, sur la Manche, une voie maritime très importante, une riche artère commerciale, un lien essentiel dans le commerce qui constituait la base de l'économie croissante du monde occidental. D'autre part, c'était aussi une frontière politique »)***
(F)	**✓ Monarchs would use piracy to undermine the enemy powers.**	**= Les monarques utilisaient la piraterie pour saper les pouvoirs ennemis.** ***« ... it was beyond the means of any monarch to continue declared, open warfare for more than a few years. It was much cheaper, and more effective, to operate unofficially. One means of doing so was to encourage piracy. »*** ***(= « ... aucun monarque n'avait les moyens de poursuivre une guerre ouverte et déclarée pendant plusieurs années. Il était beaucoup moins cher, et plus efficace, d'opérer de manière non officielle. Un moyen d'y parvenir était d'encourager la piraterie. »)***

■ Question 3 - Solution

Directions: An introductory sentence for a brief summary of the passage is provided below. Complete the summary by selecting the THREE answer choices that express the most important ideas in the passage. Some sentences do not belong in the summary because they express ideas that are not presented in the passage or are minor ideas in the passage.

- Geoffrey Chaucer used English for artistic purposes.
-
-
-

(A)	**✓ Chaucer's contribution was fundamental to the development of the English language.**	**= La contribution de Chaucer a été fondamentale pour le développement de la langue anglaise.** ***« it could be argued that he created English as a medium of art. Before him, we had a tongue, spoken and to some degree written. After him, we had a literature. »*** ***(= « on pourrait dire qu'il a créé l'anglais comme un moyen d'expression artistique. Avant lui, nous avions une langue, parlée et, dans une certaine mesure, écrite. Après lui, nous avions une littérature. »)***
(B)	Chaucer is considered to be the most creative person ever lived.	= Chaucer est considéré comme la personne la plus créative qui ait jamais vécu. *L'auteur décrit Chaucer comme « perhaps the most creative spirit ever to write in English ». (= « peut-être l'esprit le plus créatif qui ait jamais écrit en anglais »)* *Il ne dit pas qu'il était la personne la plus créative de l'histoire.*

(C) ✓ **The Hundred Years' War was the reason why the English and the French culture had separate developments.**

= La guerre de Cent Ans est la raison pour laquelle les cultures anglaise et française se sont développées séparément.

« The Hundred Years' War, which he launched five years before Chaucer was born, opened a deep chasm between England and France that made the close interaction and simultaneous development of their culture no longer possible. » "(= « La guerre de Cent Ans, qu'il a déclenchée cinq ans avant la naissance de Chaucer, a ouvert un profond gouffre entre l'Angleterre et la France qui a rendu impossible l'interaction étroite et le développement simultané de leur culture. »)

Cette information est essentielle pour comprendre comment la langue anglaise s'est développée.

(D) In Chaucer's time, English was only spoken by the lower class, while nobles would use French and Latin.

= À l'époque de Chaucer, l'anglais n'était parlé que par la classe populaire, tandis que les nobles utilisaient le français et le latin.
L'auteur décrit ce à quoi la situation linguistique ressemblait à l'époque du grand-père de Chaucer.

(E) ✓ **The use of English in official institutions represented a milestone in its development as a language.**

= L'utilisation de l'anglais dans les institutions officielles a représenté une étape importante dans son développement en tant que langue.
« The rise of English as the language of law and government... »; « It ordered that in all the courts, all cases 'shall be pleaded, showed, answered, debated and judged in the English tongue.' The following year the lord chancellor, for the first time, opened Parliament with a speech in English. A new era was about to begin. »
(= « L'essor de l'anglais comme langue de la loi et du gouvernement... » ; « Il ordonne que dans tous les tribunaux, toutes les affaires "soient plaidées, montrées, répondues, débattues et jugées en langue anglaise". L'année suivante, le lord chancelier, pour la première fois, ouvre le Parlement par un discours en anglais. Une nouvelle ère était sur le point de commencer. »)

(F) The Statue of Pleading caused a rapid decrease in the use of French.

= Le *Statue of Pleading* a entraîné une diminution rapide de l'utilisation du français.
« The Hundred Years' War, which he launched five years before Chaucer was born, opened a deep chasm between England and France that made the close interaction and simultaneous development of their culture no longer possible. The use of French in official transactions went into precipitous decline. »
(= « La guerre de Cent Ans, qu'il a déclenchée cinq ans avant la naissance de Chaucer, a ouvert un profond gouffre entre l'Angleterre et la France qui a rendu impossible l'interaction étroite et le développement simultané de leur culture. L'usage du français dans les transactions officielles connut un déclin précipité. »)

Vous avez besoin d'exercices supplémentaires ?

Le mode "premium" de la plateforme en ligne vous donne accès à des exercices inédits dont plusieurs centaines de questions de type "TOEFL".

SECTION - LISTENING

Méthode

Présentation générale

Durée	La durée varie de 41 à 57 minutes en fonction du nombre de bandes audio à écouter.
Nombre de questions	28 à 39 questions (5 à 6 questions par bande audio)
Nombre de bandes audio	5 à 7 bandes audio à écouter : • 3 ou 4 cours universitaires, chacun associé à 6 questions. • 2 ou 3 discussions sur le campus universitaire, chacune associée à 5 questions.
Durée des audios	• 3 à 5 minutes pour les cours universitaires • 3 minutes pour les discussions sur le campus universitaire.
Les accents utilisés	Accents anglais de locuteurs natifs d'Amérique du Nord, du Royaume-Uni, de Nouvelle-Zélande et d'Australie.
Déroulement de l'épreuve	Chaque bande audio est précédée d'une courte phrase d'introduction vous permettant d'identifier le contexte. Vous ne pouvez écouter la bande audio qu'une seule fois. Il n'est pas possible de mettre la bande audio en pause. Vous ne pouvez pas revenir en arrière.
Consignes officielles	*This section measures your ability to understand conversations and lectures in English.* *Audio portions of the Listening section are provided wherever you see the headphones icon:* *Listen to each recording only once. Next, answer the questions. The questions typically ask about the main idea and supporting details. Some questions ask about a speaker's purpose or attitude. Answer the questions based on what is stated or implied by the speakers.* *Answer each question before moving on. Do not return to previous questions. Give yourself 10 minutes to answer all the questions in the Listening section. Do not count the time it takes to listen to or read the conversation and lectures.* *Now begin the Listening section.* FR : Cette section mesure votre capacité à comprendre des conversations et des conférences en anglais. Les parties audio de la section *Listening* sont proposées partout où vous voyez l'icône des écouteurs : N'écoutez chaque enregistrement qu'une seule fois. Ensuite, répondez aux questions. Les questions portent généralement sur l'idée principale et sur des détails. Certaines questions portent sur l'objectif ou l'attitude du locuteur. Répondez aux questions en fonction de ce qui est dit ou sous-entendu par les locuteurs. Répondez à chaque question avant de passer à la suivante. Ne revenez pas sur les questions précédentes. Donnez-vous 10 minutes pour répondre à toutes les questions de la section *Listening*. Ne comptez pas le temps

	nécessaire pour écouter ou lire la conversation et les exposés. Commencez maintenant la section *Listening*.
Notation	0 à 30 points (25 % de la note finale)

Présentation détaillée

Tout comme la partie *Reading*, les questions ne testent pas seulement votre compréhension de l'anglais. Les questions seront beaucoup moins difficiles que celles de la partie *Reading*, mais un autre type de difficulté entrera en jeu : votre capacité à mémoriser le discours.

En effet, les bandes-son sont longues et de nombreuses questions portent sur des détails. Vos capacités de concentration et de mémorisation seront donc importantes dans cette section.

Voici une liste des principales compétences testées dans la section *Listening* :

- compréhension globale du contexte.
- mémorisation de détails.
- compréhension d'expressions idiomatiques.
- concentration pendant l'écoute de bandes-son longues.

Les questions sont sous format QCM avec 4 choix de réponse dont seulement une est correcte. Dans certaines questions, vous devez cocher deux propositions de réponse, cela sera clairement indiqué.

Environ un quart des questions vous permet de réécouter un extrait du discours. Ces questions insistent généralement sur une expression idiomatique.

N.B. : Il est possible que votre partie *Listening* comporte des questions supplémentaires. Les concepteurs introduisent en effet des exercices supplémentaires dans les parties *Reading* et *Listening* pour tester de nouvelles questions. Dans ce cas, les questions testées ne compteront pas dans le calcul de votre score. Il ne sera pas possible d'identifier les questions qui ne compteront pas, il faudra donc répondre à toutes les questions avec la même attention aux détails.

Stratégies

Conseil n°1 : Gérer sa concentration

La concentration est la clef du succès dans cette section du TOEFL. Vous êtes face à une double difficulté :

- la compréhension générale du discours.
- la mémorisation des détails pour les questions de types « informations factuelles ».

Privilégiez votre compréhension générale du texte à la mémorisation de tous les détails. En effet, les questions portant sur des détails seront beaucoup moins difficiles que leurs homologues de la partie *Reading*.

Conseil n°2 : Connaître la structure des mauvaises réponses

Il s'agit des mêmes que celles de la section *Reading* avec un panel encore plus limité de structures de mauvaises réponses.

Les mauvaises propositions de réponse sont conçues en suivant un cahier des charges précis et rigoureux. Dans la partie *Listening*, la quasi-totalité des propositions incorrectes rentre dans l'une des catégories suivantes. Bien connaître les mécanismes de création des propositions incorrectes vous permettra de vous poser les bonnes questions pour éliminer des mauvaises réponses.

- **Contresens :** Le concepteur fabrique un choix de réponse en contradiction avec ce qui est dit dans le passage. Il s'agit souvent d'une inversion entre deux choses ou deux personnes. Ces choix de réponse sont faciles à éliminer si vous avez compris le texte.
- **Inexact / Exagération :** Le choix de réponse ne correspond pas exactement à ce qui est dit dans l'audio. Ces réponses sont plus difficiles à identifier. Souvent, ce type de réponse utilise des adverbes clivants et exagérés comme : *always, any, too much, never,* etc. Dès que vous identifiez ce type de vocabulaire, vous devez vous méfier, il s'agit sans doute d'une mauvaise réponse.
- **Extrapolation :** C'est le type de réponse le plus courant et le plus facile à traiter si vous avez écouté attentivement la bande-son. Dans ces choix de réponse, le concepteur indique quelque chose qui n'est pas mentionné dans le texte.

Type de passage : Lecture (cours universitaire)

Dans ce type de passage audio, vous écouterez un professeur donner un cours universitaire (*lecture* en anglais). Il s'agit d'un long monologue, parfois coupé par quelques questions d'étudiants.

Les thèmes abordés dans ces cours universitaires sont similaires aux textes rencontrés dans la partie *Reading.* Il s'agit de vrais cours universitaires de niveau BAC+1 / BAC+2 sur des thématiques variées telles que la sociologie, l'histoire, la biologie, la littérature, etc.

Les phrases sont longues et peuvent être complexes. Le passage audio est long et souvent monotone. Cela rend ce type d'exercice très difficile. Les questions de *Listening* sont cependant beaucoup plus simples que celles que vous trouverez en *Reading*.

Exemple - Lecture (cours universitaire) - avec Script

Reportez vos réponses pour analyser votre performance.

Entraînez-vous dans les conditions d'examen.

Écoutez les fichiers audio.

prepmyfuture.com/book/68/ex/1913

Listen to part of a lecture in an anthropology class.

1) Cryptozoology

Script non affiché le jour de l'examen :

MALE PROFESSOR: It is commonly believed that every inch of our planet has been thoroughly explored, and that science possesses a complete list of every living animal species. However, this is simply not the case. Even in places such as the United States, there remain vast, unpopulated regions which, although surveyed from the air, are rarely traveled by people on the ground. The same is true on nearly every continent, save Europe. A surprising number of new species of animals are still being found each year—some 5,000 new species annually. While a great majority of these are insects, we are still discovering new mammals, fish and birds of various sizes and in various habitats. Examples range from the Kodiak bear of Alaska, the largest known bear species, which was discovered by scientists in 1899, to the largest lizard in the world, the Komodo Dragon, first captured in 1921.

In fact, there is a whole branch of science devoted to the investigation of species whose existence has been reported but not fully documented—cryptozoology. Cryptozoologists attempt to track down reports of new or unusual animals, looking for eye-witness reports, photographs and physical evidence that might lead to the discovery of a new animal species. And for cryptozoologists, evidence for the existence of one type of alleged creature is prized above all others. This creature has many names around the world—Yeti, Almas, and Sasquatch—but it is most commonly known as Bigfoot.

2) Bigfoot

Script non affiché le jour de l'examen :

Over the past two hundred years, researchers have accumulated a large amount of stories and possible evidence for the existence of Bigfoot, but even before then, images of hairy wildmen are found on art objects dating as far back as ancient Greece and Rome. During the Middle Ages, wildmen were also depicted in European art and architecture, and stories from that time told of wildmen—hairy, large creatures living in caves and forests whom the local populace did not consider humans because they could not speak. Similar stories came from the Himalayas and Central Asia in the 19th century, where wildmen had supposedly been seen, killed and even captured.

The Native Americans of the northwestern United States and western Canada still to this day believe in the reality of Bigfoot. Their folklore speaks of incredibly large and powerful human-like creatures, covered in dark fur, with long arms, and bringing with them an awful smell. The yells of these creatures are said to be low, long, eerie moans that do not sound like any other animal in those regions.

After Europeans began to explore and settle the western region of North America, reports of these monstrous, hairy creatures only grew in number, often with stories ending in death. In one famous incident included in a book written by President Teddy Roosevelt, two white men traveling through the wilderness of Montana were harassed over several days by a huge, hairy beast which walked on two feet and lingered near their camp at night. Whenever they left their camp, they would return to find the whole camp torn apart, with numerous, large human-like footprints scattered about the camp. A few days later, one of the men went far away from camp to check some animal traps they had laid—when he returned, he found his companion's dead body, his neck broken and great teeth marks on his throat; strangely, for the first time in days, all their supplies were untouched.

Speculation as to what these supposed creatures could be vary widely, and researchers examine every story and shred of evidence collected over the years to develop hypotheses on the origin of these wildmen. Perhaps they are descendants of Neanderthals, a sub-species of humans that are supposed to have gone extinct some 30,000 to 40,000 years ago—however, evidence shows that Neanderthals used tools, but in all the stories of wildmen or Bigfoot never were any of those creatures seen to be using even the most primitive tool. Perhaps they are a completely new species of human-like creature—considering the fact that no body or remains have ever been found, it is possible that these creatures have eluded science because of how they hide or bury their dead. Whatever they are, we still lack the definitive piece of evidence to prove their existence—a physical specimen.

Despite the longevity of legends of Bigfoot and creatures like it around the world, most mainstream anthropologists and zoologists still decline to even discuss their existence. However, a growing number of scientists now believe that the question of their existence is, at the very least, worthy of serious study. It is not completely outside the realm of possibility that science might someday come to fully accept the existence of wildmen. It would not be the first time that science has found examples of what have been come to be called 'living fossils'.

Question 1 What is the lecture mainly about?

(A) the usefulness in searching for new species of animals
(B) a description of creature that may or may not exist
(C) why scientists are still discovering new species every year
(D) how scientists search for evidence for new animal species

Question 2 According to the professor, why were wildmen not considered human by people living in the Middle Ages?

(A) They would attack human travelers who camped in the wilderness.
(B) They did not always walk upright.
(C) They did not seem to have the capacity to use spoken language.
(D) They lived in caves far from human settlements.

Question 3 According to the professor, why is Bigfoot, if it exists, probably not Neanderthals?

(A) The region where Bigfoot probably exists does not correspond with the location where Neanderthals lived.
(B) The physical description of Bigfoot does not fit that of Neanderthals.
(C) Bigfoot has never been observed to use objects as tools.
(D) Unlike Neanderthals, Bigfoot does not seem to possess the ability to speak.

Question 4 Why does the professor mention Greece and Rome?

(A) to point out that belief in wildmen may have existed in ancient cultures
(B) to identify which cultures first began trying to prove the existence of wildmen
(C) to argue that modern stories of wildmen are based on ancient folklore
(D) to explain why wildmen exist in different regions of the world

■ Question 5 According to the lecture, which of the following statements is true?

(A) Stories of wildmen have decreased in the last two hundred years.
(B) Interest in wildmen has grown recently in the scientific community.
(C) Europeans first heard about wildmen after they arrived in North America.
(D) There is a widespread agreement in the scientific community as to what species Bigfoot probably is.

■ Question 6 Why does the professor tell the story about the two men in Montana?

(A) To explain why Native Americans were afraid of Bigfoot.
(B) To point out that all encounters with a Bigfoot are dangerous.
(C) To describe when European settlers first encountered a Bigfoot.
(D) To provide an example of a possibly deadly encounter with a Bigfoot.

Solutions

Reportez vos réponses pour analyser votre performance.

Entraînez-vous dans les conditions d'examen.

prepmyfuture.com/book/68/ex/1913

question 1	B
question 2	C
question 3	C
question 4	A
question 5	B
question 6	D

Question 1 - Solution

What is the lecture mainly about?

FR : Quel est le sujet principal du cours ?

(A) the usefulness in searching for new species of animals
= l'utilité de la recherche de nouvelles espèces d'animaux
Le cours présente la cryptozoologie mais ne dit pas pourquoi il s'agit d'une science utile.

(B) ✓ a description of creature that may or may not exist
= la description d'une créature qui pourrait exister ou non

(C) why scientists are still discovering new species every year
= la raison pour laquelle les scientifiques découvrent encore de nouvelles espèces chaque année
Même si le cours évoque le fait que le monde entier n'a pas encore été complètement exploré, il s'agit d'un thème secondaire.

(D) how scientists search for evidence for new animal species
= la façon dont les scientifiques recherchent des preuves de l'existence de nouvelles espèces animales

Question 2 - Solution

According to the professor, why were wildmen not considered human by people living in the Middle Ages?

FR : Selon le professeur, pourquoi les hommes sauvages n'étaient pas considérés comme humains pendant le Moyen-Age ?

(A)	They would attack human travelers who camped in the wilderness.	= Ils attaquaient les voyageurs qui campaient dans les régions sauvages.
(B)	They did not always walk upright.	= Ils ne marchaient pas toujours debout.
(C) ✓	**They did not seem to have the capacity to use spoken language.**	**= Ils ne semblaient pas être capables d'utiliser le langage parlé.** ***« During the Middle Ages, wildmen were [...] whom the local populace did not consider humans because they could not speak. »*** ***(= « Au Moyen Âge, les hommes sauvages étaient [...] ceux que la population locale ne considérait pas comme des humains parce qu'ils ne pouvaient pas parler. »)***
(D)	They lived in caves far from human settlements.	= Ils ne semblaient pas être capables d'utiliser le langage parlé. *Ils habitaient effectivement dans des caves mais ce n'était pas la raison pour laquelle les gens ne les considéraient pas comme humains.*

■ Question 3 - Solution

According to the professor, why is Bigfoot, if it exists, probably not Neanderthals?

FR : Selon le professeur, pourquoi le BigFoot, s'il existe, n'était probablement pas un Neandertal ?

(A)	The region where Bigfoot probably exists does not correspond with the location where Neanderthals lived.	= La région où *Bigfoot* se trouve probablement ne correspond pas à l'endroit où vivaient les hommes de Néandertal. *Il n'est pas précisé où habitaient les hommes de Neandertal.*
(B)	The physical description of Bigfoot does not fit that of Neanderthals.	= La description physique de *Bigfoot* ne correspond pas à celle des hommes de Néandertal. *Le professeur ne donne pas d'indication relative au physique des hommes de Neandertal.*
(C) ✓	**Bigfoot has never been observed to use objects as tools.**	**= On n'a jamais pu constater que le *Bigfoot* utilisait des objets en guise d'outils.** ***« evidence shows that Neanderthals used tools, but in all the stories of wildmen or Bigfoot never were any of those creatures seen to be using even the most primitive tool. »*** ***(= « Les preuves montrent que les hommes de Neandertal utilisaient des outils, mais dans toutes les histoires d'hommes sauvages ou de Bigfoot, on n'a jamais vu aucune de ces créatures utiliser un outil, même le plus primitif. »)***
(D)	Unlike Neanderthals, Bigfoot does not seem to possess the ability to speak.	= Contrairement aux hommes de Néandertal, le *Bigfoot* ne semble pas avoir la faculté de parler.

■ Question 4 - Solution

Why does the professor mention Greece and Rome?

FR : Pourquoi le professeur mentionne-t-il la Grèce et Rome ?

(A) ✓	**to point out that belief in wildmen may have existed in ancient cultures**	**= pour souligner que la croyance en des hommes sauvages a pu exister dans des cultures anciennes** ***« evidence for the existence of Bigfoot, but even before then, images of hairy wildmen are found on art objects dating as far back as ancient Greece and Rome. »*** ***(= « [...] des preuves de l'existence de Bigfoot, mais même avant cela, on trouve des images de sauvages chevelus sur des objets d'art remontant à la Grèce et à la Rome antiques. »)***
(B)	to identify which cultures first began trying to prove the existence of wildmen	= pour souligner que la croyance en des hommes sauvages a pu exister dans des cultures anciennes *Il n'est pas précisé que la Grèce et la Rome antiques furent les premiers à donner des preuves de l'existence des hommes sauvages.*
(C)	to argue that modern stories of wildmen are based on ancient folklore	= pour soutenir que les histoires contemporaines d'hommes sauvages sont basées sur un folklore ancien *Le professeur liste de nombreuses preuves que Bigfoot a peut-être existé. Il n'essaie pas d'invalider la théorie.*
(D)	to explain why wildmen exist in different regions of the world	= pour soutenir que les histoires contemporaines d'hommes sauvages sont basées sur un folklore ancien *En mentionnant la Grèce et la Rome antiques, il n'est pas en train d'expliquer pourquoi les hommes sauvages étaient présents dans différentes parties du monde.*

▪ Question 5 - Solution

According to the lecture, which of the following statements is true?

FR : D'après le cours, laquelle de ces propositions est vraie ?

(A)	Stories of wildmen have decreased in the last two hundred years.	= Les récits d'hommes sauvages ont diminué au cours des 200 dernières années.
(B) ✓	**Interest in wildmen has grown recently in the scientific community.**	**= L'intérêt pour les hommes sauvages a récemment progressé dans la communauté scientifique.** ***« However, a growing number of scientists now believe that the question of their existence is, at the very least, worthy of serious study. »*** ***(= « Toutefois, un nombre croissant de scientifiques estiment aujourd'hui que la question de leur existence mérite, au minimum, d'être sérieusement étudiée. »)***
(C)	Europeans first heard about wildmen after they arrived in North America.	= Les Européens ont entendu parler des hommes sauvages pour la première fois après leur arrivée en Amérique du Nord. *La Grèce et la Rome antiques mentionnaient déjà l'existence d'hommes sauvages.*
(D)	There is a widespread agreement in the scientific community as to what species Bigfoot probably is.	= La communauté scientifique s'accorde largement à reconnaître de quelle espèce Bigfoot est probablement issu. *De nombreux scientifiques pensent que le Bigfoot n'existe pas.* *« mainstream anthropologists and zoologists still decline to even discuss their existence » (= « Toutefois, un nombre croissant de scientifiques estiment aujourd'hui que la question de leur existence mérite, au minimum, d'être sérieusement étudiée. »)*

- **Question 6 - Solution**

Why does the professor tell the story about the two men in Montana?

FR : Pourquoi le professeur parle-t-il de l'histoire des deux hommes dans le Montana ?

(A)	To explain why Native Americans were afraid of Bigfoot.	= pour expliquer pourquoi les Amérindiens avaient peur de *Bigfoot* *Aucun lien n'est fait par le professeur entre l'épisode du Montana et les américains autochtones. Les autochtones sont mentionnés dans une autre partie du cours car ils croient à l'existence des Bigfoot.*
(B)	To point out that all encounters with a Bigfoot are dangerous.	= pour indiquer que toute rencontre avec un Bigfoot est dangereuse *Le professeur n'insiste pas sur l'aspect dangereux du Bigfoot.*
(C)	To describe when European settlers first encountered a Bigfoot.	= pour décrire le moment où les colons européens ont rencontré un *Bigfoot* pour la première fois *Ce n'est pas présenté comme la première rencontre entre un Bigfoot et des colons américains.*
(D)	✓ **To provide an example of a possibly deadly encounter with a Bigfoot.**	**= pour donner un exemple de rencontre potentiellement mortelle avec un *Bigfoot*** ***Un des deux hommes a été tué par une créature qui aurait pu être un Bigfoot.*** ***« [...] when he returned, he found his companion's dead body, his neck broken and great teeth marks on his throat » (= « [...] à son retour, il trouva le cadavre de son compagnon, le cou brisé et de grandes marques de dents sur la gorge »)***

Type de passage : Campus conversation

Description

Dans ce type de passage, vous écoutez un dialogue entre deux ou trois personnes dans un contexte universitaire. Voici quelques exemples de situation :

- Discussion entre deux étudiants préparant un travail de groupe ou évoquant une activité parascolaire comme une association étudiante.
- Discussion entre un étudiant et un professeur. L'étudiant a des questions concernant un cours ou demande des informations concernant un examen ou un travail à réaliser.
- Discussion entre un étudiant et un membre du personnel administratif de l'école (ex : conseiller en orientation professionnelle).

Il s'agit de passages assez vivants avec peu de monologues. Les situations sont assez réalistes. Cela rend ce type de bande audio plus facile à suivre.

Stratégies

Conseil n°1 : Attention aux questions de type « détail »

Les concepteurs n'hésitent pas à poser des questions précises sur des détails du dialogue. Faites particulièrement attention aux indices spatio-temporels. Si le passage évoque une date ou un lieu, retenez-le bien, une question sera sans doute posée sur ce détail.

Conseil n°2 : Vocabulaire universitaire

Ces dialogues utilisent de nombreux mots de vocabulaire propres au champ lexical de la vie universitaire anglo-saxonne. Nous vous recommandons donc de bien maîtriser les termes liés à la vie étudiante. Cela est d'autant plus important que certains mots n'ont pas d'équivalent en français et sont propres à la culture américaine.

Être initié à la culture étudiante anglo-saxonne vous aidera à bien comprendre ces passages. Nous avons listé les mots les plus importants dans la partie vocabulaire. Tous les mots spécifiques au système universitaire américain sont associés à des mises en contexte.

Exemple - Campus conversation - avec Script

Reportez vos réponses pour analyser votre performance.

Entraînez-vous dans les conditions d'examen.

Écoutez les fichiers audio.

prepmyfuture.com/book/68/ex/1914

Listen to a discussion between a student and a professor.

Script non affiché le jour de l'examen :

FEMALE STUDENT: Good morning Dr Poplinski…

PROFESSOR: Oh hi, Sophia, come in. I was expecting you. I've looked though your resume. There are a few things you need to think about. The language is ok, but there are one or two other things. Sit down and we'll go through it together.

FEMALE STUDENT: Thanks. I had a friend read it and he said it was pretty good and that I could send it as it is.

PROFESSOR: Well, one thing about resumes is that they should always be word perfect and there are quite a few errors here. Also, if you can remember the general rule of the three Cs: your resume should be concise, complete and comprehensible. The person reading it might have a hundred or more resumes to go through in a limited time, so it's important that they can find the essential information easily. Looking at yours, it seems complete – I mean there are no years missing or anything – and it's fairly concise, one page is maximum length for an undergraduate… I'm not finding it all that easy to pick out the chronology and the essential information. The headings are quite clear, although you should really put your studies at the top, just under your name and contact details here, and your work experience second.

FEMALE STUDENT: Oh really? I was told that my work experience is what makes me different from other students, so I should begin with that.

PROFESSOR: Well I disagree. You're 21 years old and so it's only normal that your professional experience is quite limited. What you're mostly doing now is studying and the rule on a resume is that you put the most recent first. Also, why don't you put the dates of all these things in a margin on the left. That would make it much more coherent and simpler to read. Remember the last of the three Cs?

FEMALE STUDENT: Oh yeah, comprehensible.

PROFESSOR: Right. As regards the description of the School and your current studies, I won't go through all that now, but if you look at the example on the handout you received at the end of the seminar last week, that gives a fairly good template that you can adapt to your own study program. The rest of the Studies section seems fine for content, but try to make it more readable, as I said. The next part should be your work experience and it's true that this is very important because this is what makes you really different from everyone else. Everyone's studying business, everyone can speak a foreign language and use a computer, but only you have these particular experiences in these companies and it's important that you take the time to make them sound as valuable and enriching as I'm sure they are.

FEMALE STUDENT: Well, a couple of them weren't all that enriching if the truth be told…

PROFESSOR: It doesn't matter. OK, you spent 2 months selling clothes in a store, but you learnt, or you should have learnt the basics of commerce, how to deal with customers, maybe something about money and accounting… you need to find a way to express the positive aspects of your experience as concisely as possible.

FEMALE STUDENT: How about being comprehensible. Is that part easy to read?

PROFESSOR: Not really. Each experience should be in the same format: first line, in bold, what you were: assistant manager, shop assistant, bank clerk, intern, etc. Second line, the name of the organization, their type of business and the town you worked in. So you'd have Barrytown Fashions, clothing retailer, New Hampton, Maine for example. Then on the third line you need to give details of what you actually did, and you need to make this look as important and valuable as you possibly can.

FEMALE STUDENT: OK, thanks for that, Doctor. Do you think it's a good idea for me to write about my free-time activities here at the bottom?

PROFESSOR: Well yes, but it depends what you write. For me, it's a waste of time mentioning 'reading' (because who doesn't read? Really!), cinema (because, who doesn't go see a movie on the weekend, huh?). Think of the image you're giving of yourself. I've seen some resumes with 'hanging out with friends' or 'playing video games' in the 'hobbies' section. Do they really think that's going to inspire someone to hire them?

▪ Question 1 Why does the student go to see the professor?

(A) to have the professor tell her how to write a resume

(B) to give the professor her resume for a job she has applied for

(C) to discuss the content of a seminar she attended last week

(D) to have the professor review the resume she sent him previously

▪ Question 2 What can the student find in the handout she received at the end of last week's seminar?

(A) general information on how you write a resume.

(B) a template that will help her describe his current study program

(C) advice about the layout of a resume

(D) information about how to describe work experience

▪ Question 3 According to the professor, what has the student NOT done?

(A) made her resume easy to read

(B) remembered the important details of last week's seminar

(C) included all her work experience

(D) mentioned her foreign language skills

▪ Question 4 What does the professor say about the student's work experience?

(A) That some of the jobs should not have been included in her resume.

(B) That she has not told Dr Poplinsky everything she should have told him.

(C) That she should concentrate on the positive aspects of each experience.

(D) That playing video games doesn't count as work experience.

▪ Question 5 According to the professor, what should not be included in a resume?

Choose 2 answers.

(A) hobbies

(B) reading

(C) cinema

(D) free-time activities

Solutions

Reportez vos réponses pour analyser votre performance.

Entraînez-vous dans les conditions d'examen.

prepmyfuture.com/book/68/ex/1914

question 1	D	question 2	B	question 3	A	question 4	C	question 5	B C

■ **Question 1 - Solution**

Why does the student go to see the professor?

FR : Quelle est la raison pour laquelle l'étudiante va voir le professeur?

(A)	to have the professor tell her how to write a resume	= pour demander au professeur de lui expliquer comment rédiger un CV *Visiblement, pendant le séminaire de la semaine précédente, le professeur a donné des exemples de bons CVs à ses étudiants. On peut en déduire qu'il leur a déjà montré comment écrire un bon CV.* *Le but de ce rendez-vous était d'aller plus loin : le professeur est maintenant en train de corriger le CV de l'étudiante.*
(B)	to give the professor her resume for a job she has applied for	= pour donner au professeur son CV pour un emploi auquel elle a postulé *L'étudiante n'a pas l'air d'avoir encore postulé. Son ami lui a dit qu'elle pouvait envoyer son CV tel qu'il était : cela sous-entend qu'il n'avait pas encore été envoyé.* *Dans tous les cas, nous n'avons pas d'information nous confirmant qu'elle a postulé.*
(C)	to discuss the content of a seminar she attended last week	= pour discuter du contenu d'un séminaire auquel elle a assisté la semaine dernière *Le professeur fait allusion au séminaire pour laisser l'étudiante chercher les exemples qu'il lui a envoyés. Mais le but de la discussion est ailleurs.*
(D)	✓ **to have the professor review the resume she sent him previously**	**= pour demander au professeur de relire le CV qu'elle lui a envoyé précédemment** ***« I was expecting you. I've looked though your resume. There are a few things you need to think about. » (= « Je vous attendais. J'ai regardé votre CV. Il y a quelques éléments auxquels vous devez réfléchir. »)*** ***Le professeur était en train d'attendre l'étudiante et il avait pris le temps avant le rendez-vous de regarder en détail son CV.***

⇨ **explication**

FR : C'est une discussion entre un professeur et une étudiante. En écoutant la discussion, on réalise que l'étudiante a assisté au séminaire du professeur la semaine précédente. Mais la raison pour laquelle l'étudiante et le professeur ont pris rendez-vous est pour que le professeur donne des conseils à l'étudiante sur son CV.

▪ Question 2 - Solution

What can the student find in the handout she received at the end of last week's seminar?

FR : Que peut trouver l'étudiante dans le polycopié qu'elle a reçu à la fin du séminaire la semaine précédente ?

(A)	general information on how you write a resume.	= des informations générales sur la façon de rédiger un CV *On ne connaît pas le contenu du polycopié, à l'exception de l'exemple de CV.*
(B) ✓	**a template that will help her describe his current study program**	**= un modèle qui l'aidera à décrire son cursus universitaire** ***« if you look at the example on the handout you received at the end of the seminar last week, that gives a fairly good template that you can adapt to your own study program. »*** ***(= « si vous regardez l'exemple sur le polycopié qui vous a été transmis à la fin du séminaire la semaine dernière, cela donne un assez bon modèle que vous pouvez adapter à votre propre parcours scolaire. »)***
(C)	advice about the layout of a resume	= des conseils sur la mise en page d'un CV *On ne connaît pas le contenu du polycopié, à l'exception de l'exemple de CV.*
(D)	information about how to describe work experience	= des informations sur la manière de présenter l'expérience professionnelle *On ne connaît pas le contenu du polycopié, à l'exception de l'exemple de CV.*

⇨ **explication**

FR : On peut imaginer les thématiques du séminaire de la semaine passée : explications et conseils pour écrire un bon CV, sa mise en page, etc... En ce qui concerne le polycopié envoyé à la fin de celui-ci, la seule information qu'on ait est le fait qu'il contient un exemple de CV que l'étudiante pourra facilement utiliser pour décrire son parcours universitaire.

▪ Question 3 - Solution

According to the professor, what has the student NOT done?

FR : Selon le professeur, qu'est-ce que l'étudiante n'a PAS fait ?

(A)	**✓ made her resume easy to read**	**= rendu son CV facile à lire** ***Le professeur a aidé l'étudiante à rendre son CV facile à lire afin que la personne qui le lise puisse trouver facilement les informations essentielles.*** ***« That would make it much more coherent and simpler to read. » (= « Cela rendrait votre CV plus cohérent facile à lire. »)***
(B)	remembered the important details of last week's seminar	= retenu les détails importants du séminaire de la semaine dernière *Le professeur lui a suggéré de regarder le polycopié de la semaine dernière pour éviter de répéter les mêmes informations. Mais cela ne signifiait pas que l'étudiante n'était pas attentive aux détails importants du séminaire de la semaine précédente.*
(C)	included all her work experience	= mentionné toute son expérience professionnelle *L'étudiante a commencé son CV avec son expérience professionnelle car elle pensait que cela la différencierait des autres étudiants. Elle pensait également que toutes ses expériences professionnelles n'avaient pas toutes la même valeur. Mais cela ne signifie pas qu'elle ne les a pas toutes mentionnées. Le professeur était même au courant pour son travail de vendeuse. On pourrait donc penser qu'elle a tout indiqué et non l'inverse.*
(D)	mentioned her foreign language skills	= mentionné ses compétences en langues étrangères *La seule fois où il est fait allusion aux langues étrangères c'est quand le professeur dit que ce n'est pas un élément différenciant pour son CV. Cela ne signifie pas qu'il ne fallait pas le mentionner du tout ou qu'elle ne l'avait pas indiqué.*

⇒ **explication**

Le professeur donne à l'étudiante la règle des 3Cs : un CV doit être concis, complet et compréhensible. Il trouve que son CV est concis et complet. Il a challengé l'étudiante avec plusieurs exemples pour rendre le CV plus lisible.

■ Question 4 - Solution

What does the professor say about the student's work experience?

FR : Que dit le professeur concernant les expériences professionnelles de l'étudiante ?

(A)	That some of the jobs should not have been included in her resume.	= Que certains des emplois n'auraient pas dû être inclus dans son CV. *Le professeur a même insisté pour contredire cette citation : peu importe si une expérience était moins enrichissante qu'une autre, l'étudiante doit trouver des aspects positifs à son sujet.*
(B)	That she has not told Dr Poplinsky everything she should have told him.	= Qu'elle n'a pas dit au Dr Poplinsky tout ce qu'elle aurait dû lui dire. *Il n'y a aucune allusion à ce sujet dans la discussion. L'étudiante lui a seulement demandé si elle aurait dû ajouter ses loisirs ou non. Et le professeur a une réponse mitigée à ce sujet : cela dépend du loisir.*
(C)	**✓ That she should concentrate on the positive aspects of each experience.**	**= Qu'elle devrait se concentrer sur les aspects positifs de chaque expérience.** ***« you need to find a way to express the positive aspects of your experience as concisely as possible. » (= « vous devez trouver un moyen de mettre en valeur les aspects positifs de votre expérience de la manière la plus concise possible. »)***
(D)	That playing video games doesn't count as work experience.	= Que jouer à des jeux vidéo ne compte pas comme une expérience professionnelle. *Jouer aux jeux-vidéo était uniquement cité à titre d'exemple des loisirs qu'il ne faut pas mettre dans un CV.*

explication
FR : Le professeur dit qu'il est important pour elle de valoriser son expérience professionnelle. C'est quelque chose qui fera une vraie différence avec les CVs des autres étudiants.

▪ Question 5 - Solution

According to the professor, what should not be included in a resume?

Choose 2 answers.

FR :

Selon le professeur, qu'est-ce qui ne devrait pas être indiqué dans un CV ?

Choisissez deux réponses.

(A)	hobbies	= les passe-temps
(B)	**✓ reading**	**= la lecture** ***« For me, it's a waste of time mentioning 'reading' » (= « Selon moi, c'est une perte de temps de mentionner la lecture »)***
(C)	**✓ cinema**	**= le cinéma** ***« For me, it's a waste of time mentioning [...] 'cinema' » (= « Selon moi, c'est une perte de temps de mentionner [...]le cinéma »)***
(D)	free-time activities	= les loisirs *Le professeur a dit que les activités pouvaient ne pas être indiquées. Cela dépendait de l'activité.*

explication
FR : Le professeur pense que toutes les activités faites sur le temps libre ne doivent pas être indiquées dans un CV. Uniquement les moins communes.

Question type : Main idea / Gist questions

Description

Dans ce type de question, on vous demande de résumer le passage. Il y a deux grandes typologies de questions de cette catégorie :

- Idée principale : quel est le sujet du passage ?
- But : quel est l'objectif du professeur ou de l'étudiant ?

Exemple

Ces questions sont formulées sous la forme :

- *What is the lecture mainly about?*
- *What is the purpose of the lecture?*
- *Why is the student talking to the professor?*

Méthodologie

Ces questions exigent une compréhension globale du passage. Le concepteur essaiera de vous piéger en reprenant une idée mineure du passage qui ne représente pas le passage dans sa globalité.

Pour chaque passage, vous devez anticiper ce type de question et retenir l'idée principale. Faites-en un automatisme et ce type de question ne vous posera pas de problème.

Entraînement - Main idea / Gist questions

Reportez vos réponses pour analyser votre performance.

Entraînez-vous dans les conditions d'examen.

Écoutez les fichiers audio.

prepmyfuture.com/book/68/ex/1915

Listen to part of a conversation, then answer the question.

Script non affiché le jour de l'examen : So, what I want to do today is give an introductory lecture about Norse mythology: what are the basic facts; who are the basic figures, what are the basic terms that one needs to understand? What I want to do today is give an introductory lecture about Norse mythology: what are the basic facts; who are the basic figures, what are the basic terms that one needs to understand this mythology? On this channel, I've made many videos about particular subjects, particular gods, particular poems, particular sources but I realize that I've never done just an intro for someone who has just started to get into it or who wants to know the basics of what we really can know from our medieval sources, so in this video I'm going to try to do that. So first of all, I'm going to be using the forms of names in classical Old Norse, and I will be presenting them on the screen in classical Old Norse. That is going to involve using some letters that are found in Old Norse, but not in modern English. These include 'thorn', which is the 'th' sound in thin, thorn, theater, thick, etc. 'Eth', which is the sound in weather, leather, Heather, breathe, etc. Then- that is the 'th' sound in those words. There is 'ash', which is the 'a' sound in cat, or rad, or bag. There is O with a stroke, which is like Arnold Schwarzenegger saying 'bird'- it´s that 'eu' vowel, much like O with two dots in German. And there is O caudata, which is 'aw'; it is 'ahh' with rounded lips, like a northern New Jersey pronunciation of 'coffee'.

Question 1 What is the professor mainly talking about in this part of the lecture?

(A) Where Norse mythology originates from.

(B) What students need to learn in order to speak Old Norse.

(C) Why Old Norse is a difficult language.

(D) The different letters used in Old Norse that are not present in English.

Listen to part of a lecture, then answer the question.

Script non affiché le jour de l'examen : …and so I would say with regards to fiction if you take someone like Dostoyevsky or we think…it's a favorite of mine by the way, I would highly recommend that you read all five of his great novels because they are unparalleled in their psychological depth and so… if you're interested in psychology Dostoyevsky's the person for you. Tolstoy is more of a sociologist, but Dostoyevsky…man he gets right down into the bottom of the questions and messes around transformative reading. Anyways, Dostoyevsky's character, this character named Raskolnikov is a materialist rationalist I would say which was a rather new type of person back in the 1880s. One of the things that's lovely about Dostoevsky… what Dostoevsky does in his novel. The people who stand for the antithesis of what Dostoyevsky actually believes are often the strongest, smartest and sometimes most admirable people in the book.

▪ Question 2 What is the purpose of the lecture?

(A) To demonstrate why Dostoyevsky is better than Tolstoy.
(B) To explain students why they should read Dostoyevsky's work.
(C) To give an overview of Dostoyevsky's career.
(D) To analyze the character of Raskolnikov.

Listen to part of a conversation, then answer the question.

Script non affiché le jour de l'examen :

Student: Good morning Mrs Clark…I was wondering if you received my email…

Professor: Oh, good morning Jason. Please, come in. Yes, I gave it a quick read last night and I think your idea is quite interesting. Although, I'm not sure whether we'll be able to squeeze everything you want to say about Shakespeare's life in your final dissertation. After all, it's just a 5-minute speech.

Student: I understand. Uhm, do you think I would gain some more time if I did a PowerPoint presentation?

Professor: I don't think so, Jason. I'm afraid the commission doesn't allow students to prepare both a speech and a presentation. It would be too much material.

▪ Question 3 What are the student and the professor mainly discussing?

(A) the length of his final dissertation
(B) the time the student will have for his speech
(C) the irrelevance of some of the details of Shakespeare's life
(D) the commission's rejection of the student's work

Solutions

Reportez vos réponses pour analyser votre performance.

Entraînez-vous dans les conditions d'examen.

prepmyfuture.com/book/68/ex/1915

question 1	D	question 2	B	question 3	A

Question 1 - Solution

What is the professor mainly talking about in this part of the lecture?

(A)	Where Norse mythology originates from.	= L'origine de la mythologie nordique. *C'est le thème du cours dans sa globalité mais pas celui de cet extrait.*
(B)	What students need to learn in order to speak Old Norse.	= Ce que les étudiants doivent apprendre pour pouvoir parler le vieux norrois. *Le professeur n'apprend pas à ses étudiants à parler le vieux norrois.*
(C)	Why Old Norse is a difficult language.	= Les raisons pour lesquelles le vieux norrois est une langue difficile. *Le professeur ne dit pas que le vieux norrois est une langue difficile.*
(D)	✓ **The different letters used in Old Norse that are not present in English.**	**= Les différentes lettres utilisées en vieux norrois qui ne sont pas présentes en anglais.** ***Le professeur liste une série de lettres qui n'existent pas dans la langue anglaise mais celles-ci correspondent à des phonèmes déjà connus par les étudiants.*** ***« That is going to involve using some letters that are found in Old Norse, but not in modern English. » (= « Cela va impliquer l'utilisation de certaines lettres que l'on trouve en vieux norrois, mais pas en anglais moderne. »)***

Question 2 - Solution

What is the purpose of the lecture?

FR : Quel est le but de cette conférence ?

(A)	To demonstrate why Dostoyevsky is better than Tolstoy.	= montrer pourquoi Dostoïevski est supérieur à Tolstoï *Le professeur ne fait pas de comparaison qualitative entre les deux auteurs.*
(B)	✓ **To explain students why they should read Dostoyevsky's work.**	**= expliquer aux élèves pourquoi ils devraient lire l'œuvre de Dostoïevski** ***Le professeur dit que Dostoïevski est l'un de ses auteurs préférés et conseille aux étudiants de lire ses ouvrages car les aspects psychologiques de ses romans sont intéressants.*** ***« I would highly recommend that you read all five of his great novels » (= « Je vous recommande vivement de lire ses cinq grands romans. »)***
(C)	To give an overview of Dostoyevsky's career.	= donner un aperçu de la carrière de Dostoïevski *Le principal sujet de la lecture pas la carrière de Dostoïevski mais la profondeur psychologique de ses romans.*
(D)	To analyze the character of Raskolnikov.	= analyser le personnage de Raskolnikov *Le personnage de Raskolnikov est seulement mentionné à titre d'exemple.*

■ Question 3 - Solution

What are the student and the professor mainly discussing?

FR : De quoi l'étudiant et le professeur discutent-ils principalement ?

(A)	✓ **the length of his final dissertation**	**= la longueur de son mémoire de fin d'études** ***« I'm not sure whether we'll be able to squeeze everything you want to say about Shakespeare's life in your final dissertation. »*** ***(= « Je ne suis pas sûr que nous pourrons faire tenir tout ce que vous voulez dire sur la vie de Shakespeare dans votre mémoire de fin d'études. »)*** ***Ils repensent donc la longueur totale de la thèse de Jason.***
(B)	the time the student will have for his speech	= le temps dont disposera l'étudiant pour son exposé *Ce n'est le sujet principal de la discussion.*
(C)	the Irrelevance of some of the details of Shakespeare's life	= la non-pertinence de certains détails de la vie de Shakespeare *Le professeur et Jason n'expriment aucun jugement sur la vie de Shakespeare.*
(D)	the commission's rejection of the student's work	= le rejet par la commission du projet de l'étudiant *Le professeur ne fait qu'informer Jason sur les limitations imposées par la commission.*

Question type : Detail questions

Description

Dans ces questions, on vous demande de vous rappeler d'un détail du discours. La bonne réponse est une reformulation de ce qui est dit explicitement dans la bande-son. Ainsi la bonne réponse ne reprendra pas exactement les mêmes mots que le texte, mais exprimera la même idée.

Exemple

Ce type de question est formulé sous la forme :

- *According to the lecture, which of the following is true?*
- *What does the professor say about…?*

> ***NARRATOR:*** *Listen to part of a conversation. Then answer the questions.*
>
> ***FEMALE:*** *Each day, we'll be going anywhere from 40 to 60 miles, and some of that will mean biking up and over some pretty high hills. Luckily, we don't need to have our own luggage on our bikes—that goes in the tour van which follows behind us and meets us each afternoon at the next hotel.*
>
> ***MALE:*** *Cool! I think I can manage that. I've been doing a lot of biking around town, so I should be able to keep up with the group.*
>
> ***What are the two people mainly talking about?***
> *(A) a bike race around town*
> *(B) a bike tour in a town*
> *(C) a tour of a hotel*
> *(D) a tour outside of town*

Solution

(A) Ce n'est pas mentionné dans le dialogue.
Il n'est pas précisé qu'il s'agit d'une course.

(B) Inexact
La distance parcourue chaque jour est supérieure à 49 miles. Il ne semble pas s'agir d'une visite de la ville en vélo.

(C) Contresens
Les hôtels sont mentionnés, car le groupe va s'arrêter tous les soirs dans un hôtel.

La bonne réponse est (D).

Méthodologie

<u>Ce type de question demande :</u>

- une bonne compréhension du discours dans son ensemble et un bon sens logique pour éliminer les choix de réponse non compatibles avec le sens du texte ;
- une bonne mémoire « sélective ».

<u>Procéder par élimination et déduction logique</u>
Les questions de type détail / information factuelle sont conçues pour être plus faciles dans la partie *Listening* que leurs homologues de la partie *Reading*. Le concepteur prend en compte le fait que vous ne pouvez pas réécouter le passage pour répondre. Les questions portent donc sur des détails importants du discours. Souvent, vous pourrez trouver la bonne réponse par déduction logique ou par élimination des mauvaises réponses.

Stratégies

Conseil n°1 : La prise de note

La prise de note est très importante pour ce type de question, mais demande du savoir-faire. En effet, la prise de note peut nuire à votre concentration. Si vous réfléchissez trop à ce que vous allez écrire, vous allez perdre le fil de la conversation.

Il faut que vous vous comportiez comme si vous suiviez un cours universitaire. Si vous avez du mal à comprendre, alors investissez toute votre énergie sur la compréhension. Si vous êtes à l'aise alors, prenez des notes au fur et à mesure.

Conseil n°2 : La mémoire sélective

Vous devez rester très concentré tout au long de la bande-son et retenir le maximum d'éléments. Cependant, les extraits sont longs (plus de 700 mots) et vous ne pourrez pas tout retenir, il faut donc développer une écoute sélective. Certains détails sont secondaires tandis que d'autres seront clefs pour une compréhension générale du passage. Concentrez-vous sur l'idée principale et les arguments principaux. Même si la question porte sur un détail secondaire, ce qui est peu probable, vous pourrez sans doute trouver la bonne réponse par raisonnement logique (cf. conseil n°1).

Conseil n°3 : Pièges

Souvent, les mauvaises propositions de réponse reprennent des mots-clefs du passage. Le fait qu'un choix de réponse reprenne un mot du passage n'en fait pas nécessairement une bonne réponse. Les concepteurs utilisent cette méthode pour piéger les candidats débutants qui, faute d'avoir compris le passage, essaient de deviner les bonnes réponses par identification de mot-clef.

Entraînement - Detail questions

Reportez vos réponses pour analyser votre performance.

Entraînez-vous dans les conditions d'examen.

Écoutez les fichiers audio.

prepmyfuture.com/book/68/ex/1916

Listen to part of a lecture. Then answer the questions.

Script non affiché le jour de l'examen : FEMALE PROFESSOR: Most people around the world have a twisted, often racist picture of the Mongol Empire, thinking of the Mongols as crude, murderous "barbarians" who created an empire through luck and violence and nothing more. However, in the recent times, historians unearthed some fascinating information about them and are now giving them more respect. Despite this new view of the Mongols, we need to keep one thing in mind: aside from Communist China under Mao Zedong, no single nation or empire in the history of the world has had more blood on its hands.

Question 1 According to the lecture, which of the following is true?

(A) New information is changing how people think about the Mongol Empire.
(B) Historians have recently found Mongol artefacts in tombs or ancient sites.
(C) The Mongol Empire was one of the longest-lasting empires in history.
(D) The new information about the Mongol Empire was found in China.

Listen to part of a conversation. Then answer the questions.

Script non affiché le jour de l'examen :

MALE: So what do I need to do in order to be in your next production? I assume I'll need to audition.

FEMALE: Yes. We have auditions at our club's board meetings every few weeks. We are planning to have more at our next one in two weeks' time, on the 13th of March, to be precise.

MALE: I should be able to make that. And if I don't get an acting part in the play, I'm happy to do whatever else you may need help with. I've done set design and publicity before.

FEMALE: Great! We're very short of people who can do that sort of thing.

Question 2 According to the conversation, what does the man want?

(A) to have a leadership role in a club

(B) to try out for a role in a play

(C) to help set up a meeting

(D) to help publicize auditions for a play

Listen to part of a lecture. Then answer the questions.

Script non affiché le jour de l'examen : MALE PROFESSOR: The British archaeologist Arthur Evans was drawn to the island of Crete by tales and legends of King Minos and the minotaur — a half-man, half-bull creature that lived in a maze where it hunted and killed victims placed there by King Minos. In 1900, after much excavation, Evans unearthed a huge, maze-like palace, built some 3,500 years ago. The palace was filled with images of bulls painted on walls and pottery. From this, Arthur Evans concluded that the story of the minotaur must have come from this palace. Further support for his theory could be seen in many of the images, which showed young Greeks attempting to jump — sometimes successfully but more likely not — over the sharp horns of the bulls during some kind of religious festival.

Question 3 According to the lecture, which of the following is true?

(A) Arthur Evans found support for his theory of the origin of the minotaur legend in an ancient building.

(B) Arthur Evans found a maze under an ancient palace.

(C) Arthur Evans found images of a minotaur on the walls of an ancient palace.

(D) Arthur Evans was the first scientist to conduct excavations on the island of Crete.

Solutions

ılıl Reportez vos réponses pour analyser votre performance.

⏰ Entraînez-vous dans les conditions d'examen.

prepmyfuture.com/book/68/ex/1916

question 1	A

question 2	B

question 3	A

■ Question 1 - Solution

According to the lecture, which of the following is true?

FR : Selon le discours, laquelle de ces propositions est vraie ?

(A)	**✓ New information is changing how people think about the Mongol Empire.**	**= De nouvelles données changent la perception que l'on a de l'Empire mongol.** ***« However, in the recent times, historians unearthed some fascinating information about them and are now giving them more respect. »*** ***(= « Cependant, ces derniers temps, les historiens ont découvert des informations fascinantes à leur sujet et leur accordent désormais plus de respect. »)***
(B)	Historians have recently found Mongol artefacts in tombs or ancient sites.	= Les historiens ont récemment trouvé des artefacts mongols dans des tombes ou des sites anciens.
(C)	The Mongol Empire was one of the longest-lasting empires in history.	= L'empire mongol était l'un des empires les plus pérennes de l'histoire.
(D)	The new information about the Mongol Empire was found in China.	= Les nouvelles découvertes sur l'empire mongol ont été faites en Chine. *La Chine est mentionnée pour faire une comparaison entre la violence de l'Empire Mongol et celle de la Chine communiste de Mao Zedong.*

■ Question 2 - Solution

According to the conversation, what does the man want?

FR : D'après la conversation, que souhaite l'homme ?

(A)	to have a leadership role in a club	= avoir un rôle de responsable dans un club *Il veut jouer un rôle dans la prochaine pièce de théâtre. Il est explicitement dit qu'il postule à un rôle d'acteur et pas à un poste de responsable car il dit : « if I don't get an acting part in the play. » (= « si je n'ai pas de rôle dans la pièce. »)*
(B) ✓	**to try out for a role in a play**	**= auditionner pour un rôle dans une pièce de théâtre** ***« what do I need to do in order to be in your next production? » (= « Que dois-je faire pour jouer dans votre prochaine pièce ? »)***
(C)	to help set up a meeting	= aider à organiser une réunion *Il veut rejoindre le club de théâtre.*
(D)	to help publicize auditions for a play	= aider à faire connaître les auditions pour une pièce de théâtre *Son but principal est d'obtenir un rôle d'acteur dans la prochaine pièce de théâtre. S'il n'obtient pas un rôle, il veut tout de même aider l'association grâce à ses compétences en communication et design.* *Cet objectif secondaire ne consiste pas à vouloir faire la promotion des auditions du club de théâtre mais du club de théâtre dans son ensemble.*

■ Question 3 - Solution

According to the lecture, which of the following is true?

FR : D'après le cours, laquelle de ces propositions est vraie ?

(A) ✓	**Arthur Evans found support for his theory of the origin of the minotaur legend in an ancient building.**	**= Arthur Evans a trouvé dans un bâtiment ancien un élément qui confirme sa théorie sur l'origine de la légende du minotaure.** ***« Evans unearthed a huge, maze-like palace; The palace was filled with images of bulls painted on walls and pottery. »*** ***(= « Evans a déterré un immense palais en forme de labyrinthe ; Le palais était rempli d'images de taureaux peintes sur les murs et les poteries. »)***
(B)	Arthur Evans found a maze under an ancient palace.	= Arthur Evans a trouvé un labyrinthe sous un ancien palais. *Il a trouvé un ancien palais qui ressemblait à un labyrinthe. Il n'y a pas de labyrinthe sous le palais.*
(C)	Arthur Evans found images of a minotaur on the walls of an ancient palace.	= Arthur Evans a trouvé des représentations d'un minotaure sur les murs d'un ancien palais. *Il a trouvé des représentations de taureaux (l'animal) mais pas de Minotaure (créature mystique mi-homme, mi-taureau).*
(D)	Arthur Evans was the first scientist to conduct excavations on the island of Crete.	= Arthur Evans a été le premier scientifique à mener des fouilles sur l'île de Crète.

Question type : Rhetoric questions

Description

Dans ces questions, on vous demande de comprendre un sous-entendu à un moment précis du passage. Pour la plupart de ces questions, vous pourrez réécouter l'extrait du passage qui contient le sous-entendu.

Dans ces questions, la réponse n'est pas formulée explicitement dans la bande-son. Il faut prendre en compte le contexte et les intonations pour choisir la bonne réponse.

Exemple

Ce type de question est formulé sous la forme :

- *What does the professor imply when he says this: …* (suivi de l'extrait à écouter)
- *Listen again to part of the conversation. Then, answer the question: What does the student imply when he says …?* (comprend l'extrait à écouter + 2^{e} écoute avec seulement l'expression sur laquelle porte la question)
- *What does the speaker mean about… ?* (non suivi de l'extrait)

NARRATOR: *Listen to part of a conversation. Then answer the questions.*

FEMALE: *Each day, we'll be going anywhere from 40 to 60 miles, and some of that will mean biking up and over some pretty high hills. Luckily, we don't need to have our own luggage on our bikes—that goes in the tour van which follows behind us and meets us each afternoon at the next hotel.*

MALE: *Cool! I think I can manage that. I've been doing a lot of biking around town, so I should be able to keep up with the group.*

TEXT: *What does the man mean when he says this?*

MALE: *I think I can manage that.*

(A) He feels he can effectively supervise the tour.
(B) He thinks he will be able to carry his own luggage to each hotel.
(C) He believes the tour is not too difficult.
(D) He wants to be in the van instead of riding a bike.

Solution

(A) Contresens
La femme encadre l'excursion, pas l'homme.

(B) Contresens
La valise est dans le van.

(C) Il pense pouvoir parcourir les distances estimées tous les jours.

(D) Ce n'est pas mentionné dans le dialogue.

La bonne réponse est (C).

Méthodologie

Vous faites face à une double difficulté :

- votre connaissance des expressions idiomatiques employées ;
- votre compréhension du contexte pour interpréter l'expression idiomatique.

Souvent, l'un de ces deux points vous permet de répondre correctement à la question. Plus rarement, vous devrez à la fois comprendre l'expression idiomatique ET le contexte.

Entraînement - Rhetoric questions

Reportez vos réponses pour analyser votre performance.

Entraînez-vous dans les conditions d'examen.

Écoutez les fichiers audio.

prepmyfuture.com/book/68/ex/1917

Listen to part of a lecture. Then answer the questions.

Script non affiché le jour de l'examen : FEMALE PROFESSOR: Most people around the world have a twisted, often racist picture of the Mongol Empire, thinking of the Mongols as crude, murderous "barbarians" who created an empire through luck and violence and nothing more. However, in the recent times, historians unearthed some fascinating information about them and are now giving them more respect. Despite this new view of the Mongols, we need to keep one thing in mind: aside from Communist China under Mao Zedong, no single nation or empire in the history of the world has had more blood on its hands.

▪ Question 1 Listen again to part of the lecture. Then answer the question.

What does the woman mean when she says this?

Script non affiché le jour de l'examen : FEMALE PROFESSOR: Most people around the world have a twisted, often racist picture of the Mongol Empire.

(A) Most people in the world think the Mongols were racist.

(B) Many people feel the Mongols suffered from racism.

(C) Popular beliefs about the Mongol Empire are not completely accurate.

(D) People's racist opinions of the Mongols are based on depictions of them in artwork.

Listen to part of a conversation. Then answer the questions.

Script non affiché le jour de l'examen :

MALE: So what do I need to do in order to be in your next production? I assume I'll need to audition.

FEMALE: Yes. We have auditions at our club's board meetings every few weeks. We are planning to have more at our next one in two weeks' time, on the 13th of March, to be precise.

MALE: I should be able to make that. And if I don't get an acting part in the play, I'm happy to do whatever else you may need help with. I've done set design and publicity before.

FEMALE: Great! We're very short of people who can do that sort of thing.

▪ **Question 2** Listen again to part of the discussion. Then answer the question.

> **Script non affiché le jour de l'examen :**
> **FEMALE:** Yes. We have auditions at our club meetings every few weeks. We are planning to have more at our next one in two weeks' time, on the 13th of March, to be precise.
>
> **MALE:** I should be able to make that.

What does the man mean when he says this?

> **Script non affiché le jour de l'examen :**
> **NARRATOR:** What does the man mean when he says this?
>
> **MALE:** I should be able to make that.

(A) He is probably able to attend the next audition.

(B) He can probably help run the next club meeting.

(C) He is worried he will not do well at the audition.

(D) He is confident he will do well at the audition.

Listen to part of a lecture. Then answer the questions.

> **Script non affiché le jour de l'examen : MALE PROFESSOR:** The British archaeologist Arthur Evans was drawn to the island of Crete by tales and legends of King Minos and the minotaur—a half-man, half-bull creature that lived in a maze where it hunted and killed victims placed there by King Minos. In 1900, after much excavation, Evans unearthed a huge, maze-like palace, built some 3,500 years ago. The palace was filled with images of bulls painted on walls and pottery. From this, Arthur Evans concluded that the story of the minotaur must have come from this palace. Further support for his theory could be seen in many of the images, which showed young Greeks attempting to jump—sometimes successfully but more likely not--over the sharp horns of the bulls during some kind of religious festival.

■ **Question 3** **NARRATOR:** Listen again to part of the conversation. Then answer the question.

> **Script non affiché le jour de l'examen : MALE PROFESSOR:** Further support for his theory could be seen in many of the images, which showed young Greeks attempting to jump—sometimes successfully but more likely not--over the sharp horns of the bulls.

TEXT: What does the professor probably mean when he says this?

> **Script non affiché le jour de l'examen :**
> **MALE PROFESSOR:** Sometimes successfully but more likely not.

(A) It is unlikely that people jumped over bulls as portrayed in the ancient artwork on Crete.

(B) It is likely that bulls were harmed due to the way people were shown to jump over them.

(C) It was dangerous to attempt to interact with bulls as depicted in the artwork discovered from ancient Crete.

(D) Arthur Evan's theory regarding the origin of the minotaur legend is likely to be proven to be incorrect.

Solutions

Reportez vos réponses pour analyser votre performance.

Entraînez-vous dans les conditions d'examen.

prepmyfuture.com/book/68/ex/1917

question 1	C	question 2	A	question 3	C

■ Question 1 - Solution

Listen again to part of the lecture. Then answer the question.

What does the woman mean when she says this?

Script non affiché le jour de l'examen : FEMALE PROFESSOR: Most people around the world have a twisted, often racist picture of the Mongol Empire.

FR :

NARRATEUR : *Que veut dire la femme quand elle dit cela ?*

PROFESSEUR : *La plupart des personnes, partout dans le monde, ont une vision souvent raciste de l'Empire Mongol.*

(A)	Most people in the world think the Mongols were racist.	= La plupart des gens dans le monde pensent que les Mongols étaient racistes. *C'est la vision que les gens ont de l'Empire Mongol qui est qualifiée de raciste, pas les Mongols eux-mêmes.*
(B)	Many people feel the Mongols suffered from racism.	= Beaucoup de gens pensent que les Mongols ont été victimes de racisme. *C'est l'opinion du professeur. Rien n'indique qu'il s'agit de l'opinion d'autres personnes.*
(C)	**✓ Popular beliefs about the Mongol Empire are not completely accurate.**	**= Les croyances populaires sur l'empire mongol ne sont pas tout à fait exactes.**
(D)	People's racist opinions of the Mongols are based on depictions of them in artwork.	= Les opinions racistes des gens à l'égard des Mongols sont basées sur leurs représentations dans les œuvres d'art. *Rien n'est précisé à propos de la cause de l'opinion publique.*

■ Question 2 - Solution

Listen again to part of the discussion. Then answer the question.

Script non affiché le jour de l'examen :

FEMALE: Yes. We have auditions at our club meetings every few weeks. We are planning to have more at our next one in two weeks' time, on the 13th of March, to be precise.

MALE: I should be able to make that.

What does the man mean when he says this?

Script non affiché le jour de l'examen :

NARRATOR: What does the man mean when he says this?

MALE: I should be able to make that.

(A)	✔ **He is probably able to attend the next audition.**	**= Il est probablement en mesure de participer à la prochaine audition.**
(B)	He can probably help run the next club meeting.	= Il peut probablement aider à diriger la prochaine réunion du club.
(C)	He is worried he will not do well at the audition.	= Il a peur de ne pas réussir à l'audition. *contresens*
(D)	He is confident he will do well at the audition.	= Il est confiant et pense qu'il va réussir l'audition. *Il parle de sa présence à l'audition, pas de sa performance.*

▪ Question 3 - Solution

NARRATOR: Listen again to part of the conversation. Then answer the question.

Script non affiché le jour de l'examen : MALE PROFESSOR: Further support for his theory could be seen in many of the images, which showed young Greeks attempting to jump—sometimes successfully but more likely not--over the sharp horns of the bulls.

TEXT: What does the professor probably mean when he says this?

Script non affiché le jour de l'examen :

MALE PROFESSOR: Sometimes successfully but more likely not.

(A)	It is unlikely that people jumped over bulls as portrayed in the ancient artwork on Crete.	= Il est peu probable que les gens sautaient par-dessus les taureaux, comme le montrent les œuvres d'art antiques en Crète.
(B)	It is likely that bulls were harmed due to the way people were shown to jump over them.	= Il est probable que les taureaux aient été blessés en raison de la façon dont les gens étaient représentés en train de sauter par-dessus eux.
(C)	✔ **It was dangerous to attempt to interact with bulls as depicted in the artwork discovered from ancient Crete.**	**= Il était dangereux de tenter d'interagir avec les taureaux comme le montre l'œuvre d'art découverte en Crète antique.** ***Le professeur insiste sur le danger lié à cette pratique.***
(D)	Arthur Evan's theory regarding the origin of the minotaur legend is likely to be proven to be incorrect.	= Il est probable que la théorie d'Arthur Evan concernant l'origine de la légende du minotaure s'avère incorrecte.

⇨ **explication**
FR : *Sometimes successfully but more likely not* = de temps en temps, les jeunes Grecs arrivaient à sauter au-dessus des cornes du taureau sans se blesser mais la plupart du temps ces tentatives devaient probablement échouer.

Question type : Inference / Prediction questions

Description

Dans ces questions, on vous demande de déduire quelque chose du discours. La réponse n'est pas formulée explicitement dans le passage, mais est sous-entendue.

Ces questions vous demandent régulièrement de faire une prédiction sur ce qui va probablement se passer à la fin du discours.

Exemple

Ce type de question est formulé sous la forme :

- *What is inferred …?*
- *What will the professor probably do next?*

> ***NARRATOR:*** *Listen to part of a lecture. Then answer the questions.*
>
> ***FEMALE PROFESSOR:*** *Most people around the world have a twisted, often racist picture of the Mongol Empire, thinking of the Mongols as crude, murderous "barbarians" who created an empire through luck and violence and nothing more. However, in the recent times, historians unearthed some fascinating information about them and are now giving them more respect. Despite this new view of the Mongols, we need to keep one thing in mind: aside from Communist China under Mao Zedong, no single nation or empire in the history of the world has had more blood on its hands.*
>
> ***What can be Inferred from the lecture?***
> *(A) Communist China under Mao Zedong likely killed more people than the Mongol Empire did.*
> *(B) Most people now have a favorable view of the Mongol Empire.*
> *(C) At the time of the Mongol Empire, it was likely viewed positively by many people.*
> *(D) The Mongol Empire was arguably the most successful empire in history.*

Solution

(A) *« aside from Communist China under Mao Zedong, no single nation or empire in the history of the world has had more blood on its hands. »*
blood on its hands = du sang sur les mains = de nombreuses personnes ont été tuées.

(B) Contresens
« Most people around the world have a twisted, often racist picture of the Mongol Empire »
L'opinion générale a une opinion négative. Seuls les historiens ont récemment changé d'avis et ont maintenant une opinion positive de l'Empire mongol.

(C) Ce n'est pas mentionné dans le discours.

(D) **Ce n'est pas mentionné dans le discours.**

La bonne réponse est (A).

Méthodologie

Ce type de question teste avant tout votre compréhension globale du passage. La mémoire jouera ici un rôle moins important que vos capacités de raisonnement logique.

À propos des questions de type prédiction
Même si ce type de question est plutôt rare, vous y serez sans doute confronté au moins une fois sur l'ensemble des passages. Il est donc important de bien retenir la conclusion de chaque passage. C'est une habitude que vous prendrez au cours de votre entraînement.

En général, on devine dès l'écoute de la bande audio que l'exercice comprendra une question de ce type. Si la conclusion du passage se prête à ce type de question alors vous pouvez être presque certain qu'une des questions sera de type prédiction, retenez donc bien la conclusion du passage.

Entraînement - Inference / Prediction questions

Reportez vos réponses pour analyser votre performance.

Entraînez-vous dans les conditions d'examen.

Écoutez les fichiers audio.

prepmyfuture.com/book/68/ex/1918

NARRATOR: Listen to part of a conversation. Then answer the questions.

Script non affiché le jour de l'examen :

FEMALE: Each day, we'll be going anywhere from 40 to 60 miles, and some of that will mean biking up and over some pretty high hills. Luckily, we don't need to have our own luggage on our bikes—that goes in the tour van which follows behind us and meets us each afternoon at the next hotel.

MALE: Cool! I think I can manage that. I've been doing a lot of biking around town, so I should be able to keep up with the group.

Question 1 According to the conversation, which of the following can be inferred?

(A) People on the tour will carry their luggage on their bikes.
(B) The woman will be riding a bike on the tour.
(C) Some of the hotels are on top of hills.
(D) The man is from a town which has hills.

NARRATOR: Listen to part of a conversation. Then answer the questions.

Script non affiché le jour de l'examen :

MALE: So what do I need to do in order to be in your next production? I assume I'll need to audition.

FEMALE: Yes. We have auditions at our club's board meetings every few weeks. We are planning to have more at our next one in two weeks' time, on the 13th of March, to be precise.

MALE: I should be able to make that. And if I don't get an acting part in the play, I'm happy to do whatever else you may need help with. I've done set design and publicity before.

FEMALE: Great! We're very short of people who can do that sort of thing.

▪ **Question 2** Based on the conversation, what kind of club are the two people probably talking about?

(A) a board game club
(B) a mathematics club
(C) a graphic design club
(D) a drama club

NARRATOR: Listen to part of a lecture. Then answer the questions.

Script non affiché le jour de l'examen : MALE PROFESSOR: The British archaeologist Arthur Evans was drawn to the island of Crete by tales and legends of King Minos and the minotaur—a half-man, half-bull creature that lived in a maze where it hunted and killed victims placed there by King Minos. In 1900, after much excavation, Evans unearthed a huge, maze-like palace, built some 3,500 years ago. The palace was filled with images of bulls painted on walls and pottery. From this, Arthur Evans concluded that the story of the minotaur must have come from this palace. Further support for his theory could be seen in many of the images, which showed young Greeks attempting to jump—sometimes successfully but more likely not--over the sharp horns of the bulls during some kind of religious festival.

▪ **Question 3** What can be inferred from the lecture?

(A) Bulls were likely sacrificed during religious festivals in ancient Crete.
(B) Many thousands of people probably died while trying to jump over bulls in ancient Crete.
(C) Reports of the minotaur may be based on stories of an extinct animal.
(D) The legend of the minotaur likely comes from an ancient religious ritual.

Solutions

Reportez vos réponses pour analyser votre performance.

Entraînez-vous dans les conditions d'examen.

prepmyfuture.com/book/68/ex/1918

question 1	B	question 2	D	question 3	D

Question 1 - Solution

According to the conversation, which of the following can be inferred?

FR : Qu'est-ce qui est sous-entendu dans la conversation ?

(A)	People on the tour will carry their luggage on their bikes.	= Les participants à l'excursion porteront leurs bagages sur leur vélo. *Les valises sont transportées par la camionnette. « we don't need to have our own luggage on our bikes » (= « nous n'avons pas besoin d'avoir nos bagages sur nos vélos »)*
(B)	**✓ The woman will be riding a bike on the tour.**	**= La femme fera du vélo pendant le circuit.** ***Elle utilise la 1re personne du pluriel, elle s'inclue donc dans le groupe quand elle dit : « we'll be going anywhere from 40 to 60 miles » (= « nous ferons entre 40 et 60 miles. »)***
(C)	Some of the hotels are on top of hills.	= Certains des hôtels sont situés en haut des collines. *Les collines sont mentionnées car le groupe va devoir en traverser quelques unes, ce qui rendra la randonnée plus difficile. Aucun lien n'est fait avec la localisation des hôtels.*
(D)	The man is from a town which has hills.	= L'homme vient d'une ville où il y a des collines. *Les collines sont mentionnées car le groupe va devoir en traverser quelques unes, ce qui rendra la randonnée plus difficile. Aucun lien n'est fait avec l'origine de l'homme.*

Question 2 - Solution

Based on the conversation, what kind of club are the two people probably talking about?

FR : D'après la conversation, de quel type d'association les étudiants parlent-ils ?

(A)	a board game club	= un club de jeux de société
(B)	a mathematics club	= un club de mathématiques
(C)	a graphic design club	= un club de graphisme
(D)	**✓ a drama club**	**= une troupe de théâtre (association)**

⟹ explication

FR : L'homme postule à un un rôle dans une pièce de théâtre (*« acting part in the play »*). Il s'agit donc de la troupe de théâtre de l'école.

Question 3 - Solution

What can be inferred from the lecture?

FR : Qu'est-ce qui est sous-entendu dans le cours ?

(A)	Bulls were likely sacrificed during religious festivals in ancient Crete.	= Les taureaux étaient probablement sacrifiés lors des célébrations religieuses de la Crète antique.
(B)	Many thousands of people probably died while trying to jump over bulls in ancient Crete.	= Plusieurs milliers de personnes sont probablement mortes en essayant de sauter par-dessus des taureaux en Crète antique. *"which showed young Greeks attempting to jump — sometimes successfully but more likely not — over the sharp horns of the bulls"* *(= « qui montrait de jeunes Grecs tentant de sauter - parfois avec succès mais le plus souvent sans succès - par-dessus les cornes acérées des taureaux »)* *Il est vrai que de nombreux grecs se sont blessés, voire tués en sautant au-dessus de taureaux mais le professeur ne précise pas le nombre de morts lié à cette pratique. Le nombre de plusieurs milliers semble exagéré.*
(C)	Reports of the minotaur may be based on stories of an extinct animal.	= Les récits du minotaure sont peut-être basés sur des histoires d'une espèce disparue.
(D)	✓ **The legend of the minotaur likely comes from an ancient religious ritual.**	**= La légende du minotaure provient probablement d'un ancien rituel religieux.** ***Les peintures dans le palais du roi Minos valident cette théorie.***

Vous avez besoin d'exercices supplémentaires ?

Le mode "premium" de la plateforme en ligne vous donne accès à des exercices inédits dont plusieurs centaines de questions de type "TOEFL".

SECTION - SPEAKING

Méthode

Présentation générale

Durée	17 minutes, comprenant : • 15 à 30 secondes de temps de préparation avant chaque réponse • 45 à 60 secondes pour répondre
Nombre de tâches	4 tâches : • 1 tâche *independent question* • 3 tâches *integrated Speaking questions*
Les accents utilisés dans les bandes audios	Accents anglais de locuteurs natifs d'Amérique du Nord, du Royaume-Uni, de Nouvelle-Zélande et d'Australie.
Déroulement de l'épreuve	L'épreuve s'effectue entièrement sur ordinateur, vous parlez dans un microphone. Les bandes-son enregistrées seront ensuite corrigées par un correcteur accrédité par ETS, l'administrateur de l'examen.
Notation	0 à 30 points (25 % de la note finale)

Présentation détaillée

Le TOEFL iBT a le mérite d'évaluer les 4 compétences (compréhension écrite et orale, expression écrite et orale). Contrairement aux autres tests évaluant l'expression orale, l'épreuve s'effectue entièrement sur ordinateur, vous parlez dans un microphone. Les bandes-son enregistrées seront ensuite corrigées par un correcteur accrédité par ETS, l'administrateur de l'examen. Pour chacune des questions, vous répondez donc sous la forme d'un court monologue, il n'y a pas de discussion avec un examinateur.

La section est composée de 4 questions indépendantes. Il y a deux types de questions :

- La première est une question indépendante et ouverte, où on demande de raconter une expérience ou de donner votre opinion sur un sujet.
- Les trois questions qui suivent sont accompagnées de passage à lire et de bandes audio sur lesquelles porteront les questions.

Cette section n'évalue donc pas uniquement votre capacité à parler. Pour la majorité des questions, vous devez comprendre un texte ou un passage audio pour pouvoir répondre correctement.

Stratégies

1) S'habituer au format de l'épreuve

Le format de l'épreuve est déstabilisant : vous devez parler dans un microphone face à l'ordinateur. De plus, les autres candidats passeront l'épreuve en même temps que vous, avec des décalages de quelques minutes, cela ajoutera une gêne supplémentaire le jour du test.

Enfin, le format met souvent en difficulté les Français, car nous avons moins l'habitude de nous exprimer à l'oral pendant nos études. Le format est de type monologue avec une préparation courte de 15 à 30 secondes suivant les questions. Vous n'avez donc pas le temps d'écrire ce que vous allez dire. Vous avez tout juste le temps de faire un plan avec quelques idées. Après, il vous faudra improviser.

Vous devez vous entraîner dans le format de l'examen, s'entraîner à parler en anglais n'est pas suffisant. En effet, une discussion vous laisse le temps de rebondir sur une réplique et de trouver vos mots. Dans un monologue, vous devez à la fois structurer votre propos, trouver des idées et parler de manière fluide, en évitant les fautes. Ciblez votre entraînement sur la gestion du temps de préparation et sur votre vitesse d'élocution.

2) S'adapter aux critères d'évaluation

Une bonne compréhension des critères de notation vous permettra d'éviter les erreurs et de vous autoévaluer.

Voici un exemple de grille de notation utilisée par les correcteurs :

4 points	On retrouve toutes les caractéristiques suivantes : • débit rythmé et fluide, les fautes mineures d'intonation ou prononciation n'empêchent pas la compréhension ; • vocabulaire varié et maîtrise des structures complexes, les erreurs mineures n'empêchent pas la compréhension ; • utilisation de l'ensemble du temps imparti, les liens entre les idées sont clairs.
3 points	On retrouve au moins 2 des caractéristiques suivantes : • débit assez fluide, les fautes d'intonation ou prononciation rendent plus difficile la compréhension, mais le discours reste intelligible ; • les fautes de vocabulaire et de grammaire ne portent pas atteinte à l'intelligibilité du discours ; • utilisation de l'essentiel du temps imparti, le développement de la réponse est limité, mais la réponse est globalement cohérente.
2 points	On retrouve au moins 2 des caractéristiques suivantes : • rythme saccadé, le discours reste intelligible mais n'est pas clair par endroit ; • maîtrise limitée de la grammaire et du vocabulaire, seules les structures simples sont maîtrisées ; • la réponse correspond à la question, mais n'est pas assez développée, le nombre des idées est limité avec des propos vagues et répétitifs.
1 point	On retrouve au moins 2 des caractéristiques suivantes : • difficultés de prononciation et hésitations, rythme très saccadé ; • les fautes de grammaire et de vocabulaire rendent difficile la compréhension ; • discours court et répétitions.
0 point	Pas de réponse ou réponse hors sujet.

Comme vous pouvez le remarquer, le plus important n'est pas d'éviter à tout prix de faire des fautes. En réalité, vous avez intérêt à utiliser l'intégralité du temps imparti et à avoir un débit de parole fluide même si pour y parvenir vous faites quelques erreurs d'anglais. À partir du moment où votre discours reste compréhensible, vous pouvez obtenir la note maximale même en faisant quelques fautes mineures. Si vous avez trop peur de faire des fautes, vous allez rapidement perdre les points alloués aux autres critères de notation.

Enfin, gardez votre propos simple et bien organisé. Évitez les phrases trop longues et utilisez des connecteurs logiques pour structurer votre discours. Il est recommandé d'associer un exemple à vos arguments, cela rendra votre propos mieux organisé et vous permettra d'utiliser l'ensemble du temps imparti sans faire trop de répétitions.

Question type : Independent question

Présentation

La première question de la section *Speaking* est de ce type. Vous avez 15 secondes de préparation après la lecture de la question, puis 45 secondes pour répondre à la question. Vous devez essayer de parler pendant la totalité du temps alloué.

Cette tâche peut vous demander de décrire une préférence, une personne, un lieu ou une expérience.

Exemple : *What kinds of movies do you most like to watch in your free time? Explain why you like this kind of movie.*

Ou bien, cette tâche peut vous demander d'exprimer votre opinion sur un sujet.

Exemple : *Some students would prefer to study at the library. Others would prefer to study at their flat. Which option would you prefer and why?*

Stratégies

1) Évitez d'utiliser des réponses génériques, mémorisées à l'avance

Certains candidats apprennent des réponses toutes faites, généralement trouvées sur Internet. Nous vous déconseillons d'aborder cette épreuve de cette manière. Les correcteurs savent généralement reconnaître les réponses non naturelles grâce au rythme et à l'intonation. Exercez-vous à produire des réponses spontanées.

2) Entraînez-vous à structurer votre réponse

Ces questions peuvent être intimidantes, car le temps de préparation est très faible et vous devez faire preuve de créativité pour construire votre réponse au fil de l'eau.

Cette question, suivant son type (parler d'une expérience personnelle ou exprimer une opinion), a toujours la même structure : vous pouvez donc vous entraîner en utilisant l'un de ces schémas :

Exemple de schéma 1 : expérience personnelle

1. Idée principale : présentez la chose/personne dont vous allez parler.
2. Détails : donnez plus d'informations.
3. Justifiez votre choix : expliquez pourquoi vous avez choisi cette chose/personne. Faites un rapprochement entre vos goûts et une caractéristique de la chose/personne.

Exemple de schéma 2 : exprimer une opinion

1. Idée principale : présentez votre opinion pour apporter une réponse directe à la question.
2. Argument + Exemple : vous pouvez détailler 1 argument en plusieurs phrases ou utiliser plusieurs arguments. Essayez de donner plus de poids à votre argument à l'aide d'un exemple.
3. Courte conclusion : vous pouvez rappeler que les deux choix présentent des avantages et réaffirmer votre choix. Évitez d'utiliser une phrase générique et réemployez le vocabulaire lié au thème.

Pour le second type de question, évitez un plan de type « Thèse, Antithèse, synthèse » ou même de présenter les avantages des deux choix. Concentrez-vous sur l'option que vous avez choisie. Cela rendra votre discours plus clair.

3) Apprenez les accroches qui permettent de présenter votre opinion

Pour le deuxième type de question, vous devez utiliser des connecteurs logiques pour structurer votre réponse, introduire des exemples et présenter votre point de vue.

Pour introduire son opinion :	Pour introduire un exemple :
• *In my opinion, …*	• *For example…*
• *To my mind, …*	• *For instance…*
• *In my view, …*	• *In particular…*
• *I am convinced that…*	• *Among others…*

Entraînement - Independent question

Reportez vos réponses pour analyser votre performance.

Entraînez-vous dans les conditions d'examen.

prepmyfuture.com/book/68/ex/1928

▪ Question 1

DIRECTIONS: In this question, you will be asked to give your opinion about a familiar topic. After you hear the question, you have 15 seconds to prepare your response and 45 seconds to speak.

QUESTION: Some students believe that it is better to attend a university near their hometown. Others believe that to truly become independent they should enroll in a university far from home. Which do you think is better for students in general and why? Use specific details in your explanation.

Preparation Time: 15 seconds
Response Time: 45 seconds

▪ Question 2

DIRECTIONS: In this question, you will be asked to give your opinion about a familiar topic. After you hear the question, you have 15 seconds to prepare your response and 45 seconds to speak.

QUESTION: Do you agree or disagree with the following statement?

It is more important for students to study objective subjects, like math and science, than it is to study creative subjects, such as art and literature.

Preparation Time: 15 seconds
Response Time: 45 seconds

▪ Question 3

DIRECTIONS: In this question, you will be asked to speak about a familiar topic. After you hear the question, you have 15 seconds to prepare your response and 45 seconds to speak.

QUESTION: When you experience high levels of stress, what do you do to help yourself reduce that stressful feeling? Use specific details in your explanation.

Preparation Time: 15 seconds
Response Time: 45 seconds

▪ Question 4

DIRECTIONS: In this question, you will be asked to give your opinion about a familiar topic. After you hear the question, you have 15 seconds to prepare your response and 45 seconds to speak.

QUESTION: Some people prefer to go on holiday alone or with only one other close friend or relative. Others enjoy going on vacation with a group of friends and family. What do you prefer and why? Use specific details in your explanation.

Preparation Time: 15 seconds
Response Time: 45 seconds

Réponses types - Independent question

ılıl Reportez vos réponses pour analyser votre performance.

⏰ Entraînez-vous dans les conditions d'examen.

🎧 Écoutez les fichiers audio.

prepmyfuture.com/book/68/ex/1928

question 1	q. ouverte

question 2	q. ouverte

question 3	q. ouverte

question 4	q. ouverte

- **Question 1 - Solution**

DIRECTIONS: In this question, you will be asked to give your opinion about a familiar topic. After you hear the question, you have 15 seconds to prepare your response and 45 seconds to speak.

QUESTION: Some students believe that it is better to attend a university near their hometown. Others believe that to truly become independent they should enroll in a university far from home. Which do you think is better for students in general and why? Use specific details in your explanation.

Preparation Time: 15 seconds
Response Time: 45 seconds

⟹ **explication**

Exemple de réponse

In general, the most important is for students to feel comfortable at the university where they are studying. There's no harm in wanting to stay near to your hometown if it makes you happy as you are already familiar with the environment and you are close to your family and friends. However, to consider studying away from home can be really beneficial, especially when you go abroad. It allows people to become more independent, but also to discover other cultures and to become more open-minded.

Évaluation de l'exemple de réponse

Remarques générales / niveau CECRL	Le candidat répond à la question présentée dans la consigne de manière bien structurée et complète, montrant ainsi une maîtrise avancée de la langue anglaise. Le niveau de compétence du candidat correspond approximativement au niveau C1 du CECRL et la qualité de la production orale serait égale à un 4/4 dans le système de score du TOEFL iBT.
Respect des consignes	Le candidat répond correctement à la question, sans répéter plus d'une fois le même concept.
Structure de la réponse	Le candidat avance des arguments pour défendre les deux aspects de la question, sans toutefois se contredire. La réponse est correctement structurée, preuve que l'étudiant a une pensée bien construite.
Maîtrise de la langue	Le candidat fait preuve d'une maîtrise avancée de la langue anglaise tout au long de sa production orale. Il emploie des termes avancés tels que *hometown, beneficial* et *open-minded*.
Pour aller plus loin	Bien que le candidat ne fournisse aucun exemple personnel pour soutenir la thèse principale, sa réponse est tout de même un texte oral bien structuré, cohérent et homogène. Si la production orale du candidat aurait gagné à être appuyée par des exemples tirés de sa vie personnelle, cette absence est toutefois compensée par des références à des vérités générales, qui participent à la cohérence du propos.

▪ Question 2 - Solution

DIRECTIONS: In this question, you will be asked to give your opinion about a familiar topic. After you hear the question, you have 15 seconds to prepare your response and 45 seconds to speak.

QUESTION: Do you agree or disagree with the following statement?

It is more important for students to study objective subjects, like math and science, than it is to study creative subjects, such as art and literature.

Preparation Time: 15 seconds
Response Time: 45 seconds

⇒ **explication**

Exemple de réponse

No, I do not think that objective subjects are more important than others. I believe a student must integrate both types of studies in order to have a well-balanced education. While math is an important part of intellectual growth and professionalism, studying literature and the arts allows a person to be cultivated. Education should not be focused only on creating employees. A person must find a balance between independent thinking and social employment in order to function in society.

Évaluation de l'exemple de réponse

Remarques générales / niveau CECRL	Le candidat répond à la question présentée dans la consigne de manière bien structurée et complète, montrant ainsi une maîtrise avancée de la langue anglaise. Le niveau de compétence du candidat correspond approximativement au niveau C1 du CECRL et la qualité de la production orale serait égale à un 4/4 dans le système de score du TOEFL iBT.
Respect des consignes	Le candidat répond correctement à la question, sans répéter plus d'une fois le même concept.
Structure de la réponse	Le candidat a fait le choix de ne défendre qu'un seul aspect de la réponse, plutôt que de donner les points positifs de chacun. Cela lui permet de développer davantage son propos.
Maîtrise de la langue	Le candidat fait preuve d'une maîtrise avancée de la langue anglaise tout au long de sa production orale. Il emploie des termes avancés tels que *well-balanced* et *independent thinking*.
Pour aller plus loin	Bien que le candidat ne fournisse aucun exemple personnel pour soutenir la thèse principale, sa réponse est tout de même un texte oral bien structuré, cohérent et homogène. Le fait de défendre son point de vue sans chercher à en donner les limites permet à l'étudiant de montrer qu'il a un avis sur la question et qu'il est capable de le défendre.

- **Question 3 - Solution**

DIRECTIONS: In this question, you will be asked to speak about a familiar topic. After you hear the question, you have 15 seconds to prepare your response and 45 seconds to speak.

QUESTION: When you experience high levels of stress, what do you do to help yourself reduce that stressful feeling? Use specific details in your explanation.

Preparation Time: 15 seconds
Response Time: 45 seconds

⇨ **explication**

Exemple de réponse

I use several techniques to reduce my stress. The first is simple: I go outside to get some fresh air to clear my head, and I go for a walk. If this doesn't work, I sit down and concentrate on my breathing with my eyes closed. Sometimes, I also listen to soothing music. As a last resort, I eat chocolate. I will take my time to chew and concentrate on how it will make me feel better.

Évaluation de l'exemple de réponse

Remarques générales / niveau CECRL	Le candidat répond à la question présentée dans la consigne de manière bien structurée et complète, montrant ainsi une maîtrise avancée de la langue anglaise. Le niveau de compétence du candidat correspond approximativement au niveau C1 du CECRL et la qualité de la production orale serait égale à un 3/4 dans le système de score du TOEFL iBT.
Respect des consignes	Le candidat répond correctement à la question, sans répéter plus d'une fois le même concept. Cependant, l'étudiant aurait eu le temps de développer un ou deux arguments supplémentaires : il s'agit d'utiliser la totalité du temps alloué, cela fait partie intégrante de l'exercice.
Structure de la réponse	Le candidat répond correctement à la question posée, en listant une à une les techniques qu'il utilise pour réduire son stress. Une phrase de conclusion aurait permis de structurer davantage sa réponse.
Maîtrise de la langue	Le candidat réussi en quelques secondes à prouver sa bonne maîtrise de la langue anglaise. Il emploie des termes avancés tels que *soothing music, as a last resort*.
Pour aller plus loin	Si le candidat répond correctement à la question posée, il ne respecte pas le temps alloué à la réponse : sa production est un peu courte, ce qui le pénalise.

■ Question 4 - Solution

DIRECTIONS: In this question, you will be asked to give your opinion about a familiar topic. After you hear the question, you have 15 seconds to prepare your response and 45 seconds to speak.

QUESTION: Some people prefer to go on holiday alone or with only one other close friend or relative. Others enjoy going on vacation with a group of friends and family. What do you prefer and why? Use specific details in your explanation.

Preparation Time: 15 seconds
Response Time: 45 seconds

⇨ **explication**

Exemple de réponse

I do not enjoy going on holiday with my family because there are always moments of tension as we can't agree on the activities. Our desires are too different. That's why I prefer to go on holiday with my friends, who share the same interests as me and with whom I have a great time. We like to relax on the beach in the afternoon, go to concerts in the evening and meet other people to party with.

Évaluation de l'exemple de réponse

Remarques générales / niveau CECRL	Le candidat répond à la question présentée dans la consigne de manière bien structurée et complète, montrant ainsi une maîtrise avancée de la langue anglaise. Le niveau de compétence du candidat correspond approximativement au niveau C1 du CECRL et la qualité de la production orale serait égale à un 3/4 dans le système de score du TOEFL iBT.
Respect des consignes	Le candidat répond correctement à la question, sans répéter plus d'une fois le même concept. Cependant, l'étudiant aurait eu le temps de développer un ou deux arguments supplémentaires : il s'agit d'utiliser la totalité du temps alloué, cela fait partie intégrante de l'exercice.
Structure de la réponse	Le candidat répond correctement à la question posée, en donnant son avis sur les personnes avec qui il préfère partir en vacances, et les activités auxquelles il s'adonne une fois là-bas. Une phrase de conclusion aurait permis de structurer davantage sa réponse.
Maîtrise de la langue	Le candidat réussi en quelques secondes à prouver sa bonne maîtrise de la langue anglaise. Il emploie des termes avancés tels que *with whom, people to party with* (bon placement de la préposition).
Pour aller plus loin	Si le candidat répond correctement à la question posée, il ne respecte pas le temps alloué à la réponse : sa production est un peu courte, ce qui le pénalise.

Question type : Integrated Speaking questions

Présentation

Les trois autres questions de la section *Speaking* sont de ce type. Vous devez d'abord lire et/ou écouter une bande-son et ensuite répondre à une question en utilisant le microphone. Vous avez 30 secondes pour préparer et 60 pour parler. Vous devez essayer de parler pendant la totalité du temps alloué.

Le temps alloué à la lecture des textes est limité à 45 secondes. Vous ne pourrez donc lire les textes qu'une seule fois. Comme pour le reste du TOEFL, vous ne pourrez écouter les bandes-son qu'une seule fois.

Les questions peuvent vous demander :

- de résumer les documents de contexte ;
- de donner votre opinion par rapport au débat introduit dans le contexte ;
- de décrire les points communs et les différences entre deux concepts présentés dans les documents de contexte.

Stratégies

1) Apprenez des expressions permettant d'introduire vos idées

Comme pour les questions isolées, n'essayez pas d'apprendre des phrases par cœur, le correcteur s'en rendra compte et vous pénalisera fortement. De plus, vous devez varier vos expressions d'une question à l'autre pour mettre en avant l'étendue de votre vocabulaire. Cela permettra aussi au concepteur de constater que vous n'utilisez pas toujours la même accroche que vous auriez apprise par cœur pour le TOEFL.

Présenter le sujet	• *The issue is that…* • *The problem the professor discusses…*
Faire référence à une source	• *According to…* • *In the professor's point of view…* • *The student states that…* • *From the lecture, we saw that…*
Introduire des éléments de réponse	• *First of all,…* • *Moreover…* • *More importantly, …*
Opposer deux idées	• In contrast,… • Meanwhile… • On the other hand, …

2) Entraînez-vous à structurer votre réponse

Ces questions sont relativement standardisées, vous pouvez donc construire des plans génériques pour structurer vos réponses. Votre entraînement vous permettra de répartir votre temps de manière efficace entre les différentes parties de votre plan.

Exemple de schéma 1 :

1. Idée principale : présentez la chose/personne dont vous allez parler.
2. Détails : donnez plus d'informations.
3. Justifiez votre choix : expliquez pourquoi vous avez choisi cette chose/personne. Faites un rapprochement entre vos goûts et une caractéristique de la chose/personne.

Exemple de schéma 2 :

1. Idée principale : présentez votre opinion pour apporter une réponse directe à la question.
2. Argument + Exemple : vous pouvez détailler 1 argument en plusieurs phrases ou utiliser plusieurs arguments. Essayez de donner plus de poids à votre argument à l'aide d'un exemple.
3. Courte conclusion : vous pouvez rappeler que les deux choix présentent des avantages et réaffirmer votre choix. Évitez d'utiliser une phrase générique et réemployez le vocabulaire lié au thème.

Entraînement - Integrated Speaking questions - Audio

Reportez vos réponses pour analyser votre performance.

Entraînez-vous dans les conditions d'examen.

Écoutez les fichiers audio.

prepmyfuture.com/book/68/ex/1929

DIRECTIONS: In this question, you will read a short passage and listen to a conversation on the same topic. You will then be asked a question about them. You may take notes while you read the passage and listen to the lecture. You may use your notes to help prepare your response. After you hear the question, you have 30 seconds to prepare your response and 60 seconds to speak.

Reading Time: 45 seconds

Become a Resident Assistants for a Campus Dormitory

The University Housing Department is now accepting applications from students for the position of residential assistant (RA) for the upcoming fall term. Resident assistants must be full-time students not in their first year at this college, and must hold at least a 2.5 GPA. Working directly under the guidance of the Director of Housing, RAs live and work with a group of 20 to 30 students in one of our on-campus dormitories. The primary purpose of the position is to promote school functions and events, assist in resolving routine dormitory problems, enforce university policies, and do other related duties connected to dorm living. Benefits include work experience and free residence in a private dormitory room.

Listen to two students discuss the announcement.

- **Question 1** **QUESTION:** The woman expresses her opinion about the job opportunity described in the article. Briefly summarize the announcement. Then state her opinion about the announcement and explain the reasons she gives for holding that opinion.

Preparation Time: 30 seconds
Response Time: 60 seconds

DIRECTIONS: In this question, read a short passage and listen to a lecture on the same topic. You will then be asked a question about them. You may take notes while you read the passage and listen to the lecture. You may use your notes to help prepare your response. After you hear the question, you have 30 seconds to prepare your response and 60 seconds to speak.

Reading Time: 50 seconds

Clouds

A cloud is a mass of condensed water vapor or ice floating in the atmosphere, typically high above ground. This water vapor is the result of evaporation or transpiration—where plants "sweat" water in the air. As the water vapor rises into the atmosphere, it adheres to microscopic particles in the air, such as dust, dirt or sea salt. When enough of the invisible water vapor in the air condenses into visible water droplets or, ice crystals at higher altitudes, clouds can then form. Clouds are categorized according to their shape and the altitude at which they occur.

Now listen to part of a lecture on this topic in a meteorology class.

▪ **Question 2** **QUESTION:** Describe the three basic types of clouds and explain how they are different from each other.

Preparation Time: 30 seconds
Response Time: 60 seconds

DIRECTIONS: In this question, you will listen to part of a conversation. You will then be asked a question about them. You may take notes while you listen to the conversation. You may use your notes to help prepare your response. After you hear the question, you have 20 seconds to prepare your response and 60 seconds to speak.

Listen to a conversation between two students.

▪ **Question 3** **QUESTION:** Describe the woman's dilemma and the suggestions the man makes about what she should do. What do you think the woman should do, and why?

Preparation Time: 20 seconds
Response Time: 60 seconds

DIRECTIONS: In this question, you will listen to a short lecture. You will then be asked to summarize important information from the lecture. You may take notes while you listen to the lecture. You may use your notes to help prepare your response. After you hear the question, you have 20 seconds to prepare your response and 60 seconds to speak.

▪ Question 4 **QUESTION:** Describe Frederic Edwin Church's style of painting and how this style can be seen in the example of his art provided in the lecture.

Preparation Time: 20 seconds
Response Time: 60 seconds

DIRECTIONS: In this question, you will listen to part of a conversation. You will then be asked a question about them. You may take notes while you listen to the conversation. You may use your notes to help prepare your response. After you hear the question, you have 20 seconds to prepare your response and 60 seconds to speak.

Listen to a conversation between a student and a professor.

▪ Question 5 **QUESTION:** Briefly summarize the problem the speakers are discussing. Then state which of the two solutions from the conversation you would recommend. Explain the reasons for your recommendation.

Preparation Time: 20 seconds
Response Time: 60 seconds

Entraînement - Integrated Speaking questions - Script

Reportez vos réponses pour analyser votre performance.

Entraînez-vous dans les conditions d'examen.

Écoutez les fichiers audio.

prepmyfuture.com/book/68/ex/1929

DIRECTIONS: In this question, you will read a short passage and listen to a conversation on the same topic. You will then be asked a question about them. You may take notes while you read the passage and listen to the lecture. You may use your notes to help prepare your response. After you hear the question, you have 30 seconds to prepare your response and 60 seconds to speak.

Reading Time: 45 seconds

Become a Resident Assistants for a Campus Dormitory

The University Housing Department is now accepting applications from students for the position of residential assistant (RA) for the upcoming fall term. Resident assistants must be full-time students not in their first year at this college, and must hold at least a 2.5 GPA. Working directly under the guidance of the Director of Housing, RAs live and work with a group of 20 to 30 students in one of our on-campus dormitories. The primary purpose of the position is to promote school functions and events, assist in resolving routine dormitory problems, enforce university policies, and do other related duties connected to dorm living. Benefits include work experience and free residence in a private dormitory room.

Listen to two students discuss the announcement.

Script non affiché le jour de l'examen :

MAN: I think I'll apply for the RA position. It sounds like a great opportunity!

WOMAN: Are you sure about that? It may not be such a great deal.

MAN: What do you mean? I'd have my own room, which would really be nice to have after sharing a tiny dorm with someone for the last two years. And free rent? How can you go wrong with that?

WOMAN: I only know what I saw my friend go through last year. She was an RA at another college and found it took up a lot of her free time, much more than her housing director let on when she interviewed for the job. You can't imagine what a headache managing other students can be. She was always dealing with 'routine problems'; students would come to her when they were homesick or if they had any little complaint about another dorm student. There were times where it was impossible for her to do any studying in her room because there were so many interruptions.

MAN: It was really that bad? My RA doesn't seem like he's that stressed out.

WOMAN: Well, my friend told me that part of her job was to basically always be cheerful when dealing with the students she was in charge of—it was like she was always doing customer service in a store, 24/7. Besides that, making sure students didn't break rules kind of made it hard for her to make any friends with the students she was living with—no one enjoys being told what to do, or to have to enforce rules about noise or alcohol.

MAN: Now that you put it that way, maybe I should talk to some RAs here to find out what it's really like.

WOMAN: That sounds like a good idea. I'm also kind of suspicious about that job description. What does 'other related duties' mean?

■ **Question 1** **QUESTION:** The woman expresses her opinion about the job opportunity described in the article. Briefly summarize the announcement. Then state her opinion about the announcement and explain the reasons she gives for holding that opinion.

Preparation Time: 30 seconds
Response Time: 60 seconds

DIRECTIONS: In this question, read a short passage and listen to a lecture on the same topic. You will then be asked a question about them. You may take notes while you read the passage and listen to the lecture. You may use your notes to help prepare your response. After you hear the question, you have 30 seconds to prepare your response and 60 seconds to speak.

Reading Time: 50 seconds

Clouds

A cloud is a mass of condensed water vapor or ice floating in the atmosphere, typically high above ground. This water vapor is the result of evaporation or transpiration—where plants "sweat" water in the air. As the water vapor rises into the atmosphere, it adheres to microscopic particles in the air, such as dust, dirt or sea salt. When enough of the invisible water vapor in the air condenses into visible water droplets or, ice crystals at higher altitudes, clouds can then form. Clouds are categorized according to their shape and the altitude at which they occur.

Now listen to part of a lecture on this topic in a meteorology class.

Script non affiché le jour de l'examen :

PROFESSOR: While scientists divide clouds into many types, these types are based on three basic categories of clouds.

The first type, cirrus clouds, are made of ice crystals high up in the atmosphere—around 4 to 8 miles above the surface of the Earth—and look like long, thin, wispy white streamers or bands. This is due to the fact that that high up in the atmosphere there is much less water vapor available for cloud formation. Cirrus clouds usually indicate that a change in weather is about to happen, and they generally occur in fair weather and point in the direction of air movement at their elevation.

Cumulus clouds, on the other hand, are puffy clouds that look like floating cotton balls. The word "cumulus" means 'heaped' or 'piled', as in the word 'accumulate'. Unlike cirrus clouds, cumulus clouds are fairly dense, and their size can indicate what kind of weather patterns may develop. For example, if they are small and scattered, it is usually a sign that nice weather is in on its way. But larger cumulus clouds have a very dramatic appearance, with the upper sunlit parts a brilliant white while their bases are relatively dark; these cumulus clouds are a common source of both thunder and lightning.

The last type, stratus clouds, appear fairly low in the sky. The name 'stratus' actually means layers, which is fairly appropriate for this type because it often stretches from horizon to horizon like a blanket. In fact, stratus clouds kind of look like a grey fog suspended up in the air. These clouds usually indicate it is going to be an overcast day, with light mist or drizzle sometimes falling from them. Stratus clouds may stay in one place for several days.

■ **Question 2** **QUESTION:** Describe the three basic types of clouds and explain how they are different from each other.

Preparation Time: 30 seconds
Response Time: 60 seconds

DIRECTIONS: In this question, you will listen to part of a conversation. You will then be asked a question about them. You may take notes while you listen to the conversation. You may use your notes to help prepare your response. After you hear the question, you have 20 seconds to prepare your response and 60 seconds to speak.

Listen to a conversation between two students.

Script non affiché le jour de l'examen :

MAN: Hey, did you hear about the political science department's special panel discussion tonight?

WOMAN: Tonight? No. What's it about?

MAN: They've got three or four guest speakers, journalists, politicians, and lobbyists…not just professors like they normally have. It's even going to be televised live tonight on Channel 6! I saw the news crews driving up just now to set things up inside the student center. It going to be about efforts of the local government to fight poverty. You should definitely come to this!

WOMAN: I'd love to! I'm writing a paper on that for one of my classes. Oh, wait…tonight I already have plans. I'm meeting my tutor. She's going to help me with my next Poli-Sci test.

MAN: Can't you cancel or reschedule the meeting? I mean this panel is going to be on politics. Your tutor might actually think it is good for you to go.

WOMAN: I don't know. She's pretty busy. She's working on her Masters and it's kind of hard to find a time that works for the two of us. My test is in a few days, and I really need the extra help.

MAN: Why don't you ask her anyway? It never hurts.

WOMAN: You think so? Isn't it kind of short notice?

MAN: You really want to miss the panel discussion? They are going to be taking questions from the audience, so you might even get to ask them a question!

WOMAN: I don't know. I'd really like to go, but…

MAN: Hmm…I'm pretty sure the school is going to record it, so instead of going maybe you could contact the Poli-Sci department and ask if you can borrow their recording.

WOMAN: I guess that's possible.

■ **Question 3** **QUESTION:** Describe the woman's dilemma and the suggestions the man makes about what she should do. What do you think the woman should do, and why?

Preparation Time: 20 seconds
Response Time: 60 seconds

DIRECTIONS: In this question, you will listen to a short lecture. You will then be asked to summarize important information from the lecture. You may take notes while you listen to the lecture. You may use your notes to help prepare your response. After you hear the question, you have 20 seconds to prepare your response and 60 seconds to speak.

Script non affiché le jour de l'examen :

Frederic Edwin Church was a central figure in the Hudson River School, a nineteenth-century group of artists best known for their large, panoramic depictions of the American landscape. Church, like the other Hudson School painters, focused a majority of his paintings on mountains, waterfalls, and sunsets, but, due to the wealth of his family, Church was able to travel around the world to draw inspiration from more exotic locales. Despite their differences, Frederic Church and other Hudson School painters were very much products of the Romantic Era of the 1800s, with its emphasis on idealized natural scenes.

Some aspects of Church's work, however, set him apart from the other painters of his time. He would incorporate several brilliant, almost blinding sources of light in his paintings, a technique he referred to as "luminism", to highlight the beauty and intricate detail of the landscapes he painted. He also used various methods to attempt to "hide brushstrokes," which make the scenes seem more realistic and lessen evidence of the artificial origin of his works.

Inspired by scientific reports of South America, Church took two trips to that continent to see first-hand how it was different from the landscapes he had grown up around in New England. From his travels there, he produced several major works, most notably "Heart of the Andes". First displayed in 1859, "Heart of the Andes" brought him instant fame for its vibrant colors, crystal-clear details, and scientific accuracy. When first put on display, "Heart of the Andes" was set up in a room and presented as if it were a large window, with curtains hung to each side, and South American plants set in pots to each side. The room was purposefully darkened, with a spotlight positioned to shine on his painting. The effect of all this took people's breath away—those who viewed it remarked that it was as if they were truly looking out through a window upon an astonishing view of a South American jungle.

▪ **Question 4** **QUESTION:** Describe Frederic Edwin Church's style of painting and how this style can be seen in the example of his art provided in the lecture.

Preparation Time: 20 seconds
Response Time: 60 seconds

DIRECTIONS: In this question, you will listen to part of a conversation. You will then be asked a question about them. You may take notes while you listen to the conversation. You may use your notes to help prepare your response. After you hear the question, you have 20 seconds to prepare your response and 60 seconds to speak.

Listen to a conversation between a student and a professor.

Script non affiché le jour de l'examen :

MAN: Um, Professor Paulson, are you busy?

WOMAN: Well, I got a few minutes before I have to head off to class. What can I do for you?

MAN: I think I need to talk to someone about my class schedule. I know I should talk with the Registration Office at some point, but I was hoping you might be able to give me some advice on what I should do.

WOMAN: Oh? Have a seat. What's going on?

MAN: I…I mean, I'm just feeling like I've bitten off more than I can chew this term. I decided to take an extra class this term so that I could get one more required class done and be able to concentrate solely on my major starting next term. At first, it wasn't too bad—I didn't have as much free time on the weekends, but I was okay with that. But as the term has come along, it seems like I'm falling farther and farther behind in homework and reading.

WOMAN: I see. You know, you're not the first student take on too much work. Have you thought about dropping one of your classes? That would be the easiest thing to do. What was the class you added on?

MAN: Introduction to Chemistry. I know I could drop it, but if I did, that means I'm going to have to take it at some point in the future. I was really hoping to get it out of the way so that I could focus more of my time on my major.

WOMAN: I can see how that might be an attractive idea, but are you really willing to risk getting poor grades this term in order to do that?

MAN: I know, I know.

WOMAN: You know, that chemistry class is offered all year 'round. Have you considered taking it in the summer?

MAN: I could? I didn't think about that. Maybe…but that would mean I'd have to be here at college most of the summer. I was kind of thinking I would be able to go back home, or even take a road trip with some friends. And wouldn't that mean I'd have to pay for an extra class? Summer term isn't covered by the annual tuition I'm already paying.

WOMAN: That's true. Well, if you're set on continuing with the class this term, what about seeing if you can find a study group for one or two of your current classes? If you had some support from some of your classmates, that might make it possible for you to keep up with all the reading and class assignments. When I was in graduate school, that's probably the only thing that kept me from going crazy from all the work I had to do. I wouldn't be surprised if there were other students in your Introduction to Chemistry class who are struggling with the course just like you—most of the people taking that class are probably not chemistry majors.

MAN: That's probably true. It's just a question of whether I can find a study group that fits my schedule. I'm pretty busy as it is.

■ **Question 5** **QUESTION:** Briefly summarize the problem the speakers are discussing. Then state which of the two solutions from the conversation you would recommend. Explain the reasons for your recommendation.

Preparation Time: 20 seconds
Response Time: 60 seconds

Réponses types - Integrated Speaking questions

Reportez vos réponses pour analyser votre performance.

Entraînez-vous dans les conditions d'examen.

Écoutez les fichiers audio.

prepmyfuture.com/book/68/ex/1929

question 1	q. ouverte

question 2	q. ouverte

question 3	q. ouverte

question 4	q. ouverte

question 5	q. ouverte

- **Question 1 - Solution**

QUESTION: The woman expresses her opinion about the job opportunity described in the article. Briefly summarize the announcement. Then state her opinion about the announcement and explain the reasons she gives for holding that opinion.

Preparation Time: 30 seconds
Response Time: 60 seconds

⟹ **explication**

Exemple de réponse

The announcement comes from the University Housing Department. They are offering positions as Residential Assistants on their campus for the following school year. The ad states the requirements for the position, the duties that it entails as well as its benefits.

The woman lets her friend know that being an RA might not be as nice as he thinks. She refers to the personal experience of a friend of hers at another college. First, she emphasizes how time consuming this position can be. Then, she highlights the struggle an RA's duties can be. What's more, she talks about how this job had an impact on her friend's academic results. Finally, she mentions the negative impact it can have on one's social life on campus.

Overall, the woman is trying to warn her friend about the negative aspects of the job that he does not seem to have taken into account.

Évaluation de l'exemple de réponse

Remarques générales / niveau CECRL	Le candidat parvient à produire une réponse courte, mais claire et satisfaisante à la question incluse dans les instructions. Il n'y a que quelques imperfections et formulations inappropriées qui ne nuisent cependant pas à la clarté de la production orale du candidat. Le niveau de compétence du candidat correspond approximativement au niveau B2+/C1 du CECRL et la qualité de la production orale serait égale à un 3/4 dans le système de score du TOEFL iBT.
Respect des consignes	Le candidat explique avec succès le contenu de l'enregistrement et respecte le temps alloué à la réponse.
Structure de la réponse	Même s'il s'agit d'une production orale, le candidat structure correctement sa réponse en trois parties (introduction, 1er paragraphe, conclusion) afin de ne pas omettre de détail important.
Maîtrise de la langue	Le candidat démontre une aisance avec la langue anglaise. Il rapporte les propos du document audio sans paraphraser constamment les propos des narrateurs. Cela prouve à la fois sa capacité à structurer sa pensée et sa capacité à comprendre une conversation de tous les jours.
Pour aller plus loin	Le candidat parvient à rapporter les principaux éléments de la conversation, sans se perdre dans des détails futiles, ce qui est un bon point.

■ Question 2 - Solution

QUESTION: Describe the three basic types of clouds and explain how they are different from each other.

Preparation Time: 30 seconds
Response Time: 60 seconds

⟹ **explication**

Exemple de réponse

The professor describes three different types of clouds. Their categorization mainly depends on their shape and the altitude they are found at.

First, let's sum up the pieces of information referring to their shapes. While cirrus clouds and stratus clouds are both long and thin, cumulus clouds are puffier they look like cotton balls floating in the sky. When it comes to density, cirrus clouds tend to be thin and wispy and stratus clouds are more like some type of fog, whereas cumulus clouds are quite dense.

Now, let us have a look at the differences regarding their altitude. On the one hand, cirrus clouds are usually extremely high in the sky, thus being composed of ice crystals. On the other hand, stratus clouds tend to be low in the sky.

Finally, they are associated with specific types of weather. To begin with, cirrus clouds indicate a change of weather, while stratus clouds simply are an indication that the day is most likely going to be overcast. The situation is more complicated regarding cumulus clouds. Depending on their size and the way they look, they can indicate that a nice weather is coming, or on the contrary that a storm is on its way.

Évaluation de l'exemple de réponse

Remarques générales / niveau CECRL	Le candidat parvient à produire une réponse claire et satisfaisante à la question incluse dans les instructions. Le niveau de compétence du candidat correspond approximativement au niveau B2+/C1 du CECRL et la qualité de la production orale serait égale à un 3/4 dans le système de score du TOEFL iBT.
Respect des consignes	Le candidat explique avec succès le contenu de l'enregistrement et respecte le temps alloué à la réponse.
Structure de la réponse	Même s'il s'agit d'une production orale, le candidat structure correctement sa réponse en quatre parties (introduction, 1er paragraphe, 2e paragraphe, conclusion) afin de ne pas omettre de détail important.
Maîtrise de la langue	Le candidat démontre une aisance avec la langue anglaise. Il rapporte les propos du document audio sans paraphraser constamment les propos des narrateurs. Cela prouve à la fois sa capacité à structurer sa pensée et sa capacité à comprendre une conférence sur un sujet avec lequel il n'est pas forcément familier.
Pour aller plus loin	Le candidat parvient à rapporter les principaux éléments du cours, sans se perdre dans des détails futiles, ce qui est un bon point.

▪ Question 3 - Solution

QUESTION: Describe the woman's dilemma and the suggestions the man makes about what she should do. What do you think the woman should do, and why?

Preparation Time: 20 seconds
Response Time: 60 seconds

FR :

***QUESTION :** Décrivez le dilemme de la femme et les suggestions de l'homme sur ce qu'elle devrait faire. Que pensez-vous que la femme devrait faire, et pourquoi ?*

Temps de préparation : 20 secondes
Temps de réponse : 60 secondes

⇒ **explication**

Exemple de réponse

The woman has a clash in her schedule. In the evening, she is supposed to meet up with her tutor but there is a panel discussion happening on campus. She is unsure whether she should miss the panel discussion or ask her tutor to reschedule their appointment.

The man first advises her to get in touch with her tutor to try to get their meeting rescheduled. She is unsure if it will be possible because of how soon her test is and how little free time her tutor has. The man also mentions that the woman could contact the political science department to know whether the panel discussion will be recorded.

From my point of view, the woman should attend the panel discussion. Indeed, it is likely that she will be able to reschedule her meeting with her tutor, whether it be face-to-face or by planning a video call. Moreover, the panel discussion is about politics, which could be extremely helpful to her in the frame of her class. Lastly, even if her result to the test is not as good as she wants it to be, this would have a short-term impact, whereas what she might learn at the panel discussion may bring her more in the frame of her personal and professional development.

Évaluation de l'exemple de réponse

Remarques générales / niveau CECRL	Le candidat parvient à produire une réponse claire et satisfaisante à la question incluse dans les instructions. Le niveau de compétence du candidat correspond approximativement au niveau B2+/C1 du CECRL et la qualité de la production orale serait égale à un 4/4 dans le système de score du TOEFL iBT.
Respect des consignes	Le candidat explique avec succès le contenu de l'audio et respecte le temps alloué à la réponse. Il répond ainsi à chaque partie de la consigne.
Structure de la réponse	Même s'il s'agit d'une production orale, le candidat structure correctement sa réponse en trois parties (introduction, résumé de l'enregistrement, expression de son point de vue sur la situation) afin de ne pas omettre de détail important.
Maîtrise de la langue	Le candidat démontre une aisance avec la langue anglaise. Il rapporte les propos du document audio sans paraphraser constamment les propos des narrateurs. Cela prouve à la fois sa capacité à structurer sa pensée et sa capacité à comprendre une conférence sur un sujet avec lequel il n'est pas forcément familier. Il donne enfin son avis sur la situation en donnant des exemples pour illustrer pourquoi il avance tel ou tel argument.
Pour aller plus loin	Le candidat parvient à rapporter les principaux éléments du cours, sans se perdre dans des détails futiles, ce qui est un bon point. Il donne son avis de manière claire, ce qui démontre qu'il est capable d'improviser et d'avoir une opinion sur un sujet ou une situation précise.

■ **Question 4 - Solution**

QUESTION: Describe Frederic Edwin Church's style of painting and how this style can be seen in the example of his art provided in the lecture.

Preparation Time: 20 seconds
Response Time: 60 seconds

⇒ **explication**

Exemple de réponse

Frederic Edwin Church's painting style has been influenced both by the Hudson River School, which he was a part of, and by the Romantic Era of the 1800s. He painted natural landscapes in an idealized way.

He differentiated himself from his fellow members of the Hudson River School in three ways. First, he painted scenes from around the world since he was able to travel internationally because of his wealth. Second, he was known to play with brilliance in his painting, using a technique called "luminism." Finally, he pushed the realism of his pieces even further than any other member of the Hudson River School.

The professor mentions his painting called "Heart of the Andes" which he painted in South America in 1859. Him being able to paint worldwide scenes is the first aspect of his work that can be seen here. Furthermore, the quality of this work exemplifies how realistic his paintings were. It was so much so that some viewers believed it was as if they were looking through a window. Lastly, the example that is mentioned here also exemplifies the use of light and brilliance in his work.

Évaluation de l'exemple de réponse

Remarques générales / niveau CECRL	Le candidat parvient à produire une réponse claire et satisfaisante à la question incluse dans les instructions. Le niveau de compétence du candidat correspond approximativement au niveau B2+/C1 du CECRL et la qualité de la production orale serait égale à un 4/4 dans le système de score du TOEFL iBT.
Respect des consignes	Le candidat explique avec succès le contenu de l'enregistrement et respecte le temps alloué à la réponse. Il répond ainsi à chaque partie de la consigne.
Structure de la réponse	Même s'il s'agit d'une production orale, le candidat structure correctement sa réponse en trois parties (introduction, résumé de la conférence en trois points, illustration par un exemple donné dans le cours) afin de ne pas omettre de détail important.
Maîtrise de la langue	Le candidat démontre une aisance avec la langue anglaise. Il rapporte les propos du document audio sans paraphraser constamment les propos des narrateurs. Cela prouve à la fois sa capacité à structurer sa pensée et sa capacité à comprendre une conférence sur un sujet avec lequel il n'est pas forcément familier.
Pour aller plus loin	Le candidat parvient à rapporter les principaux éléments du cours, sans se perdre dans des détails futiles, ce qui est un bon point.

▪ Question 5 - Solution

QUESTION: Briefly summarize the problem the speakers are discussing. Then state which of the two solutions from the conversation you would recommend. Explain the reasons for your recommendation.

Preparation Time: 20 seconds
Response Time: 60 seconds

⟹ **explication**

Exemple de réponse

A student is having difficulty handling the work load of the extra class he decided to take this semester. He has asked his professor for advice on his class schedule and whether he should drop his introduction to chemistry class.

I think it is best for him to drop the class. First, if he is already overbooked, it will be hard to find more time to study with other classmates. Furthermore, he could risk failing the class and having to take it again and pay the course twice. Not to mention the impact on the other classes. Getting classes out of the way is not the right way to go through college. While summer school will be more expensive, it will allow him to completely focus on the course.

Évaluation de l'exemple de réponse

Remarques générales / niveau CECRL	Le candidat parvient à produire une réponse claire et satisfaisante à la question incluse dans les instructions. Le niveau de compétence du candidat correspond approximativement au niveau B2+/C1 du CECRL et la qualité de la production orale serait égale à un 3/4 dans le système de score du TOEFL iBT.
Respect des consignes	Le candidat explique avec succès le contenu de l'enregistrement mais ne respecte pas le temps alloué à la réponse : cette dernière est trop courte.
Structure de la réponse	Même s'il s'agit d'une production orale, le candidat structure correctement sa réponse en deux parties (exposition du problème soulevé dans l'audio, avis de l'étudiant sur la situation et la solution qu'il envisagerait).
Maîtrise de la langue	Le candidat démontre une aisance avec la langue anglaise. Il rapporte les propos du document audio sans paraphraser constamment les propos des narrateurs. Cela prouve à la fois sa capacité à structurer sa pensée et sa capacité à comprendre une conférence sur un sujet avec lequel il n'est pas forcément familier.
Pour aller plus loin	La réponse du candidat est un peu courte, ce qui fait qu'il a omis plusieurs détails qu'il aurait été judicieux de rapporter dans sa production orale. De ce fait, il se retrouve pénalisé.

SECTION - WRITING

Méthode

Présentation générale

Durée	50 minutes : • 20 minutes pour la première tâche • 30 minutes pour la seconde tâche
Nombre de tâches	2 tâches : • 1 tâche *integrated writing task* • 1 tâche *independent writing task*
Consignes officielles	*This section measures your ability to use writing to communicate in an academic environment. There will be two writing tasks.* *For the first writing task, you will read a passage and listen to a lecture and then answer a question based on what you have read and heard. For the second task, you will answer a question based on your own knowledge and experience.* FR : Cette section mesure votre capacité à utiliser l'écriture pour communiquer dans un environnement académique. Il y aura deux tâches d'écriture. Pour la première tâche d'écriture, vous lirez un passage et écouterez une conférence, puis répondrez à une question basée sur ce que vous avez lu et entendu. Pour la deuxième tâche, vous répondrez à une question basée sur vos propres connaissances et expériences.
Notation	0 à 30 points (25 % de la note finale)

Présentation détaillée

L'épreuve Writing dure 50 minutes et compte 2 types de questions que vous devez obligatoirement traiter :

- integrated writing task (= synthèse) : vous écoutez une bande audio puis lisez un texte. Vous devez ensuite réaliser une synthèse des deux (150 à 225 mots) ;
- independent writing task (= essai) : Vous répondez à une question posée (300 à 440 mots).

La réponse à ces questions est sous forme de dissertation. Elle ne nécessite pas de connaissances particulières dans un domaine précis. En revanche, structurer votre réponse est primordial. Vous êtes évalué sur la richesse de votre vocabulaire et la manière dont vous présentez vos idées.

Stratégies

Conseil n°1 : Bien connaître les questions types

Les concepteurs des questions officielles doivent suivre un cahier des charges précis pour créer les questions. Il y a donc un nombre limité de types de question. Les questions de même type sont toutes structurées de la même façon. Connaître les différents types de questions et les méthodes qui permettent de les résoudre vous permettra de gagner des points et du temps.

Au cours de votre entraînement, vous allez développer des automatismes qui vous permettront de gagner en efficacité. Au début, ces méthodes vous paraîtront rébarbatives, mais avec l'entraînement, vous les appliquerez rapidement sans même réfléchir.

Conseil n°2 : Savoir prendre des notes pour l'*integrated writing task*

Au cours de la lecture, vous devez prendre des notes et essayer de comprendre :

1. **l'idée principale :** souvent en rapport avec une politique, une pratique, un problème ou sur la proposition d'une hypothèse sur la manière dont fonctionne un processus ou une procédure ou sur le fonctionnement d'un phénomène naturel ;
2. **comment cette idée est développée :** soit les arguments sont énoncés en faveur de l'idée principale, soit les arguments s'opposent à l'idée principale.

> **Attention !** Après l'écoute de l'audio, le texte réapparait. Vous n'êtes donc pas obligé de le mémoriser.

Au cours de l'écoute, il est par contre primordial de prendre des notes et de mémoriser certains passages. Vous devez identifier et noter les éléments qui expliquent ou contredisent les le texte. Ces éléments vous permettront de définir votre plan.

Conseil n°3 : Structurer vos idées

La section *Writing* n'évalue pas vos connaissances sur un sujet précis, mais votre expression écrite ainsi que votre capacité à structurer vos idées.

Que ce soit pour la synthèse ou l'essai, vous devez maîtriser les mots de liaison que vous pourrez retrouver dans la partie « Grammaire ». Ils vont vous permettre d'exprimer facilement vos idées et de segmenter votre rédaction.

La question de synthèse est en lien avec un sujet précis. Votre opinion n'est pas nécessaire. Vous devez vous appliquer à reprendre uniquement les éléments du texte et du cours pour créer vos arguments. Le texte oppose ou renforce les arguments soulignés dans le passage audio.

Conseil n°4 : S'adapter aux critères d'évaluation

Une bonne compréhension des critères de notation vous permettra d'éviter les erreurs et de vous autoévaluer. Les deux parties sont notées sur 5 points chacune.

Voici un exemple de grille de notation utilisée par les correcteurs :

5 points	On retrouve toutes les caractéristiques suivantes : • réponse efficace à la question ; • bien organisés et développés, les arguments sont expliqués et soutenus par des détails/exemples ; • vocabulaire et grammaire variés. Bon niveau d'anglais même si le texte contient quelques erreurs mineures.
4 points	On retrouve toutes les caractéristiques suivantes : • réponse efficace à la question même si certains points ne sont pas élaborés. Le texte peut être un peu redondant ; • bien organisés et développés, les arguments sont expliqués et soutenus par des détails/exemples ; • vocabulaire et grammaire variés. Le texte contient des erreurs mineures qui n'empêchent pas la compréhension.
3 points	On retrouve au moins l'une des caractéristiques suivantes : • réponse à la question avec des explications développées et des détails/exemples ; • le texte est cohérent et organisé même si certaines idées ne sont pas bien liées entre elles ; • les mauvaises formations syntaxiques rendent certains passages difficiles à comprendre ; • la grammaire et le vocabulaire sont corrects, mais avec peu de variété.
2 points	On retrouve au moins l'une des faiblesses suivantes : • réponse courte et peu développée ; • texte mal organisé, mauvaises connexions entre les idées ; • arguments non développés, peu de détails/exemples. Trop de généralisations ; • vocabulaire inexact ou inapproprié ; • nombreuses erreurs de grammaire.
1 point	On retrouve au moins l'une des faiblesses suivantes : • texte complètement désorganisé ; • détails inexistants ou hors-sujets ; • erreurs grammaticales fréquentes et graves.
0 point	• pas de réponse ou réponse hors sujet ; • recopiage de quelques mots du sujet ; • écrit dans une autre langue que l'anglais.

Question type : Integrated essay

Présentation

L'épreuve écrite d'expression dirigée est une synthèse d'un texte et d'une bande-son. Cette partie se découpe en plusieurs étapes :

1. Vous avez 3 minutes pour lire un passage sur un sujet universitaire.
2. Vous entendrez l'extrait d'un cours sur le même sujet que le texte.
3. Une question s'affiche.
4. Vous devez réaliser une synthèse du cours en mettant en lien les éléments du texte pour répondre à la question.

Vous serez confronté à deux types de questions :

- La question qui met en opposition le cours et le texte :

> *Summarize the points made in the lecture, being sure to explain how they oppose specific points made in the reading passage.*

- La question qui soutient les informations du texte :

> *Summarize the points made in the lecture, being sure to explain how they answer the specific problems presented in the reading passage.*

Méthodologie

Pour les deux types de questions, la réponse est simple à structurer. Il faut résumer le cours en différents arguments en expliquant comment chaque argument s'oppose au texte ou le soutient.

Entraînement - Integrated essay - Audio

Reportez vos réponses pour analyser votre performance.

Entraînez-vous dans les conditions d'examen.

Écoutez les fichiers audio.

prepmyfuture.com/book/68/ex/1930

DIRECTIONS: For this task, you will write a response to a question about a reading passage and a lecture. You may take notes, and you may use your notes to help you write your response. Your response will be scored on the quality of your writing and on how well you connect the points in the lecture with points in the reading.

Reading Time – 3 minutes

The Mayans, an ancient society centered in the Yucatan peninsula of Central America, were arguably the most advanced Mesoamerican civilization to have existed before the arrival of the European explorers and colonists. They were the only ancient American culture to have fully developed a writing system and were masters of art, architecture, mathematics, and astronomy. They reached their height beginning in 250 A.D., but the collapse of Maya society began around 800 A.D., with millions of Mayans leaving their ancestral lands. Scientists have speculated on the reasons for why the Mayan civilization fell apart so dramatically.

Natural Disasters

One of the most common theories is that the Mayan civilization collapsed due to a sudden natural catastrophe. Many researchers have noted that Mayan ruins look as if they were hurriedly abandoned, their populations seeming to have fled, never to return. The ruins also show signs of earthquake damage that went unrepaired. In addition, hurricanes frequently sweep over the Mayan lowlands, destroying large areas of farmland. These hurricanes could have brought diseases that can wipe out whole crops, a danger that even modern farmers in that region of the Americas face.

Loss of Trade

Another intriguing possibility is that changes in trade patterns with other cultures may have brought about the fall of the Mayans. Because the Mayans lived in the lowlands of the Yucatan peninsula, they were dependent on the Mexican kingdom of the Toltecs for construction materials for their extensive building projects. There is evidence that at some point during the 9th Century, trade routes with the Toltecs shifted away from some of the larger Mayan cities--possibly the result of new sea routes being discovered—which led to their economic decline and a subsequent loss of population.

Overpopulation

While the above theories have their supporters, it is now widely accepted that in all likelihood the ever-growing Mayan population itself was the cause of its fall. With more and more people to feed, the Mayans had to begin to use less productive farmland which had soil more susceptible to disease or drought. Records show that the Mayan leaders, instead of seeking new innovations in agricultural production, focused their time and energy—and the labor of their people—on building monuments to their gods in a doomed attempt at divine intervention.

Now listen to part of a lecture on the topic you just read about.

■ Question 1

DIRECTIONS: You have 20 minutes to plan and write your response. Your response will be evaluated on the quality of your writing on how well you present the points in the lecture and their relationship to the reading passage. Typically, an effective response will have 150 to 225 words.

Response Time: 20 minutes

QUESTION: Summarize the points made in the lecture, explaining how they contrast with points made in the reading.

Entraînement - Integrated essay - Script

Reportez vos réponses pour analyser votre performance.

Entraînez-vous dans les conditions d'examen.

Écoutez les fichiers audio.

prepmyfuture.com/book/68/ex/1930

DIRECTIONS: For this task, you will write a response to a question about a reading passage and a lecture. You may take notes, and you may use your notes to help you write your response. Your response will be scored on the quality of your writing and on how well you connect the points in the lecture with points in the reading.

Reading Time – 3 minutes

The Mayans, an ancient society centered in the Yucatan peninsula of Central America, were arguably the most advanced Mesoamerican civilization to have existed before the arrival of the European explorers and colonists. They were the only ancient American culture to have fully developed a writing system and were masters of art, architecture, mathematics, and astronomy. They reached their height beginning in 250 A.D., but the collapse of Maya society began around 800 A.D., with millions of Mayans leaving their ancestral lands. Scientists have speculated on the reasons for why the Mayan civilization fell apart so dramatically.

Natural Disasters

One of the most common theories is that the Mayan civilization collapsed due to a sudden natural catastrophe. Many researchers have noted that Mayan ruins look as if they were hurriedly abandoned, their populations seeming to have fled, never to return. The ruins also show signs of earthquake damage that went unrepaired. In addition, hurricanes frequently sweep over the Mayan lowlands, destroying large areas of farmland. These hurricanes could have brought diseases that can wipe out whole crops, a danger that even modern farmers in that region of the Americas face.

Loss of Trade

Another intriguing possibility is that changes in trade patterns with other cultures may have brought about the fall of the Mayans. Because the Mayans lived in the lowlands of the Yucatan peninsula, they were dependent on the Mexican kingdom of the Toltecs for construction materials for their extensive building projects. There is evidence that at some point during the 9th Century, trade routes with the Toltecs shifted away from some of the larger Mayan cities--possibly the result of new sea routes being discovered—which led to their economic decline and a subsequent loss of population.

Overpopulation

While the above theories have their supporters, it is now widely accepted that in all likelihood the ever-growing Mayan population itself was the cause of its fall. With more and more people to feed, the Mayans had to begin to use less productive farmland which had soil more susceptible to disease or drought. Records show that the Mayan leaders, instead of seeking new innovations in agricultural production, focused their time and energy—and the labor of their people—on building monuments to their gods in a doomed attempt at divine intervention.

Now listen to part of a lecture on the topic you just read about.

Script non affiché le jour de l'examen :

PROFESSOR: While these theories about the cause of the demise of the Mayans have some evidence supporting them, each fails to take into account all that is known about the Mayans.

The idea that even the strongest of hurricanes could lead to the collapse of a whole civilization is hard to accept. For one, the destruction of a forest in the path of a hurricane's path might actually be beneficial for farmers, clearing away trees and foliage and creating new land for agricultural use. And while the idea of diseases being a major killer of Mayan people, no direct evidence, either from examination of Mayan skeletons or in the form of mass graves, has been found to support this hypothesis.

And what about a decline in trade? Well, there is some archeological evidence that island trading did increase around the 9th Century. However, there's also fairly strong evidence that at this same time the Mayans experienced dramatic changes in pottery, architecture and sculptures, leading experts to conclude that an outside culture—quite likely the Toltecs of Mexico--actually came to have greater influence on—and, as a result, trade with—Mayan society during the 9th Century. Furthermore, researchers now believe that the Mayan civilization did not seem to be as dependent on trade as was once thought—aside from stone, the region in which the Mayans lived had and still has an abundance of natural resources.

Now the idea of there being too many Mayans sounds logical, when examined more closely it really doesn't make much sense. First, there is no modern example of soil degradation leading to malnutrition. When famine strikes a country these days, it often has a political cause, and is not due to a lack of food. Instead of leading to the decline of its civilization, a huge fall in population such as the Mayans experienced would more likely have helped to bring a better balance between the people and the land.

▪ Question 1

DIRECTIONS: You have 20 minutes to plan and write your response. Your response will be evaluated on the quality of your writing on how well you present the points in the lecture and their relationship to the reading passage. Typically, an effective response will have 150 to 225 words.

Response Time: 20 minutes

QUESTION: Summarize the points made in the lecture, explaining how they contrast with points made in the reading.

Réponse type - Integrated essay - Solutions

Reportez vos réponses pour analyser votre performance.

Entraînez-vous dans les conditions d'examen.

Écoutez les fichiers audio.

prepmyfuture.com/book/68/ex/1930

question 1	q. ouverte

■ Question 1 - Solution

DIRECTIONS: You have 20 minutes to plan and write your response. Your response will be evaluated on the quality of your writing on how well you present the points in the lecture and their relationship to the reading passage. Typically, an effective response will have 150 to 225 words.

Response Time: 20 minutes

QUESTION: Summarize the points made in the lecture, explaining how they contrast with points made in the reading.

⟹ **explication**

Exemple de réponse

The professor, in his lecture, debunks the theories exposed in the text one by one.

First, he explains that natural disasters, far from being able to bring about the fall of an entire civilization as the reading would have us believe, could actually have had a beneficial impact on **their** farming habits. He also states that the spreading of diseases as an explanation for the end of the Mayan civilization cannot be supported by any hard scientific evidence.

Besides, he puts the evolution of the trade into perspective. He highlights that the Mayans' economic decline may not have been as harsh as the reading seems to indicate. The professor even states that it might be quite the opposite.

Lastly, the content of the lecture dismisses the idea that overpopulation has brought about the demise of the Mayans. It is even described as not making much sense. Although he acknowledges the change in the Mayan's population size, he concludes that it would actually have been beneficial to some extent.

Accordingly, the lecture and the reading contrast with each other regarding the reasons that led **to** the Mayan civilization to fall apart so dramatically.

Évaluation de l'exemple de réponse

Remarques générales / niveau CERCL	Le candidat rédige une analyse bien structurée, cohérente et convaincante des arguments avancés par le conférencier concernant les raisons de la disparition de la civilisation Maya. En résumant de manière appropriée les points soulevés par le conférencier et en les comparant à ceux du passage lu, le candidat prouve qu'il a une maîtrise adéquate des principales compétences analytiques (lecture et écoute). Le niveau de compétence du candidat correspond approximativement au niveau C1 du CECRL et la qualité du texte écrit serait égale à un 5/5 dans le système de score du TOEFL iBT.
Forme	Le court essai est divisé de manière appropriée en cinq parties (introduction ; 1er argument ; 2e argument ; 3e argument ; conclusion). Le candidat utilise un registre essentiellement standard avec quelques exceptions formelles qui confirment l'adéquation de la production écrite en fonction de son objectif et du sujet.
Variété et précision du vocabulaire	Le candidat utilise un éventail relativement large d'options qui témoignent d'un vocabulaire varié et approprié, sans copier des expressions ou des phrases entières du passage lu. Des termes comme *demise*, *beneficial* ou encore *scientific evidence* montrent une maîtrise avancée de la langue anglaise et permettent au candidat d'être précis et détaillé.
Grammaire, cohésion et cohérence	Le candidat emploie une série de solutions pour relier chaque paragraphe au suivant (*First*, *Besides*, *Lastly*, *Accordingly*). Pour cette raison, le texte est à la fois cohésif et cohérent, puisque le candidat ne formule pas d'affirmations contradictoires qui entravent l'efficacité de l'argument principal de la dissertation.
Pour aller plus loin	Le candidat parvient à rapporter objectivement le contenu du texte et de l'exposé sans laisser ses opinions personnelles sur le sujet (dans ce cas, les raisons de la disparition de la civilisation Maya) influencer la structure ou le contenu de sa production écrite.

Réponse corrigée

The professor, in his lecture, debunks the theories exposed in the text one by one.

First, he explains that natural disasters, far from being able to bring about the fall of an entire civilization as the reading would have us believe, could actually have had a beneficial impact on the people's farming habits. He also states that the spreading of diseases as an explanation for the end of the Mayan civilization cannot be supported by any hard scientific evidence.

Besides, he puts the evolution of the trade into perspective. He highlights that the Mayans' economic decline may not have been as harsh as the reading seems to indicate. The professor even states that it might be quite the opposite.

Lastly, the content of the lecture dismisses the idea that overpopulation has brought about the demise of the Mayans. It is even described as not making much sense. Although he acknowledges the change in the Mayan's population size, he concludes that it would actually have been beneficial to some extent.

Accordingly, the lecture and the reading contrast with each other regarding the reasons that led the Mayan civilization to fall apart so dramatically.

Question type : Independent question

Présentation

L'épreuve d'expression libre est une épreuve de rédaction où vous devez répondre à une question grâce à vos connaissances personnelles et vos idées.

Exemples

Quelques questions types :

- *Do you agree or disagree* : Vous devez donner une opinion sur un sujet. Le sujet sera détaillé par quelques phrases à la suite de la question.
- Préférence pour A ou B : Vous avez la description de deux choses. Vous devez exprimer votre préférence pour l'une ou l'autre.
- Description : en lien avec un sujet, vous décrivez une expérience personnelle ou une situation imaginée.
- Comparaison : vous devez comparer les deux éléments du sujet.

Méthodologie

Votre réponse doit être structurée sous la forme :

- introduction : synthèse du sujet en une ou deux phrases puis l'annonce du plan ;
- argument 1 + exemple ;
- argument 2 + exemple ;
- conclusion qui résume votre réponse avec une ouverture du sujet.

Entraînement - Independent question

Reportez vos réponses pour analyser votre performance.

Entraînez-vous dans les conditions d'examen.

prepmyfuture.com/book/68/ex/1931

Question 1

DIRECTIONS: Read the question below. You have 30 minutes to plan, write, and revise your essay. Typically, an effective response will contain a minimum of 300 words.

Response Time: 30 minutes

QUESTION: Do you agree or disagree with the following statement?

Novels or fictional stories cannot teach us anything useful.

Use specific reasons and examples to support your answer.

Réponse type - Independent question - Solutions

Reportez vos réponses pour analyser votre performance.

Entraînez-vous dans les conditions d'examen.

Écoutez les fichiers audio.

prepmyfuture.com/book/68/ex/1931

question 1	q. ouverte

Question 1 - Solution

DIRECTIONS: Read the question below. You have 30 minutes to plan, write, and revise your essay. Typically, an effective response will contain a minimum of 300 words.

Response Time: 30 minutes

QUESTION: Do you agree or disagree with the following statement?

Novels or fictional stories cannot teach us anything useful.

Use specific reasons and examples to support your answer.

⇝ **explication**

Exemple de réponse

As a proud bookworm, I could not disagree more with this statement. I strongly believe that novels, and all fictional stories in general, can teach us a lot.

Firstly, I believe fictional pieces of literature can teach important lessons. The most obvious example, in my opinion, is the genre of the fable, such as the works by Jean de la Fontaine. They all contain a moral that comes at the end, whether implicitly or explicitly, and that **are** designed to teach people how to behave on multiple subjects. The very fact that these are used in schools is a very telling aspect of how fiction can be used to teach, and hence be useful.

Furthermore, I am convinced that novels can be **useful in bringing** people together. Having cultural references in common helps people connect and interact. For instance, almost every single person from my generation has read the Harry Potter novels. They might not be extremely well-written, nor do they teach us a lot about our world, yet they allow people to have shared knowledge and experiences. While living abroad, I often used these as an icebreaker, as a way to ease into a conversation with someone I had just met, regardless of their country of origin.

To finish with, fictional stories allow us to escape our reality. In a world dominated by political scandals, economic difficulties, and environmental issues, being able to immerse oneself in a fictional world can be a necessary getaway for many folks. For instance, I did not like the book series Fifty Shades, but its success proves my point: people need to escape their reality and dive into an alternate **reality [repetition]** to feel better and unwind after a long day at work.

All in all, I find novels and fictional stories not only useful, but necessary to our everyday lives. If I ever met anyone who did not share my point of view, I would be interested in hearing their arguments, but I certainly would defend my position because reading is a passion of mine.

Évaluation de l'exemple de réponse

Remarques générales / niveau CERCL	Le candidat rédige un essai structuré et répond de manière claire à la question posée. Le niveau de compétence du candidat correspond approximativement au niveau C1 du CECRL et la qualité du texte écrit serait égale à un 5/5 dans le système de score du TOEFL iBT.
Forme	L'essai est divisé de manière appropriée en cinq paragraphes (introduction ; 1er argument ; 2e argument ; 3e argument ; 4e argument ; conclusion). Le candidat développe ses idées de façon claire, permettant ainsi aux différents arguments de s'imbriquer de manière fluide les uns avec les autres. De plus, le candidat n'a pas cherché à soutenir deux positions contradictoires, et a pris position en faveur d'un argument (ici, contredire la thèse qui voudrait que la fiction ne nous enseigne rien), ce qui lui a permis de le développer correctement.
Variété et précision du vocabulaire	Le candidat utilise un éventail relativement large d'options qui témoignent d'un vocabulaire varié et approprié. Il parvient à trouver des synonymes afin d'éviter les répétitions, ce qui démontre une maîtrise avancée de la langue anglaise et permet au candidat d'être précis et détaillé.
Grammaire, cohésion et cohérence	Le candidat emploie une série de connecteurs logiques pour relier les arguments entre eux (*Firstly*, *All in all*, *While*, *To finish with*). Pour cette raison, le texte est cohérent, puisque le candidat ne formule pas d'affirmations contradictoires qui entraveraient l'efficacité de l'argument principal de la dissertation.
Pour aller plus loin	Le candidat parvient à répondre à la question posée mais aurait pu nuancer son propos dans la conclusion, avec une ouverture, par exemple. Il aurait par exemple pu évoquer le genre littéraire de la fiction historique, qui enseigne l'histoire par le biais de la fiction.

Réponse corrigée

As a proud bookworm, I could not disagree more with this statement. I strongly believe that novels, and all fictional stories in general, can teach us a lot.

Firstly, I believe fictional pieces of literature can teach important lessons. The most obvious example, in my opinion, is the genre of the fable, such as the works by Jean de la Fontaine. They all contain a moral that comes at the end, whether implicitly or explicitly, and that is designed to teach people how to behave on multiple subjects. The very fact that these are used in schools is a very telling aspect of how fiction can be used to teach, and hence be useful.

Furthermore, I am convinced that novels can be a useful tool to bring people together. Having cultural references in common helps people connect and interact. For instance, almost every single person from my generation has read the Harry Potter novels. They might not be extremely well-written, nor do they teach us a lot about our world, yet they allow people to have shared knowledge and experiences. While living abroad, I often used these as an icebreaker, as a way to ease into a conversation with someone I had just met, regardless of their country of origin.

To finish with, fictional stories allow us to escape our reality. In a world dominated by political scandals, economic difficulties, and environmental issues, being able to immerse oneself in a fictional world can be a necessary getaway for many folks. For instance, I did not like the book series Fifty Shades, but its success proves my point: people need to escape their reality and dive into an alternate world [repetition] to feel better and unwind after a long day at work.

All in all, I find novels and fictional stories not only useful, but necessary to our everyday lives. If I ever met anyone who did not share my point of view, I would be interested in hearing their arguments, but I certainly would defend my position because reading is a passion of mine. Besides, books can be an effective way to learn more about history without effort, through historical fiction books, for instance.

Vocabulaire TOEFL

MODULE 1

Vocabulaire - Liste 1

Adjectifs

- **coarse** = grossier
  rough or loose in texture
  Ex: *This year's grains are a bit too coarse, cooking with them will be impossible.*

L'adjectif « *coarse* » peut s'employer dans des situations diverses : il désigne aussi bien des matériaux (*coarse hair* = des cheveux rêches) que le caractère d'une personne vulgaire, grossière.

- **disturbing** = troublant
  causing anxiety, interfering with the normal functioning of something
  Ex: *This Japanese director's movies are often quite disturbing.*

- **immense** = immense, gigantesque
  very large in scale and degree
  Ex: *They gave him an immense thank you for his courage and hard work.*

- **mundane** = banal
  something that lacks excitement and interest
  Ex: *Her book was quite mundane, addressing a common story without excitement.*

Attention ! C'est un faux-ami. En anglais, quelqu'un de *mundane* n'est pas quelqu'un de « mondain » mais bien quelqu'un d'ennuyeux, sans intérêt. C'est un adjectif péjoratif.

- **ongoing** = continu
  continuing, still in the progress
  Ex: *His erratic behavior is an ongoing issue for the family.*

- **sturdy** = vigoureux
  a person who is strongly and solidly built
  Ex: *To be a successful athlete, you must be both sturdy and hard-working.*

- **well-suited** = bien-adapté
  made well and adequately for
  Ex: *This outfit is unfortunately not well-suited for a job interview.*

Verbes

- **alter** = modifier
  to change or cause something to change
  Ex: *In order to improve my grades, I had to alter my studying methods.*

- **assert** = affirmer
  state a fact or belief with confidence
  Ex: *Throughout the trial, she continued to assert her innocence.*

- **baffle** = laisser perplexe
  leaving someone feeling perplex
  Ex: *Jenny was left baffled by her husband's sudden disappearance.*

- **bear** = supporter
  to endure a difficulty
  Ex: *During the war, my grandfather had to bear many hardships.*

- **crush** = écraser
  to deform or pulverize by pressing with force
  Ex: *In order to complete this salad, we will have to crush the cashew nuts in advance.*

> Dans le langage familier, *a crush* est un nom commun qui s'utilise pour exprimer que l'on craque, que l'on a un faible pour quelqu'un.
> Exemple : *Emily has a crush on Coby: every time she talks about him, she won't stop smiling!*
> FR : Emily a un faible pour Coby : à chaque fois qu'elle parle de lui, elle ne peut s'empêcher de sourire !

- **cultivate** = cultiver
  to develop a particular quality OR to prepare something (grains)
  Ex: *Learning Chinese was extremely difficult, I had to cultivate patience and deep serenity.*

- **dictate** = dicter
  to lay down the authority OR to say or read aloud
  Ex: *The mayor's secretary dictated this year's new laws to the people.*

- **distinguish** = distinguer
  to recognize or treat differently
  Ex: *This mother often distinguished between her two sons.*

- **embody** = incarner
  to give a visible and tangible form to something concrete or abstract
  Ex: *His art embodies the essence of passion and dedication.*

- **emit** = émettre
  to discharge or produce something
  Ex: *These new speakers emit a fantastic sound.*

- **enhance** = améliorer
  to increase or improve the quality or value of something
  Ex: *Drinking coffee can sometimes enhance productivity.*

> Il est important de trouver des synonymes pour éviter au maximum les répétitions, notamment dans les productions écrites. De fait, *to enhance* vous permettra de varier du verbe *to improve*, souvent employé.
> Exemple : *She enhanced her chances of getting accepted to her dream university by improving her resume.*
> FR : Elle a augmenté ses chances d'être acceptée dans l'université de ses rêves en améliorant son CV.

- **evolve** = évoluer
  to develop gradually
  Ex: *This company evolved quite rapidly. They now have offices in multiple countries.*

- **extinguish** = éteindre
  to cease to burn or shine
  Ex: *The fire crew successfully extinguished the ravaging forest fires.*

- **instigate** = susciter
  to bring about or initiate something
  Ex: *I hope to obtain your help in order to instigate this year's scholarship applications.*

- **relinquish** = renoncer
  to give up something voluntarily
  Ex: *My husband chose to relinquish his boss's proposal to become the school's president.*

- **work out** = faire du sport
  to take part in physical exercises
  Ex: *Working-out has both physical and psychological benefits.*

Adverbes

- **chiefly** = principalement
  mainly, mostly, or above all
  Ex: *My work chiefly consists of writing and correcting.*

- **exceedingly** = extrêmement
  to a great extent
  Ex: *I am exceedingly excited about my upcoming trip to Columbia.*

- **instantaneous** = instantané
  done or happening in an instant or immediately
  Ex: *Fortunately, the results of the exam were instantaneous.*

- **deceptively** = trompeusement
  done in a way that gives a misleading impression
  Ex: *This house is deceptively small, we will not proceed with the purchase.*

Attention à l'orthographe de l'adjectif dérivé de cet adverbe : on dit ainsi d'une personne malhonnête ou d'un discours trompeur qu'ils sont *deceitful*.
Exemple : *He is such a deceitful person! His speech was so deceitful!*
FR : C'est une personne tellement malhonnête ! Son discours était tellement trompeur !

Noms

- **petition** = pétition
  a written request to appeal for a cause
  Ex: *Thankfully, they all signed the petition to keep the local store open at night.*

- **shed** = abri, hangar
  a wood or metal structure used for storage
  Ex: *Max is such a handyman, he built his own shed twice in a row.*

Entraînements - Module 1

Exercice 1 - Synonymes / Antonymes

Reportez vos réponses pour analyser votre performance.

Entraînez-vous dans les conditions d'examen.

prepmyfuture.com/book/68/ex/1932

Question 1 Find the synonym for:

Delirious

(A) Smart
(B) Pragmatic
(C) Vulgar
(D) Insane

Question 2 Find the synonym for:

Vigilant

(A) Boring
(B) Attentive
(C) Biased
(D) Volatile

Question 3 Find the synonym for:

Fleeting

(A) Rapid
(B) Dedicated
(C) Slow
(D) Torrid

■ **Question 4** Find the synonym for:

Pompous

(A) Weak
(B) Arrogant
(C) Determined
(D) Solitary

■ **Question 5** Find the synonym for:

Helpful

(A) Useless
(B) Elusive
(C) Charitable
(D) Healthy

■ **Question 6** Find the antonym for:

Inspiring

(A) Distant
(B) Encouraging
(C) Poor
(D) Boring

■ **Question 7** Find the antonym for:

Disgusting

(A) Touching
(B) Abominable
(C) Beautiful
(D) Cheap

■ **Question 8** Find the antonym for:

Integrity

(A) Honesty
(B) Sympathy
(C) Corruption
(D) Empathy

Question 9 Find the antonym of:

Desperate

(A) Fragile
(B) Afraid
(C) Enthusiastic
(D) Dangerous

Question 10 Find the antonym for

Introspective

(A) Intelligent
(B) Fabulous
(C) Pensive
(D) Shallow

Exercice 2 - Trouver la définition

Reportez vos réponses pour analyser votre performance.

Entraînez-vous dans les conditions d'examen.

prepmyfuture.com/book/68/ex/1933

Question 1 To "Work-out" means....

(A) To work outside of your home in a public place
(B) To take part in physical exercises
(C) To work for someone without getting paid
(D) To do any kind of work to earn money

Question 2 The word "mundane" means....

(A) Very small and shiny
(B) Dull and colorless
(C) Very interesting
(D) Lacking interest and excitement

Question 3 The word "petition" means …

(A) A written request to appeal for a cause
(B) A written request to get married
(C) A written request to join the army
(D) A written request to close a bank account

Question 4 The word "emit" means…

(A) To hit someone really hard
(B) To discharge, produce or make a sound
(C) To reduce the speed
(D) To leave a place in a hurry

Question 5 Enduring an unexpected difficulty is…

(A) to receive
(B) to forgive
(C) to bear
(D) to handle

Question 6 When something is perfectly adequate it is…

(A) well-suited
(B) adaptable
(C) well kept
(D) portable

Question 7 A place under which you can store certain things is a…

(A) caravan
(B) shed
(C) pool
(D) fridge

Question 8 When you do something in continuum.

(A) Lastly
(B) Chiefly
(C) Ongoing
(D) Slowly

Question 9 It was done in a way that was misleading.

(A) Deceptively
(B) Aggressively
(C) Emotionally
(D) Sporadically

Question 10 When you improve the quality of your life.

(A) Change
(B) Revoke
(C) Maintain
(D) Enhance

Question 11 To love someone madly is to love…

(A) Partially
(B) Exceedingly
(C) Spontaneously
(D) Conditionally

Question 12 When you are confused about something, you are…

(A) Saddened
(B) Scared
(C) Baffled
(D) Joyful

Question 13 Try to acquire or develop a skill or quality.

(A) Promote
(B) Cultivate
(C) Obsess
(D) Demonstrate

Question 14 The action of reducing to small pieces is…

(A) To crush
(B) To fold
(C) To destroy
(D) To force

Exercice 3 - Mots TOEFL

Reportez vos réponses pour analyser votre performance.

Entraînez-vous dans les conditions d'examen.

prepmyfuture.com/book/68/ex/1934

Question 1 This year, the university of Colorado is home to some of the best professors in the world. From philosophy and history, to mathematics and chemistry, the quality of the lectures is excellent. Not only do the professors teach well, but they never **dictate** the students what to do. To them, learning is an individual process which should not require authority.

The word " **dictate** " in the passage is closest in meaning to:

(A) To read aloud

(B) To lay authority

(C) To allow to do

(D) To tell the truth

Question 2 The city's hospital seems to function effectively. Their emergency department, however, is often very crowded and chaotic. The hospital has, in the past few weeks, held meetings with hopes to find a working solution. The chief suggested that they **alter** their internal operational strategy.

The word " **alter** " in the passage is closest in meaning to:

(A) To preserve

(B) To keep the same

(C) To ignore

(D) To modify or change

Question 3 Marie always wanted to have a big family. At 41 years old, she is the mother of four beautiful children. However, being a mother isn't a simple task. You must, love, cook, play and always be present. However, what Marie finds the most difficult is to never **distinguish** between the four of them. Jealously is a common emotion, and Marie wants to avoid conflict of any kind.

The word " **distinguish** " in the passage is closest in meaning to:

(A) To treat differently

(B) To act differently

(C) To remember differently

(D) To doubt differently

■ Question 4 The town has a new attraction park. With some of the most exciting rollercoasters of the state, it became popular rather quickly. However, after a fatal accident, the police **instigated** a meticulous investigation.

The word " **instigate** " in the passage is closest in meaning to:

(A) To force
(B) To inaugurate
(C) To initiate
(D) To prove

Exercice 4 - Grammaire

Reportez vos réponses pour analyser votre performance.
Entraînez-vous dans les conditions d'examen.
prepmyfuture.com/book/68/ex/1935

■ Question 1 His life was ________ mundane ________ he had trouble finding a partner.

(A) that, this
(B) so, that
(C) this, so
(D) too, this

■ Question 2 In this class, there is no reason ________ a teacher would emit such a harsh sound.

(A) which
(B) that
(C) why
(D) because

■ Question 3 Everyone had immense respect for this single mother, she did all kinds of jobs ________.

(A) from living
(B) for a living
(C) to live
(D) so as to live

Question 4 Since we bought these new speakers from the store, the sound they emit is so clear, we can say ________ they work rather well

(A) as
(B) how
(C) why
(D) that

Question 5 Stephanie said she would promptly return the keys when she ________.

(A) came back
(B) should come back
(C) would come back
(D) comes back

Exercice 5 - Trouver l'erreur

Reportez vos réponses pour analyser votre performance.

Entraînez-vous dans les conditions d'examen.

prepmyfuture.com/book/68/ex/1936

Question 1 Choose the one underlined word or phrase that must be changed for the sentence to be correct.

Living in New York is a constant hustle. You have to find an apartment, earn a loade of money and endure the constant attitude of the people.

(A) Hustle
(B) Apartment
(C) loade
(D) Endure

Question 2 Success is never instantaeneous, you have to study avidly, work hard and never lose your objective. Life is a struggle and one must never give up.

(A) Instantaeneous
(B) Avidly
(C) Objective
(D) Struggle

Question 3 I have always liked eating cereals. Since my youth, mother always gave me the best quality. However, since moving to a new country, I have found that the grains are more coorse and hard to digest.

(A) Cereals

(B) Quality

(C) Grains

(D) Coorse

Question 4 After five years in the army, he was offered to become chief officer of a new division. However, he had to rellinquish the offer as his family was now his first priority.

(A) Army

(B) Chief

(C) Rellinquish

(D) Priority

Question 5 His art is quite special. It ambodies grace, style and decadence perfectly. His talent has earned him prestigious titles worldwide.

(A) Ambodies

(B) Decadence

(C) Earned

(D) Prestigious

Entraînements - Module 1 - Solutions

Exercice 1 - Synonymes / Antonymes - Solutions

Reportez vos réponses pour analyser votre performance.

Entraînez-vous dans les conditions d'examen.

prepmyfuture.com/book/68/ex/1932

question 1	D	question 3	A	question 5	C	question 7	C	question 9	C
question 2	B	question 4	B	question 6	D	question 8	C	question 10	D

Question 1 - Solution

Find the synonym for:

Delirious

FR : Trouver le synonyme de :

(A) Smart = Intelligent

(B) Pragmatic = Pragmatique

(C) Vulgar = Grossier

(D) ✓ Insane = Fou / insensé / démentiel

explication
« Delirious » (= délirant) : une personne qui délire ou qui perd la tête, dépassant les limites du raisonnable.

Question 2 - Solution

Find the synonym for:

Vigilant

FR : Trouver le synonyme de :

(A) Boring = Ennuyeux

(B) ✓ Attentive = Attentif

(C) Biased = Partial

(D) Volatile = Volatile

explication
« Vigilant » (= Vigilant) signifie faire preuve d'une attention dévouée, faire très attention.

▪ Question 3 - Solution

Find the synonym for:

Fleeting

FR : Trouver le synonyme de :

(A) ✓ Rapid = Rapide

(B) Dedicated = Dévoué

(C) Slow = Lent

(D) Torrid = Torride

⇢ **explication**
« Fleeting » (= Fugace) signifie éphémère ou bien impermanent.

▪ Question 4 - Solution

Find the synonym for:

Pompous

FR : Trouver le synonyme de :

(A) Weak = Faible

(B) ✓ Arrogant = Arrogant

(C) Determined = Déterminé

(D) Solitary = Solitaire

⇢ **explication**
« Pompous » (= Pompeux) signifie être d'une vanité excessive.

▪ Question 5 - Solution

Find the synonym for:

Helpful

FR : Trouver un synonyme de :

(A) Useless = Inutile

(B) Elusive = Insaisissable

(C) ✓ Charitable = Charitable

(D) Healthy = En bonne santé

⇢ **explication**
« Helpful » (= Utile) signifie apporter de l'aide.

▪ Question 6 - Solution

Find the antonym for:

Inspiring

FR : Trouver l'antonyme de :

Inspirant

(A) Distant = Distant

(B) Encouraging = Encourageant

(C) Poor = Pauvre

(D) ✓ Boring = Ennuyeux

⇝ **explication**
« Inspiring » (= Inspirant) signifie propre à inspirer, à donner de l'inspiration.

▪ Question 7 - Solution

Find the antonym for:

Disgusting

FR : Trouver l'antonyme de :

(A) Touching = Touchant

(B) Abominable = Abominable

(C) ✓ Beautiful = Beau / superbe

(D) Cheap = Pas cher

⇝ **explication**
« Disgusting » (= Répugnant) signifie inspirer un vif dégoût physique.

▪ Question 8 - Solution

Find the antonym for:

Integrity

FR : Trouver l'antonyme de :

(A) Honesty = Honnêteté

(B) Sympathy = Sympathie

(C) ✓ Corruption = Corruption

(D) Empathy = Empathie

⇝ **explication**
« Intégrity » (= Intégrité) signifie être honnête.

▪ Question 9 - Solution

Find the antonym of:

Desperate

FR : Trouver l'antonyme de :

(A)	Fragile	= Fragile
(B)	Afraid	= Peureux
(C)	✓ **Enthusiastic**	**= Enthousiaste**
(D)	Dangerous	= Dangereux

⇝ **explication**
« Desperate » (= Désespéré) est une personne qui s'abandonne au désespoir.

▪ Question 10 - Solution

Find the antonym for

Introspective

FR : Trouver l'antonyme de :

(A)	Intelligent	= Intelligent
(B)	Fabulous	= Fabuleux
(C)	Pensive	= Pensif
(D)	✓ **Shallow**	**= Superficiel**

⇝ **explication**
« Introspective » (= Introspectif) signifie conduire une observation méthodique de soi-même.

Exercice 2 - Trouver la définition- Solutions

Reportez vos réponses pour analyser votre performance.
Entraînez-vous dans les conditions d'examen.
prepmyfuture.com/book/68/ex/1933

question 1	B	question 4	B	question 7	B	question 10	D	question 13	B
question 2	D	question 5	C	question 8	C	question 11	B	question 14	A
question 3	A	question 6	A	question 9	A	question 12	C		

▪ Question 1 - Solution

To “Work-out” means….

FR : “To work-out” signifie :

(A)	To work outside of your home in a public place	= travailler hors de chez soi
(B) ✓	**To take part in physical exercises**	**= pratiquer une activité physique**
(C)	To work for someone without getting paid	= travailler sans attente de rémunération
(D)	To do any kind of work to earn money	= faire n'importe quel travail afin de gagner de l'argent

⟹ **explication**
« To work-out » est un verbe qui signifie pratiquer une activité physique ou bien faire du sport.

▪ Question 2 - Solution

The word "mundane" means….

FR : Le mot « mundane » signifie…

(A)	Very small and shiny	= Très petit et brillant
(B)	Dull and colorless	= Terne et incolore
(C)	Very interesting	= Très intéressant
(D) ✓	**Lacking interest and excitement**	**= Peu intéressant ou peu passionnant**

⟹ **explication**
Le mot "mundane" (= banal) signifie peu intéressant.

▪ Question 3 - Solution

The word "petition" means …

FR : Le mot "petition" signifie …

(A) ✓	**A written request to appeal for a cause**	**= Une plainte ou demande écrite**
(B)	A written request to get married	= Une demande en mariage écrite
(C)	A written request to join the army	= Une demande écrite pour rejoindre l'armée
(D)	A written request to close a bank account	= Une demande écrite pour clôturer un compte en banque

⟹ **explication**
Le mot "petition" (= pétition) signifie une plainte, ou une demande écrite qui fait appel à une cause.

▪ Question 4 - Solution

The word "emit" means…

FR : Le mot "emit" signifie…

(A)	To hit someone really hard	= Frapper quelqu'un violemment
(B) ✓	**To discharge, produce or make a sound**	**= Produire et libérer un son ou une substance telle que du gaz**
(C)	To reduce the speed	= Réduire la vitesse
(D)	To leave a place in a hurry	= Quitter un endroit rapidement

⇝ **explication**
Le mot « emit » (= émettre) signifie produire et libérer un son ou une substance telle que du gaz.

■ Question 5 - Solution

Enduring an unexpected difficulty is…

FR : Rencontrer une difficulté inattendue signifie…

(A) to receive = recevoir

(B) to forgive = pardonner

(C) ✓ to bear = supporter

(D) to handle = gérer

⇝ **explication**
Quand vous rencontrez une difficulté inattendue, il faut la supporter (= to bear).

■ Question 6 - Solution

When something is perfectly adequate it is…

FR : Quand quelque chose est totalement adéquat c'est…

(A) ✓ well-suited = adapté

(B) adaptable = adaptable

(C) well kept = conservé

(D) portable = portable / portatif

⇝ **explication**
On peut dire, quand quelque chose est totalement adéquat, que c'est bien adapté.

■ Question 7 - Solution

A place under which you can store certain things is a…

FR : Un endroit où l'on peut garder certaines choses est un …

(A) caravan = une caravane

(B) ✓ shed = un abri

(C) pool = une piscine

(D) fridge = un réfrigérateur

⇝ **explication**
Un abri est un endroit où l'on peut conserver certaines choses. Un abri peut être en bois ou en métal.

■ Question 8 - Solution

When you do something in continuum.

FR : Faire quelque chose "en continu"

(A) Lastly = en dernier

(B) Chiefly = principalement

(C) ✓ Ongoing = en continu

(D) Slowly = lentement

⇝ **explication**
Faire quelque chose "en continu", c'est le faire sans interruption, c'est de ce fait en cours ou "en continu".

▪ Question 9 - Solution

It was done in a way that was misleading.

FR : Cela a été fait d'une façon trompeuse

(A) ✓ Deceptively = De manière trompeuse

(B) Aggressively = Agressivement

(C) Emotionally = Émotionnellement

(D) Sporadically = Sporadiquement

▪ Question 10 - Solution

When you improve the quality of your life.

FR : Quand vous enrichissez la qualité de votre vie.

(A) Change = Changer

(B) Revoke = Retirer / révoquer / abroger / annuler

(C) Maintain = Maintenir / entretenir

(D) ✓ Enhance = Améliorer

⇝ **explication**
Quand vous enrichissez la qualité de votre vie, vous l'améliorez.

▪ Question 11 - Solution

To love someone madly is to love...

FR : Aimer quelqu'un à la folie, c'est aimer...

(A) Partially = partiellement

(B) ✓ Exceedingly = extrêmement

(C) Spontaneously = spontanément

(D) Conditionally = sous condition

⇝ **explication**
Quand vous aimez quelqu'un à la folie, vous l'aimé extrêmement.

▪ Question 12 - Solution

When you are confused about something, you are...

FR : Quand vous êtes confus ou troublé par quelque chose, vous êtes...

(A) Saddened = Attristé

(B) Scared = Effrayé

(C) ✓ Baffled = Perplexe

(D) Joyful = Joyeux

⟹ **explication**
Quand vous êtes troublé ou confus par quelque chose, vous êtes perplexe.

▪ Question 13 - Solution

Try to acquire or develop a skill or quality.

FR : Essayer d'acquérir ou développer une compétence ou qualité.

(A) Promote = Promouvoir

(B) ✓ Cultivate = Cultiver

(C) Obsess = Obséder

(D) Demonstrate = Démontrer

⟹ **explication**
Quand quelqu'un essaye d'acquérir ou développer une compétence, il/elle la cultive

▪ Question 14 - Solution

The action of reducing to small pieces is…

FR : L'action de réduire en petits morceaux est…

(A) ✓ To crush = Écraser

(B) To fold = Plier

(C) To destroy = Détruire

(D) To force = Forcer

⟹ **explication**
Quand on réduit des choses en petits morceaux, on les écrase.

Exercice 3 - Mots TOEFL - Solutions

Reportez vos réponses pour analyser votre performance.

Entraînez-vous dans les conditions d'examen.

prepmyfuture.com/book/68/ex/1934

question 1	B	question 2	D	question 3	A	question 4	C

■ Question 1 - Solution

This year, the university of Colorado is home to some of the best professors in the world. From philosophy and history, to mathematics and chemistry, the quality of the lectures is excellent. Not only do the professors teach well, but they never **dictate** the students what to do. To them, learning is an individual process which should not require authority.

The word " **dictate** " in the passage is closest in meaning to:

FR : Que signifie le mot "dictate" dans le passage?

(A) To read aloud = Lire à haute voix

(B) ✓ To lay authority = Imposer son autorité

(C) To allow to do = Autoriser à faire

(D) To tell the truth = Dire la vérité

⟹ **explication**

Le verbe "dictate" (= dicter) signifie imposer son autorité ou lire un texte à haute voix.

■ Question 2 - Solution

The city's hospital seems to function effectively. Their emergency department, however, is often very crowded and chaotic. The hospital has, in the past few weeks, held meetings with hopes to find a working solution. The chief suggested that they **alter** their internal operational strategy.

The word " **alter** " in the passage is closest in meaning to:

FR : Que signifie le mot "alter" dans le passage?

(A) To preserve = Préserver

(B) To keep the same = Garder le même

(C) To ignore = Ignorer

(D) ✓ To modify or change = Modifier ou changer

⟹ **explication**

"Alter" (= modifier) signifie changer quelque chose.

■ Question 3 - Solution

Marie always wanted to have a big family. At 41 years old, she is the mother of four beautiful children. However, being a mother isn't a simple task. You must, love, cook, play and always be present. However, what Marie finds the most difficult is to never **distinguish** between the four of them. Jealously is a common emotion, and Marie wants to avoid conflict of any kind.

The word " **distinguish** " in the passage is closest in meaning to:

FR : Dans le passage ci-dessus, que signifie le mot « distinguish » ?

(A) ✓ To treat differently = Traiter différemment

(B) To act differently = Agir différemment

(C) To remember differently = Se souvenir différemment

(D) To doubt differently = Douter différemment

⟹ **explication**

Le verbe « distinguish » (= distinguer) signifie différencier quelque chose ou quelqu'un. Faire une différence entre plusieurs personnes.

■ **Question 4 - Solution**

The town has a new attraction park. With some of the most exciting rollercoasters of the state, it became popular rather quickly. However, after a fatal accident, the police **instigated** a meticulous investigation.

The word " **instigate** " in the passage is closest in meaning to:

FR : Le verbe "instigate" signifie :

(A)		To force	= Forcer
(B)		To inaugurate	= Inaugurer
(C)	✓	**To initiate**	**= Initier**
(D)		To prove	= Prouver

⇨ **explication**
Le verbe "instigate" signifie initier une action ou évènement ou inciter quelqu'un à faire quelque chose.

Exercice 4 - Grammaire - Solutions

Reportez vos réponses pour analyser votre performance.

Entraînez-vous dans les conditions d'examen.

prepmyfuture.com/book/68/ex/1935

question 1	B	question 2	C	question 3	B	question 4	D	question 5	A

■ **Question 1 - Solution**

His life was ________ mundane ________ he had trouble finding a partner.

FR : Sa vie était tellement banale qu'il n'arrivait pas à trouver de conjoint.

(A)		that, this	= si, ceci
(B)	✓	**so, that**	**= tellement, que**
(C)		this, so	= comme ci, donc
(D)		too, this	= trop, ceci

■ **Question 2 - Solution**

In this class, there is no reason ________ a teacher would emit such a harsh sound.

FR : Il n'y a aucune raison pour qu'un professeur émette un tel son dans cette salle de classe.

(A)		which	= que
(B)		that	= que
(C)	✓	**why**	**= pour que**
(D)		because	= parce que

■ **Question 3 - Solution**

Everyone had immense respect for this single mother, she did all kinds of jobs ________.

FR : Tout le monde avait beaucoup de respect pour cette mère célibataire, elle occupait toute sorte d'emplois dans la vie .

(A) from living = de vivre

(B) ✓ for a living = dans la vie

(C) to live = pour vivre

(D) so as to live = afin de vivre

■ **Question 4 - Solution**

Since we bought these new speakers from the store, the sound they emit is so clear, we can say ________ they work rather well

FR : Depuis que nous avons acheté ces nouveaux haut-parleurs du magasin, le son qu'ils émettent est tellement clair, qu'on peut dire qu'ils fonctionnent plutôt bien.

(A) as = puisque

(B) how = comment

(C) why = pourquoi

(D) ✓ that = que

■ **Question 5 - Solution**

Stephanie said she would promptly return the keys when she ________.

FR : Stéphanie a dit qu'elle rendrait les clés immédiatement quand elle reviendrait.

(A) ✓ came back = est revenue

(B) should come back = devrait revenir

(C) would come back = reviendrait

(D) comes back = revient

⇨ **explication**

Attention, les conjonctions de subordination temporelles telles que **"when"** NE PEUVENT PAS ETRE SUIVIES D'UN FUTUR.

Par concordance de temps, le conditionnel sera remplacé par un prétérit.

Exercice 5 - Trouver l'erreur - Solutions

Reportez vos réponses pour analyser votre performance.

Entraînez-vous dans les conditions d'examen.

prepmyfuture.com/book/68/ex/1936

question 1	C	question 2	A	question 3	D	question 4	C	question 5	A

Question 1 - Solution

Choose the one underlined word or phrase that must be changed for the sentence to be correct.

Living in New York is a constant hustle. You have to find an apartment, earn a loade of money and endure the constant attitude of the people.

FR : Vivre à New York est un éternel combat. Il faut trouver un appartement, gagner beaucoup d'argent et supporter le comportement des citadins.

(A) Hustle

(B) Apartment

(C) ✓ loade **Le mot "Loade" n'est pas écrit correctement. Il s'écrit LOAD.**

(D) Endure

explication
Le mot « Loade » n'est pas écrit correctement, il s'écrit sans E : LOAD.

Question 2 - Solution

Success is never instantaeneous, you have to study avidly, work hard and never lose your objective. Life is a struggle and one must never give up.

FR : Le succès n'est jamais immédiat, il faut étudier avec avidité, travailler dur et ne jamais perdre son objectif de vue. La vie est un combat qu'il ne faut jamais abandonner.

(A) ✓ Instantaeneous **Le mot "instantanaeous" n'est pas écrit correctement. INSTANTANEOUS.**

(B) Avidly

(C) Objective

(D) Struggle

explication
Le mot "Instantaenous" n'est pas écrit correctement. Il s'écrit "Instantaneous".

Question 3 - Solution

I have always liked eating cereals. Since my youth, mother always gave me the best quality. However, since moving to a new country, I have found that the grains are more coorse and hard to digest.

FR : J'ai toujours aimé manger des céréales. Depuis mon plus jeune âge, ma mère m'a toujours donné la meilleure qualité. Cependant, depuis mon arrivée dans un nouveau pays, je trouve les graines plus grosses et difficiles à digérer.

(A) Cereals

(B) Quality

(C) Grains

(D) ✓ Coorse **"Coorse" n'est pas écrit correctement. Il s'écrit avec un A : COARSE.**

⟹ **explication**
Le mot « coorse » n'est pas écrit correctement. Il s'écrit avec un A : « coarse ».

▪ Question 4 - Solution

After five years in the army, he was offered to become chief officer of a new division. However, he had to rellinquish the offer as his family was now his first priority.

FR : Après cinq ans dans l'armée, on lui proposa de devenir chef d'une nouvelle division. Cependant, il refusa l'offre, car sa famille était désormais sa seule priorité.

(A) Army

(B) Chief

(C) ✓ Rellinquish

(D) Priority

⟹ **explication**
« Rellinquish » s'écrit avec un seul L: Relinquish.

▪ Question 5 - Solution

His art is quite special. It ambodies grace, style and decadence perfectly. His talent has earned him prestigious titles worldwide.

FR : Ces œuvres d'art sont très particulières. Elles incarnent la grâce, le style et la décadence. Son talent lui a valu plusieurs titres prestigieux dans le monde entier.

(A) ✓ Ambodies **"Ambodies" s'écrit avec un E : "EMBODIES".**

(B) Decadence

(C) Earned

(D) Prestigious

⟹ **explication**
Le mot "ambodies" ne s'écrit pas avec un A mais avec un E : "embodies" et non "ambodies".

MODULE 2

Vocabulaire - Liste 2

Adjectifs et adverbes

- **constantly** = constamment, continuellement
  all the time, or often
  Ex: *We are constantly updating our database.*
- **distinct** = distinct, séparé
  clearly noticeable, easy to identify
  Ex: *I distinctly heard the voice of my brother coming from the neighbor's kitchen.*
- **dormant** = dormant, inactif
  inactive, but which could become active in the future
  Ex: *Her talent remained dormant for many years before her music teacher encouraged her to perform in public.*
- **drab** = morne, terne
  boring, without bright color
  Ex: *On drab winter days like these, it is good to think of the sunny days of summer.*
- **dramatic** = dramatique
  full of action and excitement
  Ex: *His winning try in the last minute of the match ensured a dramatic victory for Ireland.*

Attention ! C'est un faux-ami. En anglais, s'il n'est pas utilisé dans un sens théâtral, *dramatic* aura plutôt le sens de quelque chose de spectaculaire, un changement que l'on remarque facilement. De plus, on dit qu'une personne est *dramatic* lorsqu'elle en fait trop, qu'elle en rajoute.
Exemple : *It is not such a dramatic change! You are being so dramatic!*
FR : Ce n'est pas un changement si spectaculaire que ça ! Tu en fais des tonnes !

- **elaborate** = détaillé, élaboré ; développer
  (adj.) containing a lot of detail; (verb) to work out or explain in detail
  Ex: *He invented an elaborate plan to steal the crown jewels. If you need more information I would be happy to elaborate.*
- **elementary** = élémentaire
  basic
  Ex: *I have an elementary knowledge of chemistry.*
- **erratic** = inégal, irrégulier
  in a way that is not regular, certain or expected
  Ex: *The passengers became increasingly frightened by the erratic driving of the bus driver.*
- **genuine** = véritable, authentique
  real, honest, sincere
  Ex: *Marius' feelings for Cosette were genuine: he truly loved her.*

Si l'adjectif *genuine* peut désigner le caractère d'une personne franche, dont les sentiments sont sincères, *genuine* s'emploie aussi pour parler des matériaux. On traduira ainsi « du cuir véritable » par l'expression *« genuine leather »*.

- **mammoth** = colossal, titanesque
  huge, very big
  Ex: *Solving the city's crime problem will be a mammoth task for the new mayor.*
- **overbearing** = autoritaire, dominateur/dominatrice
  telling other people what to do in an excessively authoritarian manner
  Ex: *He made many enemies because of his overbearing personality.*
- **prime** = premier, principal ; la fleur (de l'âge)
  (adj) main, most important or best quality; (noun) the best, most successful part of a life
  Ex: *When I go to the butcher, I expect him to sell me a prime cut of beef. When he was in his prime, he was an excellent swimmer.*
- **rudimentary** = rudimentaire, élémentaire
  basic
  Ex: *Living conditions in the camps are, at best, rudimentary.*

Verbes

- **derive** = extraire, dériver, tirer
  to obtain something from something else
  Ex: *She derives great satisfaction from her charity work.*
- **disperse** = (se) disperser, diffuser
  to spread over a large area
  Ex: *When the police arrived, the angry crowd started to disperse.*
- **eliminate** = éliminer, faire disparaître
  to remove or take away
  Ex: *We have eliminated most of the problems that were slowing us down.*
- **encircle** = encercler, entourer
  to surround, make a circle around something
  Ex: *The rich, central part of the city is encircled by poorer, more dilapidated districts.*
- **engender** = engendrer
  to make something exist
  Ex: *The government's security measures have engendered a lot of controversy.*
- **engross** = absorber
  to be so interesting as to absorb someone completely
  Ex: *I am totally engrossed in Stephen King's new novel.*
- **manage** = arriver à (faire quelque chose) ; gérer, diriger
  1) to succeed in doing something; 2) to be responsible for controlling people or things
  Ex: *I managed to persuade my boss to give me a rise. He manages a small company.*

Attention à la construction des phrases avec ce verbe ! Lorsqu'il est employé pour dire que l'on arrive à faire quelque chose, *« to manage »* est toujours suivi d'une base verbale à laquelle

on ajoute la préposion « *to* ». Ainsi, on dira toujours *to manage **to do** something.*
Exemple : *She managed **to catch** her train.*
FR : Elle a réussi à attraper son train.

- **mortify** = mortifier, blesser
  to make someone very embarrassed
  Ex: *I was mortified when I saw the photos of me at the party.*
- **obtain** = obtenir
  to get something
  Ex: *We have obtained 10 new computers for the new academic year.*
- **reject** = refuser, rejeter
  to refuse to accept, believe or use
  Ex: *We rejected all the candidates who did not send a letter with their resume.*
- **justify** = justifier, légitimer
  to be a good reason for
  Ex: *Our increased prices can be justified by the rise in production costs.*

Noms

- **accolade** = accolade
  (noun) a touch on a person's shoulders or an award or privilege granted for a person's good actions
  Ex: *His hard word paid off rather quickly. He received an accolade from the boss after just a few weeks' work.*
- **amenity** = aménagement, service
  a place that is designed to make life more pleasant or comfortable for its users
  Ex: *This prison, built over a century ago, is overcrowded and lacking in basic amenities.*
- **flaw** = un défaut, une imperfection
  a fault, mistake or weakness that causes something or someone to be less than perfect
  Ex: *Your report is full of flaws, you'll have to write it again.*
- **harvest** – la moisson, la récolte
  the cutting, picking or collecting crops from fields on a farm, etc.
  Ex: *The farm is hiring new workers to help with this year's grape harvest.*
- **idol** = idole
  a person who is much admired and respected
  Ex: *The real lives of Hollywood idols of the 50s were often very different from what their fans imagined.*
- **particle** = une particule
  an extremely small amount of something
  Ex: *If you have a particle of dust in your eye, you can usually remove it with the corner of a tissue.*

Entraînements - Module 2

Exercice 1 - Synonymes / Antonymes

Reportez vos réponses pour analyser votre performance.

Entraînez-vous dans les conditions d'examen.

prepmyfuture.com/book/68/ex/1937

Question 1

Some forms of toys probably derive from magical artifacts and fetishes that played a prominent part in primitive religions. Even today, during the Mexican festival of the Day of the Dead, sugar is formed into **elaborate** and beautiful skulls, tombs, and angels.

The word "**elaborate**" could best be replaced by:

(A) Detailed

(B) Ornamental

(C) Decorative

(D) Ostentatious

Question 2

The problems indicate that there are many **flaws** in need of urgent rectification before it is too late.

The word "**flaws**" is closest in meaning to:

(A) Suppositions

(B) Underlings

(C) Subtractions

(D) Faults

Question 3

When Taft arrived in Washington in February 1890, the office had been vacant for two months, with work piling up. He worked to **eliminate** the backlog, while simultaneously educating himself on federal law.

The word "**eliminate**" is closest in meaning to:

(A) Reduce

(B) Expel

(C) Reject

(D) Remove

▪ Question 4 The famous Wellington boot became a **staple** of hunting and outdoor wear for the British aristocracy in the early 19th century.

The word "**staple**" in the text is closest in meaning to:

(A) A fastener
(B) A simple garment
(C) A main product
(D) A bent hook

▪ Question 5 It is thought that the sperm whale can **stun** prey with its vocalized clicks, which are among the most powerful sounds in the animal kingdom.

The word "**stun**" in the text is closest in meaning to:

(A) Harm
(B) Kill
(C) Paralyse
(D) Deafen

▪ Question 6 They would like to **retrieve** the missing information, but they remain doubtful whether this will be possible.

Which of the following words is the **opposite** in meaning to the word "**retrieve**"?

(A) Recover
(B) Lose
(C) Dissipate
(D) Deplore

▪ Question 7 Mauna Kea in Hawaii, not having erupted in the past 10,000 years is an example of a volcano considered to be **dormant**.

Which of the following words is **opposite** in meaning to the word "**dormant**"?

(A) Active
(B) Conscious
(C) Awake
(D) Lively

▪ Question 8 There is considerable evidence that the perception of faces and objects is accomplished by **distinct** neural systems.

Which of the following words is **opposite** in meaning to the word " **distinct** "?

(A) Vague
(B) Normal
(C) Ambiguous
(D) Combined

▪ Question 9 The old doctor had been convinced of his own infallibility and had **managed** to persuade his patients of the same.

Which of the following words is **opposite** in meaning to the word " **managed** "?

(A) Failed
(B) Mismanaged
(C) Neglected
(D) Refused

▪ Question 10 The elephant was part of a circus, and his behaviour became so **erratic** that it was considered to be dangerous.

Which of the following words is **opposite** in meaning to the word " **erratic** "?

(A) Stationary
(B) Light
(C) Requisite
(D) Regular

Exercice 2 - Trouver la définition

Reportez vos réponses pour analyser votre performance.

Entraînez-vous dans les conditions d'examen.

prepmyfuture.com/book/68/ex/1938

▪ Question 1 Which of the following words can be defined as follows: "a person whose job is to solve problems for a company or an organization"?

(A) A rainmaker
(B) A diviner
(C) A whistleblower
(D) A troubleshooter

Question 2 Which of the following words can be defined as follows: “a period of ten years” ?

(A) A decal
(B) A decagon
(C) A decade
(D) A decay

Question 3 Which of the following words is defined as follows: “to cause something to exist or develop”?

(A) To enliven
(B) To engineer
(C) To endow
(D) To engender

Question 4 Which of the following words is defined as follows: “A place that is designed to make life more pleasant or comfortable for its users”.

(A) Convenience
(B) Commodity
(C) Juncture
(D) Amenity

Question 5 I was extremely embarrassed, in fact I was…
M…

Question 6 If you are totally absorbed in something, like a book or an activity, then you are:
E…

Question 7 My knowledge of the subject Is not very advanced. In fact it is very basic
R…

Question 8 This part of your life is when you are at your best at everything.
P…

Question 9 In the field of pop music, movies or sport these people are admired and venerated by their fans
I…

Question 10 To promote, develop, improve something or simply to grow plants
C…

Question 11 The time of the year when crops on the farm are cut, gathered and put into storage
H…

▪ Question 12 To come from an origin, like a word which comes originally from another language.
D...

▪ Question 13 A fault, mistake or weakness that causes something to be less than perfect.
F...

▪ Question 14 One of the basic units of matter or energy (a molecule, atom, proton, electron...)
P...

Exercice 3 - Mots TOEFL

Reportez vos réponses pour analyser votre performance.

Entraînez-vous dans les conditions d'examen.

prepmyfuture.com/book/68/ex/1939

▪ Question 1 The 1963 Clean Air Act gave authorization for research into techniques for **monitoring** and controlling air pollution.

The word **"monitoring"** in the passage is closest in meaning to...

(A) Banning
(B) Cleaning up
(C) Measuring
(D) Scrutinizing

▪ Question 2 The Bandeirantes were 17th century Portuguese settlers in Brazil who led expeditions into the Brazilian interior to enslave indigenous peoples and **expand** Portuguese control of the country.

The word **"expand"** in the passage is closest in meaning to...

(A) Consolidate
(B) Celebrate
(C) Improve
(D) Make bigger

Question 3 Andy Warhol's early commercial drawings were often comic, decorative and **"whimsical"**, and their tone was entirely different from his later work.

The word **"whimsical"** in the passage is closest in meaning to…

(A) Imaginative
(B) Ingenious
(C) Fanciful
(D) Controversial

Question 4 Many details of the life of Robert Johnson, the Mississippi delta blues singer, remain **sketchy**, none more so than the circumstances of his death at the age of 27.

The word **"sketchy"** in the passage is closest in meaning to…

(A) Controversial
(B) Unfortunate
(C) Dark
(D) Unclear

Exercice 4 - Grammaire

Reportez vos réponses pour analyser votre performance.
Entraînez-vous dans les conditions d'examen.
prepmyfuture.com/book/68/ex/1940

Question 1 There was _____ for such behavior.

(A) no justification
(B) no justifying
(C) unjustified
(D) not justifiable

Question 2 When you are sure of your answer, you _________ the letter corresponding to the correct response: A, B, C or D.

(A) should encircle
(B) will be encircling
(C) would encircle
(D) going to encircle

Question 3 Dumping in rubbish tips causes mercury to infiltrate waste water and ________ into the environment.

(A) dispersed

(B) To be dispersed

(C) dispersing

(D) To be dispersing

Question 4 It is understood that the government intends to support the amendments to the first bill, ________ those to the second.

(A) and be rejecting

(B) while rejecting

(C) as to reject

(D) although reject

Question 5 ________ to hear that he was obese after completing the medical examination.

(A) He was mortifying

(B) It was mortified

(C) He mortified

(D) It was mortifying

Exercice 5 - Trouver l'erreur

Reportez vos réponses pour analyser votre performance.

Entraînez-vous dans les conditions d'examen.

prepmyfuture.com/book/68/ex/1941

Question 1 *Choose the one underlined word or phrase that must be changed for the sentence to be correct.*

Behind the Lincoln memorial to the west lies Arlington National <u>cemetary</u>, to the east the Washington Monument and Capitol Hill. The massive <u>sculpture</u> of Lincoln faces east.The peaceful atmosphere <u>belies</u> the years of <u>disagreement</u> over what kind of monument to build and where.

(A) cemetary

(B) sculpture

(C) belies

(D) disagreement

■ Question 2 *Choose the one underlined word or phrase that must be changed for the sentence to be correct.*

In 1825, the convict and noted architect Francis Greenway wrote a letter to "The Australian" newspaper stating that a bridge spanning Sydney harbour would "give an idea of strenght and magnificence that would reflect credit and glory on the colony and the Mother Country"

(A) convict
(B) architect
(C) strenght
(D) magnificence

■ Question 3 *Choose the one underlined word or phrase that must be changed for the sentence to be correct.*

The University offers a guarantee of accommodation for the majority of students that are beginning their studies. This means that students will recieve an offer which takes into consideration the information and preferences they have provided in their application.

(A) guarantee
(B) accommodation
(C) recieve
(D) preferences

■ Question 4 *Choose the one underlined word or phrase that must be changed for the sentence to be correct.*

In 1940, the comic actor, W.C. Fields wrote a book entitled, Fields for President, consisting of humourous essays in the form of a campaign speech.

(A) comic
(B) entitled
(C) humourous
(D) campaign

■ Question 5 *Choose the one underlined word or phrase that must be changed for the sentence to be correct.*

By awarding the George Cross to Malta, King George VI expressed how greatful the British nation was for the island's gallantry during the Second World War.

(A) awarding
(B) expressed
(C) greatful
(D) gallantry

Entraînements - Module 2 - Solutions

Exercice 1 - Synonymes / Antonymes - Solutions

Reportez vos réponses pour analyser votre performance.

Entraînez-vous dans les conditions d'examen.

prepmyfuture.com/book/68/ex/1937

question 1	A	question 3	D	question 5	C	question 7	A	question 9	A
question 2	D	question 4	C	question 6	B	question 8	D	question 10	D

Question 1 - Solution

Some forms of toys probably derive from magical artifacts and fetishes that played a prominent part in primitive religions. Even today, during the Mexican festival of the Day of the Dead, sugar is formed into **elaborate** and beautiful skulls, tombs, and angels.

The word "**elaborate**" could best be replaced by:

FR : Dans le texte, le mot « elaborate » veut dire…

(A) ✓ Detailed = Détaillé

(B) Ornamental = Ornamental, décoratif

(C) Decorative = Décoratif, joli

(D) Ostentatious = Ostentatoire

explication
L'adjectif « elaborate » veut dire « élaboré », « détaillé », « recherché ».

Question 2 - Solution

The problems indicate that there are many **flaws** in need of urgent rectification before it is too late.

The word "**flaws**" is closest in meaning to:

FR : Dans le texte, le mot « flaws » veut dire…

(A) Suppositions = Suppositions

(B) Underlings = Subalternes, sous-fifres

(C) Subtractions = Soustractions

(D) ✓ Faults = Défauts, imperfections

explication
« A flaw » est un défaut ou une imperfection.

■ Question 3 - Solution

When Taft arrived in Washington in February 1890, the office had been vacant for two months, with work piling up. He worked to **eliminate** the backlog, while simultaneously educating himself on federal law.

The word "**eliminate**" is closest in meaning to:

FR : Dans le texte, le mot « eliminate » veut dire…

(A) Reduce = Réduire

(B) Expel = Expulser, renvoyer

(C) Reject = Rejeter, refuser

(D) ✓ Remove = Éliminer, enlever

⇝ **explication**
« Eliminate » veut dire éliminer, faire disparaître.

■ Question 4 - Solution

The famous Wellington boot became a **staple** of hunting and outdoor wear for the British aristocracy in the early 19th century.

The word "**staple**" in the text is closest in meaning to:

FR : Dans le texte, le mot « staple » veut dire…

(A) A fastener = Une fermeture, une fixation

(B) A simple garment = Un vêtement simple

(C) ✓ A main product = Un produit courant

(D) A bent hook = Un crochet tordu

⇝ **explication**
A "staple" peut être une agrafe ou un aliment de base, mais ici il est un élément ou produit principal.

■ Question 5 - Solution

It is thought that the sperm whale can **stun** prey with its vocalized clicks, which are among the most powerful sounds in the animal kingdom.

The word "**stun**" in the text is closest in meaning to:

FR : Dans le texte, le mot « stun » veut dire:

(A) Harm = Nuire, faire du mal, endommager

(B) Kill = Tuer

(C) ✓ Paralyse = Paralyser

(D) Deafen = Assourdir

⇝ **explication**
To « stun » veut dire étourdir, mais aussi assommer ou paralyser. C'est ce que fait le cachalot à sa proie.

▪ Question 6 - Solution

They would like to **retrieve** the missing information, but they remain doubtful whether this will be possible.

Which of the following words is the **opposite** in meaning to the word "**retrieve**"?

FR : Lequel des mots qui suivent est le contraire du mot « retrieve » ?

(A) Recover = Retrouver, donc c'est le synonyme de « retrieve »

(B) ✓ Lose = Rerdre, l'antonyme de « retrieve »

(C) Dissipate = (se) Dissiper, donc l'antonyme serait : accumuler

(D) Deplore = Déplorer, donc son antonyme serait « approuver »

⇒ **explication**
Retrieve veut dire « récupérer », donc l'antonyme serait : « perdre », « détruire », etc.

▪ Question 7 - Solution

Mauna Kea in Hawaii, not having erupted in the past 10,000 years is an example of a volcano considered to be **dormant**.

Which of the following words is **opposite** in meaning to the word "**dormant**"?

FR : Lequel des mots qui suivent est le contraire du mot « dormant » ?

(A) ✓ Active = Actif

(B) Conscious = Conscient, volontaire

(C) Awake = Éveillé

(D) Lively = Vivant, animé

⇒ **explication**
Bien que tous les quatre mots puissent être considérés comme l'antonyme de « dormant », le seul qui est acceptable dans le contexte des volcans est « active ».

▪ Question 8 - Solution

There is considerable evidence that the perception of faces and objects is accomplished by **distinct** neural systems.

Which of the following words is **opposite** in meaning to the word "**distinct**"?

FR : Lequel des mots qui suivent est le contraire du mot « distinct » ?

(A) Vague = Vague, imprécis

(B) Normal = Normal, habituel

(C) Ambiguous = Ambigu, équivoque

(D) ✓ Combined = Combiné, mélangé

⇒ **explication**
Le sens du mot « distinct » ici est séparé ou mis à part, et non clairement perceptible. Son antonyme serait donc uni, ou combiné.

▪ Question 9 - Solution

The old doctor had been convinced of his own infallibility and had **managed** to persuade his patients of the same.

Which of the following words is **opposite** in meaning to the word "**managed**"?

FR : Lequel des mots qui suivent est le contraire du mot « managed » ?

(A) ✓ Failed = A échoué

(B) Mismanaged = A mal géré

(C) Neglected = A négligé

(D) Refused = A refusé

explication
« To manage » peut avoir plusieurs sens, mais ici cela veut dire réussir (à faire quelque chose). Le contraire serait, donc, échouer.

▪ Question 10 - Solution

The elephant was part of a circus, and his behaviour became so **erratic** that it was considered to be dangerous.

Which of the following words is **opposite** in meaning to the word "**erratic**"?

FR : Lequel des mots qui suivent est le contraire du mot "erratic" ?

(A) Stationary = Stationnaire

(B) Light = Clair, léger, faible

(C) Requisite = Nécessaire, requis

(D) ✓ Regular = Régulier, constant

explication
« Erratic » veut dire inégal, irrégulier, ici un comportement imprévisible ou irrégulier. L'antonyme serait, donc, régulier.

Exercice 2 - Trouver la définition- Solutions

Reportez vos réponses pour analyser votre performance.

Entraînez-vous dans les conditions d'examen.

prepmyfuture.com/book/68/ex/1938

question 1	D	question 4	D	question 7	rudimentary
question 2	C	question 5	mortified	question 8	prime
question 3	D	question 6	engrossed	question 9	idols

question 10	**cultivate**
question 11	**harvest**
question 12	**derive**

question 13	**flaw**
question 14	**particle**

■ Question 1 - Solution

Which of the following words can be defined as follows: "a person whose job is to solve problems for a company or an organization"?

FR : Lequel des mots qui suivent est défini comme : « Une personne dont la fonction est de résoudre des problèmes d'une société ou d'une organisation »

(A) A rainmaker = Un faiseur de pluie, quelqu'un qui attire les affaires pour une société

(B) A diviner = Un sourcier, un devin

(C) A whistleblower = Un lanceur/se d'alerte, quelqu'un qui tire la sonnette d'alarme

(D) ✓ A troubleshooter = Un expert/e, conciliateur/trice, médiateur/trice

⟹ **explication**
« A troubleshooter » veut dire littéralement : quelqu'un qui résout des problèmes.

■ Question 2 - Solution

Which of the following words can be defined as follows: "a period of ten years" ?

FR : Lequel des mots qui suivent est défini comme : « une période de dix ans ».

(A) A decal = Un décalc

(B) A decagon = Un décagone

(C) ✓ A decade = Une décennie

(D) A decay = Une écomposition, pourrissement

⟹ **explication**
« A decade » est une periode de dix ans.

■ Question 3 - Solution

Which of the following words is defined as follows: "to cause something to exist or develop"?

FR : Lequel des mots qui suivent est défini comme : « causer l'existence ou le développement de quelque chose ».

(A) To enliven = animer

(B) To engineer = construire, concevoir, orchestrer

(C) To endow = doter

(D) ✓ To engender = engendrer

⟹ **explication**
« Engender » veut dire « engendrer ».

■ Question 4 - Solution

Which of the following words is defined as follows: "A place that is designed to make life more pleasant or comfortable for its users".

FR : Lequel des mots qui suivent est défini comme : « Un endroit conçu pour rendre la vie de ses utilisateurs plus agréable ou confortable ».

(A)	Convenience	= Utilité, commodité
(B)	Commodity	= Produit, article, merchandise, denrée
(C)	Juncture	= Moment (critique), tournant
(D)	✓ **Amenity**	**= Équipement, installation**

■ Question 5 - Solution

I was extremely embarrassed, in fact I was...
M...
Réponse(s) : mortified

■ Question 6 - Solution

If you are totally absorbed in something, like a book or an activity, then you are:
E...
Réponse(s) : engrossed

■ Question 7 - Solution

My knowledge of the subject is not very advanced. In fact it is very basic
R...
Réponse(s) : rudimentary

■ Question 8 - Solution

This part of your life is when you are at your best at everything.
P...
Réponse(s) : prime

■ Question 9 - Solution

In the field of pop music, movies or sport these people are admired and venerated by their fans
I...
Réponse(s) : idols

■ Question 10 - Solution

To promote, develop, improve something or simply to grow plants
C...
Réponse(s) : cultivate

■ Question 11 - Solution

The time of the year when crops on the farm are cut, gathered and put into storage
H...
Réponse(s) : harvest

■ Question 12 - Solution

To come from an origin, like a word which comes originally from another language.
D...
Réponse(s) : derive

Question 13 - Solution

A fault, mistake or weakness that causes something to be less than perfect.
F…
Réponse(s) : flaw

Question 14 - Solution

One of the basic units of matter or energy (a molecule, atom, proton, electron…)
P…
Réponse(s) : particle

Exercice 3 - Mots TOEFL - Solutions

Reportez vos réponses pour analyser votre performance.
Entraînez-vous dans les conditions d'examen.
prepmyfuture.com/book/68/ex/1939

question 1	D	question 2	D	question 3	C	question 4	D

Question 1 - Solution

The 1963 Clean Air Act gave authorization for research into techniques for **monitoring** and controlling air pollution.

The word **"monitoring"** in the passage is closest in meaning to…

FR : Le sens du mot « monitoring » se rapproche le plus de…

(A) Banning = interdisant

(B) Cleaning up = nettoyant

(C) Measuring = mesurant

(D) ✓ Scrutinizing = examinant, scrutant

explication
To monitor veut dire surveiller ou suivre. Ici il s'agit de la pollution, donc le mot scrutinize (= examiner, scruter) a le sens le plus proche.

Question 2 - Solution

The Bandeirantes were 17th century Portuguese settlers in Brazil who led expeditions into the Brazilian interior to enslave indigenous peoples and **expand** Portuguese control of the country.

The word **"expand"** in the passage is closest in meaning to…

FR : Le sens du mot « expand » se rapproche le plus de…

(A)	Consolidate	= Consolider, fusionner
(B)	Celebrate	= Célébrer, fêter
(C)	Improve	= Améliorer
(D)	✓ **Make bigger**	**= Élargir, accroître, étendre**

⟹ **explication**
"To expand" veut dire élargir ou étendre, ce qui se rapproche le plus du sens de "make bigger".

▪ Question 3 - Solution

Andy Warhol's early commercial drawings were often comic, decorative and **"whimsical"**, and their tone was entirely different from his later work.

The word **"whimsical"** in the passage is closest in meaning to…

FR : FR: Le sens du mot "whimsical" se rapproche le plus de…

(A)	Imaginative	= Imaginatif, créatif
(B)	Ingenious	= Ingénieux, génial
(C)	✓ **Fanciful**	**= Capricieux, fantasque**
(D)	Controversial	= Polémique, controversé

⟹ **explication**
Le mot "whimsical" veut dire capricieux ou fantasque. "Fanciful" se rapproche donc le plus du sens de "whimsical".

▪ Question 4 - Solution

Many details of the life of Robert Johnson, the Mississippi delta blues singer, remain **sketchy**, none more so than the circumstances of his death at the age of 27.

The word **"sketchy"** in the passage is closest in meaning to…

FR : Le sens du mot "sketchy" se rapproche le plus de…

(A)	Controversial	= Controversé, polémique
(B)	Unfortunate	= Malheureux
(C)	Dark	= Sombre
(D)	✓ **Unclear**	**= Pas clair, obscur**

⟹ **explication**
"Sketchy" du nom "sketch" : ébauche, esquisse, veut dire inachevé, sommaire, incomplet. "Unclear" se rapproche donc le plus du sens de "sketchy".

Exercice 4 - Grammaire - Solutions

Reportez vos réponses pour analyser votre performance.
Entraînez-vous dans les conditions d'examen.
prepmyfuture.com/book/68/ex/1940

question 1	A	question 2	A	question 3	B	question 4	B	question 5	D

Question 1 - Solution

There was _____ for such behavior.

FR : Il n'y avait _____ pour un tel comportement.

(A) ✓ **no justification** **= Aucune justification**

(B) no justifying — Pas de traduction
Avec la préposition "for", cette option n'est pas possible.

(C) unjustified — = Injustifié
"Unjustified" est un adjectif, mais ici c'est un nom qui est exigé.

(D) not justifiable — = Pas justifiable
Adjectif au négatif, ce qui n'est pas possible ici.

⇨ **explication**
"There was" doit être suivi d'un substantif. Ici "justification" est précédé du déterminant "no".

Question 2 - Solution

When you are sure of your answer, you _________ the letter corresponding to the correct response: A, B, C or D.

FR : Quand vous serez certains de votre réponse, vous _________ la lettre qui correspond à la bonne réponse : A, B, C ou D.

(A) ✓ **should encircle** **= Devriez encercler**

(B) will be encircling — = Serez en train d'encercler
Il n'a ya aucune notion de continuité ici.

(C) would encircle — = Encercleriez
"Would" exprime une condition, mais il n'y en a pas ici.

(D) going to encircle — Pas de traduction possible
Il nous faudrait l'auxiliaire "are" pour compléter la forme future "going to".

⇨ **explication**
Le verbe "should" exprime un conseil et il est suivi de la forme de l'infinitif sans "to".

Question 3 - Solution

Dumping in rubbish tips causes mercury to infiltrate waste water and _________ into the environment.

FR : La mise en décharge provoque l'infiltration de mercure dans les eaux usées et _________ dans l'environnement.

(A)	dispersed	= A dispersé *Le prétérit ou le participe passé n'est pas suffisant ici.*
(B)	✓ **To be dispersed**	**= Sa dispersion (pas de traduction littérale)**
(C)	dispersing	= Dispersant *Le gérondif n'est pas approprié ici.*
(D)	To be dispersing	Pas de traduction *Forme progressive, pas approprié ici.*

⇒ **explication**
Ici le verbe "causes" doit être suivi de la forme infinitive ainsi que la voix passive du verbe "disperse".

▪ Question 4 - Solution

It is understood that the government intends to support the amendments to the first bill, ________ those to the second.

FR : C'est entendu que le gouvernement veut soutenir les amendements portant sur le premier projet de loi, ________ ceux du deuxième.

(A)	and be rejecting	= Et être en train de rejeter *La forme progressive n'est pas possible ici.*
(B)	✓ **while rejecting**	**= Tout en rejetant**
(C)	as to reject	= Afin de rejeter *"As" n'est pas approprié ici.*
(D)	although reject	= Bien que rejeter *"Although" serait possible s'il était suivi de "it intends to reject those to the second".*

⇒ **explication**
"While" ici indique un contraste. Lorsqu'il est suivi d'un verbe, ce verbe s'emploie à la forme -ing.

▪ Question 5 - Solution

________ to hear that he was obese after completing the medical examination.

FR : ________ d'entendre qu'il était obèse après avoir passé l'examen médical.

(A)	He was mortifying	= Il mortifiait *La forme passive au "past simple" and et pas la forme active au "past continuous" est nécessaire ici.*
(B)	It was mortified	= Ce fut mortifié / c'était mortifié *"He was mortified" est possible, mais pas "it was mortified".*
(C)	He mortified	= Il a mortifié *La forme passive et pas la forme active est nécessaire ici.*
(D)	✓ **It was mortifying**	**C'était mortifiant (traduction littérale) = il fut mortifié**

⇒ **explication**
Ici le verbe "mortify" ne peut pas être employé qu'à la voix passive ("He was mortified") ou à la forme -ing avec le sujet "it" ("It was mortifying" (for him)).

Exercice 5 - Trouver l'erreur - Solutions

Reportez vos réponses pour analyser votre performance.

Entraînez-vous dans les conditions d'examen.

prepmyfuture.com/book/68/ex/1941

question 1	A	question 2	C	question 3	C	question 4	C	question 5	C

Question 1 - Solution

Choose the one underlined word or phrase that must be changed for the sentence to be correct.

Behind the Lincoln memorial to the west lies Arlington National cemetary, to the east the Washington Monument and Capitol Hill. The massive sculpture of Lincoln faces east.The peaceful atmosphere belies the years of disagreement over what kind of monument to build and where.

(A) ✓ cemetary

(B) sculpture

(C) belies

(D) disagreement

explication
L'orthographe correcte du mot est « cemetery » (= cimetière).

Question 2 - Solution

Choose the one underlined word or phrase that must be changed for the sentence to be correct.

In 1825, the convict and noted architect Francis Greenway wrote a letter to "The Australian" newspaper stating that a bridge spanning Sydney harbour would "give an idea of strenght and magnificence that would reflect credit and glory on the colony and the Mother Country"

(A) convict

(B) architect

(C) ✓ strenght

(D) magnificence

explication
L'orthographe correcte du mot est « strength » (= force).

Question 3 - Solution

Choose the one underlined word or phrase that must be changed for the sentence to be correct.

The University offers a guarantee of accommodation for the majority of students that are beginning their studies. This means that students will recieve an offer which takes into consideration the information and preferences they have provided in their application.

(A) guarantee

(B) accommodation

(C) ✓ recieve

(D) preferences

⟹ **explication**
L'orthographe correcte du mot est receive (= recevoir). (Règle générale à noter: "i" avant "e" sauf après "c").

Question 4 - Solution

Choose the one underlined word or phrase that must be changed for the sentence to be correct.

In 1940, the comic actor, W.C. Fields wrote a book entitled, Fields for President, consisting of humourous essays in the form of a campaign speech.

(A) comic

(B) entitled

(C) ✓ humourous

(D) campaign

⟹ **explication**
L'orthographe correcte du mot est "humorous" (= humoristique).

Question 5 - Solution

Choose the one underlined word or phrase that must be changed for the sentence to be correct.

By awarding the George Cross to Malta, King George VI expressed how greatful the British nation was for the island's gallantry during the Second World War.

(A) awarding

(B) expressed

(C) ✓ greatful

(D) gallantry

⟹ **explication**
L'orthographe correcte du mot est « grateful » (= reconnaissant).

MODULE 3

Vocabulaire - Liste 3

Adjectifs

- **ample** = abondant
  enough or more than enough, plentiful
  Ex: *While you start at the bottom of the line, there remains ample room for growth.*
- **arid** = aride, sec
  having no rain, very dry
  Ex: *New Mexico is a beautiful State, especially Santa Fe, where the lifestyle is frugal. However, the land remains a bit arid for my agricultural projects.*
- **blind** = aveugle
  unable to see, having no sight
  Ex: *Her blind brother decided to move to a city with adequate accommodation for the disabled community.*
- **deficient** = défectueux
  not having enough of a specified quality or ingredient
  Ex: *His new computer worked well for a few months. However, it grew deficient rather quickly.*
- **evident** = apparent
  plain or obvious; clearly seen or understood
  Ex: *After just a few months in his new house, it was evident he would never leave the city again.*
- **oblivious** = inconscient
  not being aware or concerned about what is happening around you
  Ex: *The news report said the man was quite oblivious when the accident happened.*
- **prevalent** = fréquent
  widespread in a particular area at a particular time
  Ex: *It is said that his academic success was due to his prevalent intelligence in complex mathematics.*
- **suitable** = approprié
  right or appropriate for a particular person, purpose or situation
  Ex: *This outfit is unfortunately not suitable for this event. You will have to return home and change your clothes.*
- **susceptible** = susceptible
  likely to be able to be influenced or harmed by a particular thing
  Ex: *Their relationship was rather unsuccessful. His girlfriend was both jealous and highly susceptible.*

Verbes

- **avert** = éviter, prévenir
  to turn away one's eyes or one's attention
  Ex: *As a gesture to his good intentions, his father averted many of his sons mistakes.*

- **broaden** = élargir
  become larger in distance from side to side; widen
  Ex: *In order to adapt to his new environment, he had to broaden his perspectives and be more open-minded.*

- **carry out** = effectuer
  to put through or follow up on something
  Ex: *Their decision to move to Canada was well prepared. They had to carry out various administrative steps in a meticulous way.*

- **defy** = braver, défier
  openly resist or refuse to obey
  Ex: *He lacked both tact and discipline, and constantly wanted to defy his teachers.*

Une expression couramment utilisée en anglais est « *to defy the odds* », qui signifie littéralement « défier les probabilités ». Cela signifie que quelqu'un a réussi quelque chose qui semblait peu probable, alors que la chance n'était pas vraiment de son côté (= *the odds were stacked against them*).
Exemple : *She defied all the odds when she found the cure for this rare disease: the odds were stacked against her!*
FR : Elle a défié tous les pronostics en trouvant le remède à cette maladie rare : tous les éléments étaient réunis contre elle !

- **enact** = promulguer
  make a bill or a law pass; to act out (on stage)
  Ex: *The new president was very enthusiastic and well versed. In less than a year, he managed to enact several new laws.*

- **erode** = éroder
  to gradually wear away
  Ex: *Although the pipe seemed of good quality, I saw them erode in a rather quick period.*

- **exhaust** = épuiser
  to drain someone, to tire out or to use up
  Ex: *Having children is both an intense and beautiful experience. While they are full of joy, they can exhaust you rather quickly.*

- **feign** = simuler
  pretend to be affected by (a feeling, state, or injury)
  Ex: *most men would rather feign strength than being viewed as sensitive people.*

- **recover** = récupérer
  return to a normal state of health, mind, or strength
  Ex: *Max's surgery went surprisingly well. After just a few weeks, he had already recovered.*

- **release** = relâcher
  to allow or enable; to set free
  Ex: *Although he had an excellent and famous lawyer on his side, the judge did not accept this prisoner's release.*

- **shift** = déplacer
  move or cause to move from one place to another
  Ex: *This museum is beautiful. It seems they have shifted a few things around rather successfully.*

- **surpass** = dépasser
  to exceed or be greater than
  Ex: *In order to achieve greater things, we must surpass our capacities. We must learn more, act often and persevere.*

Adverbes

- **entirely** = totalement
  completely (used for emphasis)
  Ex: *As a past employee, I am not entirely sure of the efficiency of this company's human resources department.*

- **freshly** = nouvellement
  newly, recently
  Ex: *The freshly installed coffee machine works perfectly, however, the coffee they use is of poor quality.*

- **obviously** = évidemment
  in a way that is easily perceived or understood; clearly.
  Ex: *While I don't recall ever seeing her shop here, I am obviously not one hundred percent certain.*

- **predictably** = prévisible / de façon prévisible
  in a way that can be predicted; as expected.
  Ex: *She predictably told the authorities the truth after being caught with large amounts of illegal substances.*

Entraînements - Module 3

Exercice 1 - Synonymes / Antonymes

Reportez vos réponses pour analyser votre performance.

Entraînez-vous dans les conditions d'examen.

prepmyfuture.com/book/68/ex/1942

Question 1 Find the synonym for:
Predictable

(A) Uncertain
(B) Volatile
(C) Expected
(D) Unsure

Question 2 Find the synonym for:
Surpass

(A) Transcend
(B) Mitigate
(C) Cheat
(D) Overlook

Question 3 Find the synonym of:
Suitable

(A) Possible
(B) Predictable
(C) Fit
(D) Manageable

Question 4 Find the synonym for:
Ample

(A) Sparse
(B) Little
(C) Scarce
(D) Sufficient

Question 5 Find the synonym for:
Arduous

(A) Effortful
(B) Lazy
(C) Stubborn
(D) Ancient

Question 6 Find the antonym for:
Arid

(A) Dry
(B) Sparkly
(C) Wet
(D) Shiny

Question 7 Find the antonym for:
Avert

(A) Reject
(B) Prevent
(C) Neglect
(D) Assist

Question 8 Find the antonym for:
Defy

(A) Disoblige
(B) Surrender
(C) Invite
(D) Settle

Question 9 Find the antonym for:
Recover

(A) Heal
(B) Mend
(C) Collapse
(D) Bleach

▪ **Question 10** Find the antonym for:
Prevalent

(A) Customary
(B) Exceptional
(C) Widespread
(D) Possible

Exercice 2 - Trouver la définition

Reportez vos réponses pour analyser votre performance.
Entraînez-vous dans les conditions d'examen.
prepmyfuture.com/book/68/ex/1943

▪ **Question 1** "Obviously" means…

(A) In a way that is easily perceived or understood
(B) In a way that is incomprehensible
(C) In a way that hurts other people
(D) In a way that takes others into consideration

▪ **Question 2** "Prevalent" means …

(A) Incomprehensible
(B) Hard to judge
(C) Easy to discern and judge
(D) Widespread in a particular area at a particular time

▪ **Question 3** "Secluded" means...

(A) Not purchased or used by many people
(B) Not seen or visited by many people
(C) Not understood or seen by many people
(D) Not viewed or liked by many people

▪ **Question 4** "Gregarious" means...

(A) Very sociable and convivial
(B) Very introverted and sad
(C) Very intelligent and ambitious
(D) Very angry and mean

Question 5 What you would give your best friend at his wedding

(A) A phone call
(B) An accolade
(C) A slap
(D) A postcard

Question 6 Not being honest about how we feel

(A) To feign
(B) To run
(C) To lie
(D) To fly

Question 7 What happened to the roads because the traffic was too heavy.

(A) Reduced
(B) Broadened
(C) Destroyed
(D) Repainted

Question 8 The girl who could never take a joke.

(A) Shy
(B) Tired
(C) Susceptible
(D) Lazy

Question 9 What he did to his computer screen to avoid the rays of the sun.

(A) Shift
(B) Destroy
(C) Clean
(D) Push

Question 10 The reasons she has had many car accidents

(A) Oblivious
(B) Poor
(C) Nice
(D) Careful

Question 11 She had enough to give away to others

(A) Fluent
(B) Ample
(C) Liquid
(D) Heavy

Question 12 The land did not produce any vegetables this year

(A) Wet
(B) Dirty
(C) Arid
(D) Moldy

Question 13 Her personality was so rebellious

(A) She is shy.
(B) She defies convention.
(C) She is smart.
(D) She is vague.

Question 14 The pain of the work was very intense.

(A) Arduous
(B) Exciting
(C) Vivid
(D) Priceless

Exercice 3 - Mots TOEFL

Reportez vos réponses pour analyser votre performance.

Entraînez-vous dans les conditions d'examen.

prepmyfuture.com/book/68/ex/1944

Having lived and worked in the United States for almost ten years, I must say I learned so much about myself. Before moving here, I was always a bit lazy and full of hesitations. In only five years, I learned that one must **surpass** themselves in order to grow and succeed.

■ **Question 1** The word **"surpass"** in the passage above is closest in meaning to:

(A) Be greater than
(B) Be equal to
(C) Be almost the same as
(D) Be very different from

James had to endure many surgeries after last year's fatal accident. Today, he is doing quite well, walking, living and enjoying life as he did before. However, according to specialists, it will take him about three years to fully **recover**.

■ **Question 2** The word **"recover"** in the passage above is closest in meaning to:

(A) Return to a normal state of affairs
(B) Return to a normal state of peace
(C) Return to a normal state of health
(D) Return to a normal state of social status

Cindy had a lot of trouble finding a job. She went from interview to interview for months without much success. However, last week, a recruiter contacted her for a position as an office clerk. They had asked her to come that same afternoon, however, she was not able to go as she did not have a **suitable** outfit for the interview.

■ **Question 3** The word **"suitable"** in the passage above is closest in meaning to:

(A) Appropriate for the person
(B) Appropriate for the situation
(C) Appropriate for the masses
(D) Appropriate for the judges

In the end, they decided to take their vacation in August. While the car rental prices were **predictably** expensive, the children would not have further vacations during the year. Plus, the weather was quite warm and the roads rather clear.

■ **Question 4** The word **"predictably"** in the passage above is closest in meaning to:

(A) As mentioned
(B) As understood
(C) As previously
(D) As expected

Exercice 4 - Grammaire

ılıl Reportez vos réponses pour analyser votre performance.

⏰ Entraînez-vous dans les conditions d'examen.

prepmyfuture.com/book/68/ex/1945

Question 1 If you were in so much trouble, why ________ you call me?

(A) hadn't
(B) didn't
(C) wouldn't
(D) will not

Question 2 Unfortunately the parking lot seems quite full. Where ________ I park the car?

(A) should
(B) have
(C) don't
(D) would

Question 3 He ________ watching her from afar for quite some time. After a few hours, he ________ to go and talk to her.

(A) was / had decided
(B) had been / decided
(C) had been / decides
(D) was / was deciding

Question 4 If the water ________ too hot, it will complicate the baking process.

(A) has gotten
(B) will get
(C) gets
(D) got

Question 5 I ________ playing the piano if I ________ not broken my wrist.

(A) will be / had
(B) would have been / had
(C) had been / had
(D) will be / would

Exercice 5 - Trouver l'erreur

Reportez vos réponses pour analyser votre performance.

Entraînez-vous dans les conditions d'examen.

prepmyfuture.com/book/68/ex/1946

Question 1 Which word is spelled incorrectly?

As a famous entertainer, it was evidant he earned a lot of money. However, it was not until last year that his status became clearer. Indeed, he was ranked one of Hollywood's best paid actor.

(A) entertainer
(B) evidant
(C) earned
(D) hollywood

Question 2 Which word is spelled incorrectly?

Traveling can be both an excitement and a challenge. First, you have to have great plans, then you must not axhaust your money rapidly. And finally, you must try and make the best of the adventure.

(A) excitement
(B) axhaust
(C) rapidly
(D) adventure

Question 3 Which word is spelled incorrectly?

Although the environment was exquisite and the surroundings magnificent, living in Thailand was often a challenge. Aside from the language barrier, I had to broadan my perspective in order to get along with the locals. They were, however, mush more open-minded than I expected, and my experience was fantastic.

(A) environment
(B) surroundings
(C) barrier
(D) broadan

Question 4 Which word is spelled incorrectly?

Samantha's new house was huge and decadent. She worked hard to purchase it and was quite certain the quality would be exquisite. However, within a few years, the pipes started to errode. She had to spend an additional ten thousand dollars to renovate them.

(A) decadent

(B) exquisite

(C) errode

(D) renovate

Question 5 Which word is spelled incorrectly?

Freshlly out of jail, he was behaving quite well. However, within a few months, he was again a delinquent. It only took one year for him to return to jail.

(A) freshlly

(B) behaving

(C) delinquent

(D) return

Entraînements - Module 3 - Solutions

Exercice 1 - Synonymes / Antonymes - Solutions

Reportez vos réponses pour analyser votre performance.

Entraînez-vous dans les conditions d'examen.

prepmyfuture.com/book/68/ex/1942

question 1	C	question 3	C	question 5	A	question 7	D	question 9	C
question 2	A	question 4	D	question 6	C	question 8	B	question 10	B

■ Question 1 - Solution

Find the synonym for:
Predictable

FR : Trouver le synonyme de : Predictable

(A) Uncertain = Incertain

(B) Volatile = Volatile

(C) ✓ Expected = Attendu, prévu

(D) Unsure = Peu sûr

explication
"Predictable" signifie qui peut être prévu ou prévisible.

■ Question 2 - Solution

Find the synonym for:
Surpass

*FR : Trouver le synonyme de :
Surpass*

(A) ✓ Transcend = Transcender, surpasser

(B) Mitigate = Atténuer, réduire, minimiser

(C) Cheat = Tricher, tromper

(D) Overlook = Laisser passer, ne pas voir, ignorer

explication
"Surpass" signifie dépasser, aller au-delà d'une certaine limite ou franchir une épreuve.

■ Question 3 - Solution

Find the synonym of:
Suitable

FR : Trouver le synonyme de :
Suitable

(A) Possible = Possible

(B) Predictable = Prévisible

(C) ✓ Fit = Adapté, digne, capable, approprié

(D) Manageable = Maniable, maîtrisable

⇨ **explication**
"Suitable" signifie "adapté", "convenant" ou "approprié".

▪ Question 4 - Solution

Find the synonym for:
Ample

FR : Trouver le synonyme de :
Ample

(A) Sparse = Rare, maigre, clairsemé

(B) Little = Peu

(C) Scarce = Rare, limité

(D) ✓ Sufficient = Suffisant, assez

⇨ **explication**
"Ample" signifie en grande quantité, assez ou abondant.

▪ Question 5 - Solution

Find the synonym for:
Arduous

FR : Trouver le synonyme de :
Arduous

(A) ✓ Effortful = Pénible, qui demande de l'effort

(B) Lazy = Paresseux

(C) Stubborn = Obstiné, têtu

(D) Ancient = Ancien, antique, très vieux

⇨ **explication**
"Arduous" signifie qui demande beaucoup d'efforts, laborieux ou pénible.

▪ Question 6 - Solution

Find the antonym for:
Arid

FR : Trouver l'antonyme de :
Arid

(A)	Dry	= Sec
(B)	Sparkly	= Étincelant, brillant, éclatant
(C)	**✓ Wet**	**= Humide, mouillé**
(D)	Shiny	= Brillant

⇢ **explication**
"Arid" signifie pas humide, très sec ou aride.

▪ Question 7 - Solution

Find the antonym for:
Avert

FR : Trouver l'antonyme de :
Avert

(A)	Reject	= Éjecter
(B)	Prevent	= Prévenir, éviter, empêcher
(C)	Neglect	= Négliger
(D)	**✓ Assist**	**= Assister, aider**

⇢ **explication**
"Avert" signifie détourner le regard ou éviter.

▪ Question 8 - Solution

Find the antonym for:
Defy

FR : Trouver l'antonyme de :
Defy

(A)	Disoblige	= Désobliger, offenser
(B)	**✓ Surrender**	**= Livrer à, céder, capituler**
(C)	Invite	= Inviter
(D)	Settle	= Régler, s'installer

⇢ **explication**
"Defy" signifie affronter le danger, braver, refuser d'obéir ou défier.

▪ Question 9 - Solution

Find the antonym for:
Recover

FR : Trouver l'antonyme de :
Recover

(A)	Heal	= Guérir, apaiser
(B)	Mend	= Réparer
(C)	**✓ Collapse**	**= S'effondrer, s'écrouler**
(D)	Bleach	= Décolorer, blanchir

⟹ **explication**
"Recover" signifie retourner à un état normal de santé ou récupérer, retrouver.

▪ **Question 10 - Solution**

Find the antonym for:
Prevalent

FR : Trouver l'antonyme de :
Prevalent

(A) Customary = Habituel, coutumier

(B) ✓ Exceptional = Exceptionnel

(C) Widespread = Généralisé, étendu, répandu

(D) Possible = Possible

⟹ **explication**
"Prevalent" signifie fréquent, qui arrive plusieurs fois ou souvent.

Exercice 2 - Trouver la définition- Solutions

Reportez vos réponses pour analyser votre performance.
Entraînez-vous dans les conditions d'examen.
prepmyfuture.com/book/68/ex/1943

question 1	A	question 4	A	question 7	B	question 10	A	question 13	B
question 2	D	question 5	B	question 8	C	question 11	B	question 14	A
question 3	B	question 6	A	question 9	A	question 12	C		

▪ **Question 1 - Solution**

"Obviously" means…

FR : "Obviously" signifie…

(A) ✓ In a way that is easily perceived or understood

(B) In a way that is incomprehensible

(C) In a way that hurts other people

(D) In a way that takes others into consideration

⟹ **explication**
"Obviously" signifie de manière évidente ou facilement compréhensible.

▪ **Question 2 - Solution**

"Prevalent" means …

FR : "Prevalent" signifie…

(A) Incomprehensible

(B) Hard to judge

(C) Easy to discern and judge

(D) ✓ Widespread in a particular area at a particular time

⇒ **explication**
"Prevalent" signifie fréquent, qui arrive plusieurs fois ou souvent.

▪ Question 3 - Solution

"Secluded" means...

FR : "Secluded" signifie…

(A) Not purchased or used by many people

(B) ✓ Not seen or visited by many people

(C) Not understood or seen by many people

(D) Not viewed or liked by many people

⇒ **explication**
"Secluded" signifie isolé, retiré, qui est à l'écart des autres ou pas souvent visité.

▪ Question 4 - Solution

"Gregarious" means...

FR : "Gregarious" signifie…

(A) ✓ Very sociable and convivial

(B) Very introverted and sad

(C) Very intelligent and ambitious

(D) Very angry and mean

⇒ **explication**
"Gregarious" signifie sociable, grégaire, très ouvert ou amicale.

▪ Question 5 - Solution

What you would give your best friend at his wedding

FR : Ce que vous donneriez à votre meilleur ami le jour de son mariage.

(A) A phone call

(B) ✓ An accolade

(C) A slap

(D) A postcard

⇒ **explication**
"Accolade" signifie toucher les épaules de quelqu'un pour féliciter quelqu'un.

▪ Question 6 - Solution

Not being honest about how we feel

FR : Faire semblant ou ne pas être honnête avec ses sentiments

(A) ✓ To feign

(B) To run

(C) To lie

(D) To fly

⟹ **explication**
"Feign" signifie faire semblant, simuler ou ne pas être honnête avec ses sentiments.

▪ Question 7 - Solution

What happened to the roads because the traffic was too heavy.

FR : Ce qui est arrivé aux routes car il y avait trop d'embouteillages.

(A) Reduced

(B) ✓ Broadened

(C) Destroyed

(D) Repainted

⟹ **explication**
"Broadened" signifie élargi ou agrandi des côtés.

▪ Question 8 - Solution

The girl who could never take a joke.

(A) Shy

(B) Tired

(C) ✓ Susceptible

(D) Lazy

⟹ **explication**
"Susceptible" signifie facilement influencé par les sentiments ou émotions, sensible.

▪ Question 9 - Solution

What he did to his computer screen to avoid the rays of the sun.

FR : Ce qu'il a fait à son écran pour éviter les rayons du soleil

(A) ✓ Shift

(B) Destroy

(C) Clean

(D) Push

⟹ **explication**
"Shift" signifie déplacer ou bouger d'un endroit à un autre.

▪ Question 10 - Solution

The reasons she has had many car accidents

FR : La raison pour laquelle elle a eu plusieurs accidents de la route

(A) ✓ **Oblivious**

(B) Poor

(C) Nice

(D) Careful

⟹ **explication**
"Oblivious" signifie inconscient, ne pas faire attention ou ne pas se rendre compte de ce qui se passe autour de soi.

■ Question 11 - Solution

She had enough to give away to others

FR : Elle en avait assez pour les autres

(A) Fluent

(B) ✓ **Ample**

(C) Liquid

(D) Heavy

⟹ **explication**
"Ample" signifie beaucoup, assez ou suffisant.

■ Question 12 - Solution

The land did not produce any vegetables this year

FR : La terre n'a produit aucun légume cette année.

(A) Wet

(B) Dirty

(C) ✓ **Arid**

(D) Moldy

⟹ **explication**
« Aride » signifie sans eau, extrêmement sec.

■ Question 13 - Solution

Her personality was so rebellious

FR : Elle avait une personnalité très rebelle.

(A) She is shy.

(B) ✓ **She defies convention.**

(C) She is smart.

(D) She is vague.

⟹ **explication**
« Défier » signifie résister, refuser d'obéir.

■ **Question 14 - Solution**

The pain of the work was very intense.

(A) ✓ Arduous

(B) Exciting

(C) Vivid

(D) Priceless

⇢ **explication**
"Arduous" signifie laborieux, impliquent des efforts intenses, fatiguant et difficile.

Exercice 3 - Mots TOEFL - Solutions

Reportez vos réponses pour analyser votre performance.

Entraînez-vous dans les conditions d'examen.

prepmyfuture.com/book/68/ex/1944

question 1	A	question 2	C	question 3	B	question 4	D

■ **Question 1 - Solution**

The word **"surpass"** in the passage above is closest in meaning to:

FR : Dans le passage ci-dessus, que signifie le mot "surpass" ?

(A) ✓ Be greater than

(B) Be equal to

(C) Be almost the same as

(D) Be very different from

⇢ **explication**
"Surpass" dans le passage signifie dépasser ou aller au-delà de ses capacités.

■ **Question 2 - Solution**

The word **"recover"** in the passage above is closest in meaning to:

FR : Dans le passage ci-dessus, que signifie le mot "recover" ?

(A) Return to a normal state of affairs

(B) Return to a normal state of peace

(C) ✓ Return to a normal state of health

(D) Return to a normal state of social status

⇢ **explication**
"Recover" dans le passage signifie retourner à un état de santé normal.

▪ Question 3 - Solution

The word **"suitable"** in the passage above is closest in meaning to:

FR : Dans le passage ci-dessus, que signifie le mot "suitable" ?

(A) Appropriate for the person

(B) ✓ Appropriate for the situation

(C) Appropriate for the masses

(D) Appropriate for the judges

explication
"Suitable" dans le passage signifie approprié, adéquat, bien ou correct pour la situation.

▪ Question 4 - Solution

The word **"predictably"** in the passage above is closest in meaning to:

FR : Dans le passage ci-dessus, que signifie le mot "predictably" ?

(A) As mentioned

(B) As understood

(C) As previously

(D) ✓ As expected

explication
"Predictably" dans le passage signifie qui peut être prévu.

Exercice 4 - Grammaire - Solutions

Reportez vos réponses pour analyser votre performance.

Entraînez-vous dans les conditions d'examen.

prepmyfuture.com/book/68/ex/1945

question 1	B	question 2	A	question 3	B	question 4	C	question 5	B

▪ Question 1 - Solution

If you were in so much trouble, why ________ you call me?

(A) hadn't

(B) ✓ didn't

(C) wouldn't

(D) will not

explication
La meilleure option ici c'est d'utiliser le passé simple du verbe: "Si tu avais autant de problèmes, pourquoi tu ne m'as pas appelé ?"

Le passé simple du verbe "to call" est construit avec l'auxiliaire au passé "did".

Question 2 - Solution

Unfortunately the parking lot seems quite full. Where ________ I park the car?

(A) ✓ **should**

(B) have

(C) don't

(D) would

Question 3 - Solution

He ________ watching her from afar for quite some time. After a few hours, he ________ to go and talk to her.

(A) was / had decided

(B) ✓ **had been / decided**

(C) had been / decides

(D) was / was deciding

Question 4 - Solution

If the water ________ too hot, it will complicate the baking process.

(A) has gotten

(B) will get

(C) ✓ **gets**

(D) got

Question 5 - Solution

I ________ playing the piano if I ________ not broken my wrist.

(A) will be / had

(B) ✓ **would have been / had**

(C) had been / had

(D) will be / would

Exercice 5 - Trouver l'erreur - Solutions

Reportez vos réponses pour analyser votre performance.

Entraînez-vous dans les conditions d'examen.

prepmyfuture.com/book/68/ex/1946

question 1	B	question 2	B	question 3	D	question 4	C	question 5	A

■ Question 1 - Solution

Which word is spelled incorrectly?

As a famous entertainer, it was evidant he earned a lot of money. However, it was not until last year that his status became clearer. Indeed, he was ranked one of Hollywood's best paid actor.

(A) entertainer

(B) ✓ evidant

(C) earned

(D) hollywood

⇨ **explication**
Evidant s'écrit avec un E. EVIDENT

■ Question 2 - Solution

Which word is spelled incorrectly?

Traveling can be both an excitement and a challenge. First, you have to have great plans, then you must not axhaust your money rapidly. And finally, you must try and make the best of the adventure.

(A) excitement

(B) ✓ axhaust

(C) rapidly

(D) adventure

⇨ **explication**
EXHAUST

■ Question 3 - Solution

Which word is spelled incorrectly?

Although the environment was exquisite and the surroundings magnificent, living in Thailand was often a challenge. Aside from the language barrier, I had to broadan my perspective in order to get along with the locals. They were, however, mush more open-minded than I expected, and my experience was fantastic.

(A) environment

(B) surroundings

(C) barrier

(D) ✓ broadan

⇨ **explication**
Broadan s'écrit avec un E. BROADEN

■ Question 4 - Solution

Which word is spelled incorrectly?

Samantha's new house was huge and decadent. She worked hard to purchase it and was quite certain the quality would be exquisite. However, within a few years, the pipes started to errode. She had to spend an additional ten thousand dollars to renovate them.

(A) decadent

(B) exquisite

(C) ✓ errode

(D) renovate

⟹ **explication**
Errode s'écrit avec un seul R. Erode

■ Question 5 - Solution

Which word is spelled incorrectly?

Freshlly out of jail, he was behaving quite well. However, within a few months, he was again a delinquent. It only took one year for him to return to jail.

(A) ✓ freshlly

(B) behaving

(C) delinquent

(D) return

⟹ **explication**
Freshlly s'écrit avec un seul L. FRESHLY

Vocabulaire - Vie universitaire

Présentation

Dans la section Listening, la plupart des exercices de type « discussion » se basent sur le vocabulaire de la vie universitaire. Les mots les plus courants sont faciles à apprendre, il s'agit donc d'un très bon investissement. Nous vous recommandons d'accorder une attention particulière à la liste « cours universitaires », il s'agit de la liste la plus importante pour le TOEFL.

Vous passez sans doute le TOEFL avec pour objectif de partir étudier à l'étranger. Ce vocabulaire vous sera utile pour votre intégration et votre vie universitaire dans votre pays d'accueil. Nous avons intégré des précisions culturelles sur la vie universitaire anglo-saxonne pour faciliter votre intégration.

COURS UNIVERSITAIRE

Vocabulaire

Les bases

- **a course** = un cours
  refers to the course as a whole with all its lectures, homework and exams during one term.
  Ex: *This anthropology course was the hardest I have ever taken.*
- **a compulsory course** = un cours obligatoire
  a course that is mandatory, that one must enroll in
  Ex: *My accounting degree is composed of many compulsory courses such as a math course, a law course, and a public speaking course.*
- **to attend a course** = assister à un cours
  to show up for, to take part in a course
  Ex: *I attended this course last year, that is why my schedule is less busy this semester.*
- **a subject** = une matière
  a discipline, an academic field
  Ex: *At school, my favorite subject was history.*
- **syllabus** = le programme d'un cours
  the topics covered by a course
  Ex: *During the first class, the professor handed out the syllabus of the course so we'd know what we would be doing during the semester.*
- **a lecture** = un cours magistral
  a class, a specific section of a course
  Ex: *I had a psychology lecture this morning that I thought was fascinating*
- **lecture hall** = amphithéâtre
  the place where the lecture takes place, usually similar, but bigger than, a regular classroom
  Ex: *So many students enrolled in this course that the university had to move it to a larger lecture hall.*
- **textbook** = manuel scolaire
  a book that is the basis of a class and that students use to study a specific subject
  Ex: *My anatomy textbook is very big, I struggle to take it with me every time I have to go to class.*

Les manuels de l'enseignement supérieur peuvent être très chers aux États-Unis. La plupart d'entre eux coûtent entre 100 et 300 dollars. Pour cette raison, de nombreux étudiants achètent des manuels d'occasion ou les louent.

Le temps

- **a period** = une heure de cours
  the time unit of the university, the normal duration of a lecture. In some universities, it will last 55

minutes while others will have periods of 3 hours.
Ex: *Today is Monday. My son's first period is math and then his second is English literature.*

- **a break** = une pause, une récréation
  a pause
  Ex: *I will call you when I'm on my lunch break.*
- **a timetable / a schedule** = un emploi du temps
  the list of all activities and classes with their dates, times, and places
  Ex: *I have registered for next year's classes. My schedule is actually really nice, I will be free every afternoon!*
- **homework** = les devoirs
  the work one has to do on one's own time, outside of the classroom
  Ex: *I'm sorry, I cannot go out with you tonight because I'm swamped. I have so much homework to do before tomorrow…*
- **office hours** = les heures de permanence
  in the U.S., teachers and their assistants (TAs - Teaching Assistants) are available each week at fixed time slots. Students can meet them in their office in order to ask them some questions.
  Ex: *I have questions about next week's sociology test. I will go and see the professor during her office hours to get more information.*
- **a term** = un trimestre
  the duration of a course (most universities have two main terms (fall and spring) and an optional summer term for retakes and optional courses)
  Ex: *This will be my last term in college before I graduate. I'm a bit anxious about what will happen next.*

Les examens

- **a mark / a grade** = une note
  a score
  Ex: *The teacher gave us our presentation grades. I passed even though I had barely prepared it.*

Aux États-Unis, les notes des cours sont souvent des lettres allant de A à F. Les étudiants obtiennent des crédits pour chaque cours dont la note est supérieure à C. La plupart des enseignants donnent des notes supérieures à 100 points et la note est ensuite convertie en lettre.

- **to sit an exam** = passer un examen
  to take an exam
  Ex: *I have to sit an exam and I am really stressed about it. This course is so hard!*
- **to resit an exam** = repasser un examen
  when someone sits an exam for the second time
  Ex: *I failed one of my finals last term, so I had to resit the exam. Luckily, I passed the second time around, so I was really relieved.*
- **to pass (an exam)** = réussir (un examen)
  to do it successfully
  Ex: *I passed my senior year exams! I am officially graduated.*
- **to fail (an exam)** = échouer (à un examen)
  to do it unsuccessfully
  Ex: *Sadly, my sister failed her exams, so we will not have much to celebrate this weekend…*
- **midterms (US)** = examens de milieu de semestre académique
  exams that take place at the middle of the term, usually followed by one week of holiday

Ex: *I had my midterms last week, I had to study so much… I'm so glad I have a full week to relax now.*

- **finals** = examen de fin de semestre
  exams that take place at the end of the term, usually the most important of the course grade which is usually based on many components: finals, midterms, quizzes, homework, presentations, participation, etc.
  Ex: *Since finals are just around the corner, the university library is always packed.*

- **to assess sth/sb** = évaluer (quelque chose ou quelqu'un)
  to evaluate, judge, rate
  Ex: *The professor will assess his students with 2 quizzes and 1 oral presentation. The workload is quite manageable for this course.*

- **to mark a paper** = noter un devoir
  to grade a paper, to score it, evaluate it
  Ex: *The professor marked my paper and was thrilled about it. She gave me an A!*

- **a mock exam (uk) / a practice test (us)** = un examen blanc
  a way to prepare an exam by completing exercises that mirror the actual exam
  Ex: *I have to sit an exam next week. The teacher posted a mock exam online to help us review the course content.*

Les protagonistes

- **teaching assistant (T.A.)** = assistant du professeur / chargé de TD
  a person, usually an advanced student, who assists the professor with their responsibilities
  Ex: *When I was a graduate student, I was Professor Mangold's teaching assistant. I learned so much from his experience.*

Dans le monde anglophone, il est courant que les professeurs d'université aient des assistants. Ces assistants sont généralement des étudiants de deuxième ou troisième cycle. Ils ont des « heures de bureau » pendant lesquelles ils se rendent disponibles pour aider les étudiants de premier cycle et répondre aux questions qu'ils peuvent se poser. Ils sont aussi parfois chargés de corriger les examens et d'animer des ateliers.

- **lecturer** = le conférencier
  a person who delivers a lecture (e.g. a class that is similar to a presentation with fewer interactions)
  Ex: *I have applied to be a Spanish lecturer at the local community college. I should hear back from them within 10 days.*

- **classmate** = camarade de classe
  a person who attends the same class as you
  Ex: *I get along really well with my classmates. We usually hang out at the weekend and we organized a study group to get better grades.*

Entraînement - Cours universitaire

Reportez vos réponses pour analyser votre performance.

Entraînez-vous dans les conditions d'examen.

prepmyfuture.com/book/68/ex/1947

▪ Question 1 How can you translate “a grade” at university?

(A) Une note
(B) Un grade
(C) Un échelon
(D) Un test

▪ Question 2 What does the expression “to sit an exam” means?

(A) S' asseoir à un examen
(B) Passer un examen
(C) Rater un examen
(D) Réussir un examen

▪ Question 3 What is a “textbook”?

(A) Un bloc-note
(B) Un manuel scolaire
(C) Un cahier
(D) Un livret

▪ Question 4 What is "a compulsory class"?

(A) Un cours obligatoire
(B) Un cours facultatif
(C) Un cours complexe
(D) Une course compétitive

▪ Question 5 What is “a lecture hall”?

(A) Une salle de lecture
(B) Un amphithéâtre
(C) Une salle de théâtre
(D) Une bibliothèque

Question 6 What is a "term"?

(A) La fin d'année
(B) Une fin de contrat
(C) Un terminal
(D) Un trimestre

Question 7 What does "to assess" mean?

(A) Examiner
(B) Accéder
(C) Saisir
(D) Evaluer

Question 8 Comment appelle-t-on un "examen blanc" en anglais ?

(A) A white exam
(B) A discretional test
(C) A mock exam
(D) A graded test

Question 9 What is a "syllabus" ?

(A) Une syllabe
(B) Un résumé
(C) Une thèse
(D) Un programme de cours

Question 10 What does the word "lecture" means?

(A) Une lecture
(B) Un cours magistral
(C) Lire
(D) Un devoir maison

Solutions

Reportez vos réponses pour analyser votre performance.

Entraînez-vous dans les conditions d'examen.

prepmyfuture.com/book/68/ex/1947

question 1	A	question 3	B	question 5	B	question 7	D	question 9	D
question 2	B	question 4	A	question 6	D	question 8	C	question 10	B

Question 1 - Solution

How can you translate “a grade” at university?

(A) ✓	**Une note**	**A grade**
(B)	Un grade	A rank
(C)	Un échelon	A level / a stage
(D)	Un test	A test

Question 2 - Solution

What does the expression “to sit an exam” means?

(A)	S' asseoir à un examen	To sit at an exam
(B) ✓	**Passer un examen**	**To sit an exam**
(C)	Rater un examen	To fail an exam
(D)	Réussir un examen	To pass an exam

Question 3 - Solution

What is a “textbook”?

(A)	Un bloc-note	A notepad
(B) ✓	**Un manuel scolaire**	**A textbook**
(C)	Un cahier	A notebook
(D)	Un livret	A booklet

Question 4 - Solution

What is "a compulsory class"?

(A)	✓	**Un cours obligatoire**	**A compulsory class**
(B)		Un cours facultatif	An optional class
(C)		Un cours complexe	A complex class
(D)		Une course compétitive	A competitive race

⇝ **explication**

Un cours (FR) = a class (En)
Un programme / un cursus / des cours (FR) = a course (En)

Ex: This class on statistics is only available for the students from the microeconomics course.
FR : Ce cours de statistiques n'est ouvert qu'aux étudiants du programme de micro-économie.

■ Question 5 - Solution

What is "a lecture hall"?

(A)		Une salle de lecture	A reading room
(B)	✓	**Un amphithéâtre**	**A lecture hall**
(C)		Une salle de théâtre	A theater
(D)		Une bibliothèque	A library

■ Question 6 - Solution

What is a "term"?

(A)		La fin d'année	The end of the year
(B)		Une fin de contrat	A contract's end
(C)		Un terminal	A terminal
(D)	✓	**Un trimestre**	**A term**

■ Question 7 - Solution

What does "to assess" mean?

(A)		Examiner	to examine
(B)		Accéder	to reach
(C)		Saisir	to grasp
(D)	✓	**Evaluer**	**to assess**

■ Question 8 - Solution

Comment appelle-t-on un "examen blanc" en anglais ?

(A)		A white exam
(B)		A discretional test
(C)	✓	**A mock exam**
(D)		A graded test

■ Question 9 - Solution

What is a “syllabus” ?

(A)	Une syllabe	A syllabe
(B)	Un résumé	A summary
(C)	Une thèse	A thesis (UK) / a dissertation (US)
(D)	✓ **Un programme de cours**	**A syllabus**

■ Question 10 - Solution

What does the word "lecture" means?

(A)	Une lecture	A reading
(B)	✓ **Un cours magistral**	**A lecture**
(C)	Lire	To read
(D)	Un devoir maison	A homework

ADMINISTRATION / CURSUS DE FORMATION

Vocabulaire

Les niveaux universitaires

- **A-levels (U.K.)** = le baccalauréat
  final exam before college in the U.K.
  Ex: *I was accepted at the university of my choice but my admission will only be confirmed when I receive my A levels' grades.*

- **freshman** = étudiant de 1re année
  first year student
  Ex: *My cousin is a freshman at Arizona State University. He started college less than 2 months ago.*

- **sophomore** = étudiant de 2e année
  second year student
  Ex: *Being a sophomore is not great. I was told that the hardest classes of my degree take place during the second year.*

- **junior** = étudiant de 3e année
  third year student
  Ex: *I just graduated in French and Spanish. I'm glad I chose that path because it allowed me to study abroad when I was a junior, during my third year in college.*

- **senior** = étudiant de 4e année
  fourth year student
  Ex: *I started university not long ago. My sister who's only one year younger is currently a senior in high school.*

- **undergraduate student** = étudiant en licence
  college student / student enrolled in a bachelor's program
  Ex: *When I was an undergraduate student, it took me almost two years to decide what my major would be. I hesitated between religious studies and philosophy.*

- **graduate student** = étudiant en master
  master's student
  Ex: *After I finished my bachelor's degree, I did not want to start working straight away. This is why I kept studying. My years as a graduate student were the best of my life.*

- **post-graduate student** = doctorant
  PhD student
  Ex: *My cousin just got her PhD. She is relieved because she felt lonely when she was a postgraduate student.*

Diplômes

- **a degree / a diploma** = un diplôme
  what one receives when they complete their studies
  Ex: *In the U.S., students receive their diploma during a huge graduation ceremony.*

- **cum laude** = mention « avec honneur »
  graduating "with honours"
  Ex: *My brother graduated cum laude while my sister didn't. He was so proud his GPA was higher than hers.*

- **magna cum laude** = mention « avec grand honneur »
  graduating "with great honours"
  Ex: *Graduating magna cum laude is not as easy as it sounds. It takes a lot of time and energy.*

- **summa cum laude** = mention « avec le plus grand honneur »
  graduating "with the greatest honours"
  Ex: *I worked really hard in college because I knew I needed to graduate summa cum laude to be accepted in my dream graduate school.*

- **valedictorian** = major de promotion
  the best student of the class
  Ex: *Every year, the valedictorian gives a speech during the graduation ceremony. This year, it will be me.*

- **to drop out of university** = abandonner ses études universitaires
  to stop attending university
  Ex: *My best friend dropped out of university because of financial reasons. He simply couldn't pay the tuition fees anymore.*

Lieux

- **library** = bibliothèque
  where you can borrow and read books
  Ex: *When I was a student, I spent many a night studying at the library because my dorm was way too noisy.*

- **bookstore** = librairie
  where you buy the books
  Ex: *I traveled to Italy and discovered a small bookstore that sold comics and mangas. It was so cool I spent a full afternoon in there.*

- **career center** = centre d'orientation professionnelle
  the office where you can get help regarding your professional goals
  Ex: *Most high schools have a career service to help their students figure out what they want to do for a living.*

- **athletic facilities / recreational center** = centre sportif
  where athletes go to work out and practice sports
  Ex: *The basketball team meets up at 6 am every Monday, Wednesday and Friday at the recreational center to improve and be more competitive.*

Inscription à un programme

- **application** = candidature
  the file containing documents that you need to send to a college in order to become a student there
  Ex: *I have sent applications to five colleges. I am waiting to hear back from them and it stresses me out.*

- **to apply** = candidater, postuler
  the act of trying to become a student at a university
  Ex: *When applying for colleges, you should always include a "safety school". This is a university that you know will likely accept your application, but where you do not really want to go.*

- **SAT (Scholastic Aptitude Test)** = test d'aptitude
  standardized U.S. test used for college applications
  Ex: *Most U.S. high school students take the SAT during the spring semester of their junior year. If they are not happy with the result, they resit it in the fall of the senior year.*

Le SAT et les admissions à l'université

Ce test standardisé est utilisé pour sélectionner les élèves qui veulent aller à l'université. Il constitue une partie très importante du dossier de candidature. Il représente généralement 25 à 50% de la décision finale avec le relevé de notes, la lettre de motivation, les lettres de recommandation et les activités extrascolaires. L'utilisation de tests standardisés est beaucoup plus développée aux États-Unis qu'en Europe.

- **orientation week** = semaine d'intégration
  the first week during which one discovers the campus, its activities and resources, and meets classmates
  Ex: *I met my college best friend on the very first day. We were teamed up for a game during orientation week and never left each other after that.*

- **tuition fees** = frais d'inscription (à une formation)
  the amount one has to pay to attend college
  Ex: *Some believe tuition fees in the U.S. are extortionate. However, it is true that most students get scholarships and don't pay the entire amount.*

- **a scholarship** = une bourse
  an amount of money that is given to a student to help pay for their studies (usually on the basis of their results, their athletic abilities, or any other remarkable feature of their admission file)
  Ex: *My cousin would never have been able to go to college and afford the tuition fees if she had not received multiple scholarships.*

- **to win a scholarship** = obtenir une bourse
  to receive / get / be granted a certain amount of money to study
  Ex: *I applied to a scholarship that was offered by a private company. I never thought I would get it but I just learned I won the scholarship! I'm so thrilled!*

- **a university's admission requirements** = les critères d'admission d'une université
  the prerequisites to attend a specific college
  Ex: *I've heard of a college which is lowering its admission requirements because it is struggling financially. I understand the need for money, but I don't think this is a sensible solution.*

Les facultés

- **college, university** = la fac
  a higher learning institution
  Ex: *Grinnell College is one of the most famous liberal arts colleges. It is located in Grinnell, Iowa.*
- **school of fine arts** = la Faculté des beaux-arts
  the arts department of a college
  Ex: *I have always been passionate about drawing and painting. In college, I almost spent more time in the building of the school of fine arts than in my dorm.*
- **school of humanities/liberal arts** = La Faculté de lettres et des sciences humaines
  the department of a college where one studies literature, history, philosophy…
  Ex: *The school of humanities stopped offering majors in French and German because there was not enough of a demand. Now, you can only minor in these fields.*
- **school of medicine / med school** = la Faculté de médecine
  the department of a college where one studies to become a doctor, a nurse…
  Ex: *You better be very motivated if you want to attend med school. Classes are hard and it is very competitive.*
- **law school** = la Faculté de droit
  the department of a college where one studies to become a lawyer, a judge…
  Ex: *In the U.S., you need to obtain a bachelor's degree, preferably in political science or history, before you can go to law school.*
- **business school** = école de commerce
  where one studies to learn about management, trading, banking, being a business executive…
  Ex: *I never attended business school and yet I decided to create a company from scratch. It was a bumpy ride but it's a successful adventure so far!*

Entraînement - Administration / Cursus de formation

Reportez vos réponses pour analyser votre performance.

Entraînez-vous dans les conditions d'examen.

prepmyfuture.com/book/68/ex/1948

Question 1 What is a "freshman"?

(A) A first-year student

(B) A second-year student

(C) A student that has just graduated

(D) A popular student

Question 2 What does the student mean when he says: "I am dropping out of university"?

(A) Je suis diplômé de l'université.

(B) J'abandonne l'université.

(C) Je passe d'une université à une autre.

(D) Je vais dans une université d'un niveau supérieur.

Question 3 What does "tuition fees" mean?

(A) les frais de logement

(B) une fête de fin d'année

(C) une bourse universitaire

(D) les frais de scolarité

Question 4 What is the best translation for the word "scholarship"?

(A) Une bourse universitaire

(B) Une bourse d'échange

(C) Une faculté

(D) Un prix du meilleur étudiant

- **Question 5** What are the "universty's admission requirements" ?

(A) Les frais d'inscription à l'université
(B) Les critères d'admission de l'université
(C) Un tests d'entrée à l'université
(D) Une épreuve d'entrée à l'université

- **Question 6** What does "orientation week" mean?

(A) Semaine d'orientation
(B) Semaine d'intégration
(C) Semaine de vacances
(D) Semaine d'examens

- **Question 7** What does "valedictorian" mean?

(A) Un major de promotion
(B) Un étudiant de 1ère année
(C) Un étudiant en école de droit
(D) Un étudiant en école de médecine

- **Question 8** What does the word "degree" mean?

(A) Un diplôme
(B) Un niveau
(C) Une certification
(D) Une température

- **Question 9** Qu'est ce qu'un "undergraduate student"?

(A) Un étudiant pas encore diplomé
(B) Un étudiant en licence
(C) Un étudiant redoublant
(D) Un lycéen

- **Question 10** What is the « SAT » ?

(A) A disease
(B) An admission test
(C) A scholarship
(D) A grade

Solutions

Reportez vos réponses pour analyser votre performance.

Entraînez-vous dans les conditions d'examen.

prepmyfuture.com/book/68/ex/1948

question 1	A	question 3	D	question 5	B	question 7	A	question 9	B
question 2	B	question 4	A	question 6	B	question 8	A	question 10	B

Question 1 - Solution

What is a "freshman"?

FR : Qu'est ce qu'un "fresman" ?

(A) ✓ A first-year student — **Un étudiant de 1ère année**

(B) A second-year student — Un étudiant de 2ème année

(C) A student that has just graduated — Un étudiant qui vient juste d'être diplômé

(D) A popular student — Un étudiant populaire

explication

- Freshman : étudiant de 1ère année
- Sophomore : étudiant de 2ème année
- Junior : étudiant de 3ème année
- Senior : étudiant de 4ème année

Question 2 - Solution

What does the student mean when he says: "I am dropping out of university"?

FR : Que signifie « to drop out of university » ?

(A) Je suis diplômé de l'université. — I graduated from University.

(B) ✓ J'abandonne l'université. — **I am dropping out of University.**

(C) Je passe d'une université à une autre. — I am transferring University.

(D) Je vais dans une université d'un niveau supérieur. — I am going to a better university.

Question 3 - Solution

What does "tuition fees" mean?

(A)		les frais de logement	The accommodation charges
(B)		une fête de fin d'année	Prom night
(C)		une bourse universitaire	A scholarship / a study grant
(D)	✓	**les frais de scolarité**	**The tuition fees**

▪ Question 4 - Solution

What is the best translation for the word "scholarship"?

(A)	✓	**Une bourse universitaire**	**A scholarship**
(B)		Une bourse d'échange	A mobility grant / an exchange grant
(C)		Une faculté	A faculty
(D)		Un prix du meilleur étudiant	A student award

▪ Question 5 - Solution

What are the "universty's admission requirements" ?

(A)		Les frais d'inscription à l'université	The application fees
(B)	✓	**Les critères d'admission de l'université**	**The universty's admission requirements**
(C)		Un tests d'entrée à l'université	A test to enter university
(D)		Une épreuve d'entrée à l'université	A test to enter university

▪ Question 6 - Solution

What does "orientation week" mean?

(A)		Semaine d'orientation	Pas de traduction
(B)	✓	**Semaine d'intégration**	**Orientation week**
(C)		Semaine de vacances	One-week break / week's break
(D)		Semaine d'examens	Midterms or finals

▪ Question 7 - Solution

What does "valedictorian" mean?

(A)	✓	**Un major de promotion**	**A valedictorian**
(B)		Un étudiant de 1ère année	A freshman
(C)		Un étudiant en école de droit	A law school student
(D)		Un étudiant en école de médecine	A med school student

▪ Question 8 - Solution

What does the word "degree" mean?

(A)	✓	**Un diplôme**	**A degree (licence) / a certificate / a diploma**
(B)		Un niveau	A level
(C)		Une certification	A certification
(D)		Une température	A temperature

■ Question 9 - Solution

Qu'est ce qu'un "undergraduate student"?

(A)		Un étudiant pas encore diplomé	A student that has not graduated yet
(B)	✓	**Un étudiant en licence**	**An undergraduate**
(C)		Un étudiant redoublant	A student retaking the year
(D)		Un lycéen	A high schooler

■ Question 10 - Solution

What is the « SAT » ?

(A) A disease

(B) ✓ An admission test

(C) A scholarship

(D) A grade

CAMPUS / VIE ÉTUDIANTE

Vocabulaire

Organisations

- **student clubs** = associations étudiantes
  groups on campus to which students can become a part of and contribute
  Ex: *There was a fair organized during the first week of classes so that new students could join the student clubs they were interested in.*

- **fraternity** = fraternité
  an all-male group on campus that shares similar interests, mainly on U.S. and Canadian campuses
  Ex: *Theo joined a fraternity because he believed this was the only way one can fully experience college life.*

- **sorority** = sororité
  an all-female group on campus that shares similar interests, mainly on U.S. and Canadian campuses
  Ex: *My niece's sorority is hosting an event this weekend. She and her sorority sisters want to raise money for a good cause.*

Temps forts

- **spring break** = vacances de printemps
  a week-long holiday that usually takes place after the midterm exams during the second semester
  Ex: *It is common for U.S. students to go to Florida or Mexico during spring break. That is a way of relaxing and partying before the end of the semester.*

- **orientation week** = semaine d'intégration
  the first week during which one discovers the campus, its activities and resources, and meets classmates
  Ex: *If I had missed orientation week, I would have never met my college best friend this early on.*

- **graduation** = obtention du diplôme
  the ceremony where you receive your diploma
  Ex: *Graduation will take place on May 17th this year. My entire family will come to see me walk and receive my diploma.*

- **graduation night** = soirée de remise des diplômes
  This night follows the graduation ceremony and usually takes the form of a formal reception and/or ball.
  Ex: *Graduation night was a little bittersweet. Everybody had so much fun, and at the same time we knew it would be the last time we all were together.*

- **exchange program** = échange universitaire
  program that allows students to go and study abroad
  Ex: *I participated in an exchange program last year. I was able to go and study in Mexico for a semester. It was the best experience ever!*

Lieux

- **on-campus** = sur le campus
  used to describe what happens on the university grounds
  Ex: *Living on-campus is a unique experience. You get all the facilities you can dream of and rent is much cheaper than if you rent a house off-campus.*

- **off-campus** = hors du campus
  used to describe what happens outside of the university grounds
  Ex: *My boyfriend and I decided to move together. Though we are still studying, we decided to live off-campus to have more privacy and quiet.*

- **student center** = foyer étudiant
  central place of the university where students can gather (for club or other reasons)
  Ex: *We are both on the campus activity board, so we hang out a lot at the student center. This is where we have the room where we plan all our events.*

Sports

- **football** = football américain
  this can refer to American football (in the U.S.) or to European football (in the U.K.)
  Ex: *Playing football in college can allow you to get a scholarship in the U.S.*

Aux États-Unis, ce terme fait référence au football américain. Au Royaume-Uni, ce terme fait référence au football « européen ».

Aux États-Unis, il s'agit du principal sport universitaire. Chaque université possède sa propre équipe et participe à des championnats intercollégiaux. La ligue NCAA (college football league) est presque aussi populaire et diffusée que la NFL (la National Football League professionnelle). Les universités tentent d'attirer les joueurs les plus prometteurs en leur offrant des bourses sportives. Aux États-Unis, le fait d'être un athlète permet d'être accepté plus facilement dans les universités, même les plus prestigieuses.

- **rowing** = aviron
  sport that is practiced on a lake or on a river, on thin and long boats that one moves using oars
  Ex: *Rowing is extremely physical. I tried once and I was sore for a full week afterwards.*

Les compétitions d'aviron sont particulièrement importantes pour les universités les plus prestigieuses, telles que les universités « Ivy League » aux États-Unis, et Oxford et Cambridge au Royaume-Uni.

- **soccer** = football
  the name that is given to the "European" football in the U.S., it is a marginal sport there
  Ex: *When I first moved to the U.S., I always got confused between football and soccer, but not anymore.*

- **sailing** = voile (bateau)
  an aquatic sport that usually takes place on lakes or on the sea
  Ex: *My dream holiday is to sail from the coast of California all the way to Hawaii. I don't know if I'll ever be able to do it, but one can dream.*

- **fencing** = escrime
  a sport where two people face each other with some type of sword and aim at touching the other contestant before they get touched
  Ex: *The French are really good at fencing, that's the reason why I want to study abroad there. I'm obsessed with that sport.*

Entraînement - Campus / Vie étudiante

Reportez vos réponses pour analyser votre performance.

Entraînez-vous dans les conditions d'examen.

prepmyfuture.com/book/68/ex/1949

Question 1 What is the best translation for the word "bibliothèque" ?

(A) A book store
(B) A publishing house
(C) A library
(D) A bookshop

Question 2 What are the "athletic Facilities" ?

(A) Piste d'athlétisme
(B) Equipe d'athlétisme
(C) Salle de sport
(D) Activités sportives

Question 3 What is a "sorority"?

(A) It's a college social organization gathering only girls.
(B) It's a place where all the students meet.
(C) It's the name of the university's football team.
(D) It's a university that admits only girls.

Question 4 What does "exchange program" mean?

(A) Une admission parallèle
(B) Un échange universitaire
(C) Un changement de programme
(D) Un changement d'emploi du temps

Question 5 What does "off-campus" mean?

(A) The campus is closed.
(B) Outside the campus
(C) The access to the campus is forbidden.
(D) You are not a student of the campus.

Question 6 What is a "recreational center"?

(A) Un foyer d'étudiants
(B) Un bar étudiants
(C) Un bibliothèque
(D) Un centre sportif

Question 7 What is a "student club"?

(A) Une association étudiante
(B) Un groupe d'anciens étudiants
(C) Un groupe de travail
(D) Un syndicat d'étudiants

Question 8 Among the following propositions, which one is a sport?

(A) Sales
(B) Sailing
(C) Tailoring
(D) Boating

Question 9 What does "fencing" mean?

(A) Chic
(B) Escrime
(C) Joute
(D) Aviron

Question 10 What is the specific term used in English to refer to the higher level university sport?

(A) University sport
(B) Sport
(C) NCAA
(D) Athletics

Solutions

ılıl Reportez vos réponses pour analyser votre performance.

⏰ Entraînez-vous dans les conditions d'examen.

prepmyfuture.com/book/68/ex/1949

question 1	C	question 3	A	question 5	B	question 7	A	question 9	B
question 2	C	question 4	B	question 6	D	question 8	B	question 10	D

▪ Question 1 - Solution

What is the best translation for the word "bibliothèque" ?

(A) A book store — Une librairie

(B) A publishing house — Une maison d'édition

(C) ✓ A library — Une bibliothèque

(D) A bookshop — Une librairy

▪ Question 2 - Solution

What are the "athletic Facilities" ?

(A) Piste d'athlétisme

(B) Equipe d'athlétisme

(C) ✓ Salle de sport

(D) Activités sportives

▪ Question 3 - Solution

What is a "sorority"?

(A) ✓ It's a college social organization gathering only girls. — ***C'est une organisation sociale universitaire ne regroupant que des filles.***

(B) It's a place where all the students meet. — *C'est un endroit où les étudiants se rencontrent.*

(C) It's the name of the university's football team. — *C'est le nom de l'équipe de football de l'université.*

(D) It's a university that admits only girls. — *C'est une université qui accepte seulement des filles.*

▪ Question 4 - Solution

What does "exchange program" mean?

(A) Une admission parallèle

(B) ✓ Un échange universitaire

(C) Un changement de programme

(D) Un changement d'emploi du temps

▪ Question 5 - Solution

What does "off-campus" mean?

(A) The campus is closed.

(B) ✓ Outside the campus

(C) The access to the campus is forbidden.

(D) You are not a student of the campus.

⇒ **explication**
It's the specific word to say that you or an activity is outside of the campus.

▪ Question 6 - Solution

What is a "recreational center"?

(A)	Un foyer d'étudiants	A students' hostel
(B)	Un bar étudiants	A student bar
(C)	Un bibliothèque	A library
(D)	**✓ Un centre sportif**	**A recreational center**

▪ Question 7 - Solution

What is a "student club"?

(A)	**✓ Une association étudiante**	**A student club**
(B)	Un groupe d'anciens étudiants	An alumni association
(C)	Un groupe de travail	A working group
(D)	Un syndicat d'étudiants	A student union

▪ Question 8 - Solution

Among the following propositions, which one is a sport?

(A)	Sales	Les ventes
(B)	**✓ Sailing**	**La voile**
(C)	Tailoring	Une adaption / la confection (textile)
(D)	Boating	N'existe pas

▪ Question 9 - Solution

What does "fencing" mean?

(A)		Chic	Fancy
(B)	✓	**Escrime**	**Fencing**
(C)		Joute	Joust
(D)		Aviron	Rowing

▪ Question 10 - Solution

What is the specific term used in English to refer to the higher level university sport?

FR : Comment nomme-t-on le sport universitaire de haut niveau ?

(A)		University sport	
(B)		Sport	
(C)		NCAA	*La NCAA est l'association nationale qui organise et gère les athlètes et les compétitions universitaires.*
(D)	✓	**Athletics**	***"Athletics" est le terme spécifique pour désigner le sport universitaire de haut niveau.***

LOGEMENT

Vocabulaire

Sur le campus

- **dormitory / dorm** = résidence étudiante
  (often shared) student accommodation
  Ex: *I lived in a dorm on campus when I was a freshman, but I started sharing a house off campus as early as my sophomore year.*

- **roommate** = colocataire, camarade de chambre
  the person you share your dorm room with
  Ex: *My sister's roommate is not clean at all. I don't know how my sister keeps her calm, I wouldn't be able to live with a person like that.*

- **flatmate** = colocataire
  the person you share an apartment with (used especially in the U.K.)
  Ex: *My flatmates are throwing a party this weekend. I'm not sure I'll be home for this since I might be out of town for work.*

Le terme « colocataire » est utilisé littéralement lorsque deux personnes partagent une chambre. Aux États-Unis, les dortoirs sont très souvent partagés. Étant utilisé très régulièrement, ce mot a également commencé à être utilisé pour décrire les personnes partageant un appartement, même si elles ont chacune leur propre chambre.

Toutefois, si vous voyagez au Royaume-Uni, il est probable que vous entendiez le terme « flatmate » pour désigner les personnes qui partagent un appartement ou « housemate » pour parler des personnes qui partagent une maison.

- **furnished** = meublé
  said of an apartment in which there already are pieces of furniture (couch, table, chairs…)
  Ex: *Since I am moving to another country, I will not be able to take any large item with me. I really need to find a furnished apartment, otherwise I will need to spend a lot of money to turn it into a home.*

- **security deposit** = dépôt de garantie/ caution
  an amount of money that is set aside while you rent a place, you get it back at the end of the rental period unless something happened and damaged the place
  Ex: *Because of his roommate's carelessness, my brother did not get his security deposit back. The oven was broken and the fridge did not close properly.*

Autres

- **downtown** = centre-ville
  the city center

Ex: *Downtown Los Angeles is fairly dirty and dangerous, you should try living in the suburbs instead.*

- **suburbs** = banlieue
  the parts surrounding the city center, the outskirts of town
  Ex: *The southside of Chicago is one of the most dangerous suburbs in the U.S.*

- **blocks** = pâté de maison
  a group of buildings surrounded by roads on all four sides, this has become a unit of measurement that is used to calculate distances.
  Ex: *We had to park six blocks away from the restaurant because there were very few parking spots available downtown.*

- **estate agency** = agence immobilière
  a place where you can be advised professionally to find a place to live
  Ex: *When they decided to buy a house, my parents used an estate agency because they were afraid of scams and wanted to be safe. The professional who helped them did not disappoint.*

- **household insurance** = assurance habitation
  an insurance that covers your place of residence, the items within it and the people who live there
  Ex: *The monthly fee I pay for my household insurance has gone up and I cannot afford it anymore. I need to find a new one ASAP.*

- **lease, leasehold** = bail
  the official paper that states the terms of a rental (length, rent, conditions…)
  Ex: *Martha has signed the lease to her new apartment yesterday! She is so thrilled to have found a place.*

- **mortgage** = prêt immobilier
  a loan that was taken out for accommodation purposes
  Ex: *I got a raise a couple months ago, but since my mortgage is really big I don't really see the difference. Most of my salary goes to the bank to pay it back.*

- **to take out a mortgage** = prendre un prêt immobilier
  the act of borrowing money for accommodation purposes
  Ex: *Sarah and John took out a mortgage about a year ago in order to be able to afford this lovely house. Apparently, it was the best decision ever.*

- **housewarming party** = pendaison de crémaillère
  a celebration where you invite your friends over shortly after having moved to a new place to show them the place and start making memories in it
  Ex: *My sister moved into her new flat last month. She is throwing a housewarming party this weekend and has invited several of her friends.*

- **condo / condominium** = appartement
  a large apartment located in a collectively-owned building and in which the owner lives
  Ex: *Living in a condo in New York City was my dream as a kid. Now that I am a grown-up, I realize that it is easier to dream about it than to be able to afford it.*

Entraînement - Logement

Reportez vos réponses pour analyser votre performance.

Entraînez-vous dans les conditions d'examen.

prepmyfuture.com/book/68/ex/1950

Question 1 What is a “security deposit"?

(A) Une assurance habitation
(B) Un bureau de sécurité
(C) Un dépot de garantie
(D) Une garantie

Question 2 How can we translate “une agence immobilière"?

(A) A housing agency
(B) A housing shop
(C) An estate agency
(D) A house store

Question 3 What does the word "lease” mean?

(A) Un bail
(B) Un emprunt
(C) Un prêt
(D) Emprunter

Question 4 What is a “mortgage”?

(A) Une résidence étudiante
(B) Un prêt immobilier
(C) Une assurance habitation
(D) Une petite maison

Question 5 What is an “estate agency”?

(A) Une agence immobilière
(B) Une ambassade
(C) Une banque
(D) Un centre commercial

■ Question 6 What does “a block” mean?

(A) Un pâté de maison
(B) Un immeuble
(C) Un quartier
(D) Un chemin

■ Question 7 How would you translate the French expression "une pendaison de crémaillère"?

(A) A hanging cog party
(B) A house warming party
(C) A house party
(D) A house moving party

■ Question 8 What is a “household insurance”?

(A) Une assurance habitation
(B) Une assurance propriétaire
(C) Une assurance vie
(D) Une assurance locataire

■ Question 9 What would be the translation of the word “bail”?

(A) A bail
(B) A lease
(C) A rent
(D) A household

■ Question 10 What does “furnished” mean?

(A) Plein
(B) Meublé
(C) Fourni
(D) Sur le campus

Solutions

Reportez vos réponses pour analyser votre performance.

Entraînez-vous dans les conditions d'examen.

prepmyfuture.com/book/68/ex/1950

question 1	C	question 3	A	question 5	A	question 7	B	question 9	B
question 2	C	question 4	B	question 6	A	question 8	A	question 10	B

Question 1 - Solution

What is a "security deposit"?

(A) Une assurance habitation — A house insurance

(B) Un bureau de sécurité — A security office

(C) ✓ Un dépot de garantie — A security deposit

(D) Une garantie — A warranty

Question 2 - Solution

How can we translate "une agence immobilière"?

(A) A housing agency — Ne se dit pas

(B) A housing shop — Ne se dit pas

(C) ✓ An estate agency

(D) A house store — Ne se dit pas

Question 3 - Solution

What does the word "lease" mean?

(A) ✓ Un bail — A lease

(B) Un emprunt — A loan

(C) Un prêt — A loan

(D) Emprunter — To borrow

Question 4 - Solution

What is a "mortgage"?

(A)	Une résidence étudiante	A student house
(B)	**✓ Un prêt immobilier**	**A mortgage**
(C)	Une assurance habitation	A housing insurance
(D)	Une petite maison	A cottage

▪ Question 5 - Solution

What is an “estate agency”?

(A)	**✓ Une agence immobilière**	**An estate agency / a letting agency**
(B)	Une ambassade	An embassy
(C)	Une banque	A bank
(D)	Un centre commercial	A mall

▪ Question 6 - Solution

What does “a block” mean?

(A)	**✓ Un pâté de maison**	**A block**
(B)	Un immeuble	A building
(C)	Un quartier	A district / an area
(D)	Un chemin	A path

▪ Question 7 - Solution

How would you translate the French expression "une pendaison de crémaillère"?

(A)	A hanging cog party	Ne veut rien dire
(B)	**✓ A house warming party**	**Expression spécifique pour dire pendaison de crémaillère**
(C)	A house party	Une réception / soirée à la maison
(D)	A house moving party	Une dépendaison crémaillère

▪ Question 8 - Solution

What is a “household insurance”?

(A)	**✓ Une assurance habitation**	**A household insurance**
(B)	Une assurance propriétaire	An owner insurance
(C)	Une assurance vie	A life insurance
(D)	Une assurance locataire	A tenant insurance

▪ Question 9 - Solution

What would be the translation of the word “bail”?

(A)	A bail	Une caution (prison)
(B)	✓ **A lease**	**Un bail**
(C)	A rent	Une location
(D)	A household	Un ménage / une famille

▪ Question 10 - Solution

What does “furnished” mean?

(A)	Plein	Full
(B)	✓ **Meublé**	**Furnished**
(C)	Fourni	Supplied / provided
(D)	Sur le campus	On campus

Vocabulaire - Académique

RECHERCHE ACADÉMIQUE

Vocabulaire

- **accuracy** = précision
(noun) the degree to which the result of a measurement, calculation, or specification conforms to the correct value or standard
Ex: *Each experiment is performed twice to ensure accuracy.*

- **assumption** = hypothèse
(noun) a thing that is accepted as true or as certain to happen, without proof
Ex: *This assumption might be addressed in future studies.*

- **cite** = citer
(verb) make reference to
Ex: *authors who are highly regarded by their peers tend to be cited.*

- **compile** = compiler
(verb) collect (information) in order to produce a list or book
Ex: *The local authority must compile a list of the names and addresses of taxpayers.*

- **correlation** = corrélation
(noun) a mutual relationship or connection between two or more things
Ex: *research showed a clear correlation between recession and levels of property crime.*

- **data collection** = collecte de données
(noun) the activity of collecting information that can be used to find out about a particular subject
Ex: *The majority of data collection will be undertaken by interview.*

- **empirical** = empirique
(adj.) based on, concerned with, or verifiable by observation or experience rather than theory or pure logic
Ex: *They provided considerable empirical evidence to support their argument.*

- **extensively** = largement
(adverb) in a way that covers or affects a large area
Ex: *The house was extensively damaged by the fire.*

- **field** = domaine
(noun) a particular branch of study or sphere of activity or interest
Ex: *He talked to professionals in various fields.*

- **knowledge** = connaissance
(noun) facts, information, and skills acquired through experience or education; the theoretical or practical understanding of a subject
Ex: *The transmission of knowledge.*

- **qualitative** = qualitatif
(adj.) relating to, measuring, or measured by the quality of something rather than its quantity
Ex: *There has been a qualitative change in the relationship between the public and the government.*

- **quantitative** = quantitatif
(adj.) relating to, measuring, or measured by the quantity of something rather than its quality
Ex: *Our employees receive a quantitative rating based on the dollar value of their sales.*

- **margin of error** = marge d'erreur
  (noun) an extra amount of something, such as time or money, that youallow because there might be a mistake in your calculations
  Ex: *When archaeologists date objects that are thousands of years old, they allow a margin of error of several hundred years.*

- **normative** = normatif
  (adj.) relating to rules, or making people obey the rules, especially rules of behavior
  Ex: *Because normative behaviors in these two cultures vary, it should also be expected that their cultural scripts would also vary.*

- **theoretical** = théorique
  (adj.) concerned with or involving the theory of a subject or area of study rather than its practical application
  Ex: *The idea is purely theoretical at this point.*

- **reliability** = fiabilité
  (noun) the quality of being trustworthy or of performing consistently well
  Ex: *These data throw doubt on the reliability of national statistics.*

- **sample** = échantillon
  (noun) a small part or quantity intended to show what the whole is like
  Ex: *The sample group is very small.*

- **statistical** = statistique
  (adj.) relating to the use of statistics
  Ex: *A statistical comparison.*

Entraînement - Recherche Académique

Reportez vos réponses pour analyser votre performance.

Entraînez-vous dans les conditions d'examen.

prepmyfuture.com/book/68/ex/1951

Question 1 the degree to which the result of a measurement, calculation, or specification conforms to the correct value or a standard.

(A) assumption
(B) accuracy
(C) correlation
(D) empirical

Question 2 a particular branch of study or sphere of activity or interest

(A) knowledge
(B) assumption
(C) normative
(D) field

Question 3 a thing that is accepted as true or as certain to happen, without proof

(A) assumption
(B) correlation
(C) margin of error
(D) reliability

Question 4 a small part or quantity intended to show what the whole is like

(A) margin of error
(B) normative
(C) sample
(D) knowledge

Question 5 based on, concerned with, or verifiable by observation or experience rather than theory or pure logic.

(A) accuracy
(B) compilation
(C) data collection
(D) empirical

Question 6 make reference to

(A) cite
(B) collect
(C) analyse
(D) sample

Question 7 the quality of being trustworthy or of performing consistently well

(A) normative
(B) reliability
(C) qualitative
(D) extensively

Question 8 a mutual relationship or connection between two or more things

(A) cite
(B) compile
(C) data collection
(D) correlation

Question 9 a mutual relationship or connection between two or more things

(A) correlation
(B) data collection
(C) extensively
(D) reliability

Question 10 concerned with or involving the theory of a subject or area of study rather than its practical application.

(A) reliability
(B) theoretical
(C) quantitative
(D) statistical

Solutions

Reportez vos réponses pour analyser votre performance.

Entraînez-vous dans les conditions d'examen.

prepmyfuture.com/book/68/ex/1951

question 1	B	question 3	A	question 5	D	question 7	B	question 9	A
question 2	D	question 4	C	question 6	A	question 8	D	question 10	B

Question 1 - Solution

the degree to which the result of a measurement, calculation, or specification conforms to the correct value or a standard.

(A) assumption FR = hypothèse

(B) ✓ accuracy FR = précision

(C) correlation FR = corrélation

(D) empirical FR = empirique

Question 2 - Solution

a particular branch of study or sphere of activity or interest

(A) knowledge FR = hypothèse

(B) assumption FR = connaissance

(C) normative FR = normatif

(D) ✓ field FR = domaine

Question 3 - Solution

a thing that is accepted as true or as certain to happen, without proof

(A) ✓ assumption FR = hypothèse

(B) correlation FR = corrélation

(C) margin of error FR = marge d'erreur

(D) reliability FR = fiabilité

Question 4 - Solution

a small part or quantity intended to show what the whole is like

(A) margin of error FR = marge d'erreur

(B) normative FR = normatif

(C) ✓ sample FR = échantillon

(D) knowledge FR = connaissance

▪ Question 5 - Solution

based on, concerned with, or verifiable by observation or experience rather than theory or pure logic.

(A) accuracy FR = précision

(B) compilation FR = compilation

(C) data collection FR = collecte de données

(D) ✓ empirical FR = empirique

▪ Question 6 - Solution

make reference to

(A) ✓ cite FR = citer

(B) collect FR = collecter

(C) analyse FR = analyser

(D) sample FR = échantillon

▪ Question 7 - Solution

the quality of being trustworthy or of performing consistently well

(A) normative FR = normatif

(B) ✓ reliability FR = fiabilité

(C) qualitative FR = qualitatif

(D) extensively FR = largement

▪ Question 8 - Solution

a mutual relationship or connection between two or more things

(A) cite FR = citer

(B) compile FR = compiler

(C) data collection FR = collecte de données

(D) ✓ correlation FR = corrélation

▪ Question 9 - Solution

a mutual relationship or connection between two or more things

(A) ✓ **correlation** **FR = corrélation**

(B) data collection FR = collecte de données

(C) extensively FR = largement

(D) reliability FR = fiabilité

■ Question 10 - Solution

concerned with or involving the theory of a subject or area of study rather than its practical application.

(A) reliability FR = fiabilité

(B) ✓ **theoretical** **FR = théorique**

(C) quantitative FR =quantitatif

(D) statistical FR = statistique

SOCIOLOGIE

Vocabulaire

- **affluent** = riche
  (adj.) having a great deal of money; wealthy
  Ex: *He is affluent and can afford to send his children to the best schools.*
- **alienation** = aliénation
  (noun) the feeling that you have no connection with the people around you
  Ex: *Depressed people frequently feel a sense of alienation from those around them.*
- **behavior** = comportement
  (noun) the way in which one acts or conducts oneself, especially towards others
  Ex: *The stupid behavior of one pupil has brought discredit on the whole school.*
- **contextual** = contextuel
  (adj.) relating to the set of facts surrounding a situation
  Ex: *They offered a lot of contextual clues to understand the language.*
- **consumerism** = consumérisme
  (noun) the theory that an increasing consumption of goods is economically desirable
  Ex: *Exeperts are concerned about increasing consumerism among teenagers.*
- **ethnicity** = ethnicité
  (noun) an affiliation resulting from racial or cultural ties
  Ex: *A university that aggressively recruits a student body of diverse ethnicities.*
- **globalization** = mondialisation
  (noun) the process by which businesses or other organizations develop international influence or start operating on an international scale
  Ex: Experts fear that the globalization of the world's economy will keep increasing in the coming years.
- **indigent** = pauvre
  (adj.) poor, needy
  Ex: *He founded a charity for the relief of indigent artists.*
- **interdependency** = interdépendance
  (noun) the dependence of two or more people or things on each other
  Ex: *The new economic interdependence of the two nations.*
- **means of production** = moyens de production
  the facilities and resources for producing goods
  Ex: *In this society, the means of production are communally owned.*
- **opulent** = opulent
  (adj.) ostentatiously costly and luxurious, wealthy
  Ex: He appreciated the opulent comfort of a limousine.
- **paradigm** = paradigme
  (noun) a set of assumptions, theories, and perspectives, that make up a way of understanding social reality
  Ex: *They released a new study that challenges the current evolutionary paradigm.*
- **pluralism** = pluralisme

(noun) the holding of two or more offices or positions (such as benefices) at the same time
Ex: *He spoke of the benefits of cultural pluralism.*

- **urbanization** = urbanisation
(noun) the process of making an area more urban
Ex: *Online sales in the world's second most-populous nation are growing about 35 percent a year, according to data tracker Euromonitor, fueled by a rising middle class and urbanization that present an attractive environment for e-commerce.*

- **scapegoat (noun) / make a scapegoat of (verb)** = bouc émissaire
a person who is blamed for the wrongdoings, mistakes, or faults of others, especially for reasons of expediency
Ex: *Secret police scapegoated a few of the ringleaders to put an end to the issue.*

- **secularization** = sécularisation
(noun) removal of religion as a control or influence over something
Ex: *Secularization was in harmony with the growth of republican ideas.*

- **social stratification** = stratification sociale
(noun) a kind of social differentiation whereby a society groups people into socioeconomic strata, based upon their occupation and income, wealth and social status, or derived power (social and political)
Ex: *Social stratification is found in every society.*

- **sociologist** = sociologue
(noun) an expert of the development, structure, and functioning of human society
Ex: *The sociologist Michael Mann called this process by which wars create larger and more productive societies "caging".*

Entraînement - Sociologie

Reportez vos réponses pour analyser votre performance.

Entraînez-vous dans les conditions d'examen.

prepmyfuture.com/book/68/ex/1952

Question 1 The process by which businesses or other organizations develop international influence or start operating on an international scale.

(A) consumerism
(B) alienation
(C) globalization
(D) secularization

Question 2 the feeling that you have no connection with the people around you

(A) scapegoat
(B) secularization
(C) affluent
(D) alienation

Question 3 an expert in or student of the development, structure, and functioning of human society.

(A) interdependency
(B) means of Production
(C) scapegoat
(D) sociologist

Question 4 the way in which one acts or conducts oneself, especially towards others

(A) behaviour
(B) secularization
(C) pluralism
(D) paradigm

Question 5 poor; needy

(A) affluent
(B) opulent
(C) indigent
(D) consumerism

Question 6 a set of assumptions, theories, and perspectives, that make up a way of understanding social reality

(A) social stratification
(B) paradigm
(C) globalization
(D) behaviour

Question 7 relating to the set of facts surrounding a situation

(A) behaviour
(B) contextual
(C) interdependency
(D) paradigm

Question 8 the holding of two or more offices or positions (such as benefices) at the same time

(A) pluralism
(B) ethnicity
(C) contextual
(D) alienation

Question 9 a person who is blamed for the wrongdoings, mistakes, or faults of others, especially for reasons of expediency.

(A) indigent
(B) opulent
(C) scapegoat
(D) affluent

Question 10 having a great deal of money; wealthy

(A) affluent
(B) indigent
(C) paradigm
(D) secularization

Solutions

Reportez vos réponses pour analyser votre performance.

Entraînez-vous dans les conditions d'examen.

prepmyfuture.com/book/68/ex/1952

question 1	C	question 3	D	question 5	C	question 7	B	question 9	C
question 2	D	question 4	A	question 6	B	question 8	A	question 10	A

Question 1 - Solution

The process by which businesses or other organizations develop international influence or start operating on an international scale.

(A) consumerism FR = consumérisme

(B) alienation FR = aliénation

(C) ✓ globalization FR = mondialisation

(D) secularization FR = sécularisation

Question 2 - Solution

the feeling that you have no connection with the people around you

(A) scapegoat FR = bouc émissaire

(B) secularization FR = sécularisation

(C) affluent FR = riche

(D) ✓ alienation FR = aliénation

Question 3 - Solution

an expert in or student of the development, structure, and functioning of human society.

(A) interdependency FR = interdépendance

(B) means of Production FR = moyens de production

(C) scapegoat FR = bouc émissaire

(D) ✓ sociologist FR = sociologue

Question 4 - Solution

the way in which one acts or conducts oneself, especially towards others

(A) ✓ **behaviour** **FR = comportement**

(B) secularization FR = sécularisation

(C) pluralism FR = pluralisme

(D) paradigm FR = paradigme

▪ Question 5 - Solution

poor; needy

(A) affluent FR = riche

(B) opulent FR = opulent

(C) ✓ **indigent** **FR = pauvre**

(D) consumerism FR = consumérisme

▪ Question 6 - Solution

a set of assumptions, theories, and perspectives, that make up a way of understanding social reality

(A) social stratification

(B) ✓ **paradigm** **FR = paradigme**

(C) globalization FR = mondialisation

(D) behaviour FR = comportement

▪ Question 7 - Solution

relating to the set of facts surrounding a situation

(A) behaviour

(B) ✓ **contextual**

(C) interdependency

(D) paradigm

▪ Question 8 - Solution

the holding of two or more offices or positions (such as benefices) at the same time

(A) ✓ **pluralism**

(B) ethnicity FR = ethnicité

(C) contextual FR = contextuel

(D) alienation FR = aliénation

▪ Question 9 - Solution

a person who is blamed for the wrongdoings, mistakes, or faults of others, especially for reasons of expediency.

(A)		indigent	FR = pauvre
(B)		opulent	FR = opulent
(C)	✓	**scapegoat**	**FR = bouc émissaire**
(D)		affluent	FR = riche

▪ Question 10 - Solution

having a great deal of money; wealthy

(A)	✓	**affluent**	**FR = riche**
(B)		indigent	FR = pauvre
(C)		paradigm	FR = paradigme
(D)		secularization	FR = sécularisation

LITTÉRATURE

Vocabulaire

- **abstract** = abstrait / résumé
  1) (adj.) existing in thought or as an idea but not having a physical or concrete existence ; 2) (noun) a summary of the contents of a book, article, or speech
  Ex: *Love and beauty are such abstract concepts! / She allowed me to read an abstract of her speech.*
- **allegory** = allégorie
  (noun) a symbol, a story, poem, or picture that can be interpreted to reveal a hidden meaning, typically a moral or political one
  Ex: *Augustine's "City of God" is an allegory of the triumph of Good over Evil.*
- **catharsis** = catharsis
  (noun) the experience of expressing strong emotions that were previously blocked
  Ex: *It's the director's hope that Germans who see his movie will go through a catharsis similar to his own.*
- **connotation** = connotation
  (noun) a feeling or idea that is suggested by a particular word although it needs not be a part of the word's meaning, or something suggested by an object or situation
  Ex: *The word "lady" has connotations of refinement and excessive femininity that some women find offensive.*
- **denotation** = dénotation, signification
  (noun) the literal or primary meaning of a word, in contrast to the feelings or ideas that the word suggests
  Ex: *Beyond their immediate denotation, the words have a connotative power.*
- **dialect** = dialecte
  (noun) a particular form of a language which is peculiar to a specific region or social group
  Ex: *The Lancashire dialect seemed like a foreign language.*
- **drama** = un drame, une pièce de théâtre, une tragédie
  (noun) a play for theatre, radio, or television; an exciting, emotional, or unexpected event or circumstance
  Ex: *I prefer drama to comedy.*
- **euphemism** = euphémisme
  (noun) a word or phrase used to avoid saying an unpleasant or offensive word
  Ex: *"Senior citizen" is a euphemism for "old person".*
- **idiomatic** = idiomatique
  (adj.) idiomatic also means natural in expression, correct without being too formal
  Ex: *His English is fluent and idiomatic.*
- **figure of speech** = figure de style
  (noun) an expression that uses words to mean something different from their ordinary meaning
  Ex: *"Break a leg" is a figure of speech, meaning "good luck".*
- **foreshadow** = annoncer
  (verb) to act as a warning or sign of a future event
  Ex: *The recent outbreak of violence was foreshadowed by isolated incidents in the city earlier this year.*

- **masterpiece** = chef d'œuvre
(noun) a work of art such as a painting, film, or book that is made with great skill
Ex: *Leonardo's "Last Supper" is widely regarded as a masterpiece.*

- **narrative** = narratif
(noun) a story or a description of a series of events
Ex: *It's a moving narrative of wartime adventure.*

- **nemesis** = ennemi juré
(noun) someone's nemesis is a person or thing that is very difficult for them to defeat; punishment or defeat that is deserved and cannot be avoided
Ex: *Will Harry Potter finally defeat his nemesis, Voldemort?*

- **outcome** = résultat
(noun) the way a thing turns out; a consequence
Ex: *It is the outcome of the vote that counts.*

- **plot** = intrigue
(noun) the main events of a play, novel, film, or similar work, devised and presented by the writer as an interrelated sequence
Ex: *The plot consists almost entirely of a man and woman falling in love.*

- **publisher** = éditeur
(noun) a company or person that prepares and issues books, journals, or music for sale
Ex: *It was not easy to find a publisher for her first novel.*

- **purpose** = objectif
the reason for which something is done or created or for which something exists
Ex: *The purpose of the meeting is to appoint a trustee.*

- **prominent** = important
(noun) important; famous
Ex: *She was a prominent member of the city council.*

- **protagonist** = protagoniste
(noun) the leading character or one of the major characters in a play, film, novel, etc.
Ex: *The novel's main protagonist is an American intelligence officer.*

- **thesaurus** = thésaurus
(noun) a book that lists words in groups of synonyms and related concepts
Ex: *To find synonyms, I regularly use the thesaurus.*

- **rhetoric** = rhétorique
(noun) the art of effective or persuasive speaking or writing, especially the exploitation of figures of speech and other compositional techniques
Ex: *He was considered to excel in this form of rhetoric.*

- **setting** = cadre
(noun) the place and time at which a play, novel, or film is taking place
Ex: *It is a short stories with a contemporary setting.*

- **simile** = comparaison
(noun) a figure of speech involving the comparison of one thing with another thing of a different kind, used to make a description more emphatic or vivid (e.g. as brave as a lion).
Ex: *His audacious deployment of similes and metaphors contributed to making his essay all the more convincing.*

Entraînement - Littérature

Reportez vos réponses pour analyser votre performance.

Entraînez-vous dans les conditions d'examen.

prepmyfuture.com/book/68/ex/1953

Question 1 To act as a warning or sign of a future event

(A) abstract

(B) denotation

(C) foreshadow

(D) outcome

Question 2 The way a thing turns out; a consequence.

(A) catharsis

(B) denotation

(C) masterpiece

(D) outcome

Question 3 A company or person that prepares and issues books, journals, or music for sale.

(A) dialect

(B) foreshadow

(C) publisher

(D) thesaurus

Question 4 An expression that uses words to mean something different from their ordinary meaning.

(A) idiomatic

(B) figure of speech

(C) narrative

(D) plot

■ **Question 5** important; famous

(A) nemesis
(B) prominent
(C) protagonist
(D) setting

■ **Question 6** A figure of speech involving the comparison of one thing with another thing of a different kind, used to make a description more emphatic or vivid (e.g. as brave as a lion).

(A) simile
(B) euphemism
(C) nemesis
(D) rhetoric

■ **Question 7** A particular form of a language which is peculiar to a specific region or social group.

(A) idiomatic
(B) dialect
(C) figure of speech
(D) narrative

■ **Question 8** A work of art such as a painting, film, or book that is made with great skill

(A) masterpiece
(B) outcome
(C) publisher
(D) purpose

■ **Question 9** A book that lists words in groups of synonyms and related concepts

(A) nemesis
(B) plot
(C) publisher
(D) thesaurus

■ **Question 10** A person or thing that is very difficult for someone to defeat

(A) allegory
(B) drama
(C) nemesis
(D) simile

Solutions

ılıl Reportez vos réponses pour analyser votre performance.

⏰ Entraînez-vous dans les conditions d'examen.

prepmyfuture.com/book/68/ex/1953

question 1	C	question 3	C	question 5	B	question 7	B	question 9	D
question 2	D	question 4	B	question 6	A	question 8	A	question 10	C

▪ Question 1 - Solution

To act as a warning or sign of a future event

(A) abstract FR = abstrait (adj.) // résumé (nom)

(B) denotation FR = dénotation / signification

(C) ✓ foreshadow FR = annoncer

(D) outcome FR = résultat

▪ Question 2 - Solution

The way a thing turns out; a consequence.

(A) catharsis

(B) denotation FR = dénotation / signification

(C) masterpiece FR = chef d'oeuvre

(D) ✓ outcome FR = résultat

▪ Question 3 - Solution

A company or person that prepares and issues books, journals, or music for sale.

(A) dialect FR = dialecte

(B) foreshadow FR = annoncer

(C) ✓ publisher FR = éditeur

(D) thesaurus FR = dictionnaire

▪ Question 4 - Solution

An expression that uses words to mean something different from their ordinary meaning.

(A)	idiomatic	FR = idiomatique
(B)	**✓ figure of speech**	**FR = figure de style**
(C)	narrative	
(D)	plot	FR = intrigue

▪ Question 5 - Solution

important; famous

(A)	nemesis	
(B)	**✓ prominent**	**FR = important**
(C)	protagonist	FR = protagoniste
(D)	setting	FR = cadre

▪ Question 6 - Solution

A figure of speech involving the comparison of one thing with another thing of a different kind, used to make a description more emphatic or vivid (e.g. as brave as a lion).

(A)	**✓ simile**	**FR = comparaison**
(B)	euphemism	FR = euphémisme
(C)	nemesis	
(D)	rhetoric	FR = rhétorique

▪ Question 7 - Solution

A particular form of a language which is peculiar to a specific region or social group.

(A)	idiomatic	FR = idiomatique
(B)	**✓ dialect**	**FR = dialecte**
(C)	figure of speech	FR = figure de style
(D)	narrative	

▪ Question 8 - Solution

A work of art such as a painting, film, or book that is made with great skill

(A)	**✓ masterpiece**	**FR = chef d'oeuvre**
(B)	outcome	FR = résultat
(C)	publisher	FR = éditeur
(D)	purpose	FR = objectif

▪ Question 9 - Solution

A book that lists words in groups of synonyms and related concepts

(A) nemesis

(B) plot FR = intrigue

(C) publisher FR = éditeur

(D) ✓ thesaurus FR = dictionnaire

▪ Question 10 - Solution

A person or thing that is very difficult for someone to defeat

(A) allegory FR = allégorie

(B) drama FR = drame

(C) ✓ nemesis

(D) simile FR = comparaison

HISTOIRE

Vocabulaire

- **archaeology** = archéologue
  (noun) the study of human history and prehistory through the excavation of sites and the analysis of artefacts and other physical remains
  Ex: *An archaeology professor helped by extracting core samples from the soil with a long, narrow metal cylinder.*

- **ballot (noun); ballot (verb)** = scrutin (nom) ; bulletin de vote
  a system of voting secretly
  Ex: *A strike ballot; the union is preparing to ballot its members on industrial action.*

- **Bill Of Rights** = Déclaration des droits
  (noun) a formal declaration of the legal and civil rights of the citizens of any state, country, federation, etc.
  Ex: *International law and the New Zealand Bill of Rights say that everyone has the right to seek asylum if they are found to be persecuted.*

- **century** = siècle
  (noun) a period of one hundred years
  Ex: Gandhi was born in the nineteenth century in India.

- **federal** = fédéral
  (adj.) having or relating to a system of government in which several states form a unity but remain independent in internal affairs
  Ex: *The health ministry has sole federal responsibility for health care.*

- **foreign policy** = politique extérieure
  (noun) a government's strategy in dealing with other nations
  Ex: *A scathing critic of US foreign policy.*

- **free trade** = libre échange
  (noun) international trade left to its natural course without tariffs, quotas, or other restrictions
  Ex: *An agreement intended to introduce free trade in marine products.*

- **palaeontology** = paléontologie
  (noun) the branch of science concerned with fossil animals and plants
  Ex: *Ross Geller in Friends studied paleontology.*

- **tariff** = droit de douane
  (noun) a tax or duty to be paid on a particular class of imports or exports
  Ex: *The reduction of trade barriers and import tariffs had consequences on the nation's economy.*

- **trade union** = syndicat
  (noun) an organized association of workers in a trade, group of trades, or profession, formed to protect and further their rights and interests
  Ex: *Not only did a trade union have to be recognized by the employers, but it also had to be 'representative'.*

- **tribe** = tribu
  (noun) a social division in a traditional society consisting of families or communities linked by social, economic, religious, or blood ties, with a common culture and dialect, typically having a recognized leader

Ex: *Native people generally prefer to be referred to by the specific name of their tribe.*

- **segregation** = ségrégation, séparation
  (noun) the action or state of setting someone or something apart from others
  Ex: *He stood up against the segregation of pupils with learning difficulties.*
- **senate** = sénat
  (noun) the smaller upper assembly in the US, US states, France, and other countries
  Ex: *The senate must ratify any treaty with a two-thirds majority.*
- **settler** = colon
  (noun) a person who settles in an area, typically one with no or few previous inhabitants
  Ex: *The settlers had come to America to look for land.*

Entraînement - Histoire

Reportez vos réponses pour analyser votre performance.

Entraînez-vous dans les conditions d'examen.

prepmyfuture.com/book/68/ex/1954

Question 1 The smaller upper assembly in the US, US states, France, and other countries.

(A) segregation
(B) senate
(C) settler
(D) tribe

Question 2 A tax or duty to be paid on a particular class of imports or exports

(A) foreign policy
(B) free trade
(C) tariff
(D) trade union

Question 3 Having or relating to a system of government in which several states form a unity but remain independent in internal affairs

(A) federal
(B) free trade
(C) segregation
(D) settler

Question 4 A social division in a traditional society consisting of families or communities linked by social, economic, religious, or blood ties, with a common culture and dialect, typically having a recognized leader

(A) federal
(B) trade union
(C) tribe
(D) segregation

▪ Question 5 A formal declaration of the legal and civil rights of the citizens of any state, country, federation, etc.

(A) Bill Of Rights
(B) foreign Policy
(C) tariff
(D) senate

▪ Question 6 A system of voting secretly and in writing on a particular issue.

(A) ballot
(B) Bill Of Rights
(C) tariff
(D) senate

▪ Question 7 The action or state of setting someone or something apart from others

(A) segregation
(B) tribe
(C) settler
(D) foreign policy

▪ Question 8 International trade left to its natural course without tariffs, quotas, or other restrictions.

(A) foreign policy
(B) trade union
(C) free trade
(D) tariff

▪ Question 9 An organized association of workers in a trade, group of trades, or profession, formed to protect and further their rights and interests.

(A) balot
(B) tribe
(C) segregation
(D) trade union

▪ Question 10 The branch of science concerned with fossil animals and plants

(A) archaeology
(B) paleontology
(C) sociology
(D) biology

Solutions

ılıl Reportez vos réponses pour analyser votre performance.

⏰ Entraînez-vous dans les conditions d'examen.

prepmyfuture.com/book/68/ex/1954

question 1	B	question 3	A	question 5	A	question 7	A	question 9	D
question 2	C	question 4	C	question 6	A	question 8	C	question 10	B

▪ Question 1 - Solution

The smaller upper assembly in the US, US states, France, and other countries.

(A) segregation FR = ségrégation

(B) ✓ senate FR = sénat

(C) settler FR = colon

(D) tribe FR = tribu

▪ Question 2 - Solution

A tax or duty to be paid on a particular class of imports or exports

(A) foreign policy FR = politique extérieure

(B) free trade FR = libre échange

(C) ✓ tariff FR = droit de douane

(D) trade union FR = syndicat

▪ Question 3 - Solution

Having or relating to a system of government in which several states form a unity but remain independent in internal affairs

(A) ✓ federal FR = fédéral

(B) free trade FR = libre échange

(C) segregation FR = ségrégation

(D) settler FR = colon

▪ Question 4 - Solution

A social division in a traditional society consisting of families or communities linked by social, economic, religious, or blood ties, with a common culture and dialect, typically having a recognized leader

(A) federal FR = fédéral

(B) trade union FR = syndicat

(C) ✓ tribe FR = tribu

(D) segregation FR = ségrégation

▪ Question 5 - Solution

A formal declaration of the legal and civil rights of the citizens of any state, country, federation, etc.

(A) ✓ Bill Of Rights FR = Déclaration des droits

(B) foreign Policy FR = politique extérieure

(C) tariff FR = droits de douane

(D) senate FR = sénat

▪ Question 6 - Solution

A system of voting secretly and in writing on a particular issue.

(A) ✓ ballot FR = scrutin (nom); voter au scrutin secret (verbe)

(B) Bill Of Rights FR = Déclaration des droits

(C) tariff FR = droits de douane

(D) senate FR = sénat

▪ Question 7 - Solution

The action or state of setting someone or something apart from others

(A) ✓ segregation FR = ségrégation

(B) tribe FR = tribu

(C) settler FR = colon

(D) foreign policy FR = politique extérieure

▪ Question 8 - Solution

International trade left to its natural course without tariffs, quotas, or other restrictions.

(A) foreign policy FR = politique extérieure

(B) trade union FR = syndicat

(C) ✓ free trade FR = libre échange

(D) tariff FR = droit de douane

▪ Question 9 - Solution

An organized association of workers in a trade, group of trades, or profession, formed to protect and further their rights and interests.

(A) balot FR = scrutin

(B) tribe FR = tribu

(C) segregation FR = ségrégation

(D) ✓ trade union FR = syndicat

▪ Question 10 - Solution

The branch of science concerned with fossil animals and plants

(A) archaeology FR = archéologie

(B) ✓ paleontology FR = paléontologie

(C) sociology FR = sociologie

(D) biology FR = biologie

SCIENCES (MATHÉMATIQUES, BIOLOGIE, ETC.)

Vocabulaire

- **catalyst** = catalyseur
  (noun) a substance that increases the rate of a chemical reaction without undergoing any permanent chemical change itself
  Ex: *Chlorine acts as a catalyst promoting the breakdown of ozone.*
- **cell** = cellule
  (noun) the smallest structural and functional unit of an organism, which is typically microscopic and consists of cytoplasm and a nucleus enclosed in a membrane
  Ex: *The doctors discovered cancerous cells.*
- **chemistry** = chimie
  (noun) the scientific study of the basic characteristics of substances and the ways in which they react or combine
  Ex: *She studied chemistry and physics at college.*
- **climate** = climat
  (noun) the general weather conditions usually found in a particular place
  Ex: *The Mediterranean climate is good for growing citrus fruits and grapes.*
- **engineering** = ingénierie
  (noun) the branch of science and technology concerned with the design, building, and use of engines, machines, and structures
  Ex: *The Eiffel Tower is a remarkable feat of engineering.*
- **exponentially** = de façon exponentielle
  (adverb) (with reference to an increase) more and more rapidly
  Ex: *Our business has been growing exponentially.*
- **formula** = formule
  (noun) a mathematical relationship or rule expressed in symbols
  Ex: *It is so hard to memorize all those formulas for chemistry class!*
- **matter** = matière
  (noun) physical substance in general, as distinct from mind and spirit; (in physics) that occupies space and possesses rest mass, especially as distinct from energy
  Ex: *The structure and properties of matter.*
- **measure** = mesurer
  (verb) ascertain the size, amount, or degree of (something) by using an instrument or device marked in standard units
  Ex: *The amount of water collected is measured in pints.*
- **scientist** = scientifique
  (noun) a person who is studying or has expert knowledge of one or more of the natural or physical sciences
  Ex: *She is a research scientist.*
- **standard deviation** = écart type

(noun) a quantity expressing by how much the members of a group differ from the mean value of the group
Ex: *A fund's performance is measured using its standard deviation from the average profits of all the funds in its category.*

- **slope** = pente
(noun) The (measure of the) inclination of a line
Ex: *The children will soon realize that the steeper the slope the greater the effort required.*

- **rate** = taux
(noun) the speed at which something happens or changes, or the amount or number of times it happens or changes in a particular period
Ex: *I told my assistants to work at their own rate.*

- **wildlife** = vie sauvage
(noun) animals and plants that grow independently of people, usually in natural conditions
Ex: *I watched a documentary on Peruvian wildlife.*

Entraînement - Sciences (mathématiques, biologie, etc.)

Reportez vos réponses pour analyser votre performance.

Entraînez-vous dans les conditions d'examen.

prepmyfuture.com/book/68/ex/1955

Question 1 The branch of science and technology concerned with the design, building, and use of engines, machines, and structures.

(A) mathematics

(B) engineering

(C) scientist

(D) physics

Question 2 Ascertain the size, amount, or degree of (something) by using an instrument or device marked in standard

(A) engineering

(B) formula

(C) matter

(D) measure

Question 3 The scientific study of the basic characteristics of substances and the ways in which they react or combine

(A) engineering

(B) physics

(C) chemistry

(D) biology

Question 4 Physical substance in general, as distinct from mind and spirit; (in physics) that which occupies space and possesses rest mass, especially as distinct from energy

(A) matter

(B) formula

(C) slope

(D) wildlife

■ **Question 5** The speed at which something happens or changes, or the amount or number of times it happens or changes in a particular period

(A) measure
(B) slope
(C) rate
(D) standard deviation

■ **Question 6** A quantity expressing by how much the members of a group differ from the mean value for the group

(A) measure
(B) rate
(C) slope
(D) standard deviation

■ **Question 7** The general weather conditions usually found in a particular place

(A) climate
(B) formula
(C) matter
(D) standard deviation

■ **Question 8** A measure of how steep a line is

(A) rate
(B) slope
(C) measure
(D) formula

■ **Question 9** A person who is studying or has expert knowledge of one or more of the natural or physical sciences

(A) scientist
(B) mathematics
(C) catalyst
(D) architect

■ **Question 10** a substance that increases the rate of a chemical reaction without itself undergoing any permanent chemical change

(A) chemistry
(B) cell
(C) catalyst
(D) wildlife

Solutions

Reportez vos réponses pour analyser votre performance.
Entraînez-vous dans les conditions d'examen.
prepmyfuture.com/book/68/ex/1955

question 1	B	question 3	C	question 5	C	question 7	A	question 9	A
question 2	D	question 4	A	question 6	D	question 8	B	question 10	C

■ Question 1 - Solution

The branch of science and technology concerned with the design, building, and use of engines, machines, and structures.

(A) mathematics FR = mathématiques

(B) ✓ engineering FR = ingénierie

(C) scientist FR = scientifique (nom)

(D) physics FR = physique

■ Question 2 - Solution

Ascertain the size, amount, or degree of (something) by using an instrument or device marked in standard

(A) engineering FR = ingénierie

(B) formula FR = formule

(C) matter FR = matière

(D) ✓ measure FR = mesurer

■ Question 3 - Solution

The scientific study of the basic characteristics of substances and the ways in which they react or combine

(A) engineering FR = ingénierie

(B) physics FR = physique

(C) ✓ chemistry FR = chimie

(D) biology FR = biologie

■ Question 4 - Solution

Physical substance in general, as distinct from mind and spirit; (in physics) that which occupies space and possesses rest mass, especially as distinct from energy

(A) ✓ matter FR = matière

(B) formula FR = formule

(C) slope FR = pente

(D) wildlife FR = vie sauvage

▪ Question 5 - Solution

The speed at which something happens or changes, or the amount or number of times it happens or changes in a particular period

(A) measure FR = mesurer

(B) slope FR = pente

(C) ✓ rate FR = taux

(D) standard deviation FR = écart type

▪ Question 6 - Solution

A quantity expressing by how much the members of a group differ from the mean value for the group

(A) measure FR = mesurer

(B) rate FR = taux

(C) slope FR = pente

(D) ✓ standard deviation FR = écart type

▪ Question 7 - Solution

The general weather conditions usually found in a particular place

(A) ✓ climate FR = climat

(B) formula FR = formule

(C) matter FR = matière

(D) standard deviation FR = écart type

▪ Question 8 - Solution

A measure of how steep a line is

(A) rate FR = taux

(B) ✓ slope FR = pente

(C) measure FR = mesurer

(D) formula FR = formule

▪ Question 9 - Solution

A person who is studying or has expert knowledge of one or more of the natural or physical sciences

(A) ✓ scientist FR = scientifique (nom)

(B) mathematics FR = mathématiques

(C) catalyst FR = catalyseur

(D) architect FR = architecte

■ Question 10 - Solution

a substance that increases the rate of a chemical reaction without itself undergoing any permanent chemical change

(A) chemistry FR = chimie

(B) cell FR = cellule

(C) ✓ catalyst FR = catalyseur

(D) wildlife FR = vie sauvage

Grammaire

MOTS DE LIAISON

Rappel de cours

Il n'y a pas de règle fixe pour l'utilisation des mots de liaison. Il faut donc les mémoriser, ou au moins les comprendre en contexte. Quand vous devez insérer ou comprendre un mot de liaison, vous devez d'abord saisir le lien qui unit les idées à lier. Par exemple, dans la phrase suivante, il y a une opposition entre les deux idées, donc il faut savoir comment exprimer ce contraste :

idée 1 idée 2
The children went out to play ________ it was raining.
(A) although
(B) despite
(C) whereas
(D) instead

Ayant compris quel genre de mot ou phrase convient, il faut choisir celui qui convient grammaticalement. Dans la liste ci-dessus, il y a plusieurs possibilités pour exprimer cette opposition (*instead, whereas, despite, although*). La compréhension de la fonction grammaticale du mot ou de la phrase est nécessaire pour savoir que le seul mot qui convient ici est *« although »*.

The children went out to play ________ the rain.

Cet exemple présente la même notion d'opposition, mais grammaticalement, la réponse correcte ici serait *« despite »* car il s'agit d'un mot qui est toujours suivi par un nom, tandis que *« although »* est toujours suivi par un sujet et un verbe.

Vous trouverez ci-dessous une liste de mots de liaison pour exprimer d'autres notions, telles que l'addition, la cause, la conséquence, l'exemplarité, etc.

Addition

mot de liaison	traduction	exemple
moreover	de plus	The alarm will ring if there is a robbery. Moreover, it will discourage people from trying to rob the bank.
furthermore	en outre, par ailleurs	They reject our accusations. Furthermore, they claim that the loss is our responsibility.
besides	d'ailleurs, en plus de	Do you play other sports besides football? / She won't mind you being late – besides, it's not your fault.
in addition	de plus	In addition, there were parallel meetings with management.
in addition to	en plus de	In addition to being a great painter, he knows how to make beautiful video clips.
also	aussi, de même	This is also extremely interesting.
as well as	ainsi que	We have invited friends as well as family to the wedding.
too	aussi, de même	I'll support you. Bob will too.

Contraste / Opposition

mot de liaison	traduction	exemple
but	mais	I don't know you but I trust you.
instead (of)	au lieu de / à la place	There's no coffee. Will you have some tea instead?
on the one hand…	d'une part	On the one hand, your proposal doesn't include our suggestions…
on the other hand…	d'autre part, en revanche	…but on the other hand, it has some very positive points.
however	cependant, pourtant	This is one possible solution to the problem. However, there are others.
nevertheless / nonetheless	néanmoins, toutefois	I already knew most of the points she made, but her talk was interesting nevertheless / nonetheless.
yet	cependant	He didn't study at all, and yet he passed his exams easily.
on the contrary	au contraire	I never said I was against the idea. On the contrary, I spoke in favour of it.
either… or…	soit… soit…	Either you sign now or the deal is off.
in spite of / despite	malgré	Despite the weather, the event attracted a big crowd.
although / even though	bien que	Although / Even though it was raining, the event attracted a big crowd.
neither… nor…	ni…ni…	This is neither the time nor the place for such discussions.
still	cependant / malgré cela	He made a mess of it. Still, it was a difficult thing to try and do.
whereas	tandis que	Humans are capable of making errors, whereas computers are not.
while	tandis que	While I accept that she is not perfect, I must admit that I do like her.
otherwise	autrement, sinon	I'd better write it down, otherwise I'll forget it.
unlike	à la difference de, contrairement à…	Unlike his brother, he hates working.

Cause

mot de liaison	traduction	exemple
as	parce que	She bought herself a car as she felt she couldn't keep borrowing Alan's.
due to	dû à	The crash was due to a faulty steering mechanism.
owing to	en raison de	Owing to a lack of interest, the picnic has been cancelled.
because of	à cause de	Production has gone down sharply because of the strikes last month.
since	puisque	Since you can't stay late this evening, perhaps you can arrive earlier tomorrow morning.
thanks to	grâce à	Thanks to your hard work, we have achieved all our goals this year.

Condition

mot de liaison	traduction	exemple
as long as	tant que	As long as you do what we tell you, you'll be ok.
even if	même si	Even if you find it too difficult, keep on trying.
(just) in case…	au cas où…	You should read it again in case you misunderstood something.
in the event of…	dans le cas de	In the event of a fire, please use this extinguisher.
unless	à moins que	Unless we hear from you in the next two weeks, we shall be forced to take legal action.
whether	si (oui ou non)	I don't know whether to laugh or cry.
on condition that	à condition	She has agreed on condition that there is no publicity involved.
provided / providing (that)	pourvu que	He'll help us provided (that) he can bring his dog with him.

Comparaison

mot de liaison	traduction	exemple
in comparison (with)	en comparaison	In comparison with some companies, ours isn't too bad at all.
similarly	de même, parallèlement	Cars have to stop at red lights; similarly, bicycles should also stop.
likewise	également, de même	He had a very hostile attitude towards the police; likewise to his parents.

Degré

mot de liaison	traduction	exemple
in many ways	à bien des égards	She seemed like the perfect partner, and in many ways she was.
in some respects	à certains égards	He was like his father in some respects; in others he was totally different.
one way or another	d'une façon ou d'une autre	I will have my revenge on him one way or another.
to some extent	dans une certaine mesure	We can recuperate our losses to some extent by selling what we don't need.
to a large extent	en grande partie	Life will always be to a large extent what we make of it.
thus	ainsi, donc	A rise in income will increase purchasing power, thus stimulting the economy.
somehow	d'une certaine façon, d'une façon ou d'une autre	You look somehow different. / We must finish the job by tomorrow evening somehow.

Exemple / Précision

mot de liaison	traduction	exemple
insofar as	en ce sens que	I believe in God insofar as I feel sure there is a power guiding the universe.
i.e. (id est) / that is to say	c'est à dire	Keeping a dog will cost you a lot of money, i.e. £200.
namely	à savoir	I'm thinking of three U.S. presidents, namely Roosevelt, Eisenhower and Kennedy.
e.g. (exempli gratia) / for example	par exemple	Many US fast-food chains (e.g. Pizza Hut) are well established in Europe.
e.g. (exempli gratia = for example)	par exemple	Many companies have used our services, e.g. Renault, Cisco, Nokia.
such as	comme, tel que	Brands such as Nike and Adidas are the essence of fashionable sportswear.
for instance = for example	par exemple	Take you mother for instance.

But

mot de liaison	traduction	exemple
in order that	afin que	In order that you can complete your task, we have installed 24-hour surveillance.
(in order) to	afin de	This is what we must do (in order) to help them.
in such a way as to	de telle façon à / de manière à ce que	We have organised things in such a way as to make sure that nobody loses.
so as to	afin de	They went ahead on foot so as not to be heard.
by way of	en lieu de	By way of introduction, let me tell you something about my recent experiences in Borneo.
so that	de sorte que	He needs to earn a good salary so that he can keep paying his bills.

Résultat

mot de liaison	traduction	exemple
as a result	par conséquent	As a result of your incompetence, the whole switchboard has now been destroyed.
consequently	par conséquent	We spent most of the money in the first quarter and consequently had none left in the final one.
so	ainsi, donc	This is very easy so I expect you to finish before 4 o'clock.
then	puis	Do this first, then come and see me.
therefore	par conséquent, donc	The new car is smaller and therefore cheaper than our old one.
thus	ainsi, donc	A rise in income will increase purchasing power, thus stimulting the economy.
hence	d'où	His mother was Italian, hence the name – Giulio.
accordingly	en conséquence	When we receive your instructions, we shall act accordingly.

Généralités

mot de liaison	traduction	exemple
usually	d'habitude, avoir l'habitude de	I usually play badminton on Sunday afternoon.
for the most part	pour la plupart	The factory operatives are, for the most part, hard-working, honest people.
on the whole	en gros	There were a few problems, but on the whole, the event went very well.
as a rule	en règle générale	As a rule, we disbelieve all the facts and theories that are of no use to us.

Identification

mot de liaison	traduction	exemple
in the case of	dans le cas de	In the case of young Harry though, we will have to make an exception.
as for…	quant à…	As for the meeting, it will have to be cancelled.
elsewhere	autre part, ailleurs	We still have problems here, but elsewhere everything is under control.
wherever	partout où	Wherever you look these days, there is a McDonald's and a Starbucks.

Temps

mot de liaison	traduction	exemple
prior to	préalablement à	Prior to signing the agreement, we must read the small print.
once	une fois que	Once you have finished your test, you may leave the room.
since	depuis (moment)	It has been this way since 1947.
for	depuis, pendant (period)	It has been this way for 80 years.
for the time being	pour l'instant	For the time being we will have to continue with the old method.
until/till	jusqu'à ce que	They didn't find her until the following day.
whenever	chaque fois que	"Whenever I hear the word 'culture' I reach for my revolver" (H. Goering).
while	pendant que	It happened while I was out of the room.

Entraînement

Exercice 1

Reportez vos réponses pour analyser votre performance.

Entraînez-vous dans les conditions d'examen.

prepmyfuture.com/book/68/ex/1956

Question 1 ________ people who enjoy their work need time to relax, it is hard for them to forget about their job.

(A) Also
(B) However
(C) Even though
(D) Despite

Question 2 ________ the successful summer season, the manager doesn't think he can afford to add a new wing to the hotel.

(A) Although
(B) Because
(C) Due to
(D) Despite

Question 3 Sadly, the newspaper had to either cut its editorial staff ________ reduce the salary of every employee.

(A) nor
(B) but
(C) and
(D) or

Question 4 ________ recent developments in aviation technology, flight safety has increased dramatically for all airlines.

(A) Resulting in
(B) Because
(C) Due to
(D) Despite

■ Question 5 ________ recent news reports, it is very likely the central bank will raise interest rates next month.

(A) According
(B) According to
(C) About to
(D) Accounting for

■ Question 6 ________ we have now received all the brochures we ordered, we shall settle the balance by the end of this week.

(A) Although
(B) Except
(C) Since
(D) Despite

■ Question 7 ________ it is expected to snow this weekend, we should not delay the company Christmas party.

(A) Although
(B) However
(C) Because of
(D) Because

■ Question 8 This trade magazine has some great articles which could really help us ________ our brainstorming sessions.

(A) while
(B) on
(C) during
(D) about

■ Question 9 The company is legally obliged to consult the works council ________ to the announcement of any decisions concerning staff cuts.

(A) before
(B) once
(C) prior
(D) seldom

■ **Question 10** According to a report in the financial press, a company can only change its name ________ a special resolution has been passed by the Board of Directors.

(A) once
(B) despite
(C) though
(D) hence

■ **Question 11** During the summer vacation, certain staff members will be unavailable; ________, all important issues should be resolved before the beginning of July.

(A) nevertheless
(B) moreover
(C) however
(D) consequently

■ **Question 12** He is not our best worker. ________ he has done a good job today.

(A) In spite of
(B) As well as
(C) Nevertheless
(D) Namely

■ **Question 13** ________ all your papers in order, we will send off the application form.

(A) Provided
(B) Or
(C) Whereas
(D) Instead of

■ **Question 14** He has failed many times, ________ he never gives up.

(A) on the one hand
(B) or
(C) yet
(D) futhermore

■ **Question 15** ________ repeated warnings, the client has still not paid the bill.

(A) Namely
(B) Similarly
(C) Although
(D) Despite

Exercice 2

ılıl Reportez vos réponses pour analyser votre performance.

⏰ Entraînez-vous dans les conditions d'examen.

prepmyfuture.com/book/68/ex/1957

Fill in the gap with a suitable linking word or phrase.
(There may be more than one possible answer)

- **Question 1** You should learn the vocabulary ________ you will have trouble in the test next week.

- **Question 2** The passengers received ________ food nor drink during the flight.

- **Question 3** ________ of typing out all the text, why don't you just photocopy it.

- **Question 4** The train has been delayed ________ snow on the tracks.

- **Question 5** There is a conference in Berlin ________ the one in Frankfurt.

- **Question 6** In the morning I drink coffee,________ in the evening I drink herbal tea.

- **Question 7** Our opponents have won their last four matches.________ we feel confident of a win tomorrow.

- **Question 8** ________ the number of people eating at the canteen is increasing, the management has decided to hire a new chef and two part time counter staff.

- **Question 9** Our prices are relatively low ________ our competitors, which means we should sell more products.

- **Question 10** We are laying off staff ________ the increase in profits this year.

Solutions

Exercice 1 - Solution

Reportez vos réponses pour analyser votre performance.

Entraînez-vous dans les conditions d'examen.

prepmyfuture.com/book/68/ex/1956

question 1	C	question 4	C	question 7	A	question 10	A	question 13	A
question 2	D	question 5	B	question 8	C	question 11	D	question 14	C
question 3	D	question 6	C	question 9	C	question 12	C	question 15	D

Question 1 - Solution

________ people who enjoy their work need time to relax, it is hard for them to forget about their job.

FR : ________ les gens qui aiment leur travail ont besoin de temps pour se détendre, il est difficile pour eux d'oublier leur travail.

(A) Also = Aussi

(B) However = Cependant

(C) ✓ Even though = Même si

(D) Despite = Malgré

Question 2 - Solution

________ the successful summer season, the manager doesn't think he can afford to add a new wing to the hotel.

FR : ________ la réussite de la saison estivale, le manager ne pense pas pouvoir se permettre d'ajouter une nouvelle aile à l'hôtel.

(A) Although = Mais

(B) Because = Parce que

(C) Due to = Grâce à

(D) ✓ Despite = Malgré

Question 3 - Solution

Sadly, the newspaper had to either cut its editorial staff ________ reduce the salary of every employee.

FR : Malheureusement, le journal devait soit réduire son équipe éditoriale,________ réduire le salaire de chaque employé.

(A)	nor	= ni
(B)	but	= mais
(C)	and	= et
(D)	✓ **or**	**= soit**

explication
« either-or » voir cours *linking words*

■ Question 4 - Solution

_________ recent developments in aviation technology, flight safety has increased dramatically for all airlines.

FR : _________ développements récents dans les technologies de l'aviation, la sécurité des vols a augmenté pour toutes les compagnies aériennes.

(A)	Resulting in	= Causant/ Provoquant
(B)	Because	= Parce que
(C)	✓ **Due to**	**= Grâce aux**
(D)	Despite	= Bien que

■ Question 5 - Solution

_________ recent news reports, it is very likely the central bank will raise interest rates next month.

FR : _________ les récentes nouvelles, il est très probable que la banque centrale augmente ses taux d'intérêt le mois prochain.

(A)	According	= Accorder
(B)	✓ **According to**	**= Selon**
(C)	About to	= Sur le point de
(D)	Accounting for	= Représentant

■ Question 6 - Solution

_________ we have now received all the brochures we ordered, we shall settle the balance by the end of this week.

FR : _________ nous avons reçu toutes les brochures que nous avons commandées, nous allons régler le solde restant d'ici la fin de la semaine.

(A)	Although	= Malgré
(B)	Except	= Excepté
(C)	✓ **Since**	**= Comme, Puisque**
(D)	Despite	= Malgré

■ Question 7 - Solution

_________ it is expected to snow this weekend, we should not delay the company Christmas party.

FR : _________ de la neige est prévue ce weekend, nous ne devrions pas reporter la fête de Noël de l'entreprise.

(A) ✓ **Although** **= Même si**

(B) However = Cependant

(C) Because of = À cause de

(D) Because = Parce que

▪ Question 8 - Solution

This trade magazine has some great articles which could really help us ________ our brainstorming sessions.

FR : Ce magazine d'affaire comporte des articles qui peuvent vraiment nous aider ________ nos sessions de brainstorming.

(A) while = pendant que / alors que

(B) on = sur

(C) ✓ **during** **= pendant**

(D) about = à propos

▪ Question 9 - Solution

The company is legally obliged to consult the works council ________ to the announcement of any decisions concerning staff cuts.

FR : La société a pour obligation légale de consulter le comité d'entreprise ________ d'annoncer une quelconque décision concernant des licenciements.

(A) before = avant

(B) once = une fois

(C) ✓ **prior** **= avant (*« prior to »*)**

(D) seldom = rarement

▪ Question 10 - Solution

According to a report in the financial press, a company can only change its name ________ a special resolution has been passed by the Board of Directors.

FR : Selon un rapport publié dans la presse financière, une société ne peut changer sa raison sociale que ________ une résolution a été adoptée par le Conseil d'Administration.

(A) ✓ **once** **= une fois que**

(B) despite = malgré

(C) though = bien que

(D) hence = d'où

▪ Question 11 - Solution

During the summer vacation, certain staff members will be unavailable; ________, all important issues should be resolved before the beginning of July.

FR : Pendant les vacances d'été, certains collaborateurs ne seront pas disponibles ; ________, toutes les questions importantes devront être résolues avant début juillet.

(A)	nevertheless	= cependant
(B)	moreover	= De plus
(C)	however	= cependant
(D)	**✓ consequently**	**= par conséquent**

▪ Question 12 - Solution

He is not our best worker. ________ he has done a good job today.

FR : Il n'est pas notre meilleur employé. ________ il a bien travaillé aujourd'hui.

(A)	In spite of	En dépit de quoi
(B)	As well as	Aussi bien que
(C)	**✓ Nevertheless**	**Cependant, néanmoins**
(D)	Namely	A savoir

▪ Question 13 - Solution

________ all your papers in order, we will send off the application form.

FR : ________ tous vos papiers soient en règle, nous enverrons le formulaire d'inscription.

(A)	**✓ Provided**	**Pourvu que**
(B)	Or	Ou
(C)	Whereas	Tandis que
(D)	Instead of	A la place de

▪ Question 14 - Solution

He has failed many times, ________ he never gives up.

FR : Il a échoué beaucoup de fois, ________ il n'abandonne jamais.

(A)	on the one hand	d'une part
(B)	or	ou
(C)	**✓ yet**	**cependant**
(D)	futhermore	de plus

▪ Question 15 - Solution

________ repeated warnings, the client has still not paid the bill.

FR : ________ des rappels à répétition, le client n'a toujours pas payé la note.

(A)	Namely	A savoir
(B)	Similarly	De la même façon
(C)	Although	Bien que
(D)	**✓ Despite**	**Malgré**

Exercice 2 - Solution

Reportez vos réponses pour analyser votre performance.

Entraînez-vous dans les conditions d'examen.

prepmyfuture.com/book/68/ex/1957

question 1	otherwise
question 2	neither

question 3	Instead
question 4	due to / because of / owing to

question 5	Besides / as well as
question 6	whereas / but / though / although

question 7	Nevertheless / nonetheless
question 8	As / Since / Because

question 9	In comparison with / compared to / compared with
question 10	despite / in spite of

Question 1 - Solution

You should learn the vocabulary _________ you will have trouble in the test next week.
Réponse(s) : otherwise

Question 2 - Solution

The passengers received _________ food nor drink during the flight.
Réponse(s) : neither

Question 3 - Solution

_________ of typing out all the text, why don't you just photocopy it.
Réponse(s) : Instead

Question 4 - Solution

The train has been delayed _________ snow on the tracks.
Réponse(s) : due to / because of / owing to

Question 5 - Solution

There is a conference in Berlin _________ the one in Frankfurt.
Réponse(s) : Besides / as well as

Question 6 - Solution

In the morning I drink coffee,_________ in the evening I drink herbal tea.
Réponse(s) : whereas / but / though / although

Question 7 - Solution

Our opponents have won their last four matches._________ we feel confident of a win tomorrow.
Réponse(s) : Nevertheless / nonetheless

■ Question 8 - Solution

________ the number of people eating at the canteen is increasing, the management has decided to hire a new chef and two part time counter staff.
Réponse(s) : As / Since / Because

■ Question 9 - Solution

Our prices are relatively low ________ our competitors, which means we should sell more products.
Réponse(s) : In comparison with / compared to / compared with

■ Question 10 - Solution

We are laying off staff ________ the increase in profits this year.
Réponse(s) : despite / in spite of

LA POSSESSION – DÉTERMINANTS ET PRONOMS

Rappel de cours

Utilisation des pronoms

Certains pronoms peuvent remplacer un sujet ou un objet dans une phrase, souvent pour éviter de répéter le mot.

> I bought a new computer and I love editing films on ~~the computer~~ it.

D'autres peuvent montrer l'idée de possession. Les déterminants possessifs s'utilisent avec un nom, les pronoms possessifs remplacent le nom.

> Where is their book?
> The bag is ours.

Liste des pronoms

Sujets	Objets	Déterminants possessifs (Utilisés avec un nom)	Pronoms possessifs (Utilisés seuls)	Pronoms réflexifs
I	Me	My	Mine	Myself
You	You	Your	Yours	Yourself
He	Him	His	His	Himself
She	Her	Her	Hers	Herself
It	It	Its	Its	Itself
We	Us	Our	Ours	Ourselves
You	You	Your	Yours	Yourselves
They	Them	Their	Theirs	Themselves

Quelques exemples :

- I saw **them** in the park (Je **les** ai vus dans le parc)
- He gave us **his** book (Il nous a donné **son** livre)
- That pen is not **mine** (Le stylo n'est pas à **moi**)
- She painted the house **herself** (Elle a peint la maison **elle-même**)

Piège

En anglais les objets ne peuvent pas être masculins ou féminins et les pronoms/déterminants possessifs se basent sur la personne (possesseur), pas sur l'objet.

Quelques exemples :

- Robert has arrived with **his** sister. (Robert est arrivé avec **sa** sœur)
- Where is **my** dog? (Où est **mon** chien ?)
- Where is **my** chair? (Où est **ma** chaise ?)
- Where are **my** shoes? (Où sont **mes** chaussures ?)

Entraînement

Reportez vos réponses pour analyser votre performance.

Entraînez-vous dans les conditions d'examen.

prepmyfuture.com/book/68/ex/1958

Question 1 It is very likely that because Mr. Wright cannot attend the meeting ________ company will not receive the contract.

(A) himself
(B) his
(C) he
(D) him

Question 2 Mr. Garrison is best known for having started an international shipping company all on ________ at the age of 25.

(A) his
(B) his own
(C) him
(D) himself own

Question 3 These computers look great, but are you sure we can afford ________ yearly service plan?

(A) their
(B) these
(C) those
(D) them

Question 4 The employees can take ________ breaks at any time.

(A) they
(B) their
(C) theirs
(D) them

Question 5 I will ask ________ suppliers if they can deliver the goods a day earlier than usual.

(A) ourselves
(B) us
(C) our
(D) ours

Question 6 He contacted all the people ________.

(A) he
(B) him
(C) his
(D) himself

Question 7 She is going to spend most of the night writing ________ reports.

(A) her
(B) his
(C) hers
(D) she

Question 8 This way is shorter. Yes ________ is.

(A) he
(B) she
(C) it
(D) they

Question 9 The population in this area is expected to double ________ size in the next twenty years.

(A) their
(B) his
(C) her
(D) its

Question 10 The boutique ________ is well-situated, but many customers would like to be in a shopping mall.

(A) it
(B) its
(C) her
(D) itself

Question 11 Do you think ________ are better than mine.

(A) his song
(B) his songs
(C) her song
(D) their song

Question 12 You can't blame ________ for trying.

(A) her
(B) herself
(C) hers
(D) she

Question 13 My sister's friends are arriving around three o'clock. Could you pick ________ up at the airport please?

(A) her
(B) hers
(C) them
(D) their

Question 14 We thought it was ours, but in fact it's ________.

(A) ourselves
(B) you
(C) yours
(D) yourself

Question 15 Great Expectations is a novel about a boy called Pip, ________ is profoundly affected by his encounter with Magwitch, an escaped convict.

(A) whose life
(B) who's life
(C) which life
(D) what life

Solutions

ıll Reportez vos réponses pour analyser votre performance.

⏰ Entraînez-vous dans les conditions d'examen.

prepmyfuture.com/book/68/ex/1958

question 1	B
question 2	B
question 3	A

question 4	B
question 5	C
question 6	D

question 7	A
question 8	C
question 9	D

question 10	D
question 11	B
question 12	A

question 13	C
question 14	C
question 15	A

▪ Question 1 - Solution

It is very likely that because Mr. Wright cannot attend the meeting ________ company will not receive the contract.

FR : Puisque monsieur Wright ne pourra pas venir à la réunion, il est très probable que ________ compagnie ne reçoive pas le contrat.

(A) himself = lui-même (pronom)

(B) ✓ his = sa (déterminant)

(C) he = il (pronom)

(D) him = lui (pronom)

▪ Question 2 - Solution

Mr. Garrison is best known for having started an international shipping company all on ________ at the age of 25.

FR : Monsieur Garrison est surtout connu pour avoir commencé une entreprise de transport ________ à l'âge de 25 ans.

(A) his = sa

(B) ✓ his own = tout seul

(C) him = lui

(D) himself own = lui-même possède

⇝ **explication**
Ici, la locution adverbiale « *all on his own* » doit être utilisée.

▪ Question 3 - Solution

These computers look great, but are you sure we can afford ________ yearly service plan?

FR : Ces ordinateurs ont l'air bien, mais es-tu sûr que nous pouvons nous permettre ________ offre de service annuelle ?

(A)	✓	**their**	**= leur**
(B)		these	= ces
(C)		those	= ceux-ci
(D)		them	= les

⇒ **explication**
Ici, nous devons utiliser un déterminant possessif. Il n'y en a qu'un seul parmi les propositions de réponse.

▪ Question 4 - Solution

The employees can take ________ breaks at any time.

FR : Les employés peuvent prendre ________ pauses n'importe quand.

(A)		they	ils
(B)	✓	**their**	**leurs**
(C)		theirs	la leur
(D)		them	eux

▪ Question 5 - Solution

I will ask ________ suppliers if they can deliver the goods a day earlier than usual.

FR : Je vais demander à ________ fournisseurs s'ils peuvent nous livrer les biens un jour plus tôt que prévu.

(A)		ourselves	nous-même
(B)		us	nous
(C)	✓	**our**	**nos**
(D)		ours	les nôtres

▪ Question 6 - Solution

He contacted all the people ________.

FR : Il a contacté toutes les personnes ________.

(A)		he	il
(B)		him	lui
(C)		his	son
(D)	✓	**himself**	**lui-même**

▪ Question 7 - Solution

She is going to spend most of the night writing ________ reports.

FR : Elle va passer le plus clair de la nuit à écrire ________ rapport.

(A) ✓ her sa (she est une fille il s'accorde avec la fille pas le rapport)

(B) his sa=on

(C) hers la sienne

(D) she elle

⟹ **explication**
En Anglais le pronom possessif s'accorde avec le sujet. réponse (A)

▪ Question 8 - Solution

This way is shorter. Yes ________ is.

FR : Ce chemin est plus court. Oui ________ l'est.

(A) he Il (une personne)

(B) she elle (une personne)

(C) ✓ it il (un objet)

(D) they ils

▪ Question 9 - Solution

The population in this area is expected to double ________ size in the next twenty years.

FR : La population de ce lieu a prévu de doubler ________ taille d'ici vingt ans.

(A) their leur

(B) his son ou sa

(C) her son ou sa

(D) ✓ its son ou sa (relatif à la population)

⟹ **explication**
En anglais le pronom s'accorde avec le sujet ici la population qui est neutre. Réponse (D)

▪ Question 10 - Solution

The boutique ________ is well-situated, but many customers would like to be in a shopping mall.

FR : La boutique ________ est bien située, mais beaucoup de clients préféreraient être dans un centre commercial.

(A) it ça

(B) its sa

(C) her elle

(D) ✓ itself elle-même

▪ Question 11 - Solution

Do you think ________ are better than mine.

FR : Penses-tu que ________ sont meilleures que les miennes.

(A)	his song	sa chanson (à lui)
(B)	✓ **his songs**	**ses chansons**
(C)	her song	sa chanson (à elle)
(D)	their song	leur chanson (à eux)

■ Question 12 - Solution

You can't blame _________ for trying.

FR : Tu ne peux pas _________ reprocher d'essayer.

(A)	✓ **her**	**lui**
(B)	herself	elle-même
(C)	hers	la sienne
(D)	she	elle

■ Question 13 - Solution

My sister's friends are arriving around three o'clock. Could you pick _________ up at the airport please?

FR : Les amis de ma sœur vont arriver vers trois heures. Peux-tu aller _________ chercher à l'aéroport s'il te plaît.

(A)	her	la
(B)	hers	la sienne
(C)	✓ **them**	**les**
(D)	their	leur(s)

⇒ **explication**

Ici nous parlons de plusieurs personnes, nous avons donc besoin du pronom personnel pluriel : *them*. *Them* est l'équivalent au COD du pronom sujet *they*.

Ex: *They arrive at noon. Could you pick them up ?*

■ Question 14 - Solution

We thought it was ours, but in fact it's _________.

FR : Nous pensions que c'était le nôtre mais en fait c'est _________.

(A)	ourselves	nous-même
(B)	you	vous
(C)	✓ **yours**	**le vôtre**
(D)	yourself	vous-même

■ Question 15 - Solution

Great Expectations is a novel about a boy called Pip, _________ is profoundly affected by his encounter with Magwitch, an escaped convict.

FR : Les Grandes Espérances est un roman au sujet d'un garçon nommé Pip, _________ est profondément affectée par sa rencontre avec Magwitch, un prisonnier évadé.

(A)	✓	**whose life**	**whose life = dont la vie**
(B)		who's life	who's life = qui est la vie
(C)		which life	which life = laquelle des vies
(D)		what life	what life = quelle vie?

⇨ **explication**
"Whose" est la forme possessive de **"who"**. A comparer avec le mot dont en français

CONJUGAISON

Rappel de cours

Conjugaison

Beaucoup d'étudiants ne sont pas à l'aise avec les différentes formes des verbes en anglais: *« he speaks, he has spoken, he is speaking, he has been speaking, he had spoken… »*. Si vous avez du mal à comprendre la différence entre toutes ces différentes formes, cette section vous sera utile.

La grille ci-dessous donne un aperçu général du système des temps en anglais. Contrairement au français, il y a très peu de conjugaisons en anglais. Prenons l'exemple du verbe "eat" (manger). En français, les formes de ce verbe sont très nombreuses (manger, mangé, mange, mangeons, manges, mangeant …), tandis que le verbe *« to eat »* en anglais n'a que cinq formes : *eat, eats, eating, ate, eaten*.

Cela est identique pour tous les verbes. Vous n'aurez jamais plus de cinq formes d'un verbe à apprendre :

- L'infinitif (*eat*, ou *to eat*)
- La troisième personne du singulier, qui prend toujours un "s" (*eats*) - sauf pour les verbes modaux
- Le gérondif ou le participe du présent (*eating*)
- Le passé (*ate*)
- Le participe passé (*eaten*)

Prenons un autre exemple, le verbe *« to have »* :

- L'infinitif (*have*, ou *to have*)
- La 3e personne du singulier (*he, she, it, etc.*), qui prend toujours un "s" (*has*)
- Le gérondif (*« gerund »*) ou le participe du présent (*having*)
- Le passé (*had*)
- Le participe passé (ici, *had* aussi)

Les temps des verbes en anglais s'expriment en ajoutant d'autres mots à ces cinq formes de base. Afin d'identifier la forme appropriée d'un verbe dans une phrase, il faut d'abord identifier l'indicateur du temps dans la phrase. En général, cet indicateur est exprimé par des phrases telles que : *at the moment, 4 days ago, since 2004, every day*, etc. Parfois, il n'y aura pas d'indicateur et il faudra saisir le contexte du temps en lisant les parties du texte qui précèdent et qui suivent le verbe.

La grille ci-dessous montre la logique des temps des verbes. Les indicateurs du temps sont marqués avec la forme affirmative dans chaque case. C'est à partir d'eux que l'on détermine la forme appropriée du verbe.

Un conseil important : quand il s'agit des temps des verbes, il ne faut jamais traduire littéralement du français. Les systèmes des temps en anglais et en français ne sont pas pareils !

	Forme simple	Forme continue Verbe *« to be »* + *« -ing »* (= être en train de)
Présent	• Every day she eats snails for breakfast. • Does she really eat snails for breakfast? • No, she doesn't eat snails for breakfast.	• She's eating snails right now. • Is she eating snails? • No, she isn't eating snails.
Futur (avec *« will »*)	• She'll eat snails if you offer her some. • Will she eat snails? • No, she won't eat snails, even if you offer her some.	• At midnight, she'll be eating snails. • Will she be eating snails then? • No, she won't be eating then.
Passé	• She ate snails last Saturday night. • Did she eat snails? • No, she didn't eat snails.	• She was eating snails when I saw her. • Was she eating snails? • No, she wasn't eating.
Present Perfect (jusqu'à maintenant)	• She has eaten a kilo of snails since she arrived. • Has she eaten a whole kilo? • No, she hasn't eaten a kilo.	• She has been eating snails since she arrived (and still is). • Has she really been eating that long? • No, she hasn't been eating that long.
Past Perfect (avant le passé)	• She had eaten two kilos of snails before she went to the restaurant. • Had she really eaten that much? • No, she hadn't really eaten two kilos.	• She had been eating for six hours before she arrived at the restaurant. • Had she been eating that long? • No, she hadn't been eating that long.

La grille contient les formes affirmative, interrogative et négative pour chaque temps en utilisant la même structure : *she / to eat / snails*.

Les particularités de l'anglais par rapport au français

Il faut noter en particulier le fait que certaines de ces formes n'existent pas en français.

Le *« present perfect »*

La structure *have/has* + le participe passé (*he has eaten/they have eaten*, etc.) est liée à un indicateur de temps qui va jusqu'au présent, même si l'action est terminée.

En français on dirait :
J'ai mangé 3 gâteaux hier soir.
et de la même façon :

J'ai mangé 3 gâteaux aujourd'hui.

Par contre, en anglais, cela donne :
I ate 3 cakes yesterday evening (indicateur du temps : le passé).
mais :
I have eaten 3 cakes today (indicateur du temps : jusqu'à maintenant).

La forme continue

En regardant la grille, on voit que chaque temps a une forme simple pour l'action complète et une forme continue qui correspond à la notion « en train de » du français.

On peut donc entendre :

I smoke, but I'm not smoking now.
FR : Je fume, mais je ne suis pas en train de fumer.

Cette différence existe également pour d'autres structures, comme le *present perfect* par exemple :

I have been writing letters; I have written 5 of them up to now.
FR : J'écris des lettres depuis un certain temps ; j'en ai écris 5 jusqu'à maintenant.

Le « *past perfect* »

La structure *had* + le participe passé (*he had eaten*, etc.) est liée à un indicateur de temps (souvent le mot *before*) qui montre que l'action s'était passée avant une autre action au passé. Autrement dit, on fait deux pas dans le passé.

En français on dirait :
Avant d'arriver à Paris, j'étais déjà resté 3 jours à Londres.
ou
Avant que je rencontre Pierre, j'avais déjà rencontré son frère.

En anglais cela donne :
Before I arrived in Paris (past tense), I had already stayed in London for 3 days (past perfect).
et
Before I met Pierre (past tense), I had already met his brother (past perfect).

Entraînement

Reportez vos réponses pour analyser votre performance.

Entraînez-vous dans les conditions d'examen.

prepmyfuture.com/book/68/ex/1959

Question 1 The new invoicing program we have just acquired ________ us to send out bills and process money more quickly compared to last year.

(A) allow

(B) will allow

(C) are allowing

(D) allowed

Question 2 Company profits ________ by 20% since we installed the new high-speed computer network.

(A) rise

(B) risen

(C) rising

(D) have risen

Question 3 In order to ________ their new line of young adult books, the publishers will conduct book-signings in various cities.

(A) promotion

(B) promoting

(C) have promoted

(D) promote

Question 4 Albion Automotive ________ a two-year guarantee on all its products.

(A) provide

(B) provides

(C) providing

(D) provision

Question 5 The CEO sent a memo ________ that his company would be implementing new pollution controls during the next quarter.

(A) states
(B) statement
(C) stated
(D) stating

Question 6 If the top half of the sample doesn't ________ the bottom half, then you should throw it away.

(A) matching
(B) match
(C) matched
(D) matches

Question 7 The airport has ________ into a city in its own right, employing 53,000 people and covering an area of over 5 square miles.

(A) growth
(B) grow
(C) growing
(D) grown

Question 8 I'm not sure where John put the paper clips, but I think he ________ them in the drawer next to the filing cabinet.

(A) might have put
(B) might put
(C) might be putting
(D) might be put

Question 9 The CEO would like to remind you that all reports ________ completed by the end of next week – this is the final deadline.

(A) might be
(B) should
(C) would have been
(D) must be

Question 10 At your time of life you _________ about your next career move, not about retiring!

(A) should have thought
(B) might think
(C) should be thinking
(D) will think

Question 11 Excuse me, but _________ open the window over there, I think this young lady is not feeling very well.

(A) could you
(B) may you
(C) must you
(D) should you

Question 12 I'm sorry to contradict you, but you couldn't possibly _________ here on Friday evening. The office was closed at that time.

(A) worked
(B) be worked
(C) have been working
(D) be working

Question 13 You _________ come in early tomorrow, Frieda. The CEO's visit has been canceled.

(A) don't have to
(B) mustn't
(C) wouldn't have to
(D) mustn't have

Question 14 Why weren't you in your office at 10 o'clock this morning? You _________ on the Campinas project – you know it has to be finished by lunch time!

(A) must have been working
(B) might have worked
(C) should have been working
(D) could be worked

Question 15 When the Manager _________ I will speak to him.

(A) comes
(B) will come
(C) would come
(D) came

Solutions

Reportez vos réponses pour analyser votre performance.

Entraînez-vous dans les conditions d'examen.

prepmyfuture.com/book/68/ex/1959

question 1	B	question 4	B	question 7	D	question 10	C	question 13	A
question 2	D	question 5	D	question 8	A	question 11	A	question 14	C
question 3	D	question 6	B	question 9	D	question 12	C	question 15	A

▪ Question 1 - Solution

The new invoicing program we have just acquired ________ us to send out bills and process money more quickly compared to last year.

FR : Le nouveau système de facturation que nous venons d'acquérir nous ________ d'envoyer les factures et de traiter l'argent plus rapidement, comparé à l'année dernière.

(A) allow = permettre / permet

(B) ✓ will allow = « va nous permettre »

(C) are allowing = « est en train de nous permettre »

(D) allowed = permettait (concordance des temps *"last year"*)

▪ Question 2 - Solution

Company profits ________ by 20% since we installed the new high-speed computer network.

FR : Les bénéfices de l'entreprise ________ de 20% depuis que nous avons installé le nouveau réseau informatique à haute vitesse.

(A) rise = s'élève / s'élèvent/ s'élever (base verbale)

(B) risen = augmenté (participe passé)

(C) rising = levant (gérondif)

(D) ✓ have risen = ont augmenté (present perfect)

▪ Question 3 - Solution

In order to ________ their new line of young adult books, the publishers will conduct book-signings in various cities.

FR : De façon à ________ leur nouvelle série de livres pour adultes, les éditeurs vont organiser des séances de dédicaces dans diverses villes.

(A) promotion = promotion (nom)

(B) promoting = promouvant (gérondif)

(C) have promoted = ont fait la promotion (verbe au present perfect)

(D) ✓ promote = promouvoir (verbe à l'infinitif)

⟹ **explication**
in order to + base verbale

▪ Question 4 - Solution

Albion Automotive ________ a two-year guarantee on all its products.

FR : Albion Automotive ________ une garantie de deux ans sur tous ses produits.

(A) provide = fournir (base verbale)

(B) ✓ provides = fournit (présent simple troisième personne)

(C) providing = qui fournit (gérondif)

(D) provision = provision (nom singulier)

▪ Question 5 - Solution

The CEO sent a memo ________ that his company would be implementing new pollution controls during the next quarter.

FR : Le directeur général a envoyé une note de service ________ que sa compagnie allait mettre en place de nouveaux contrôles de pollution pendant le prochain trimestre.

(A) states = indique (présent troisième personne)

(B) statement = déclaration (nom)

(C) stated = indiquait (prétérit)

(D) ✓ stating = indiquant (gérondif)

▪ Question 6 - Solution

If the top half of the sample doesn't ________ the bottom half, then you should throw it away.

FR : Si la partie supérieure de l'échantillon ne ________ pas avec la partie inférieure, alors vous devriez le jeter.

(A) matching = correspondant (gérondif de « correspondre ») ou nom
Doesn't ne peut pas être suivi d'un verbe conjugé.

(B) ✓ match = correspondre

(C) matched = correspondait (passé)
Doesn't ne peut pas être suivi d'un verbe conjugué.

(D) matches = il / elle correspond (présent)
The top half of the sample est bien un sujet à la troisième personne du singulier. Cependant, c'est le modal do not, et non pas le verbe, qui porte la marque de la troisième personne du singulier : do not devient does not.

⟹ **explication**
Il ne s'agit pas de savoir quelle conjugaison choisir mais plutôt s'il faut conjuger ou non le verbe *to match*.

La phrase contient déjà un verbe conjugué : *do*. Une phrase ne pouvant pas contenir deux verbes conjugués, il faut utiliser l'infinitif.

▪ Question 7 - Solution

The airport has _________ into a city in its own right, employing 53,000 people and covering an area of over 5 square miles.

FR : L'aéroport est _________ une ville à part entière qui emploie 53 000 personnes et qui occupe une surface de plus de 5 miles carrés.

(A) growth = croissance (nom)

(B) grow = devient (présent)

(C) growing = devenant (gérondif)

(D) ✓ grown = devenu (participe passé)
auxiliaire suivi du participe passé

▪ Question 8 - Solution

I'm not sure where John put the paper clips, but I think he _________ them in the drawer next to the filing cabinet.

FR : Je ne suis pas sûr de l'endroit où John a mis les trombones, mais je pense qu'il _________ dans le tiroir à côté du meuble d'archivage.

(A) ✓ might have put a pu les mettre

(B) might put pourrait mettre

(C) might be putting pourrait être en train de les mettre

(D) might be put pu être mis

▪ Question 9 - Solution

The CEO would like to remind you that all reports _________ completed by the end of next week – this is the final deadline.

FR : Le PDG voudrait vous rappeler que tous les rapports _________ terminés pour la fin de la semaine prochaine - c'est la date limite définitive.

(A) might be peuvent être

(B) should devraient être

(C) would have been auraient été

(D) ✓ must be doivent être
Ce que demande le PDG est un ordre non une indication cette réponse est la seule qui permet l'intimation d'un ordre dans la phrase, elle est donc la bonne.

▪ Question 10 - Solution

At your time of life you _________ about your next career move, not about retiring!

FR : À ton âge tu _________ à la prochaine étape de ta carrière, pas à prendre ta retraite !

(A)	should have thought	aurais dû penser
(B)	might think	pourrais penser
(C)	**✓ should be thinking**	**devrais (être en train de) penser** ***réponse au présent continu***
(D)	will think	vas penser

▪ Question 11 - Solution

Excuse me, but _________ open the window over there, I think this young lady is not feeling very well.

FR : Excusez-moi mais _________ ouvrir la fenêtre là-bas, j'ai l'impression que cette jeune femme ne se sent pas très bien.

(A)	**✓ could you**	**pouvez-vous**
(B)	may you	puissiez-vous *May you n'est pas une formulation idiomatique à l'inverse de may I.* *Cette formuation est correcte : May I ask you to open the window [...] ?* *May you est généralement utilisé pour exprimer un souhait, un vœu : May you be happy always." (= puissiez-vous être toujours heureux.)*
(C)	must you	êtes-vous obligés d'
(D)	should you	devriez-vous

▪ Question 12 - Solution

I'm sorry to contradict you, but you couldn't possibly _________ here on Friday evening. The office was closed at that time.

FR : Je suis désolé mais vous ne pouviez pas _________ ici vendredi. Les bureaux étaient fermés à cette heure-là.

(A)	worked	travaillé
(B)	be worked	être travaillé
(C)	**✓ have been working**	**être en train de travailler**
(D)	be working	travaillant

⇒ **explication**
Après un modal, on n'utilise jamais le prétérit mais la forme continue.
On ne dit pas "you could came" mais "you could have come"

"You couldn't have worked here" = vous ne pouviez pas avoir un emploi / être employé ici.

"You couldn't have been working here" = vous ne pouviez pas travailler (faire des tâches ; l'action de travailler) ici.

▪ Question 13 - Solution

You _________ come in early tomorrow, Frieda. The CEO's visit has been canceled.

FR : Vous _________ arriver tôt demain, Frieda. La visite du PDG a été annulée.

(A)	✓	**don't have to**	**n'êtes pas obligée d'**
(B)		mustn't	ne devez pas
(C)		wouldn't have to	avez pas d'
(D)		mustn't have	ne devez pas avoir d'

▪ Question 14 - Solution

Why weren't you in your office at 10 o'clock this morning? You ________ on the Campinas project – you know it has to be finished by lunch time!

FR : Pourquoi n'étiez vous pas dans votre bureau à dix heures ce matin? Vous ________ sur le projet Campinas - vous savez qu'il doit être fini pour l'heure du déjeuner !

(A)		must have been working	étiez sûrement en train de travailler
(B)		might have worked	auriez pu travailler
(C)	✓	**should have been working**	**auriez dû être en train de travailler** ***Dans le sens de la phrase et l'intonation de celle-ci on comprend que seule cette réponse est possible***
(D)		could be worked	pourriez être travaillés

▪ Question 15 - Solution

When the Manager ________ I will speak to him.

FR : Quand le manager ________ je lui parlerai.

(A)	✓	**comes**	**arrivera** ***car conditionnel de type 1***
(B)		will come	va arriver
(C)		would come	arriverait
(D)		came	arriva

COMPARATIF / SUPERLATIF

Rappel de cours

Définitions

Un comparatif compare deux choses.

> John is **taller than** Peter.

Un superlatif compare plus de deux choses.

> Everest is **the highest** mountain in the world.
> Jane is **the nicest** girl in the class.

Les règles

Adectifs courts

Si l'adjectif comporte deux syllabes ou moins :

- Comparatif : ajoutez -er à l'adjectif.
- Superlatif : ajoutez -est à l'adjectif, l'adjectif sera précédé de « the ».

> fast/faster/the fastest
> big/bigger/the biggest

Lorsqu'un adjectif se termine avec une seule consonne, il faut souvent la doubler.

> hot/hotter/the hottest

Adjectifs terminant par -y

Si l'adjectif termine par un « y », remplacez le « y » avec un « i », puis ajoutez –er/est.

happy/happier/the happiest
shy/shier/the shiest

Adjectifs longs

Si l'adjectif fait plus de deux syllabes :

- Comparatif : l'adjectif sera précédé de « more ».
- Superlatif : l'adjectif sera précédé de « the most ».

intelligent/more intelligent/the most intelligent
beautiful/more beautiful/the most beautiful

Quelques exceptions

Good / better / the best
Bad / worse / the worst
Far / farther (further) / the farthest (the furthest)
Little (quantité) / less / the least
Much / more / the most

D'autres comparaisons à connaître

as _________ as
(aussi _________ que)

He is as fast as you. (Il est aussi rapide que vous.)

The same as
(comme/ le même _________ que)

He's the same as usual (Il est comme d'habitude)
He has the same hat as me (Il a le même chapeau que moi)

Entraînement

Reportez vos réponses pour analyser votre performance.

Entraînez-vous dans les conditions d'examen.

prepmyfuture.com/book/68/ex/1960

Question 1 Because he really understands the specifics of all our products, Allen is probably our ________ indispensable salesperson.

(A) biggest

(B) least

(C) best

(D) most

Question 2 The government is concerned that due to the economic situation, growth in tax revenues might be ________ than expected.

(A) weak

(B) weakly

(C) weaker

(D) weakens

Question 3 I got a better grade this time because I ________ last time.

(A) tried hard

(B) tried harder

(C) tried harder than

(D) tried hard then

Question 4 Tchernobyl was ________ nuclear accident of all time.

(A) worse

(B) the worse

(C) the bad

(D) the worst

Question 5 We are proud to present this chocolate which is undoubtedly ________in our range.

(A) fine
(B) the finest
(C) finer than
(D) finest

Question 6 I can't hear a word. You need ________.

(A) to speak louder
(B) to speak loudest
(C) to speak more loud
(D) to speak the loudest

Question 7 We are having ________ last year.

(A) the same delivery problems as
(B) more delivery problems as
(C) the most delivery problem as
(D) the same delivery problems than

Question 8 I don't want him working in my team because he is ________ person I know.

(A) more unreliable
(B) the more unreliable
(C) most unreliable
(D) the most unreliable

Question 9 We all agree that the Mona Lisa is ________ painting in the world.

(A) as famous as
(B) more famous than
(C) the most famous
(D) the most famous than

Question 10 Despite the accident, business is ________ usual.

(A) the same than
(B) the same as
(C) best than
(D) the best than

Solutions

ılıl Reportez vos réponses pour analyser votre performance.

⏰ Entraînez-vous dans les conditions d'examen.

prepmyfuture.com/book/68/ex/1960

question 1	D	question 3	C	question 5	B	question 7	A	question 9	C
question 2	C	question 4	D	question 6	A	question 8	D	question 10	B

▪ Question 1 - Solution

Because he really understands the specifics of all our products, Allen is probably our ________ indispensable salesperson.

FR : Car il comprend vraiment les spécificités de tous nos produits, Allen est probablement notre vendeur ________ indispensable.

(A) biggest = plus gros

(B) least = moins

(C) best = meilleur

(D) ✓ most = le plus

▪ Question 2 - Solution

The government is concerned that due to the economic situation, growth in tax revenues might be ________ than expected.

FR : Le gouvernement s'inquiète que, en raison de la situation économique, l'augmentation des recettes fiscales risque d'être ________ que prévu.

(A) weak = faible (adjectif)

(B) weakly = faiblement (adverbe)

(C) ✓ weaker = plus faible (comparatif)

(D) weakens = affaibli (troisième personne du singulier)

▪ Question 3 - Solution

I got a better grade this time because I ________ last time.

FR : J'ai eu une meilleure note cette fois-ci car j'ai ________ la dernière fois.

(A) tried hard

(B) tried harder

(C) ✓ tried harder than

(D) tried hard then

➾ **explication**

FR : *« To try harder »* signifie « se donner plus de mal, travailler plus ».

▪ Question 4 - Solution

Tchernobyl was ________ nuclear accident of all time.

FR : Tchernobyl est ________ accident nucléaire de tous les temps.

(A)	worse	= moins bien
(B)	the worse	= le moins bien
(C)	the bad	= le mauvais
(D)	✓ **the worst**	**= le pire**

▪ Question 5 - Solution

We are proud to present this chocolate which is undoubtedly ________in our range.

FR : Nous sommes fiers de vous présenter ce chocolat qui est à n'en pas douter ________ de notre collection.

(A)	fine	très bien
(B)	✓ **the finest**	**le meilleur**
(C)	finer than	mieux que
(D)	finest	le mieux

▪ Question 6 - Solution

I can't hear a word. You need ________.

FR : Je n'entends pas un mot. Vous devez ________.

(A)	✓ **to speak louder**	**parler plus fort**
(B)	to speak loudest	parler le plus fort (mais *loudest* doit être précédé de *the*)
(C)	to speak more loud	parler plus fort (mais *loud* est un adjectif court, donc il prend *–er* pour former le comparatif).
(D)	to speak the loudest	parler le plus fort (de tous)

▪ Question 7 - Solution

We are having ________ last year.

FR : Nous avons ________ l'année dernière.

(A)	✓ **the same delivery problems as**	**les mêmes problèmes de livraison que**
(B)	more delivery problems as	plus de problèmes de livraison que
(C)	the most delivery problem as	le plus de problèmes de livraison que (une confusion entre les deux structures *'more... than...'*, et *'the same... as...'*)
(D)	the same delivery problems than	les mêmes problèmes de livraison que (une confusion entre les deux structures *'more... than...'*, et *'the same... as...'*)

▪ Question 8 - Solution

I don't want him working in my team because he is ________ person I know.

FR : Je ne veux pas qu'il travaille dans mon équipe car il est ________ personne que je connaisse.

(A)	more unreliable	"moins fiable" *(less reliable = more unreliable)*
(B)	the more unreliable	"il manque plus de sérieux que" (on ne compare pas 2 personnes)
(C)	most unreliable	"il manque plus de sérieux que je connaisse" (le superlatif, mais il doit être précédé par *the*)
(D)	✓ **the most unreliable**	**"c'est la personne la moins fiable que je connaisse"**

▪ Question 9 - Solution

We all agree that the Mona Lisa is ________ painting in the world.

FR : Nous sommes tous d'accord que la Mona Lisa est le tableau ________ au monde.

(A)	as famous as	aussi célèbre que
(B)	more famous than	plus célèbre que
(C)	✓ **the most famous**	**le plus célèbre**
(D)	the most famous than	(le superlatif n'est pas suivi par *than*)

▪ Question 10 - Solution

Despite the accident, business is ________ usual.

FR : Malgré l'accident, le business est ________ d'habitude.

(A)	the same than	le même que
(B)	✓ **the same as**	**le même que**
(C)	best than	une confusion entre *the best* et *better than*
(D)	the best than	une confusion entre *the best* et *better than*)

Épreuves d'expression
Erreurs courantes

PHRASES INTERROGATIVES AVEC DO/DOES/DID

Rappel de cours

DO/DOES/DID + SUJET + INFINITIF

Le **verbe** inclus dans la question est **toujours à l'infinitif**. La marque de la troisième personne du singulier au présent ou la marque du passé se retrouve uniquement dans le DO/DOES/DID.

> Illustration :
>
> On ne dira PAS « *Does he ~~HEARS~~ me?* », mais « *Does he **HEAR** me?* ».
> FR : M'entend-il ?
>
> On ne dira PAS « *Did you ~~WATCHED~~ television?* », mais « *Did he **WATCH** television?* ».
> FR : As-tu regardé la télévision ?

DO, DOES ou DID ?

DO s'utilise au présent avec les sujets suivants : I, you, we, they.

DOES s'utilise au présent avec les sujets suivants : he, she, it.

DID s'utilise au passé avec tous les sujets.

> Exemples :
>
> ***DO** you think you can make it?*
> FR : Penses-tu y arriver ?
>
> ***DOES** it seem likely?*
> FR : Cela semble-t-il probable ?

***DID** they contact you <u>yesterday</u>?*
FR : T'ont-ils contacté hier ?

Entraînement

Reportez vos réponses pour analyser votre performance.
Entraînez-vous dans les conditions d'examen.
prepmyfuture.com/book/68/ex/1963

Question 1 _________ he come to work yesterday? I'm sure I saw him.

(A) Does
(B) Did

Question 2 *Is the following sentence correct?*

Did they walked all the way here?

(A) Yes
(B) No

Question 3 _________ we need to leave now?

(A) Does
(B) Don't

Question 4 _________ they win the football match last week?

(A) Do
(B) Did

Question 5 _________ she leave without saying good-bye last night? But of course she did!

(A) Didn't
(B) Did

Solutions

Reportez vos réponses pour analyser votre performance.

Entraînez-vous dans les conditions d'examen.

prepmyfuture.com/book/68/ex/1963

question 1	B	question 2	B	question 3	B	question 4	B	question 5	A

Question 1 - Solution

________ he come to work yesterday? I'm sure I saw him.

FR : Est-il venu travailler hier ? Je suis certaine de l'avoir vu.

(A) Does

(B) ✓ Did

explication
FR : Le mot *yesterday* (hier) requiert le prétérit. *DID* est l'auxiliaire utilisé au prétérit.

Question 2 - Solution

Is the following sentence correct?

Did they walked all the way here?

FR : La phrase suivante est-elle correcte ? Ont-ils marché jusqu'ici ?

(A) Yes

(B) ✓ No

explication
FR : La marque de la troisième personne du singulier au présent ou la marque du passé se retrouve **uniquement** dans le DO/DOES/DID.

Question 3 - Solution

________ we need to leave now?

FR : N'a-t-on pas besoin de partir maintenant ?

(A) Does

(B) ✓ Don't

explication
FR : *We* est un pronom pluriel, qui exige l'auxiliaire pluriel *DON'T*, la forme raccourcie de *DO NOT*.

Question 4 - Solution

________ they win the football match last week?

FR : Ont-ils gagné le match de football la semaine dernière ?

(A) Do

(B) ✓ Did

⇝ **explication**
FR : *Last week* (la semaine dernière) implique le passé, donc l'auxiliaire *DID* est celui qui est le plus adéquat.

■ Question 5 - Solution

_________ she leave without saying good-bye last night? But of course she did!

FR : N'est-elle pas partie sans dire au revoir hier ? Mais si, elle l'a fait !

(A) ✓ Didn't

(B) Did

⇝ **explication**
FR : La deuxième phrase « *But of course she did!* » signifie « Mais si, elle l'a fait ». Ceci implique que la phrase interrogative doit être au négatif : *DIDN'T SHE*.

WHEN

Rappel de cours

Cette fiche se concentre sur le **temps du verbe** situé dans la proposition suivant directement la conjonction ***when***.

WHEN + FUTUR N'EXISTE PAS

La conjonction *when* ne peut **jamais** être suivie par un verbe conjugué **au futur**.

Illustration :

On ne dira PAS « *When you ~~WILL GET~~ home, you will do the dishes* », mais « *When you **GET** home, you will do the dishes* »
FR : Quand tu arriveras à la maison, tu feras la vaisselle.

WHEN + PRÉSENT SIMPLE

La conjonction *when* est le plus souvent suivie par un verbe au **présent simple**. La phrase exprime alors la **simultanéité**.

Exemples :

*I want to be a teacher when I **am** older.*
FR : Je veux être professeur quand je serai grand.

*We will have dinner when I **arrive** home.*
FR : Nous dînerons quand j'arriverai à la maison.

⇒ Les deux actions se déroulent simultanément.

POUR ALLER PLUS LOIN

La conjonction *when* peut parfois être suivie par un verbe au ***present perfect***. La phrase parle alors d'**actions successives**. Cette utilisation est plus rare et la différence est subtile. Elle ne deviendra utile que lorsque vous aurez atteint un niveau de langue avancé.

Exemples :

*I will move in after I **have graduated**.*
FR : J'emménagerai quand j'aurai obtenu mon diplôme.

⇒ La seconde action doit être accomplie et révolue avant que la première proposition ne puisse être réalisée.

Entraînement

Reportez vos réponses pour analyser votre performance.

Entraînez-vous dans les conditions d'examen.

prepmyfuture.com/book/68/ex/1964

Question 1 Let me know when you ________ ready to eat.

(A) are
(B) will be

Question 2 Will you come and visit me when I ________ to France next year?

(A) come
(B) will come

Question 3 Submit your bank details when ________ the registration process.

(A) you completed
(B) you've completed

Question 4 We'll call you when we ________ the estimate.

(A) have received
(B) will receive

■ **Question 5** If all goes well, when the train ________ at the station, ________ there waiting for you.

(A) arrives / we'll be there

(B) has arrived / we were there

Solutions

Reportez vos réponses pour analyser votre performance.

Entraînez-vous dans les conditions d'examen.

prepmyfuture.com/book/68/ex/1964

question 1	A	question 2	A	question 3	B	question 4	A	question 5	A

Question 1 - Solution

Let me know when you ________ ready to eat.

FR : Dis-moi quand tu seras prête à manger.

(A) ✓ are

(B) will be

explication

FR : *When* est suivi du présent simple dans la proposition subordonnée, si la proposition principale est au futur en anglais.

Question 2 - Solution

Will you come and visit me when I ________ to France next year?

FR : Viendras-tu me rendre visite quand tu seras en France l'année prochaine ?

(A) ✓ come

(B) will come

explication

FR : *When* est suivi du présent simple dans la proposition subordonnée, si la proposition principale est au futur en anglais.

Question 3 - Solution

Submit your bank details when ________ the registration process.

FR : Soumettez vos coordonnées bancaires lorsque vous aurez complété votre inscription.

(A) you completed

(B) ✓ you've completed

explication

FR : *When* peut être suivi du *present perfect* dans la proposition subordonnée, si la proposition principale est au présent.

Dans ce cas, il s'agit de **deux actions consécutives**. La première action est au *present perfect*, et la seconde à l'impératif.

▪ Question 4 - Solution

We'll call you when we ________ the estimate.

FR : On vous appellera lorsqu'on aura reçu le devis.

(A) ✓ **have received**

(B) will receive

⟹ **explication**

FR : *When* peut être suivi du *present perfect* dans la proposition subordonnée, si la proposition principale est au présent.

Dans ce cas, il s'agit de **deux actions consécutives**. La première action est rendue au *present perfect*, et la seconde au présent simple.

▪ Question 5 - Solution

If all goes well, when the train ________ at the station, ________ there waiting for you.

FR : Si tout va bien, lorsque le train arrivera en gare, il y aura quelqu'un en train de vous attendre.

(A) ✓ **arrives / we'll be there**

(B) has arrived / we were there

⟹ **explication**

FR : Cette phrase contient deux propositions subordonnées: *« If all goes well »* + *« when the train arrives »*. Ces deux propositions doivent être au même temps verbal, car elles impliquent toutes les deux le même type d'action. Elles sont donc toutes les deux au présent simple.

La proposition subordonnée qui commence par *when* n'est jamais suivi du futur. Il faut utiliser le présent simple.

THE MAJORITY OF

Rappel de cours

Cette expression veut dire « **plus de 50 %** ». Elle est souvent utilisée pour parler d'enquêtes, de sondages ou de résultats d'élections.

The majority of + dénombrable pluriel + verbe au pluriel

Cette expression est utilisée la plupart du temps avant un nom **dénombrable au pluriel**. Le verbe s'accorde avec le nom, qui est le sujet de la phrase, et est donc au pluriel aussi.

Exemple (le nom qui détermine la conjugaison est souligné) :

The vast majority of *our cheeses are made with pasteurised milk.*
FR : La vaste majorité de nos fromages sont fabriqués à partir de lait pasteurisé.

The majority of + indénombrable + verbe au singulier

Cette expression peut aussi être utilisée avant un nom **indénombrable**. Le verbe s'accorde avec le nom, qui est le sujet de la phrase, et est donc au **singulier**.

Exemple (le nom qui détermine la conjugaison est souligné) :

The majority of *the wine is from Argentina.*
FR : La majorité du vin provient d'Argentine.

Astuce

Commencez toujours par regarder le nom que vous utilisez :

Cas numéro 1 : c'est un nom **dénombrable**.
⇒ vous savez alors que vous devez mettre le nom au pluriel et conjuguer le verbe en conséquence.

Cas numéro 2 : c'est un **indénombrable**.
⇒ vous savez que le nom sera au singulier, et donc le verbe aussi.

Entraînement

Reportez vos réponses pour analyser votre performance.

Entraînez-vous dans les conditions d'examen.

prepmyfuture.com/book/68/ex/1965

Question 1 The overwhelming majority of people of African and Asian descent ________ brown eyes, but on rare occasions, they can indeed have blue eyes.

(A) have

(B) has

Question 2 The majority of politicians, on the evidence available to us, ________ interested not in truth but in power and maintenance of that power.

(A) are

(B) is

Question 3 The majority of the rocket fuel ________ used in this acceleration phase.

(A) are

(B) is

Question 4 As at the 2018 census, the majority of New Zealand's population ________ of European descent (70 percent), with the indigenous Māori being the largest minority (16.5 percent).

(A) is

(B) are

Question 5 In both sexes, the majority of time ________ spent sedentary, and the least time was spent in moderate and vigorous physical activity.

(A) were

(B) was

Solutions

Reportez vos réponses pour analyser votre performance.

Entraînez-vous dans les conditions d'examen.

prepmyfuture.com/book/68/ex/1965

question 1	A	question 2	A	question 3	B	question 4	A	question 5	B

Question 1 - Solution

The overwhelming majority of people of African and Asian descent ________ brown eyes, but on rare occasions, they can indeed have blue eyes.

FR : L'écrasante majorité des personnes d'origine africaine et asiatique ________ les yeux bruns, mais dans de rares cas, elles peuvent avoir les yeux bleus.

(A) ✓ have = ont

(B) has = a
Le sujet people est au pluriel, le verbe ne peut donc pas être au singulier.

explication
FR : Le verbe s'accorde avec le nom, qui est le sujet de la phrase.

Question 2 - Solution

The majority of politicians, on the evidence available to us, ________ interested not in truth but in power and maintenance of that power.

FR : La majorité des politiciens, d'après les preuves dont nous disposons, ne ________ pas intéressés par la vérité mais par le pouvoir et le maintien de ce pouvoir.

(A) ✓ are = sont

(B) is = est
Le sujet politicians est au pluriel, le verbe ne peut donc pas être au singulier.

explication
FR : Le verbe s'accorde avec le nom, qui est le sujet de la phrase.

Question 3 - Solution

The majority of the rocket fuel ________ used in this acceleration phase.

FR : La majeure partie du carburant de la fusée ________ utilisée dans cette phase d'accélération.

(A) are = sont
Le sujet rocket fuel est au singulier, donc la bonne réponse ne peut pas être le pluriel du verbe.

(B) ✓ is = est

explication
FR : Le verbe s'accorde avec le nom, qui est le sujet de la phrase.

▪ Question 4 - Solution

As at the 2018 census, the majority of New Zealand's population ________ of European descent (70 percent), with the indigenous Māori being the largest minority (16.5 percent).

FR : Au recensement de 2018, la majorité de la population néo-zélandaise ________ d'origine européenne (70 %), les autochtones Maori constituant la principale minorité (16,5 %).

(A) ✓ is = est

(B) are = sont
Le sujet population est au singulier. La réponse ne peut pas être la forme plurielle du verbe.

⇒ **explication**
FR : Le verbe s'accorde avec le nom, qui est le sujet de la phrase.

▪ Question 5 - Solution

In both sexes, the majority of time ________ spent sedentary, and the least time was spent in moderate and vigorous physical activity.

FR : Chez les deux sexes, la majorité du temps ________ consacrée à la sédentarité, et le moins de temps était consacré à une activité physique modérée ou vigoureuse.

(A) were = étaient
Le sujet time est au singulier, donc la bonne réponse ne peut pas être le pluriel du verbe.

(B) ✓ was = était

⇒ **explication**
FR : Le verbe s'accorde avec le nom, qui est le sujet de la phrase.

A LOT OF / LOTS OF

Rappel de cours

Ces expressions sont utilisées en anglais **informel**. Elles signifient **« une grande quantité de »** ou « **un grand nombre de** ». *Lots of* est plus informel que *a lot of*.

A lot of/Lots of + dénombrable pluriel + verbe au pluriel

Ces expressions peuvent être utilisées avant un nom **dénombrable au pluriel**. Le verbe s'accorde avec le nom, qui est le sujet de la phrase, et est donc au pluriel aussi.

Exemples (le nom qui détermine la conjugaison est souligné) :

A lot of *my friends live abroad.*
FR : Beaucoup de mes amis vivent à l'étranger.

Lots of *my clothes are blue.*
FR : J'ai plein de vêtements qui sont bleus.

A lot of/Lots of + indénombrable + verbe au singulier

Ces expressions peuvent aussi être utilisées avant un nom **indénombrable**. Le verbe s'accorde avec le nom, qui est le sujet de la phrase, et est donc au **singulier**.

Exemples (le nom qui détermine la conjugaison est souligné) :

A lot of *my family lives in England.*
FR : Une grande partie de ma famille vit en Angleterre.

There is ***lots of*** *tea left in the pot.*
FR : Il y a encore plein de thé dans la théière.

Astuce

Commencez toujours par regarder le nom que vous utilisez :

Cas numéro 1 : c'est un nom **dénombrable**.
⇒ vous savez alors que vous devez mettre le nom au pluriel et conjuguer le verbe en conséquence.

Cas numéro 2 : c'est un **indénombrable**.
⇒ vous savez que le nom sera au singulier, et donc le verbe aussi.

Entraînement

Reportez vos réponses pour analyser votre performance.

Entraînez-vous dans les conditions d'examen.

prepmyfuture.com/book/68/ex/1966

Question 1 Lots of people in the world ________ English.

(A) speaks
(B) speak

Question 2 There ________ a lot of cars on the roads today.

(A) are
(B) is

Question 3 A lot of fruits ________ a high amount of sugar.

(A) contain
(B) contains

Question 4 ________ there a lot of people at the football match yesterday?

(A) Were
(B) Was

Question 5 A lot of water ________ wasted when you have a bath.

(A) are
(B) is

Solutions

Reportez vos réponses pour analyser votre performance.

Entraînez-vous dans les conditions d'examen.

prepmyfuture.com/book/68/ex/1966

question 1	B	question 2	A	question 3	A	question 4	A	question 5	B

■ Question 1 - Solution

Lots of people in the world ________ English.

FR : Beaucoup de personnes dans le monde ________ anglais.

(A) speaks = parle

People est un nom pluriel. Le verbe to speak ne peut donc pas être à la 3e personne du singulier.

(B) ✓ speak = parlent

explication

FR : Si *a lot of / lots of* précèdent un sujet pluriel, le verbe est au pluriel. Si ces expressions précèdent un nom singulier, le verbe est au singulier.

■ Question 2 - Solution

There ________ a lot of cars on the roads today.

FR : Il y a beaucoup de voitures sur la route aujourd'hui.

(A) ✓ are = il y a + pluriel

(B) is = il y a + singulier

Le sujet cars est au pluriel. Le verbe to be ne peut donc pas être conjugué au singulier.

explication

FR : Quand *a lot of / lots of* précèdent un sujet pluriel, le verbe est au pluriel. Si ces expressions précèdent un nom singulier, le verbe est au singulier.

■ Question 3 - Solution

A lot of fruits ________ a high amount of sugar.

FR : Beaucoup de fruits ________ une grande quantité de sucre.

(A) ✓ contain = contiennent

(B) contains = contient

Le sujet fruits est au pluriel. Le verbe to contain ne peut donc pas être conjugué au singulier.

explication

FR : Quand *a lot of / lots of* précèdent un sujet pluriel, le verbe est au pluriel. Si ces expressions précèdent un nom singulier, le verbe est au singulier.

▪ Question 4 - Solution

________ there a lot of people at the football match yesterday?

FR : Est-ce qu'il y avait beaucoup de monde au match de foot hier ?

(A) ✓ Were = il y avait + pluriel

(B) Was = il y avait + singulier
Le sujet people est pluriel. Le verbe to be ne peut donc pas être conjugué au singulier.

⤳ **explication**
FR : Quand *a lot of / lots of* précèdent un sujet pluriel, le verbe est au pluriel. Si ces expressions précèdent un nom singulier, le verbe est au singulier.

▪ Question 5 - Solution

A lot of water ________ wasted when you have a bath.

FR : Beaucoup d'eau ________ gaspillée losqu'on prend un bain.

(A) are = sont
Le sujet water est singulier et indénombrable. Le verbe to be ne peut donc pas être au pluriel.

(B) ✓ is = est

⤳ **explication**
FR : Quand *a lot of / lots of* précèdent un sujet pluriel, le verbe est au pluriel. Si ces expressions précèdent un nom singulier, le verbe est au singulier.

PLENTY OF

Rappel de cours

Plenty of signifie **« en grand nombre »** d'un nom. Cette expression s'emploie dans une **phrase affirmative**.

Plenty of + dénombrable pluriel + verbe au pluriel

Cette expression peut être utilisée avant un nom **dénombrable au pluriel**. Le verbe s'accorde avec le nom, qui est le sujet de la phrase, et est donc au pluriel aussi.

Exemple (le nom qui détermine la conjugaison est souligné) :

Plenty of *jobs are available, but no one wants them, because they're so poorly paid.*
FR : Beaucoup d'emplois sont disponibles mais personne n'en veut parce qu'ils sont tellement mal payés.

Plenty of + indénombrable + verbe au singulier

Cette expression peut aussi être utilisée avant un nom **indénombrable**. Le verbe s'accorde avec le nom, qui est le sujet de la phrase, et est donc au **singulier**.

Exemple (le nom qui détermine la conjugaison est souligné) :

There is ***plenty of*** *toner left in this cartridge.*
FR : Il y a encore largement assez de toner dans cette cartouche.

Astuce

Commencez toujours par regarder le nom que vous utilisez :

Cas numéro 1 : c'est un nom **dénombrable**.
⇒ vous savez alors que vous devez mettre le nom au pluriel et conjuguer le verbe en conséquence.

Cas numéro 2 : c'est un **indénombrable**.
⇒ vous savez que le nom sera au singulier, et donc le verbe aussi.

Entraînement

Reportez vos réponses pour analyser votre performance.

Entraînez-vous dans les conditions d'examen.

prepmyfuture.com/book/68/ex/1967

Question 1 There ________ plenty of other fish in the sea.

(A) is

(B) are

Question 2 There ________ still plenty of time before the train leaves.

(A) is

(B) are

Question 3 There ________ still plenty of room for improvement.

(A) is

(B) are

Question 4 Plenty of satisfied customers ________ written to Booking.com and given a five star rating.

(A) has

(B) have

Question 5 If plenty of fruits and vegetables ________ included in your diet, you should stay healthy.

(A) are

(B) is

Solutions

Reportez vos réponses pour analyser votre performance.

Entraînez-vous dans les conditions d'examen.

prepmyfuture.com/book/68/ex/1967

question 1	B	question 2	A	question 3	A	question 4	B	question 5	A

Question 1 - Solution

There _________ plenty of other fish in the sea.

FR : Il y a beaucoup d'autres poissons dans la mer.

(A) is = il y a + singulier
Le sujet fish est pluriel. Le verbe to be ne peut donc pas être conjugué au singulier.

(B) ✓ are = il y a + pluriel

explication
FR : Si *plenty of* précède un sujet pluriel, le verbe est pluriel.

Question 2 - Solution

There _________ still plenty of time before the train leaves.

FR : Il y a encore largement le temps avant que le train ne parte.

(A) ✓ is = il y a + singulier

(B) are = il y a + pluriel
Le sujet time est singulier, le verbe ne peut donc pas être au pluriel.

explication
FR : Si cette expression précède un sujet singulier, le verbe est singulier.

Question 3 - Solution

There _________ still plenty of room for improvement.

FR : Il y a encore des axes d'amélioration.

(A) ✓ is = il y a + singulier

(B) are = il y a + pluriel
Le sujet room est singulier, le verbe ne peut donc pas être au pluriel.

explication
FR : Si cette expression précède un sujet singulier, le verbe est singulier.

Question 4 - Solution

Plenty of satisfied customers _________ written to Booking.com and given a five star rating.

FR : Énormément de clients satisfaits _________ écrit à Booking.com et ont donné une note 5 étoiles.

(A) has = a
Le sujet customers est pluriel. Le verbe ne peut donc pas être conjugué au singulier.

(B) ✓ have = ont

⇨ **explication**
FR : Si *plenty of* précède un sujet pluriel, le verbe est pluriel.

▪ Question 5 - Solution

If plenty of fruits and vegetables ________ included in your diet, you should stay healthy.

FR : Si plus qu'assez de fruits et légumes ________ inclus dons votre régime alimentaire, vous devriez rester en bonne santé.

(A) ✓ are = sont

(B) is = est
Le sujet fruits and vegetables est pluriel. Le verbe ne peut donc pas être conjugué au singulier.

⇨ **explication**
FR : Si *plenty of* précède un sujet pluriel, le verbe est pluriel.

A COUPLE OF

Rappel de cours

A couple of est une façon informelle de dire **« deux ou plus »** ou « **quelques** ». Cette expression est utilisée avant une **phrase affirmative**.

A couple of + nom dénombrable pluriel

Cette expression peut seulement précéder un nom **dénombrable** et uniquement au **pluriel**.

Exemple :

I've only known her for ***a couple of*** *weeks.*
FR : Je ne la connais que depuis quelques semaines.

A couple of + verbe au pluriel

A couple of précède uniquement un sujet pluriel et **le verbe est au pluriel**.

Exemples :

A couple of *years* *<u>have</u>* *gone by since the last film in the* Fifty Shades *trilogy.*
FR : Quelques années ont passé depuis le dernier film dans la trilogie *Cinquante Nuances*.

There *<u>are</u>* ***a couple of*** *beers left in the fridge if you want one.*
FR : Il y a encore quelques bières dans le frigo si tu en veux une.

Entraînement

Reportez vos réponses pour analyser votre performance.

Entraînez-vous dans les conditions d'examen.

prepmyfuture.com/book/68/ex/1968

Question 1 Here ________ a couple of examples of eight syllable words.

(A) are

(B) is

Question 2 If you are hosting an event, there ________ a couple of things you can do to ensure it is safe and fun for all guests.

(A) is

(B) are

Question 3 Here ________ a couple of things that you can do or use as basic ideas on e-campaigning.

(A) are

(B) is

Question 4 A couple of shocks to the marketing system ________ occurred in the past few weeks.

(A) has

(B) have

Question 5 Greene highlighted how she and "a couple of my colleagues" on the House Freedom Caucus ________ able to reduce 28 suspension bills on Congress' docket down to just five.

(A) was

(B) were

Solutions

Reportez vos réponses pour analyser votre performance.

Entraînez-vous dans les conditions d'examen.

prepmyfuture.com/book/68/ex/1968

question 1	A	question 2	B	question 3	A	question 4	B	question 5	B

Question 1 - Solution

Here ________ a couple of examples of eight syllable words.

FR : Ici, ________ quelques exemples de mots à huit syllabes.

(A) ✓ are = voici + pluriel

(B) is = voici + singulier
Is est la troisième personne du singulier du verbe to be. Le verbe doit s'accorder avec le sujet pluriel donc ce n'est pas la bonne réponse.

explication
FR : Cette expression peut seulement précéder un nom dénombrable au pluriel.

Question 2 - Solution

If you are hosting an event, there ________ a couple of things you can do to ensure it is safe and fun for all guests

FR : Si vous organisez un événement, il y a quelques mesures que vous pouvez prendre pour vous assurer qu'il est à la fois sécurisé et amusant pour tous les invités.

(A) is = il y a + singulier
Is est la troisième personne du singulier du verbe to be. Le verbe doit s'accorder avec le sujet pluriel donc ce n'est pas la bonne réponse.

(B) ✓ are = il y a + pluriel

explication
FR : Cette expression peut seulement précéder un nom dénombrable au pluriel.

Question 3 - Solution

Here ________ a couple of things that you can do or use as basic ideas on e-campaigning.

FR : Voici deux ou trois choses que vous pouvez faire ou utiliser comme idées de base sur l'e-campagne.

(A) ✓ are = voici + pluriel

(B) is = voici + singulier
Is est la troisième personne du singulier du verbe to be. Le verbe doit s'accorder avec le sujet pluriel donc ce n'est pas la bonne réponse.

explication
FR : Cette expression peut seulement précéder un nom dénombrable au pluriel.

▪ Question 4 - Solution

A couple of shocks to the marketing system ________ occurred in the past few weeks.

FR : Le système de commercialisation a subi quelques chocs au cours des dernières semaines.

(A) has = a
Has est la troisième personne du singulier du verbe to have. Le verbe doit s'accorder avec le sujet pluriel donc ce n'est pas la bonne réponse.

(B) ✓ have = ont

⇒ **explication**
FR : Cette expression peut seulement précéder un nom dénombrable au pluriel.

▪ Question 5 - Solution

Greene highlighted how she and "a couple of my colleagues" on the House Freedom Caucus ________ able to reduce 28 suspension bills on Congress' docket down to just five.

FR : Mme Greene a souligné comment elle et « deux de mes collègues » du House Freedom Caucus ________ pu réduire à cinq seulement les 28 projets de loi de suspension inscrits au programme du Congrès.

(A) was = avait
Was est le singulier du prétérit du verbe to be, ce n'est donc pas la bonne réponse.

(B) ✓ were = avaient

⇒ **explication**
FR : Cette expression peut seulement précéder un nom dénombrable au pluriel.

A GREAT DEAL OF / A LARGE AMOUNT OF

Rappel de cours

A great deal of/A large amount of = formel

A great deal of et *a large amount of* sont utilisés pour dire **« une grande quantité de »**. Ce sont des expressions plutôt **formelles**.

Exemples :

I told my boss I was under ***a great deal of*** *stress.* (formel)
⇒ *I told my boss I was under a lot of stress.* (moins formel)
FR : J'ai dit à mon patron que je ressentais beaucoup de stress.

When my mother passed, I inherited ***a large amount of*** *money.* (formel)
⇒ *When my mum died, I inherited lots of money.* (moins formel)
FR : Quand ma mère est décédée, j'ai hérité d'une grande somme d'argent.

A great deal of/A large amount of + indénombrable + verbe au singulier

Ces expressions ne peuvent être utilisées que devant un nom **indénombrable** et donc uniquement **au singulier**.

Exemples :

A great deal of *research has been done already.*
FR : De nombreuses recherches ont déjà été effectuées.

There is also, inevitably, ***a large amount of*** *overlap between articles.*
FR : Il y a aussi, inévitablement, un grand nombre de chevauchements entre les articles.

Entraînement

Reportez vos réponses pour analyser votre performance.

Entraînez-vous dans les conditions d'examen.

prepmyfuture.com/book/68/ex/1969

Question 1 Even with the damper closed, a great deal of heat still ________ up the chimney.

(A) escape

(B) escapes

Question 2 A great deal of time ________ spent on the project.

(A) was

(B) were

Question 3 The man listened quietly to the end, and said at the corner where we parted: "And yet there ________ a great deal of money made here, good morning, sir."

(A) are

(B) is

Question 4 A large amount of money ________ invested for me for my retirement.

(A) was

(B) were

Question 5 A great deal of effort ________ gone into making the software reliable.

(A) have

(B) has

Solutions

Reportez vos réponses pour analyser votre performance.

Entraînez-vous dans les conditions d'examen.

prepmyfuture.com/book/68/ex/1969

question 1	B	question 2	A	question 3	B	question 4	A	question 5	B

Question 1 - Solution

Even with the damper closed, a great deal of heat still ________ up the chimney.

FR : Même lorsque le clapet est fermé, une grande partie de la chaleur ________ par la cheminée.

(A) escape = s'échappent
Le sujet heat est au singulier. La réponse ne peut pas être le pluriel du verbe.

(B) ✓ escapes = s'échappe

explication
FR : Cette expression ne peut être utilisée que devant un nom indénombrable et donc singulier. Le verbe s'accorde avec le sujet (le nom).

Question 2 - Solution

A great deal of time ________ spent on the project.

FR : Beaucoup de temps ________ consacré à ce projet.

(A) ✓ was = a été

(B) were = ont été
Le sujet time est au singulier. La réponse ne peut pas être le pluriel du verbe.

explication
FR : Cette expression ne peut être utilisée que devant un nom indénombrable et donc singulier. Le verbe s'accorde avec le sujet (le nom).

Question 3 - Solution

The man listened quietly to the end, and said at the corner where we parted: "And yet there ________ a great deal of money made here, good morning, sir."

FR : L'homme écouta tranquillement jusqu'au bout, et dit au coin de la rue où nous nous séparâmes : « Et pourtant, ils ont fait beaucoup d'argent ici, bonne journée, monsieur. »

(A) are = il y a + pluriel
Le sujet money est au singulier. La réponse ne peut pas être le pluriel du verbe.

(B) ✓ is = il y a + singulier

explication
FR : Cette expression ne peut être utilisée que devant un nom indénombrable et donc singulier. Le verbe s'accorde avec le sujet (le nom).

▪ Question 4 - Solution

A large amount of money _________ invested for me for my retirement.

FR : Une grosse somme d'argent _________ investie pour moi en vue de ma retraite.

(A) ✓ was = a été

(B) were = ont été
Le sujet money est au singulier. La réponse ne peut pas être le pluriel du verbe.

⇨ **explication**
FR : Cette expression ne peut être utilisée que devant un nom indénombrable et donc singulier. Le verbe s'accorde avec le sujet (le nom).

▪ Question 5 - Solution

A great deal of effort _________ gone into making the software reliable.

FR : De nombreux efforts _________ consentis pour rendre le logiciel fiable.

(A) have = ont
Le sujet effort est au singulier. La réponse ne peut pas être le pluriel du verbe.

(B) ✓ has = a

⇨ **explication**
FR : Cette expression ne peut être utilisée que devant un nom indénombrable et donc singulier. Le verbe s'accorde avec le sujet (le nom).

SEVERAL

Rappel de cours

Several signifie **plusieurs**, **différents**. Cette expression s'utilise dans les phrases **affirmatives**.

Several + dénombrable pluriel

Cette expression ne s'utilise qu'avec des noms **dénombrables** au **pluriel**.

Exemples :

I decided to start exercising more ***several*** *weeks ago. It hasn't been very successful so far…*
FR : J'ai décidé de commencer à faire du sport il y a plusieurs semaines. Je n'ai pas encore réussi…

I tried ***several*** *local dishes when I visited Nigeria. They were so good!*
FR : J'ai essayé différents plats locaux quand j'ai visité le Nigéria. Ils étaient tellement bons !

Several + verbe au pluriel

Several ne peut être suivi que d'un nom pluriel qui, quand il est sujet de la phrase, implique que **le verbe sera lui aussi conjugué au pluriel**.

Exemples :

Several *stores have closed in the past year.*
FR : Plusieurs magasins ont fermé cette année.

There are ***several*** *expired yogurts in the fridge.*
FR : Il y a plusieurs yaourts périmés dans le frigo.

Pour aller plus loin

Lorsque l'on utilise *several* pour parler d'une **partie ou d'une fraction d'un groupe**, il est nécessaire d'y ajouter *of* ⇒ ***several of***.

Exemples :

***Several of** my friends have already told me they wouldn't be able to make it to the party.*
FR : Plusieurs de mes amis m'ont déjà dit qu'ils ne pourraient pas venir à la fête.

*A friend of mine ate here last week and she told me that **several of** the customers returned their dish.*
FR : Une de mes amis a mangé ici la semaine dernière et elle m'a dit que plusieurs clients avaient renvoyé leurs plats.

Entraînement

Reportez vos réponses pour analyser votre performance.

Entraînez-vous dans les conditions d'examen.

prepmyfuture.com/book/68/ex/1970

Question 1 There were several ________ of sun last autumn.

(A) day

(B) days

Question 2 Several days ________ since the accident.

(A) have gone by

(B) has gone by

Question 3 I cannot believe several people ________ in this tiny house.

(A) live

(B) lives

Question 4 I take care of several ________ on a daily basis.

(A) kid

(B) children

Question 5 ________ the colleagues I work with are off today.

(A) Several of

(B) Several

Solutions

Reportez vos réponses pour analyser votre performance.

Entraînez-vous dans les conditions d'examen.

prepmyfuture.com/book/68/ex/1970

question 1	B	question 2	A	question 3	A	question 4	B	question 5	A

Question 1 - Solution

There were several _________ of sun last autumn.

FR : Il y a eu quelques _________ ensoleillés l'automne dernier.

(A) day = jour
Day est au singulier ici. Cela ne fonctionne pas après several.

(B) ✓ days = jours

explication
FR : *Several* ne s'utilise qu'avec des noms dénombrables au pluriel.

Question 2 - Solution

Several days _________ since the accident.

FR : Plusieurs jours _________ depuis l'accident.

(A) ✓ have gone by = sont passés

(B) has gone by = est passé
Has est la conjugaison du verbe to have au singulier. Cela ne peut pas être utilisé dans une phrase après l'utilisation de several.

explication
FR : *Several* ne peut être suivi que d'un nom pluriel qui, quand il est sujet de la phrase, implique que le verbe sera conjugué au pluriel.

Question 3 - Solution

I cannot believe several people _________ in this tiny house.

FR : Je ne peux pas croire que plusieurs personnes _________ dans cette petite maison.

(A) ✓ live = vivent

(B) lives = vive
Lives est la conjugaison du verbe to live au singulier. Cela ne peut pas être utilisé dans une phrase après l'utilisation de several.

explication
FR : *Several* ne peut être suivi que d'un nom pluriel qui, quand il est sujet de la phrase, implique que le verbe sera conjugué au pluriel.

■ **Question 4 - Solution**

I take care of several ________ on a daily basis.

FR : Je m'occupe de plusieurs ________ quotidiennement.

(A) kid = enfant
Kid est au singulier ici. Cela ne fonctionne pas après several.

(B) ✓ children = enfants

⇒ **explication**
FR : *Several* ne s'utilise qu'avec des noms dénombrables au pluriel.

■ **Question 5 - Solution**

________ the colleagues I work with are off today.

FR : ________ collègues avec qui je travaille sont en congé aujourd'hui.

(A) ✓ Several of = Plusieurs des

(B) Several = Plusieurs

⇒ **explication**
FR : Lorsque l'on utilise *several* pour parler d'une partie ou d'une fraction d'un groupe, il est nécessaire d'y ajouter *of* ⇒ *several of.*

MANY / MUCH

Rappel de cours

Many

Many est un adjectif utilisé pour exprimer une quantité avec les noms **dénombrables**. Il signifie qu'il y a une grande quantité de ces objets/sujets.

> Exemples :
>
> *I have **many** friends.*
> FR : J'ai de nombreux amis.
>
> ***Many** people would like to travel abroad this summer.*
> FR : Beaucoup de personnes voudraient partir à l'étranger cet été.

Much

Much est un adjectif utilisé pour exprimer une quantité avec les noms **indénombrables**. Il signifie « beaucoup de ».

> Exemples :
>
> *I don't have **much** money left… I am really looking forward to my next paycheck.*
> FR : Il ne me reste pas beaucoup d'argent… J'ai vraiment hâte de recevoir mon prochain salaire.
>
> ***Much** strength is needed to lift this bed frame.*
> FR : Beaucoup de force est nécessaire pour soulever ce sommier.

Astuce pour les différencier

Ces deux mots peuvent être source de nombreux malentendus, donc pour différencier les deux, rappelez-vous que :

⇒ *Many* est utilisé avec les noms **dénombrables** tels que des objets et des personnes, alors que *much* est utilisé avec les noms **indénombrables**. **Si vous pouvez remplacer l'adjectif par un nombre**, vous devrez alors utiliser *many*, sinon vous devrez utiliser *much*.

Exemples :

***Many** people showed up.* ⇒ ***Five** people showed up.*
La phrase a du sens = on utilise *many*.
FR : Beaucoup de personnes sont venues.

*I don't feel **much** joy when winning.* ⇒ *I don't feel **four** joy when winning.*
La phrase n'a pas de sens = on utilise *much*.
FR : Je ne ressens pas beaucoup de joie quand je gagne.

Entraînement

Reportez vos réponses pour analyser votre performance.
Entraînez-vous dans les conditions d'examen.
prepmyfuture.com/book/68/ex/1971

Question 1 I don't have ________ time to talk to you.

(A) many
(B) much

Question 2 ________ people have attended my webinar.

(A) Many
(B) Much

Question 3 How ________ food do you need to buy?

(A) many
(B) much

Question 4 I am just under too ________ stress at the moment, I need a break.

(A) many
(B) much

Question 5 You are in so ________ trouble, young boy!

(A) many
(B) much

Solutions

Reportez vos réponses pour analyser votre performance.

Entraînez-vous dans les conditions d'examen.

prepmyfuture.com/book/68/ex/1971

question 1	B	question 2	A	question 3	B	question 4	B	question 5	B

Question 1 - Solution

I don't have ________ time to talk to you.

FR : Je n'ai pas ________ temps pour te parler

(A) many = beaucoup de + dénombrable
Ici, time est un nom indénombrable. On ne peut donc pas utiliser many.

(B) ✓ much = beaucoup de + indénombrable

explication
FR : *Many* est un adjectif utilisé pour exprimer une quantité avec les noms dénombrables. *Much* est un adjectif utilisé pour exprimer une quantité avec les noms indénombrables.

Question 2 - Solution

________ people have attended my webinar.

FR : ________ personnes ont assisté à mon webinaire.

(A) ✓ Many = De nombreuses + dénombrable

(B) Much = De nombreuses + indénombrable
Ici, people est un nom dénombrable. On ne peut donc pas utiliser much.

explication
FR : *Many* est un adjectif utilisé pour exprimer une quantité avec les noms dénombrables. *Much* est un adjectif utilisé pour exprimer une quantité avec les noms indénombrables.

Question 3 - Solution

How ________ food do you need to buy?

FR : ________ nourriture as-tu besoin d'acheter ?

(A) many = Combien de + dénombrable
Ici, food est un nom indénombrable. On ne peut donc pas utiliser many.

(B) ✓ much = Combien de + indénombrable

explication
FR : *Many* est un adjectif utilisé pour exprimer une quantité avec les noms dénombrables. *Much* est un adjectif utilisé pour exprimer une quantité avec les noms indénombrables.

▪ Question 4 - Solution

I am just under too ________ stress at the moment, I need a break.

FR : Je ressens simplement ________ pression en ce moment. Il faut que je fasse une pause.

(A) many = trop de + dénombrable
Ici, stress est un nom indénombrable. On ne peut donc pas utiliser many.

(B) ✓ much = trop de + indénombrable

⇒ **explication**
FR : *Many* est un adjectif utilisé pour exprimer une quantité avec les noms dénombrables. *Much* est un adjectif utilisé pour exprimer une quantité avec les noms indénombrables.

▪ Question 5 - Solution

You are in so ________ trouble, young boy!

FR : Tu vas avoir ________ ennuis, jeune homme !

(A) many = beaucoup d' + dénombrable
Ici, trouble est un nom indénombrable. On ne peut donc pas utiliser many.

(B) ✓ much = beaucoup d' + indénombrable

⇒ **explication**
FR : *Many* est un adjectif utilisé pour exprimer une quantité avec les noms dénombrables. *Much* est un adjectif utilisé pour exprimer une quantité avec les noms indénombrables.

EVERY DAY VS EVERYDAY

Rappel de cours

Les mots **everyday** et **every day** sont facilement et couramment confondus en anglais, même par les locuteurs natifs. La meilleure façon de comprendre la différence entre ces deux mots est de regarder quelle fonction ils remplissent dans la phrase. **S'agit-il d'adjectifs, de noms, d'adverbes, etc. ?**

Everyday

Everyday, lorsqu'il est utilisé en un seul mot, est un adjectif qui signifie quotidien, banal, habituel ou adapté aux jours ordinaires. Comme il s'agit d'un adjectif, il modifie un nom dans une phrase, vous devez donc vous attendre à ce qu'il apparaisse près d'un nom.

Exemples (le nom modifié est souligné) :

These shoes are great for ***everyday*** *<u>use</u>.*
FR : Ces chaussures sont parfaites pour un usage quotidien.

Don't use <u>the</u> ***everyday*** *<u>dishes</u> – it's a special occasion.*
FR : N'utilisez pas la vaisselle de tous les jours – c'est une occasion spéciale.

Every day

Every day, lorsqu'il est utilisé en deux mots, est une phrase adverbiale, signifiant chaque jour, tous les jours, ou quotidiennement. Le premier mot every est un adjectif et le deuxième mot day est un nom, et ensemble ils fonctionnent comme une phrase adverbiale. Par conséquent, il n'a pas la même fonction que everyday.

Puisqu'il est utilisé comme adverbe, every day (deux mots) modifie les adjectifs, les verbes ou d'autres adverbes, mais pas les noms. Seuls les adjectifs modifient les noms.

Exemples (le verbe modifié est souligné dans chaque phrase) :

*I go to the gym **every day**.*
FR : Je vais à la salle de sport tous les jours.

*I used to run **every day**, but I stopped after my surgery.*
FR : J'avais l'habitude de courir tous les jours, mais j'ai arrêté après mon opération.

Astuce pour les différencier

Essayez de **remplacer everday / every day par each day**. Si la phrase fonctionne toujours, on utilise every day (en deux mots).

Exemples:

*You shouldn't wear an ~~**each day**~~ outfit to the wedding.*
FR : Tu ne devrais pas porter une tenue de tous les jours pour le mariage.

Incorrect: you want to use everyday = You shouldn't wear an **everyday** outfit to the wedding.

---

*I get up for work **each day** at six.*
FR : Je me lève pour aller travailler tous les jours à six heures.

Correct: you want to use every day = I get up for work **every day** at six.

Entraînement

Reportez vos réponses pour analyser votre performance.
Entraînez-vous dans les conditions d'examen.
prepmyfuture.com/book/68/ex/1972

Question 1 Stress is just a part of ________ life.

(A) everyday
(B) every day

Question 2 For most people, ________ crime is a much more imminent threat than terrorism.

(A) everyday
(B) every day

Question 3 But people do it all across the globe ________.

(A) everyday
(B) every day

Question 4 Noland makes sculptures out of ________ objects.

(A) everyday
(B) every day

Question 5 She commutes from Oxford to London ________ by train and never tires of the scenery.

(A) everyday
(B) every day

Solutions

Reportez vos réponses pour analyser votre performance.

Entraînez-vous dans les conditions d'examen.

prepmyfuture.com/book/68/ex/1972

question 1	A	question 2	A	question 3	B	question 4	A	question 5	B

■ Question 1 - Solution

Stress is just a part of ________ life.

FR : Le stress fait partie de la vie ________.

(A) ✓ **everyday** **= quotidienne**

(B) every day = tous les jours
La phrase requiert un adjectif, every day est une locution adverbiale.

explication
FR : *Everyday* est un adjectif que l'on utilise pour décrire quelque chose que l'on voit ou utilise tous les jours. Il signifie « ordinaire » ou « typique ».

■ Question 2 - Solution

For most people, ________ crime is a much more imminent threat than terrorism.

FR : Pour la plupart des gens, la criminalité ________ constitue une menace bien plus imminente que le terrorisme.

(A) ✓ **everyday** **= quotidienne**

(B) every day = tous les jours
La phrase requiert un adjectif, every day est une locution adverbiale.

explication
FR : *Everyday* est un adjectif que l'on utilise pour décrire quelque chose que l'on voit ou utilise tous les jours. Il signifie « ordinaire » ou « typique ».

■ Question 3 - Solution

But people do it all across the globe ________.

FR : Mais les gens le font ________ dans le monde entier.

(A) everyday = quotidien
Everyday est un adjectif que l'on utilise pour décrire quelque chose que l'on voit ou utilise tous les jours. Il signifie « ordinaire » ou « typique ».

(B) ✓ **every day** **= tous les jours**

explication
FR : Cette phrase nécessite un adverbe ; *every day* est une location adverbiale qui signifie simplement « chaque jour ».

■ Question 4 - Solution

Noland makes sculptures out of ________ objects.

FR : Noland réalise des sculptures à partir d'objets du ________.

(A) ✓ everyday = quotidien

(B) every day = tous les jours
La phrase requiert un adjectif, every day est une locution adverbiale.

⇝ **explication**
FR : *Everyday* est un adjectif que l'on utilise pour décrire quelque chose que l'on voit ou utilise tous les jours. Il signifie « ordinaire » ou « typique ».

■ Question 5 - Solution

She commutes from Oxford to London ________ by train and never tires of the scenery.

FR : Elle fait ________ la navette entre Oxford et Londres en train et ne se lasse pas du paysage.

(A) everyday = quotidien
Everyday est un adjectif que l'on utilise pour décrire quelque chose que l'on voit ou utilise tous les jours. Il signifie « ordinaire » ou « typique ».

(B) ✓ every day = tous les jours

⇝ **explication**
FR : Cette phrase nécessite un adverbe ; *every day* est une location adverbiale qui signifie simplement « chaque jour ».

HISTORIC VS HISTORICAL

Rappel de cours

Historic et ***historical*** sont tous deux des adjectifs et sont souvent traduits en français par le mot « historique ». **Le contexte de la phrase définit le mot correct** en anglais.

Historic

Historic est un adjectif utilisé pour parler d'un **événement marquant** de l'histoire ou d'une personne importante historiquement. Il est parfois traduit en français par « marquant », « mémorable » ou « sans précédent ». Il modifie un nom dans une phrase et est souvent lié à des événements, des personnes, des lieux ou des objets importants dans le passé ou le présent, ou en relation avec une prédiction sur un événement dans un avenir proche.

Exemples (le nom modifié est souligné) :

*We are standing on a **historic** site; this is where the battle of Gettysburg took place.*
FR : Nous nous trouvons sur un site historique ; c'est ici qu'a eu lieu la bataille de Gettysburg.

*When the Berlin wall came down, it was a **historic** occasion.*
FR : La chute du mur de Berlin a été un événement historique.

*Next month's election will be a **historic** event for the new democracy.*
FR : L'élection du mois prochain sera un événement historique pour la nouvelle démocratie.

Historical

Historical est un adjectif utilisé pour décrire quelque chose qui est lié à l'étude des choses du passé ou qui est **relatif à l'histoire**. C'est également un adjectif et il est utilisé pour décrire toute chose du passé, importante ou non.

Exemples (le nom modifié est souligné) :

*The new law removed **historical** protections that were given to small businesses.*
FR : La nouvelle loi a supprimé les protections historiques qui étaient accordées aux petites entreprises.

*Countless **historical** documents and artifacts were destroyed during the bombing of Berlin.*

FR : D'innombrables documents et objets historiques ont été détruits lors du bombardement de Berlin.

*This powerful new **historical** drama tells the story of England from the time of the Romans until today.*
FR : Ce nouveau drame historique puissant raconte l'histoire de l'Angleterre depuis l'époque des Romains jusqu'à aujourd'hui.

Entraînement

Reportez vos réponses pour analyser votre performance.

Entraînez-vous dans les conditions d'examen.

prepmyfuture.com/book/68/ex/1973

Question 1 I love reading ________ novels.

(A) historic

(B) historical

Question 2 When the Berlin wall came down, it was a ________ occasion.

(A) historic

(B) historical

Question 3 I visited numerous ________ sites during my trip.

(A) historic

(B) historical

Question 4 Public spending has reached ________ levels.

(A) historic

(B) historical

Question 5 However, it is clear that, from a ________, political and legal perspective, a 'deal' will never be satisfactory.

(A) historic

(B) historical

Solutions

Reportez vos réponses pour analyser votre performance.

Entraînez-vous dans les conditions d'examen.

prepmyfuture.com/book/68/ex/1973

question 1	B	question 2	A	question 3	B	question 4	A	question 5	B

Question 1 - Solution

I love reading ________ novels.

FR : J'adore lire des romans ________.

(A) historic = mémorables
Fait référence à quelque chose de très mémorable, peut-être sans précédent.

(B) ✓ historical = historiques

explication
FR : *Historical* se rapporte au passé ou ayant existé dans le passé.

Question 2 - Solution

When the Berlin wall came down, it was a ________ occasion.

FR : La chute du mur de Berlin a été un événement ________.

(A) ✓ historic = marquant

(B) historical = historique

explication
FR : La phrase fait référence à quelque chose de très mémorable, peut-être sans précédent. En anglais, seul le mot *historic* est correct.

Question 3 - Solution

I visited numerous ________ sites during my trip.

FR : J'ai visité de nombreux sites ________ pendant mon voyage.

(A) historic = sans précédent
Fait référence à quelque chose, normalement un événement, de très mémorable.

(B) ✓ historical = historique

explication
FR : *Historical* se rapporte au passé ou ayant existé dans le passé.

Question 4 - Solution

Public spending has reached ________ levels.

FR : Les dépenses publiques ont atteint des niveaux ________.

(A) ✓ historic = sans précédent

(B) historical = historiques

⇨ **explication**
FR : La phrase fait référence à quelque chose de très mémorable, peut-être sans précédent. En anglais, seul le mot *historic* est correct.

- **Question 5 - Solution**

However, it is clear that, from a ________, political and legal perspective, a 'deal' will never be satisfactory.

FR : Toutefois, il est clair que, d'un point de vue ________, politique et juridique, une « transaction » ne sera jamais satisfaisante.

(A) historic = sans précédent
Fait référence à quelque chose, normalement un événement, de très mémorable.

(B) ✓ historical = historique

⇨ **explication**
FR : *Historical* se rapporte au passé ou ayant existé dans le passé.

THAN VS THEN

Rappel de cours

Then

Then a un certain nombre de fonctions différentes, mais il est le plus souvent utilisé comme un adverbe. Voici quatre utilisations différentes de *then* comme adverbe.

⇒ À ce moment-là (dans le passé ou dans le futur).
*I was at work **then**.*
FR : J'étais au travail à ce moment-là.
*Come over this afternoon; I'll be ready **then**.*
FR : Venez cet après-midi ; je serai prêt à ce moment-là.

⇒ Après dans le temps, l'espace ou l'ordre ; immédiatement après.
*We saw a movie and **then** went out for dinner.*
FR : Nous avons vu un film, puis nous sommes sortis dîner.
*We filled up the car and **then** began the trip.*
FR : Nous avons fait le plein de la voiture, puis nous avons commencé le voyage.

⇒ En plus.
*The glasses are $100, and **then** there is sales tax.*
FR : Les lunettes coûtent 100 $, et en plus il y a la taxe de vente.

⇒ Dans ce cas, en conséquence.
*If the weather is bad, **then** my flight will get canceled.*
FR : Si le temps est mauvais, (dans ce cas) mon vol sera annulé.
*If there is heavy traffic, **then** I might be late.*
FR : S'il y a beaucoup de circulation, (dans ce cas) je risque d'être en retard.

Than

Than, traduit en français par « que », est une conjonction qui est utilisée pour faire des comparaisons entre des éléments, des objets, des personnes, etc.

*He is taller **than** I am.*
FR : Il est plus grand que moi.

*She can run faster **than** I can.*

FR : Elle peut courir plus vite que moi.

*Your meal looks better **than** mine does.*
FR : Votre repas est meilleur que le mien.

*Coca-Cola is better **than** Pepsi.*
FR : Le Coca-Cola est meilleur que le Pepsi.

Astuce pour les différencier

Dans tous les cas, *than* est utilisé pour introduire une comparaison entre deux choses. Il est important de garder cela à l'esprit. Peu importe ce que vous comparez, que ce soit le temps, l'argent, la vitesse, **si une comparaison a lieu, *than* est le bon choix de mot**.

Entraînement

Reportez vos réponses pour analyser votre performance.

Entraînez-vous dans les conditions d'examen.

prepmyfuture.com/book/68/ex/1974

Question 1 He is taller ________ his older brother.

(A) then
(B) than

Question 2 If you cannot come, ________ we will have to postpone the meeting.

(A) then
(B) than

Question 3 My two sisters are younger ________ me.

(A) then
(B) than

Question 4 I finally found the location of the site visit, and ________ I saw that the meeting had already started!

(A) then
(B) than

▪ Question 5 For weaker readers, this may take a bit longer ________ it would for children who are already reading at grade level expectations.

(A) then

(B) than

Solutions

Reportez vos réponses pour analyser votre performance.

Entraînez-vous dans les conditions d'examen.

prepmyfuture.com/book/68/ex/1974

question 1	B	question 2	A	question 3	B	question 4	A	question 5	B

Question 1 - Solution

He is taller ________ his older brother.

FR : Il est plus grand ________ son frère aîné.

(A) then = puis
Then est couramment utilisé comme adverbe pour indiquer le temps.

(B) ✓ than = que

explication
FR : *Than* est utilisé pour faire des comparaisons.

Question 2 - Solution

If you cannot come, ________ we will have to postpone the meeting.

FR : Si vous ne pouvez pas venir, ________ nous devrons reporter la réunion.

(A) ✓ then = alors

(B) than = que
Than est utilisé pour faire des comparaisons.

explication
FR : *Then* est utilisé comme un adverbe pour indiquer la conséquence d'une clause précédente.

Question 3 - Solution

My two sisters are younger ________ me.

FR : Mes deux sœurs sont plus jeunes ________ moi.

(A) then = puis
Then est couramment utilisé comme adverbe pour indiquer le temps.

(B) ✓ than = que

explication
FR : *Than* est utilisé pour faire des comparaisons.

Question 4 - Solution

I finally found the location of the site visit, and ________ I saw that the meeting had already started!

FR : J'ai finalement trouvé le lieu de la visite du site, et ________ j'ai vu que la réunion avait déjà commencé !

(A) ✓ then = puis

(B) than = que
Than est utilisé pour faire des comparaisons.

⟹ **explication**
FR : *Then* est couramment utilisé comme adverbe pour indiquer le temps

▪ Question 5 - Solution

For weaker readers, this may take a bit longer ________ it would for children who are already reading at grade level expectations.

FR : Cela peut prendre un peu plus de temps chez les lecteurs les plus faibles ________ chez les élèves qui ont déjà atteint le niveau de lecture escompté dans leur année.

(A) then = puis
Then est couramment utilisé comme adverbe pour indiquer le temps.

(B) ✓ than = que

⟹ **explication**
FR : *Than* est utilisé pour faire des comparaisons.

ITS VS IT'S

Rappel de cours

Le mot ***it*** est un pronom de la troisième personne du singulier, non genré, utilisé (entre autres) pour désigner **des choses ou des idées inanimées** (comme une maison, une entreprise ou un pays). Il est également utilisé pour désigner **des animaux**, mais pas les animaux domestiques. Les animaux domestiques sont souvent désignés par les pronoms personnels sexués « il » ou « elle ».

It's

It's est une contraction qui signifie à la fois ***it is*** (c'est, « il est » ou « elle est ») et ***it has*** (« il a » ou « elle a »).

Exemples de ***« it's »*** :

It's *a beautiful day today!*
FR : C'est une belle journée aujourd'hui !
⇒ *It's* = *it is* ; cette phrase requiert un verbe.

It's *so nice to see you!* ***It's*** *been so long since we last saw each other.*
FR : C'est un plaisir de te voir ! Cela fait si longtemps que nous ne nous sommes pas vus.
⇒ Dans la première phrase : *it is* (le présent simple) ; dans la deuxième phrase : *it has been* (le *present perfect*).

She lost her phone, but she thinks ***it's*** *in the car.*
FR : Elle a perdu son téléphone, mais elle pense qu'il est dans la voiture.
⇒ *It's* = *it is* ; « il » fait référence au téléphone et la deuxième clause requiert un verbe.

Its

Its est un adjectif possessif, ce qui signifie que c'est la **forme possessive** du pronom *it*, c'est-à-dire qu'il lui appartient.

Exemples de ***« its »*** (son, sa, ses) :

*The house is quite beautiful, but **its** windows are ugly.*
FR : La maison est très belle, mais ses fenêtres sont laides.
⇒ ses = *its* ; ses fenêtres = les fenêtres de la maison.

*The furniture store celebrated **its** tenth anniversary.*
FR : Le magasin de meubles a fêté son dixième anniversaire.
⇒ son = *its* ; « son » concerne le magasin de meubles.

Astuce pour les différencier

Si vous hésitez entre *it's* et *its*, **remplacez-les par *it is* ou *it has***. Si la phrase a toujours du sens avec l'une ou l'autre de ces substitutions, on utilise *it's*. Sinon, on utilise *its*.

Entraînement

Reportez vos réponses pour analyser votre performance.

Entraînez-vous dans les conditions d'examen.

prepmyfuture.com/book/68/ex/1975

Question 1 I have to go, ________ late.

(A) its
(B) it's

Question 2 The company pays ________ workers on Fridays.

(A) its
(B) it's

Question 3 A chain is as strong as ________ weakest link.

(A) its
(B) it's

Question 4 If you spot something really rude, or get someone bothering you on-line, ________ not your fault.

(A) its
(B) it's

Question 5 For him ________ over because it is just, it is right.

(A) its
(B) it's

Solutions

Reportez vos réponses pour analyser votre performance.

Entraînez-vous dans les conditions d'examen.

prepmyfuture.com/book/68/ex/1975

question 1	B	question 2	A	question 3	A	question 4	B	question 5	B

Question 1 - Solution

I have to go, ________ late.

FR : Je dois y aller, ________ tard.

(A) its = son
« Its » est la forme possessive de la troisième personne. La deuxième clause de la phrase nécessite un sujet et un verbe.

(B) ✓ it's = il est

explication
FR : La deuxième clause de la phrase nécessite un sujet et un verbe.

Question 2 - Solution

The company pays ________ workers on Fridays.

FR : L'entreprise paie ________ travailleurs le vendredi.

(A) ✓ its = ses

(B) it's = c'est
Cette phrase nécessite un adjectif possessif.

explication
FR : « *Its* » est la forme possessive de la troisième personne. Cette phrase nécessite un adjectif possessif.

Question 3 - Solution

A chain is as strong as ________ weakest link.

FR : Une chaîne est aussi forte que ________ maillon le plus faible.

(A) ✓ its = son

(B) it's = il est
Cette phrase nécessite un adjectif possessif.

explication
FR : « *Its* » est la forme possessive de la troisième personne. « *Its* » fait référence à la chaîne.

Question 4 - Solution

If you spot something really rude, or get someone bothering you on-line, ________ not your fault.

FR : Si vous tombez sur un message choquant ou si quelqu'un vous ennuie sur Internet, ________ votre faute.

(A) its = ses pas
« Its » est la forme possessive de la troisième personne. La clause finale de la phrase nécessite un sujet et un verbe.

(B) ✓ it's = ce n'est pas

⇨ **explication**
FR : La clause finale de la phrase nécessite un sujet et un verbe.

▪ Question 5 - Solution

For him ________ over because it is just, it is right.

FR : Pour lui ________ fini parce que c'est juste ; c'est droit.

(A) its = son
« Its » est la forme possessive de la troisième personne. La phrase nécessite un sujet et un verbe.

(B) ✓ it's = c'est

⇨ **explication**
FR : La phrase nécessite un sujet et un verbe.

BETWEEN VS AMONG

Rappel de cours

Between

Between est un adverbe et une préposition utilisé pour décrire la localisation d'une personne ou d'un objet entre d'autres.

> Exemple :
>
> *We cannot put the table here. There is not enough room* ***between*** *the door and the wall.*
> FR : Nous ne pouvons pas mettre la table ici. Il n'y a pas assez de place entre la porte et le mur.

Among

Among est une préposition utilisée pour parler d'une personne ou d'un objet situé parmi un groupe (au milieu d'autres personnes ou objets ou entourés par eux).

> Exemple :
>
> *Who* ***among*** *us would agree to speak in front of the president tomorrow?*
> FR : Qui parmi nous accepterait de parler devant le président demain ?

Astuce pour les différencier

Ces deux mots peuvent causer beaucoup de confusion et ils sont source de nombreux malentendus. Pour différencier les deux, vous pouvez utiliser la technique suivante :

⇒ *Between* est utilisé pour parler d'**éléments distincts et individuels**(deux ou plus) contrairement à *among* qui est utilisé pour parler d'**éléments qui font partie d'un groupe et qui ne sont pas spécifiquement nommés** (voir exemples ci-dessus).

Entraînement

Reportez vos réponses pour analyser votre performance.

Entraînez-vous dans les conditions d'examen.

prepmyfuture.com/book/68/ex/1976

Question 1 I'm happy you're ________ us tonight.

(A) between

(B) among

Question 2 There was a fine line ________ being frugal and being a miser.

(A) between

(B) among

Question 3 Divide it ________ the poor people who need it so badly.

(A) between

(B) among

Question 4 When choosing our holiday destination, we were having a hard time choosing ________ Spain and Italy.

(A) between

(B) among

Question 5 He strolled ________ the self-conscious pets and people, smiling and looking until he was sure she wasn't there.

(A) between

(B) among

Solutions

Reportez vos réponses pour analyser votre performance.

Entraînez-vous dans les conditions d'examen.

prepmyfuture.com/book/68/ex/1976

question 1	B	question 2	A	question 3	B	question 4	A	question 5	A

Question 1 - Solution

I'm happy you're ________ us tonight.

FR : Je suis heureux que tu sois ________ nous ce soir.

(A) between = entre
Between est un adverbe et une préposition signifiant dans ou dans l'espace qui sépare deux lieux, personnes ou objets.

(B) ✓ among = parmi

explication
FR : Suivant les règles grammaticales, la phrase a besoin d'une préposition et non d'un adverbe.

Question 2 - Solution

There was a fine line ________ being frugal and being a miser.

FR : Il y avait une ligne fine ________ être frugal et être avare.

(A) ✓ between = entre

(B) among = parmi
Among est une préposition signifiant au milieu ou entourée d'autres choses.

explication
FR : Suivant les règles grammaticales, la phrase a besoin d'un adverbe et non d'une préposition.

Question 3 - Solution

Divide it ________ the poor people who need it so badly.

FR : Répartissez-le ________ les pauvres qui en ont tellement besoin.

(A) between = entre
Between est un adverbe et une préposition signifiant dans ou dans l'espace qui sépare deux lieux, personnes ou objets.

(B) ✓ among = parmi

explication
FR : Suivant les règles grammaticales, la phrase a besoin d'une préposition et non d'un adverbe.

Question 4 - Solution

When choosing our holiday destination, we were having a hard time choosing ________ Spain and Italy.

FR : Lors du choix de notre destination de vacances, nous avions du mal à choisir ________ l'Espagne et l'Italie.

(A) ✓ **between** **= entre**

(B) among = parmi
Among est une préposition signifiant au milieu ou entourée d'autres choses.

⟹ **explication**
FR : Suivant les règles grammaticales, la phrase a besoin d'un adverbe et non d'une préposition.

▪ Question 5 - Solution

He strolled ________ the self-conscious pets and people, smiling and looking until he was sure she wasn't there.

FR : Il se promenait ________ les animaux et les gens conscients de lui-même, souriant et regardant jusqu'à ce qu'il soit sûr qu'elle n'était pas là.

(A) ✓ **between** **= entre**

(B) among = parmi
Among est une préposition signifiant au milieu ou entourée d'autres choses.

⟹ **explication**
FR : Suivant les règles grammaticales, la phrase a besoin d'un adverbe et non d'une préposition.

LOOSE VS LOSE

Rappel de cours

Loose

Loose est un adjectif qui signifie que quelque chose n'est pas attaché, ou est mal attaché et est donc instable ou bancal.

Exemple :

*The nail came **loose**, that's why the painting fell from the wall.*
FR : La vis est mal fixée, c'est la raison pour laquelle le tableau est tombé du mur.

Lose

Lose est un verbe que l'on utilise pour dire qu'on a perdu quelque chose, qu'on l'a égaré.

Exemple:

*My worst nightmare is to **lose** my child in a crowd.*
FR : Mon pire cauchemar est de perdre mon enfant dans une foule.

Astuce pour les différencier

Ces deux mots peuvent entraîner beaucoup de confusion et ils sont source de nombreux malentendus. Pour les différencier, vous pouvez utiliser deux techniques :

⇒ **Prononcez** les deux : *loose* /luːs/ rime avec les mots *moose* et *goose* alors que ce n'est pas le cas pour *lose* /luːz/.
⇒ Pour vous assurer d'avoir à utiliser le mot *lose*, vous pouvez **mettre le verbe au passé** pour confirmer que la phrase a du sens.

Exemples :

I often ***lose*** *my car keys.*
⇒ *I often* ***lost*** *my car keys.* La phrase a du sens = on utilise *lose*.
FR : Je perds souvent mes clés de voiture.

The screws from my bed frame came ***loose****.*
⇒ *The screws from my bed frame came* ***lost****.* La phrase n'a plus de sens = on utilise *loose*.
FR : Les boulons de mon sommier se sont dévissés.

Entraînement

Reportez vos réponses pour analyser votre performance.

Entraînez-vous dans les conditions d'examen.

prepmyfuture.com/book/68/ex/1977

Question 1 I don't like to ________ at games I play.

(A) loose

(B) lose

Question 2 The movie is a rather ________ interpretation of the original story.

(A) lose

(B) loose

Question 3 The wheel was ________ and I nearly fell off the bicycle.

(A) lose

(B) loose

Question 4 ________ clothes are my favourite.

(A) Lose

(B) Loose

Question 5 With this placemat, you will never ________ napkin rings again.

(A) lose

(B) loose

Solutions

Reportez vos réponses pour analyser votre performance.

Entraînez-vous dans les conditions d'examen.

prepmyfuture.com/book/68/ex/1977

question 1	B	question 2	B	question 3	B	question 4	B	question 5	A

Question 1 - Solution

I don't like to ________ at games I play.

FR : Je n'aime pas ________ aux jeux auxquels je joue.

(A) loose = détaché
Etant un adjectif, c'est impossible comme option dans cette phrase.

(B) ✓ lose = perdre

explication
FR : Cette phrase serait incorrecte avec un adjectif comme « détaché » donc elle nécessite le verbe « perdre ».

Question 2 - Solution

The movie is a rather ________ interpretation of the original story.

FR : Le film est une interprétation assez ________ de l'histoire originale.

(A) lose = perdre
Etant un verbe, c'est impossible comme option dans cette phrase.

(B) ✓ loose = détachée

explication
FR : Cette phrase serait incorrecte avec un verbe comme « perdre » donc elle nécessite l'adjectif « détachée ».

Question 3 - Solution

The wheel was ________ and I nearly fell off the bicycle.

FR : La roue était ________ et j'ai failli tomber de la bicyclette.

(A) lose = perdre
Etant un verbe, c'est impossible comme option dans cette phrase.

(B) ✓ loose = détachée

explication
FR : Cette phrase serait incorrecte avec un verbe comme « perdre » après le verbe conjugué « était » donc elle nécessite l'adjectif « détachée ».

▪ Question 4 - Solution

________ clothes are my favourite.

FR : Les vêtements ________ sont mes préférés.

(A) Lose = perdre
Etant un verbe, c'est impossible comme option dans cette phrase.

(B) ✓ Loose = ample

⇒ explication
FR : Cette phrase serait incorrecte avec un verbe comme « perdre » après le nom commun « vêtements » donc elle nécessite l'adjectif « ample ».

▪ Question 5 - Solution

With this placemat, you will never ________ napkin rings again.

FR : Avec ce set de table, vous ne ________ plus jamais les ronds de serviette.

(A) ✓ lose = perdrez

(B) loose = détaché
Dans cette phrase l'adjectif n'est pas une option après le pronom « vous » qui attend un verbe conjugué.

⇒ explication
FR : D'après les règles grammaticales cette phrase a besoin un verbe après le pronom « vous » et non un adjectif.

DESPITE / EVEN THOUGH / ALTHOUGH / THOUGH / IN SPITE OF

Rappel de cours

Although / even though / though et despite / in spite of sont tous utilisés pour **lier deux idées contrastées** ou montrer qu'**un fait rend l'autre surprenant**. Ils peuvent tous être utilisés au début ou au milieu de la phrase.

Although / Even though

Although et *even though* sont suivis d'un **sujet** et d'un **verbe** et ils signifient « bien que / quoique » [+ subjonctif] ou « même si/alors que/alors même que » [+ indicatif].

Even though est une forme légèrement plus forte de *although*.

Exemples :

***Although / Even though** Amy was wearing glasses, she couldn't read the notice.*
FR : Bien qu'Amy porte des lunettes, elle n'a pas pu lire l'avis.

***Although / Even though** Jack had worked hard, he failed the exam.*
FR : Bien que Jack ait travaillé dur, il a échoué à l'examen.

*You're still playing loud music **although/even though** I've asked you several times not to.*
FR : Tu continues à mettre de la musique à fond, bien que je t'aie demandé plusieurs fois d'arrêter.

Though

Though peut être utilisé de la même manière que *although*. *Though* est moins formel que *although*. Il peut également se placer à la fin de la deuxième phrase. Cette façon d'exprimer des idées contrastées est courante en anglais parlé.

Exemple :

*We waited ages for our food. The waiter was really nice, **though**.*
FR : Nous avons attendu longtemps pour notre repas. Le serveur était très gentil, pourtant.

In spite of / Despite

Après *in spite of* et *despite*, on utilise un **nom**, un **gérondif** (forme en -ing d'un verbe) ou un **pronom**.

Exemples :

*They never made much money, **in spite of** their success.*
FR : Ils n'ont jamais gagné beaucoup d'argent, malgré leur succès.

***In spite of** the pain in his leg, he completed the marathon.*
FR : Malgré la douleur dans sa jambe, il a terminé le marathon.

***Despite** having a headache, I had a great birthday.*
FR : Malgré un mal de tête, j'ai passé un excellent anniversaire.

*The train was cancelled. **Despite** that, we arrived on time.*
FR : Le train a été annulé. Malgré cela, nous sommes arrivés à l'heure.

Astuces

⇒ Notez qu'il est courant d'utiliser ***in spite of*** et ***despite*** avec l'expression ***the fact that*** (le fait que), suivie d'un sujet et d'un verbe.

Exemples :

***In spite of the fact that** he worked very hard, he didn't pass the exam.*
FR : Malgré le fait qu'il ait travaillé très dur, il n'a pas réussi l'examen.

*He didn't pass the exam, **despite the fact that** he worked very hard.*
FR : Il n'a pas réussi l'examen, malgré le fait qu'il ait travaillé très dur.

⇒ **Attention !** *Despite of* n'existe pas !

Entraînement

Reportez vos réponses pour analyser votre performance.

Entraînez-vous dans les conditions d'examen.

prepmyfuture.com/book/68/ex/1978

Question 1 He enjoys his job ________ the low salary.

(A) despite

(B) even though

Question 2 ________ my careful planning, we ended up staying in a really bad hotel.

(A) In spite of

(B) Although

Question 3 My partner snores really loudly, but ________ that I sleep well.

(A) though

(B) in spite of

Question 4 You keep making that stupid noise ________ I've asked you to stop three times.

(A) despite

(B) although

Question 5 ________ he had enough money, he refused to buy a new car.

(A) Even though

(B) In spite of

Solutions

ılıl Reportez vos réponses pour analyser votre performance.

⏰ Entraînez-vous dans les conditions d'examen.

prepmyfuture.com/book/68/ex/1978

question 1	A	question 2	A	question 3	B	question 4	B	question 5	A

Question 1 - Solution

He enjoys his job ________ the low salary.

FR : Il aime son travail ________ le faible salaire.

(A) ✓ despite = malgré

(B) even though = bien que
Even though est suivi d'un sujet et d'un verbe.

explication
FR : Après *despite*, on utilise un nom, un gérondif (forme en -ing d'un verbe) ou un pronom.

Question 2 - Solution

________ my careful planning, we ended up staying in a really bad hotel.

FR : ________ ma planification minutieuse, nous avons fini par séjourner dans un très mauvais hôtel.

(A) ✓ In spite of = Malgré

(B) Although = Bien que
Although est suivi d'un sujet et d'un verbe.

explication
FR : Après *in spite of*, on utilise un nom, un gérondif (forme en -ing d'un verbe) ou un pronom.

Question 3 - Solution

My partner snores really loudly, but ________ that I sleep well.

FR : Mon conjoint ronfle très fort, mais ________ cela, je dors bien.

(A) though = bien que
Though est suivi directement d'un sujet et d'un verbe.

(B) ✓ in spite of = malgré

explication
FR : Après *in spite of*, on utilise un nom, un gérondif (forme en -ing d'un verbe) ou un pronom.

Question 4 - Solution

You keep making that stupid noise ________ I've asked you to stop three times.

FR : Tu continues à faire ce bruit stupide ________ je t'ai demandé d'arrêter trois fois.

(A) despite = malgré
Après despite, on utilise un nom, un gérondif (forme en -ing d'un verbe) ou un pronom.

(B) ✓ although = alors que

explication
FR : *Although* est suivi d'un sujet et d'un verbe.

■ Question 5 - Solution

________ he had enough money, he refused to buy a new car.

FR : ________ il avait assez d'argent, il a refusé d'acheter une nouvelle voiture.

(A) ✓ Even though = Même si

(B) In spite of = Malgré
Après in spite of, on utilise un nom, un gérondif (forme en -ing d'un verbe) ou un pronom.

explication
FR : *Even though* est suivi d'un sujet et d'un verbe.

BECAUSE / BECAUSE OF

Rappel de cours

Because of et *because* sont tous deux utilisés pour expliquer les **causes** ou les **raisons** d'un événement ou d'une situation.

Because of

Because of est une préposition, elle est généralement suivie d'un **gérondif** (forme en -ing d'un verbe), d'un **nom** ou d'un **pronom**.

Exemples :

Because of *her illness, Maria didn't go to the supermarket.*
FR : À cause de sa maladie, Maria n'est pas allée au supermarché.

Maria didn't go to the supermarket ***because of*** *her illness.*
FR : Maria n'est pas allée au supermarché à cause de sa maladie.

Because of *feeling sick, Maria didn't go to the supermarket.*
FR : À cause de son malaise, Maria n'est pas allée au supermarché.

Because

Because est une conjonction, elle est suivie d'un **sujet** et d'un **verbe**.

Exemples :

Because *Maria was feeling sick, she didn't go to the supermarket.*
FR : Parce que Maria se sentait malade, elle n'est pas allée au supermarché.

Maria didn't go to the supermarket, ***because*** *she was feeling sick.*
FR : Maria n'est pas allée au supermarché, parce qu'elle se sentait malade.

Astuce

Because of peut aussi être remplacé par ***due to***.

Exemples :

Due to *her illness, Maria didn't go to the supermarket.*
FR : À cause de sa maladie, Maria n'est pas allée au supermarché.

Maria didn't go to the supermarket ***due to*** *her illness.*
FR : Maria n'est pas allée au supermarché à cause de sa maladie.

Due to *feeling sick, Maria didn't go to the supermarket.*
FR : À cause de sa maladie, Maria n'est pas allée au supermarché.

Entraînement

Reportez vos réponses pour analyser votre performance.

Entraînez-vous dans les conditions d'examen.

prepmyfuture.com/book/68/ex/1979

Question 1 The exam was easy ________ he knew all the answers.

(A) because
(B) because of

Question 2 He sat down ________ he was feeling dizzy.

(A) because
(B) because of

Question 3 Their new product didn't sell well ________ its poor quality.

(A) because
(B) because of

Question 4 We hurried indoors ________ it was raining.

(A) because
(B) because of

Question 5 It is ________ your mother that we got into this mess.

(A) because of
(B) because

Solutions

Reportez vos réponses pour analyser votre performance.

Entraînez-vous dans les conditions d'examen.

prepmyfuture.com/book/68/ex/1979

question 1	A	question 2	A	question 3	B	question 4	A	question 5	A

Question 1 - Solution

The exam was easy ________ he knew all the answers.

FR : L'examen était facile ________ il connaissait toutes les réponses.

(A) ✓ because = car

(B) because of = à cause de
Because of est une préposition, elle est généralement suivie d'un gérondif (verbe + ing), d'un nom ou d'un pronom.

⇒ **explication**
FR : *Because* est une conjonction, elle est suivie d'un sujet et d'un verbe.

Question 2 - Solution

He sat down ________ he was feeling dizzy.

FR : Il s'est assis ________ il avait des vertiges.

(A) ✓ because = car

(B) because of = à cause de
Because of est une préposition, elle est généralement suivie d'un gérondif (verbe + ing), d'un nom ou d'un pronom.

⇒ **explication**
FR : *Because* est une conjonction, elle est suivie d'un sujet et d'un verbe.

Question 3 - Solution

Their new product didn't sell well ________ its poor quality.

FR : Leur nouveau produit ne s'est pas bien vendu ________ sa mauvaise qualité.

(A) because = parce que
Because est une conjonction, elle est suivie d'un sujet et d'un verbe.

(B) ✓ because of = en raison de

⇒ **explication**
FR : *Because of* est une préposition, elle est généralement suivie d'un gérondif (verbe + ing), d'un nom ou d'un pronom.

Question 4 - Solution

We hurried indoors ________ it was raining.

FR : Nous nous sommes précipités à l'intérieur ________ il pleuvait.

(A)	**✓**	**because**	**= parce qu'**
(B)		because of	= à cause d' *Because of est une préposition, elle est généralement suivie d'un gérondif (verbe + ing), d'un nom ou d'un pronom.*

⇨ **explication**
FR : *Because* est une conjonction, elle est suivie d'un sujet et d'un verbe.

Question 5 - Solution

It is ________ your mother that we got into this mess.

FR : C'est ________ ta mère qu'on s'est mis dans ce pétrin.

(A)	**✓**	**because of**	**= à cause de**
(B)		because	= car *Because est une conjonction, elle est suivie d'un sujet et d'un verbe.*

⇨ **explication**
FR : *Because of* est une préposition, elle est généralement suivie d'un gérondif (verbe + ing), d'un nom ou d'un pronom.

THANKS TO VS THANKS FOR

Rappel de cours

Thanks to

Thanks to est utilisé pour indiquer qu'un effet ou un résultat (généralement **positif**) est dû à une **cause spécifique** et il est généralement suivi d'un **nom** ou d'un **pronom**. *Thanks to* peut généralement être remplacé par *because of. Thanks to* est l'utilisation du verbe *to thank* (remercier), et non la forme abrégée de *thank you* (merci).

Exemple :

***Thanks to** your lessons, my English has improved a lot.*
= ***Because of** your lessons, my English has improved a lot.*
FR : Grâce à vos leçons, mon anglais s'est beaucoup amélioré.

Thanks for

Thanks for est utilisé pour **montrer son appréciation** pour quelque chose et est utilisé avec un **nom** ou un **gérondif** (forme en -ing d'un verbe). *Thanks for* (merci pour) est l'abréviation de *thank you for* (merci à vous pour).

Exemples :

***Thanks for** the help! = **Thank you for** the help!*
FR : Merci (à vous) pour le coup de main !

***Thanks for** helping me! = **Thank you for** helping me!*
FR : Merci (à vous) de m'avoir aidé !

*I just wanted to say **thanks for** adding me to the online group.*
= *I just wanted to say **thank you for** adding me to the online group.*
FR : Je voulais juste (vous) dire merci de m'avoir ajouté au groupe en ligne.

Entraînement

Reportez vos réponses pour analyser votre performance.

Entraînez-vous dans les conditions d'examen.

prepmyfuture.com/book/68/ex/1980

Question 1 ________ the coffee, I was able to stay awake during the meeting.

(A) Thanks to

(B) Thanks for

Question 2 The improvement was achieved ________ massive state support for the financial sector.

(A) thanks to

(B) thanks for

Question 3 We all know that we have achieved a great deal together, and it is mainly ________ her that we did so.

(A) thanks to

(B) thanks for

Question 4 ________ a sustained effort and a high level of expenditure on research and development, they are able to offer their customers the best product range on the market.

(A) Thanks to

(B) Thanks for

Question 5 I do, however, wish to express my heartfelt ________ the interest you have shown in this debate.

(A) thanks to

(B) thanks for

Solutions

ılıl Reportez vos réponses pour analyser votre performance.

⏰ Entraînez-vous dans les conditions d'examen.

prepmyfuture.com/book/68/ex/1980

question 1	A	question 2	A	question 3	A	question 4	A	question 5	B

▪ Question 1 - Solution

________ the coffee, I was able to stay awake during the meeting.

FR : ________ café, j'ai pu rester éveillé pendant la réunion.

(A) ✓ Thanks to = Grâce au

(B) Thanks for = Merci pour le
Thanks for est utilisé pour montrer son appréciation par rapport à quelque chose et est utilisé avec un nom ou un gérondif (verbe + ing). Thanks for (merci pour) est l'abréviation de thank you for (merci à vous pour).

⇝ **explication**
FR : *Thanks to* est utilisé pour indiquer qu'un effet ou un résultat (généralement positif) est dû à une cause spécifique et il est généralement suivi d'un nom ou d'un pronom.

▪ Question 2 - Solution

The improvement was achieved ________ massive state support for the financial sector.

FR : Cette amélioration a pu avoir lieu ________ aides massives de l'État au secteur financier.

(A) ✓ thanks to = grâce aux

(B) thanks for = merci pour des
Thanks for est utilisé pour montrer son appréciation par rapport à quelque chose et est utilisé avec un nom ou un gérondif (verbe + ing). Thanks for (merci pour) est l'abréviation de thank you for (merci à vous pour).

⇝ **explication**
FR : *Thanks to* est utilisé pour indiquer qu'un effet ou un résultat (généralement positif) est dû à une cause spécifique et il est généralement suivi d'un nom ou d'un pronom.

▪ Question 3 - Solution

We all know that we have achieved a great deal together, and it is mainly ________ her that we did so.

FR : Nous savons tous que nous avons effectué ensemble des progrès considérables et ce, principalement ________ elle.

(A) ✓ **thanks to** **= grâce à**

(B) thanks for = merci pour
Thanks for est utilisé pour montrer son appréciation par rapport à quelque chose et est utilisé avec un nom ou un gérondif (verbe + ing). Thanks for (merci pour) est l'abréviation de thank you for (merci à vous pour).

⇒ **explication**
FR : *Thanks to* est utilisé pour indiquer qu'un effet ou un résultat (généralement positif) est dû à une cause spécifique et il est généralement suivi d'un nom ou d'un pronom.

■ Question 4 - Solution

________ a sustained effort and a high level of expenditure on research and development, they are able to offer their customers the best product range on the market.

FR : ________ un effort constant et un investissement important en matière de recherche et développement, ils sont en mesure d'offrir à leurs clients la meilleure gamme de produits du marché.

(A) ✓ **Thanks to** **= Grâce à**

(B) Thanks for = Merci pour
Thanks for est utilisé pour montrer son appréciation par rapport à quelque chose et est utilisé avec un nom ou un gérondif (verbe + ing). Thanks for (merci pour) est l'abréviation de thank you for (merci à vous pour).

⇒ **explication**
FR : *Thanks to* est utilisé pour indiquer qu'un effet ou un résultat (généralement positif) est dû à une cause spécifique et il est généralement suivi d'un nom ou d'un pronom.

■ Question 5 - Solution

I do, however, wish to express my heartfelt ________ the interest you have shown in this debate.

FR : Mais je tiens à vous dire un grand ________ l'intérêt que vous portez à ce débat.

(A) thanks to = grâce à
Thanks to est utilisé pour indiquer qu'un effet ou un résultat (généralement positif) est dû à une cause spécifique et il est généralement suivi d'un nom ou d'un pronom.

(B) ✓ **thanks for** **= merci pour**

⇒ **explication**
FR : *Thanks for* est utilisé pour montrer son appréciation par rapport à quelque chose et est utilisé avec un nom ou un gérondif (verbe + ing). *Thanks for* (merci pour) est l'abréviation de *thank you for* (merci à vous pour).

FROM MY POINT OF VIEW VS ACCORDING TO

Rappel de cours

According to

According to est utilisé pour donner la **source d'une idée ou d'une information**. Cette source ne doit pas être vous.

Exemples :

***According to** Sir Isaac Newton, there are three laws of motion.*
FR : Selon Sir Isaac Newton, il existe trois lois du mouvement.

*The term 'VIP' means Very Important Person **according to** the dictionary.*
FR : Selon le dictionnaire, le terme "VIP" signifie Very Important Person.

***According to** my roommate, recycling is a waste of time.*
FR : D'après mon colocataire, le recyclage est une perte de temps.

From my point of view

From my point of view (de mon point de vue) est souvent utilisé pour introduire une **opinion** et peut être remplacé par *in my opinion* (à mon avis). Il est généralement utilisé en début de phrase.

Exemples :

***From my point of view**, I can't understand why he doesn't quit his job.*
FR : De mon point de vue, je ne comprends pas pourquoi il ne quitte pas son emploi.

***From my point of view**, I don't think she should talk to her anymore.*
FR : De mon point de vue, je pense qu'elle ne devrait plus lui parler.

Astuces

⇒ Avec *according to*, si la source est une personne, il s'agit souvent d'un **expert** (par exemple : Selon le professeur Barton...). L'expression *according to me* (selon moi) est étrange. Lorsque vous dites *according to me*, vous sous-entendez que vous êtes un expert du sujet. Dans la plupart des cas, vous n'êtes probablement pas un expert et, par conséquent, l'expression ne devrait pas être utilisée. Utilisez plutôt *from my point of view* ou *in my opinion*.

⇒ L'expression ***in accordance with*** est utilisée pour signifier en accord avec. Elle signifie qu'une règle ou une idée est conforme, en accord ou compatible avec quelque chose d'autre (par exemple, une loi, un règlement ou les désirs de quelqu'un). Cette expression est généralement utilisée en anglais formel ou juridique.

> Exemple :
>
> *The company's policies are* ***in accordance with*** *federal regulations.*
> FR : Les politiques de l'entreprise sont conformes à la réglementation fédérale.

⇒ **Attention !** L'expression *in my point of view* n'existe pas. Utilisez *from my point of view* ou *in my opinion*.

Entraînement

Reportez vos réponses pour analyser votre performance.

Entraînez-vous dans les conditions d'examen.

prepmyfuture.com/book/68/ex/1981

Question 1 Well, ________, it's going to be fun either way.

(A) according to
(B) from my point of view

Question 2 ________, we can't let Richard control the project budget anymore.

(A) According to
(B) From my point of view

Question 3 ________, you should never trust Jared to tell the truth.

(A) According to
(B) From my point of view

▪ Question 4 ________ a recent study, the number of people suffering from health problems has increased drastically.

(A) According to

(B) From my point of view

▪ Question 5 The size of the network may vary ________ the areas and subjects involved.

(A) according to

(B) from my point of view

Solutions

ılıl Reportez vos réponses pour analyser votre performance.

⏰ Entraînez-vous dans les conditions d'examen.

prepmyfuture.com/book/68/ex/1981

question 1	B	question 2	B	question 3	B	question 4	A	question 5	A

▪ Question 1 - Solution

Well, _________, it's going to be fun either way.

FR : Eh bien, _________, ça va être amusant de toute façon.

(A)	according to	= selon *According to est utilisé pour indiquer la source d'une idée ou d'une information.*
(B)	✓ **from my point of view**	**= de mon point de vue**

⇨ **explication**

FR : *From my point of view* est souvent utilisé pour introduire une opinion et peut être remplacé par *in my opinion*.

▪ Question 2 - Solution

_________, we can't let Richard control the project budget anymore.

FR : _________, on ne peut plus laisser Richard contrôler le budget du projet.

(A)	According to	= Selon *According to est utilisé pour indiquer la source d'une idée ou d'une information.*
(B)	✓ **From my point of view**	**= De mon point de vue**

⇨ **explication**

FR : *From my point of view* est souvent utilisé pour introduire une opinion et peut être remplacé par *in my opinion*.

▪ Question 3 - Solution

_________, you should never trust Jared to tell the truth.

FR : _________, vous ne devriez jamais faire confiance à Jared pour dire la vérité.

(A)	According to	= Selon *According to est utilisé pour indiquer la source d'une idée ou d'une information.*
(B)	✓ **From my point of view**	**= De mon point de vue**

⇝ **explication**
FR : *From my point of view* est souvent utilisé pour introduire une opinion et peut être remplacé par *in my opinion.*

▪ Question 4 - Solution

________ a recent study, the number of people suffering from health problems has increased drastically.

FR : ________ une étude récente, le nombre de personnes souffrant de problèmes de santé a considérablement augmenté.

(A)	✓	**According to**	**= Selon**
(B)		From my point of view	= De mon point de vue *From my point of view est souvent utilisé pour introduire une opinion et peut être remplacé par in my opinion.*

⇝ **explication**
FR : *According to* est utilisé pour indiquer la source d'une idée ou d'une information.

▪ Question 5 - Solution

The size of the network may vary ________ the areas and subjects involved.

FR : La taille du réseau pourra varier ________ les domaines et les sujets concernés.

(A)	✓	**according to**	**= selon**
(B)		from my point of view	= de mon point de vue *From my point of view est souvent utilisé pour introduire une opinion et peut être remplacé par in my opinion.*

⇝ **explication**
FR : *According to* est utilisé pour indiquer la source d'une idée ou d'une information.

TOEFL iBT #1

TOEFL iBT #1 - READING

READING SECTION DIRECTIONS

The Reading section measures your ability to understand academic passages in English. You will read passages and answer questions about them. Answer all questions based on what is stated or implied in the passage.

There are three passages in a full TOEFL iBT test. You should allow 20 minutes to read each passage and answer the questions about it.

Reportez vos réponses pour analyser votre performance.

Entraînez-vous dans les conditions d'examen.

prepmyfuture.com/book/68/ex/1982

Development of Sociology

[P1] In 1873, the English philosopher Herbert Spencer (1820–1903) published The Study of Sociology, the first book with the term "sociology" in the title. Much of Comte's philosophy was rejected by Spencer as well as Marx's theory of class struggle and his support of communism. Instead, he favored a form of government that allowed market forces to control capitalism. His work influenced many early sociologists including Émile Durkheim (1858–1917).

[P2] Durkheim helped establish sociology as a formal academic discipline by establishing the first European department of sociology at the University of Bordeaux in 1895. His Rules of the Sociological Method (1895) was another step in the development of sociology as an academic discipline. In another important work, Division of Labour in Society (1893), Durkheim laid out his theory on how societies transformed from a primitive state into a capitalist, industrial society. According to Durkheim, people rise to their proper level in society based on merit. Durkheim believed that sociologists could study objective "social facts" (Poggi 2000). He also believed that through such studies it would be possible to determine if a society was "healthy" or "pathological." He saw healthy societies as stable, while pathological societies experienced a **breakdown** in social norms between individuals and society. In 1897, Durkheim attempted to demonstrate the effectiveness of his rules of social research when he published a work titled Suicide. Durkheim examined suicide statistics in different police districts to research differences between Catholic and Protestant communities. He attributed the differences to socio-religious forces rather than to individual or psychological causes.

[P3] Meanwhile in Germany, prominent sociologist Max Weber (1864–1920) established a sociology department at the Ludwig Maximilians University of Munich in 1919. Weber wrote on many topics related to sociology including political change in Russia and social forces that affect factory workers. He is known best for his 1904 book, The Protestant Ethic and the Spirit of Capitalism. Weber remains controversial to this very day. It is thought that Weber was arguing that the beliefs of many Protestants, especially Calvinists, led to the creation of capitalism. Some interpret it as simply claiming that the ideologies of capitalism and Protestantism are **complementary**. Weber also made a major contribution to the methodology of sociological research. Along with other researchers such as Wilhelm Dilthey (1833–1911) and Heinrich Rickert (1863–1936), Weber believed that it was difficult if not impossible to use standard scientific methods to accurately predict the behavior of groups as people hoped to do. They argued that the influence of culture on human behavior had to be taken into account. This even applied to the researchers themselves, who, they believed, should be aware of how their own cultural biases could influence their research. To deal with this problem, Weber and Dilthey introduced the concept of *verstehen*, a German verb that means to understand in a deep way. In seeking *verstehen*, outside observers of a social world—an entire culture or a small setting—attempt to understand it from an insider's point of view.

[P4] **In his book The Nature of Social Action (1922), Weber described sociology as striving to "interpret the meaning of social action and thereby give a causal explanation of the way in which action proceeds and the effects it produces."** He and other like-minded sociologists proposed a philosophy of anti-positivism whereby social researchers would strive for subjectivity as they worked to represent social processes, cultural norms, and societal values. This approach led to some research methods whose aim was not to generalize or predict (traditional in science), but to systematically gain an in-depth understanding of social worlds.

[P5] The different approaches to research based on positivism or anti-positivism are often considered the foundation for the differences found today between quantitative sociology and qualitative sociology. Quantitative sociology uses statistical methods such as surveys with large numbers of participants. Researchers analyze data using statistical techniques to see if they can uncover patterns of human behavior. Qualitative sociology seeks to understand human behavior by learning about it through in-depth interviews, focus groups, and analysis of content sources (like books, magazines, journals, and popular media).

■ Question 1 Paragraph 1 implies that:

(A) The discipline of sociology was founded in 1873.

(B) Marx discarded Comte's philosophy.

(C) Before Spencer, the word "sociology" hadn't appeared on any book cover.

(D) Durkheim was Spencer's mentor.

■ Question 2 Based on information in paragraph 2, which of the following statements is true concerning Durkheim's sociological contribution?

(A) Durkheim saw pathological societies as stable, while healthy societies were perceived as a collective system of social norms between the individual and society.

(B) Durkheim laid out his theory on how capitalist, industrial societies transformed into a collective of primitive communities

(C) Durkheim claimed that people rise to their proper level in society based on financial background.

(D) Durkheim was directly responsible for making sociology a formal academic discipline

■ Question 3 According to Durkheim, studying sociology is important because:

(A) Sociology can help us better understand and tolerate capitalist, industrial societies.

(B) Sociology could help us understand suicide statistics in different police districts.

(C) Sociology could help scientists research the differences between Catholic and Protestant communities.

(D) Sociology could help us better understand and identify the underlying factors that lead a society to become either "healthy" or "pathological."

■ Question 4 The word "breakdown" in the passage is closest in meaning to:

(A) collapse

(B) decomposition

(C) loss of mental health

(D) analysis

■ Question 5 According to paragraph 3, which of the following is true about Max Weber (1864–1920)?

(A) He is mostly known for his sociological contributions to the research conducted into far-reaching social forces affecting factory workers in Russia.

(B) He is best known for his 1904 book as well as for giving birth to a unique methodology of sociological research

(C) Weber had controversial views on both Protestants and Calvinists whom all had different views on the topic of capitalism

(D) He single-handedly introduced the concept of *verstehen*

■ Question 6 Which of the following sentences best describes the highlighted sentence in the passage? The other choices change the meaning or leave out information.

In his book The Nature of Social Action (1922), Weber described sociology as striving to "interpret the meaning of social action and thereby give a causal explanation of the way in which action proceeds and the effects it produces."

(A) The Nature of Social Action (1922) is Weber's attempt at comprehending the deeper values of social actions in order to provide a way for a better understanding of people's actions and the consequences of those actions.

(B) Weber's book is simply about finding explanations to people's actions and looking at the results in a way that would enable sociologists to draw vague conclusions.

(C) Weber's book is solely about interpreting the meaning of social actions without any extra attempt to give a causal explanation of the way in which action are carried out or what consequences those actions might carry in themselves.

(D) Weber's book provides a general introduction to the study of sociology.

■ Question 7 According to paragraph 6, qualitative sociology investigate human behavior through all of the following methods EXCEPT.

(A) focus groups

(B) content source analysis

(C) in-depth interviews

(D) statistical techniques to uncover patterns of human behavior

■ Question 8 In paragraph 3, the term "complementary" is closer in meaning to:

(A) accessory

(B) interrelated

(C) mandatory

(D) permissive

▪ Question 9 Look at the four squares in paragraph 3, A, B, C, and D, which indicate where the following sentence could be added to the passage. Where would the sentence best fit?

Weber, in fact, inferred that psychological insecurity that Calvin's doctrine had imposed was such that people began to live by an ethic of unceasing commitment to one's worldly calling and ascetic abstinence from any enjoyment, focused on the accumulation of capital.

[P3] Meanwhile in Germany, prominent sociologist Max Weber (1864–1920) established a sociology department at the Ludwig Maximilians University of Munich in 1919. Weber wrote on many topics related to sociology including political change in Russia and social forces that affect factory workers. **A** He is known best for his 1904 book, The Protestant Ethic and the Spirit of Capitalism. **B** Weber remains controversial to this very day. It is thought that Weber was arguing that the beliefs of many Protestants, especially Calvinists, led to the creation of capitalism. **C** Some interpret it as simply claiming that the ideologies of capitalism and Protestantism are complementary. Weber also made a major contribution to the methodology of sociological research. **D** Along with other researchers such as Wilhelm Dilthey (1833–1911) and Heinrich Rickert (1863–1936), Weber believed that it was difficult if not impossible to use standard scientific methods to accurately predict the behavior of groups as people hoped to do. They argued that the influence of culture on human behavior had to be taken into account. This even applied to the researchers themselves, who, they believed, should be aware of how their own cultural biases could influence their research. To deal with this problem, Weber and Dilthey introduced the concept of verstehen, a German verb that means to understand in a deep way. In seeking verstehen, outside observers of a social world—an entire culture or a small setting—attempt to understand it from an insider's point of view.

(A) **A**
(B) **B**
(C) **C**
(D) **D**

■ **Question 10** Directions:

An introductory sentence for a brief summary of the passage is provided below.

Complete the summary by selecting the THREE answer choices that express the most important ideas in the passage. Some sentences do not belong in the summary because they express ideas that are not presented in the passage or are minor ideas in the passage.

This question is worth 2 points.

- From the second half of the nineteenth century, new approaches toward sociology started developing and it also began to be formally studied at university.
- ________
- ________
- ________

(A) In its early stages, sociology was associated with capitalism, because Comte's theories had been proven wrong by Herbert Spencer.

(B) Durkheim set out to determine the evolutionary process of societies, establishing different categories through an objective approach towards social phenomena.

(C) Durkheim realized that, unlike he previously believed, the Protestant doctrine was a result of both pathological and healthy societies.

(D) Further studies established the influence of factors such as culture and ideologies in society, and, therefore, the impossibility to adopt an ordinary objective approach.

(E) By studying groups of Russian factory workers, Max Weber could develop the theory that led him to redefine the methodology of sociological research.

(F) The dispute between scholars proposing a scientific approach against those suggesting the adoption of an internal perspective, led to the modern diversification in the field of sociology.

“Music and Meter”

[P1] The meter of a piece of music is the arrangement of its rhythms in a repetitive pattern of strong and weak beats. This does not necessarily mean that the rhythms themselves are repetitive, but they do strongly suggest a repeated pattern of pulses. It is on these pulses, the beat of the music, that you tap your foot, clap your hands, dance, etc. Some music does not have a meter. Ancient music, such as Gregorian chants; new music, such as some experimental twentieth-century art music; and Non-Western music, such as some native American flute music, may not have a strong, repetitive pattern of beats. Other types of music, such as traditional Western African drumming, may have very complex meters that can be difficult for the beginner to identify. The influence of incidental exposure to varied metrical patterns from different musical cultures is thought to have an influence on the perception of complex metrical structures from an unfamiliar musical culture. Adults with some exposure to non-Western music that is unmetered or metrically complex successfully detect meter-violating changes in non-Western music with both simple and complex meters.

[P2] But most Western music has simple, repetitive patterns of beats. This makes meter a very useful way to organize the music. Common notation, for example, divides the written music into small groups of beats called measures, or bars. The lines dividing each measure from the next help the musician reading the music to keep track of the rhythms. A piece (or section of the piece) is assigned a time signature that tells the performer how many beats to expect in each measure, and what type of note should get one beat.

[P3] Conducting also depends on the meter of the piece; conductors use different conducting patterns for the different meters. These patterns emphasize the differences between the stronger and weaker beats to help the performers keep track of where they are in the music. But the conducting patterns depend only on the **pattern** of strong and weak beats. In other words, they only depend on "how many beats there are in a measure", not "what type of note gets a beat". So even though the time signature is often called the "meter" of a piece, one can talk about meter without worrying about the time signature or even being able to read music.

[P4] Meters can be classified by counting the number of beats from one strong beat to the next. For example, if the meter of the music feels like "strong-weak-strong-weak", it is in duple meter. "strong-weak-weak-strong-weak-weak" is triple meter, and "strong-weak-weak-weak" is quadruple. (Most people don't bother classifying the more unusual meters, such as those with five beats in a measure.)

[P5] Meters can also be classified as either simple or compound. In a simple meter, each beat is basically divided into halves. In compound meters, each beat is divided into thirds. A borrowed division occurs whenever the basic meter of a piece is **interrupted** by some beats that sound like they are "borrowed" from a different meter. One of the most common examples of this is the use of triplets to add some compound meter to a piece that is mostly in a simple meter.

[P6] To learn to recognize meter, remember that (in most Western music) the beats and the subdivisions of beats are all equal and even. So, you are basically listening for a running, even pulse underlying the rhythms of the music. For example, if it makes sense to count along with the music "ONE-and-Two-and-ONE-and-Two-and" (with all the syllables very evenly spaced) then you probably have a simple duple meter. But if it's more comfortable to count "ONE-and-a-Two-and-a-ONE-and-a-Two-and-a", it's probably compound duple meter. (Make sure numbers always come on a pulse, and "one" always on the strongest pulse.)

[P7] This may take some practice if you're not used to it, but it can be useful practice for anyone who is learning about music. To help you get started, you may also want to listen to some examples of music that is in simple duple, simple triple, simple quadruple to then slowly move to more the more complex compound duple and compound triple meters.

■ Question 11 According to paragraph 1, which is true about a meter?

(A) The meter of a music is the repeated tapping of your foot and clapping of your hands

(B) The meter of a music is a traditional Western African drumming

(C) The meter of a music is a repetitive pattern of beats

(D) The meter of a music is nothing else but a measure of enjoyment

■ Question 12 It can be inferred that some music does not have a meter because:

(A) they would be extremely boring to listen to

(B) not all music has such a powerful repetitive pattern of beats

(C) ancient music, such as Gregorian chants, had a huge effect on today's musical taste

(D) some traditional music consists of complex meters that would be too difficult for the beginner to identify

■ Question 13 The word "pattern" in paragraph 3 is closest in meaning to:

(A) presence

(B) range

(C) choice

(D) sequence

■ Question 14 Why does the author go on listing the different meters of music in paragraph 4?

(A) to prove why counting the number of beats from one strong beat to the next is so troublesome

(B) to argue that meters can be classified by counting the number of beats, but the majority of people just don't really bother classifying these more unusual meters

(C) to make the readers realize that there is no practical reason for counting meters in a musical picoo

(D) to drive a sharper wedge between simple and compound meters

■ Question 15 According to paragraph 6, what could be the most useful method of identifying underlying meters?

(A) by watching out for a running, even pulse underlying the rhythms of the music

(B) by watching out for an equal and even "click" sound underlying the rhythms of the music

(C) by making sure that you count the rhythm on a pulse, and you do that always on the weakest pulse

(D) by counting the evenly spaced syllables, for they serve as excellent pointers to whether we are listening to a music with a simple duple meter or a compound duple meter

Question 16 Which of the following statements most accurately reflects the author's opinion about music and meter in general?

(A) Recognizing, classifying and organizing meters should be the first step for anyone who is seriously considering learning more about music

(B) There is no way anyone can enjoy listening to music before learning more about music

(C) The only way for anyone to improve his/her conducting patterns is by being able to recognize, classify and identify meters.

(D) Given the fact that it could take some practice to successfully identify meters, especially if you're not used to the process, those who have no musical affinity whatsoever will surely fail.

Question 17 According to paragraph 4, what is considered a triple meter?

(A) strong-weak-weak-weak-strong-weak

(B) strong- strong-weak-weak-weak-weak

(C) strong-weak-weak-strong-weak-weak

(D) strong-weak-weak

Question 18 The word "interrupted" in paragraph 5 is closest in meaning to:

(A) discontinued

(B) encouraged

(C) promoted

(D) expedited

Question 19 Look at the four squares in paragraph 3, A, B, C, and D, which indicate where the following sentence could be added to the passage. Where would the sentence best fit?

As a matter of fact, adults who are just familiar with Western music usually detect meter-violating changes in non-Western music with simple meter only.

The meter of a piece of music is the arrangement of its rhythms in a repetitive pattern of strong and weak beats. This does not necessarily mean that the rhythms themselves are repetitive, but they do strongly suggest a repeated pattern of pulses. It is on these pulses, the beat of the music, that you tap your foot, clap your hands, dance, etc. Some music does not have a meter. **A** Ancient music, such as Gregorian chants; new music, such as some experimental twentieth-century art music; and Non-Western music, such as some native American flute music, may not have a strong, repetitive pattern of beats. **B** Other types of music, such as traditional Western African drumming, may have very complex meters that can be difficult for the beginner to identify. The influence of incidental exposure to varied metrical patterns from different musical cultures is thought to have an influence on the perception of complex metrical structures from an unfamiliar musical culture. **C** Adults with some exposure to non-Western music that is unmetered or metrically complex successfully detect meter-violating changes in non-Western music with both simple and complex meters. **D**

(A) **A**

(B) **B**

(C) **C**

(D) **D**

■ Question 20 Directions:

An introductory sentence for a brief summary of the passage is provided below.

Complete the summary by selecting the THREE answer choices that express the most important ideas in the passage. Some sentences do not belong in the summary because they express ideas that are not presented in the passage or are minor ideas in the passage.

This question is worth 2 points.

- By individuating the strong and weak beats in a piece of music and keeping track of their frequency, we can determine the meter of a piece of music.
- ________
- ________
- ________

(A) Musicians rely on meter. Conductors do the same, basing their indications more on the rhythmic aspect than on the melodic one, when approaching a piece of music.

(B) Meter does not belong to every single music genre. In fact, Gregorian chants, native American flute music and Western African drumming represent the best examples of music without meter.

(C) The distance that separates two strong beats is used as a criterion of classification for different types of meter.

(D) It is possible to have simple and more complex meters. Beginners should start from the ones with a regular beat subdivision if they want to learn to recognize the different varieties of meter

(E) Triplet meter differ from duplet meter for the addition of two more "weak" beats in its metric pattern.

(F) The separation of syllables while counting is the most important element in order to recognize, count and learn any meter. If we can count all numbers on a beat, then we know we have a simple duple meter.

"Mapping and measuring the Ocean"

[P1] Distances on earth are measured in many different units, the most common are degrees of latitude or longitude, meters, miles, and nautical miles. Latitude is the angle between the local vertical and the equatorial plane. A meridian is the intersection at earth's surface of a plane **perpendicular** to the equatorial plane and passing through earth's axis of rotation. Longitude is the angle between the standard meridian and any other meridian, where the standard meridian is the one that passes through a point at the Royal Observatory at Greenwich, England. Thus, longitude is measured east or west of Greenwich.

[P2] A degree of latitude is not the same length as a degree of longitude except at the equator. Because distance in degrees of longitude is not constant, oceanographers measure distance on maps using degrees of latitude. Nautical miles and meters are connected historically to the size of earth. Gabriel Mouton proposed in 1670 a decimal system of measurement based on the length of an arc that is one minute of a great circle of earth. This eventually became the **nautical** mile. Mouton's decimal system eventually became the metric system based on a different unit of length, the meter, which was originally intended to be one ten-millionth the distance from the Equator to the pole along the Paris meridian.

[P3] Although the tie between nautical miles, meters, and earth's radius was soon abandoned because it was not practical, the approximations are very good. For example, earth's polar circumference is approximately 40,008 km. Therefore, one ten-millionth of a quadrant is 1.0002 m. Similarly, a nautical mile should be 1.8522 km, which is very close to the official definition of the international nautical mile: 1 nm = 1.8520 km.

[P4] Oceanic dimensions range from around 1500 km for the minimum width of the Atlantic to more than 13,000 km for the north-south extent of the Atlantic and the width of the Pacific. Typical depths are only 3–4 km. If the ocean were scaled down to a width of 8 inches it would have depths about the same as the thickness of a piece of paper. As a result, the velocity field in the ocean is nearly 2-dimensional. Vertical velocities are much smaller than horizontal velocities.

[P5] There are only three official oceans. The volume of ocean water exceeds the capacity of the ocean basins, and the ocean overflows on to the continents creating continental shelves. A few of the more important shelves are: the East China Sea, the Bering Sea, the North Sea, the Grand Banks, the Patagonian Shelf, the Arafura Sea and Gulf of Carpentaria, and the Siberian Shelf. **The shallow seas help dissipate tides, they are often areas of high biological productivity, and are usually included in the exclusive economic zone of adjacent countries.**

[P6] The depths of the oceans are mapped by echo sounders which measure the time required for a sound pulse to travel from the surface to the bottom and back. Depths measured by ship-based echo sounders have been used to produce maps of the sea floor. The maps have poor horizontal resolution in some regions because the regions are seldom visited by ships and ship tracks are far apart. The depths of the oceans are also measured by satellite altimeter systems, which profile the shape of the sea surface. The local shape of the surface is influenced by changes in gravity due to sub-sea features. Recent maps based on satellite altimeter measurements of the shape of the sea surface combined with ship data have depth accuracy of ±100 m and horizontal resolutions of ±3 km.

[P7] With our recently acquired ability to travel into space, we now see the earth and its oceans as a whole. A new NASA satellite, ICESat2, was launched in September 2018. Using satellite cameras, we can locate storms and guide ships out of harm's way. We can count the phytoplankton that fuel the fisheries and direct fishermen to fertile grounds. Our sensors detect climatic anomalies as they begin, allowing us to predict their consequences. These are exciting times for humankind's interactions with the sea.

Glossary

Velocity field: a distribution of velocity in a given region

Question 21 According to paragraph 1, which of the following statements is true about a meridian?

(A) It is an imaginary great circle on the Earth's surface passing through the North and South geographic poles.

(B) It is a curve on a surface of revolution, formed by the intersection of the surface with a plane containing the axis of revolution.

(C) It is a vertical equatorial plane passing through Earth's axis of rotation.

(D) It is the angle between the local vertical and the equatorial plane.

Question 22 The word "perpendicular" in paragraph 1 is closest in meaning to:

(A) vertical

(B) horizontal

(C) parallel

(D) principal

Question 23 The word "nautical" in paragraph 2 is closest in meaning to:

(A) military

(B) tactical

(C) empirical

(D) maritime

Question 24 According to paragraph 3, the tie between nautical miles, meters, and Earth's radius was soon abandoned because:

(A) They were impractical, and the rough estimations were also lagging behind.

(B) They were impractical to use although the estimations were quite correct.

(C) They were not only practical but also 100% correct in terms of approximations.

(D) They were practical, and the approximations were very good.

Question 25 According to paragraph 4, what can be inferred about maps of the sea floor?

(A) Maps of the sea floor are of high-quality horizontal resolution because the regions in question are seldom visited by ships.

(B) Maps of the sea floor created by ship-based echo sounders produce fairly low-resolution maps due to large distances and inconsistencies between ships visiting a certain area and the number of ship tracks being far apart from one another.

(C) Maps of the sea floor are produced by equipments found on seldom visiting ships and ship tracks.

(D) Maps of the sea floor are ship-based echo sounders designed to scare ships away from a given territory.

■ Question 26 Which of the following sentences best describes the highlighted sentence in the passage? The other choices change the meaning or leave out information.

The shallow seas help dissipate tides, they are often areas of high biological productivity, and are usually included in the exclusive economic zone of adjacent countries.

(A) Shallow seas dissipate tides, biological productivity and economic zones.

(B) Shallow seas are important centers of biochemical productivity, especially in economic zones where dissipating tides is more troublesome.

(C) Shallow seas not only contribute to breaking up tides, but they also serve as an important hub for organic productivity and economic territorial division.

(D) Shallow seas have tremendous consequences to biological productivity and tidal dissipation.

■ Question 27 All of the following statements are correct EXCEPT:

(A) The current number of official oceans is 3.

(B) There are 7 continental shelves all over the world.

(C) Shallow seas disperse tides.

(D) Continental shelves can serve economic purposes.

■ Question 28 It can be concluded that echo sounders:

(A) map approximate ocean depth by measuring the time necessary for the sound to get to the surface from the bottom

(B) map approximate ocean depth by measuring the speed of sound from one end of the ocean to the other

(C) map approximate ocean depth by giving off a sound pulse

(D) map approximate ocean depth by factoring in the time required for the sound to reach the sky

■ Question 29 Look at the four squares in paragraph 7, **A**, **B**, **C**, and **D**, which indicate where the following sentence could be added to the passage. Where would the sentence best fit?

It is expected to gauge future changes of the Greenland and Antarctic ice sheets at an accuracy of the width of a pencil.

[P7] With our recently acquired ability to travel into space, we now see the earth and its oceans as a whole. **A** A new NASA satellite, ICESat2, was launched in September 2018. **B** Using satellite cameras, we can locate storms and guide ships out of harm's way. **C** We can count the phytoplankton that fuel the fisheries and direct fishermen to fertile grounds. Our sensors detect climatic anomalies as they begin, allowing us to predict their consequences. **D** These are exciting times for humankind's interactions with the sea.

(A) **A**

(B) **B**

(C) **C**

(D) **D**

■ Question 30 Directions:

An introductory sentence for a brief summary of the passage is provided below.

Complete the summary by selecting the THREE answer choices that express the most important ideas in the passage. Some sentences do not belong in the summary because they express ideas that are not presented in the passage or are minor ideas in the passage.

This question is worth 2 points.

- Distances on Earth are measured thanks to systems, each using different parameters, with points of reference such as the equatorial plan and Greenwich.
- ________
- ________
- ________

(A) The irregularity of the Earth's shape led to the adoption of different measuring systems, some of which, albeit valid, are no longer used due to being impractical.

(B) Thanks to Gabriel Mouton's work, the whole world could start using the metric system for different kinds of measurements.

(C) The echo-sound measurement allows oceanographers to locate storms and guide ships while at sea.

(D) The new NASA satellite will allow the experts to better study continental shelves and control climate changes.

(E) Although oceans have irregular dimensions, it is possible to state that they are generally wider than they are deep.

(F) The development of new technologies allows to measure and examine an ocean's depth and surface through sound waves and space satellites in much greater detail.

TOEFL iBT #1 - LISTENING (AUDIO)

LISTENING SECTION DIRECTIONS

The Listening section measures your ability to understand conversations and lectures in English. You will hear a conversation or lecture **only one time**, and you will answer some questions about them. The questions typically ask about the main idea and supporting details of the conversation and lecture. Some questions will ask about a speaker's purpose or attitude. Answer the questions based on what the speakers state or imply.

You may take notes while you listen. You may use your notes to help you answer the questions. Your notes will not be scored.

In some question, you will see an audio icon. This means that you will hear, but not see, part of the question.

You should answer each question, even if you must guess the answer.

Reportez vos réponses pour analyser votre performance.

Entraînez-vous dans les conditions d'examen.

Écoutez les fichiers audio.

prepmyfuture.com/book/68/ex/1983

Listen to part of a lecture in an engineering class.

1) The Great Pyramid

2) Long Ramp Theory

3) Spiral Ramp Theory

Question 1 What is the lecture mainly about?

(A) A presentation of alternate theories about the purpose of the Great Pyramid.

(B) A summary of some competing ideas on how the Great Pyramid was constructed.

(C) A discussion on who the original builder of the Great Pyramid might be.

(D) A debate about when the Great Pyramid may have been built.

▪ Question 2 According to the lecture, what is one problem with the Long Ramp Theory?

(A) It would have taken an estimated 3 years to complete.
(B) It would have involved transporting stone blocks from Aswan.
(C) It does not explain how steep the ramp would need to be in order to reach the top of the pyramid.
(D) There are no indications for the existence of a long ramp near the Great Pyramid.

▪ Question 3 What evidence did Houdin use to create his "Spiral Ramp" theory?

(A) a pathway of stones circling the Great Pyramid
(B) an old map showing something unusual inside the Great Pyramid
(C) a recently discovered structural weakness in the interior of the Great Pyramid
(D) records from ancient builders describing the removal of an external ramp

▪ Question 4 Why does the professor mention stone blocks when discussing problems with the Long Ramp Theory?

(A) To emphasize the magnitude of transporting and setting the large stones.
(B) To explain why a long ramp probably would collapse under the weight of the heaviest stones.
(C) To highlight the difficulty of finding an adequate source of stone.
(D) To point out that sleds or rolling logs would not have been able to support their weight.

▪ Question 5 What might have been a benefit in building the Great Pyramid using spiral ramps?

(A) It would have required a less steep ramp.
(B) It would have shortened the time needed to finish the pyramid.
(C) It would have helped the pyramid builders move blocks around 90-degree turns.
(D) It would have eliminated the possibility of any collapses during construction.

▪ Question 6 Listen again to part of the lecture. Then answer the question.

(A) Scientists had to search a different part of the Great Pyramid for evidence.
(B) Scientists had to return to more traditional theories on pyramid construction.
(C) Scientists had to do research at pyramids from different parts of Egypt.
(D) Scientists had to be more creative in explaining the pyramid's construction.

Listen to part of a discussion in an anthropology class.

1) Introduction

2) Sympathetic Magic

3) Shamanism

Question 7 What is the main purpose of the lecture?

(A) To compare the symbols in prehistoric art to those in modern art.
(B) To describe the hunting rituals of ancient people as seen in cave art.
(C) To argue that ancient hunters believed in evil spirits living in animals.
(D) To contrast two possible explanations for the creation of prehistoric cave art.

Question 8 Listen again to part of the lecture. Then answer the question.

(A) Images with dark lines on them are rarely seen.
(B) There are several possible explanations for the dark lines.
(C) The dark lines on the cave paintings are very faint.
(D) The best interpretation for the dark marks is that they are weapons.

Question 9 Why does the professor mention sports team mascots in the lecture?

(A) To show that ancient people played games similar to modern people.
(B) To provide a modern-day example of a type of Sympathetic Magic ritual.
(C) To explain why Sympathetic Magic rituals were probably not very effective.
(D) To point out how cave paintings could teach ancient people how to hunt as a group.

Question 10 Listen again to part of the lecture. Then answer the question.

(A) The student probably did see a cave painting of a lion in the documentary.
(B) The cave painting the student had seen had probably been vandalized.
(C) The cave painting was probably of a different type of animal than the student thought.
(D) The cave painting probably looked as the artist originally intended.

Question 11 What kind of cave paintings seem to support the Shamanism theory of cave art?

(A) images with dark marks appearing to come out of the animal's mouth
(B) images showing half-man, half-animal figures
(C) images that display groups of animals together
(D) images hidden deep inside caves that are not easy to reach

■ **Question 12** According to the Shamanism theory of cave art, what is the main purpose of ancient cave paintings?

(A) to create a deeper state of awareness of the world
(B) to assist ancient people in hunting for food
(C) to give respect to the animals they saw in nature
(D) to help ancient people connect with their dead ancestors

Listen to part of a discussion in a world history class.

■ **Question 13** What are the main topics of the lecture?

Click on 2 answers.

(A) Why ancient China was the source of many inventions
(B) How technology moved from medieval Europe to other parts of the world
(C) How China kept the process for making silk secret for centuries
(D) How Chinese innovations were picked up by other cultures in ancient times

■ **Question 14** According to the professor, all of the following are examples of Chinese technology or knowledge that reached Europe before the 13th century EXCEPT:

(A) creating items out of iron
(B) gunpowder
(C) medicine
(D) silk weaving

■ **Question 15** According to the lecture, how did the loom most likely come to be used in the Middle East?

(A) Roman travelers saw a loom being used in China.
(B) Chinese craftsmen were captured and taken to the Middle East.
(C) Chinese merchants sold diagrams of the loom to people in the Middle East.
(D) Buddhist monks brought the loom with them while on pilgrimage.

■ **Question 16** What does the professor imply by this statement?

(A) Europe benefited from the fact that China was the only source for silk.
(B) Europe and the Middle East sought for many centuries to find a way to travel to China by sea.
(C) After discovering a sea route to China, European no longer used the Silk Road.
(D) Silk was the only commodity which both Europe and the Middle East desired from China.

▪ Question 17 According to the lecture, why was China the originator of many devices?

(A) It had the largest population in the ancient world.
(B) It heavily restricted access to Chinese technology.
(C) It had a strong central government.
(D) It maintained tight control over merchants traveling the Silk Road.

▪ Question 18 Which of the following statements is true?

(A) It is well understood how all Chinese technologies and ideas reached Europe.
(B) Ancient China did not seek out technology from other countries.
(C) Peaceful immigration was the primary method for Chinese technology reaching Europe in ancient times.
(D) Ancient China was well-suited for large-scale building projects.

Listen to a discussion between a student and a professor.

▪ Question 19 Why does the student want to talk with the professor?

(A) to explain why she feels a project in a class is too difficult
(B) to get help preparing for a test
(C) to interview him for a project
(D) to get advice on how to do an assignment

▪ Question 20 Why is the student having trouble with the assignment?

(A) She doesn't know any business leaders who are looking to hire college students.
(B) She's not familiar with anyone who fits a certain criteria.
(C) She doesn't think anyone would want to do an interview with her.
(D) She didn't conduct an interview in time for a deadline.

▪ Question 21 How does the professor help the student?

(A) Suggesting a method for looking for someone to interview.
(B) Giving her the name of a business leader to contact to set up an interview.
(C) Offering an alternate project for the final assignment.
(D) Telling a story of how he found a local business person to interview.

Question 22 According to the professor, what are some of the goals of the class they are discussing?

Click on 2 answers.

(A) To explore the types of industries students may want to work in
(B) To examine how business leaders are viewed in the local community
(C) To understand what business leaders do to promote the general welfare of the community
(D) To learn how to effectively manage a company

Question 23 Listen again to part of the lecture. Then answer the question.

What does the professor mean when he says this?

(A) He feels that the student should find a student partner to help her with the project.
(B) He thinks the student should ask a local business to help her find someone to interview.
(C) He feels that the project may be too difficult for the student to complete.
(D) He believes that the student won't have any further problems completing her project.

Listen to a conversation between a students and a counselor at a university career center.

Question 24 Why did the student go to the Career Center?

(A) to ask for more information about an upcoming job fair
(B) to get advice on which field of study he should pursue
(C) to get a list of questions to ask companies attending a fair
(D) to inquire about a particular job opportunity

Question 25 The student thinks he can't go to the career fair for the following reasons EXCEPT:

(A) He is not in his final year of college.
(B) He is not yet an international business student.
(C) He is planning getting a science or language degree.
(D) He is a male student.

Question 26 According to the counselor, companies attend the career fair for the following reasons EXCEPT:

(A) To encourage students to get international business degrees.
(B) To explain how other field of study may be related to international business.
(C) To encourage students to get a graduate degree.
(D) To meet upcoming graduates interested in a business career.

▪ **Question 27** Why does the counselor suggest that the student visit the university website next week before the career fair begins?

(A) There may be changes to which companies are attending the fair.

(B) There will be a list of questions that the companies will be asking students.

(C) The schedule and location of the fair may change.

(D) Students can schedule an interview with companies in which they are interested.

▪ **Question 28** What does the counselor recommend the student do before the career fair?

(A) talk to some seniors who are going to the fair to look for a job

(B) print out a map of the fair to see which companies are attending

(C) make a list of which fields of study he is interested in studying

(D) visit the websites of companies attending the career fair to learn more about them

TOEFL iBT #1 - LISTENING (SCRIPT)

LISTENING SECTION DIRECTIONS

The Listening section measures your ability to understand conversations and lectures in English. You will hear a conversation or lecture **only one time**, and you will answer some questions about them. The questions typically ask about the main idea and supporting details of the conversation and lecture. Some questions will ask about a speaker's purpose or attitude. Answer the questions based on what the speakers state or imply.

You may take notes while you listen. You may use your notes to help you answer the questions. Your notes will not be scored.

In some question, you will see an audio icon. This means that you will hear, but not see, part of the question.

You should answer each question, even if you must guess the answer.

Reportez vos réponses pour analyser votre performance.

Entraînez-vous dans les conditions d'examen.

Écoutez les fichiers audio.

prepmyfuture.com/book/68/ex/1983

Listen to part of a lecture in an engineering class.

1) The Great Pyramid

Script non affiché le jour de l'examen :

MALE PROFESSOR: Egypt's Great Pyramid at Giza is one of the world's most amazing achievements of engineering. Built during one of the early dynasties of Egypt around 2500 B.C., it is among the world's top tourist attractions, and the subject of both serious study and wild speculation. But how was it built? To this day, the method used by ancient Egyptians to construct the Great Pyramid is an archeological and engineering mystery.

2) Long Ramp Theory

Script non affiché le jour de l'examen :

For years, the consensus among archaeologists, historians, and Egyptologists was that the stone blocks used to build it had been quarried from as far as 900 kilometers away in Aswan and then transported to Giza, probably on rafts which could float down the Nile. At Giza, the stones could have then been pulled on sleds or over rolling logs up to the pyramids along a stone causeway, after which they would have been pulled up long earthen ramps to the various heights on the pyramid for placement. This theory presumes that tens of thousands of workers—either slaves or freemen—labored for decades to quarry, transport, and place the over 2.3 million blocks used to erect the Great Pyramid.

Though this "Long Ramp" theory of pyramid construction has existed for decades, recently scientists from various disciplines have begun to question some of its aspects. For one, in order to complete the pyramid within the generally-accepted time frame for construction of 20 years, workers would have had to maneuver into place one stone block every 3 minutes—an impossible feat considering the average weight of the blocks is over 2 metric tons, and with some blocks as heavy as 80 tons. Another problem with this theory is that in order to pull the stone blocks up to the highest levels of the pyramid, workers would have needed to build a steep ramp over a mile in length; despite extensive examinations of the surrounding plateau, no trace of such a ramp has ever been found. Over the years, scientists tried to come up with various explanations to either downplay or discount these problems with the Long Ramp theory…all to no avail. So, historians and engineers had to begin to think outside the box, because the traditional ideas weren't actually in sync with what people were seeing in the field.

3) Spiral Ramp Theory

Script non affiché le jour de l'examen :

In the 2000's, a French architect, Jean-Pierre Houdin, developed a new theory regarding the manner in which the ancient Egyptians may have constructed the Great Pyramid. It involved the construction of two ramps—one interior and one exterior—which spiral up and around the pyramid. He found support for this his theory from an old survey of the pyramid showing a "spiral anomaly" inside the pyramid—a strange pathway of stones that seemed to be shaped like a corridor snaking around the pyramid just underneath the exterior surface. This 'spiral' would have enabled the pyramid-builders to create a ramp of a much easier grade, making it possible to haul large granite blocks to the very top of the Great Pyramid. Once the pyramid was complete, the interior ramp could have then been filled with stone and other material, and with the external ramp also removed, any evidence of its existence would be erased.

Even though there is growing interest in Houdin's "Spiral Ramp" theory, skeptics have pointed out some serious issues with it. In order for Houdin's theory to work, a method must be given for how ancient workers could pull 80-ton blocks around the 90-degree turns posited by Houdin's spiral ramp. Another complication is caused by the interplay of the interior and exterior ramps; the interior ramp, because it is empty space inside the pyramid, would create structural weaknesses in the pyramid, making the possibility of collapses very likely due the hundreds of tons of rock pressing down on it. While Houdin remains confident that his theory is correct, he has been unable to corroborate it due to lack of access to the interior of the Great Pyramid in order to conduct further research.

▪ Question 1 What is the lecture mainly about?

(A) A presentation of alternate theories about the purpose of the Great Pyramid.
(B) A summary of some competing ideas on how the Great Pyramid was constructed.
(C) A discussion on who the original builder of the Great Pyramid might be.
(D) A debate about when the Great Pyramid may have been built.

▪ Question 2 According to the lecture, what is one problem with the Long Ramp Theory?

(A) It would have taken an estimated 3 years to complete.
(B) It would have involved transporting stone blocks from Aswan.
(C) It does not explain how steep the ramp would need to be in order to reach the top of the pyramid.
(D) There are no indications for the existence of a long ramp near the Great Pyramid.

▪ Question 3 What evidence did Houdin use to create his "Spiral Ramp" theory?

(A) a pathway of stones circling the Great Pyramid
(B) an old map showing something unusual inside the Great Pyramid
(C) a recently discovered structural weakness in the interior of the Great Pyramid
(D) records from ancient builders describing the removal of an external ramp

▪ Question 4 Why does the professor mention stone blocks when discussing problems with the Long Ramp Theory?

(A) To emphasize the magnitude of transporting and setting the large stones.
(B) To explain why a long ramp probably would collapse under the weight of the heaviest stones.
(C) To highlight the difficulty of finding an adequate source of stone.
(D) To point out that sleds or rolling logs would not have been able to support their weight.

▪ Question 5 What might have been a benefit in building the Great Pyramid using spiral ramps?

(A) It would have required a less steep ramp.

(B) It would have shortened the time needed to finish the pyramid.

(C) It would have helped the pyramid builders move blocks around 90-degree turns.

(D) It would have eliminated the possibility of any collapses during construction.

▪ Question 6 Listen again to part of the lecture. Then answer the question.

> **Script non affiché le jour de l'examen :**
> **MALE PROFESSOR:** Over the years, scientists tried to come up with various explanations to either downplay or discount these problems with the Long Ramp theory…all to no avail. So, historians and engineers had to begin to think outside the box, because the traditional ideas weren't actually in sync with what people were seeing in the field.
>
> **NARRATOR:** What does the professor mean when he says this?
>
> **MALE PROFESSOR:** So, historians and engineers had to begin to think outside the box.

(A) Scientists had to search a different part of the Great Pyramid for evidence.

(B) Scientists had to return to more traditional theories on pyramid construction.

(C) Scientists had to do research at pyramids from different parts of Egypt.

(D) Scientists had to be more creative in explaining the pyramid's construction.

Listen to part of a discussion in an anthropology class.

1) Introduction

Script non affiché le jour de l'examen :

FEMALE PROFESSOR: In the Paleolithic era, long before written history, humans had painted images in caves for tens of thousands of years. Scientists have attempted to explain the meaning behind this cave art in a number of ways. Today, I want to talk about two of the most popular categories of theories: “Sympathetic Magic” and “Shamanism”.

2) Sympathetic Magic

Script non affiché le jour de l'examen :

Proponents of the Sympathetic Magic theory assert that the animals in the cave paintings were created to control or influence real animals. One of the most popular of the sympathetic magic theories is the idea of "hunting magic"—the idea that Paleolithic art sprung from the hunter's anxieties about the availability of game in the wild. The most compelling proof for this theory comes from researchers noting that some animals painted on cave walls appear to have been killed by missiles or attacked by hand-held weapons.

What do I mean by this? Well, in many ancient caves circles are painted to cover some of the depicted animals, which might indicate that the animal had been stoned to death. Dark marks at the animals' mouth or nose appear to be blood being vomited by the dying beasts. In a cave in Montespan, France scientists found a depiction of a bear that seems to be riddled with holes and to have been stabbed with long dark lines—possibly images of spears—in a ritual attack. If you've ever seen images of cave paintings, it's hard to see what else those long dark lines could be.

MALE STUDENT: I've seen some of those. They were in a documentary I saw last year. There was one—I think it was a painting of a lion—and it had so many lines drawn over it, it looked like someone had tried to vandalize it. But I guess that's not the case, huh?

FEMALE PROFESSOR: That's probably a safe bet. It has been suggested that ancient man used the paintings again and again, as a kind of imagination…um, I mean visualization exercise before going out on hunts, kind of like nowadays when rival college sports teams burn a wooden statue of the other team's mascot before an important game. Other archaeologists, however, note that often the "holes" are actually simply the natural texture of the cave wall. These scientists feel that proponents of the Sympathetic Magic Theory are over-interpreting images and marks on cave walls, and are stretching evidence to fit their theory.

MALE STUDENT: So all those lines and circles might just be ancient people decorating the wall.

FEMALE PROFESSOR: Well, probably more than just decoration for the sake of decoration, but less than some type of magic ritual. For example, it could have been part of a game, like a kind of target practice, or even something like an instructional diagram, helping ancient hunters teach a new generation of hunters how to kill an animal, where to strike it with a spear, or something like that.

3) Shamanism

Script non affiché le jour de l'examen :

In contrast to all those possibilities, the old theory of Shamanism seems to be returning in popularity. This concept involves a complex view of the world in which two “worlds”—one being the physical world and another being spiritual, like as heaven or hell—coexist as different levels of reality. These worlds are thought to interact with and influence one another. Thus, in our own world, most events are believed to be the consequence of some phenomena from the other world—a modern day equivalent of this would be the belief that praying to a Catholic saint can help someone recover from an illness or overcome some problem. Supporters of the Shamanism theory of cave painting claim that the paintings exist to help certain elite members of primitive societies—priest or magicians called "shamans"—enter a deeper state of consciousness in order to form a closer connection to or deeper understanding of the world.

Support for this theory come from cave paintings which show one animal seemingly combined with another, like some kind of hybrid creature, or in painting showing an animal head painted on a human body, clearly displaying a creature that does not exist in the real world but is based on some symbolic meaning. These hybrid animals could be "spirit animals", spirits from the other world who take the shape of strange beasts or half-human/half-animal creatures in our world to help people with matters of survival or health. Proponents of the Shamanism Theory look at those animal paintings which have a dark substance coming out of their mouths as representations of "evil spirits"—not blood—being cast out of the bodies of animals or people here in the real world.

This debate continues to this day, with new books and papers being published that advance one idea or the other for why ancient man painted cave walls, but there probably was no single reason for making art that spanned this huge stretch of time and space; just like how all artists today create for different reasons. All of these hypotheses are probably true to a certain extent. Regardless of the ultimate explanation, they remain a beautiful and fascinating link to our long-gone heritage.

▪ Question 7 What is the main purpose of the lecture?

(A) To compare the symbols in prehistoric art to those in modern art.
(B) To describe the hunting rituals of ancient people as seen in cave art.
(C) To argue that ancient hunters believed in evil spirits living in animals.
(D) To contrast two possible explanations for the creation of prehistoric cave art.

▪ Question 8 Listen again to part of the lecture. Then answer the question.

Script non affiché le jour de l'examen :
FEMALE PROFESSOR: In a cave in Montespan, France scientists found a depiction of a bear that seems to be riddled with holes and to have been stabbed with long dark lines—possibly images of spears—in a ritual attack. If you've ever seen images of cave paintings, it's hard to see what else those long dark lines could be.

NARRATOR: What does the professor mean by this statement?

FEMALE PROFESSOR: If you've ever seen images of cave paintings, it's hard to see what else those long dark lines could be.

(A) Images with dark lines on them are rarely seen.
(B) There are several possible explanations for the dark lines.
(C) The dark lines on the cave paintings are very faint.
(D) The best interpretation for the dark marks is that they are weapons.

Question 9 Why does the professor mention sports team mascots in the lecture?

(A) To show that ancient people played games similar to modern people.
(B) To provide a modern-day example of a type of Sympathetic Magic ritual.
(C) To explain why Sympathetic Magic rituals were probably not very effective.
(D) To point out how cave paintings could teach ancient people how to hunt as a group.

Question 10 Listen again to part of the lecture. Then answer the question.

> **Script non affiché le jour de l'examen :**
> **MALE STUDENT:** I've seen some of those! They were in a documentary I saw last year. There was one--I think it was a painting of a lion—and it had so many lines drawn over it, it looked like someone had tried to vandalize it. But I guess that's not the case, huh?
>
> **FEMALE PROFESSOR:** That's probably a safe bet.
>
> **NARRATOR:** What does the professor mean by this statement?
>
> **FEMALE PROFESSOR:** That's probably a safe bet.

(A) The student probably did see a cave painting of a lion in the documentary.
(B) The cave painting the student had seen had probably been vandalized.
(C) The cave painting was probably of a different type of animal than the student thought.
(D) The cave painting probably looked as the artist originally intended.

Question 11 What kind of cave paintings seem to support the Shamanism theory of cave art?

(A) images with dark marks appearing to come out of the animal's mouth
(B) images showing half-man, half-animal figures
(C) images that display groups of animals together
(D) images hidden deep inside caves that are not easy to reach

Question 12 According to the Shamanism theory of cave art, what is the main purpose of ancient cave paintings?

(A) to create a deeper state of awareness of the world
(B) to assist ancient people in hunting for food
(C) to give respect to the animals they saw in nature
(D) to help ancient people connect with their dead ancestors

Listen to part of a discussion in a world history class.

Script non affiché le jour de l'examen :

FEMALE PROFESSOR: So, before we finish our examination of Europe in the Middle Ages, I wanted to say a little bit about how China was able to play such a vital role in introducing new technology and scientific thought to medieval Europe. While Europe's interactions with other regions—such as the Middle East and Africa—did result in some exchanges of technological know-how, by far the most important and rewarding of these cultural and technological borrowings came from China. The most isolated of the ancient civilizations, with its own characteristic cultural patterns and style of thought, China developed its science independent of Greek influence, resulting in revolutionary and wondrous—in the eyes of Europeans—inventions. Um, yes, Steve?

MALE STUDENT 1: Are you talking about stuff like gunpowder?

FEMALE PROFESSOR: Well, gunpowder didn't arrive in Europe until the 13th century. And while that is the most well-known technology Europe got from China, I want to focus on an earlier part of European history, from Roman times up through the Dark Ages. Some of the Chinese inventions that reached Europe during this era passed quickly to the West, and some took centuries. The course of transmission of several of these technologies can be traced step by step, such as paper manufacturing; but others remain frustratingly speculative. One agency of contact between China and the West that was a catalyst for the transmission of technology was silk, the most desired luxury textile of the ancient and medieval worlds. East Asia held a near-complete monopoly on silk manufacturing since its mythological origins some 5,000 years ago—

FEMALE STUDENT 1: Wait a minute, if silk was so prized in Europe, how could China have a monopoly on its production? You would think that at some point a merchant or craftsperson would have taught a foreigner how to make silk.

FEMALE PROFESSOR: For many other inventions that did happen, but silk was special. The Chinese monopoly on silk was actually from an official decree from the emperors, handed down through the centuries—anyone caught attempting to sell silkworms or instructing foreigners on how to produce silk would be put to death...and in ancient China, with its strong authoritative government, this policy could be enforced. In some ways, this monopoly of production served Europe and the Middle East well, because this combination of both desirability and monopoly provided a permanent line of interaction, first through Central Asia over the four-thousand-mile long Silk Road and later by sea, between the Far East and Europe.

Warfare was one carrier of technology, where Chinese artisans and craftsmen would be taken captive and taken back to the Middle East. In the 10th century, one Chinese officer who had been held prisoner in Persia reported finding Chinese goldsmiths and silk weavers there, and noted that the Chinese artisans were using machines like the loom—a device unknown to the local Arabic culture, but which had been invented in China centuries before.

Other carriers of technology included immigrants, such as those from a Chinese delegation who settled in Persia as early as 110 B.C. and taught their new neighbors to cast weapons, tools and utensils from iron. At about this same time, researchers believe that deserters from a Chinese army taught people in Central Asia the art of well drilling. While most of these technological transfers were accidental, sometimes armies invading China would demand hostages such as metalworkers, weavers and tailors, showing that Chinese technology was much sought after by the lesser cultures that surrounded it. Even religious pilgrims played a role in spread of technology, when Buddhist monks traveling from China to India in the early Middle Ages shared their knowledge of less-technological subjects like astrology, mineralogy, and medicine.

MALE STUDENT 1: But why China? What is it that made it so advanced compared to other ancient civilizations?

FEMALE PROFESSOR: Well, many historians believe that Chinese technological leadership was due to the strong bureaucratic government which had ruled China since the third century B.C. They point to historical records showing that most of China's engineers and master technicians were either directly employed or closely supervised by administrative representatives. On top of that, complex machines, such as the water mill, could be developed only under government sponsorship. The same was true of large-scale engineering projects, the most famous of which was the Great Wall of China, built as a defensive barrier against nomadic horsemen of Northern Asia. These massive building projects, organized by a powerful, centralized government which could assert its authority over local governments, led to massive irrigation and transportation networks to be constructed throughout the kingdom.

▪ **Question 13** What are the main topics of the lecture?

Click on 2 answers.

(A) Why ancient China was the source of many inventions
(B) How technology moved from medieval Europe to other parts of the world
(C) How China kept the process for making silk secret for centuries
(D) How Chinese innovations were picked up by other cultures in ancient times

▪ **Question 14** According to the professor, all of the following are examples of Chinese technology or knowledge that reached Europe before the 13th century EXCEPT:

(A) creating items out of iron
(B) gunpowder
(C) medicine
(D) silk weaving

▪ **Question 15** According to the lecture, how did the loom most likely come to be used in the Middle East?

(A) Roman travelers saw a loom being used in China.
(B) Chinese craftsmen were captured and taken to the Middle East.
(C) Chinese merchants sold diagrams of the loom to people in the Middle East.
(D) Buddhist monks brought the loom with them while on pilgrimage.

Question 16 What does the professor imply by this statement?

> **Script non affiché le jour de l'examen :**
> **FEMALE PROFESSOR:** In some ways, this monopoly of production served Europe and the Middle East well, because this combination of both desirability and monopoly provided a permanent line of interaction, first through Central Asia over the four-thousand-mile Silk Road and later by sea, between the Far East and Europe.

(A) Europe benefited from the fact that China was the only source for silk.
(B) Europe and the Middle East sought for many centuries to find a way to travel to China by sea.
(C) After discovering a sea route to China, European no longer used the Silk Road.
(D) Silk was the only commodity which both Europe and the Middle East desired from China.

Question 17 According to the lecture, why was China the originator of many devices?

(A) It had the largest population in the ancient world.
(B) It heavily restricted access to Chinese technology.
(C) It had a strong central government.
(D) It maintained tight control over merchants traveling the Silk Road.

Question 18 Which of the following statements is true?

(A) It is well understood how all Chinese technologies and ideas reached Europe.
(B) Ancient China did not seek out technology from other countries.
(C) Peaceful immigration was the primary method for Chinese technology reaching Europe in ancient times.
(D) Ancient China was well-suited for large-scale building projects.

Listen to a discussion between a student and a professor.

Script non affiché le jour de l'examen :

FEMALE STUDENT: Um, Professor Clauson? Do you have minute?

MALE PROFESSOR: Sure, but I don't have a lot of time. I've got a department meeting to get to across campus.

FEMALE STUDENT: I shouldn't take a minute. I'm wondering if you might be able to help me with something about our final project.

MALE PROFESSOR: The business leader interview, huh? Are you having trouble coming up with interview questions?

FEMALE STUDENT: It's not that. I...well, maybe I've lived a sheltered life, but I don't really know anybody who I could say was a "business leader". I mean...you want us to talk with someone's who's made an impact in the community, someone who's made a difference. I've been wracking my brain all week, and even though I could probably interview any number of business owners from some of the establishments I go to here in town, I wouldn't necessarily call any them a leader of the community.

MALE PROFESSOR: I see. You're not the first student who's had this problem. I mean, unless your mom or dad knows someone or you're related to someone who fits the bill, you have to go out and find someone on your own.

FEMALE STUDENT: That's just it. I don't even know where or how to begin my search. I don't know if you knew this about me, but I'm not from around here. I don't really follow local news—too much homework, I guess--

MALE PROFESSOR: That's understandable.

FEMALE STUDENT: So, I'm wondering...

MALE PROFESSOR: Well, it wouldn't be fair to the other students in class if I just gave you the name of someone I know.

FEMALE STUDENT: (sighs) Yeah. I guess not.

MALE PROFESSOR: But I think I may be able to point you in the right direction. You know, part of this class is to not just get you to understand what it takes to run a business, but to see how companies contribute to the community in various ways—whether it's through environmentally-conscious practices, sponsorships or charitable-giving. I want you to go out into the local community and learn about it. The business leaders here in town didn't start out by knowing what they could do to help people living around them; they had to step out of their store and talk to people, make connections, understand more about the lives of the people who come into their establishment. This project allows you to develop those skills.

FEMALE STUDENT: I guess I never thought of it that way. Some of them must have felt like I do right now, not knowing where to start or where to go.

MALE PROFESSOR: Exactly! Now, a good way to find out about what's going in town is to check out the local papers.

FEMALE STUDENT: Like the Willamette Week?

MALE PROFESSOR: Or the Portland Herald. Both of them have a Business Section highlighting important news and personalities here in town. You might find someone there—it's easy enough: call them up and ask for an interview. You might even find out that one of the business owners you know about actually is a community leader.

FEMALE STUDENT: Won't they think doing an interview with me might be a little, I don't know, under them?

MALE PROFESSOR: (Chuckles) Many people, especially successful business people, enjoy telling the story of how they got to where they are now. You remember how I was saying last week that some of the best business leaders often have the same qualities as a teacher? It's in their DNA to share, if for nothing else but to make themselves seem even more interesting and successful.

FEMALE STUDENT: Yeah...you did say that.

MALE PROFESSOR: I think you'll find that with just a little bit of searching in the local news, you'll find some people who you'd enjoy interviewing, and who would get a kick out of being interviewed for a college project.

FEMALE STUDENT: Thank you so much, Professor. This is all a really big help.

MALE PROFESSOR: My pleasure. Sometimes it takes just a little help to get yourself off on the right foot. In no time you'll see it's not so hard.

Question 19 Why does the student want to talk with the professor?

(A) to explain why she feels a project in a class is too difficult
(B) to get help preparing for a test
(C) to interview him for a project
(D) to get advice on how to do an assignment

Question 20 Why is the student having trouble with the assignment?

(A) She doesn't know any business leaders who are looking to hire college students.
(B) She's not familiar with anyone who fits a certain criteria.
(C) She doesn't think anyone would want to do an interview with her.
(D) She didn't conduct an interview in time for a deadline.

Question 21 How does the professor help the student?

(A) Suggesting a method for looking for someone to interview.
(B) Giving her the name of a business leader to contact to set up an interview.
(C) Offering an alternate project for the final assignment.
(D) Telling a story of how he found a local business person to interview.

▪ Question 22 According to the professor, what are some of the goals of the class they are discussing?

Click on 2 answers.

(A) To explore the types of industries students may want to work in

(B) To examine how business leaders are viewed in the local community

(C) To understand what business leaders do to promote the general welfare of the community

(D) To learn how to effectively manage a company

▪ Question 23 Listen again to part of the lecture. Then answer the question.

> **Script non affiché le jour de l'examen :**
> **FEMALE STUDENT:** Thank you so much, Professor. This is all a really big help.
>
> **MALE PROFESSOR:** My pleasure. Sometimes it takes just a little help to get yourself off on the right foot. In no time you'll see it's not so hard.

What does the professor mean when he says this?

> **Script non affiché le jour de l'examen :**
> **MALE PROFESSOR:** Sometimes it takes just a little help to get yourself off on the right foot.

(A) He feels that the student should find a student partner to help her with the project.

(B) He thinks the student should ask a local business to help her find someone to interview.

(C) He feels that the project may be too difficult for the student to complete.

(D) He believes that the student won't have any further problems completing her project.

Listen to a conversation between a student and a counselor at a university career center.

Script non affiché le jour de l'examen :

MALE STUDENT: Hi! Do you have a minute?

FEMALE COUNSELOR: Sure. How can I help you?

MALE STUDENT: Yesterday I saw a poster for an international business career fair.

FEMALE COUNSELOR: You mean the one next week?

MALE STUDENT: Yeah. I've got a couple questions about it.

FEMALE COUNSELOR: Just a sec. Let me pull up the file on it. (pause) Ok. Here it is. What did you want to know?

MALE STUDENT: I guess first off, can I go? Someone told me it was a woman's career fair.

FEMALE COUNSELOR: Oh, no. We hold that later in the year.

MALE STUDENT: Oh, I see. Also...I'm just a sophomore—I don't even know if I want to major in international business—but I was kind of hoping to be able to meet some people at the fair and talk about what opportunities that degree may open up for me once I'm out of school. Is that okay?

FEMALE COUNSELOR: That's no problem! The career fair is open to all our students, no matter their year or major.

MALE STUDENT: Great!

FEMALE COUNSELOR: In a lot of ways, you're exactly the kind of student they are wanting to see most. Sure, there will be some seniors going to look for jobs—and companies looking to hire them right after they graduate--but most of the students that attend the fair are people who don't know much about international business jobs to begin with, like science majors or language students, or students like yourself who haven't even figured out what they want to focus on.

MALE STUDENT: I guess I won't feel so out of place then.

FEMALE COUNSELOR: What's more, the companies that attend are hoping to meet people just like you. They're there to encourage students to study international business, or to help students see how it might be related to any number of different fields of study. You'd be surprised by how many different kinds of graduates some of those businesses are looking for.

MALE STUDENT: That sounds like just what I'm looking for. And is there a list of companies that are going to be at the fair? It would be great to see that before I go, so I can plan out which booths I'll want to go to.

FEMALE COUNSELOR: I can print out a map of the fair for you right here. But keep in mind that we still have 8 days before the fair begins. We're still getting responses back from companies about whether they are coming or not. In the past years, we've even had companies pull out at the last minute, so I recommend checking out the Career Center webpage on the university website maybe the day before the fair. You might find some new companies that you might be interested in, too. There's more information about the location and times for the fair on our webpage as well, which you'll want to look at, because there will be company booths in three different campus buildings this year.

MALE STUDENT: Cool. I guess the last thing I was hoping you might help me out with is any advice on if or how I should prepare for the career fair. I mean, I already know that I should do a little research on the companies I want to talk to so that I'm not completely ignorant of what they do, but is there anything else you think might help me?

FEMALE COUNSELOR: If you really want to make the most of the fair, I can't recommend enough sitting down and coming up with a list of questions to ask each company. Maybe two or three questions for each one, just enough to get a conversation going. Ask them to talk about what the atmosphere is like at the company. Are they laid back or do they like to run things on a tight schedule? How often do people hold meetings? That can give you some good insight into whether or not you'd be kind of left on your own on projects if you worked there or if it's more of a collaborative workplace.

MALE STUDENT: Good idea. I never thought about that.

FEMALE COUNSELOR: Here's the list of companies. I recommend spending some time this weekend going to their websites and seeing which ones strike you as interesting.

MALE STUDENT: Thanks!

■ **Question 24** Why did the student go to the Career Center?

(A) to ask for more information about an upcoming job fair
(B) to get advice on which field of study he should pursue
(C) to get a list of questions to ask companies attending a fair
(D) to inquire about a particular job opportunity

■ **Question 25** The student thinks he can't go to the career fair for the following reasons EXCEPT:

(A) He is not in his final year of college.
(B) He is not yet an international business student.
(C) He is planning getting a science or language degree.
(D) He is a male student.

■ **Question 26** According to the counselor, companies attend the career fair for the following reasons EXCEPT:

(A) To encourage students to get international business degrees.
(B) To explain how other field of study may be related to international business.
(C) To encourage students to get a graduate degree.
(D) To meet upcoming graduates interested in a business career.

■ Question 27 Why does the counselor suggest that the student visit the university website next week before the career fair begins?

(A) There may be changes to which companies are attending the fair.

(B) There will be a list of questions that the companies will be asking students.

(C) The schedule and location of the fair may change.

(D) Students can schedule an interview with companies in which they are interested.

■ Question 28 What does the counselor recommend the student do before the career fair?

(A) talk to some seniors who are going to the fair to look for a job

(B) print out a map of the fair to see which companies are attending

(C) make a list of which fields of study he is interested in studying

(D) visit the websites of companies attending the career fair to learn more about them

TOEFL iBT #1 - SPEAKING (AUDIO)

SPEAKING SECTION DIRECTIONS

The Speaking section measures your ability to speak in English about a variety of topics.

In this question, you will listen to a short lecture. You will then be asked to summarize important information from the lecture. You may take notes while you listen to the lecture. You may use your notes to help prepare your response. After you hear the question, you have 20 seconds to prepare your response and 60 seconds to speak.

Reportez vos réponses pour analyser votre performance.

Entraînez-vous dans les conditions d'examen.

Écoutez les fichiers audio.

prepmyfuture.com/book/68/ex/1984

Question 1

DIRECTIONS: *In this question, you will be asked to speak about a familiar topic. After you hear the question, you have 15 seconds to prepare your response and 45 seconds to speak.*

If you could spend 2 weeks traveling to anywhere in the world, where would you go and why? Use specific details and examples in your explanation.

Preparation Time: 15 seconds
Response Time: 45 seconds

DIRECTIONS: In this question, you will read a short passage and listen to a conversation on the same topic. You will then be asked a question about them. You may take notes while you read the passage and listen to the lecture. You may use your notes to help prepare your response. After you hear the question, you have 30 seconds to prepare your response and 60 seconds to speak.

Reading Time: 45 seconds

Proposal to Change Terms to Trimester Schedule

Western State University is considering changing its term schedule from a semester (two-term per year) system to a trimester (three-term per year) system, and is looking for student input on this proposed change. For universities using trimesters, their students benefit from greater flexibility in scheduling required courses, more variety of course offerings, and the option for a fourth "summer" term. With trimesters, students would reduce their minimum course load from four to three classes per term. There will be a question-answer session in the Student Center main hall on Tuesday, May 3rd at 7:00 PM—all students are welcome to attend.

Listen to two students discuss the proposal.

▪ **Question 2**

QUESTION: The woman expresses her opinion about the proposal described in the article. Briefly summarize the proposal. Then state her opinion about the proposal and explain the reasons she gives for holding that opinion.

Preparation Time: 30 seconds
Response Time: 60 seconds

DIRECTIONS: In this question, read a short passage and listen to a lecture on the same topic. You will then be asked a question about them. You may take notes while you read the passage and listen to the lecture. You may use your notes to help prepare your response. After you hear the question, you have 30 seconds to prepare your response and 60 seconds to speak.

Reading Time: 50 seconds

Geysers

A geyser is a vent or crack in surface of the Earth that from time to time ejects a column of hot water and steam. Geysers vary in size, with some blasting thousands of gallons of boiling hot water hundreds of feet in the air. Geysers are extremely rare features; most of the world's geysers are be found in just a few locations--most notably in Yellowstone Park in the United States--because geysers require a combination of unusual geological and hydrological conditions.

Now listen to part of a lecture on this topic in a geology class.

▪ **Question 3**

QUESTION: Using details from the reading and lecture, describe the conditions and processes necessary for geyser formation.

Preparation Time: 30 seconds
Response Time: 60 seconds

DIRECTIONS: In this question, you will listen to a short lecture. You will then be asked to summarize important information from the lecture. You may take notes while you listen to the lecture. You may use your notes to help prepare your response. After you hear the question, you have 20 seconds to prepare your response and 60 seconds to speak.

Listen to part of a lecture in an oceanography class. The professor is talking about ocean currents.

■ **Question 4**

QUESTION: Using points and details from the lecture, explain the various ways in which ocean currents affect climate conditions in various parts of the world.

Preparation Time: 20 seconds
Response Time: 60 seconds

TOEFL iBT #1 - SPEAKING (SCRIPTS)

SPEAKING SECTION DIRECTIONS

The Speaking section measures your ability to speak in English about a variety of topics.

In this question, you will listen to a short lecture. You will then be asked to summarize important information from the lecture. You may take notes while you listen to the lecture. You may use your notes to help prepare your response. After you hear the question, you have 20 seconds to prepare your response and 60 seconds to speak.

Reportez vos réponses pour analyser votre performance.

Entraînez-vous dans les conditions d'examen.

Écoutez les fichiers audio.

prepmyfuture.com/book/68/ex/1984

Question 1

DIRECTIONS: *In this question, you will be asked to speak about a familiar topic. After you hear the question, you have 15 seconds to prepare your response and 45 seconds to speak.*

If you could spend 2 weeks traveling to anywhere in the world, where would you go and why? Use specific details and examples in your explanation.

Preparation Time: 15 seconds
Response Time: 45 seconds

DIRECTIONS: In this question, you will read a short passage and listen to a conversation on the same topic. You will then be asked a question about them. You may take notes while you read the passage and listen to the lecture. You may use your notes to help prepare your response. After you hear the question, you have 30 seconds to prepare your response and 60 seconds to speak.

Reading Time: 45 seconds

Proposal to Change Terms to Trimester Schedule

Western State University is considering changing its term schedule from a semester (two-term per year) system to a trimester (three-term per year) system, and is looking for student input on this proposed change. For universities using trimesters, their students benefit from greater flexibility in scheduling required courses, more variety of course offerings, and the option for a fourth "summer" term. With trimesters, students would reduce their minimum course load from four to three classes per term. There will be a question-answer session in the Student Center main hall on Tuesday, May 3rd at 7:00 PM—all students are welcome to attend.

Listen to two students discuss the proposal.

Script non affiché le jour de l'examen :

MAN: This trimester idea sounds pretty exciting, don't you think?

WOMAN: I hope they decide not to switch. I don't want the added stress of a trimester schedule.

MAN: But I heard that with trimesters, we only need to take three classes per term, instead of the four we do now. I kind of like the idea of being able to focus on only 3 classes.

WOMAN: It sounds nice, but my brother is at a college that uses a trimester schedule and he tells me he has a hard time keeping up with all the material he has to learn. He has to learn in 10 weeks everything that I study in 15 weeks. Even though he got better grades in high school than I did, I'm now getting a better GPA. He's worried this is going to affect his ability to get into the graduate programs he looking at, and might even affect his scholarship.

MAN: Really? It sounds like he's got his work cut out for him.

WOMAN: I know! He tells me that just a few weeks into a term he is already trying to get ready for mid-terms. It's like he's being asked to master a subject he only started learning about. Last week he was sick but still went to class, because he knows if he misses even one lesson, he'll fall behind. I also remember that he had to start school earlier in the fall, and because of the way his school set up vacations, he's getting out of school around the end of June, about two weeks later than me.

MAN: Hmm. Well, maybe that's true for his school, but perhaps we can ask the administration to set up a different vacation schedule.

WOMAN: Maybe, but whatever schedule they come up with, I would suspect it would be pretty close to what my brother has now.

Question 2 **QUESTION:** The woman expresses her opinion about the proposal described in the article. Briefly summarize the proposal. Then state her opinion about the proposal and explain the reasons she gives for holding that opinion.

Preparation Time: 30 seconds
Response Time: 60 seconds

DIRECTIONS: In this question, read a short passage and listen to a lecture on the same topic. You will then be asked a question about them. You may take notes while you read the passage and listen to the lecture. You may use your notes to help prepare your response. After you hear the question, you have 30 seconds to prepare your response and 60 seconds to speak.

Reading Time: 50 seconds

Geysers

A geyser is a vent or crack in surface of the Earth that from time to time ejects a column of hot water and steam. Geysers vary in size, with some blasting thousands of gallons of boiling hot water hundreds of feet in the air. Geysers are extremely rare features; most of the world's geysers are be found in just a few locations--most notably in Yellowstone Park in the United States--because geysers require a combination of unusual geological and hydrological conditions.

Now listen to part of a lecture on this topic in a geology class.

Script non affiché le jour de l'examen :

PROFESSOR: So what do we actually need for a geyser to form? Clearly, a geyser needs a large amount of water. Many geysers are actually located near rivers or lakes, and are linked to them through underground fissures. Others are fed from rain or snowfall from the surrounding land.

Besides water, a geyser needs a subsurface water transporting system, like the water pipes in a house. Some of these underground systems are a single, long vertical vent, while others are miles long with many side branches—and geysers need this system to be connected to a pocket of molten rock--known as magma--far below the surface of the Earth. This magma, while relatively close to the Earth's surface when compared with the total depth of the Earth's crust, is a common phenomenon near the edges of Earth's tectonic plates. These tectonic plates, which form the top layer of the Earth's surface and are connected to each other like the pieces of a giant jigsaw puzzle, are always in motion, creating cracks and faults, and generating enormous energy and friction, resulting in underground reservoirs of magma, volcanic vents, and--when all the necessary pieces are in place--geysers.

To really comprehend how geysers result from the interaction of water and heat under the surface, one must first understand the relationship between water and steam. Under normal conditions, steam is produced when water is heated to its boiling point—but when water is heated deep in the Earth's surface, the weight of the water above also pushes down on the slowly heating water, preventing it from turning into steam. This phenomenon is called "superheating". The water is hot enough to become steam, but it can't due to the weight of the water above.

At some point, the deep, superheated water reaches a point where the pressure from the water above it less than the pressure of the superheated water, and it explodes, instantly turning into steam. This "steam explosion" blasts the confined water out of the vent as a geyser.

Question 3 **QUESTION:** Using details from the reading and lecture, describe the conditions and processes necessary for geyser formation.

Preparation Time: 30 seconds
Response Time: 60 seconds

DIRECTIONS: In this question, you will listen to a short lecture. You will then be asked to summarize important information from the lecture. You may take notes while you listen to the lecture. You may use your notes to help prepare your response. After you hear the question, you have 20 seconds to prepare your response and 60 seconds to speak.

Listen to part of a lecture in an oceanography class. The professor is talking about ocean currents.

Script non affiché le jour de l'examen :

PROFESSOR: Ocean water is continuously circulating across the planet, due to numerous surface and deepwater currents, which act as giant conveyor belts moving water in various directions.

The surface currents are driven by prevailing winds, sometimes called trade winds, which circulate warm water away from the equator and cold water toward it. Coastal desert areas, such as in Morocco along the West African coast, are the result of these cold ocean currents creating cold air masses above the ocean. These masses prevent moisture from rising up into the atmosphere, inhibiting cloud formation and rain.

In contrast, warm ocean currents warm the air over the nearby land. One example of this is the Gulf Stream in the Atlantic Ocean, which has dramatic effects on the regional climate. As the Gulf Stream pushes warm water from the Caribbean Sea north along the East Coast of the United States and eventually all the way to Western Europe, it warms the air of the coastlines it passes. This results in the region's unusually mild climate, when compared with similar latitudes around the world, such as in Canada, which experiences markedly colder temperatures through much of the year. The relatively mild regional climate created by the Gulf Stream allows palm trees to grow in Ireland and keeps the coast of Norway ice-free all year.

While the surface currents are driven by wind, deepwater currents are driven by density and temperature variations. For example, when warm water currents such as the Gulf Stream reach the North Polar region, its waters are cooled by the frigid Arctic winds, become denser, and sink deeper into the ocean until they reach the ocean floor. There, they begin to move southward along the ocean floor, gradually warming as they pass the equator, eventually rising to the surface once more as it reaches South Africa, where it is picked up by a circulating current and routed back to the Caribbean to start its journey all over again.

■ Question 4 **QUESTION:** Using points and details from the lecture, explain the various ways in which ocean currents affect climate conditions in various parts of the world.

Preparation Time: 20 seconds
Response Time: 60 seconds

TOEFL iBT #1 - WRITING (AUDIO)

WRITING SECTION DIRECTIONS

The Writing section measures your ability to use writing to communicate in an academic environment.

For this task, you will write a response to a question about a reading passage and a lecture. You may take notes, and you may use your notes to help you write your response. Your response will be scored on the quality of your writing and on how well you connect the points in the lecture with points in the reading.

Reportez vos réponses pour analyser votre performance.

Entraînez-vous dans les conditions d'examen.

Écoutez les fichiers audio.

prepmyfuture.com/book/68/ex/1985

DIRECTIONS: For this task, you will write a response to a question about a reading passage and a lecture. You may take notes, and you may use your notes to help you write your response. Your response will be scored on the quality of your writing and on how well you connect the points in the lecture with points in the reading.

Reading Time – 3 minutes

Perched atop a low hill in Newport, Rhode Island, an old, 3-story-tall, stone tower stands as one of North America's longest enduring architectural mysteries. The tower itself is made completely of stone and mortar, with its ground floor formed from eight rounded columns separated by an equal number of arches. Known as the Newport Tower, debate has raged over the identity of the builder of the structure. While most historians believe it was built in the 17th century by English colonists to serve as a windmill, there is now mounting evidence that the Newport Tower is actually the remains of a 12th century Viking expedition to the New World, making the Newport Tower the oldest European structure in North America.

Ancient Sea Voyages

Researchers were able to reach this conclusion partly through analysis of several medieval Viking sagas (stories which recount the histories of famous Viking heroes). In these stories, written between the 10th and 14th Centuries, Viking ships, either by design or accident, reached a distant land to the west they named "Vinland". It was a land rich in natural resources and ideal for colonization. Indeed, one expedition attempted to set up a settlement in 1025, but failed due to conflict with the native peoples of Vinland. Because neither Iceland nor Greenland fit this description, historians now agree that Vinland must be located somewhere along the eastern coast of North America.

Architectural Style

Another reason the Newport Tower is likely a Viking construct is the fact that the tower does not resemble other 17th-century structures, which were commonly square or rectangular and built of wood. Other structural elements, such as the eight base pillars which jut out slightly from the wall, are features common to medieval European churches. The pillars themselves are connected by Romanesque arches, a style of architecture which reached its peak in popularity in the 11th century in Europe.

Not a windmill

The eight-pillar design of the Newport Tower also makes it highly unlikely it could have been used as a windmill. Windmills are subject to the strong force of the moving blades; a heavy stone second floor on top of eight rather narrow columns is a very poor design for such a purpose. An even more glaring problem with the idea of the Newport Tower being a windmill is the presence of a fireplace built into the second story wall of the tower. A fireplace in a windmill is quite hazardous, due to the highly flammable dust produced when grinding grain.

Now listen to part of a lecture on the topic you just read about.

■ Question 1

DIRECTIONS: You have 20 minutes to plan and write your response. Your response will be evaluated on the quality of your writing on how well you present the points in the lecture and their relationship to the reading passage. Typically, an effective response will have 150 to 225 words.

Response Time: 20 minutes

QUESTION: Summarize the points made in the lecture, being sure to explain how they contradict specific points made in the reading passage.

■ Question 2

DIRECTIONS: Read the question below. You have 30 minutes to plan, write, and revise your essay. Typically, an effective response will contain a minimum of 300 words.

Response Time: 30 minutes

QUESTION: More and more people are choosing a vegetarian diet due to its personal health and environmental benefits. Despite this, many people feel that vegetarianism has several drawbacks that make it not an ideal way of eating. Which of these views do you think is correct and why? Use details and examples to support your opinion.

TOEFL iBT #1 - WRITING (SCRIPTS)

WRITING SECTION DIRECTIONS

The Writing section measures your ability to use writing to communicate in an academic environment.

For this task, you will write a response to a question about a reading passage and a lecture. You may take notes, and you may use your notes to help you write your response. Your response will be scored on the quality of your writing and on how well you connect the points in the lecture with points in the reading.

Reportez vos réponses pour analyser votre performance.

Entraînez-vous dans les conditions d'examen.

Écoutez les fichiers audio.

prepmyfuture.com/book/68/ex/1985

DIRECTIONS: For this task, you will write a response to a question about a reading passage and a lecture. You may take notes, and you may use your notes to help you write your response. Your response will be scored on the quality of your writing and on how well you connect the points in the lecture with points in the reading.

Reading Time – 3 minutes

Perched atop a low hill in Newport, Rhode Island, an old, 3-story-tall, stone tower stands as one of North America's longest enduring architectural mysteries. The tower itself is made completely of stone and mortar, with its ground floor formed from eight rounded columns separated by an equal number of arches. Known as the Newport Tower, debate has raged over the identity of the builder of the structure. While most historians believe it was built in the 17th century by English colonists to serve as a windmill, there is now mounting evidence that the Newport Tower is actually the remains of a 12th century Viking expedition to the New World, making the Newport Tower the oldest European structure in North America.

Ancient Sea Voyages

Researchers were able to reach this conclusion partly through analysis of several medieval Viking sagas (stories which recount the histories of famous Viking heroes). In these stories, written between the 10th and 14th Centuries, Viking ships, either by design or accident, reached a distant land to the west they named "Vinland". It was a land rich in natural resources and ideal for colonization. Indeed, one expedition attempted to set up a settlement in 1025, but failed due to conflict with the native peoples of Vinland. Because neither Iceland nor Greenland fit this description, historians now agree that Vinland must be located somewhere along the eastern coast of North America.

Architectural Style

Another reason the Newport Tower is likely a Viking construct is the fact that the tower does not resemble other 17th-century structures, which were commonly square or rectangular and built of wood. Other structural elements, such as the eight base pillars which jut out slightly from the wall, are features common to medieval European churches. The pillars themselves are connected by Romanesque arches, a style of architecture which reached its peak in popularity in the 11th century in Europe.

Not a windmill

The eight-pillar design of the Newport Tower also makes it highly unlikely it could have been used as a windmill. Windmills are subject to the strong force of the moving blades; a heavy stone second floor on top of eight rather narrow columns is a very poor design for such a purpose. An even more glaring problem with the idea of the Newport Tower being a windmill is the presence of a fireplace built into the second story wall of the tower. A fireplace in a windmill is quite hazardous, due to the highly flammable dust produced when grinding grain.

Now listen to part of a lecture on the topic you just read about.

Script non affiché le jour de l'examen :

PROFESSOR: It is intriguing to think of a medieval Viking colony in North America, but careful examination of the evidence used to make this claim show this theory is based on a limited understanding of both history and engineering.

How can we say this? Well, while it is accepted by most historians that Vikings did reach the east coast of North America at various times during the Middle Ages, archaeological finds actually point to Vinland being located far to the north in Canada, over 1000 miles from the Newport Tower. Despite its current cold climate and proximity to the Arctic, this area had a much warmer climate in medieval times, and would have been an ideal location for Viking colonization.

On top of that, the supposed medieval architectural style and building techniques of the Newport Tower are actually found in other buildings from the colonial New England time period. The Romanesque style of architecture was still in use in Europe in the 17th century, so it is only natural for colonists to bring that style with them to the New World. It is also true that most colonial buildings were made of wood, but records show that stone buildings were built throughout the colonies as defense against attacks by Native Americans, storehouses, or even windmills. In fact, a 1632 petition by New England colonists to a local government official shows the community requesting a round, stone tower--a description that fits the Newport Tower quite well.

And what about the impossibility of a fireplace in a windmill? Well, though there is logic behind this thinking, one can find numerous examples throughout Europe of fireplaces installed in mills. The type of fireplace installed in most of these windmills is also similar to the fireplace in the Newport Tower—where the chimney is built into the wall and exits through the side wall, rather than the roof. This side-exit for the chimney is the most practical design for a fireplace in a windmill, because it keeps smoke and ash away from the turning blades of the windmill, greatly reducing the danger of accidental fires.

▪ Question 1

DIRECTIONS: You have 20 minutes to plan and write your response. Your response will be evaluated on the quality of your writing on how well you present the points in the lecture and their relationship to the reading passage. Typically, an effective response will have 150 to 225 words.

Response Time: 20 minutes

QUESTION: Summarize the points made in the lecture, being sure to explain how they contradict specific points made in the reading passage.

▪ Question 2

DIRECTIONS: Read the question below. You have 30 minutes to plan, write, and revise your essay. Typically, an effective response will contain a minimum of 300 words.

Response Time: 30 minutes

QUESTION: More and more people are choosing a vegetarian diet due to its personal health and environmental benefits. Despite this, many people feel that vegetarianism has several drawbacks that make it not an ideal way of eating. Which of these views do you think is correct and why? Use details and examples to support your opinion.

TOEFL iBT #1 - SOLUTIONS

TOEFL iBT #1 - READING - Solutions

Reportez vos réponses pour analyser votre performance.

Entraînez-vous dans les conditions d'examen.

prepmyfuture.com/book/68/ex/1982

question 1	C
question 2	D
question 3	D
question 4	A
question 5	B
question 6	A

question 7	D
question 8	B
question 9	C
question 10	B D F
question 11	C
question 12	B

question 13	D
question 14	B
question 15	A
question 16	A
question 17	C
question 18	A

question 19	C
question 20	A C D
question 21	A
question 22	A
question 23	D
question 24	B

question 25	B
question 26	C
question 27	B
question 28	A
question 29	B
question 30	A E F

■ **Question 1 - Solution**

Paragraph 1 implies that:

FR : Le paragraphe 1 laisse entendre que :

(A) The discipline of sociology was founded in 1873.

= La sociologie en tant que discipline a été fondée en 1873.
Le passage mentionne seulement que le mot « sociologie » n'avait pas été utilisé comme titre de livre à date. Cela ne veut pas dire que la discipline n'existait pas.

(B) Marx discarded Comte's philosophy.

= Marx rejetait la philosophie de Comte.
L'auteur écrit seulement que les idées de Spencer ne reflètent pas celles de Comte ou Marx.

(C) ✓ Before Spencer, the word "sociology" hadn't appeared on any book cover.

= Avant Spencer, le terme « sociologie » n'apparaissait sur aucune couverture de livre.
« In 1873, the English philosopher Herbert Spencer (1820–1903) published The Study of Sociology, the first book with the term "sociology" in the title. »
(« En 1873, le philosophe britannique Herbert Spencer (1820 - 1903) a publié Etude de la Sociologie, le premier livre dont le titre contenait le terme sociologie. »)

(D) Durkheim was Spencer's mentor.

= Durkheim était le mentor de Spencer.
Durkheim a été influencé par Spencer.

■ Question 2 - Solution

Based on information in paragraph 2, which of the following statements is true concerning Durkheim's sociological contribution?

FR : D'après les informations données dans le paragraphe 2, lequel des énoncés suivants est vrai concernant les contributions sociologiques de Durkheim ?

(A)	Durkheim saw pathological societies as stable, while healthy societies were perceived as a collective system of social norms between the individual and society.	= Durkheim considérait les sociétés pathologiques comme stables, tandis que les sociétés saines étaient perçues comme un système collectif de normes sociales entre l'individu et la société. *Contresens : c'est l'inverse.* *« He saw healthy societies as stable, while pathological societies experienced a breakdown in social norms between individuals and society. »* *(« Il voyait les sociétés saines comme des sociétés stable, tandis que les sociétés pathologiques ont vu leurs normes sociales s'effondrer entre les individus et la société. »)*
(B)	Durkheim laid out his theory on how capitalist, industrial societies transformed into a collective of primitive communities	= Durkheim a élaboré sa théorie sur la façon dont les sociétés industrielles capitalistes se sont transformées en un collectif de communautés primitives. *Contresens : c'est l'inverse.* *« Durkheim laid out his theory on how societies transformed from a primitive state into a capitalist, industrial society. »* *(« Durkheim a élaboré sa théorie sur la façon dont les sociétés se sont transformées d'un état primitif à une société capitaliste industrielle. »)*
(C)	Durkheim claimed that people rise to their proper level in society based on financial background.	= Durkheim a soutenu que les individus s'élèvent à leur juste niveau dans la société en fonction de leur situation financière. *« According to Durkheim, people rise to their proper level in society based on merit »* *(= « Selon Durkheim, les individus s'élèvent à leur juste position dans la société par le mérite. »)*
(D)	✓ **Durkheim was directly responsible for making sociology a formal academic discipline**	**= Durkheim a directement participé à faire de la sociologie une discipline académique à part entière.** ***« Durkheim helped establish sociology as a formal academic discipline [...]» (= « Durkheim a participé à faire de la sociologie une discipline académique à part entière. »)***

■ Question 3 - Solution

According to Durkheim, studying sociology is important because:

FR : Selon Durkheim, étudier la sociologie est important car :

(A)	Sociology can help us better understand and tolerate capitalist, industrial societies.	= La sociologie peut nous permettre de mieux comprendre et supporter les sociétés industrielles capitalistes. *Inexact : Durkheim ne demande pas de tolérer le capitalisme.*
(B)	Sociology could help us understand suicide statistics in different police districts.	= La sociologie peut nous permettre de mieux comprendre les statistiques liées au suicide dans différents quartiers de la police. *Inexact : l'utilisation des statistiques sur le suicide avait pour seul but de démontrer l'efficacité de ses recherches. La compréhension des taux de suicide n'est pas l'objectif de la recherche.*
(C)	Sociology could help scientists research the differences between Catholic and Protestant communities.	= La sociologie pourrait permettre aux scientifiques de comprendre les différences entre les communautés Catholique et Protestante. *Insuffisant : aider les scientifiques à étudier les différences entre les communautés catholiques et protestantes est l'une des utilisations possibles des recherches de Durkheim sur la sociologie mais pas la plus importante.*
(D)	✓ **Sociology could help us better understand and identify the underlying factors that lead a society to become either "healthy" or "pathological."**	**= La sociologie peut nous permettre de mieux comprendre les facteurs sous-jacents qui ont contribué au passage d'une société « saine » à une société dite « pathologique ».** ***« He [Durkheim] also believed that through such studies it would be possible to determine if a society was healthy or pathological. »*** ***(= « Il [Durkheim] croyait aussi que de telles études permettraient de déterminer si une société était pathologique ou non. »)***

■ **Question 4 - Solution**

The word "breakdown" in the passage is closest in meaning to:

FR : Le sens du mot « breakdown » dans le passage se rapproche le plus de :

(A)	✓ **collapse**	**= chute**
(B)	decomposition	= décomposition
(C)	loss of mental health	= perte de la santé mentale
(D)	analysis	= analyse

⇒ **explication**

Le mot « *breakdown* » signifie, entre autres, un effondrement, une chute.

Attention au sens de la phrase car « *breakdown* » peut également signifier la perte de la santé mentale (« *nervous breakdown* ») comme stipulé dans la réponse c) ou une toute autre signification selon le contexte.

■ **Question 5 - Solution**

According to paragraph 3, which of the following is true about Max Weber (1864–1920)?

FR : D'après le paragraphe 3, lequel des énoncés suivants est vrai à propos de Max Weber (1864 – 1920) ?

(A)	He is mostly known for his sociological contributions to the research conducted into far-reaching social forces affecting factory workers in Russia.	= Il est surtout connu pour ses contributions sociologiques aux recherches menées sur les forces sociales profondes qui touchent les ouvriers d'usine en Russie. *Ce n'est pas mentionné dans le texte. Weber a effectivement écrit sur les forces sociales affectant les ouvriers russes mais le texte ne dit pas s'il est connu pour cela.*
(B) ✓	**He is best known for his 1904 book as well as for giving birth to a unique methodology of sociological research**	**= Il est surtout connu pour son livre de 1904 ainsi que pour sa méthodologie unique de recherche sociologique.** ***« He is known best for his 1904 book […]. » / « Weber also made a major contribution to the methodology of sociological research. » (« Il est surtout connu pour son ouvrage de 1904 » / « Weber a également largement contribué à la méthodologie de la recherche en sociologie »)***
(C)	Weber had controversial views on both Protestants and Calvinists whom all had different views on the topic of capitalism	= Weber avait des opinions controversées sur les protestants et les calvinistes, qui avaient chacun des points de vue différents sur le capitalisme. *Contresens - Énoncé trompeur* *Les calvinistes font partie de l'église protestante. De plus, Weber n'avait pas lui-même d'idées controversées mais était sujet à controverse sur l'interprétation de sa pensée sur le capitalisme et le protestantisme.*
(D)	He single-handedly introduced the concept of *verstehen*	= Il a introduit à lui seul le concept de *verstehen*. *Inexact* *Durkheim a introduit le concept de verstehen avec l'aide d'un autre chercheur, Wilhelm Dilthey.*

▪ Question 6 - Solution

Which of the following sentences best describes the highlighted sentence in the passage? The other choices change the meaning or leave out information.

In his book The Nature of Social Action (1922), Weber described sociology as striving to "interpret the meaning of social action and thereby give a causal explanation of the way in which action proceeds and the effects it produces."

FR : Lequel des énoncés suivants décrit le mieux la phrase surlignée dans le passage ? Les autres choix changent le sens de la phrase ou omettent des informations.

(A)	✓ **The Nature of Social Action (1922) is Weber's attempt at comprehending the deeper values of social actions in order to provide a way for a better understanding of people's actions and the consequences of those actions.**	**= La nature de l'action sociale est la façon dont Weber tente de comprendre les causes profondes des actions sociales afin de mieux comprendre les actions des gens et les conséquences de ces actions.** ***« The deeper values of social actions » = « the meaning of social action »*** ***« A better understanding of people's actions and the consequences of those actions" = "a causal explanation of the way in which action proceeds and the effects it produces. » (= « la cause profonde des actions sociales » / « mieux comprendre les actions des individus et les conséquences de ces actions »)***
(B)	Weber's book is simply about finding explanations to people's actions and looking at the results in a way that would enable sociologists to draw vague conclusions.	= Le livre de weber consiste simplement à trouver des explications aux actions des individus et à examiner les résultats d'une manière qui permettrait aux sociologues de tirer de vagues conclusions. *Le but de Weber est de mieux comprendre la sociologie. Il ne cherche pas à être « vague ».*
(C)	Weber's book is solely about interpreting the meaning of social actions without any extra attempt to give a causal explanation of the way in which action are carried out or what consequences those actions might carry in themselves.	= Le livre de weber se contente d'interpréter la signification des actions sociales sans chercher à donner une explication causale de la manière dont les actions sont menées ou des conséquences que ces actions pourraient avoir en elles-mêmes. *La phrase stipule que Weber n'a pas essayé de donner une explication causale alors que la phrase surlignée le souligne de façon explicite.*
(D)	Weber's book provides a general introduction to the study of sociology.	= Le livre de Weber constitue une introduction générale à l'étude de la sociologie. *Dans son livre, Weber essaie d'interpréter le sens des actions sociales, un sujet bien spécifique qui n'a rien à voir avec une introduction générale sur la sociologie.*

⟹ **explication**

FR : Dans son livre *The Nature of Social Action* (1922), Weber décrit la sociologie comme cherchant à « interpréter le sens de l'action sociale et ainsi donner une explication causale sur la manière dont se déroule l'action et les effets qu'elle produit. »

▪ Question 7 - Solution

According to paragraph 6, qualitative sociology investigate human behavior through all of the following methods EXCEPT:

FR : D'après le paragraphe 6, les méthodes de sociologie qualitative explorent le comportement humain à travers tous les moyens suivants SAUF un. Lequel ?

(A) focus groups = des groupes de discussion

(B) content source analysis = de l'analyse de données

(C) in-depth interviews = des entretiens approfondis

(D) ✓ statistical techniques to uncover patterns of human behavior **= des données staistiques pour mettre au jour des schémas comportementaux**
Ce n'est pas mentionné dans le texte.

⇝ **explication**
FR : *« Qualitative sociology seeks to understand human behavior by learning about it through in-depth interviews, focus groups, and analysis of content sources [...]. »*
(= « La sociologie qualitative cherche à comprendre le comportement humain en l'appréhendant par des entretiens approfondis, des groupes de discussion et l'analyse de sources de données [...]. »)

▪ Question 8 - Solution

In paragraph 3, the term "complementary" is closer in meaning to:

FR : Dans le paragraphe 3, la signification du terme « complementary » se rapproche de :

(A) accessory = accessoire

(B) ✓ Interrelated = lié

(C) mandatory = obligatoire

(D) permissive = permissif

⇝ **explication**
FR : Comme rapporté dans le passage, Weber pense que le protestantisme a joué un rôle dans le développement des sociétés capitalistes. Il est donc correct de dire que les deux éléments sont liés et complémentaires.

▪ Question 9 - Solution

Look at the four squares in paragraph 3, A, B, C, and D, which indicate where the following sentence could be added to the passage. Where would the sentence best fit?

Weber, in fact, inferred that psychological insecurity that Calvin's doctrine had imposed was such that people began to live by an ethic of unceasing commitment to one's worldly calling and ascetic abstinence from any enjoyment, focused on the accumulation of capital.

[P3] Meanwhile in Germany, prominent sociologist Max Weber (1864–1920) established a sociology department at the Ludwig Maximilians University of Munich in 1919. Weber wrote on many topics related to sociology including political change in Russia and social forces that affect factory workers. **A** He is known best for his 1904 book, The Protestant Ethic and the Spirit of Capitalism. **B** Weber remains controversial to this very day. It is thought that Weber was arguing that the beliefs of many Protestants, especially Calvinists, led to the creation of capitalism. **C** Some interpret it as simply claiming that the ideologies of capitalism and Protestantism are complementary. Weber also made a major contribution to the methodology of sociological research. **D** Along with other researchers such as Wilhelm Dilthey (1833–1911) and Heinrich Rickert (1863–1936), Weber believed that it was difficult if not impossible to use standard scientific methods to accurately predict the behavior of groups as people hoped to do. They argued that the influence of culture on human behavior had to be taken into account. This even applied to the researchers themselves, who, they believed, should be aware of how their own cultural biases could influence their research. To deal with this problem, Weber and Dilthey introduced the concept of verstehen, a German verb that means to understand in a deep way. In seeking verstehen, outside observers of a social world—an entire culture or a small setting—attempt to understand it from an insider's point of view.

(A) **A** *Cela ne serait pas correct car l'auteur est sur le point d'introduire les travaux de Weber les plus importants. Cela n'aurait pas de sens de placer des explications détaillées sur le point de vue de Weber avant d'avoir mentionné à quel livre l'auteur fait référence.*

(B) **B** *La phrase contient des explications détaillées qui clarifient la pensée de Weber sur le rôle important joué par le protestantisme sur le développement du capitalisme, elle doit donc être placée après la présentation de l'idée principale.*

(C) ✓ **C** ***L'auteur vient de présenter le lien entre protestantisme et capitalisme. Le lecteur est donc prêt pour lire des explications détaillées sur cette théorie.***

(D) **D** *L'auteur est passé sur un autre sujet, il est trop tard pour placer cette information. L'auteur est maintenant en train d'évoquer la contribution de Weber aux méthodes de recherche en sociologie.*

▪ Question 10 - Solution

Directions:

An introductory sentence for a brief summary of the passage is provided below.

Complete the summary by selecting the THREE answer choices that express the most important ideas in the passage. Some sentences do not belong in the summary because they express ideas that are not presented in the passage or are minor ideas in the passage.

This question is worth 2 points.

- From the second half of the nineteenth century, new approaches toward sociology started developing and it also began to be formally studied at university.
- ________
- ________
- ________

(A)	In its early stages, sociology was associated with capitalism, because Comte's theories had been proven wrong by Herbert Spencer.	= À ses débuts, la sociologie était associée au capitalisme, car les théories de Comte avaient été démenties par Herbert Spencer. *Cette phrase donne une information inexacte. Personne n'a prouvé que la théorie de Comte était fausse. Sa théorie est simplement en opposition avec celle de Spencer.*
(B) ✓	**Durkheim set out to determine the evolutionary process of societies, establishing different categories through an objective approach towards social phenomena.**	**= Durkheim a cherché à déterminer le processus d'évolution des sociétés, en établissant différentes catégories par une approche objective des phénomènes sociaux.** ***Bon résumé du paragraphe 2.***
(C)	Durkheim realized that, unlike he previously believed, the Protestant doctrine was a result of both pathological and healthy societies.	= Durkheim se rend compte que, contrairement à ce qu'il croyait auparavant, la doctrine protestante est le résultat de sociétés à la fois pathologiques et saines. *Cette informations n'est pas mentionnée dans le passage.*
(D) ✓	**Further studies established the influence of factors such as culture and ideologies in society, and, therefore, the impossibility to adopt an ordinary objective approach.**	**= D'autres études ont démontré l'influence de facteurs tels que la culture et les idéologies dans la société, et donc l'impossibilité d'adopter une approche objective ordinaire.** ***Bon résumé du paragraphe 3.***
(E)	By studying groups of Russian factory workers, Max Weber could develop the theory that led him to redefine the methodology of sociological research.	= En étudiant des groupes d'ouvriers russes, Max Weber a pu développer la théorie qui l'a amené à redéfinir la méthodologie de la recherche sociologique. *Une partie de cette phrase mentionne des informations secondaires. De plus, l'autre partie est fausse, les recherches de Weber sur les ouvriers russes constituent seulement une partie de ses travaux.*
(F) ✓	**The dispute between scholars proposing a scientific approach against those suggesting the adoption of an internal perspective, led to the modern diversification in the field of sociology.**	**= Le conflit entre les chercheurs proposant une approche scientifique et ceux suggérant l'adoption d'une perspective interne a conduit à la diversification moderne du champ de la sociologie.** ***Bon résumé des paragraphes 4 et 5.***

■ **Question 11 - Solution**

According to paragraph 1, which is true about a meter?

FR : D'après le paragraphe n°1, lequel des énoncés suivants est vrai à propos du rythme ?

(A)	The meter of a music is the repeated tapping of your foot and clapping of your hands	= La mesure d'une musique est le battement répété du pied et des mains. *Contresens - Énoncé trompeur* *C'est sur le rythme que l'on tape du pied et des mains.*
(B)	The meter of a music is a traditional Western African drumming	= La mesure d'une musique est un tambour traditionnel de l'Afrique de l'Ouest. *Extrapolation* *Les percussions traditionnelles de l'Afrique de l'Ouest sont uniquement un type de musique qui a un rythme très complexe.*
(C) ✓	**The meter of a music is a repetitive pattern of beats**	**= La mesure d'une musique est un schéma répétitif de rythmes.** ***« The meter of a piece of music is the arrangement of its rhythms in a repetitive pattern of strong and weak beats. » (= « Le métrage d'un morceau de musique est la disposition de ses rythmes selon un schéma répétitif de temps forts et de temps faibles. »)***
(D)	The meter of a music is nothing else but a measure of enjoyment	= La mesure d'une musique n'est rien d'autre qu'une mesure de plaisir. *Même s'il est vrai que c'est sur le rythme musical que l'on tape du pied et des mains, le texte ne précise pas si cela mesure le plaisir que ressent individu à l'écoute d'un morceau de musique.*

▪ Question 12 - Solution

It can be inferred that some music does not have a meter because:

FR : Il peut être conclu que certaines musiques n'ont pas de métrique musicale (rythme) car :

(A)	they would be extremely boring to listen to	= Elles seraient extrêmement ennuyeuses à écouter. *Cela n'est pas mentionné dans le texte.*
(B) ✓	**not all music has such a powerful repetitive pattern of beats**	**= Toutes les musiques n'ont pas un rythme répétitif aussi puissant.** ***Certaines musiques n'ont pas de rythme car elles n'ont pas une répartition des temps forts et des temps faibles très soutenue ou répétitive. C'est par exemple le cas des chants grégoriens.***
(C)	ancient music, such as Gregorian chants, had a huge effect on today's musical taste	= La musique ancienne, comme les chants grégoriens, a eu un effet considérable sur les goûts musicaux d'aujourd'hui. *Cela n'est pas mentionné dans le texte.* *Les chants grégoriens et la musique expérimentale sont de nos jours pris comme deux exemples de musiques qui n'ont pas de rythme. Le texte ne mentionne pas une quelconque influence.*
(D)	some traditional music consists of complex meters that would be too difficult for the beginner to identify	= Certaines musiques traditionnelles comportent des mesures complexes qui seraient trop difficiles à identifier pour un débutant. *Inexact - Pas de corrélation entre les deux parties de la phrase.* *Ce n'est pas parce que certaines musiques ont des rythmes complexes que d'autres n'ont pas de rythme du tout.*

▪ Question 13 - Solution

The word "pattern" in paragraph 3 is closest in meaning to:

FR : Le mot « pattern » dans le paragraphe 3 est plus proche du sens de :

(A) presence = une présence

(B) range = une gamme

(C) choice = un choix

(D) ✓ sequence = une séquence
Une séquence de battements forts et faibles peuvent former un « pattern ».

⟹ **explication**
FR : Le mot *« pattern »* n'a pas d'équivalent français dans ce contexte. Il s'agit de la répétition de quelque chose : un motif, une séquence, etc.

▪ Question 14 - Solution

Why does the author go on listing the different meters of music in paragraph 4?

FR : Dans le paragraphe 4, pourquoi l'auteur énumère-t-il les différents rythmes de musique ?

(A) to prove why counting the number of beats from one strong beat to the next is so troublesome — = pour prouver pourquoi il est si difficile de compter le nombre de battements d'un temps fort à l'autre
Cela n'est pas mentionné dans le texte.
Même si le texte indique que la plupart des gens ne s'embêtent pas à classer les rythmes plus inhabituels, le texte n'indique pas que compter les mesures soit particulièrement pénible.

(B) ✓ to argue that meters can be classified by counting the number of beats, but the majority of people just don't really bother classifying these more unusual meters — **= pour soutenir que les mesures peuvent être classées en comptant le nombre de battements, mais que la majorité des gens ne prennent pas vraiment la peine de classer ces mesures plus inhabituelles**
« Meters can be classified by counting the number of beats from one strong beat to the next.[…] Most people don't bother classifying the more unusual meters […]. »
(= « Les mesures peuvent être classées en comptant le nombre de battements entre un temps fort et le suivant [...] la plupart des gens ne prennent pas la peine de classer les mesures les plus inhabituelles [...]. »)

(C) to make the readers realize that there is no practical reason for counting meters in a musical piece — = pour faire comprendre aux lecteurs qu'il n'y a aucune raison pratique de compter les mesures dans un morceau de musique
Cela n'est pas mentionné dans le texte.
La raison pour laquelle quelqu'un compterait les rythmes d'un morceau de musique n'est pas donnée dans le texte.

(D) to drive a sharper wedge between simple and compound meters — = pour établir une distinction plus nette entre les mesures simples et les mesures composées
Les rythmes simples et les rythmes composés ne sont pas mentionnés dans le paragraphe 4.

▪ Question 15 - Solution

According to paragraph 6, what could be the most useful method of identifying underlying meters?

FR : Selon le paragraphe 6, quelle serait la méthode la plus efficace pour identifier les rythmes sous-jacents ?

(A)	**✓ by watching out for a running, even pulse underlying the rhythms of the music**	**= en recherchant une pulsation régulière et constante dans les rythmes de la musique** ***« So you are basically listening for a running, even pulse underlying the rhythms of the music. »*** ***(= « Il s'agit donc essentiellement d'écouter une pulsation régulière et régulière qui sous-tend les rythmes de la musique. »)***
(B)	by watching out for an equal and even "click" sound underlying the rhythms of the music	= en veillant à ce que les rythmes de la musique soient sous-tendus par un « clic » égal et régulier *Cela n'est pas mentionné dans le texte.*
(C)	by making sure that you count the rhythm on a pulse, and you do that always on the weakest pulse	= en veillant à compter le rythme sur une pulsation, et ce toujours sur la pulsation la plus faible *« Make sure numbers always come on a pulse, and "one" is always on the strongest pulse. »* *(= « Assurez-vous que les chiffres sont toujours sur une impulsion, et que un" est toujours sur l'impulsion la plus forte. »)*
(D)	by counting the evenly spaced syllables, for they serve as excellent pointers to whether we are listening to a music with a simple duple meter or a compound duple meter	= en comptant les syllabes régulièrement espacées, car elles sont d'excellents indicateurs pour savoir si nous écoutons une musique avec une double mesure simple ou une double mesure composée *Le texte n'indique pas si compter les syllabes à intervalles réguliers servirait à identifier les rythmes sous-jacents.*

■ **Question 16 - Solution**

Which of the following statements most accurately reflects the author's opinion about music and meter in general?

FR : Lequel des énoncés suivants résume le mieux la pensée de l'auteur au sujet de la musique et du rythme en général ?

(A) ✓	**Recognizing, classifying and organizing meters should be the first step for anyone who is seriously considering learning more about music**	**= Reconnaître, classer et organiser les mesures devrait être la première étape pour toute personne qui envisage sérieusement d'en apprendre davantage sur la musique.** ***« This may take some practice if you're not used to it, but it can be useful practice for anyone who is learning about music. » (= « Cela peut demander un peu d'entraînement si vous n'avez pas l'habitude, mais cela peut être un entraînement utile pour toute personne qui s'initie à la musique. »)*** ***De plus, reconnaître, classer et organiser les rythmes musicaux sont des sujets qui ont été abordés dans le corps du texte.***
(B)	There is no way anyone can enjoy listening to music before learning more about music	= Il est impossible de prendre plaisir à écouter de la musique avant d'en savoir plus sur la musique. *Il n'est pas obligatoire de s'y connaître en musique pour en apprécier la qualité.*
(C)	The only way for anyone to improve his/her conducting patterns is by being able to recognize, classify and identify meters.	= La seule façon pour quiconque d'améliorer sa façon de faire la musique est d'être capable de reconnaître, de classer et d'identifier les mesures. *Le texte stipule que savoir reconnaître, classer et organiser les rythmes est une pratique utile afin d'en apprendre plus sur la musique mais ce n'est pas la seule façon de le faire.*
(D)	Given the fact that it could take some practice to successfully identify meters, especially if you're not used to the process, those who have no musical affinity whatsoever will surely fail.	= Étant donné que l'identification des mesures peut demander un certain entraînement, surtout si vous n'êtes pas habitué à ce processus, ceux qui n'ont aucune affinité musicale échoueront certainement. *Il n'est pas nécessaire de s'y connaître en solfège et en métrique musicale pour savoir en jouer (ex: prodiges).*

▪ Question 17 - Solution

According to paragraph 4, what is considered a triple meter?

FR : Selon le paragraphe 4, qu'est-ce qu'une mesure à trois temps ?

(A)	strong-weak-weak-weak-strong-weak	= fort - faible - faible - faible- fort
(B)	strong- strong-weak-weak-weak-weak	= fort - fort - faible- faible- faible - faible
(C) ✓	**strong-weak-weak-strong-weak-weak**	**= fort - faible - faible - fort - faible - faible**
(D)	strong-weak-weak	= fort - faible - faible

⇒ **explication**

FR : *« strong-weak-weak-strong-weak-weak is triple meter »* (= « fort - faible - faible - fort - faible - faible est une mesure en trois temps »)

▪ Question 18 - Solution

The word "interrupted" in paragraph 5 is closest in meaning to:

FR : Le sens du mot « interrupted » dans le paragraphe 5 se rapproche le plus de :

(A) ✓ discontinued = discontinué

(B) encouraged = encouragé

(C) promoted = promu

(D) expedited = accéléré

⇝ **explication**

FR : *« Interrupted »* (= interrompu) signifie rompre la continuité. Alors, le mot qui se rapproche le plus de celui-ci dans les propositions est le verbe *« discontinued »* – Le préfixe 'dis-' indiquant une négation.

▪ Question 19 - Solution

Look at the four squares in paragraph 3, A, B, C, and D, which indicate where the following sentence could be added to the passage. Where would the sentence best fit?

As a matter of fact, adults who are just familiar with Western music usually detect meter-violating changes in non-Western music with simple meter only.

The meter of a piece of music is the arrangement of its rhythms in a repetitive pattern of strong and weak beats. This does not necessarily mean that the rhythms themselves are repetitive, but they do strongly suggest a repeated pattern of pulses. It is on these pulses, the beat of the music, that you tap your foot, clap your hands, dance, etc. Some music does not have a meter. **A** Ancient music, such as Gregorian chants; new music, such as some experimental twentieth-century art music; and Non-Western music, such as some native American flute music, may not have a strong, repetitive pattern of beats. **B** Other types of music, such as traditional Western African drumming, may have very complex meters that can be difficult for the beginner to identify. The influence of incidental exposure to varied metrical patterns from different musical cultures is thought to have an influence on the perception of complex metrical structures from an unfamiliar musical culture. **C** Adults with some exposure to non-Western music that is unmetered or metrically complex successfully detect meter-violating changes in non-Western music with both simple and complex meters. **D**

(A) **A** *Le sujet du rythme mis en relation avec les influences culturelles et la capacité à le reconnaitre n'a pas encore été introduit à ce stade dans le texte, il serait donc incorrect de placer la phrase ici.*

(B) **B** *La phrase n'appartient pas à cette section du paragraphe car elle ne suit pas la progression logique utilisée par l'auteur. Il cite d'abord différents cas dans lesquels la musique peut avoir un rythme simple, complexe voire inexistant. Ce n'est qu'après qu'il commence à décrire la relation que les gens peuvent avoir avec la musique, en fonction de leur origine culturelle.*

(C) ✓ C ***C'est la seule option possible. La phrase que le candidat doit insérer illustre la corrélation entre «incidental exposure to varied metrical patterns from different musical cultures» et «the perception of complex metrical structures from an unfamiliar musical culture.».***

(D) **D** *La présence de la structure « as a matter of fact » (= en fait) dans la phrase qui doit être placée dans le texte, est un indice supplémentaire qui nous dit qu'une exemplification est nécessaire peu de temps après l'illustration du concept de « influence of incidental exposure to varied metrical patterns from different musical cultures ». L'auteur du passage présente les concéquences pour les adultes qui ne connaissent que la musique occidentale. C'est seulement après cela qu'il mentionne que ceux qui ont également écouté de la musique non occidentale sont capables de reconnaître une plus grande variété de rythmes.*

▪ Question 20 - Solution

Directions:

An introductory sentence for a brief summary of the passage is provided below.

Complete the summary by selecting the THREE answer choices that express the most important ideas in the passage. Some sentences do not belong in the summary because they express ideas that are not presented in the passage or are minor ideas in the passage.

This question is worth 2 points.

- By individuating the strong and weak beats in a piece of music and keeping track of their frequency, we can determine the meter of a piece of music.
- ________
- ________
- ________

(A) ✓ **Musicians rely on meter. Conductors do the same, basing their indications more on the rhythmic aspect than on the melodic one, when approaching a piece of music.**

= Les musiciens s'appuient sur le métrage. Les chefs d'orchestre font de même, en basant leurs indications sur l'aspect rythmique plus que sur l'aspect mélodique, lorsqu'ils appréhendent un morceau de musique.

« The lines dividing each measure from the next help the musician reading the music to keep track of the rhythms. A piece (or section of the piece) is assigned a time signature that tells the performer how many beats to expect in each measure »
(« Les lignes qui séparent chaque mesure de la suivante aident le musicien qui lit la musique à suivre les rythmes. Un morceau (ou une section du morceau) se voit attribuer une signature temporelle qui indique à l'interprète le nombre de battements à attendre dans chaque mesure. »)

« the conducting patterns depend only on the pattern of strong and weak beats. In other words, they only depend on "how many beats there are in a measure", not "what type of note gets a beat. »
(« les motifs de direction de la musique dépendent uniquement du motif des temps forts et des temps faibles. En d'autres termes, ils ne dépendent que du "nombre de temps qu'il y a dans une mesure", et non du "type de note qui reçoit un temps". »)

(B) Meter does not belong to every single music genre. In fact, Gregorian chants, native American flute music and Western African drumming represent the best examples of music without meter.

= La mesure n'appartient pas à tous les genres musicaux. En fait, les chants grégoriens, la musique des flûtes amérindiennes et les tambours d'Afrique occidentale sont les meilleurs exemples de musique sans mesure.
Les informations de cette phrase ne sont pas entièrement correctes. En effet, les percussions de l'Afrique de l'ouest « may have very complex meters that can be difficult for the beginner to identify. » (= « peuvent avoir des mesures très complexes qui peuvent être difficiles à identifier pour un débutant. »)

(C) ✓ **The distance that separates two strong beats is used as a criterion of classification for different types of meter.**

= La distance qui sépare deux temps forts est utilisée comme critère de classification des différents types de mesure.
« Meters can be classified by counting the number of beats from one strong beat to the next. »
(= « Les mesures peuvent être classées en comptant le nombre de battements entre un temps fort et le suivant.»)

(D) ✓ **It is possible to have simple and more complex meters. Beginners should start from the ones with a regular beat subdivision if they want to learn to recognize the different varieties of meter**

= Il est possible d'avoir des mesures simples et plus complexes. Les débutants devraient commencer par celles avec une subdivision régulière du rythme s'ils veulent apprendre à reconnaître les différentes variétés de mesure.

« Meters can also be classified as either simple or compound »

« To help you get started, you may also want to listen to some examples of music that is in simple duple, simple triple, simple quadruple to then slowly move to more the more complex compound duple and compound triple meters. »
(« Les mesures peuvent aussi être classées comme simples ou composées. »
« Pour vous aider à démarrer, vous pouvez également écouter des exemples de musique en mesure simple, triple ou quadruple, puis passer lentement aux mesures composées plus complexes, en mesure double ou triple. »)

(E) Triplet meter differ from duplet meter for the addition of two more “weak” beats in its metric pattern.

= La mesure en trois temps diffère de la mesure en deux temps par l'ajout de deux temps "faibles" supplémentaires dans son schéma métrique.

« strong-weak-strong-weak, it is in duple meter. strong-weak-weak-strong-weak-weak is triple meter. » (« Fort-faible-fort-faible, c'est en deux temps. Fort-faible-faible-fort-faible-faible est en trois temps. »)

Même si la distinction entre les rythmes en deux temps et en trois temps avait été correcte, la phrase ne contient que des informations d'importance secondaire.

(F) The separation of syllables while counting is the most important element in order to recognize, count and learn any meter. If we can count all numbers on a beat, then we know we have a simple duple meter.

= La séparation des syllabes pendant le comptage est l'élément le plus important pour reconnaître, compter et apprendre n'importe quelle mesure. Si nous pouvons compter tous les chiffres sur un temps, nous savons que nous avons une mesure simple en deux temps.
Cela n'est pas mentionné dans le texte.

▪ Question 21 - Solution

According to paragraph 1, which of the following statements is true about a meridian?

FR : D'après le paragraphe 1, lequel des énoncés suivants est vrai à propos d'un méridien ?

(A) ✓ It is an imaginary great circle on the Earth's surface passing through the North and South geographic poles.

= C'est un grand cercle imaginaire à la surface de la Terre qui passe par les pôles géographiques Nord et Sud.

« A meridian is the intersection at earth's surface of a plane perpendicular to the equatorial plane and passing through earth's axis of rotation. »
(= « Un méridien est l'intersection à la surface de la Terre d'un plan perpendiculaire au plan équatorial et passant par l'axe de rotation de la Terre. »)

Les axes de rotation de la Terre sont le pôle Nord et le pôle Sud.

(B) It is a curve on a surface of revolution, formed by the intersection of the surface with a plane containing the axis of revolution.

= C'est une courbe sur une surface de révolution, formée par l'intersection de la surface avec un plan contenant l'axe de révolution.
Il n'est pas question de surface de révolution dans le paragraphe 1.

(C) It is a vertical equatorial plane passing through Earth's axis of rotation.

= C'est un plan équatorial vertical passant par l'axe de rotation de la Terre.
Un méridien correspond à <u>l'intersection</u> entre le plan perpendiculaire et le plan équatorial traversant l'axe de rotation de la Terre.

(D) It is the angle between the local vertical and the equatorial plane.

= C'est l'angle entre la verticale locale et le plan équatorial
« Latitude is the angle between the local vertical and equatorial plane. »
(= « La latitude est l'angle entre la verticale locale et le plan équatorial. »)

▪ Question 22 - Solution

The word "perpendicular" in paragraph 1 is closest in meaning to:

FR : Le sens du mot « perpendicular » dans le paragraphe 1 se rapproche le plus de :

(A) ✓ vertical = vertical

(B) horizontal = horizontal

(C) parallel = parallèle

(D) principal = principal

⇨ explication
FR : Le mot *« equatorial »* faisant référence à l'horizontalité, il est alors logique que le mot *« perpendicular »* fasse allusion à la verticalité car on parle ici d'une intersection entre ces deux plans (le méridien).

▪ Question 23 - Solution

The word "nautical" in paragraph 2 is closest in meaning to:

FR : Le sens du mot « nautical » dans le paragraphe 2 se rapproche le plus de :

(A)	military	= militaire
(B)	tactical	= tactique
(C)	empirical	= empirique
(D)	**✓ maritime**	**= maritime**

explication

FR : Le mot « *nautical* » (= nautique) est un terme relatif à la navigation, c'est pourquoi le mot « *maritime* » est le mot dont le sens s'en rapproche le plus.

■ Question 24 - Solution

According to paragraph 3, the tie between nautical miles, meters, and Earth's radius was soon abandoned because:

FR : D'après le paragraphe 3, le lien entre les milles marins, les mètres et le rayon de la Terre a été vite abandonné parce que :

(A)	They were impractical, and the rough estimations were also lagging behind.	= Ils n'étaient pas pratiques, et les estimations approximatives étaient également défaillantes. *contresens* *Les estimations, même approximatives, étaient plutôt précises.*
(B)	**✓ They were impractical to use although the estimations were quite correct.**	**= Ils n'étaient pas pratiques à utiliser, bien que les estimations soient tout à fait correctes.** ***« Although the tie between nautical miles, meters, and earth's radius was soon abandoned because it was not practical, the approximations are very good. »*** ***(= « Bien que le lien entre les milles nautiques, les mètres et le rayon de la Terre ait été rapidement abandonné parce qu'il n'était pas pratique, les approximations sont très justes. »)***
(C)	They were not only practical but also 100% correct in terms of approximations.	= Ils étaient non seulement pratiques mais aussi 100% corrects en termes d'approximations. *Contresens - Le texte mentionne le contraire.* *Cette réponse prétend que cette méthode était pratique lorsque le texte dit le contraire. De plus, les estimations n'étaient pas correctes à 100% selon l'exemple donné dans le paragraphe 3.*
(D)	They were practical, and the approximations were very good.	= Ils étaient pratiques, et les approximations étaient très justes. *inexact - réponse partiellement erronée.* *Les estimations étaient bel et bien très bonnes, mais la méthode peu pratique.*

■ Question 25 - Solution

According to paragraph 4, what can be inferred about maps of the sea floor?

FR : Selon le paragraphe 4, que peut-on conclure des cartes des fonds marins ?

(A) Maps of the sea floor are of high-quality horizontal resolution because the regions in question are seldom visited by ships.

= Les cartes des fonds marins ont une résolution horizontale de haute qualité car les régions en question sont rarement visitées par des navires.
contresens
Les cartes des fonds marins ne peuvent pas être de haute qualité si des bateaux ne visitent que rarement ces régions.

(B) ✓ Maps of the sea floor created by ship-based echo sounders produce fairly low-resolution maps due to large distances and inconsistencies between ships visiting a certain area and the number of ship tracks being far apart from one another.

= Les cartes des fonds marins créées par les échosondeurs des navires produisent des cartes à résolution assez faible en raison des grandes distances et des incohérences entre les navires qui visitent une certaine zone et du fait que les traces des navires sont très éloignées les unes des autres.
« The maps have poor horizontal resolution in some regions because the regions are seldom visited by ships and ship tracks are far apart. »
(= « Les cartes ont une mauvaise résolution horizontale dans certaines régions parce que les régions sont rarement visitées par les navires et que les traces des navires sont très éloignées les unes des autres. »)

(C) Maps of the sea floor are produced by equipments found on seldom visiting ships and ship tracks.

= Les cartes des fonds marins sont produites par des équipements trouvés sur des navires rarement visités et des traces de navires.
Les équipements se trouvent sur des bateaux qui visitent souvent les régions en question.

(D) Maps of the sea floor are ship-based echo sounders designed to scare ships away from a given territory.

= Les cartes des fonds marins sont produites par des échosondeurs embarqués sur des navires et conçus pour faire fuir les navires d'un territoire donné.
Les cartes des fonds marins sont dessinées à l'aide d'échosondeurs se trouvant sur les bateaux qui traversent les océans.

▪ Question 26 - Solution

Which of the following sentences best describes the highlighted sentence in the passage? The other choices change the meaning or leave out information.

The shallow seas help dissipate tides, they are often areas of high biological productivity, and are usually included in the exclusive economic zone of adjacent countries.

FR : Lequel des énoncés suivants décrit le mieux la phrase surlignée dans le passage ? Les autres choix changent le sens de la phrase ou omettent des informations.

(A)	Shallow seas dissipate tides, biological productivity and economic zones.	= Les mers peu profondes dissipent les marées, la productivité biologique et les zones économiques. *Les mers peu profondes dissipent les vagues, mais pas la productivité biologique ni les zones économiques.*
(B)	Shallow seas are important centers of biochemical productivity, especially in economic zones where dissipating tides is more troublesome.	= Les mers peu profondes sont des centres importants de productivité biochimique, surtout dans les zones économiques où la dissipation des marées est plus problématique. *On parle de productivité biologique et non biochimique. De plus, le texte ne dit pas si dissiper les vagues est plus difficile dans les zones économiques.*
(C) ✓	**Shallow seas not only contribute to breaking up tides, but they also serve as an important hub for organic productivity and economic territorial division.**	**= Les mers peu profondes contribuent non seulement à dissiper les marées, mais elles constituent également un centre important de productivité biochimique et de division territoriale et économique.** ***« Breaking up tides » fait référence à « help dissipate tides » dans la phrase surlignée.*** ***« Shallow seas […] also serve as an important hub for organic productive and economic territorial division. » (= « Les mers peu profondes [...] servent également de plaque tournante importante pour la division territoriale biologique productive et économique. ») fait référence au passage suivant dans la phrase surlignée : « The shallow seas […] are often areas of high biological productivity, and are usually included in the exclusive economic zone of adjacent countries. » (= « Les mers peu profondes [...] sont souvent des zones de haute productivité biologique, et sont généralement incluses dans la zone économique exclusive des pays adjacents. »)***
(D)	Shallow seas have tremendous consequences to biological productivity and tidal dissipation.	= Les mers peu profondes ont des conséquences considérables sur la productivité biologique et la dissipation des marées. *Le texte ne dit pas si les mers peu profondes ont des « conséquences énormes » sur la productivité biologique et la dissipation des vagues. De plus, pour refléter parfaitement la phrase surlignée, il aurait dû y avoir une mention des zones économiques.*

■ Question 27 - Solution

All of the following statements are correct EXCEPT:

FR : Tous les énoncés suivants sont corrects, sauf un. Lequel ?

(A)	The current number of official oceans is 3.	= Le nombre actuel d'océans officiellement reconnus est de 3. *« There are only three official oceans. » (= « Il n'y a officiellement que 3 océans »)*
(B) ✓	**There are 7 continental shelves all over the world.**	**= Il y a 7 plateaux continentaux dans le monde.** ***L'auteur liste une partie des plateaux continentaux importants mais le passage ne mentionne pas qu'il s'agit des seuls plateaux continentaux existants. « A few of the more important shelves are [...] »*** ***(= « Quelques-uns des plateaux les plus importants sont [...] »)***
(C)	Shallow seas disperse tides.	= Les mers peu profondes dispersent les marées. *« shallow seas help dissipate tides. » (= « Les mers peu profondes aident à dissiper les marées. »)*
(D)	Continental shelves can serve economic purposes.	= Les plateaux continentaux peuvent servir à des fins économiques. *« [the shallow seas, characterizing continental shelves] are usually included in the exclusive economic zone of adjacent countries. »* *(= « [les mers peu profondes, qui caractérisent les plateaux continentaux] sont généralement incluses dans la zone économique exclusive des pays adjacents. »)*

▪ Question 28 - Solution

It can be concluded that echo sounders:

FR : Il peut en être conclu que les échosondeurs :

(A) ✓	**map approximate ocean depth by measuring the time necessary for the sound to get to the surface from the bottom**	**= cartographient la profondeur approximative de l'océan en mesurant le temps nécessaire au son pour atteindre la surface depuis le fond de l'océan** ***« The depths of the oceans are mapped by echo sounders which measure the time required for a sound pulse to travel from the surface to the bottom and back. »*** ***(« Les profondeurs des océans sont cartographiées par des échosondeurs qui mesurent le temps nécessaire à une impulsion sonore pour se déplacer de la surface au fond et inversement. »)***
(B)	map approximate ocean depth by measuring the speed of sound from one end of the ocean to the other	= cartographient la profondeur approximative des océans en mesurant la vitesse du son d'un bout à l'autre de l'océan *La vitesse du son n'est pas la fonction utilisée pour le calcul de la profondeur des océans mais plutôt le temps que le son met à faire l'aller-retour entre le fond de l'océan et la surface. De plus, "d'un bout à l'autre de l'océan" est techniquement incorrect (plutôt du fond de l'océan vers la surface).*
(C)	map approximate ocean depth by giving off a sound pulse	= cartographient de la profondeur approximative des océans en émettant une impulsion sonore *Envoyer uniquement une impulsion sonore serait inutile pour calculer les profondeurs de l'océan. Le signal doit revenir à l'émetteur afin de calculer la profondeur estimée.*
(D)	map approximate ocean depth by factoring in the time required for the sound to reach the sky	= cartographient la profondeur approximative des océans en tenant compte du temps nécessaire au son pour atteindre le ciel *Utiliser le ciel pour calculer la profondeur des océans n'a pas de sens.*

▪ Question 29 - Solution

Look at the four squares in paragraph 7, **A**, **B**, **C**, and **D**, which indicate where the following sentence could be added to the passage. Where would the sentence best fit?

It is expected to gauge future changes of the Greenland and Antarctic ice sheets at an accuracy of the width of a pencil.

[P7] With our recently acquired ability to travel into space, we now see the earth and its oceans as a whole. **A** A new NASA satellite, ICESat2, was launched in September 2018. **B** Using satellite cameras, we can locate storms and guide ships out of harm's way. **C** We can count the phytoplankton that fuel the fisheries and direct fishermen to fertile grounds. Our sensors detect climatic anomalies as they begin, allowing us to predict their consequences. **D** These are exciting times for humankind's interactions with the sea.

(A) **A** *La phrase n'aurait aucun sens à cet endroit.*

(B) ✓ **B** ***La phrase apporte alors des détails à propos du satellite lancé par la NASA, on peut donc l'insérer ici juste après l'évocation de ce satellite.***

(C) **C** *La phrase précédente a un sujet au pluriel (« satellite cameras »). Pour cette raison, il n'est pas possible d'insérer la phrase à cet endroit.*

(D) **D** *La phrase précédente a un sujet au pluriel (« sensors »). Pour cette raison, il n'est pas possible d'insérer la phrase à cet endroit.*

▪ Question 30 - Solution

Directions:

An introductory sentence for a brief summary of the passage is provided below.

Complete the summary by selecting the THREE answer choices that express the most important ideas in the passage. Some sentences do not belong in the summary because they express ideas that are not presented in the passage or are minor ideas in the passage.

This question is worth 2 points.

- Distances on Earth are measured thanks to systems, each using different parameters, with points of reference such as the equatorial plan and Greenwich.
- ________
- ________
- ________

(A)	**✓ The irregularity of the Earth's shape led to the adoption of different measuring systems, some of which, albeit valid, are no longer used due to being impractical.**	**= L'irrégularité de la forme de la Terre a conduit à l'adoption de différents systèmes de mesure, dont certains, bien que valides, ne sont plus utilisés en raison de leur manque de praticité.** ***Bon résumé des paragraphes 2 et 3.***
(B)	Thanks to Gabriel Mouton's work, the whole world could start using the metric system for different kinds of measurements.	= Grâce aux travaux de Gabriel Mouton, le monde entier a pu commencer à utiliser le système métrique pour différents types de mesures. *Même si il est vrai que les travaux de Mouton ont été importants, l'information n'a qu'une importance secondaire si l'on considère le passage dans son ensemble. En effet, le thème du texte est l'océan et la manière dont on les mesure. Il ne s'agit pas d'un texte sur l'histoire des systèmes de mesure.*
(C)	The echo-sound measurement allows oceanographers to locate storms and guide ships while at sea.	= La technique de l'écho-son permet aux océanographes de localiser les tempêtes et de guider les navires en mer. *L'information est incorrecte. Les satellites permettent aux océanographes de localiser les tempêtes et de guider les bateaux.*
(D)	The new NASA satellite will allow the experts to better study continental shelves and control climate changes.	= Le nouveau satellite de la NASA permettra aux experts de mieux étudier les plateaux continentaux et de contrôler les changements climatiques. *Cela n'est pas mentionné dans le passage.*
(E)	**✓ Although oceans have irregular dimensions, it is possible to state that they are generally wider than they are deep.**	**= Bien que les océans aient des dimensions irrégulières, on peut affirmer qu'ils sont généralement plus larges que profonds.** ***La phrase donne un aperçu correct des principales caractéristiques des océans.***
(F)	**✓ The development of new technologies allows to measure and examine an ocean's depth and surface through sound waves and space satellites in much greater detail.**	**= Le développement de nouvelles technologies permet de mesurer et d'examiner de façon beaucoup plus détaillée la profondeur et la surface d'un océan grâce aux ondes sonores et aux satellites spatiaux.** ***Bon résumé des paragraphes 6 et 7 sur les procédures de mesure des océans.***

Conversion de votre résultat en score TOEFL iBT sur 30

Votre nombre de points (maximum 36 points avec les questions valant deux points)	Estimation score TOEFL iBT
35-36	30
34	29
33	28
32	27
31	26
30	25
29	24
28	23
27	22
26	21
25	20
24	19
23	18
22	17
21	16
20	15
19	14
18	13
17	12
16	11
15	10
14	9
13	8
12	7
11	6
10	5
9	4
8	3
7	2
5-6	1
0-4	0

TOEFL iBT #1 - LISTENING - Solutions

Reportez vos réponses pour analyser votre performance.

Entraînez-vous dans les conditions d'examen.

Écoutez les fichiers audio.

prepmyfuture.com/book/68/ex/1983

question 1	B
question 2	D
question 3	B
question 4	A
question 5	A
question 6	D

question 7	D
question 8	D
question 9	B
question 10	D
question 11	B
question 12	A

question 13	A D
question 14	B
question 15	B
question 16	A
question 17	C
question 18	D

question 19	D
question 20	B
question 21	A
question 22	C D
question 23	D

question 24	A
question 25	C
question 26	C
question 27	A
question 28	D

■ **Question 1 - Solution**

What is the lecture mainly about?

FR : Quel est le sujet principal du cours ?

(A)	A presentation of alternate theories about the purpose of the Great Pyramid.	= Une présentation des théories alternatives sur le rôle de la Grande Pyramide. *Le cours se concentre sur la façon dont la grande Pyramide a été construite, pas sur sur l'utilité de cette dernière.*
(B)	**✓ A summary of some competing ideas on how the Great Pyramid was constructed.**	**= Un résumé de quelques idées divergentes sur la façon dont la Grande Pyramide a été construite.** ***« But how was it built? To this day, the method used by ancient Egyptians to construct the Great Pyramid is an archeological and engineering mystery. »*** ***(= « Mais comment a-t-elle été construite ? À ce jour, la méthode utilisée par les Égyptiens de l'Antiquité pour construire la Grande Pyramide est un mystère à la fois archéologique et technique. »)***
(C)	A discussion on who the original builder of the Great Pyramid might be.	= Une discussion sur l'identité du constructeur originel de la Grande Pyramide. *Les travailleurs sont mentionnés comme élément de détail lorsque le professeur parle de la pyramide.*
(D)	A debate about when the Great Pyramid may have been built.	= Un débat sur la date à laquelle la Grande Pyramide aurait été construite. *Le professeur donne la date de construction de la Grande Pyramide et ne remet pas en question cette date. « Built during one of the early dynasties of Egypt around 2500 B.C » (= « Construite au cours de l'une des premières dynasties d'Égypte, vers 2500 av. »)*

■ Question 2 - Solution

According to the lecture, what is one problem with the Long Ramp Theory?

FR : D'après le cours, quel est l'un des problèmes posé par la théorie de la longue rampe ?

(A)	It would have taken an estimated 3 years to complete.	= Il aurait fallu environ 3 ans pour le réaliser. *Le temps de construction de la rampe n'est pas mentionné, il est simplement dit que la durée estimée des travaux est de 20 ans.* *« generally-accepted time frame for construction of 20 years, workers would have had to maneuver into place one stone block every 3 minutes—an impossible feat »* *(= « Le délai généralement admis pour la construction est de 20 ans, les ouvriers auraient dû mettre en place un bloc de pierre toutes les 3 minutes - un exploit impossible. »)*
(B)	It would have involved transporting stone blocks from Aswan.	= Il aurait fallu transporter des blocs de pierre depuis Assouan. *Cela n'est pas énoncé comme un problème par rapport à la théorie de la longue rampe. Les blocs étaient transportés par bateau à partir d'Assouan, cela n'a rien à voir avec la théorie de construction.*
(C)	It does not explain how steep the ramp would need to be in order to reach the top of the pyramid.	= Elle n'explique pas le degré d'inclinaison de la rampe nécessaire pour atteindre le sommet de la pyramide. *Les scientifiques n'ont pas estimé l'inclinaison de la rampe mais seulement le fait qu'elle aurait dû mesurer 1 mile de long.*
(D) ✓	**There are no indications for the existence of a long ramp near the Great Pyramid.**	**= Il n'y a aucune indication de l'existence d'une longue rampe près de la Grande Pyramide.** ***« no trace of such a ramp has ever been found » (= « aucune trace d'une telle rampe n'a jamais été retrouvée »)***

▪ Question 3 - Solution

What evidence did Houdin use to create his "Spiral Ramp" theory?

FR : Quelle preuve Houdin a-t-il utilisé pour mettre au point sa théorie de la « Rampe en Spirale » ?

(A)	a pathway of stones circling the Great Pyramid	= un chemin de pierres autour de la Grande Pyramide
(B) ✓	**an old map showing something unusual inside the Great Pyramid**	**= une vieille carte montrant quelque chose d'inhabituel à l'intérieur de la Grande Pyramide** ***« He found support for this theory from an old survey of the pyramid showing a "spiral anomaly" inside the pyramid »*** ***(= « Il a trouvé un argument en faveur de cette théorie dans une ancienne étude de la pyramide montrant une "anomalie en spirale" à l'intérieur de la pyramide. »)***
(C)	a recently discovered structural weakness in the interior of the Great Pyramid	= une fragilité structurelle récemment découverte à l'intérieur de la Grande Pyramide *Ils n'ont pas trouvé de fragilité dans la structure mais un ancien couloir comblé avec des pierres.*
(D)	records from ancient builders describing the removal of an external ramp	= des documents provenant d'anciens bâtisseurs décrivant la démolition d'une rampe extérieure

■ Question 4 - Solution

Why does the professor mention stone blocks when discussing problems with the Long Ramp Theory?

FR : Pourquoi le professeur mentionne-t-il les blocs de pierre quand il parle des problèmes de théorie de la longue rampe ?

(A) ✓ To emphasize the magnitude of transporting and setting the large stones. **= Pour souligner l'ampleur du processus de transport et de pose des grosses pierres.**
« For one, in order to complete the pyramid within the generally-accepted time frame for construction of 20 years, workers would have had to maneuver into place one stone block every 3 minutes—an impossible feat considering the average weight of the blocks is over 2 metric tons, and with some blocks as heavy as 80 tons. »
(= « D'une part, pour achever la pyramide dans le délai généralement admis pour la construction, soit 20 ans, les ouvriers auraient dû manipuler un bloc de pierre toutes les 3 minutes - un exploit impossible si l'on considère que le poids moyen des blocs est supérieur à 2 tonnes métriques, et que certains blocs peuvent peser jusqu'à 80 tonnes. »)

(B) To explain why a long ramp probably would collapse under the weight of the heaviest stones. = Pour expliquer pourquoi une longue rampe s'effondrerait probablement sous le poids des pierres les plus lourdes.

(C) To highlight the difficulty of finding an adequate source of stone. = Pour mettre en évidence la difficulté de trouver une réserve de pierres suffisante.
La source d'approvisionnement des pierres est mentionnée (Assouan).

(D) To point out that sleds or rolling logs would not have been able to support their weight. = Pour souligner que les traîneaux ou les rondins de bois n'auraient pas pu supporter leur poids.

⇨ **explication**

FR : Le nombre de blocs et leur poids est l'argument principal pour remettre en question la théorie de la longue rampe. Cette technique de construction était peut-être réalisable mais les travaux auraient duré plus de 20 ans.

■ Question 5 - Solution

What might have been a benefit in building the Great Pyramid using spiral ramps?

FR : Qu'est-ce qui aurait pu procurer un avantage dans la construction de la Grande Pyramide en utilisant la méthode des rampes en spirale ?

(A)	**✓ It would have required a less steep ramp.**	**= Cela aurait nécessité une rampe moins raide.** ***« This 'spiral' would have enabled the pyramid-builders to create a ramp of a much easier grade » (= « Cette "spirale" aurait permis aux bâtisseurs de pyramides de créer une rampe beaucoup plus facile à gravir »)***
(B)	It would have shortened the time needed to finish the pyramid.	= Cela aurait raccourci le temps nécessaire pour terminer la pyramide.
(C)	It would have helped the pyramid builders move blocks around 90-degree turns.	= Cela aurait aidé les bâtisseurs de pyramides à déplacer les blocs en faisant des virages à 90 degrés. *Les tournants à 90-degrés auraient été une contrainte.*
(D)	It would have eliminated the possibility of any collapses during construction.	= Cela aurait empêché tout effondrement pendant la construction. *Cette méthode de construction aurait rendu un effondrement encore plus probable.* *« the interior ramp, because it is empty space inside the pyramid, would create structural weaknesses in the pyramid, making the possibility of collapses very likely »* *(« La rampe intérieure, parce qu'elle constitue un espace vide à l'intérieur de la pyramide, créerait des faiblesses structurelles dans la pyramide, rendant très probable la possibilité d'un effondrement. »)*

▪ Question 6 - Solution

Listen again to part of the lecture. Then answer the question.

> **Script non affiché le jour de l'examen :**
>
> **MALE PROFESSOR:** Over the years, scientists tried to come up with various explanations to either downplay or discount these problems with the Long Ramp theory...all to no avail. So, historians and engineers had to begin to think outside the box, because the traditional ideas weren't actually in sync with what people were seeing in the field.
>
> **NARRATOR:** What does the professor mean when he says this?
>
> **MALE PROFESSOR:** So, historians and engineers had to begin to think outside the box.

FR :

Que veut dire le professeur quand il dit :

« So, historians and engineers had to begin to think outside the box. »

(A)	Scientists had to search a different part of the Great Pyramid for evidence.	= Les scientifiques ont dû chercher des preuves dans une autre partie de la Grande Pyramide. *Ils cherchent une nouvelle théorie.*
(B)	Scientists had to return to more traditional theories on pyramid construction.	= Les scientifiques ont dû revenir à des théories plus traditionnelles sur la construction des pyramides. *Les scientifiques recherchent une nouvelle théorie moins traditionnelle. La théorie de la longue rampe est considérée comme traditionnelle.*
(C)	Scientists had to do research at pyramids from different parts of Egypt.	= Les scientifiques ont dû faire des recherches sur des pyramides de différentes régions d'Egypte. *Les autres pyramides ne sont pas mentionnées.*
(D)	✓ **Scientists had to be more creative in explaining the pyramid's construction.**	**= Les scientifiques ont dû être plus créatifs pour expliquer la construction de la pyramide.** ***L'expression « think outside the box » signifie « penser au-delà des idées reçues ».***

■ Question 7 - Solution

What is the main purpose of the lecture?

FR . Quel est le but principal de ce cours ?

(A)	To compare the symbols in prehistoric art to those in modern art.	= Comparer les symboles de l'art préhistorique à ceux de l'art moderne. *Lorsque le professeur fait une référence à l'art moderne, il ne compare pas les peintures préhistoriques à l'art moderne. Il dit simplement que les artistes du Paléolithique avaient de nombreuses raisons de peindre, tout comme les artistes d'aujourd'hui. De plus, l'allusion à l'art moderne est une idée mineure dans le texte.*
(B)	To describe the hunting rituals of ancient people as seen in cave art.	= Décrire les rituels de chasse des peuples anciens tels qu'ils apparaissent dans l'art rupestre. *Le professeur décrit les rituels de chasse dans le but de présenter la théorie de la magie par empathie.*
(C)	To argue that ancient hunters believed in evil spirits living in animals.	= Soutenir que les chasseurs primitifs croyaient aux mauvais esprits vivant dans les animaux. *Le professeur décrit cette théorie dans le but de présenter le Chamanisme.*
(D)	✓ **To contrast two possible explanations for the creation of prehistoric cave art.**	**= Comparer deux explications possibles de la création de l'art rupestre préhistorique.** ***« Scientists have attempted to explain the meaning behind this cave art in a number of ways. Today, I want to talk about two of the most popular categories of theories: Sympathetic Magic and Shamanism. »*** ***(= « Les scientifiques ont tenté d'expliquer la signification de cet art rupestre de plusieurs manières. Aujourd'hui, je veux parler de deux des catégories de théories les plus populaires : la magie sympathique et le chamanisme. »)***

■ Question 8 - Solution

Listen again to part of the lecture. Then answer the question.

> **Script non affiché le jour de l'examen :**
>
> **FEMALE PROFESSOR:** In a cave in Montespan, France scientists found a depiction of a bear that

seems to be riddled with holes and to have been stabbed with long dark lines—possibly images of spears—in a ritual attack. If you've ever seen images of cave paintings, it's hard to see what else those long dark lines could be.

NARRATOR: What does the professor mean by this statement?

FEMALE PROFESSOR: If you've ever seen images of cave paintings, it's hard to see what else those long dark lines could be.

FR :

Que veut dire le professeur quand elle déclare :

« If you've ever seen images of cave paintings, it's hard to see what else those long dark lines could be. »

(A)	Images with dark lines on them are rarely seen.	= Les images comportant des lignes de couleur sombre sont rares. *« Scientists found a depiction of a bear that seems to be riddled with holes and to have been stabbed with long dark lines—possibly images of spears—in a ritual attack. [...] it's hard to see what else those long dark lines could be. »* *(= « Les scientifiques ont découvert la représentation d'un ours qui semble être criblé de trous et avoir été poignardé par de longues lignes sombres - peut-être des images de lances - lors d'une attaque rituelle. [...] il est difficile de voir ce que ces longues lignes sombres pourraient représenter d'autre. »)*
(B)	There are several possible explanations for the dark lines.	= Il y a plusieurs explications possibles pour expliquer les lignes sombres.
(C)	The dark lines on the cave paintings are very faint.	= Les lignes sombres sur les peintures rupestres sont très peu marquées.
(D)	✓ **The best interpretation for the dark marks is that they are weapons.**	**= La meilleure interprétation des marques sombres est qu'il s'agit d'armes.**

⇨ **explication**
FR : Elle dit qu'il est très clair que les lignes représentent des lances lorsque l'on voit les peintures.

▪ Question 9 - Solution

Why does the professor mention sports team mascots in the lecture?

FR : Pourquoi la professeur mentionne-t-elle les mascottes d'équipes de sport dans son cours ?

(A)	To show that ancient people played games similar to modern people.	= Pour montrer que les peuples anciens jouaient à des jeux similaires à ceux des peuples modernes.
(B) ✓	**To provide a modern-day example of a type of Sympathetic Magic ritual.**	**= Pour fournir un exemple moderne d'un rituel de magie sympathique.** ***« ancient man used the paintings again and again, as a kind of imagination…um, I mean visualization exercise before going out on hunts, kind of like nowadays when rival college sports teams burn a wooden statue of the other team's mascot before an important game. » (= « L'homme des temps anciens utilisait les peintures encore et encore, comme une sorte d'exercice d'imagination... hum, je veux dire de visualisation avant de partir à la chasse, un peu comme de nos jours lorsque des équipes sportives universitaires concurrentes brûlent une statue en bois de la mascotte de l'autre équipe avant un match important. »)***
(C)	To explain why Sympathetic Magic rituals were probably not very effective.	= Pour expliquer pourquoi les rituels de magie sympathique n'étaient probablement pas très efficaces.
(D)	To point out how cave paintings could teach ancient people how to hunt as a group.	= Pour indiquer comment les peintures rupestres pouvaient enseigner aux peuples anciens comment chasser en groupe. *Le professeur mentionne effectivement le fait que les peintures auraient été utilisées à des fins d'enseignement mais aucun lien n'est fait avec les équipes de sport lorsqu'elle mentionne ce fait.*

■ Question 10 - Solution

Listen again to part of the lecture. Then answer the question.

Script non affiché le jour de l'examen :

MALE STUDENT: I've seen some of those! They were in a documentary I saw last year. There was one--I think it was a painting of a lion—and it had so many lines drawn over it, it looked like someone had tried to vandalize it. But I guess that's not the case, huh?

FEMALE PROFESSOR: That's probably a safe bet.

NARRATOR: What does the professor mean by this statement?

FEMALE PROFESSOR: That's probably a safe bet.

FR :

Que veut dire la professeur quand elle dit :

« That's probably a safe bet. »

(A)	The student probably did see a cave painting of a lion in the documentary.	= L'étudiant a probablement vu une peinture rupestre représentant un lion dans le documentaire.
(B)	The cave painting the student had seen had probably been vandalized.	= La peinture rupestre que l'étudiant avait vue avait probablement été vandalisée.
(C)	The cave painting was probably of a different type of animal than the student thought.	= La peinture rupestre représentait probablement un type d'animal différent de celui auquel l'étudiant pensait.
(D)	✓ **The cave painting probably looked as the artist originally intended.**	**= La peinture rupestre ressemblait probablement à ce que l'artiste avait imaginé à l'origine.**

⇝ **explication**
FR : *« That's a safe bet »* signifie littéralement que c'est un pari peu risqué, qu'il y a fort à parier. Ainsi, le professeur implique que ce qu'affirme l'étudiant est probablement vrai (ici, que les caves n'ont pas été vandalisées).

▪ Question 11 - Solution

What kind of cave paintings seem to support the Shamanism theory of cave art?

FR : Quel type de peinture rupestre semble justifier la théorie chamaniste ?

(A)	images with dark marks appearing to come out of the animal's mouth	= des images avec des marques sombres semblant sortir de la bouche de l'animal *Ces images sont surtout utilisées pour soutenir la première théorie.* *« Dark marks at the animals' mouth or nose appear to be blood being vomited by the dying beasts. »* *(= « Les marques sombres au niveau de la bouche ou du nez des animaux semblent être du sang vomi par les bêtes mourantes. »)*
(B)	✓ **images showing half-man, half-animal figures**	**= des images montrant des figures mi-homme, mi-animal** ***« Support for this theory come from cave paintings which show one animal seemingly combined with another, like some kind of hybrid creature, or in painting showing an animal head painted on a human body »*** ***(= « Cette théorie est étayée par des peintures rupestres qui montrent un animal apparemment mélangé à un autre, comme une sorte de créature hybride, ou par des peintures montrant une tête d'animal peinte sur un corps humain. »)***
(C)	images that display groups of animals together	= des images montrant des groupes d'animaux ensemble
(D)	images hidden deep inside caves that are not easy to reach	= des images cachées au fond de grottes difficilement accessibles

▪ Question 12 - Solution

According to the Shamanism theory of cave art, what is the main purpose of ancient cave paintings?

FR : Selon la théorie chamaniste de l'art rupestre, quel est le principal objectif des peintures préhistoriques ?

(A)	✓ **to create a deeper state of awareness of the world**	**= créer un état de conscience plus profond du monde** ***« priest or magicians called "shamans"—enter a deeper state of consciousness in order to form a closer connection to or deeper understanding of the world. »*** ***(= « Les prêtres ou les magiciens appelés "chamans" - entrent dans un état de conscience plus profond afin d'établir un lien plus intime avec le monde ou pour mieux le comprendre. »)***
(B)	to assist ancient people in hunting for food	= aider les peuples anciens à chasser pour se nourrir *C'est le cas pour la première théorie.*
(C)	to give respect to the animals they saw in nature	= témoigner du respect aux animaux qu'ils voyaient dans la nature
(D)	to help ancient people connect with their dead ancestors	= aider les anciens à se connecter avec leurs ancêtres défunts

■ **Question 13 - Solution**

What are the main lupics of the lecturc?

Click on 2 answers.

FR : Quels sont les principaux thèmes du cours ?
Choisissez 2 réponses.

(A)	✓ **Why ancient China was the source of many inventions**	**= la raison pour laquelle la Chine ancienne a été la source de nombreuses inventions** ***Le professeur donne une explication principale (le fonctionnement bureaucratique du gouvernement chinois) à la dernière question. C'est un des thèmes importants car cela nous donne beaucoup de clés de compréhension (et notamment pourquoi cette civilisation isolée a donné naissance à tant de technologies).***
(B)	How technology movod from medieval Europe to other parts of the world	= la façon dont la technologie s'est déplacée de l'Europe médiévale vers d'autres parties du monde *Le professeur ne fait allusion aux échanges de technologie européens que pour mettre en exergue la situation isolée de la Chine. Le centre de cette discussion est la Chine et non l'Europe.*
(C)	How China kept the process for making silk secret for centuries	= la façon dont la Chine a gardé secret le processus de fabrication de la soie pendant des siècles *Le professeur fait allusion à la soie uniquement à titre d'exemple pour illustrer les échanges commerciaux entre l'Europe et la Chine.*
(D)	✓ **How Chinese innovations were picked up by other cultures in ancient times**	**= la façon dont les innovations de la Chine ont été reprises par d'autres cultures dans les temps anciens** ***Après avoir donné des exemples de technologie chinoise, le professeur explique quels ont été selon lui les principaux vecteurs d'échange de technologie (la guerre et l'immigration).***

⇨ **explication**
FR : Les réponses A et D sont les 2 thèmes principaux du cours. Les autres parties du cours sont plus orientées autour d'exemples.

■ **Question 14 - Solution**

According to the professor, all of the following are examples of Chinese technology or knowledge that reached Europe before the 13th century EXCEPT:

FR : Selon le professeur, les phrases suivantes sont des exemples de technologie ou de savoir chinois qui ont atteint l'Europe avant le 13e siècle, sauf un. Lequel ?

(A)	creating items out of iron	= la création d'objets en fer *« [...]a Chinese delegation who settled in Persia as early as 110 B.C. [...] taught their new neighbors to cast weapons, tools and utensils from iron. »* *(= « [...] une délégation chinoise qui s'est installée en Perse dès 110 avant J.-C. [...] a appris à ses nouveaux voisins à mouler des armes, des outils et des ustensiles en fer. »)*
(B)	**✓ gunpowder**	**= la poudre à canon** ***« [...] gunpowder didn't arrive in Europe until the 13th century. »(= « la poudre à canon n'est arrivée en Europe qu'au 13e siècle. »)***
(C)	medicine	= la médecine *« Buddhist monks traveling from China to India in the early Middle Ages shared their knowledge of [...] medicine. » (= « Les moines bouddhistes qui voyageaient de la Chine à l'Inde au début du Moyen Âge partageaient leurs connaissances de [...] la médecine. »)*
(D)	silk weaving	= le tissage de la soie *« In the 10th century, one Chinese officer who had been held prisoner in Persia reported finding Chinese [...] silk weavers there » (= « Au 10e siècle, un officier chinois qui avait été retenu prisonnier en Perse a rapporté y avoir trouvé [...] des tisserands de soie chinois »)*

⟹ **explication**

FR : Le professeur explique en répondant à la première question que la poudre à canon (réponse B) est un exemple de technologie qui a pris plus de temps que les autres à atteindre l'Europe.

Il choisit à la suite de ce propos de ne se concentrer que sur les technologies ou savoirs qui ont atteint l'Europe avant ou pendant le Moyen Âge (ce qui est le cas des 3 autres choix A, C ou D).

▪ Question 15 - Solution

According to the lecture, how did the loom most likely come to be used in the Middle East?

FR : FR : D'après le cours, comment le métier à tisser est-il venu à être utilisé au Moyen-Orient ?

(A)	Roman travelers saw a loom being used in China.	= Les voyageurs romains ont vu un métier à tisser utilisé en Chine.
(B) ✓	**Chinese craftsmen were captured and taken to the Middle East.**	**= Des artisans chinois ont été capturés et emmenés au Moyen-Orient.** ***« Warfare was one carrier of technology, where Chinese artisans and craftsmen would be taken captive and taken back to the Middle East. » (= « La guerre était l'un des vecteurs de la technologie, les artisans chinois étant capturés et ramenés au Moyen-Orient. »)***
(C)	Chinese merchants sold diagrams of the loom to people in the Middle East.	= Les marchands chinois ont vendu des schémas du métier à tisser aux populations du Moyen-Orient. *Cela ne peut être vrai car dans l'exemple que le professeur donne, des orfèvres chinois et des tisseurs de soie semblent être détenus en Perse. On peut en déduire qu'ils n'étaient pas là par choix : ils ont été capturés et ont dû montrer leur savoir.*
(D)	Buddhist monks brought the loom with them while on pilgrimage.	= Les moines bouddhistes ont apporté le métier à tisser avec eux lors de leurs pèlerinages. *Les moines bouddhistes ont partagé leur savoir sur des sujets moins technologiques (astrologie, minéralogie, médecine).*

⇒ **explication**

FR : Durant la conférence, le professeur explique que la guerre a été l'une des principales raisons pour lesquelles la technologie chinoise a été exportée. Le métier à tisser est un exemple d'échange de technologies non souhaité.

■ Question 16 - Solution

What does the professor imply by this statement?

> **Script non affiché le jour de l'examen :**
>
> **FEMALE PROFESSOR:** In some ways, this monopoly of production served Europe and the Middle East well, because this combination of both desirability and monopoly provided a permanent line of interaction, first through Central Asia over the four-thousand-mile Silk Road and later by sea, between the Far East and Europe.

FR : Que suggère le professeur dans ce paragraphe?

(A)	✓	**Europe benefited from the fact that China was the only source for silk.**	**= L'Europe a bénéficié du fait que la Chine était la seule source de soie.** ***« [...] this monopoly of production served Europe and the Middle East well, because this combination of both desirability and monopoly provided a permanent line of interaction, first through Central Asia over the four-thousand-mile long Silk Road and later by sea, between the Far East and Europe. »*** ***(= « Ce monopole de production a bien servi l'Europe et au Moyen-Orient, car cette combinaison de désirabilité et de monopole a fourni une ligne d'interaction permanente, d'abord à travers l'Asie centrale sur la route de la soie longue de quatre mille miles, puis par voie maritime, entre l'Extrême-Orient et l'Europe. »)***
(B)		Europe and the Middle East sought for many centuries to find a way to travel to China by sea.	= L'Europe et le Moyen-Orient ont cherché pendant plusieurs siècles à trouver un moyen de se rendre en Chine par la mer. *La route de la soie a été remplacée par un itinéraire maritime qui a fonctionné pendant plusieurs siècles. Il n'est pas précisé que l'Europe et le Moyen-Orient étaient à l'origine de ce changement.*
(C)		After discovering a sea route to China, European no longer used the Silk Road.	= Après avoir découvert une route maritime vers la Chine, les Européens n'ont plus utilisé la route de la soie. *L'itinéraire par la mer était une alternative à la route de la soie. Mais le texte n'est pas explicite sur le fait que les Européens n'aient plus utilisé la route de la soie par la suite.*
(D)		Silk was the only commodity which both Europe and the Middle East desired from China.	= La soie était la seule marchandise que l'Europe et le Moyen-Orient désiraient obtenir de la Chine. *La Chine avait un monopole sur la soie. C'est pourquoi l'Europe et le Moyen-Orient étaient dépendants de ce pays. Cela ne signifie pas qu'ils n'étaient pas intéressés par d'autres achats.*

⇨ **explication**

Le monopole de la Chine sur la soie a bénéficé à l'Europe car celui-ci à été à l'origine d'échanges réguliers entre les 2 partenaires. Ces échanges ont eu lieu le long d'une longue route commerciale partant d'Europe et traversant l'Asie : d'abord par la Route de la soie puis par la mer.

▪ Question 17 - Solution

According to the lecture, why was China the originator of many devices?

FR : Selon le cours, pourquoi la Chine était-elle à l'origine de tant d'innovations?

(A)	It had the largest population in the ancient world.	= Elle avait la plus grande population du monde antique. *Il n'y a aucune référence dans le texte à la taille de la population chinoise.*
(B)	It heavily restricted access to Chinese technology.	= Elle limitait fortement l'accès à la technologie chinoise. *Pendant le cours, l'accès restreint aux technologies chinoises est mentionné uniquement pour souligner la situation isolée du pays.*
(C)	**✓ It had a strong central government.**	**= Elle avait un gouvernement central fort.** ***Des grands projets immobiliers, organisés par un gouvernement fort, centralisé, ont mené à une irrigation massive et à un réseau de transports. Cela a donné à la Chine une avance nette sur les autres pays.***
(D)	It maintained tight control over merchants traveling the Silk Road.	= Elle exerçait un contrôle étroit sur les marchands qui empruntaient la route de la soie. *Suite à un décret officiel des empereurs, quiconque était pris en train de vendre des vers à soie ou en train d'apprendre aux étrangers comment produire de la soie était mis à mort. C'est un cas particulier : ce n'était pas le cas pour d'autres innovations.*

⇒ **explication**

FR : *« [...] many historians believe that Chinese technological leadership was due to the strong bureaucratic government which had ruled China since the third century B.C. »* (= « De nombreux historiens pensent que la domination technologique chinoise est due au gouvernement bureaucratique fort qui régnait en Chine depuis le troisième siècle avant Jésus-Christ. »)"

▪ Question 18 - Solution

Which of the following statements is true?

FR : Laquelle de ces propositions est vraie ?

(A)	It is well understood how all Chinese technologies and ideas reached Europe.	= On comprend bien comment toutes les technologies et idées chinoises sont parvenues en Europe. *Le professeur commence son cours en précisant que la transmission à l'Europe de certaines technologies s'est faite de manière spéculative.*
(B)	Ancient China did not seek out technology from other countries.	= La Chine antique n'a pas cherché à obtenir des technologies d'autres pays. *Le cours se concentre sur la façon dont l'Europe ou le Moyen Orient se sont appropriés des technologies de Chine. Et non l'inverse.*
(C)	Peaceful immigration was the primary method for Chinese technology reaching Europe in ancient times.	= L'immigration pacifique était la meilleure manière pour la technologie chinoise d'atteindre l'Europe à l'époque antique. *L'immigration était une raison parmi d'autres de la fuite des technologies chinoises vers l'Europe. Par ailleurs, les exemples du professeur vont plus dans le sens d'une immigration de guerre que celle d'une immigration paisible.*
(D) ✓	**Ancient China was well-suited for large-scale building projects.**	**= La Chine antique était bien adaptée à la construction de bâtiments à grande échelle.** ***« These massive building projects, organized by a powerful, centralized government which could assert its authority over local governments, led to massive irrigation and transportation networks to be constructed throughout the kingdom. »*** ***(= « Ces projets de construction massifs, organisés par un gouvernement puissant et centralisé qui pouvait affirmer son autorité sur les gouvernements locaux, ont conduit à la construction de réseaux d'irrigation et de transport massifs dans tout le royaume. »)***

⇒ **explication**

La réponse D est la plus appropriée car elle utilise des extraits clairs du texte. Les réponses A, B ou C sont soit fausses soit proposent des déclarations qui n'étaient pas précisées ou même suggérées dans le texte.

▪ Question 19 - Solution

Why does the student want to talk with the professor?

FR : Pourquoi l'étudiante veut-elle parler au professeur ?

(A)	to explain why she feels a project in a class is too difficult	= pour expliquer pourquoi elle estime qu'un projet pour un cours est trop difficile *Elle ne parle pas au professeur pour se plaindre. Elle parle au professeur pour obtenir de l'aide.*
(B)	to get help preparing for a test	= pour obtenir de l'aide pour préparer un examen
(C)	to interview him for a project	= pour l'interviewer pour un projet *Le professeur est celui qui demande à l'étudiante d'interviewer quelqu'un. Elle doit interviewer un dirigeant d'entreprise, pas son professeur.*
(D) ✓	**to get advice on how to do an assignment**	**= pour obtenir des conseils sur la façon de faire un devoir** ***« I'm wondering if you might be able to help me with something about our final project. » (= « Je me demandais si vous pouviez m'aider sur un point concernant notre travail de fin de semestre. »)***

⇒ **explication**

Le professeur a demandé aux étudiants d'interviewer un dirigeant d'entreprise. L'étudiante n'a pas réussi à trouver quelqu'un à interviewer. Elle demande donc au professeur de l'aider à trouver un dirigeant d'entreprise qui acceptera de se faire interviewer.

■ Question 20 - Solution

Why is the student having trouble with the assignment?

FR : Pour quelle raison l'étudiante a-t-elle du mal à réaliser le projet donné par le professeur ?

(A)	She doesn't know any business leaders who are looking to hire college students.	= Elle ne connaît aucun dirigeant d'entreprise qui chercherait à embaucher des étudiants. *Elle ne recherche pas un emploi.*
(B)	✓ **She's not familiar with anyone who fits a certain criteria.**	**= Elle ne connaît personne qui réponde à certains critères.** ***« I don't really know anybody who I could say was a business leader » (= « Je ne connais personne dont je pourrais dire qu'il est chef d'entreprise »)***
(C)	She doesn't think anyone would want to do an interview with her.	= Elle pense que personne n'accepterait de la rencontrer pour un entretien. *Ce n'est pas la raison pour laquelle elle a du mal à réaliser le projet. Elle soulève ce problème seulement dans la deuxième partie de la conversation.*
(D)	She didn't conduct an interview in time for a deadline.	= Elle n'a pas réussi à obtenir un entretien dans les temps.

⇒ **explication**

FR : Elle est nouvelle dans la région et ne connaît aucun dirigeant d'entreprise important. Elle ne sait même pas qui sont les dirigeants importants de la région.

■ Question 21 - Solution

How does the professor help the student?

FR : Comment le professeur aide-t-il l'étudiante ?

(A)	**✓ Suggesting a method for looking for someone to interview.**	**= En suggérant une méthode pour rechercher une personne à interviewer.**
(B)	Giving her the name of a business leader to contact to set up an interview.	= En lui donnant le nom d'un chef d'entreprise à contacter pour organiser un entretien. *« Now, a good way to find out about what's going in town is to check out the local papers. […] You might find someone there—it's easy enough call them up and ask for an interview. »* *(= « Maintenant, un bon moyen de savoir ce qui se passe en ville est de consulter les journaux locaux. [...] Vous pourriez y trouver quelqu'un - il est assez facile de l'appeler et de lui demander de vous accorder un entretien. »)*
(C)	Offering an alternate project for the final assignment.	= En lui proposant un projet alternatif pour le travail final.
(D)	Telling a story of how he found a local business person to interview.	= En racontant comment il a trouvé un homme d'affaires local à interviewer. *Il n'est pas à la recherche d'un dirigeant d'entreprise à interviewer. Il est simplement en train de donner des conseils de méthodologie à l'étudiante.*

▪ Question 22 - Solution

According to the professor, what are some of the goals of the class they are discussing?

Click on 2 answers.

FR : Selon le professeur, quels sont les objectifs du cours dont ils sont en train de parler ?

Sélectionnez 2 réponses

(A)	To explore the types of industries students may want to work in	= Étudier les types d'industries dans lesquelles les étudiants pourraient vouloir travailler.
(B)	To examine how business leaders are viewed in the local community	= Examiner comment les chefs d'entreprise sont perçus dans la communauté locale. *Le professeur est davantage intéressé par ce que les dirigeants d'entreprises apportent à leur communauté locale.*
(C)	**✓ To understand what business leaders do to promote the general welfare of the community**	**= Comprendre ce que font les chefs d'entreprise pour promouvoir le bien-être général de la communauté.** ***« [...] part of this class is to [...] see how companies contribute to the community in various ways » (= « [...] une partie de ce cours consiste à [...] voir comment les entreprises apportent leur contribution à la communauté de diverses manières. »)***
(D)	**✓ To learn how to effectively manage a company**	**= Apprendre à gérer efficacement une entreprise.** ***« The business leaders here in town [...] had to step out of their store and talk to people, make connections, understand more about the lives of the people who come into their establishment. This project allows you to develop those skills. »*** ***(= « Les chefs d'entreprise ici en ville [...] ont dû sortir de leur commerce et parler aux gens, établir des liens, comprendre davantage la vie des personnes qui viennent dans leur établissement. Ce projet vous permet de développer ces compétences. »)***

▪ Question 23 - Solution

Listen again to part of the lecture. Then answer the question.

Script non affiché le jour de l'examen :

FEMALE STUDENT: Thank you so much, Professor. This is all a really big help.

MALE PROFESSOR: My pleasure. Sometimes it takes just a little help to get yourself off on the right foot. In no time you'll see it's not so hard.

What does the professor mean when he says this?

Script non affiché le jour de l'examen :

MALE PROFESSOR: Sometimes it takes just a little help to get yourself off on the right foot.

FR : Que veut dire le professeur quand il dit la phrase suivante :
« Sometimes it takes just a little help to get yourself off on the right foot. » ?

(A) He feels that the student should find a student partner to help her with the project.	= Il estime que l'étudiante devrait trouver un binôme pour l'aider dans son projet.
(B) He thinks the student should ask a local business to help her find someone to interview.	= Il pense que l'étudiante devrait demander à une entreprise locale de l'aider à trouver une personne à interviewer.
(C) He feels that the project may be too difficult for the student to complete.	= Il pense que le projet est peut-être trop difficile à réaliser pour l'étudiante.
(D) ✓ He believes that the student won't have any further problems completing her project.	**= Il pense que l'étudiante n'aura plus de problème pour terminer son projet.**

⟹ **explication**

FR : Cette expression idiomatique veut dire « parfois, il suffit d'un petit coup de pouce pour repartir sur le bon pied ». Le professeur dit que grâce au conseil qu'il a donné, l'étudiante devrait pouvoir réussir le projet.

▪ Question 24 - Solution

Why did the student go to the Career Center?

FR : Pourquoi l'étudiant s'est-il rendu au centre d'orientation professionnelle ?

(A) ✓ to ask for more information about an upcoming job fair	**= pour demander de plus amples informations sur un salon de l'emploi organisé prochainement** ***« Yesterday I saw a poster for an international business career fair. [...] Yeah. I've got a couple questions about it. » (= « Hier, j'ai vu une affiche pour un salon des carrières en commerce international. [...] J'ai quelques questions à ce sujet. »)***
(B) to get advice on which field of study he should pursue	= pour obtenir des conseils sur le domaine d'études qu'il devrait poursuivre *L'étudiant ne sait pas dans quel domaine il va se spécialiser mais ce n'est pas la raison de sa visite au centre de gestion de carrière.*
(C) to get a list of questions to ask companies attending a fair	= pour obtenir une liste de questions à poser aux entreprises qui participent à un salon *La conseillère recommande à l'étudiant de préparer une liste de questions. L'étudiant ne demande pas cette liste.*
(D) to inquire about a particular job opportunity	= pour se renseigner sur une offre d'emploi particulière

▪ Question 25 - Solution

The student thinks he can't go to the career fair for the following reasons EXCEPT:

FR : L'étudiant pense qu'il ne peut pas aller au salon de recrutement pour les raisons suivantes à l'exception de :

(A)	He is not in his final year of college.	= Il n'est pas en dernière année d'études. *« I'm just a sophomore. » (= « Je suis juste un étudiant de deuxième année. »)*
(B)	He is not yet an international business student.	= Il n'est pas encore étudiant en commerce international. *« I don't even know if I want to major in international business. » (= « Je ne sais même pas si je veux me spécialiser dans le commerce international. »)*
(C) ✓	**He is planning getting a science or language degree.**	**= Il envisage d'obtenir un diplôme en sciences ou en langues.** ***Il ne sait pas encore quelle spécialité choisir.*** ***« I don't even know if I want to major in international business » (= « Je ne sais même pas si je veux me spécialiser dans le commerce international. »)***
(D)	He is a male student.	= C'est un garçon. *« Someone told me it was a woman's career fair. » (= « On m'a dit que c'était un salon de l'emploi pour les femmes. »)*

▪ Question 26 - Solution

According to the counselor, companies attend the career fair for the following reasons EXCEPT:

FR : Selon la conseillère, les entreprises participent au salon de recrutement pour les raisons suivantes à l'exception de :

(A)	To encourage students to get international business degrees.	= Encourager les étudiants à obtenir des diplômes en commerce international. *« They're there to encourage students to study international business. » (= « Ils sont là pour encourager les étudiants à étudier le commerce international. »)*
(B)	To explain how other field of study may be related to international business.	= Expliquer comment d'autres domaines d'études peuvent être liés au commerce international. *« help students see how it might be related to any number of different fields of study » (= « aider les étudiants à voir comment [le commerce international] peut être lié à un certain nombre de domaines d'études différents. »)*
(C) ✓	**To encourage students to get a graduate degree.**	**= Encourager les étudiants à obtenir un diplôme d'études supérieures.**
(D)	To meet upcoming graduates interested in a business career.	= Rencontrer les futurs diplômés intéressés par une carrière commerciale. *« the companies that attend are hoping to meet people just like you. They're there to encourage students to study international business »* *(= « Les entreprises présentes espèrent rencontrer des personnes comme vous. Elles sont là pour encourager les étudiants à étudier le commerce international. »)*

▪ Question 27 - Solution

Why does the counselor suggest that the student visit the university website next week before the career fair begins?

FR : Pourquoi la conseillère suggère-t-elle à l'étudiant d'aller sur le site internet de l'université la semaine prochaine avant que le salon de recrutement commence ?

(A)	✓ **There may be changes to which companies are attending the fair.**	**= Il peut y avoir des changements dans les entreprises présentes au salon.** ***« we've even had companies pull out at the last minute, so I recommend checking out the Career Center webpage on the university website maybe the day before the fair. You might find that some new companies that you might be interested in, too. »*** ***(= « Nous avons même eu des entreprises qui se sont retirées à la dernière minute. Je vous recommande donc de consulter la page Web du centre des carrières sur le site de l'université, peut-être la veille du salon. Vous pourriez découvrir de nouvelles entreprises qui pourraient vous intéresser. »)***
(B)	There will be a list of questions that the companies will be asking students.	= Il y aura une liste de questions que les entreprises poseront aux étudiants. *La conseillère mentionne effectivement une liste de questions. Ces questions doivent être préparées par l'étudiant dans le but de débuter des conversations avec les entreprises.*
(C)	The schedule and location of the fair may change.	= L'horaire et le lieu du salon peuvent changer.
(D)	Students can schedule an interview with companies in which they are interested.	= Les étudiants peuvent planifier un entretien avec les entreprises qui les intéressent. *Les étudiants peuvent préparer leur visite du salon. Il n'est pas mentionné qu'ils puissent prendre un rendez-vous à partir du site internet.*

▪ Question 28 - Solution

What does the counselor recommend the student do before the career fair?

FR : Qu'est-ce la conseillère recommande à l'étudiant de faire avant le salon de recrutement ?

(A)	talk to some seniors who are going to the fair to look for a job	= parler à des étudiants de dernière annéequi vont au salon pour chercher un emploi *Les étudiants de dernière année (EN : seniors) sont mentionnés uniquement pour dire que ceux-ci participent au salon pour obtenir un emploi.*
(B)	print out a map of the fair to see which companies are attending	= imprimer un plan du salon pour voir quelles entreprises y seront présentes *La conseillère propose d'imprimer le plan du salon pour l'étudiant.* *« I can print out a map of the fair for you (= « Je peux vous imprimer un plan du salon. »)*
(C)	make a list of which fields of study he is interested in studying	= faire une liste des domaines d'études qui l'intéressent
(D)	✓ **visit the websites of companies attending the career fair to learn more about them**	**= visiter les sites web des entreprises présentes au salon de l'emploi pour en savoir plus sur elles** ***« Here's the list of companies. I recommend spending some time this weekend going to their websites and seeing which ones strike you as interesting. »*** ***(= « Voici la liste des entreprises. Je vous recommande de passer un peu de temps ce week-end à visiter leurs sites web et à voir celles qui vous semblent intéressantes. »)***

Conversion de votre résultat en score TOEFL iBT sur 30

Votre nombre de bonnes réponses	Estimation score TOEFL iBT
27-28	30
26	29
25	28
24	27
23	26
22	25
21	24
20	23
19	22
18	21
17	20
16	19
15	18
14	17
13	16
12	15
11	14
10	13
9	11
8	9
7	7
6	5
5	3
4	1
0-3	0

TOEFL iBT #1 - SPEAKING - Solutions

Utilisez la grille ci-dessous pour vous auto-évaluer sur chaque exercice. Additionnez vos scores et multipliez le résultat par 30/16 pour obtenir une note sur 30.

4 points	On retrouve toutes les caractéristiques suivantes : • débit rythmé et fluide, les fautes mineures d'intonation ou prononciation n'empêchent pas la compréhension • vocabulaire varié et maîtrise des structures complexes, les erreurs mineures n'empêchent pas la compréhension • utilisation de l'ensemble du temps imparti, les liens entre les idées sont clairs
3 points	On retrouve au moins 2 des caractéristiques suivantes : • débit assez fluide, les fautes d'intonation ou prononciation rendent plus difficile la compréhension mais le discours reste intelligible • les fautes de vocabulaire et de grammaire ne portent pas atteinte à l'intelligibilité du discours • utilisation de l'essentiel du temps imparti, le développement de la réponse est limité mais la réponse est globalement cohérente
2 points	On retrouve au moins 2 des caractéristiques suivantes : • rythme saccadé, mais le discours reste intelligible mais n'est pas clair par endroit • maîtrise limitée de la grammaire et du vocabulaire, seules les structures simples sont maîtrisées • la réponse correspond à la question mais n'est pas assez développée, le nombre des idées est limité avec des propos vagues et répétitifs
1 point	On retrouve au moins 2 des caractéristiques suivantes : • difficultés de prononciation et hésitations, rythme très saccadé. • les fautes de grammaire et de vocabulaire rendent difficile la compréhension • discours court et répétitions
0 point	Pas de réponse ou réponse hors-sujet

Nous avons pour projet de mettre en ligne un service de correction personnalisée pour les épreuves d'expression orale et écrite. Ce service fera appel à des correcteurs expérimentés qui vous attribueront une note en suivant les critères du TOEFL iBT. La correction détaillée incluera des conseils personnalisés pour vous améliorer. À l'heure où vous lirez ce manuel, le service sera peut-être déjà en ligne sur http://www.prepmyfuture.com/toefl

Réponses types

ıl Reportez vos réponses pour analyser votre performance.

⏰ Entraînez-vous dans les conditions d'examen.

🎧 Écoutez les fichiers audio.

prepmyfuture.com/book/68/ex/1984

question 1	q. ouverte

question 2	q. ouverte

question 3	q. ouverte

question 4	q. ouverte

- **Question 1 - Solution**

DIRECTIONS: *In this question, you will be asked to speak about a familiar topic. After you hear the question, you have 15 seconds to prepare your response and 45 seconds to speak.*

If you could spend 2 weeks traveling to anywhere in the world, where would you go and why? Use specific details and examples in your explanation.

Preparation Time: 15 seconds
Response Time: 45 seconds

FR :

DIRECTIONS : *Dans cette question, on vous demandera de donner votre opinion sur un sujet familier. Après avoir entendu la question, vous avez 15 secondes pour préparer votre réponse et 45 secondes pour parler.*

Si vous pouviez passer 2 semaines à voyager n'importe où dans le monde, où iriez-vous et pourquoi ? Donnez des détails et des exemples précis dans votre réponse.

Temps de préparation : 15 secondes
Temps de réponse : 45 secondes

⇒ **explication**

Exemple de réponse qui aurait obtenu le score maximum

If I could spend two weeks traveling anywhere in the world, I would definitely go to China. I believe China has a multitude of rich experiences to offer. Since forever, I have always been fascinated with its culture, its language and famous landmarks. My first stop would have to be Beijing, a pulsating city and a melting pot. I dream of wandering in its small streets and devour the local foods. A trip to the summer palace is a must. The summer palace is renowned for its artworks and lavish temples, which I adore.

Then, after an exciting visit to the Great Wall, I would take a local train to Yunnan Province, so as to visit the enchanting and mystical small city named Dali, where my best friend is from.

Évaluation de l'exemple de réponse

Remarques générales / niveau CECRL	Le candidat répond à la question présentée dans la consigne de manière bien structurée et complète, montrant ainsi une maîtrise avancée de la langue anglaise. Le niveau de compétence du candidat correspond approximativement au niveau C1 du CECRL et la qualité de la production orale serait égale à un 4/4 dans le système de score du TOEFL iBT.
Respect des consignes	Le candidat répond correctement à la question en se concentrant sur les thèmes introduits et sans répéter plus d'une fois le même concept.
Structure de la réponse	Le candidat commence par introduire le sujet, puis expose des arguments qui soutiennent sa thèse. Même s'il s'agit d'une courte production, l'étudiant utilise des connecteurs logiques pour structurer son propos, preuve qu'il maîtrise les exigences de cette épreuve.
Maîtrise de la langue	Le candidat fait preuve d'une maîtrise avancée de la langue anglaise tout au long de sa production orale. Le vocabulaire est riche et varié (*melting pot, artworks and lavish temples, wandering*).
Pour aller plus loin	Comme le demande la question, l'étudiant utilise des exemples personnels pour développer son propos. Sa production est bien structurée, cohérente et homogène.

▪ Question 2 - Solution

QUESTION: The woman expresses her opinion about the proposal described in the article. Briefly summarize the proposal. Then state her opinion about the proposal and explain the reasons she gives for holding that opinion.

Preparation Time: 30 seconds
Response Time: 60 seconds

FR :

DIRECTIONS: *Donnez-vous 30 secondes pour préparer votre réponse à la question suivante. Puis enregistrez-vous en train de parler pendant 60 secondes.*

La femme exprime son opinion sur la proposition décrite dans l'article. Résumez brièvement la proposition. Énoncez ensuite son opinion sur la proposition et expliquez les raisons pour lesquelles elle est de cet avis.

Temps de préparation : 30 secondes
Temps de réponse : 60 secondes

⇨ **explication**

Exemple de réponse

Western state University is thinking of changing its term schedule from one semester to three trimesters. The trimester option would give students more flexibility and options. Some students have been asked to give their opinion on the subject.

The woman's opinion is not positive. She fears the change to a new schedule will resemble that of her brother's. She thinks there will be too much stress, making it hard for students to keep up with homework. Furthermore, she fears this new stress could affect the performances of the students and potentially impact college and scholarship applications.

Évaluation de l'exemple de réponse

Remarques générales / niveau CECRL	Le candidat répond à la question présentée dans la consigne de manière bien structurée et complète, montrant ainsi une maîtrise avancée de la langue anglaise. Le niveau de compétence du candidat correspond approximativement au niveau C1 du CECRL et la qualité de la production orale serait égale à un 4/4 dans le système de score du TOEFL iBT.
Respect des consignes	Le candidat répond correctement à la question en se concentrant sur les thèmes introduits et sans répéter plus d'une fois le même concept.
Structure de la réponse	Le candidat commence par introduire le sujet, puis expose des arguments développés dans l'enregistrement. Même s'il s'agit d'une courte production, l'étudiant utilise des connecteurs logiques pour structurer son propos, preuve qu'il maîtrise les exigences de cette épreuve.
Maîtrise de la langue	Le candidat fait preuve d'une maîtrise avancée de la langue anglaise tout au long de sa production orale. Le vocabulaire est riche et varié (*to fear the change, to keep up with, scholarship applications*).
Pour aller plus loin	Comme le demande la question, l'étudiant rapporte les propos de l'oratrice, preuve de sa bonne compréhension du document. Sa production est bien structurée, cohérente et homogène.

- **Question 3 - Solution**

QUESTION: Using details from the reading and lecture, describe the conditions and processes necessary for geyser formation.

Preparation Time: 30 seconds
Response Time: 60 seconds

FR :

DIRECTIONS: *Donnez-vous 30 secondes pour préparer votre réponse à la question suivante. Puis enregistrez-vous en train de parler pendant 60 secondes.*

> ***En utilisant les détails de l'article et de la conférence, décrivez les conditions et les processus nécessaires à la formation des geysers.***

Temps de préparation : 30 secondes
Temps de réponse : 60 secondes

⇨ **explication**

Exemple de réponse

In order to form, a geyser requires a combination of unusual geological and hydrological conditions. First, geysers need a lot of water. They also need a subsurface water transporting system, like a house water pipe, which should be connected to a pocket of magma below the surface of the Earth. Geysers are the direct result of the relationship with water and heat. The imbalance of pressure between the superheating water and the layer above, finally explodes into a steam explosion, blasting the water out of the vent as a geyser.

Évaluation de l'exemple de réponse

Remarques générales / niveau CECRL	Le candidat répond à la question présentée dans la consigne de manière bien structurée et complète, montrant ainsi une maîtrise avancée de la langue anglaise. Le niveau de compétence du candidat correspond approximativement au niveau C1 du CECRL et la qualité de la production orale serait égale à un 4/4 dans le système de score du TOEFL iBT.
Respect des consignes	Le candidat répond correctement à la question en se concentrant sur les thèmes introduits et sans répéter plus d'une fois le même concept.
Structure de la réponse	Le candidat commence par introduire le sujet, puis expose des arguments développés dans les supports écrit et audio. Même s'il s'agit d'une courte production, l'étudiant utilise des connecteurs logiques pour structurer son propos, preuve qu'il maîtrise les exigences de cette épreuve.
Maîtrise de la langue	Le candidat fait preuve d'une maîtrise avancée de la langue anglaise tout au long de sa production orale. Le vocabulaire est riche et varié (*subsurface water, water pipe, imbalance, blasting the water*).
Pour aller plus loin	Comme le demande la question, l'étudiant reprend et résume les propos exposés dans les documents, preuve de sa bonne compréhension du document. « Sa production est bien structurée, cohérente et homogène.

▪ Question 4 - Solution

QUESTION: Using points and details from the lecture, explain the various ways in which ocean currents affect climate conditions in various parts of the world.

Preparation Time: 20 seconds
Response Time: 60 seconds

FR :

DIRECTIONS: *Donnez-vous 20 secondes pour préparer votre réponse à la question suivante. Puis enregistrez-vous en train de parler pendant 60 secondes.*

> ***En utilisant les arguments et les détails de la conférence, expliquez les différentes façons dont les courants océaniques affectent les conditions climatiques dans diverses parties du monde.***

Temps de préparation : 30 secondes
Temps de réponse : 60 secondes

⟹ **explication**

Exemple de réponse

The weather of our planet is highly affected by surface and deep water currents. Their movement either away or towards the water will determine the temperatures of a land area.

For example, desert weather is often the result of cold air masses above the ocean. These masses do not allow the moisture to rise and inhibit cloud formation. Making the weather very dry. In the same way, warm currents will warm the air over the nearby land.

The Gulf Stream, for example, affects the weather of its coast line by pushing the warm water along the coast. The area's weather becomes milder than other places on the same latitude. Both cold and warm water currents can alter the vegetation and weather of an area. Removing ice and snow where it should be and putting palm trees where they should not be.

Évaluation de l'exemple de réponse

Remarques générales / niveau CECRL	Le candidat répond à la question présentée dans la consigne de manière bien structurée et complète, montrant ainsi une maîtrise avancée de la langue anglaise. Le niveau de compétence du candidat correspond approximativement au niveau C1 du CECRL et la qualité de la production orale serait égale à un 4/4 dans le système de score du TOEFL iBT.
Respect des consignes	Le candidat répond correctement à la question en se concentrant sur les thèmes introduits et sans répéter plus d'une fois le même concept.
Structure de la réponse	Le candidat commence par introduire le sujet, puis expose des arguments développés durant la conférence. Même s'il s'agit d'une courte production, l'étudiant utilise des connecteurs logiques pour structurer son propos, preuve qu'il maîtrise les exigences de cette épreuve.
Maîtrise de la langue	Le candidat fait preuve d'une maîtrise avancée de la langue anglaise tout au long de sa production orale. Le vocabulaire est riche et varié (*moisture, milder, coast line*).
Pour aller plus loin	Comme le demande la question, l'étudiant reprend et résume les propos exposés dans le support, preuve de sa bonne compréhension du document. Sa production est bien structurée, cohérente et homogène.

TOEFL iBT #1 - WRITING - Solutions

Utilisez la grille ci-dessous pour vous auto-évaluer sur chaque exercice. Additionnez vos scores et multipliez le résultat par 3 pour obtenir une note sur 30.

5 points	On retrouve toutes les caractéristiques suivantes : • réponse efficace à la question • bien organisés et développés, les arguments sont expliqués et soutenus par des détails/exemples • vocabulaire et grammaire variés. Bon niveau d'anglais même si le texte contient quelques erreurs mineures
4 points	On retrouve toutes les caractéristiques suivantes : • réponse efficace à la question même si certains points ne sont pas élaborés. Le texte peut être un peu redondant • bien organisés et développés, les arguments sont expliqués et soutenus par des détails/exemples • vocabulaire et grammaire variés. Le texte contient des erreurs mineures qui n'empèchent pas la compréhension
3 points	On retrouve au moins l'une des caractéristiques suivantes : • réponse à la question avec des explications développées et des détails/exemples • le texte est cohérent et organisé même si certaines idées ne sont pas bien liées entre elles • les mauvaises formations syntaxiques rendent certains passages difficiles à comprendre • la grammaire et le vocabulaire sont corrects mais avec peu de variété
2 points	On retrouve au moins l'une des faiblesses suivantes : • réponse courte et peu développée • texte mal organisé, mauvaises connexions entre les idées • arguments non développés, peu de détails/exemples. Trop de généralisations • vocabulaire inexacte ou inapproprié • nombreuses erreurs de grammaire
1 point	On retrouve au moins l'une des faiblesses suivantes : • texte complétement désorganisé • détails inexistants ou hors-sujets • erreurs grammaticales fréquentes et graves
0 point	• pas de réponse ou réponse hors-sujet • recopiage de quelques mots du sujet • écrit dans une autre langue que l'anglais

Nous avons pour projet de mettre en ligne un service de correction personnalisée pour les épreuves d'expression orale et écrite. Ce service fera appel à des correcteurs expérimentés qui vous attribueront une note en suivant les critères du TOEFL iBT. La correction détaillée incluera des conseils personnalisés pour vous améliorer. À l'heure où vous lirez ce manuel, le service sera peut-être déjà en ligne sur http://www.prepmyfuture.com/toefl

Réponse type

Reportez vos réponses pour analyser votre performance.

Entraînez-vous dans les conditions d'examen.

Écoutez les fichiers audio.

prepmyfuture.com/book/68/ex/1985

question 1	q. ouverte

question 2	q. ouverte

▪ Question 1 - Solution

DIRECTIONS: You have 20 minutes to plan and write your response. Your response will be evaluated on the quality of your writing on how well you present the points in the lecture and their relationship to the reading passage. Typically, an effective response will have 150 to 225 words.

Response Time: 20 minutes

QUESTION: Summarize the points made in the lecture, being sure to explain how they contradict specific points made in the reading passage.

FR :

CONSIGNES : *Donnez-vous 20 minutes pour planifier et rédiger votre réponse. Votre réponse sera jugée sur la qualité de l'écriture et sur la façon dont elle présente les points du cours et leur relation avec le passage lu. En général, une réponse efficace comptera entre 150 et 225 mots. Vous pouvez consulter le passage à lire pendant que vous répondez.*

Temps de réponse : 20 minutes

QUESTION : *Résumez les points soulevés dans la conférence, en veillant à expliquer comment ils remettent en question certains points spécifiques du passage lu.*

⟹ **explication**

Exemple de réponse

A theory that Viking colonies were at some time present in North America is **accepted**.

However, some archeological facts show Vinland, in the far north of Canada, was a most probable place of colonization. Although Vinland's climate is today quite cold, its temperatures were much milder back then. Additionally, the medieval building style of the Newport tower **are** also found in other **building** of the colonial New England time period. This particular Romanesque style of architecture was still used in Europe around the 17th century. Thus, it seems normal for colonists **to import** that style into the New World. While it is also true that colonial buildings were made out of wood, records show that stone buildings were built out of stone to protect from Native Americans' attacks. In fact, a 1632 petition by the New England colonists requesting a round stone tower similar to the Newport Tower was signed.

There is some logic in the impossibility of a fireplace to be built in a windmill. However, windmills did exist in fireplaces in Europe. That type of fireplace, similar to the one in the Newport Tower, has a chimney built inside the wall but exits through the side wall instead of the roof. A very practical and safe design for a windmill, keeping smoke and ashes away from the turn blades of the windmill.

Évaluation de l'exemple de réponse

Remarques générales / niveau CERCL	Le candidat rédige un essai structuré et répond correctement à la question posée. Les idées manquent toutefois de structure, ce qui peut entraver la compréhension du texte à certains moments. Le niveau de compétence du candidat correspond approximativement au niveau C1 du CECRL et la qualité du texte écrit serait égale à un 4/5 dans le système de score du TOEFL iBT.
Forme	L'essai est divisé de manière appropriée en quatre paragraphes (introduction ; 1er argument ; 2e argument ; 3e argument). Le candidat reprend les éléments des supports écrit et audio et en fait une synthèse. Un paragraphe de conclusion aurait été nécessaire pour reprendre les éléments de l'essai.
Variété et précision du vocabulaire	Le vocabulaire utilisé est correct, mais plusieurs répétitions auraient pu être évitées grâce à l'utilisation de synonymes.
Grammaire, cohésion et cohérence	Le manque de connecteurs logiques nuit à la fluidité et à la cohérence du texte. De fait, un mot de liaison aurait été le bienvenu pour relier les paragraphes deux et trois, entre autres. La concordance des temps est respectée, mais le candidat a fait une faute de grammaire dans le deuxième paragraphe (accord du singulier/ pluriel). L'essai reste cependant cohérent et répond à la question posée.

Exemple de réponse corrigée

There is a theory that says Viking colonies were at some time present in North America.

However, some archeological facts show Vinland, in the far north of Canada, was a most probable place of colonization. Although Vinland's climate is today quite cold, its temperatures were much milder back then. Additionally, the medieval building style of the Newport tower **was** also found in other **buildings** of the colonial New England time period. This particular Romanesque style of architecture was still used in Europe around the 17th century. Thus, it seems normal **that** colonists **would have imported** that style into the New World. While it is also true that colonial buildings were made out of wood, records show that stone buildings were built as a way to be protected against Native Americans' attacks. In fact, in 1632 a petition was signed by colonists from New England to request the construction of a round stone tower similar to the Newport Tower.

Furthermore, even though it sounds illogical that a fireplace would have been built in a windmill, we could actually find windmills in fireplaces in Europe. That type of fireplace, similar to the one in the Newport Tower, has a chimney built inside the wall but exits through the side wall instead of the roof. It is a very practical and safe design for a windmill, keeping smoke and ashes away from the turn blades of the windmill.

Thus, only a close examination of historical facts and engineering evidence can help unveil the mystery of the origins of Newport Tower.

- **Question 2 - Solution**

DIRECTIONS: Read the question below. You have 30 minutes to plan, write, and revise your essay. Typically, an effective response will contain a minimum of 300 words.

Response Time: 30 minutes

QUESTION: More and more people are choosing a vegetarian diet due to its personal health and environmental benefits. Despite this, many people feel that vegetarianism has several drawbacks that make it not an ideal way of eating. Which of these views do you think is correct and why? Use details and examples to support your opinion.

FR :

***DIRECTIONS :** Lisez la question ci-dessous. Vous avez 30 minutes pour planifier, rédiger et réviser votre essai. En général, une réponse efficace comprendra un minimum de 300 mots.*

Temps de réponse : 30 minutes

***QUESTION :** De plus en plus de personnes optent pour un régime végétarien en raison de ses avantages pour la santé et l'environnement. Malgré cela, de nombreuses personnes pensent que le végétarisme présente plusieurs inconvénients qui en font un mode d'alimentation non idéal. Selon vous, laquelle de ces opinions est la plus juste et pourquoi ? Utilisez des détails et des exemples pour étayer votre opinion.*

→ **explication**

Exemple de réponse

While it is true to say that a vegetarian diet has many health benefits, meat remains an important part of a diet which cannot not be ignored. A vegetarian diet allows a person to have a more **eclectic [contresens]** palate of foods from which to choose from. When we eliminate an important ingredient such as meat, we are forced to be more creative with our meals. For health reasons, being a vegetarian, if well balanced and healthy, will give us more vitality. A vegetarian is likely to introduce more vegetables, fresh dairy products as well as healthy grains into his meals. Vegetarians are also less likely to be overweight and at risk for serious heart problems. However, this is not always the case. Today, the meat industry has become quite disgusting. Animals are injected with hormones and raised in horrible conditions. Furthermore, today, most animals are fed massive amounts of drugs, reducing the quality of the meat we eat. Environmentalists make a strong case of animal protection, which I strongly support. But, it is true to say that meat remains a tradition in many cultures, where animals are grass fed and the quality of the meat is excellent. I believe meat still has its place in a healthy diet. However, we must be responsible consumers, purchase meat only on occasion and from farmers when possible. People have different needs depending on their activity and environmental conditions. We cannot tell a farmer from the mountains to stop eating meat, as it is sometimes **all he has available for food**. We can, however, as citizens living in a developed world, be more sensitive to our environment and consume with care. Unfortunately, it is also true that healthy meat is now a luxury. The organic industry is **unfortunately [repetition]** very expensive and quite political. I hope we will one day find the balance and make organic food available to everyone, everywhere and at reasonable prices.

Évaluation de l'exemple de réponse

Remarques générales / niveau CERCL	Le candidat répond à la question posée en exposant des arguments valides. Le niveau de compétence du candidat correspond approximativement au niveau C1 du CECRL et la qualité du texte écrit serait égale à un 4/5 dans le système de score du TOEFL iBT.
Forme	L'essai n'est pas structuré en paragraphes, ce qui entrave la bonne compréhension du texte. De fait, si le candidat avait organisé sa réponse en paragraphes distincts (introduction, 1er paragraphe, 2e paragraphe, 3e paragraphe, conclusion, par exemple), l'essai aurait gagné en fluidité tandis que le candidat aurait évité de se contredire.
Variété et précision du vocabulaire	Le vocabulaire utilisé est correct et démontre d'une bonne maîtrise de la langue anglaise : l'utilisation de termes tels que *eclectic palate of foods*, *fresh dairy products*, *purchase*, *to make a strong case of* le démontre. Cependant, quelques vérités générales auraient pu être évitées ou nuancées pour rendre le propos plus convaincant.
Grammaire, cohésion et cohérence	Le manque de connecteurs logiques, liés à l'absence de structure du texte, nuit à la fluidité et à la cohérence du texte. De plus, une phrase d'introduction et de conclusion aurait été les bienvenues pour annoncer le sujet et revenir sur les arguments exposés, potentiellement avec une phrase d'ouverture. Le candidat n'a fait aucune faute de grammaire majeure, ce qui est un bon point. Une réorganisation des arguments (introduction, argument 1 : les bienfaits du végétarisme, argument 2 : les limites de ce régime, conclusion) aurait rendu l'essai plus cohérent. Les propos exposés permettent toutefois de répondre correctement à la question posée.

Exemple de réponse corrigée

The recent decade has seen a rise in the number of individuals who, for various reasons, choose to opt for a vegetarian diet.

Even though a vegetarian diet restricts the palate of foods from which a person can choose from, as all animal-based aliments are banned, it is also a way for vegetarians to be more creative with their meals. For health reasons, being a vegetarian, if the diet is well balanced and healthy, will give individuals more vitality. Indeed, a vegetarian is likely to introduce more vegetables, fresh dairy products as well as healthy grains into their meals. Vegetarians are also less likely to be overweight and at risk for serious heart problems.

However, while it is true to say that a vegetarian diet has many benefits for our health, meat remains an important part of a diet which most people do not consider not eating anymore. But today, the meat industry has become quite disgusting: animals are injected with hormones and raised in horrible conditions. Furthermore, today, most animals are fed massive amounts of drugs, reducing the quality of the meat that we eat. Environmentalists make a strong case of animal protection nowadays.

But it is true to say that meat remains a tradition in many cultures, where animals are grass-fed and the quality of the meat is excellent. I believe meat still has its place in a healthy diet. However, we must be responsible consumers, purchase meat only on occasion and from farmers when possible. People have different needs depending on their activity and environmental and health conditions. We cannot tell a farmer from the mountains to stop eating meat, as it is sometimes the only food that is available to him. We can, however, as citizens living in a developed world, be more sensitive to our environment and consume with care. Unfortunately, it is also true that healthy meat is now a luxury. The organic industry is still very expensive and quite political, which prevents some people from buying organic products.

I hope we will one day find the balance between a responsible meat production and consumption, while making organic food available to everyone, everywhere and at reasonable prices. The consequence of such actions would probably dampen the fracture that sometimes exists between vegetarians, who are most often than not, environmentalists advocates, and those who aren't, who are sometimes accused of destroying the planet while hurting animals.

TOEFL iBT #2

TOEFL iBT #2 - READING

READING SECTION DIRECTIONS

The Reading section measures your ability to understand academic passages in English. You will read passages and answer questions about them. Answer all questions based on what is stated or implied in the passage.

There are three passages in a full TOEFL iBT test. You should allow 20 minutes to read each passage and answer the questions about it.

Reportez vos réponses pour analyser votre performance.

Entraînez-vous dans les conditions d'examen.

prepmyfuture.com/book/68/ex/1986

"Discovering deserts"

[P1] The world's great deserts were formed by natural processes interacting over long intervals of time. During most of these times, deserts have grown and shrunk independent of human activities. **Paleodeserts**, large sand seas now inactive because they are stabilized by vegetation, extend beyond the present margins of core deserts, such as the Sahara. In some regions, deserts are separated sharply from surrounding, less **arid** areas by mountains and other contrasting landforms that reflect basic structural differences in the regional geology. In other areas, desert fringes form a gradual transition from a dry to a more humid environment, making it more difficult to define the desert border.

[P2] These transition zones have very fragile, delicately balanced ecosystems. Desert fringes often are a mosaic of microclimates. Small hollows support vegetation that picks up heat from the hot winds and protects the land from the prevailing winds. After rainfall, the vegetated areas are distinctly cooler than the surroundings. In these marginal areas, human activity may stress the ecosystem beyond its tolerance limit, resulting in degradation of the land. By pounding the soil with their hooves, livestock compact the substrate, increase the proportion of fine material, and reduce the percolation rate of the soil, thus encouraging erosion by wind and water. Grazing and the collection of firewood reduces or eliminates plants that help to bind the soil.

[P3] This degradation of formerly productive land–desertification–is a complex process. It involves multiple causes, and it proceeds at varying rates in different climates. Desertification may intensify a general climatic trend toward greater aridity, or it may initiate a change in local climate.

[P4] Desertification does not occur in linear, easily mappable patterns. Deserts advance erratically, forming patches on their borders. Areas far from natural deserts can degrade quickly to barren soil, rock, or sand through poor land management. The presence of a nearby desert has no direct relationship to desertification. Unfortunately, an area undergoing desertification is brought to public attention only after the process is well underway. Often little or no data are available to indicate the previous state of the ecosystem or the rate of degradation. Scientists still question whether desertification, as a process of global change, is permanent or how and when it can be halted or reversed.

[P5] **While desertification has received tremendous publicity by the political and news media, there are still many things that we don't know about the degradation of productive lands and the expansion of deserts.** In 1988 Ridley Nelson pointed out in an important scientific paper that the desertification problem and processes are not clearly defined. There is no **consensus** among researchers as to the specific causes, extent, or degree of desertification. Contrary to many popular reports, desertification is actually a subtle and complex process of deterioration that may often be reversible.

[P6] In the last 25 years, satellites have begun to provide the global monitoring necessary for improving our understanding of desertification. Landsat images of the same area, taken several years apart but during the same point in the growing season, may indicate changes in the susceptibility of land to desertification. Studies using Landsat data help demonstrate the impact of people and animals on the Earth. However, other types of remote-sensing systems, land-monitoring networks, and global data bases of field observations are needed before the process and problems of desertification will be completely understood.

[P7] At the local level, individuals and governments can help to reclaim and protect their lands. Sand fences are used throughout the Middle East and the United States, in the same way snow fences are used in the north. Placement of straw grids, each up to a square meter in area, will also decrease the surface wind velocity. Shrubs and trees planted within the grids are protected by the straw until they take root. In areas where some water is available for irrigation, shrubs planted on the lower one-third of a dune's windward side will stabilize the dune. This vegetation decreases the wind velocity near the base of the dune and prevents much of the sand from moving. Higher velocity winds at the top of the dune level it off and trees can be planted atop these flattened surfaces.

Question 1 In paragraph 1, which of the following statement best describes great deserts? The other choices change the meaning or leave out information.

(A) Great deserts were created by natural processes over long time intervals.
(B) Great deserts were created by natural processes over long time intervals, and their development has been independent of human influence.
(C) Great deserts were created by natural processes and human activities.
(D) Great deserts have grown and shrunk with the help of human intervention and other natural processes.

Question 2 In paragraph 4, the author implies that:

(A) Scientists have not been doing an excellent job collecting data.
(B) People only worry about the deteriorating conditions of an area when it's too late.
(C) Particularly fertile areas are more likely to become deserts.
(D) Weather changes might be causing desertification.

Question 3 Based on information in paragraph 1, which of the following best explains the term "Paleodeserts" ? The other choices change the meaning or leave out information.

(A) A flat area of desert covered with wind-swept sand with little or no vegetal cover
(B) Large sand seas that are now inactive due to stabilized vegetation
(C) A flat area of desert covered with little or no vegetal cover
(D) Large sand seas that are still active due to stabilized vegetation

Question 4 The word "arid" is closest in meaning to:

(A) dry
(B) humid
(C) boring
(D) flat

Question 5 According to paragraph 2, which of the following best describes "transition zones"? The other choices change the meaning or leave out information.

(A) They have unstable and carefully balanced ecosystems with a variety of microclimates.
(B) They have stable and delicately imbalanced ecosystems with a variety of microclimates.
(C) They have carefully balanced ecosystems with a variety of microclimates.
(D) They have unstable ecosystems with a variety of macroclimates.

Question 6 The word "consensus" in paragraph 5 is closest in meaning to:

(A) dissension
(B) denial
(C) refusal
(D) agreement

Question 7 Which of the following sentences best describes the highlighted sentence in the passage? The other choices change the meaning or leave out information.

(A) While desertification has become a popular topic among politicians and citizens alike, there are still numerous issues that are needed to be addressed.
(B) Desertification has received tremendous publicity due to the news media because we still don't know a few things about the degradation of productive lands or the expansion of deserts.
(C) Despite the political and social publicity of the topic of desertification, there are still many things hidden from us in terms of how productive lands are degraded or how deserts manage to increase in size.
(D) Desertification is a rather popular topic among political circles because we know so much about the degradation of productive lands and the expansion of deserts.

Question 8 According to Paragraph 7, individuals and governments on a local level could reclaim and protect lands from desertification with all the following methods EXCEPT:

(A) covering the dunes with large boulders or petroleum to interrupt the wind regime
(B) placing straw grids
(C) planting vegetation inside the grids
(D) removing shrubs and trees planted within the grids

■ Question 9 Look at the four squares in paragraph 7, **A**, **B**, **C**, and **D**, which indicate where the following sentence could be added to the passage. Where would the sentence best fit?

In areas of sand dunes, covering the dunes with large boulders or petroleum will interrupt the wind regime near the face of the dunes and prevent the sand from moving.

[P7] At the local level, individuals and governments can help to reclaim and protect their lands. **A** Sand fences are used throughout the Middle East and the United States, in the same way snow fences are used in the north. Placement of straw grids, each up to a square meter in area, will also decrease the surface wind velocity. **B** Shrubs and trees planted within the grids are protected by the straw until they take root. In areas where some water is available for irrigation, shrubs planted on the lower one-third of a dune's windward side will stabilize the dune. **C** This vegetation decreases the wind velocity near the base of the dune and prevents much of the sand from moving. **D** Higher velocity winds at the top of the dune level it off and trees can be planted atop these flattened surfaces.

(A) **A**
(B) **B**
(C) **C**
(D) **D**

■ Question 10 Directions:

An introductory sentence for a brief summary of the passage is provided below.

Complete the summary by selecting the THREE answer choices that express the most important ideas in the passage. Some sentences do not belong in the summary because they express ideas that are not presented in the passage or are minor ideas in the passage.

This question is worth 2 points.

- Vast deserts have natural origin and their edges are not always clearly defined.
- ________
- ________
- ________

(A) Although some of the causes of desertification are known, it is still difficult to predict how and where it will happen.

(B) Despite the uneven pattern of the phenomenon of desertification, it is possible to predict its evolution by focusing on the different climates.

(C) Activities such as pasture and agriculture are condensed in the warmest regions of the desert fringes, causing their expansion.

(D) Studies made clear that, as we still have an incomplete knowledge of the process of desertification, it may still be possible to recover some areas.

(E) Studies revealed that the process of desertification is not reversible, but it can be prevented through constant monitoring and the use of snow fences in colder areas.

(F) Measures that include the planting of trees and their protection from wind currents, could be fundamental to start a chain mechanism of recovery.

Children's Literature

[P1] Most stories are more effective when well told than they are when read, just as most lectures and sermons are most effective when delivered without manuscript. The story-teller can look at her audience and is free to add a descriptive word or phrase occasionally to produce vividness of impression. Some stories, of course, are so constructed that they must follow closely the diction of the original form. "Henny-Penny" and Kipling's Just-So Stories are of this type. Such stories should be read. Most stories, however, are most effective when well told. The teacher, especially the teacher of one of the primary grades, should not consider herself prepared to teach literature until she has gained something of the art of story-telling.

[P2] Never attempt to tell a story that you do not like. You are not prepared to interest pupils in a story, however appropriate it otherwise may be, if you are not interested in it yourself. Try to choose stories adapted in structure and content to the age and experience of the children of your grade. For the first or second grade, choose a few simple fables, a few short, simple fairy tales, and a few short, simple nature stories, such as "Peter Rabbit," "How Johnny Chuck Finds the Best Thing in the World," and "Mr. 'Possum's Sick Spell." Remember that a story for the first or second grade should be short.

[P3] Learn to apply readily the following principles of method: First, use the past tense in telling a story except in direct quotation. The rules of grammar require this, and it is an aid to clearness and effectiveness. For example, do not say, "So he goes" or "Then he says"; but say, "So he went" or "Then he said" (or, for variety, replied, growled, mumbled, etc.) Second, use direct discourse (the exact words of the characters) rather than indirect discourse. For example, do not say, "The Troll asked who was tripping over his bridge"; but say, "'WHO'S THAT tripping over my bridge?' roared the Troll." Direct discourse always gives life and vividness to a story.

[P4] When you have selected a suitable story, read it carefully several times to learn the essential details and the order in which they should come. Keep in mind the fact that you are to use the past tense and direct discourse. If the story is a fable, you probably will see that you should add much conversation and description not in the text. A little description of the witch, giant, fairy, or castle may give vividness to your story. If the story is a long fairy tale, you may see that many details may be **omitted**. If the story is as concise and dramatic as is the version of "The Three Billy-Goats Gruff" in this book, it may be suitable for presentation without any changes. When you have the story clearly in mind as you wish to present it, tell it to the pupils several times, and then have some of them tell it.

[P5] Your story, of course, should not be told in a lifeless monotone. Some parts should be told slowly, and others rapidly. In some parts the voice should be low and soft, while in other parts it should be loud and **gruff** or harsh. The words of the princess should not sound like those of the old witch or the soldier. The daintiness and grace of elves and fairies should be indicated in the delivery.

[P6] The play spirit that leads children to play lady, doctor, church, and school will also lead them to enjoy dramatizing stories, or "playing the stories," as they call it. **Some stories, of course, are so lacking in action as to be not well suited for dramatization, and others have details of action, character, or situation that may not well be represented in the schoolroom.** The teacher may be surprised, however, to see how ingenious her pupils are in overcoming difficulties after they have had a little assistance in playing two or three stories. Unconsciously, the pupil will get from the dramatization a training in oral English, reading, and literary appreciation that can hardly be gained in any other way.

Question 11 According to paragraph 1, which is true about storytelling?

(A) Storytelling gives the possibility to operate minor changes to the text during a performance.

(B) Storytelling is more effective when delivered in the form of manuscripts.

(C) Storytelling is practiced by those who have studied literature and cannot substitute the reading.

(D) Storytelling gives the audience a unique experience through vivid and descriptive manuscripts.

Question 12 According to paragraph 2, the selection of stories should be based on the following criteria EXCEPT:

(A) Do not tell a story you do not like

(B) Do not tell a story you are not interested in yourself

(C) Stories should be chosen based on the target age group, content and structure

(D) Stories should be long for first and second grade students

Question 13 It can be concluded that following the two principles is important because:

(A) Telling a story in past tense, and with the use of direct discourse between characters, gives the story its clearness and effectiveness.

(B) Telling a story in simple tense imbued with direct quotations and indirect discourse gives the story its clearness and effectiveness.

(C) Telling a story in past tense imbued with indirect quotations and direct discourse gives the story its clearness and effectiveness.

(D) Telling a story in past tense, and with the use of direct discourse between the storytellers, gives the story its clearness and effectiveness.

Question 14 According to paragraph 4, which of the following sentences best describes what are the things that should be kept in mind when it comes to telling a fable? The other choices change the meaning or leave out information.

(A) Use past tense and direct discourse while also trying to add more conversation and descriptions of the characters in the text

(B) Use past tense and direct discourse while also adding indirect conversations and character descriptions not in the text

(C) Use past tense and direct discourse while also adding much more conversation and description that are not particularly present in the text

(D) Use past tense and indirect discourse while also adding direct conversations and character descriptions not in the text

▪ Question 15 Which of the following sentences best describes the highlighted sentence in the passage? The other choices change the meaning or leave out information.

"Some stories, of course, are so lacking in action as to be not well suited for dramatization, and others have details of action, character, or situation that may not well be represented in the schoolroom."

(A) While some stories may have a story line that lacks action suited for dramatization, others might have just too detailed characters, actions or situations to be suitable for classroom audiences.

(B) Some stories lack the action needed for dramatization, while others might have details of action, character, or situation that could be very well suited for students in the schoolroom.

(C) Some actions, characters, or situations may well be represented in the schoolroom while some story lines lack the attention suited for dramatization.

(D) Some stories have more attention-grabbing storylines than others.

▪ Question 16 The word "gruff" in paragraph 5 is closest in meaning to:

(A) cheerful

(B) tactful

(C) kind

(D) grumpy

▪ Question 17 The word "omitted" in paragraph 4 refers to:

(A) leave out

(B) include

(C) attend

(D) notice

▪ Question 18 Why does the author mention the importance of dramatization in paragraph 6?

(A) To discuss the relevance of pupils failing to face their difficulties and express their literary appreciation

(B) To argue that dramatizing stories can not only help students overcome difficulties in playing out stories, but it would also make them better speakers, readers by also developing a sense of literary appreciation in the process

(C) To prove that dramatization is the one and only tool that can help students overcome their fears of public speaking and literary appreciation

(D) To make a comparison between ingenious pupils and their process of overcoming individual difficulties

■ Question 19 Look at the four squares in paragraph 1, **A**, **B**, **C**, and **D**, which indicate where the following sentence could be added to the passage. Where would the sentence best fit?

Much of the superiority probably comes from the freedom of the "talk style" and the more appropriate use of inflection and emphasis.

[P1] **A** Most stories are more effective when well told than they are when read, just as most lectures and sermons are most effective when delivered without manuscript. **B** The story-teller can look at her audience and is free to add a descriptive word or phrase occasionally to produce vividness of impression. **C** Some stories, of course, are so constructed that they must follow closely the diction of the original form. "Henny-Penny" and Kipling's Just-So Stories are of this type. Such stories should be read. Most stories, however, are most effective when well told. The teacher, especially the teacher of one of the primary grades, should not consider herself prepared to teach literature until she has gained something of the art of story-telling. **D**

(A) **A**
(B) **B**
(C) **C**
(D) **D**

■ Question 20 Directions:

An introductory sentence for a brief summary of the passage is provided below.

Complete the summary by selecting the THREE answer choices that express the most important ideas in the passage. Some sentences do not belong in the summary because they express ideas that are not presented in the passage or are minor ideas in the passage.

This question is worth 2 points.

- The precious art of story-telling makes stories come to life and engages the audience even more.
- ________
- ________
- ________

(A) Story-tellers should pay particular attention to the use of the past tense and direct discourse, because the children listening to them will replicate their use of grammar when "playing" their own stories.

(B) Story-tellers should be passionate about the story they are telling.

(C) Story-tellers should be aware that there are certain grammar structures to use and that the type length of the story might require them to make some changes.

(D) Story-tellers should work on differentiating the voice they use for a princess from the one they use for the soldier and speak with a louder voice to avoid children from getting distracted.

(E) Teachers should give children the chance to "play" stories because it constitutes an extremely effective educational strategy.

(F) Teachers should help children dramatize the various stories, so that they can learn the rudiments of acting without getting bored.

Geothermal Resources

[P1] Geothermal energy is simply power derived from the Earth's internal heat. It is present everywhere beneath the Earth's surface, although the highest temperature, and thus the most desirable resources are concentrated in regions of active or geologically young volcanoes. There are many advantages of geothermal energy. It can be extracted without burning a fossil fuel such as coal or oil. Geothermal fields produce only about one-sixth of the carbon dioxide that a clean natural-gas-fueled power plant produces. It does have some environmental problems, namely the release of hydrogen sulfide at low concentrations. Though the resource is thermal energy rather than a physical substance such as gold or coal, many aspects of geothermal energy are **akin** to characteristics of mineral and fossil-fuel resources.

[P2] A mineral deposit is generally evaluated in terms of the quality or purity of the ore and the amount of this ore that can be mined profitably. Such grade-and-size criteria also can be applied to the evaluation of geothermal energy potential. Grade would be roughly comparable to temperature, and size would correspond to the volume of heat-containing material that can be tapped. For mineral and geothermal deposits alike, concentrations of the natural resource should be significantly higher than average (the background level) for the Earth's crust and must be at depths accessible by present-day extraction technologies before commercial development is feasible.

[P3] However, geothermal resources differ in important ways from many other natural resources. For example, the exploitation of metallic minerals generally involves digging, crushing, and processing huge amounts of rock to recover a relatively small amount of a particular element. In contrast, geothermal energy is tapped by means of a liquid carrier—the water in the pores and fractures of rocks—that either naturally reaches the surface at hot springs, or can be brought to the surface through drilled wells. **The extraction of geothermal energy is accomplished without the large-scale movement of rock involved in mining operations, such as construction of mine shafts and tunnels, open pits, and waste heaps.**

[P4] Geothermal energy is usable over a very wide spectrum of temperature and volume, whereas the benefits of other natural resources can be reaped only if a deposit exceeds some minimum size and (or) grade for profitable exploitation or efficiency of operation. For example, at the low end of the spectrum, geothermal energy can help heat and cool a single residence. To do so requires only the burial of piping a few meters underground, where the temperature fluctuates little with the changing seasons. Then, by circulating water or some other fluid through this piping using a geothermal heat pump, thermal energy is extracted from the ground during the coldest times of the year and deposited in the ground during the hottest times. Together, the heat pump and the Earth's thermal energy form a small, effective, and commercially viable heating and cooling system. Heat pump systems are already in use at more than 350,000 buildings in the United States.

[P5] Toward the high end of the spectrum, a single large spectrum, a single large volume, high-temperature deposit of geothermal energy can be **harnessed** to generate electricity sufficient to serve a city of 1 million people or more. For example, at The Geysers in northern California, fractures in rocks beneath a large area, are filled with steam of about 240°C at depths that can easily be reached using present-day drilling technology. This steam is produced through wells, piped directly to conventional turbine generators, and used to generate electricity. With a generating capacity of about 1,000 megawatts electric, The Geysers is presently the largest group of geothermally powered electrical plants in the world. At current rates of per capita consumption in the United States, 1 megawatt is sufficient to supply a community with a population of 1,000. Between these relatively extreme examples are geothermal resources that encompass a broad spectrum of grade (temperature) and tonnage (volume). The challenge, for governmental agencies and the private sector alike, is to assess the amount and distribution of these resources, to work toward new and inventive ways to use this form of energy, and to incorporate geothermal into an appropriate energy mix for the Nation and the world.

■ Question 21 In paragraph 1, which of the following is true about geothermal energy?

(A) It can be found below Earth's surface and is concentrated in regions of geologically active volcanoes.
(B) Geothermal energy has unique attributes whose characteristics are similar to those of certain geothermal activities.
(C) Geothermal energy is present everywhere above the Earth's surface.
(D) Geothermal energy includes physical substances such as gold or coal.

■ Question 22 According to paragraph 2, we can infer that:

(A) Companies would not consider selling minerals if their deposits were unreachable.
(B) The grade of mineral deposits can be compared to volume.
(C) Deposits of geothermal energy leave traces of ore.
(D) Mineral deposits need to be deep enough below Earth's crust in order to be reached.

■ Question 23 The word "akin" in the passage refers to:

(A) parallel
(B) ideal
(C) similar
(D) opposite

■ Question 24 Which of the following sentences best describes the highlighted sentence in the passage? The other choices change the meaning or leave out information.

(A) Geothermal energy extraction can be carried out without the use and construction of mine shafts, tunnels, waste heaps or open pits.
(B) Geothermal energy extraction can be facilitated without the large-scale movement of rocks and mining operations.
(C) The extraction of geothermal energy is accomplished with the help of large-scale mining operations, such as construction of mine shafts and tunnels, open pits, and waste heaps.
(D) The extraction of geothermal energy is all about the construction of mine shafts and tunnels, open pits, and waste heaps.

■ Question 25 According to the passage, geothermal energy has a number of other uses EXCEPT:

(A) It can help heat and cool a single residence.
(B) It is a commercially viable heating and cooling system currently in use in many households.
(C) It can be harnessed to generate electricity.
(D) It circulates water or some other fluid for cooling heat pump systems.

■ Question 26 Which of the following statements most accurately reflects the author's opinion about the commercial use of geothermal energy?

(A) The author sees geothermal resources as a viable source of energy and instructs governmental agencies to find new innovative ways to incorporate these energy sources into the mix for the whole world to benefit.

(B) The author sees geothermal resources as a viable source of energy and challenges governmental agencies to find new innovative ways to incorporate these energy sources into the mix for the whole world to benefit.

(C) The author sees geothermal resources as a viable source of energy and goes on to express his belief that governmental agencies need to find new innovative ways to incorporate these energy sources into the mix for the whole world to benefit.

(D) The assessment and distribution of these resources cannot take place without establishing new ways to use geothermal energy worldwide.

■ Question 27 The word "harnessed" in paragraph 5 is closest in meaning to:

(A) permit

(B) exploit

(C) liberate

(D) detach

■ Question 28 According to paragraph 4, how many heat pump systems are already in use in the United States?

(A) less than 350,000

(B) 35,000

(C) more than 350,000

(D) more than 350,000 but less than 400,000

■ Question 29 Look at the four squares in paragraph 1, **A**, **B**, **C**, and **D**, which indicate where the following sentence could be added to the passage. Where would the sentence best fit?

Alarming is also the disposal of some geothermal fluids, which may contain low levels of toxic materials.

[P1] Geothermal energy is simply power derived from the Earth's internal heat. **A** It is present everywhere beneath the Earth's surface, although the highest temperature, and thus the most desirable resources are concentrated in regions of active or geologically young volcanoes. There are many advantages of geothermal energy. **B** It can be extracted without burning a fossil fuel such as coal or oil. Geothermal fields produce only about one-sixth of the carbon dioxide that a clean natural-gas-fueled power plant produces. **C** It does have some environmental problems, namely the release of hydrogen sulfide at low concentrations. **D** Though the resource is thermal energy rather than a physical substance such as gold or coal, many aspects of geothermal energy are akin to characteristics of mineral and fossil-fuel resources.

(A) **A**
(B) **B**
(C) **C**
(D) **D**

■ Question 30 Directions:

An introductory sentence for a brief summary of the passage is provided below.

Complete the summary by selecting the THREE answer choices that express the most important ideas in the passage. Some sentences do not belong in the summary because they express ideas that are not presented in the passage or are minor ideas in the passage.

This question is worth 2 points.

- Geothermal energy is a natural resource that can be found beneath the Earth's crust.
- ________
- ________
- ________

(A) The circumstances under which geothermal energy is evaluated and eventually retrieved, are not much dissimilar from those of minerals.

(B) Being unevenly distributed beneath the Earth's surface, geothermal energy is rarer and more valuable than minerals, but also more dangerous, due to its toxic properties.

(C) Geothermal energy is often used, through a system of pumps, to heat and cool houses depending on the need.

(D) The Geysers in northern California represent the biggest deposit of geothermal energy in the world.

(E) The biggest differences between geothermal energy and other natural resources are its easier extraction process and its much more flexible employability.

(F) Better and more beneficial ways to exploit geothermal energy are yet to be found.

TOEFL iBT #2 - LISTENING (AUDIO)

LISTENING SECTION DIRECTIONS

The Listening section measures your ability to understand conversations and lectures in English. You will hear a conversation or lecture **only one time**, and you will answer some questions about them. The questions typically ask about the main idea and supporting details of the conversation and lecture. Some questions will ask about a speaker's purpose or attitude. Answer the questions based on what the speakers state or imply.

You may take notes while you listen. You may use your notes to help you answer the questions. Your notes will not be scored.

In some question, you will see an audio icon. This means that you will hear, but not see, part of the question.

You should answer each question, even if you must guess the answer.

Reportez vos réponses pour analyser votre performance.

Entraînez-vous dans les conditions d'examen.

Écoutez les fichiers audio.

prepmyfuture.com/book/68/ex/1987

Listen to part of a discussion in an English literature class.

Question 1 What is the discussion mainly about?

(A) the difficulties faced when casting a play

(B) the cost of attending a play in Shakespeare's day

(C) the 17th century theater in London

(D) the relationship between the actors and the company

■ Question 2 Listen again to part of the lecture. Then answer the question.

Why does the professor say this:

"...Anyway, let's continue from last week's lesson. Where were we? Oh yes..."

(A) He is lost and needs to find his way back to class.
(B) He wants the students to help him recall last week's class.
(C) He hopes to get the class to pay attention.
(D) He takes a pause to remember where he is in his lesson.

■ Question 3 Listen again to part of the lecture. Then answer the question.

According to the professor, what does the term "groundling" mean?

(A) audience members who paid the least for their seats
(B) part of the stage that was on the ground
(C) a small section of the seats where the gentry sat
(D) a member of the company

■ Question 4 How did the playwrights get around restrictions surrounding female performers?

(A) They wrote creative parts for the actors.
(B) Women were performing disguised as men.
(C) They eliminated female characters.
(D) They performed the play outside the city limits to avoid problems with the authorities.

■ Question 5 Why does the professor say that he checked records from the period about the theater's capacity?

(A) He is very interested in the records.
(B) He didn't know much about them.
(C) He wants the class to study like him.
(D) He wasn't sure if they were correct.

■ Question 6 What can be inferred about the professor?

(A) He is a good actor.
(B) He encourages his class to write plays.
(C) He is not very patient with his students.
(D) He is very well informed about English Renaissance theater.

Listen to a lecture in a psychology class.

▪ **Question 7** What is the lecture mainly about?

(A) how to tell the difference between a panic attack and a phobia
(B) the characteristics of anxiety disorders
(C) why psychological disorders are learned behaviors
(D) some of the psychological experiments performed on students

▪ **Question 8** Which of the following is an example of a genetic component in psychological disorders that was used in the lecture?

(A) Anxiety that is present in identical twin pairs.
(B) Phobias that are a result of problems in life.
(C) Physical stress.
(D) The ability to control the flow of carbon dioxide.

▪ **Question 9** What technique does the professor use to explain the development of a panic attack?

(A) He asks the students to perform a simulation in the lab.
(B) He performs an experiment on the class.
(C) He uses a scenario in which the students are implicated.
(D) He takes a survey of the class.

▪ **Question 10** Listen again to part of the lecture. Then answer the question.

Why does the student say this:

"Those of us who believe that we have control over the flow of carbon dioxide?"

(A) He is asking the professor a question about the previous point.
(B) He is offering a possible answer to the professor's question.
(C) He is checking his comprehension of the question.
(D) He is challenging the professor's opinion.

▪ **Question 11** According to the professor, why is OCD considered a learned pattern?

(A) Because most people with OCD know that their thoughts are irrational.
(B) Because anxiety decreases when obsessions are interrupted.
(C) Because endless rituals help to eliminate obsessive thoughts.
(D) Because often OCD is strengthen through negative reinforcement.

▪ **Question 12** How does this professor organize the lecture?

(A) He has a video to explain each point.
(B) He makes reference to the students' textbook.
(C) He uses a whiteboard and interactive instructions.
(D) He gives examples and implicates his students.

Listen to part of a discussion in an Economics class.

Question 13 According to the professor, how do governments determine what the best projects are?

(A) They look at a long list of projects.
(B) They classify projects according to urgency and cost.
(C) They choose the most inexpensive projects.
(D) They analyze which projects will be most successful with the least amount of money.

Question 14 How does the professor organize the lecture?

(A) He relates data to his own personal experiences.
(B) He presents important information in an ascending order.
(C) He refers to studies from international organizations.
(D) He compares American and foreign aid budgets.

Question 15 According to the professor, what are the most important threats to global water stability?

(A) subterranean water reserve depletion and population increase
(B) agriculture and industry
(C) mining
(D) urban areas

Question 16 Why does the professor mention the industry sector?

(A) to highlight further future complications
(B) to disguise the need for government action
(C) to eliminate other sectors
(D) to emphasize economic profits

Question 17 **Listen again to part of the lecture and answer the question.**

What does the professor imply when he say this:

"None of us are superman."

(A) He likes comic books.
(B) We have to prioritize in order to improve situations.
(C) He would like to have superhuman powers.
(D) He is not sure who is in his class.

▪ Question 18 What can be inferred about the professor?

(A) He is a water specialist.
(B) He encourages his students to get involved in research.
(C) He likes to travel to the developing world.
(D) He is an experienced policy maker.

Listen to a conversation between two students.

▪ Question 19 What is the purpose of this conversation?

(A) The man is trying to convince the woman to sign up for the debating society.
(B) The woman is encouraging the man to overcome his fear of public speaking.
(C) The woman is looking for an extra curricular activity to join.
(D) The woman is telling the man that he has to study more.

▪ Question 20 What does the man imply about the fear of public speaking?

(A) Public speaking becomes easier with practice.
(B) Public speaking can be stressful.
(C) There are classes in which public speaking is mandatory.
(D) Rules are the most important aspect.

▪ Question 21 How does the man feel about the debating society?

(A) He believes it is useful for college.
(B) He thinks students should make the rules.
(C) He hopes everyone will join.
(D) He wants it to be obligatory.

▪ Question 22 Listen again to part of the discussion and answer the question.

(A) She agrees that debating reduces anxiety.
(B) She hopes that debating will help her with public speaking.
(C) She doubts that public speaking will reduce anxiety.
(D) She would like to know how to reduce anxiety.

▪ Question 23 What will the woman probably do?

(A) Register for the debating society and attend the meeting
(B) Practice public speaking before joining the debating society
(C) Learn the rules on how to become a representative
(D) Practice public speaking during the meeting

Listen to a conversation between a professor and a student.

▪ Question 24 Why did the man go and see his professor?

(A) to borrow a biology book
(B) to ask a question about her mid-term exam
(C) to see when the professor has office hours
(D) to hand in a paper

▪ Question 25 How is mitochondrial DNA different from regular DNA?

(A) Mitochondrial DNA is located in the cytoplasm of a cell.
(B) Regular DNA makes up genes but mitochondrial DNA does not.
(C) Regular DNA and mitochondrial DNA come from both sets of parents.
(D) Mitochondrial DNA is found in the nucleus.

▪ Question 26 Listen again to part of the discussion and answer the question.

(A) He does not understand why the team analyzed placentas.
(B) He wants to clarify the reason why the researchers studied mitochondrial DNA.
(C) He is criticizing the team's analysis.
(D) He wants to pronounce the word better.

▪ Question 27 What will the student do before the next exam?

(A) take better notes in class
(B) go over class lectures with classmates
(C) see the professor before the test
(D) study harder than she did for the mid-term

▪ Question 28 What can be said about the professor?

(A) He teaches psychology.
(B) He is very strict when it comes to grading.
(C) He is often not in his office.
(D) He wants his students to come for extra help.

TOEFL iBT #2 - LISTENING (SCRIPT)

LISTENING SECTION DIRECTIONS

The Listening section measures your ability to understand conversations and lectures in English. You will hear a conversation or lecture **only one time**, and you will answer some questions about them. The questions typically ask about the main idea and supporting details of the conversation and lecture. Some questions will ask about a speaker's purpose or attitude. Answer the questions based on what the speakers state or imply.

You may take notes while you listen. You may use your notes to help you answer the questions. Your notes will not be scored.

In some question, you will see an audio icon. This means that you will hear, but not see, part of the question.

You should answer each question, even if you must guess the answer.

Reportez vos réponses pour analyser votre performance.

Entraînez-vous dans les conditions d'examen.

Écoutez les fichiers audio.

prepmyfuture.com/book/68/ex/1987

Listen to part of a discussion in an English literature class.

Script non affiché le jour de l'examen :

PROFESSOR: This is just a friendly reminder that your mid–terms are next week. Exam rooms will be posted this weekend. Please be sure to check the student platform. Are there any questions? Anyway, let's continue from last week's lesson. Where were we? Oh yes, we were talking about Shakespeare's theaters and we said that the first playhouse built as such in Elizabethan London, constructed in 1576, was called The Theater. Its co-founders were John Brayne, an investor, and James Burbage, a carpenter turned actor. Many of the theaters during that period were situated outside of the city in order to avoid conflict with the authorities. There were about six or seven public or outdoor theaters. You must remember that not only was play going considered dishonorable on moral grounds but also on political grounds. There was always risk of the plague as well. During Shakespeare's lifetime there were two major epidemics and both times the theaters were closed for long periods.

PROFESSOR: Yes.

MALE STUDENT: I read somewhere that The Theater was closed because of financial problems too?

PROFESSOR: Well actually, yes and no. In fact, The Theater was a financial success, and Shakespeare's company performed there until 1598. They had to close down the theater because there was a dispute over the lease. This forced Burbage to demolish the building. It was rebuilt though, in Southwalk, London and was called The Globe. Shakespeare, in addition to being one of the greatest writers of all time was also a savvy businessman and was one of the principal shareholders. This was very common for the period, in order to build up capital actors usually invested their own money and formed a company. The company would direct and write plays as well. A company such as The King's Men at The Globe would consist of around twenty-five actors, half of whom might be shareholders, and the rest part-timers engaged for a particular play.

Anyway, by modern standards, the Globe was small, especially externally. The octagonal building measured less than thirty meters across, but in spite of this, it could accommodate an audience between two and three thousand people. If you were to compare it to the largest of the three theaters at the National Theater complex in London today, you would find that the largest only seats 1160.

FEMALE STUDENT: How did people find out about performances? And how much were the tickets?

PROFESSOR: Good questions. Performances were advertised by means of playbills posted around the city, and the plays took place during the hours of daylight when the weather was suitable. As courtesy to the playgoer, a flag flew to let people know that it was safe and that there was no risk of contamination. In terms of the price, it wasn't very expensive. There were no reservations and it was a first come first serve basis. At entrance the doorkeeper collected one penny (about 60 cents today) for admission to the "pit". This was the cheapest price in order to see a play. The "groundlings," as they were called, stood around the three sides of the stage, in the open air. Much like today when we go to see a rock band, the best "seats" aren't seats at all but standing room in front of the stage. Unlike today however, these were not the most expensive seats. The best seats were under cover. Stairs led from the pit to the three tiers of the galleries around the walls. The higher one went, the more one paid. The best seats cost one shilling or about 7 dollars today. In theaters owned by speculators like Francis Langley and Philip Henslowe, half the gallery profits went to the landlord and half went to the company.

A full house might consist of 800 groundlings and 1500 in the galleries, with a dozen more exclusive seats on the stage itself for the gentry. When I was researching this, I couldn't believe that such a theater could hold so many people, but it must be accurate. From the records dating back to that time, I found that a mere 700 meters square was able to hold more than 2000 people, while a place like Carnegie Hall, with its 4,600 meters square can hold about 1500, not to mention the space that was needed of the seats and actors.

Usually what happened is that the acting company assembled in what was called the Tiring House at the rear of the stage. This was where they attired (or dressed) themselves. Most actors did not dress in costumes representing the period of the play, but in regular Elizabethan attire. All performances were therefore in modern dress, though no expense was spared to make the stage costumes lavish. The entire company was male. Remember that by law, actresses were not allowed, and female roles were performed by boys. Playwrights therefore devised parts to suit the actors who were available, and used creativity in order to overcome the absence of women. Shakespeare often has his heroines dress as young men, and physical contact between lovers was formal compared with the realism we expect today. Access to the stage from the Tiring House was through two doors, one on each side of the stage. Because there was no front curtain, every entrance had to have its corresponding exit, so an actor killed on stage had to be carried off. There was no scenery: the audience used its imagination, guided by the spoken word.

FEMALE STUDENT: That is incredible but how were scenes, such as ghost scenes, carried out? I was watching a documentary and I saw that they were very realistic.

PROFESSOR: Well usually a trapdoor in the stage made ghostly entrances and the grave digging scene in Hamlet possible. Behind the main stage, in between the two entrance doors, there was a curtained area, concealing a small inner stage, useful for bedroom scenes. Above this was a balcony, which served for castle walls or a domestic balcony, as in the famous scene in Romeo and Juliet.

▪ Question 1 What is the discussion mainly about?

(A) the difficulties faced when casting a play
(B) the cost of attending a play in Shakespeare's day
(C) the 17th century theater in London
(D) the relationship between the actors and the company

▪ Question 2 Listen again to part of the lecture. Then answer the question.

Script non affiché le jour de l'examen :
PROFESSOR: Please be sure to check the student platform. Are there any questions? Anyway, let's continue from last week's lesson. Where were we? Oh yes, we were talking about Shakespeare's theaters and we said [...]

Why does the professor say this:

"...Anyway, let's continue from last week's lesson. Where were we? Oh yes..."

(A) He is lost and needs to find his way back to class.
(B) He wants the students to help him recall last week's class.
(C) He hopes to get the class to pay attention.
(D) He takes a pause to remember where he is in his lesson.

▪ Question 3 Listen again to part of the lecture. Then answer the question.

> **Script non affiché le jour de l'examen :**
> **PROFESSOR:** A full house might consist of 800 groundlings and 1500 in the galleries, with a dozen more exclusive seats on the stage itself for the gentry.

According to the professor, what does the term "groundling" mean?

(A) audience members who paid the least for their seats
(B) part of the stage that was on the ground
(C) a small section of the seats where the gentry sat
(D) a member of the company

▪ Question 4 How did the playwrights get around restrictions surrounding female performers?

(A) They wrote creative parts for the actors.
(B) Women were performing disguised as men.
(C) They eliminated female characters.
(D) They performed the play outside the city limits to avoid problems with the authorities.

▪ Question 5 Why does the professor say that he checked records from the period about the theater's capacity?

(A) He is very interested in the records.
(B) He didn't know much about them.
(C) He wants the class to study like him.
(D) He wasn't sure if they were correct.

▪ Question 6 What can be inferred about the professor?

(A) He is a good actor.
(B) He encourages his class to write plays.
(C) He is not very patient with his students.
(D) He is very well informed about English Renaissance theater.

Listen to a lecture in a psychology class.

Script non affiché le jour de l'examen :

PROFESSOR: Last week we started looking at psychological disorders and their causes. Today we will specifically discuss anxiety disorders. As with all forms of psychopathology we will consider, the exact causes of anxiety disorders are a matter of debate. I am sure that this comes as no surprise to most of you. We saw how both biological and cognitive factors contribute to all psychological disorders. There is also good evidence that psychological and social factors contribute as well. Biological dispositions, distortions in thinking and learning experiences appear to be particularly important.

PROFESSOR: Can any of you name some biological dispositions?

STUDENT 1: I think I can. I remember from our last class that some anxiety disorders have a genetic component, such as in the case of twins.

PROFESSOR: Yes, very good. Research shows that if one identical twin has had an anxiety disorder, the other is more likely also to have an anxiety disorder than is the case in non-identical twin pairs. It appears that most anxiety disorders seem to run in families. So imagine someone that Inherits an autonomic nervous system that is oversensitive to stress, what might be the outcome?

STUDENT 2: They may react, due to their physiological predisposition, with anxiety to a wide range of situations.

PROFESSOR: Exactly. Although, from what we know, biological predispositions may set the stage for anxiety disorders, most researchers agree that environmental stressors and psychological factors, including cognitive processes and learning, are also involved in bringing about most anxiety disorder. So for example, people displaying an anxiety disorder may exaggerate dangers in their environment, thereby creating an unrealistic expectation that bad things are going to happen. Moreover they tend to underestimate their own capacity for dealing with threatening events. This results in experiencing anxiety and desperation when feared events do occur.

STUDENT 1: I'm not sure that I understand, would it be possible to have an example?

PROFESSOR: Sure. I want you to consider the development of a panic attack. An unexplained symptom of physical arousal may set the stage for a panic attack, but it is the person's sensitivity to, and cognitive interpretation of, those symptoms that can determine whether or not the attack actually develops. Imagine I was to tell you that you are to breathe in air rich with carbon dioxide. Some of you will have a dial that controls the flow of carbon dioxide while others of you will not. Which of you are less likely to have a severe panic attack?

STUDENT 1: Those of us who believe that we have control over the flow of carbon dioxide?

PROFESSOR: Correct. In fact, it doesn't matter if the dial has any effect for either group. The group that believes it has control will be less likely to develop an attack. In another study, panic-disorder patients who inhaled carbon dioxide in the presence of a person they associated with safety were significantly less fearful than patients whose "safe person" was not present. Results like these suggest that cognitive factors play a role in panic disorders.

This brings to my next point about phobias. Most of you have heard of someone who has arachnophobia, or fear of spiders. Well would you be surprised if I told you that this type of behavior is often a learned behavior? There are learning principles that may be involved in the acquisitions and maintenance of phobias. Problems in life such as money troubles, illness, final exams, or unhappy relationships often create upsetting thoughts and worry. And upsetting thoughts create anxiety. These thoughts become particularly difficult to dismiss when you are under stress or feel incapable of dealing effectively with the problems that you are worried about. As the thoughts become more persistent, anxiety increases. Anxiety is also at the root of obsessive-compulsive disorder. People diagnosed with this disorder are plagued by persistent, upsetting and unwanted thoughts. Many of those who display OCD recognize the irrationality of their thoughts and actions, but they still experience severe anxiety if they try to interrupt their obsessions or give up their compulsive behaviors. So if an action such as cleaning temporarily relieves the anxiety, that action may be strengthened through the process of negative reinforcement. But such actions do nothing to eliminate the obsessive thoughts, so they become compulsive endlessly repeated rituals that keep the person trapped in a vicious circle of anxiety. Thus social – learning theorists see an illness, such as obsessive- compulsive disorder, as learned pattern sparked by distressing thoughts and maintained by operant conditioning.

Question 7 What is the lecture mainly about?

(A) how to tell the difference between a panic attack and a phobia
(B) the characteristics of anxiety disorders
(C) why psychological disorders are learned behaviors
(D) some of the psychological experiments performed on students

Question 8 Which of the following is an example of a genetic component in psychological disorders that was used in the lecture?

(A) Anxiety that is present in identical twin pairs.
(B) Phobias that are a result of problems in life.
(C) Physical stress.
(D) The ability to control the flow of carbon dioxide.

Question 9 What technique does the professor use to explain the development of a panic attack?

(A) He asks the students to perform a simulation in the lab.
(B) He performs an experiment on the class.
(C) He uses a scenario in which the students are implicated.
(D) He takes a survey of the class.

■ **Question 10** Listen again to part of the lecture. Then answer the question.

> **Script non affiché le jour de l'examen :**
> **PROFESSOR:** Imagine I was to tell you that you are to breathe in air rich with carbon dioxide. Some of you will have a dial that controls the flow of carbon dioxide while others of you will not. Which of you are less likely to have a severe panic attack?
>
> **STUDENT 1:** Those of us who believe that we have control over the flow of carbon dioxide?

Why does the student say this:

"Those of us who believe that we have control over the flow of carbon dioxide?"

(A) He is asking the professor a question about the previous point.
(B) He is offering a possible answer to the professor's question.
(C) He is checking his comprehension of the question.
(D) He is challenging the professor's opinion.

■ **Question 11** According to the professor, why is OCD considered a learned pattern?

(A) Because most people with OCD know that their thoughts are irrational.
(B) Because anxiety decreases when obsessions are interrupted.
(C) Because endless rituals help to eliminate obsessive thoughts.
(D) Because often OCD is strengthen through negative reinforcement.

■ **Question 12** How does this professor organize the lecture?

(A) He has a video to explain each point.
(B) He makes reference to the students' textbook.
(C) He uses a whiteboard and interactive instructions.
(D) He gives examples and implicates his students.

Listen to part of a discussion in an Economics class.

Script non affiché le jour de l'examen :

PROFESSOR: What do you think the world's biggest problems are?

STUDENT 1: Education? Climate change?

STUDENT 2: Clean water? The food supply?

PROFESSOR: You are all right. Not to mention the plethora of other problems that are out there including drugs, conflicts and corruption. When it comes to the globe's toughest issues, policy makers have a huge list of spending possibilities akin to a gigantic menu at a restaurant. But this menu comes without prices or serving sizes. If an international agency spends $10 million on one project instead of another, how much more good will it do? Global leaders can rarely answer that question. They need better information and so do ordinary citizens. Economics gives us the tools to look at the costs of taking effective action and measure the excepted benefits. When we know the costs and benefits, it will be a lot easier to choose the best projects – the projects which do the most good with the money available.

National governments prioritize all the time. Government revenues are finite and there are many competing demands for expenditure. Responsible economic management means balancing priorities between defense, education, healthcare and welfare. This prioritization is straightforward enough in a democratic state: although there is usually debate. The result is an explicitly acknowledged trade-off between different segments of society and different problems share a finite pot of money. Do any of you remember any example of a pressing international issue from the World Health studies report?

STUDENT 1: I remember that there was a discussion about water and the water crisis in China.

PROFESSOR: Exactly. Undeniably, water is a particularly challenging problem for the near future because when you talk about change on a local level that is one thing, but when it comes to global welfare projects, the situation gets very murky. We seem to believe that we can achieve anything, that the pool of money is infinite and that everything should be tackled at once. Water, simply put, makes the existence of the human race on this planet possible. With few exceptions, water has always been a natural resource that people take for granted. Today, the situation has changed. The World Bank reports that 80 countries now have water shortages and 2 billion people lack access to clean water. More disturbingly, the World Health Organization has reported that 1 billion people lack enough water to simply meet their basic needs. Population growth and groundwater depletion present the two most significant dangers to global water stability. In the last century, the human population has increased from 1.7 billion people to 6.6 billion people, while the total amount of potable water has slightly decreased. Much of the population growth and economic development experienced in the last fifty years has been supported by subterranean water reserves called groundwater. These nonrenewable reserves, an absolutely essential aspect of the modern world, are being consumed at an unsustainable rate. To make matters even more complicated, the global supply is not distributed evenly around the planet, nor is water equally available at all times throughout the year. Many areas of the world have seriously inadequate access to water, and many places with high annual averages experience alternating seasons of drought and monsoons. Water usage also differs highly between developing countries and developed ones. Developing countries use 90% of their water for agriculture, 5% for industry, and 5% for urban areas. Developed countries use 45% of their water for agriculture, 45% for industry, and 10% for urban areas. The industrial sector accounts for 22% of global water consumption; this number will grow in the coming decades as the developing world industrializes. The needs of industry tend to take precedence over agriculture for simple economic reasons. 1,000 tons of water will produce 1 ton of wheat, which is worth $200. 1,000 tons of water in the industrial sector, however, will generate $14,000 worth of goods. On a per ton basis, industry creates 70 times more wealth. Despite its economic benefits, intense water use by industry has led to serious pollution that is beginning to create problems worldwide.

STUDENT 2: I can see why things are so difficult to address and fix. What steps can we as students make to deal with the world's problems?

PROFESSOR: That's a very good question. None of us are superman. The main obstacle is that we live in a world with limited resources and limited attention. As students you are limited in your ability to make immediate change but then again even the most sophisticated organizations such as the United Nations Environment Program or the United Nations Educational, Scientific and Cultural Organization are often faced with the same quandary. My advice is to conduct research that encourages cross-agency comparison. After all there is little to be gained and much to lose if one's organization work turns out to be costlier or less effective than that of another.

▪ **Question 13** According to the professor, how do governments determine what the best projects are?

(A) They look at a long list of projects.
(B) They classify projects according to urgency and cost.
(C) They choose the most inexpensive projects.
(D) They analyze which projects will be most successful with the least amount of money.

▪ **Question 14** How does the professor organize the lecture?

(A) He relates data to his own personal experiences.
(B) He presents important information in an ascending order.
(C) He refers to studies from international organizations.
(D) He compares American and foreign aid budgets.

▪ **Question 15** According to the professor, what are the most important threats to global water stability?

(A) subterranean water reserve depletion and population increase
(B) agriculture and industry
(C) mining
(D) urban areas

▪ **Question 16** Why does the professor mention the industry sector?

(A) to highlight further future complications
(B) to disguise the need for government action
(C) to eliminate other sectors
(D) to emphasize economic profits

■ Question 17 **Listen again to part of the lecture and answer the question.**

> **Script non affiché le jour de l'examen :**
> **STUDENT:** What steps can we as students make to deal with the world's problems?
>
> **PROFESSOR:** That's a very good question. None of us are superman. The main obstacle is that we live in a world with limited resources and limited attention.

What does the professor imply when he say this:

"None of us are superman."

(A) He likes comic books.
(B) We have to prioritize in order to improve situations.
(C) He would like to have superhuman powers.
(D) He is not sure who is in his class.

■ Question 18 What can be inferred about the professor?

(A) He is a water specialist.
(B) He encourages his students to get involved in research.
(C) He likes to travel to the developing world.
(D) He is an experienced policy maker.

Listen to a conversation between two students.

Script non affiché le jour de l'examen :

MAN: Have you heard the good news?

WOMAN: No, I haven't.

MAN: Our college dean is about to start a debating society.

WOMAN: Oh, really? Did you join?

MAN: Yes, of course. There are so many advantages to joining a debating society.

WOMAN: Really, like what? It seems like it would take time away from studying and class. I don't see any point in fact.

MAN: Well actually it's just the opposite. Debating is a good way to tackle different issues before an audience. Some students are called upon to discuss various topics before a crowd of people. You develop confidence with practice. It's an important tool for the future and it also reduces anxiety.

WOMAN: Reduces anxiety? I would think that it would increase anxiety. I am terrified when I have to speak in front of a classroom filled with people.

MAN: That is precisely why you should join the debating society.

WOMAN: Do you have to join? I heard that it is obligatory in some classes.

MAN: I don't know but it is very helpful for college. Why don't you come with me this afternoon to the first meeting, this way you can sign up and learn the rules.

WOMAN: Who makes the rules?

MAN: Ok, it's like this: there are bylaws so that no matter where you debate the rules will be the same.

WOMAN: That sounds interesting. Are there many rules to learn?

MAN: No, no. There are few rules. In any case there is always a teacher or representative that will preside over the debates and enforce the rules.

WOMAN: Are there any fees involved?

MAN: There is a small fee for materials and supplies for our weekly debates and monthly meetings. In fact, if you volunteer as a student representative your fees are waived.

WOMAN: That's great.

MAN: In college, it's important to study but also to relax and enjoy yourself. We are meeting today from 2-4pm. We'll have a snack and then a short meeting. That's when we plan our debates and pick our topics. Most people don't participate in every single debate but between 3 and 4 a year.

WOMAN: So I don't have to participate in every debate? I still think that it will be very difficult to speak in front people in the beginning.

MAN: Oh come on, you have to face your fears. It will be good for you. Anyway, after today, registration closes. Now is your last chance.

WOMAN: Ok, but if I don't like it I can always quit, right?

MAN: Yes, of course but I have a feeling that you are going to love it.

Question 19 What is the purpose of this conversation?

(A) The man is trying to convince the woman to sign up for the debating society.
(B) The woman is encouraging the man to overcome his fear of public speaking.
(C) The woman is looking for an extra curricular activity to join.
(D) The woman is telling the man that he has to study more.

Question 20 What does the man imply about the fear of public speaking?

(A) Public speaking becomes easier with practice.
(B) Public speaking can be stressful.
(C) There are classes in which public speaking is mandatory.
(D) Rules are the most important aspect.

Question 21 How does the man feel about the debating society?

(A) He believes it is useful for college.
(B) He thinks students should make the rules.
(C) He hopes everyone will join.
(D) He wants it to be obligatory.

Question 22 Listen again to part of the discussion and answer the question.

Script non affiché le jour de l'examen :
WOMAN: Reduces anxiety? I would think that it would increase anxiety. I am terrified when I have to speak in front of a classroom filled with people.

NARRATOR: What does the woman mean when she says:

WOMAN: Reduces anxiety?

(A) She agrees that debating reduces anxiety.
(B) She hopes that debating will help her with public speaking.
(C) She doubts that public speaking will reduce anxiety.
(D) She would like to know how to reduce anxiety.

Question 23 What will the woman probably do?

(A) Register for the debating society and attend the meeting
(B) Practice public speaking before joining the debating society
(C) Learn the rules on how to become a representative
(D) Practice public speaking during the meeting

Listen to a conversation between a professor and a student.

Script non affiché le jour de l'examen :

STUDENT: Hi Professor Allen, do you have a minute? I have some questions about the mid-term.

PROFESSOR: Sure. I have about 5 minutes before my next class starts.

STUDENT: I was hoping to have done better on the exam. I was confused about something before the test but didn't think to ask you about it.

PROFESSOR: You didn't do terribly. If I recall, you only got one or two questions wrong. It was not an easy exam. You did better than most people in your class.

STUDENT: I know but I still am confused by mitochondrial DNA and its links with Anatomically Modern Humans. I have in my notes that AMHs are all descendants of the same DNA.

PROFESSOR: Well not exactly, in fact when molecular geneticists looked to prove that modern humans arose fairly recently in Africa and then spread out and colonized the world, they focused only on mitochondrial DNA.

STUDENT: The genetic material located in the cytoplasm of cells?

PROFESSOR: Precisely. Ordinary DNA, which makes up the genes that determine most physical traits, is found in the nucleus and comes from both parents but only the mother contributes mitochondrial DNA to the fertilized egg.

STUDENT: Hence the reason that the team analyzed genetic markers in placentas.

PROFESSOR: Mitochondrial DNA helps to establish a genetic clock. The researchers needed to measure the variation in their 147 tissue samples. By estimating the number of mutations that had taken place in each sample since its common origin with the 146 others, the researchers drew an evolutionary tree with the help of a computer. The researchers concluded that everyone alive today has mitochondrial DNA that descends from one woman who lived in sub-Saharan Africa about 200,000 years ago.

STUDENT: So in other words, we are all descendent of the first modern woman?

PROFESSOR: Well in fact we are all descendents of a woman dubbed "Eve". She wasn't the only woman alive then; she was just the only one whose descendents have included a daughter in each generation up to the present.

STUDENT: Ok. So mtDNA can only pass from mother to daughter. Now I understand the evolutionary tree better.

PROFESSOR: That's right. Because mitochondrial DNA passes exclusively through females, mitochondrial DNA lines disappear whenever a woman has no children or only sons. The details of the Eve theory suggest that her descendants left Africa no more than 135,000 years ago and that there were two branches in the evolutionary tree. The tree started in Africa and then branched in two. One group remained in Africa, while the other split off, carrying its mitochondrial DNA to the rest of the world.

STUDENT: That is where I made my mistakes. I wasn't sure why the female line was so important nor the difference between ordinary DNA and mtDNA. But now I see that without an intact female line, there is no way to trace back to the origin of our common ancestor.

PROFESSOR: Good, I am happy you understand better. Don't worry about your grade. The mid-term only counts for 15% of your final grade. There is still your final paper and your final exam. Next time you find that you don't understand something, its best to come and see me during my office hours.

STUDENT: Next time I won't hesitate.

Question 24 Why did the man go and see his professor?

(A) to borrow a biology book
(B) to ask a question about her mid-term exam
(C) to see when the professor has office hours
(D) to hand in a paper

Question 25 How is mitochondrial DNA different from regular DNA?

(A) Mitochondrial DNA is located in the cytoplasm of a cell.
(B) Regular DNA makes up genes but mitochondrial DNA does not.
(C) Regular DNA and mitochondrial DNA come from both sets of parents.
(D) Mitochondrial DNA is found in the nucleus.

Question 26 Listen again to part of the discussion and answer the question.

Script non affiché le jour de l'examen :
STUDENT: The genetic material located in the cytoplasm of cells?

PROFESSOR: Precisely. Ordinary DNA, which makes up the genes that determine most physical traits, is found in the nucleus and comes from both parents but only the mother contributes mitochondrial DNA to the fertilized egg.

STUDENT: Hence the reason that the team analyzed genetic markers in placentas.

NARRATOR: What does the student mean when he says:

STUDENT: Hence the reason that the team analyzed genetic markers in placentas?

(A) He does not understand why the team analyzed placentas.
(B) He wants to clarify the reason why the researchers studied mitochondrial DNA.
(C) He is criticizing the team's analysis.
(D) He wants to pronounce the word better.

Question 27 What will the student do before the next exam?

(A) take better notes in class
(B) go over class lectures with classmates
(C) see the professor before the test
(D) study harder than she did for the mid-term

Question 28 What can be said about the professor?

(A) He teaches psychology.
(B) He is very strict when it comes to grading.
(C) He is often not in his office.
(D) He wants his students to come for extra help.

TOEFL iBT #2 - SPEAKING (AUDIO)

SPEAKING SECTION DIRECTIONS

The Speaking section measures your ability to speak in English about a variety of topics.

In this question, you will listen to a short lecture. You will then be asked to summarize important information from the lecture. You may take notes while you listen to the lecture. You may use your notes to help prepare your response. After you hear the question, you have 20 seconds to prepare your response and 60 seconds to speak.

Reportez vos réponses pour analyser votre performance.

Entraînez-vous dans les conditions d'examen.

Écoutez les fichiers audio.

prepmyfuture.com/book/68/ex/1988

Question 1 **DIRECTIONS:** In this question, you will be asked to speak about a familiar topic. After you hear the question, you have 15 seconds to prepare your response and 45 seconds to speak.

QUESTION: Talk about an event in your life when you were successful in accomplishing a goal. Describe the experience and explain how it affected your life. Use specific details in your explanation.

Preparation Time: 15 seconds
Response Time: 45 seconds

DIRECTIONS: In this question, you will read a short passage and listen to a conversation on the same topic. You will then be asked a question about them. You may take notes while you read the passage and listen to the lecture. You may use your notes to help prepare your response. After you hear the question, you have 30 seconds to prepare your response and 60 seconds to speak.

Reading Time: 45 seconds

Online Science Seminar

Pacific University is pleased to announce a new online science seminar course for non-science majors. In this course, we will read selected articles, hold online discussions and write about topics from various scientific fields. No previous background in science is needed for this course, nor are there any course requirements for joining. The course will explore ideas about nature, astronomy, and oceanography, as well as explore the lives of scientists from ancient times up to modern times. Students who take this course and complete all required work will receive 2 class credits; it also can fulfill the freshman "Introduction to Science" course requirement needed by all undergraduate students.

Listen to two students discuss the new seminar.

Question 2 **QUESTION:** The man expresses his opinion about the new online seminar described in the article. Briefly summarize the announcement. Then state his opinion about the announcement and explain the reasons he gives for holding that opinion.

Preparation Time: 30 seconds
Response Time: 60 seconds

DIRECTIONS: In this question, read a short passage and listen to a lecture on the same topic. You will then be asked a question about them. You may take notes while you read the passage and listen to the lecture. You may use your notes to help prepare your response. After you hear the question, you have 30 seconds to prepare your response and 60 seconds to speak.

Reading Time: 50 seconds

Frank Lloyd Wright

Frank Lloyd Wright was an American architect who in the late 19th and early 20th century was credited with developing a uniquely American style of architecture. Wright strove to create "organic" designs for homes and commercial buildings, featuring horizontal layouts with expansive, open interior spaces. However, his most notable contribution to architecture was to design buildings that enhanced or echoed elements of the natural environment around them. He felt that people were a part of nature; thus, architecture which conformed to nature would conform to the needs and desires of people.

Now listen to part of a lecture on this topic in an art history class.

▪ **Question 3** **QUESTION:** Describe Frank Lloyd Wright's style of architecture and how this style can be seen in the buildings described in the lecture.

Preparation Time: 30 seconds
Response Time: 60 seconds

DIRECTIONS: In this question, you will listen to a short lecture. You will then be asked to summarize important information from the lecture. You may take notes while you listen to the lecture. You may use your notes to help prepare your response. After you hear the question, you have 20 seconds to prepare your response and 60 seconds to speak.

Listen to part of a lecture. The professor is talking about space stations.

▪ **Question 4** **QUESTION:** Using points and examples from the lecture, explain the importance of Skylab.

Preparation Time: 20 seconds
Response Time: 60 seconds

TOEFL iBT #2 - SPEAKING (SCRIPTS)

SPEAKING SECTION DIRECTIONS

The Speaking section measures your ability to speak in English about a variety of topics.

In this question, you will listen to a short lecture. You will then be asked to summarize important information from the lecture. You may take notes while you listen to the lecture. You may use your notes to help prepare your response. After you hear the question, you have 20 seconds to prepare your response and 60 seconds to speak.

Reportez vos réponses pour analyser votre performance.

Entraînez-vous dans les conditions d'examen.

Écoutez les fichiers audio.

prepmyfuture.com/book/68/ex/1988

Question 1

DIRECTIONS: In this question, you will be asked to speak about a familiar topic. After you hear the question, you have 15 seconds to prepare your response and 45 seconds to speak.

QUESTION: Talk about an event in your life when you were successful in accomplishing a goal. Describe the experience and explain how it affected your life. Use specific details in your explanation.

Preparation Time: 15 seconds
Response Time: 45 seconds

DIRECTIONS: In this question, you will read a short passage and listen to a conversation on the same topic. You will then be asked a question about them. You may take notes while you read the passage and listen to the lecture. You may use your notes to help prepare your response. After you hear the question, you have 30 seconds to prepare your response and 60 seconds to speak.

Reading Time: 45 seconds

Online Science Seminar

Pacific University is pleased to announce a new online science seminar course for non-science majors. In this course, we will read selected articles, hold online discussions and write about topics from various scientific fields. No previous background in science is needed for this course, nor are there any course requirements for joining. The course will explore ideas about nature, astronomy, and oceanography, as well as explore the lives of scientists from ancient times up to modern times. Students who take this course and complete all required work will receive 2 class credits; it also can fulfill the freshman "Introduction to Science" course requirement needed by all undergraduate students.

Listen to two students discuss the new seminar.

Script non affiché le jour de l'examen :

MAN: Did you hear about the new online science class? I think I might sign up for it.

WOMAN: Really?

MAN: Why not? It can get a class requirement out of the way and get me some credits for graduation. I was kind of dreading having to sit through some boring 'intro to science' class.

WOMAN: But isn't that what you're going to be doing in the online course?

MAN: Sort of, but I don't mind doing online discussions—they're better than being stuck in a classroom while the professor and students talk about stuff. At least in the online course I can stand up and move around, or even have a snack—not many professors like it when you do that in a classroom. I could even be sitting in a park while the class discussions are taking place!

WOMAN: That's a good point. I never thought of it that way.

MAN: And you know how much I hate science. I just don't have the head for it—must be why I'm studying art!

WOMAN: I do remember how much you complained last term about that chemistry class.

MAN: Don't remind me! I kind of like the idea that they cover a lot of different topics in the class, too. It might actually keep me more interested in the class all the way through the term. I kind of like the idea of studying about the history of science. Who knows...knowing more about the scientists who have shaped our world just might make me appreciate it more.

▪ **Question 2** **QUESTION:** The man expresses his opinion about the new online seminar described in the article. Briefly summarize the announcement. Then state his opinion about the announcement and explain the reasons he gives for holding that opinion.

Preparation Time: 30 seconds
Response Time: 60 seconds

DIRECTIONS: In this question, read a short passage and listen to a lecture on the same topic. You will then be asked a question about them. You may take notes while you read the passage and listen to the lecture. You may use your notes to help prepare your response. After you hear the question, you have 30 seconds to prepare your response and 60 seconds to speak.

Reading Time: 50 seconds

Frank Lloyd Wright

Frank Lloyd Wright was an American architect who in the late 19th and early 20th century was credited with developing a uniquely American style of architecture. Wright strove to create "organic" designs for homes and commercial buildings, featuring horizontal layouts with expansive, open interior spaces. However, his most notable contribution to architecture was to design buildings that enhanced or echoed elements of the natural environment around them. He felt that people were a part of nature; thus, architecture which conformed to nature would conform to the needs and desires of people.

Now listen to part of a lecture on this topic in an art history class.

Script non affiché le jour de l'examen :

PROFESSOR: One building which art historians feel best exemplifies Frank Lloyd Wright's style of architecture is the Robie House, completed in 1908 at the University of Chicago. With unsupported eaves projecting dramatically from its roof, and its continuous bands of windows that wrap around the building and even around corners, the building is meant to convey the flat horizon of the American open prairies. This serene, horizontal feeling was further emphasized in the way the outer brick walls were constructed. The horizontal joints above and below the layers of bricks were filled with a cream-colored mortar while the vertical joints between them were filled with brick-colored mortar. The effect of this was that, from a distance, it looked as if it were continuous lines of horizontal color, like layers of soil.

However, Wright's greatest achievement is arguably the "Fallingwater" house in rural Pennsylvania. It's a house that doesn't even appear to stand on solid ground; instead it stretches out over a 30-foot high waterfall. The sound of its water permeates the house, especially during the spring when the snow is melting. Constructed of locally-quarried stone, Fallingwater House is a series of overlapping terraces that resemble the nearby rock formations, and it, like the Robie House, incorporates broad expanses of windows that wrap around corners, providing unobstructed views of the surround forest. Its balconies seem to reach out and float among the trees. It remains one of Wright's most celebrated works, and is a national landmark that is widely considered one of the most beautiful homes ever built.

■ Question 3 **QUESTION:** Describe Frank Lloyd Wright's style of architecture and how this style can be seen in the buildings described in the lecture.

Preparation Time: 30 seconds
Response Time: 60 seconds

DIRECTIONS: In this question, you will listen to a short lecture. You will then be asked to summarize important information from the lecture. You may take notes while you listen to the lecture. You may use your notes to help prepare your response. After you hear the question, you have 20 seconds to prepare your response and 60 seconds to speak.

Listen to part of a lecture. The professor is talking about space stations.

Script non affiché le jour de l'examen :

While the International Space Station is currently the most famous object in Earth's orbit, it was not the first attempt to have humans live and work for extended periods of time in space. America's first space station, Skylab, launched in 1973, helped pave the way for permanent habitations in low-Earth orbit. At the time, Skylab was hailed as a bold concept, building upon previous manned space missions, namely the Apollo series, which famously landed men on the Moon in 1969.

Skylab orbited the Earth from 1973 to 1979. It included a workshop, a solar observatory, multiple docking ports for various rockets that were in service by various countries at the time, and support systems to allow teams of astronauts and scientists to spend up to 3 months in space.

Some of the primary goals of the Skylab program were to study how different materials handled the extremely low gravity of Earth's orbit and to make observations of the Earth's surface. But most importantly, Skylab was NASA's attempt to prove that humans could live and work in space for extended time periods.

All in all, the three manned expeditions that lived and worked in Skylab accumulated a vast amount of data about our planet, such as its crops, weather and changes in environment. They also learned to work in space, completing a revealing study of the sun, manufacturing special alloys, growing perfect crystals and conducting a myriad of other minor experiments and studies.

After these expeditions, plans were made to refurbish and reuse Skylab, but due to delays in getting repair equipment up to it, Skylab's orbit slowly brought it closer and closer to Earth. It reentered Earth's atmosphere and disintegrated in 1979, with debris striking portions of Western Australia.

Skylab transformed the NASA space program from its focus on spectacular spaceflights into a new phase that can be characterized possibly as almost businesslike. While Skylab's discoveries and contributions were not broadcast as widely as the space missions of the previous decade, Skylab's success ultimately contributed to push toward the next phase in NASA, space shuttles.

■ Question 4 **QUESTION:** Using points and examples from the lecture, explain the importance of Skylab.

Preparation Time: 20 seconds
Response Time: 60 seconds

TOEFL iBT #2 - WRITING (AUDIO)

WRITING SECTION DIRECTIONS

The Writing section measures your ability to use writing to communicate in an academic environment.

For this task, you will write a response to a question about a reading passage and a lecture. You may take notes, and you may use your notes to help you write your response. Your response will be scored on the quality of your writing and on how well you connect the points in the lecture with points in the reading.

Reportez vos réponses pour analyser votre performance.

Entraînez-vous dans les conditions d'examen.

Écoutez les fichiers audio.

prepmyfuture.com/book/68/ex/1989

DIRECTIONS: For this task, you will write a response to a question about a reading passage and a lecture. You may take notes, and you may use your notes to help you write your response. Your response will be scored on the quality of your writing and on how well you connect the points in the lecture with points in the reading.

Reading Time – 3 minutes

Scattered across the British Isles and northern France are some of the world's most mysterious monuments, stone ruins of both simple beauty and breathtaking age. Massive tombs and huge standing stones set in circles and rows like Stonehenge, these wonders of the prehistoric world were erected between 4500 BC and 1500 BC. Over the last hundred years, debate has raged over the possibility that these "megaliths" may not have been just religious sites but may very well have been astronomical observatories of surprisingly precise construction.

Precise Alignments

Over one hundred years ago, researchers identified highly accurate alignments of rows of stones at these megalithic sites to various annual celestial events. These alignments could be found by lining up the sides or tops of stones or tunnels to far distant landmarks on the horizon. For example, one common alignment would pinpoint the place on the horizon where the sun would rise on the morning of the summer solstice. After running computer simulations, it was found that the possibility of these alignments being by chance was less than one in ten million.

Mathematically-constructed Calendar

Later, surveys of these megalithic sites revealed that nearly all of them had been laid out using the same measurement of length—2.72 feet—which came to be known as the "megalithic yard." Many of these sites formed elaborate, geometric arrangements of stones using this measurement, including egg-shapes, ellipses and arcs. It was theorized that these patterns, built using a precisely cut length of wood--the megalithic yard--as a measuring device, were constructed by ancient astronomers to create intricate celestial calendars, tracking the passage of time over the course of a year.

Astronomer-Priests

But how could these alignments and measurements be so uniform across all of Britain? Many researchers believe that the only way for this to have happened is for there to have been a class of astronomer-priests, people knowledgeable in math, geometry and astronomy who could pass their knowledge down over hundreds of years. It would have been these people who designed and maintained these megalithic sites over hundreds of years. Instead of just being ceremonial centers as was previously believed, these sites were likely also places of learning, teaching ancient man highly-sophisticated math and science.

Now listen to part of a lecture on the topic you just read about.

▪ **Question 1**

DIRECTIONS: You have 20 minutes to plan and write your response. Your response will be evaluated on the quality of your writing on how well you present the points in the lecture and their relationship to the reading passage. Typically, an effective response will have 150 to 225 words.

Response Time: 20 minutes

QUESTION: Summarize the points made in the lecture, explaining how they contrast with points made in the reading.

▪ **Question 2**

DIRECTIONS: Read the question below. You have 30 minutes to plan, write, and revise your essay. Typically, an effective response will contain a minimum of 300 words.

Response Time: 30 minutes

QUESTION: Does the success and happiness someone experiences in life depend more on the choices they make rather than factors outside their control? Use specific reasons and examples to support your opinion.

TOEFL iBT #2 - WRITING (SCRIPTS)

WRITING SECTION DIRECTIONS

The Writing section measures your ability to use writing to communicate in an academic environment.

For this task, you will write a response to a question about a reading passage and a lecture. You may take notes, and you may use your notes to help you write your response. Your response will be scored on the quality of your writing and on how well you connect the points in the lecture with points in the reading.

Reportez vos réponses pour analyser votre performance.

Entraînez-vous dans les conditions d'examen.

Écoutez les fichiers audio.

prepmyfuture.com/book/68/ex/1989

DIRECTIONS: For this task, you will write a response to a question about a reading passage and a lecture. You may take notes, and you may use your notes to help you write your response. Your response will be scored on the quality of your writing and on how well you connect the points in the lecture with points in the reading.

Reading Time – 3 minutes

Scattered across the British Isles and northern France are some of the world's most mysterious monuments, stone ruins of both simple beauty and breathtaking age. Massive tombs and huge standing stones set in circles and rows like Stonehenge, these wonders of the prehistoric world were erected between 4500 BC and 1500 BC. Over the last hundred years, debate has raged over the possibility that these "megaliths" may not have been just religious sites but may very well have been astronomical observatories of surprisingly precise construction.

Precise Alignments

Over one hundred years ago, researchers identified highly accurate alignments of rows of stones at these megalithic sites to various annual celestial events. These alignments could be found by lining up the sides or tops of stones or tunnels to far distant landmarks on the horizon. For example, one common alignment would pinpoint the place on the horizon where the sun would rise on the morning of the summer solstice. After running computer simulations, it was found that the possibility of these alignments being by chance was less than one in ten million.

Mathematically-constructed Calendar

Later, surveys of these megalithic sites revealed that nearly all of them had been laid out using the same measurement of length—2.72 feet—which came to be known as the "megalithic yard." Many of these sites formed elaborate, geometric arrangements of stones using this measurement, including egg-shapes, ellipses and arcs. It was theorized that these patterns, built using a precisely cut length of wood--the megalithic yard--as a measuring device, were constructed by ancient astronomers to create intricate celestial calendars, tracking the passage of time over the course of a year.

Astronomer-Priests

But how could these alignments and measurements be so uniform across all of Britain? Many researchers believe that the only way for this to have happened is for there to have been a class of astronomer-priests, people knowledgeable in math, geometry and astronomy who could pass their knowledge down over hundreds of years. It would have been these people who designed and maintained these megalithic sites over hundreds of years. Instead of just being ceremonial centers as was previously believed, these sites were likely also places of learning, teaching ancient man highly-sophisticated math and science.

Now listen to part of a lecture on the topic you just read about.

Script non affiché le jour de l'examen :

PROFESSOR: Despite the romantic notion of the megalithic sites in western Europe being monuments of scientific and geometrical precision, when analyzed more fully it is clear that they are in fact much more primitive in their layout and probable purposes.

Critics have pointed out that many of the supposed alignments at these megalithic sites came highly selective analyses, and that many of them may really just be coincidences. Indeed, at Stonehenge, one researcher, using a computer to help with calculations, created tens of thousands of potential alignments. It stretches belief to think that ancient man designed Stonehenge with so many "lines of sight" for so many different celestial events. Moreover, many of these "lines of sight" are not lines at all; rather they point near to, but not directly at, distant landmarks, supporting the critics' claim that these alignments are not very precise at all.

And what about the existence of a "megalithic yard"? While there is strong evidence that the stone circles and other megalithic sites were indeed laid out using a similar kind of measuring method or technique, critics have found little evidence for a highly accurate unit of measurement that was identical from one site to the other. From the variations noticed at these sites, it is now theorized that simple measuring methods, such as the average pace of a grown man, could very easily explain the similarity of measurements from one site to another; alternatively, the geometric layouts found at many sites could have been simply created by using a combination of wooden stakes and ropes to draw arcs or circles.

And as for groups of astronomer-priests passing on their Stone Age science from generation to generation, this idea seems to be merely our modern, science-oriented mind attempting to find advanced technical knowledge in the monuments of ancient Europe. Several megalithic sites are situated on uneven ground, and the stone circles at those sites are not real circles at all, but are arrangements of stones that bent or elongated to give the impression of a circle if one were to stand inside of it. From this, it is clear that these sites had a more symbolic—and thus, religious--meaning, not a scientific one.

■ Question 1

DIRECTIONS: You have 20 minutes to plan and write your response. Your response will be evaluated on the quality of your writing on how well you present the points in the lecture and their relationship to the reading passage. Typically, an effective response will have 150 to 225 words.

Response Time: 20 minutes

QUESTION: Summarize the points made in the lecture, explaining how they contrast with points made in the reading.

■ Question 2

DIRECTIONS: Read the question below. You have 30 minutes to plan, write, and revise your essay. Typically, an effective response will contain a minimum of 300 words.

Response Time: 30 minutes

QUESTION: Does the success and happiness someone experiences in life depend more on the choices they make rather than factors outside their control? Use specific reasons and examples to support your opinion.

TOEFL iBT #2 - SOLUTIONS

TOEFL iBT #2 - READING - Solutions

Reportez vos réponses pour analyser votre performance.

Entraînez-vous dans les conditions d'examen.

prepmyfuture.com/book/68/ex/1986

question 1	B
question 2	B
question 3	B
question 4	A
question 5	A
question 6	D

question 7	C
question 8	D
question 9	A
question 10	A D F
question 11	A
question 12	D

question 13	A
question 14	C
question 15	A
question 16	D
question 17	A
question 18	B

question 19	B
question 20	B C E
question 21	A
question 22	A
question 23	C
question 24	A

question 25	D
question 26	C
question 27	B
question 28	C
question 29	D
question 30	A E F

■ Question 1 - Solution

In paragraph 1, which of the following statement best describes great deserts? The other choices change the meaning or leave out information.

FR : D'après le paragraphe 1, quelle proposition décrit le mieux les grands déserts ? Les autres choix changent le sens ou omettent des informations.

(A)	Great deserts were created by natural processes over long time intervals.	= Les grands déserts ont été créés par des processus naturels sur de longs intervalles de temps. *Cette réponse est vraie mais il n'y a pas de référence à l'activité humaine.*
(B)	**✓ Great deserts were created by natural processes over long time intervals, and their development has been independent of human influence.**	**= Les grands déserts ont été créés par des processus naturels sur de longs intervalles de temps, et leur développement est indépendant de toute intervention humaine.** ***« The world's great deserts were formed by natural processes interacting over long intervals of time. During most of these times, deserts have grown and shrunk independent of human activities. »*** ***(= « Les grands déserts du monde ont été formés par des processus naturels interagissant sur de longs intervalles de temps. Pendant la plupart de ces périodes, les déserts ont grandi et reculé indépendamment des activités humaines. »)***
(C)	Great deserts were created by natural processes and human activities.	= Les grands déserts ont été créés par des processus naturels et des activités humaines. *Le texte mentionne au contraire que l'activité humaine n'a pas eu de rôle important.* *« During most of these times, deserts have grown and shrunk independent of human activities. »* *(= « Pendant la plupart de ces périodes, les déserts ont grandi et rétréci indépendamment des activités humaines. »)*
(D)	Great deserts have grown and shrunk with the help of human intervention and other natural processes.	= Les grands déserts ont progressé et reculé grâce à l'intervention de l'homme et à d'autres processus naturels. *La plupart du temps, l'intervention humaine n'a pas eu d'impact sur l'agrandissement et le rétrécissement des déserts.*

▪ Question 2 - Solution

In paragraph 4, the author implies that:

FR : Dans le paragraphe 4, l'auteur sous-entend que :

(A)	Scientists have not been doing an excellent job collecting data.	= Les scientifiques n'ont pas fait un très bon travail de collecte de données. *L'auteur n'écrit pas cela. Il mentionne simplement que les données collectées jusqu'à présent ne donnent toujours pas une explication complète du phénomène de désertification.*
(B) ✓	**People only worry about the deteriorating conditions of an area when it's too late.**	**= Les gens ne s'inquiètent de la dégradation de l'état d'une région que lorsqu'il est trop tard.** ***« Unfortunately, an area undergoing desertification is brought to public attention only after the process is well underway. »*** ***(= « Malheureusement, une zone en voie de désertification ne suscite l'attention du public qu'une fois le processus déjà bien engagé. »)***
(C)	Particularly fertile areas are more likely to become deserts.	= Les zones particulièrement fertiles sont plus susceptibles de devenir des déserts. *Ce n'est pas ce que suggère l'auteur.*
(D)	Weather changes might be causing desertification.	= Les changements climatiques peuvent être à l'origine de la désertification. *L'auteur spécifie seulement qu'avec la désertification surviennent une série de changements climatiques.*

■ Question 3 - Solution

Based on information in paragraph 1, which of the following best explains the term "Paleodeserts" ? The other choices change the meaning or leave out information.

FR : Selon les informations contenues dans le paragraphe 1, laquelle des propositions suivantes explique le mieux le terme « paléodéserts » ? Les autres choix modifient le sens ou omettent des informations.

(A)	A flat area of desert covered with wind-swept sand with little or no vegetal cover	= Une zone désertique plate, couverte de sable balayé par le vent, avec peu ou pas de végétation. *L'auteur mentionne que ces zones ont été « stabilized by vegetation » et il n'y a pas d'allusion au vent dans ce paragraphe.*
(B) ✓	**Large sand seas that are now inactive due to stabilized vegetation**	**= De grandes mers de sable qui sont maintenant inactives en raison de la végétation qui s'est installée.** ***« Paleodeserts, large sand seas now inactive because they are stabilized by vegetation. »*** ***(= « Les paléodéserts, de grandes mers de sable aujourd'hui inactives car elles ont été stabilisées par la végétation. »)***
(C)	A flat area of desert covered with little or no vegetal cover	= Une zone plate de désert recouverte de peu ou pas de végétation. *Il n'y a pas de référence dans le texte au fait que la végétation ne soit pas dense.*
(D)	Large sand seas that are still active due to stabilized vegetation	= De grandes mers de sable encore actives grâce à une végétation qui s'est installée. *L'auteur écrit qu'elles sont « now inactive » (= maintenant inactives).*

▪ Question 4 - Solution

The word "arid" is closest in meaning to:

FR : Le mot « arid » dans le paragraphe 1 a une signification proche de :

(A) ✓ **dry** **= sec**

(B) humid = humide

(C) boring = ennuyeux

(D) flat = plat

▪ Question 5 - Solution

According to paragraph 2, which of the following best describes "transition zones"? The other choices change the meaning or leave out information.

FR : D'après le paragraphe 2, qu'est-ce qui décrit le mieux les « zones de transition » ? Les autres choix changent le sens ou omettent des informations.

(A)	✓ **They have unstable and carefully balanced ecosystems with a variety of microclimates.**	**= Elles ont des écosystèmes instables et bien équilibrés avec une diversité de microclimats.** ***« Unstable » (= instable) est synonyme de « very fragile » (= très fragile) et « carefully balanced » (= délicatement équilibrés) signifie la même chose que « delicately balanced ».*** ***(= « Ces zones de transition ont des écosystèmes très fragiles et bien équilibrés. »)***
(B)	They have stable and delicately imbalanced ecosystems with a variety of microclimates.	= Elles ont des écosystèmes stables et légèrement déséquilibrés avec une diversité de microclimats. *L'écosystème est délicatement équilibré.*
(C)	They have carefully balanced ecosystems with a variety of microclimates.	= Ils ont des écosystèmes bien équilibrés avec une diversité de microclimats. *On perd la dimension de fragilité de cet écosystème.*
(D)	They have unstable ecosystems with a variety of macroclimates.	= Ils ont des écosystèmes instables avec une diversité de macroclimats. *La phrase emploie « macroclimates » (= macroclimats) à la place de « microclimates » (= microclimats).*

▪ Question 6 - Solution

The word "consensus" in paragraph 5 is closest in meaning to:

FR : Le mot « consensus » dans le paragraphe 5 a une signification proche de :

(A) dissension = discorde

(B) denial = déni

(C) refusal = refus

(D) ✓ **agreement** **= accord**

▪ Question 7 - Solution

Which of the following sentences best describes the highlighted sentence in the passage? The other choices change the meaning or leave out information.

FR : Parmi les phrases suivantes, laquelle décrit le mieux la phrase soulignée dans le passage ? Les autres choix changent le sens ou omettent des informations.

(A)	While desertification has become a popular topic among politicians and citizens alike, there are still numerous issues that are needed to be addressed.	= Si la désertification est devenue un sujet populaire parmi les politiciens et les citoyens, il reste encore de nombreux problèmes à résoudre. *La réponse sous-entend que le sujet de la désertification fait aussi bien débat auprès des politiques que des citoyens. Or si les médias font la publicité de ce phénomène, cela ne signifie pas pour autant que les citoyens en parlent.*
(B)	Desertification has received tremendous publicity due to the news media because we still don't know a few things about the degradation of productive lands or the expansion of deserts.	= La désertification a reçu une énorme publicité grâce aux médias d'information, car nous ne savons toujours pas grand-chose sur la dégradation des terres fertiles ou l'expansion des déserts. *Le phénomène de désertification a reçu beaucoup de publicité mais ce n'est pas parce qu'on connaît peu de choses sur la dégradation des terrains productifs ou sur l'expansion des déserts.*
(C) ✓	**Despite the political and social publicity of the topic of desertification, there are still many things hidden from us in terms of how productive lands are degraded or how deserts manage to increase in size.**	**= Malgré la publicité politique et sociale du thème de la désertification, on nous cache encore beaucoup de choses sur la dégradation des terres fertiles ou sur l'expansion des déserts.**
(D)	Desertification is a rather popular topic among political circles because we know so much about the degradation of productive lands and the expansion of deserts.	= La désertification est un sujet plutôt populaire dans les milieux politiques car nous savons beaucoup de choses sur la dégradation des terres fertiles et l'expansion des déserts. *Nous ne savons pas grand-chose à propos de la raison de la dégradation des terrains productifs et l'expansion des déserts.*

⇝ **explication**

FR : Alors que la désertification a été énormément couverte par les politiques et les médias, il y a toujours beaucoup de choses que nous ne savons pas au sujet de la dégradation des terrains productifs et l'expansion des déserts.

▪ Question 8 - Solution

According to Paragraph 7, individuals and governments on a local level could reclaim and protect lands from desertification with all the following methods EXCEPT:

FR : D'après le paragraphe 7, les individus et les gouvernements pourraient reprendre la main et protéger leurs terrains de la désertification avec toutes les méthodes suivantes SAUF :

(A)	covering the dunes with large boulders or petroleum to interrupt the wind regime	= recouvrir les dunes de gros rochers ou du pétrole pour interrompre le régime des vents *« In areas of sand dunes, covering the dunes with large boulders or petroleum will interrupt the wind regime near the face of the dunes and prevent the sand from moving. »* *(« Dans les zones de dunes de sable, recouvrir les dunes de gros rochers ou de pétrole bloquera les vents à la surface des dunes et empêchera le sable de se déplacer. »)*
(B)	placing straw grids	= placer des grilles de paille *« Placement of straw grids, each up to a square meter in area, will also decrease the surface wind velocity. » (= « Le placement de grilles de paille, d'une superficie pouvant atteindre un mètre carré chacune, permet également de diminuer la vitesse du vent en surface. »)*
(C)	planting vegetation inside the grids	= planter de la végétation à l'intérieur des grilles *« In areas where some water is available for irrigation, shrubs planted on the lower one-third of a dune's windward side will stabilize the dune. »* *(« Dans les régions où il y a de l'eau disponible pour l'irrigation, les arbustes plantés sur le tiers inférieur de la partie de la dune exposée au vent stabiliseront la dune entière. »)*
(D)	✓ **removing shrubs and trees planted within the grids**	**= enlever les arbustes et les arbres plantés à l'intérieur des grilles**

▪ Question 9 - Solution

Look at the four squares in paragraph 7, **A**, **B**, **C**, and **D**, which indicate where the following sentence could be added to the passage. Where would the sentence best fit?

In areas of sand dunes, covering the dunes with large boulders or petroleum will interrupt the wind regime near the face of the dunes and prevent the sand from moving.

[P7] At the local level, individuals and governments can help to reclaim and protect their lands. **A** Sand fences are used throughout the Middle East and the United States, in the same way snow fences are used in the north. Placement of straw grids, each up to a square meter in area, will also decrease the surface wind velocity. **B** Shrubs and trees planted within the grids are protected by the straw until they take root. In areas where some water is available for irrigation, shrubs planted on the lower one-third of a dune's windward side will stabilize the dune. **C** This vegetation decreases the wind velocity near the base of the dune and prevents much of the sand from moving. **D** Higher velocity winds at the top of the dune level it off and trees can be planted atop these flattened surfaces.

FR :

Où serait-il le plus juste de placer cette phrase ?
In areas of sand dunes, covering the dunes with large boulders or petroleum will interrupt the wind regime near the face of the dunes and prevent the sand from moving.

(A) ✓ **A** ***La phrase à insérer contient un exemple pour illustrer le point suivant : « individuals and governments can [do] to reclaim and protect their lands. » (= « [ce que] les individus et les gouvernements peuvent [faire] pour récupérer et protéger leurs terres. »)***

(B) **B** *La phrase n'aurait pas de sens à cet endroit, entre une phrase sur les « straw grids » et une autre sur les « shrubs and trees ».*

(C) **C** *Insérer la phrase à cet endroit couperait la description des bénéfices potentiels que l'on pourrait obtenir en plantant des arbres.*

(D) **D** *Insérer la phrase à cet endroit couperait la description sur les effets du vent sur les dunes.*

▪ Question 10 - Solution

Directions:

An introductory sentence for a brief summary of the passage is provided below.

Complete the summary by selecting the THREE answer choices that express the most important ideas in the passage. Some sentences do not belong in the summary because they express ideas that are not presented in the passage or are minor ideas in the passage.

This question is worth 2 points.

- Vast deserts have natural origin and their edges are not always clearly defined.
- ________
- ________
- ________

(A) ✓ Although some of the causes of desertification are known, it is still difficult to predict how and where it will happen.	**= Bien que certaines origines de la désertification soient connues, il est encore difficile de prévoir comment et où elle se produira.** ***Cette phrase résume les paragraphes 1 et 2.***
(B) Despite the uneven pattern of the phenomenon of desertification, it is possible to predict its evolution by focusing on the different climates.	= Malgré l'irrégularité du phénomène de la désertification, il est possible de prédire son évolution en se concentrant sur les différents climats. *L'information est incorrecte. L'auteur dit que la désertification pourrait amener des changements climatiques mais pas que ces changements rendent la désertifications possible.*
(C) Activities such as pasture and agriculture are condensed in the warmest regions of the desert fringes, causing their expansion.	= Les activités telles que le pâturage et l'agriculture sont condensées dans les régions les plus chaudes des franges du désert, ce qui provoque leur expansion. *« After rainfall, the vegetated areas are distinctly cooler than the surroundings. In these marginal areas, human activity may stress the ecosystem beyond its tolerance limit, resulting in degradation of the land. » (= « Après les pluies, les zones végétalisées sont nettement plus fraîches que les zones environnantes. Dans ces zones marginales, l'activité humaine peut stresser l'écosystème au delà de sa limite de tolérance, ce qui entraîne une dégradation des terres. »)*
(D) ✓ Studies made clear that, as we still have an incomplete knowledge of the process of desertification, it may still be possible to recover some areas.	**= Les études ont montré que, comme nous avons une connaissance encore incomplète du processus de désertification, il est peut-être encore possible de récupérer certaines zones.** ***« Contrary to many popular reports, desertification is actually a subtle and complex process of deterioration that may often be reversible. » (= « Contrairement à ce qui est couramment admis, la désertification est en fait un processus subtil et complexe de détérioration qui peut souvent être réversible. »)***
(E) Studies revealed that the process of desertification is not reversible, but it can be prevented through constant monitoring and the use of snow fences in colder areas.	= Les études ont révélé que le processus de désertification n'est pas réversible, mais qu'il peut être évité grâce à une surveillance constante et à l'utilisation de barrières à neige dans les zones plus froides. *L'auteur spécifie que, dans certains cas, la désertification pourrait être réversible. Le suivi et les barrières pour la neige ne sont pas mentionnées comme des mesures.*
(F) ✓ Measures that include the planting of trees and their protection from wind currents, could be fundamental to start a chain mechanism of recovery.	**= Des mesures comprenant la plantation d'arbres et leur protection contre les courants des vents, pourraient être fondamentales pour démarrer un mécanisme de récupération en chaîne.** ***Ce sytème presque autonome et bien illustré dans le paragraphe 7.***

■ **Question 11 - Solution**

According to paragraph 1, which is true about storytelling?

FR : D'après le paragraphe 1, qu'est-ce qui est vrai au sujet de la narration ?

(A)	**✓ Storytelling gives the possibility to operate minor changes to the text during a performance.**	**= La narration donne la possibilité d'opérer des changements mineurs au niveau du texte pendant la représentation.** ***« The story-teller can look at her audience and is free to add a descriptive word or phrase occasionally to produce vividness of impression. »*** ***(= « La narratrice peut regarder son public et est libre d'ajouter un mot ou une phrase descriptive de temps en temps pour rendre la narration plus vivante. »)***
(B)	Storytelling is more effective when delivered in the form of manuscripts.	= La narration est plus efficace lorsqu'elle est présentée sous forme de manuscrits. *Les manuscrits sont simplement mentionnés pour illustrer le fait que même une lecture simple peut se révélé moins engageante que qu'un discours sans recours à la lecture d'un texte.*
(C)	Storytelling is practiced by those who have studied literature and cannot substitute the reading.	= La narration d'histoires est pratiquée par ceux qui ont étudié la littérature et ne peut se substituer à la lecture. *Le texte dit quelque chose de différent. L'auteur suggère que ceux qui veulent enseigner la littérature aux enfants doivent d'abord être de bons narrateurs.*
(D)	Storytelling gives the audience a unique experience through vivid and descriptive manuscripts.	= La narration d'histoires permet au public de vivre une expérience unique grâce à des manuscrits vivants et descriptifs. *La narration est bien une expérience unique pour l'audience mais sans usage de manuscrits.*

- **Question 12 - Solution**

According to paragraph 2, the selection of stories should be based on the following criteria EXCEPT:

FR : D'après le paragraphe 2, la sélection des histoires devrait être basée selon les critères suivants SAUF :

(A)	Do not tell a story you do not like	= Ne racontez pas une histoire que vous n'aimez pas. *« Never attempt to tell a story that you do not like. »* *(= « N'essayez jamais de raconter une histoire que vous n'aimez pas. »)*
(B)	Do not tell a story you are not interested in yourself	= Ne racontez pas une histoire qui ne vous intéresse pas. *« You are not prepared to interest pupils in a story, however appropriate it otherwise may be, if you are not interested in it yourself. »* *(= « Vous n'êtes pas prêt à intéresser des élèves à une histoire, aussi appropriée soit-elle par ailleurs, si vous ne vous y intéressez pas vous-même. »)*
(C)	Stories should be chosen based on the target age group, content and structure	= Les histoires devraient être choisies en fonction du groupe d'âge cible, du contenu et de la structure. *« Try to choose stories adapted in structure and content to the age and experience of the children of your grade. »* *(= « Essayez de choisir des histoires dont la structure et le contenu sont adaptés à l'âge et à l'expérience des enfants de votre classe. »)*
(D)	✓ **Stories should be long for first and second grade students**	**= Les histoires doivent être longues pour des élèves de première et deuxième année de primaire.** ***« For the first or second grade, choose a few simple fables, a few short, simple fairy tales, and a few short, simple nature stories ».*** ***(= « Pour la première ou la deuxième année de primaire, choisissez quelques fables simples, quelques contes de fées et quelques récits sur la nature qui soient à la fois courts et simples. »)***

▪ Question 13 - Solution

It can be concluded that following the two principles is important because:

FR : Il peut être conclu que suivre les deux principes est important car:

(A)	**✓ Telling a story in past tense, and with the use of direct discourse between characters, gives the story its clearness and effectiveness.**	**= Raconter une histoire au passé, et avec l'utilisation du discours direct entre les personnages, donne à l'histoire clarté et efficacité.** ***« First, use the past tense in telling a story except in direct quotation. The rules of grammar require this, and it is an aid to clearness and effectiveness. »*** ***(= « Tout d'abord, utilisez le passé dans le récit d'une histoire, sauf dans les citations directes. Les règles de grammaire l'exigent, et c'est une aide à la clarté et à l'efficacité. »)***
(B)	Telling a story in simple tense imbued with direct quotations and indirect discourse gives the story its clearness and effectiveness.	= Raconter une histoire en utilisant des temps simples, mêlant discours direct et discours indirect donne à l'histoire clarté et efficacité. *L'emploi du terme « indirect discourse » est contradictoire avec ce qui est dit dans le texte où on insiste sur l'emploi du « direct discourse » (synonyme de « direct quotation »).*
(C)	Telling a story in past tense imbued with indirect quotations and direct discourse gives the story its clearness and effectiveness.	= Raconter une histoire au passé mêlant discours direct et discours indirect donne à l'histoire clarté et efficacité. *L'emploi du terme « indirect quotation » invalide cette réponse pour les mêmes raisons que la réponse (B).*
(D)	Telling a story in past tense, and with the use of direct discourse between the storytellers, gives the story its clearness and effectiveness.	= Raconter une histoire au passé, et avec l'utilisation du discours direct entre les narrateurs, donne à l'histoire clarté et efficacité. *L'emploi du discours direct n'est pas entre les narrateurs mais entre les personnages.*

▪ Question 14 - Solution

According to paragraph 4, which of the following sentences best describes what are the things that should be kept in mind when it comes to telling a fable? The other choices change the meaning or leave out information.

FR : D'après le paragraphe 4, parmi les phrases suivantes, laquelle décrit le mieux les choses à garder en tête lorsqu'on raconte une fable ? Les autres choix changent le sens ou omettent des informations.

(A) Use past tense and direct discourse while also trying to add more conversation and descriptions of the characters in the text

= Utiliser le passé et le discours direct tout en essayant d'ajouter plus de détails sur la conversation et les descriptions des personnages dans le texte.
Ici la phrase parle d'ajouter des descriptions et des conversations dans le texte. Ce n'est pas de cette façon que le texte formulait la règle. Il s'agit plutôt d'ajouter des éléments qui ne sont pas dans le texte.

(B) Use past tense and direct discourse while also adding indirect conversations and character descriptions not in the text

= Utiliser le passé et le discours direct tout en ajoutant des dialogues au discours indirect et des descriptions de personnages qui ne sont pas dans le texte.
Un des pré-requis est d'utiliser les discours directs dès qu'il s'agit de conversations. C'est contradictoire avec l'emploi du terme « conversations indirectes ».

(C) ✓ Use past tense and direct discourse while also adding much more conversation and description that are not particularly present in the text

= Utiliser le passé et le discours direct tout en ajoutant beaucoup plus de dialogues et de descriptions qui ne sont pas forcément présents dans le texte.

(D) Use past tense and indirect discourse while also adding direct conversations and character descriptions not in the text

= Utiliser le passé et le discours indirect tout en ajoutant des dialogues au discours direct et des descriptions de personnages qui ne sont pas présents dans le texte.
L'emploi du terme « discours indirect » invalide cette proposition.

⇒ **explication**
FR : *« If the story is a fable, you probably will see that you should add much conversation and description not in the text. »* (paragraphe 4) (= « Si l'histoire est une fable, vous allez probablement constater que vous devrez ajouter beaucoup de conversations et de descriptions qui ne sont pas dans le texte. »)

▪ Question 15 - Solution

Which of the following sentences best describes the highlighted sentence in the passage? The other choices change the meaning or leave out information.

"Some stories, of course, are so lacking in action as to be not well suited for dramatization, and others have details of action, character, or situation that may not well be represented in the schoolroom."

FR : Parmi les phrases suivantes, laquelle décrit le mieux la phrase soulignée dans le passage ? Les autres choix changent le sens ou omettent des informations.

(A)	**✓ While some stories may have a story line that lacks action suited for dramatization, others might have just too detailed characters, actions or situations to be suitable for classroom audiences.**	**= Alors que certaines histoires peuvent avoir une trame qui manque d'action pour une mise en scène, d'autres peuvent avoir des personnages, des actions ou des situations trop détaillées pour être adaptées en classe.**
(B)	Some stories lack the action needed for dramatization, while others might have details of action, character, or situation that could be very well suited for students in the schoolroom.	= Certaines histoires n'ont pas l'action nécessaire à une dramatisation, alors que d'autres peuvent avoir des détails sur l'action, les personnages ou les situations qui pourraient très bien convenir à des élèves en classe. *La deuxième partie de la phrase dit l'exact contraire de ce qui était affirmé.*
(C)	Some actions, characters, or situations may well be represented in the schoolroom while some story lines lack the attention suited for dramatization.	= Certaines actions, certains personnages ou certaines situations pourraient très bien être représentés dans une salle de classe, alors que certaines histoires manquent de précision pour être mises en scène. *L'opposition dans la phrase soulignée ne porte pas sur les histoires qui se prêtent à la théâtralisation contre celles qui ne le sont pas. Elle compare deux cas de figure qui se prêtent difficilement à la théâtralisation.*
(D)	Some stories have more attention-grabbing storylines than others.	= Certaines histoires ont des intrigues qui attirent plus facilement l'attention que d'autres. *La phrase ne dit pas que certaines histoires sont moins captivantes que d'autres mais qu'elles peuvent se prêter plus difficilement à une théâtralisation en classe.*

⇒ **explication**

FR : Certaines histoires, bien sûr, manquent tellement d'action qu'elles ne se prêtent pas à la théâtralisation, et d'autres présentent des détails concernant l'action, les personnages ou la situation qui pourraient ne pas être facilement mis en scène dans une salle de classe.

▪ Question 16 - Solution

The word "gruff" in paragraph 5 is closest in meaning to:

FR : Le mot « bourru » dans le paragraphe 5 a une signification plus proche de :

(A) cheerful = joyeux

(B) tactful = précautionneux

(C) kind = gentil

(D) ✓ grumpy = grincheux
On pouvait deviner que ce synonyme correspondait par élimination car les autres mots font référence à des termes plus doux. Or, le mot était positionné entre les termes « loud » (= fort) et « harsh » (= dur).

▪ Question 17 - Solution

The word "omitted" in paragraph 4 refers to:

FR : Le mot « omitted » dans le paragraphe 4 fait référence à :

(A)	**✓ leave out**	**= laisser de côté**
(B)	include	= inclure
(C)	attend	= assister à
(D)	notice	= remarquer

■ Question 18 - Solution

Why does the author mention the importance of dramatization in paragraph 6?

FR : Pourquoi l'auteur mentionne l'importance de la théâtralisation dans le paragraphe 6 ?

(A)	To discuss the relevance of pupils failing to face their difficulties and express their literary appreciation	= Pour aborder la question de la pertinence des élèves qui ne parviennent pas à faire face à leurs difficultés et à exprimer leur sensibilité littéraire. *Le texte ne mentionne pas le fait que la théâtralisation peut aider les élèves à résoudre leurs problèmes.*
(B)	**✓ To argue that dramatizing stories can not only help students overcome difficulties in playing out stories, but it would also make them better speakers, readers by also developing a sense of literary appreciation in the process**	**= Pour affirmer que la mise en scène des histoires peut non seulement aider les élèves à surmonter les difficultés qu'ils rencontrent en jouant des rôles, mais aussi faire d'eux de meilleurs orateurs et lecteurs en développant également un sens de l'appréciation littéraire par la même occasion.** ***« Unconsciously the pupil will get from the dramatization a training in oral English, reading, and literary appreciation that can hardly be gained in any other way. » (= « Inconsciemment, l'élève tirera de la mise en scène une formation à l'anglais oral, à la lecture et à la critique littéraire qui ne peut guère être acquise d'une autre manière. »)***
(C)	To prove that dramatization is the one and only tool that can help students overcome their fears of public speaking and literary appreciation	= Pour prouver que la théâtralisation est le seul et unique outil qui puisse aider les élèves à surmonter leur peur de parler en public et d'apprécier la littérature. *L'auteur dit que la théâtralisation permet d'acquérir une combinaison d'éléments (goût pour la littérature, entraînement à l'anglais oral…) qui pourrait difficilement être acquise autrement. Mais il ne dit pas que chacun de ces éléments ne peut être acquis autrement.*
(D)	To make a comparison between ingenious pupils and their process of overcoming individual difficulties	= Pour faire une comparaison entre des élèves astucieux et leur processus permettant de surmonter des difficultés individuelles. *L'auteur dit que les étudiants peuvent se montrer ingénieux via la théâtralisation mais il ne va pas plus loin à ce sujet.*

■ Question 19 - Solution

Look at the four squares in paragraph 1, **A**, **B**, **C**, and **D**, which indicate where the following sentence could be added to the passage. Where would the sentence best fit?

Much of the superiority probably comes from the freedom of the "talk style" and the more appropriate use of inflection and emphasis.

[P1] **A** Most stories are more effective when well told than they are when read, just as most lectures and sermons are most effective when delivered without manuscript. **B** The story-teller can look at her audience and is free to add a descriptive word or phrase occasionally to produce vividness of impression. **C** Some stories, of course, are so constructed that they must follow closely the diction of the original form. "Henny-Penny" and Kipling's Just-So Stories are of this type. Such stories should be read. Most stories, however, are most effective when well told. The teacher, especially the teacher of one of the primary grades, should not consider herself prepared to teach literature until she has gained something of the art of story-telling. **D**

(A) **A** *Pour l'insérer au début du paragraphe, il aurait fallu qu'il y ait au moins une brève mention au concept de supériorité dans la phrase pour que celle-ci ait du sens.*

(B) ✓ **B** ***Insérer la phrase à cet endroit ajoute de la clarté au paragraphe et apporte plus de détails à la première phrase.***

(C) **C** *Même si cela semble correct, le concept de supériorité a déjà été présenté plus tôt dans le texte.*

(D) **D** *L'auteur a déjà terminé son illustration de la puissance du storytelling par rapport à la celle de la lecture et est passé à un autre sujet, plus spécifiquement celui du storytelling dans l'enseignement de la littérature.*

⇨ **explication**

FR : Traduction de l'extrait à insérer dans le paragraphe :
(= « Une grande partie de cette supériorité vient probablement de la liberté du "language oral" et de l'utilisation plus appropriée de l'intonation et de l'accentuation. »)

▪ Question 20 - Solution

Directions:

An introductory sentence for a brief summary of the passage is provided below.

Complete the summary by selecting the THREE answer choices that express the most important ideas in the passage. Some sentences do not belong in the summary because they express ideas that are not presented in the passage or are minor ideas in the passage.

This question is worth 2 points.

- The precious art of story-telling makes stories come to life and engages the audience even more.
- ________
- ________
- ________

(A) Story-tellers should pay particular attention to the use of the past tense and direct discourse, because the children listening to them will replicate their use of grammar when "playing" their own stories.

= Les narrateurs doivent prêter une attention particulière à l'utilisation du passé et du discours direct, car les enfants qui les écoutent reproduiront leur utilisation de la grammaire lorsqu'ils « joueront » leurs propres histoires.
L'auteur mentionne les structures grammaticales et le temps des verbes à utiliser car ils sont nécessaires à la nature même des histoires "racontées". Il ne s'agit pas d'introduire ces changements pour transformer l'activité en leçon de grammaire.

(B) ✓ Story-tellers should be passionate about the story they are telling.

= Les narrateurs doivent être passionnés par l'histoire qu'ils racontent.
C'est le message le plus important du paragraphe 2.

(C) ✓ Story-tellers should be aware that there are certain grammar structures to use and that the type length of the story might require them to make some changes.

= Les conteurs doivent être conscients qu'il y a des structures grammaticales à respecter et que la longueur de l'histoire peut les obliger à apporter quelques modifications.
Cette phrase résume bien le contenu des paragraphes 3, 4 et 5. Les changements mentionnés dans la phrase incluent à la fois le ton de voix et les changements apportés au texte.

(D) Story-tellers should work on differentiating the voice they use for a princess from the one they use for the soldier and speak with a louder voice to avoid children from getting distracted.

= Les narrateurs doivent s'efforcer de différencier la voix qu'ils utilisent pour la princesse de celle qu'ils utilisent pour le soldat et parler plus fort pour éviter que les enfants ne se déconcentrent.
L'auteur mentionne la princesse et soldat comme des exemples dans le but d'illustrer l'importance des tons de voix lorsque l'on lit des histoires. De plus, l'auteur suggère que les lecteurs doivent jouer avec le volume de leur voix, par moment en parlant moins fort.

(E) ✓ Teachers should give children the chance to "play" stories because it constitutes an extremely effective educational strategy.

= Les enseignants devraient donner aux enfants la possibilité de « jouer » aux histoires car cela constitue une stratégie éducative extrêmement efficace.
C'est l'information la plus importante du paragraphe 7 : « Unconsciously, the pupil will get from the dramatization a training in oral English, reading, and literary appreciation that can hardly be gained in any other way. »
(= « Inconsciemment, l'élève tirera de la mise en scène une formation à l'anglais oral, à la lecture et à l'appréciation littéraire qui ne peut guère être acquise d'une autre manière. »)

(F) Teachers should help children dramatize the various stories, so that they can learn the rudiments of acting without getting bored.

= Les enseignants doivent aider les enfants à mettre en scène les différentes histoires, afin qu'ils puissent apprendre les rudiments du théâtre sans s'ennuyer.
Le but n'est pas d'apprendre aux élèves les rudiments du théâtre mais de la littérature.

- **Question 21 - Solution**

In paragraph 1, which of the following is true about geothermal energy?

FR : Dans le premier paragraphe, qu'est-ce qui est vrai au sujet de l'énergie géothermique ?

(A)	**✓ It can be found below Earth's surface and is concentrated in regions of geologically active volcanoes.**	**= On la trouve sous la surface de la Terre et elle est concentrée dans les régions où se trouvent des volcans géologiquement actifs.** ***« Geothermal energy is present everywhere beneath the Earth's surface, concentrated in regions of active or geologically young volcanoes ».*** ***(= « L'énergie géothermique est présente partout sous la surface de la Terre, concentrée dans les régions de volcans actifs ou géologiquement jeunes. »)***
(B)	Geothermal energy has unique attributes whose characteristics are similar to those of certain geothermal activities.	= L'énergie géothermique possède des attributs uniques dont les caractéristiques sont similaires à celles de certaines activités géothermiques. *« many aspects of geothermal energy are akin to characteristics of mineral and fossil-fuel resources. » (= « de nombreux aspects de l'énergie géothermique s'apparentent aux caractéristiques des ressources minérales et des combustibles fossiles. »)*
(C)	Geothermal energy is present everywhere above the Earth's surface.	= L'énergie géothermique est présente partout au-dessus de la surface de la Terre. *«[Geothermal energy] is present everywhere beneath the Earth's surface. » (= « [L'énergie géothermique] est présente partout sous la surface de la Terre. »)*
(D)	Geothermal energy includes physical substances such as gold or coal.	= L'énergie géothermique comprend des éléments physiques tels que l'or ou le charbon. *« Though the resource is thermal energy rather than a physical substance such as gold or coal »* *(= « Bien que la ressource soit l'énergie thermique plutôt qu'une substance physique comme l'or ou le charbon. »)*

⟹ **explication**

FR : L'idée ici était de vérifier la bonne compréhension quant à l'origine de l'énergie géothermique.

- **Question 22 - Solution**

According to paragraph 2, we can infer that:

FR : On peut déduire du paragraphe 2 que :

(A)	✓ **Companies would not consider selling minerals if their deposits were unreachable.**	**= Les entreprises n'envisageraient pas de vendre des minéraux si leurs gisements étaient inaccessibles.** ***« For mineral and geothermal deposits alike, concentrations of the natural resource should be significantly higher than average (the background level) for the Earth's crust and must be at depths accessible by present-day extraction technologies before commercial development is feasible. »*** ***(= « Pour les gisements minéraux comme pour les gisements géothermiques, les concentrations de la ressource naturelle doivent être nettement supérieures à la moyenne (le niveau de fond) de la croûte terrestre et doivent se trouver à des profondeurs accessibles par les technologies d'extraction actuelles pour que le développement commercial soit réalisable. »)***
(B)	The grade of mineral deposits can be compared to volume.	= La qualité des gisements de minéraux peut être comparée à leur volume. *« Grade would be roughly comparable to temperature. » (= « La qualité serait à peu près comparable à la température. »)*
(C)	Deposits of geothermal energy leave traces of ore.	= Les gisements d'énergie géothermique laissent des traces de minerai. *Cela n'est pas mentionné dans le paragraphe.*
(D)	Mineral deposits need to be deep enough below Earth's crust in order to be reached.	= Les gisements de minerais doivent être suffisamment profondément enfouis sous la croûte terrestre pour être atteints. *L'auteur clarifie seulement le fait que les dépôts de minéraux ainsi que ceux de l'énergie géothermique doivent être accessibles.*

▪ Question 23 - Solution

The word "akin" in the passage refers to:

FR : Le mot « akin » dans le passage fait référence à :

(A)	parallel	= parallèle
(B)	ideal	= idéal
(C) ✓	**similar**	**= similaire**
(D)	opposite	= opposé

⟹ **explication**
FR : Traduction du contexte :
« L'énergie géothermique a des attributs désirables et uniques, de plus, de nombreux aspects de l'énergie géothermique sont **proches** des caractéristiques des minéraux et autres énergies fossiles. »

▪ Question 24 - Solution

Which of the following sentences best describes the highlighted sentence in the passage? The other choices change the meaning or leave out information.

FR : Laquelle des propositions suivantes décrit le mieux la phrase surlignée dans le passage ? Les autres propositions changent le sens ou omettent des informations.

(A)	**✓ Geothermal energy extraction can be carried out without the use and construction of mine shafts, tunnels, waste heaps or open pits.**	**= L'extraction de l'énergie géothermique peut se faire sans avoir recours à la construction de puits de mine, de tunnels, de terrils ou de puits à ciel ouvert.**
(B)	Geothermal energy extraction can be facilitated without the large-scale movement of rocks and mining operations.	= L'extraction d'énergie géothermique peut être facilitée sans déplacement de roches à grande échelle et sans opérations minières. *Le terme facilitated change le sens de la phrase.*
(C)	The extraction of geothermal energy is accomplished with the help of large-scale mining operations, such as construction of mine shafts and tunnels, open pits, and waste heaps.	= L'extraction de l'énergie géothermique est réalisée à l'aide d'opérations minières à grande échelle, telles que la construction de puits et de tunnels de mine, de puits à ciel ouvert et de terrils.
(D)	The extraction of geothermal energy is all about the construction of mine shafts and tunnels, open pits, and waste heaps.	= L'extraction de l'énergie géothermique se fait par la construction de puits et de tunnels, de mines à ciel ouvert et de terrils.

⟹ **explication**

FR : Traduction de la phrase à paraphraser :

« L'extraction de l'énergie géothermique est réalisée sans avoir besoin de déplacer des grandes quantités de roche comme c'est le cas dans les opérations de minage, avec, par exemple, la construction de puits miniers, de tunnels, de fosses à ciel ouvert et de terrils. »

■ Question 25 - Solution

According to the passage, geothermal energy has a number of other uses EXCEPT:

FR : Selon le passage, l'énergie géothermique est utilisée de nombreuses autres façons à l'exception de :

(A)	It can help heat and cool a single residence.	= Elle peut contribuer à chauffer et à refroidir une seule résidence. *« geothermal energy can help heat and cool a single residence »* *(= « l'énergie géothermique peut aider à chauffer et à refroidir une seule résidence »)*
(B)	It is a commercially viable heating and cooling system currently in use in many households.	= Il s'agit d'un système de chauffage et de refroidissement commercialement viable, actuellement utilisé dans de nombreux foyers. *« the heat pump and the Earth's thermal energy form a small, effective, and commercially viable heating and cooling system. Heat pump systems are already in use at more than 350,000 buildings »* *(= « la pompe à chaleur et l'énergie thermique de la Terre forment un système de chauffage et de refroidissement petit, efficace et commercialement viable. Les systèmes de pompe à chaleur sont déjà utilisés dans plus de 350 000 bâtiments »)*
(C)	It can be harnessed to generate electricity.	= Elle peut être exploitée pour produire de l'électricité. *« a single large volume, high-temperature deposit of geothermal energy can be harnessed to generate electricity »* *(= « un seul gisement d'énergie géothermique de grand volume et à haute température peut être exploité pour produire de l'électricité »)*
(D)	**✓ It circulates water or some other fluid for cooling heat pump systems.**	**= Elle fait circuler de l'eau ou un autre fluide pour refroidir les systèmes de pompe à chaleur.** ***Elle est utilisée pour rafraîchir les maisons, pas les pompes à chaleur.***

■ Question 26 - Solution

Which of the following statements most accurately reflects the author's opinion about the commercial use of geothermal energy?

FR : Laquelle de ces propositions reflète le mieux l'opinion de l'auteur à propos de l'exploitation commerciale de l'énergie géothermique ?

(A)	The author sees geothermal resources as a viable source of energy and instructs governmental agencies to find new innovative ways to incorporate these energy sources into the mix for the whole world to benefit.	= L'auteur considère les ressources géothermiques comme une source d'énergie viable et ordonne aux agences gouvernementales de trouver de nouveaux moyens innovants d'intégrer ces sources d'énergie dans le mix pour que le monde entier en profite. *L'auteur n'est pas en train « d'ordonner » au gouvernement quoi que ce soit.*
(B)	The author sees geothermal resources as a viable source of energy and challenges governmental agencies to find new innovative ways to incorporate these energy sources into the mix for the whole world to benefit.	= L'auteur considère les ressources géothermiques comme une source d'énergie viable et met au défi les agences gouvernementales de trouver des moyens novateurs d'intégrer ces sources d'énergie dans le mix énergétique pour que le monde entier en profite. *L'auteur ne « lance pas un défi » au gouvernement. Il dit que l'énergie géothermique est un défi pour le gouvernement.*
(C)	✓ **The author sees geothermal resources as a viable source of energy and goes on to express his belief that governmental agencies need to find new innovative ways to incorporate these energy sources into the mix for the whole world to benefit.**	**= L'auteur considère les ressources géothermiques comme une source d'énergie viable et poursuit en disant qu'il pense que les agences gouvernementales doivent trouver des moyens innovants d'intégrer ces sources d'énergie dans le mix énergétique pour que le monde entier en profite.** ***L'auteur partage effectivement son point de vue et pense que le gouvernement devrait mettre en place des mesures innovantes pour exploiter au mieux l'énergie géothermique.***
(D)	The assessment and distribution of these resources cannot take place without establishing new ways to use geothermal energy worldwide.	= L'évaluation et la distribution de ces ressources ne peut se faire sans établir de nouveaux moyens d'utiliser l'énergie géothermique dans le monde entier. *L'expression « cannot take place » est exagérée. Certes l'auteur voudrait que le gouvernement mette en place de nouvelles mesures, mais il trouve que les mesures prises ont déjà un impact très positif.*

■ Question 27 - Solution

The word "harnessed" in paragraph 5 is closest in meaning to:

FR : Le mot « harnesses » dans le paragraphe 5 a un sens proche de :

(A) permit = permettre

(B) ✓ exploit = exploiter

(C) liberate = libérer

(D) detach = détacher

⇒ **explication**
FR : Littéralement, « *to harness* » veut dire exploiter quelque chose pour produire de l'énergie.

▪ Question 28 - Solution

According to paragraph 4, how many heat pump systems are already in use in the United States?

FR : D'après le paragraphe 4, combien de pompes à chaleur sont déjà utilisées aux États-Unis ?

(A)	less than 350,000	= moins de 350 000
(B)	35,000	= 35 000
(C) ✓	**more than 350,000**	**= plus de 350 000**
(D)	more than 350,000 but less than 400,000	= plus de 350 000 mais moins de 400 000 *Rien n'indique qu'il n'y ait pas plus de 400 000 pompes à chaleur aux États-Unis.*

⇒ **explication**
FR : *"Heat pump systems are already in use at more than 350,000 buildings in the United States."* (= « Les systèmes de pompe à chaleur sont déjà utilisés dans plus de 350 000 immeubles aux États-Unis. »)

▪ Question 29 - Solution

Look at the four squares in paragraph 1, **A**, **B**, **C**, and **D**, which indicate where the following sentence could be added to the passage. Where would the sentence best fit?

Alarming is also the disposal of some geothermal fluids, which may contain low levels of toxic materials.

[P1] Geothermal energy is simply power derived from the Earth's internal heat. **A** It is present everywhere beneath the Earth's surface, although the highest temperature, and thus the most desirable resources are concentrated in regions of active or geologically young volcanoes. There are many advantages of geothermal energy. **B** It can be extracted without burning a fossil fuel such as coal or oil. Geothermal fields produce only about one-sixth of the carbon dioxide that a clean natural-gas-fueled power plant produces. **C** It does have some environmental problems, namely the release of hydrogen sulfide at low concentrations. **D** Though the resource is thermal energy rather than a physical substance such as gold or coal, many aspects of geothermal energy are akin to characteristics of mineral and fossil-fuel resources.

(A) **A** *L'auteur est toujours en train de présenter les principales caractéristiques de l'énergie géothermique, cela n'aurait pas de sens d'insérer ici une phrase sur ses aspects négatifs.*

(B) **B** *En insérant la phrase ici, cela viendrait en opposition avec la phrase précédente étant donné que l'auteur vient de commencer à présenter les aspects positifs de l'énergie géothermique.*

(C) **C** *Insérer la phrase ici compromettrait la cohérence et la cohésion du paragraphe. La présence de l'adverbe « also » dans la phrase nous indique que qu'il faut que la nouvelle phrase suive la présentation d'un premier aspect négatif de l'énergie géothermique.*

(D) ✓ D ***C'est la position la plus naturelle pour la phrase à insérer. En effet, elle ajoute un aspect négatif supplémentaire avec l'adverbe « also » et il n'y a pas de conflit avec la phrase qui suit.***

▪ Question 30 - Solution

Directions:

An introductory sentence for a brief summary of the passage is provided below.

Complete the summary by selecting the THREE answer choices that express the most important ideas in the passage. Some sentences do not belong in the summary because they express ideas that are not presented in the passage or are minor ideas in the passage.

This question is worth 2 points.

- Geothermal energy is a natural resource that can be found beneath the Earth's crust.
- ________
- ________
- ________

(A)	**✓ The circumstances under which geothermal energy is evaluated and eventually retrieved, are not much dissimilar from those of minerals.**	**= Les conditions dans lesquelles l'énergie géothermique est évaluée et finalement récupérée ne sont pas très différentes de celles des minéraux.** ***Cette phrase est un bon résumé du paragraphe 2.***
(B)	Being unevenly distributed beneath the Earth's surface, geothermal energy is rarer and more valuable than minerals, but also more dangerous, due to its toxic properties.	= Étant inégalement répartie sous la surface de la Terre, l'énergie géothermique est plus rare et plus précieuse que les minéraux, mais aussi plus dangereuse, en raison de ses propriétés toxiques. *L'information est incorrecte. L'auteur ne mentionne que l'énergie géothermique est plus rare ou qu'elle est plus dangereuse.*
(C)	Geothermal energy is often used, through a system of pumps, to heat and cool houses depending on the need.	= L'énergie géothermique est souvent utilisée, par le biais d'un système de pompes, pour chauffer et refroidir les maisons en fonction des besoins. *Même si cette information est correcte, elle reste secondaire. Le sytème de pompes est juste un exemple.*
(D)	The Geysers in northern California represent the biggest deposit of geothermal energy in the world.	= Les Geysers du nord de la Californie représentent le plus grand gisement d'énergie géothermique au monde. *Cela n'est pas mentionné dans le texte. L'auteur écrit : « With a generating capacity of about 1,000 megawatts electric, The Geysers is presently the largest group of geothermally powered electrical plants in the world. » (= « Avec une capacité de production d'environ 1 000 mégawatts électriques, The Geysers est actuellement le plus grand groupe de centrales électriques alimentées par la géothermie au monde. »)*

(E) ✓ **The biggest differences between geothermal energy and other natural resources are its easier extraction process and its much more flexible employability.**

= Les plus grandes différences entre l'énergie géothermique et les autres ressources naturelles sont son processus d'extraction plus facile et son employabilité beaucoup plus flexible.

« Geothermal energy is usable over a very wide spectrum of temperature and volume, whereas the benefits of other natural resources can be reaped only if a deposit exceeds some minimum size and (or) grade for profitable exploitation or efficiency of operation. »
(= « L'énergie géothermique est utilisable sur un très large spectre de température et de volume, alors que les avantages d'autres ressources naturelles ne peuvent être récoltés que si un gisement dépasse une taille et (ou) une teneur minimales pour une exploitation rentable ou une efficacité d'exploitation. »)

En seulement quelques mots, la phrase résume les paragraphes 4 et 5.

(F) ✓ **Better and more beneficial ways to exploit geothermal energy are yet to be found.**

= Il reste à trouver des moyens plus efficaces et plus avantageux d'exploiter l'énergie géothermique.
« The challenge, for governmental agencies and the private sector alike, is to assess the amount and distribution of these resources, to work toward new and inventive ways to use this form of energy, and to incorporate geothermal into an appropriate energy mix for the Nation and the world. »
(= « Le défi, tant pour les agences gouvernementales que pour le secteur privé, est d'évaluer la quantité et la distribution de ces ressources, de travailler à des moyens novateurs d'utiliser cette forme d'énergie et d'intégrer la géothermie dans un mix énergétique approprié pour la nation et le monde. »)

Conversion de votre résultat en score TOEFL iBT sur 30

Votre nombre de points (maximum 36 points avec les questions valant deux points)	Estimation score TOEFL iBT
35-36	30
34	29
33	28
32	27
31	26
30	25
29	24
28	23
27	22
26	21
25	20
24	19
23	18
22	17
21	16
20	15
19	14
18	13
17	12
16	11
15	10
14	9
13	8
12	7
11	6
10	5
9	4
8	3
7	2
5-6	1
0-4	0

TOEFL iBT #2 - LISTENING - Solutions

Reportez vos réponses pour analyser votre performance.

Entraînez-vous dans les conditions d'examen.

Écoutez les fichiers audio.

prepmyfuture.com/book/68/ex/1987

question 1	C	question 7	B	question 13	D	question 19	A	question 24	B
question 2	D	question 8	A	question 14	C	question 20	A	question 25	A
question 3	A	question 9	C	question 15	A	question 21	A	question 26	B
question 4	A	question 10	B	question 16	A	question 22	C	question 27	C
question 5	D	question 11	D	question 17	B	question 23	A	question 28	D
question 6	D	question 12	D	question 18	B				

Question 1 - Solution

What is the discussion mainly about?

FR : Quel est le sujet principal du cours ?

(A)		the difficulties faced when casting a play	= les difficultés rencontrées lors de la distribution d'une pièce de théâtre
(B)		the cost of attending a play in Shakespeare's day	= le coût de la représentation d'une pièce de théâtre à l'époque de Shakespeare
(C)	✓	**the 17th century theater in London**	**= le coût de la représentation d'une pièce de théâtre à l'époque de Shakespeare** ***« Oh yes, we were talking about Shakespeare's theaters and we said that the first playhouse built as such in Elizabethan London… »*** ***(= « Ah oui, nous parlions des théâtres de Shakespeare et nous disions que le premier théâtre construit comme tel dans le Londres élisabéthain… »)***
(D)		the relationship between the actors and the company	= la relation entre les acteurs et la compagnie

⇨ **explication**

FR : Les réponses A, B et D font référence à des détails du discours. Il s'agit de détails mineurs, seule la réponse C résume la discussion dans son ensemble.

Question 2 - Solution

Listen again to part of the lecture. Then answer the question.

Script non affiché le jour de l'examen :

> **PROFESSOR:** Please be sure to check the student platform. Are there any questions? Anyway, let's continue from last week's lesson. Where were we? Oh yes, we were talking about Shakespeare's theaters and we said [...]

Why does the professor say this:

"...Anyway, let's continue from last week's lesson. Where were we? Oh yes..."

FR : Pourquoi le professeur dit-il ceci : "... Peu importe, continuons le cours de la semaine dernière. Où en étions-nous ? Ah oui ..."

(A)	He is lost and needs to find his way back to class.	= Il est perdu et doit retrouver le chemin de la classe. *Le professeur est dans la salle de cours. Il a déjà commencé son cours.*
(B)	He wants the students to help him recall last week's class.	= Il veut que les élèves l'aident à se souvenir du cours de la semaine dernière. *C'est une question rhétorique qui n'attend pas de réponse. Le professeur répond lui-même à sa propre question.*
(C)	He hopes to get the class to pay attention.	= Il veut que les élèves l'aident à se souvenir du cours de la semaine dernière.
(D)	✓ **He takes a pause to remember where he is in his lesson.**	**= Il veut que les élèves l'aident à se souvenir du cours de la semaine dernière.** ***Le professeur se parle à lui-même car il répond à sa propre question.***

▪ Question 3 - Solution

Listen again to part of the lecture. Then answer the question.

> **Script non affiché le jour de l'examen :**
>
> **PROFESSOR:** A full house might consist of 800 groundlings and 1500 in the galleries, with a dozen more exclusive seats on the stage itself for the gentry.

According to the professor, what does the term "groundling" mean?

FR : Selon le professeur, que signifie le terme « groundling » ?

(A)	✓ **audience members who paid the least for their seats**	**= les membres du public qui ont payé le moins cher pour leur place** ***« This was the cheapest price in order to see a play. The "groundlings," as they were called, stood around the three sides of the stage, in the open air. »*** ***(= « C'était le prix le moins cher pour voir une pièce. Les "groundlings", comme on les appelait, se tenaient autour des trois côtés de la scène, en plein air. »)***
(B)	part of the stage that was on the ground	= la partie de la scène qui était située au sol *« Groundling » n'est pas synonyme de « ground » dans ce contexte.*
(C)	a small section of the seats where the gentry sat	= la partie de la scène qui était située au sol *Ces places sont destinées aux spectateurs les plus modestes.*
(D)	a member of the company	= un membre de la compagnie *Il s'agit d'une catégorie de spectateur.*

⟹ **explication**

FR : Le professeur utilise plusieurs fois le terme « *groundling* » pour désigner une catégorie de spectateur des pièces de théâtre : ceux dont les tickets étaient les moins chers et se tenaient debout devant la scène.

▪ Question 4 - Solution

How did the playwrights get around restrictions surrounding female performers?

FR : Comment les dramaturges contournaient-ils les restrictions concernant les actrices ?

(A)	✓ **They wrote creative parts for the actors.**	**= Ils ont écrit des rôles inventifs pour les acteurs.** ***« Remember that by law, actresses were not allowed, and female roles were performed by boys. Playwrights therefore devised parts to suit the actors who were available, and used creativity in order to overcome the absence of women » (paragraphe 3)*** ***(= « Rappelons que, selon la loi, les actrices n'étaient pas autorisées et que les rôles féminins étaient interprétés par des garçons. Les dramaturges ont donc imaginé des rôles adaptés aux acteurs disponibles et ont fait preuve de créativité pour pallier l'absence de femmes. »)***
(B)	Women were performing disguised as men.	= Les femmes jouaient déguisées en hommes. *Les femmes ne sont pas autorisées à jouer. Les héroïnes de Shakespeare étaient souvent habillées comme des jeunes hommes. Cela permettait aux hommes de jouer plus facilement ces rôles.*
(C)	They eliminated female characters.	= Ils ont éliminé les personnages féminins. *Ils étaient joués par des hommes.*
(D)	They performed the play outside the city limits to avoid problems with the authorities.	= Ils ont joué la pièce en dehors des limites de la ville pour éviter les problèmes avec les autorités. *Il est bien écrit que les pièces étaient jouées en périphérie des villes pour éviter d'entrer en conflit avec les autorités. Malgré cela le professeur précise que les metteurs en scènes ne faisaient pas jouer de femmes sur scène.*

▪ Question 5 - Solution

Why does the professor say that he checked records from the period about the theater's capacity?

FR : Pourquoi le professeur dit-il qu'il a vérifié les données d'époque sur la capacité d'accueil du théâtre ?

(A)	He is very interested in the records.	= Il est très intéressé par les archives.
(B)	He didn't know much about them.	= Il est très intéressé par les archives. *Il fournit des informations factuelles à ses étudiants.*
(C)	He wants the class to study like him.	= Il veut que la classe étudie comme lui.
(D)	✓ **He wasn't sure if they were correct.**	**= Il n'était pas sûr qu'ils soient corrects.** ***« When I was researching this, I couldn't believe that such a theater could hold so many people, but it must be accurate » (paragraphe 4)*** ***(= « Lorsque j'ai fait mes recherches, je n'arrivais pas à croire qu'un tel théâtre puisse contenir autant de personnes, mais ça doit être exact... »)***

⟹ **explication**

FR : La capacité d'accueil du théâtre lui paraissait tellement importante qu'elle ne semblait pas réaliste.

■ Question 6 - Solution

What can be inferred about the professor?

FR : Qu'est-ce qui peut être déduit à propos du professeur ?

(A)	He is a good actor.	= C'est un bon acteur. *Le professeur donne un cours sur le théâtre. Nous n'avons pas d'information sur ses talents d'acteur.*
(B)	He encourages his class to write plays.	= C'est un bon acteur.
(C)	He is not very patient with his students.	= Il n'est pas très patient avec ses élèves.
(D)	**✓ He is very well informed about English Renaissance theater.**	**= Il n'est pas très patient avec ses élèves.** ***On suppose donc que le professeur a une connaissance approfondie du sujet qu'il aborde.***

■ Question 7 - Solution

What is the lecture mainly about?

FR : Quel est le sujet principal du cours ?

(A)	how to tell the difference between a panic attack and a phobia	= comment faire la différence entre une crise de panique et une phobie *Il s'agit d'aborder les troubles de l'anxiété en général.*
(B)	**✓ the characteristics of anxiety disorders**	**= les caractéristiques des troubles de l'anxiété** ***« Today we will specifically discuss anxiety disorders »*** ***(= « Aujourd'hui, nous allons discuter plus spécifiquement des troubles de l'anxiété »)***
(C)	why psychological disorders are learned behaviors	= la raison pour laquelle les troubles psychologiques sont des comportements acquis *Il existe plusieurs causes aux troubles de l'anxiété :* *Cause 1 : « biological and cognitive factors » (= « les facteurs biologiques et cognitifs »)* *Cause 2 : « psychological and social factors » (= « les facteurs psychologiques et sociaux »)*
(D)	some of the psychological experiments performed on students	= la raison pour laquelle les troubles psychologiques sont des comportements acquis

■ Question 8 - Solution

Which of the following is an example of a genetic component in psychological disorders that was used in the lecture?

FR : Laquelle de ces propositions est un exemple utilisé dans le cours de composante génétique dans les désordres psychologiques ?

(A) ✓	**Anxiety that is present in identical twin pairs.**	**= L'anxiété présente dans les paires de vrais jumeaux.** ***« Research shows that if one identical twin has had an anxiety disorder, the other is more likely also to have an anxiety disorder than is the case in non-identical twin pairs. »*** ***(= « Les recherches montrent que si l'un des vrais jumeaux a souffert d'un trouble de l'anxiété, l'autre est plus susceptible de souffrir également d'un trouble de l'anxiété que dans le cas de paires de jumeaux non identiques. »)***
(B)	Phobias that are a result of problems in life.	= Les phobies qui sont le fruit de difficultés dans la vie.
(C)	Physical stress.	= Le stress physique *Le professeur mentionne les causes physiques qui peuvent déclencher des crises de panique. Il ne fait pas de lien avec la génétique à ce moment là.*
(D)	The ability to control the flow of carbon dioxide.	= La capacité à contrôler le débit de dioxyde de carbone. *Le professeur mentionne la capacité à réguler le dioxyde de carbone pour éviter une crise de panique. Aucun lien n'est fait à la génétique avec cet exemple.*

▪ Question 9 - Solution

What technique does the professor use to explain the development of a panic attack?

FR : Quelle technique le professeur utilise-t-il pour expliquer le développement d'une crise de panique ?

(A)	He asks the students to perform a simulation in the lab.	= Il demande aux étudiants de réaliser une simulation dans le laboratoire. *Il n'est pas question de laboratoire.*
(B)	He performs an experiment on the class.	= Il réalise une expérience sur les étudiants. *Il ne s'agit pas d'une mise en pratique mais d'une simulation mentale.*
(C) ✓	**He uses a scenario in which the students are implicated.**	**= Il utilise un scénario dans lequel les élèves sont impliqués.** ***« Imagine I was to tell you that you are to breathe in air rich with carbon dioxide » (= « Imaginez que je vous dise que vous devez respirer un air riche en dioxyde de carbone. »)***
(D)	He takes a survey of the class.	= Il utilise un scénario dans lequel les élèves sont impliqués. *Les étudiants n'ont pas à remplir un formulaire.*

▪ Question 10 - Solution

Listen again to part of the lecture. Then answer the question.

> **Script non affiché le jour de l'examen :**
>
> **PROFESSOR:** Imagine I was to tell you that you are to breathe in air rich with carbon dioxide. Some of you will have a dial that controls the flow of carbon dioxide while others of you will not. Which of you are less likely to have a severe panic attack?
>
> **STUDENT 1:** Those of us who believe that we have control over the flow of carbon dioxide?

Why does the student say this:

"Those of us who believe that we have control over the flow of carbon dioxide?"

FR :

Pourquoi l'étudiant dit-il :

« Those of us who believe that we have control over the flow of carbon dioxide? »

(A) He is asking the professor a question about the previous point. = Il pose une question au professeur sur le point précédent.
Il s'agit d'une réponse à la question du professeur.

(B) ✓ He is offering a possible answer to the professor's question. **= Il propose une réponse à la question du professeur.**
« Which of you are less likely to have a severe panic attack?
Student 1: Those of us who believe that we have control over the flow of carbon dioxide?"
(= « Lesquels d'entre vous ont le moins de chances d'avoir une grave crise de panique ?
Étudiant 1 : Ceux d'entre nous qui croient pouvoir contrôler le flux de dioxyde de carbone ? »)

(C) He is checking his comprehension of the question. = Il vérifie sa compréhension de la question.
Il répond à la question.

(D) He is challenging the professor's opinion. = Il vérifie sa compréhension de la question.
Il attend la confirmation du professeur.

⇨ **explication**
Le ton de l'étudiant est interrogatif car il n'est pas sûr de sa réponse.

▪ Question 11 - Solution

According to the professor, why is OCD considered a learned pattern?

FR : Selon le professeur, pourquoi les TOC sont-ils considérés comme un comportement acquis ?

(A) Because most people with OCD know that their thoughts are irrational. = Parce que la plupart des personnes souffrant de TOC savent que leurs pensées sont irrationnelles.

(B) Because anxiety decreases when obsessions are interrupted. = Parce que l'anxiété diminue lorsque les obsessions sont interrompues.
Les TOC demeurent même après une interruption.

(C) Because endless rituals help to eliminate obsessive thoughts. = Parce que l'anxiété diminue lorsque les obsessions sont interrompues.

(D) ✓ Because often OCD is strengthen through negative reinforcement. **= Parce que les TOC sont souvent favorisés par des renforcements négatifs.**
« So if an action such as cleaning temporarily relieves the anxiety, that action may be strengthened through the process of negative reinforcement. »
(= « Ainsi, si une action telle que le fait de faire le ménage soulage temporairement l'anxiété, cette action peut être favorisée par le processus de renforcement négatif. »)

⇨ **explication**
FR : *OCD* est l'accronyme qui signifie *obsessive-compulsive disorder* (en français, ce sont les TOC).

▪ Question 12 - Solution

How does this professor organize the lecture?

FR : Comment le professeur organise-t-il son cours ?

(A)	He has a video to explain each point.	= Il présente une vidéo pour expliquer chaque point. *Il n'y a pas de vidéo.*
(B)	He makes reference to the students' textbook.	= Il fait référence au manuel scolaire des élèves. *Le manuel n'est pas mentionné.*
(C)	He uses a whiteboard and interactive instructions.	= Il utilise un tableau blanc et des consignes interactives. *Il n'est pas question de tableau.*
(D)	✓ **He gives examples and implicates his students.**	**= Il utilise un tableau blanc et des consignes interactives.** ***« I want you to consider the development of a panic attack » (= « Je veux que vous réfléchissiez au processus de déclenchement d'une crise de panique. »)***

▪ Question 13 - Solution

According to the professor, how do governments determine what the best projects are?

FR : Selon le professeur, comment les gouvernements identifient-ils quels projets sont les plus intéressants ?

(A)	They look at a long list of projects.	= Ils étudient une longue liste de projets. *Il y a une grande liste de projets mais ceux-ci ne sont pas choisis au hasard. Il y a des critères de décision.*
(B)	They classify projects according to urgency and cost.	= Ils classent les projets en fonction de leur urgence et de leur coût. *L'urgence et le coût sont juste des facteurs de décision, il ne s'agit pas des seuls facteurs de décision pris en compte.* *« The result is an explicitly acknowledged trade-off between different segments of society » (= « Le résultat est un compromis explicitement reconnu entre différents segments de la société. »)*
(C)	They choose the most inexpensive projects.	= Ils choisissent les projets les moins coûteux. *Le coût des projets n'est pas le seul facteur de décision.*
(D)	✓ **They analyze which projects will be most successful with the least amount of money.**	**= Ils choisissent les projets les moins coûteux.** ***« the projects which do the most good with the money available. » (= « les projets qui font le maximum avec les fonds disponibles. »)***

▪ Question 14 - Solution

How does the professor organize the lecture?

FR : Comment le professeur organise-t-il le cours ?

(A)	He relates data to his own personal experiences.	= Il relie les données à ses expériences personnelles.
(B)	He presents important information in an ascending order.	= Il présente les informations importantes dans un ordre croissant. *Le professeur commence par un débat général et se concentre ensuite sur un problème plus précis.*
(C)	✓ **He refers to studies from international organizations.**	**= Il présente les informations importantes dans un ordre croissant.** ***« Do any of you remember any example of a pressing international issue from the World Health studies report? »*** ***(= « L'un d'entre vous se souvient-il d'un exemple de problématique internationale urgente tirée du rapport de l'Organisation Mondiale de la Santé ? »)***
(D)	He compares American and foreign aid budgets.	Il compare les budgets d'aide américains et étrangers.

▪ Question 15 - Solution

According to the professor, what are the most important threats to global water stability?

FR : Selon le professeur, quelles sont les menaces les plus importantes pour la stabilité des réserves d'eau mondiales ?

(A)	✓ **subterranean water reserve depletion and population increase**	**= l'épuisement des nappes phréatiques et l'augmentation de la population** ***« Population growth and groundwater depletion present the two most significant dangers to global water stability. »*** ***(= « La croissance démographique et l'épuisement des nappes phréatiques représentent les deux dangers les plus importants pour la stabilité de l'eau dans le monde. »)***
(B)	agriculture and industry	= l'épuisement des nappes phréatiques et l'augmentation de la population *L'agriculture et l'industrie sont mentionnées car il s'agit des plus grandes sources de consommation d'eau. Le professeur ne dit pas qu'il s'agit d'une menace.*
(C)	mining	= l'épuisement des nappes phréatiques et l'augmentation de la population
(D)	urban areas	= les zones urbaines *Les villes sont mentionnées car leur consommation d'eau est croissante. Le professeur ne dit pas qu'il s'agit d'une menace.*

▪ Question 16 - Solution

Why does the professor mention the industry sector?

FR : Pourquoi le professeur mentionne-t-il le secteur de l'industrie ?

(A) ✓	**to highlight further future complications**	**= pour mettre en évidence des complications futures** ***« The industrial sector accounts for 22% of global water consumption; this number will grow » (= « Le secteur industriel représente 22 % de la consommation mondiale d'eau ; ce chiffre est amené à augmenter. »)*** ***Il dit cela car la croissance du secteur industriel dans les pays émergents va rendre le problème de l'eau encore plus important.***
(B)	to disguise the need for government action	= pour masquer la nécessité d'une action gouvernementale
(C)	to eliminate other sectors	= pour éliminer d'autres secteurs *Le professeur n'essaie pas d'éliminer les autres secteurs, il insiste sur l'industrie car son impact est plus important que celui de l'agriculture et des zones urbaines.*
(D)	to emphasize economic profits	= pour mettre l'accent sur les bénéfices économiques *Les profits générés par le secteur industriel sont présentés comme la cause du problème et pas sa conséquence.*

▪ Question 17 - Solution

Listen again to part of the lecture and answer the question.

> **Script non affiché le jour de l'examen :**
>
> **STUDENT:** What steps can we as students make to deal with the world's problems?
>
> **PROFESSOR:** That's a very good question. None of us are superman. The main obstacle is that we live in a world with limited resources and limited attention.

What does the professor imply when he say this:

"None of us are superman."

FR : Qu'est-ce le professeur sous-entend quand il dit : « None of us are superman. » ?

(A)	He likes comic books.	= Il aime les bandes dessinées. *La référence à superman est idiomatique. Superman fait partie de la culture américaine, il est désigné ici au sens figuré et non pour faire référence aux bandes-dessinées.*
(B) ✓	**We have to prioritize in order to improve situations.**	**= Nous devons établir des priorités afin d'améliorer les situations.** ***Il sous-entend que puisque nous n'avons pas les pouvoirs de Superman, alors nous ne pouvons pas tout régler. Par conséquent, nous devons avoir des priorités.***
(C)	He would like to have superhuman powers.	= Il aimerait avoir des pouvoirs surhumains. *Il ne parle pas de ses propres capacités.*
(D)	He is not sure who is in his class.	= Il ne sait pas qui est dans sa classe.

▪ Question 18 - Solution

What can be inferred about the professor?

FR : Qu'est-ce qui peut être déduit à propos du professeur ?

(A)	He is a water specialist.	= Il est spécialiste des problématiques liées à l'eau.
(B)	**✓ He encourages his students to get involved in research.**	**= Il encourage ses étudiants à s'impliquer dans la recherche.** ***« My advice is to conduct research » (= « Je vous recommande de faire de la recherche. »)***
(C)	He likes to travel to the developing world.	= Il aime voyager dans les pays en voie de développement.
(D)	He is an experienced policy maker.	= C'est un législateur expérimenté.

▪ Question 19 - Solution

What is the purpose of this conversation?

FR : Quel est l'objectif de cette conversation ?

(A)	**✓ The man is trying to convince the woman to sign up for the debating society.**	**= L'homme essaie de convaincre la femme de s'inscrire au club de débat.** ***« Debating is a good way to tackle different issues before an audience » (= « Le débat est un bon moyen d'aborder différentes questions devant un public »)***
(B)	The woman is encouraging the man to overcome his fear of public speaking.	= La femme encourage l'homme à surmonter sa peur de parler en public. *C'est le jeune homme qui cherche à convaincre la jeune femme.*
(C)	The woman is looking for an extra curricular activity to join.	= La femme cherche une activité extra-scolaire à laquelle s'inscrire. *La jeune femme n'est pas attirée par les sessions de débat.*
(D)	The woman is telling the man that he has to study more.	= La femme dit à l'homme qu'il doit étudier davantage.

▪ Question 20 - Solution

What does the man imply about the fear of public speaking?

FR : Qu'est-ce que l'homme sous-entend à propos de la peur de parler en public ?

(A)	**✓ Public speaking becomes easier with practice.**	**= Parler en public devient plus facile avec la pratique.** ***Le jeune homme affirme que la pratique du débat public renforce la confiance en soi, et peut donc aider à la prise de parole en public : « You develop confidence with practice. » (= « La confiance en soi s'acquiert avec la pratique. »)***
(B)	Public speaking can be stressful.	= Parler en public devient plus facile avec la pratique.
(C)	There are classes in which public speaking is mandatory.	= Il y a des cours dans lesquels il est obligatoire de parler en public.
(D)	Rules are the most important aspect.	= Les règles sont le point le plus important. *Les règles ne sont pas l'aspect le plus important d'une séance de débat public.*

▪ Question 21 - Solution

How does the man feel about the debating society?

FR : Quel est l'avis de l'homme sur le club de débat ?

(A) ✓	**He believes it is useful for college.**	**= Il pense que c'est utile pour l'université.** ***« I don't know but it is very helpful for college » (= « Je ne sais pas mais c'est très utile pour l'Université »)***
(B)	He thinks students should make the rules.	= Il pense que les étudiants devraient établir les règles. *Il dit simplement que les règles sont pré-établies. Elles sont définies dans un règlement : « there are bylaws » (= « Il y a un règlement »)*
(C)	He hopes everyone will join.	= Il espère que tout le monde participera.
(D)	He wants it to be obligatory.	= Il veut que ce soit obligatoire.

▪ Question 22 - Solution

Listen again to part of the discussion and answer the question.

Script non affiché le jour de l'examen :

WOMAN: Reduces anxiety? I would think that it would increase anxiety. I am terrified when I have to speak in front of a classroom filled with people.

NARRATOR: What does the woman mean when she says:

WOMAN: Reduces anxiety?

(A)	She agrees that debating reduces anxiety.	= Elle est d'accord pour dire que débattre réduit l'anxiété. *La jeune femme pense que les débats publics augmentent l'angoisse.*
(B)	She hopes that debating will help her with public speaking.	= Elle espère que le débat l'aidera à parler en public.
(C) ✓	**She doubts that public speaking will reduce anxiety.**	**= Elle doute que le fait de parler en public réduise son anxiété.** ***« I would think that it would increase anxiety. » (= « Je pense plutôt que cela augmenterait l'anxiété. »)***
(D)	She would like to know how to reduce anxiety.	= Elle doute que le fait de parler en public réduise son anxiété. *Cette question n'a pas pour but de demander une information mais sert à exprimer le doute.*

▪ Question 23 - Solution

What will the woman probably do?

FR : Que va probablement faire la jeune femme ?

(A)	**✓ Register for the debating society and attend the meeting**	**= s'inscrire à la société de débat et assister à la réunion** ***MAN: Oh come on, you have to face your fears. It will be good for you.*** ***WOMAN: Ok, but if I don't like it I can always quit, right?*** ***(= HOMME : « Oh allez, il faut que tu affrontes tes peurs. Ça te fera du bien.*** ***FEMME : Ok, mais si je n'aime pas ça, je peux toujours démissionner, non ? »)***
(B)	Practice public speaking before joining the debating society	= s'entraîner à parler en public avant de s'inscrire au club de débat
(C)	Learn the rules on how to become a representative	= apprendre les règles pour devenir un représentant
(D)	Practice public speaking during the meeting	= s'entraîner à parler en public durant la réunion *"We'll have a snack and then a short meeting." (= « Nous prendrons une petite collation, puis nous ferons une courte réunion. »)*

▪ Question 24 - Solution

Why did the man go and see his professor?

FR : Pourquoi l'étudiant va-t-il voir le professeur ?

(A)	to borrow a biology book	= pour emprunter un livre de biologie
(B)	**✓ to ask a question about her mid-term exam**	**= pour poser une question sur son examen de mi-semestre** ***« I have some questions about the mid-term » (= « J'ai quelques questions à propos de l'examen de mi-semestre. »)***
(C)	to see when the professor has office hours	= pour savoir quand le professeur a des heures de permanence
(D)	to hand in a paper	= pour rendre un devoir *Il s'agit de commenter les résultats de l'examen.*

▪ Question 25 - Solution

How is mitochondrial DNA different from regular DNA?

FR : En quoi l'ADN mitochondrial est-il différent de l'ADN ordinaire ?

(A)	**✓ Mitochondrial DNA is located in the cytoplasm of a cell.**	**= L'ADN mitochondrial est situé dans le cytoplasme d'une cellule.** ***« ... they focused only on mitochondrial DNA. Student: The genetic material located in the cytoplasm of cells? Professor: Precisely »*** ***(= Professeur : « ... ils se sont concentrés uniquement sur l'ADN mitochondrial. L'étudiant : Le patrimoine génétique situé dans le cytoplasme des cellules ? Professeur : Précisément »)***
(B)	Regular DNA makes up genes but mitochondrial DNA does not.	= L'ADN ordinaire constitue les gènes, mais pas l'ADN mitochondrial.
(C)	Regular DNA and mitochondrial DNA come from both sets of parents.	= L'ADN ordinaire et l'ADN mitochondrial proviennent des deux parents.
(D)	Mitochondrial DNA is found in the nucleus.	= L'ADN mitochondrial se trouve dans le noyau. *Il se trouve dans le cytoplasme.*

▪ Question 26 - Solution

Listen again to part of the discussion and answer the question.

> **Script non affiché le jour de l'examen :**
>
> **STUDENT:** The genetic material located in the cytoplasm of cells?
>
> **PROFESSOR:** Precisely. Ordinary DNA, which makes up the genes that determine most physical traits, is found in the nucleus and comes from both parents but only the mother contributes mitochondrial DNA to the fertilized egg.
>
> **STUDENT:** Hence the reason that the team analyzed genetic markers in placentas.
>
> **NARRATOR:** What does the student mean when he says:
>
> **STUDENT:** Hence the reason that the team analyzed genetic markers in placentas?

FR : Que veut dire l'étudiant quand il dit :
« Hence the reason that the team analyzed genetic markers in placentas? »

(A)	He does not understand why the team analyzed placentas.	= Il ne comprend pas pourquoi les chercheurs ont analysé les placentas. *L'étudiant a compris mais demande plus de détails.*
(B) ✓	**He wants to clarify the reason why the researchers studied mitochondrial DNA.**	**= Il veut clarifier la raison pour laquelle les chercheurs ont étudié l'ADN mitochondrial.** ***« Ok. So mitochondrial DNA can only pass from mother to daughter. Now I understand the evolutionary tree better »*** ***(= « Ok. Donc l'ADN mitochondrial ne peut être transmis que de mère en fille. Maintenant je comprends mieux l'arbre de l'évolution »)***
(C)	He is criticizing the team's analysis.	= Il critique l'analyse des chercheurs. *Il ne comprend pas tous les details des travaux de l'équipe.*
(D)	He wants to pronounce the word better.	= Il critique l'analyse des chercheurs.

▪ Question 27 - Solution

What will the student do before the next exam?

FR : Que fera l'étudiant avant le prochain examen ?

(A)	take better notes in class	= Il améliorera sa prise de notes en classe. *Il n'hésitera pas à poser plus de questions en cas de doute.*
(B)	go over class lectures with classmates	= Il reverra les cours avec ses camarades de classe.
(C) ✓	**see the professor before the test**	**= Il ira voir le professeur avant l'examen.** ***PROFESSOR: Next time you find that you don't understand something, its best to come and see me during my office hours.*** ***STUDENT: Next time I won't hesitate*** ***(= « PROFESSEUR : La prochaine fois que vous ne comprenez pas quelque chose, le mieux est de venir me voir pendant mes heures de bureau.*** ***ÉTUDIANT : La prochaine fois, je n'hésiterai pas à venir vous voir. »)***
(D)	study harder than she did for the mid-term	= Il étudiera davantage que pour l'examen de mi-semestre. *Le problème n'est pas le manque de travail.*

▪ Question 28 - Solution

What can be said about the professor?

FR : Que peut-on dire du professeur ?

(A)		He teaches psychology.	= Il enseigne la psychologie. *Les mentions répétées à la génétique et à l'ADN orientent nettement la spécialité du professeur vers la biologie.*
(B)		He is very strict when it comes to grading..	= Il est très strict en matière de notation.
(C)		He is often not in his office.	= Il est souvent absent de son bureau. *Il précise qu'il a des heures de permanence (= office hours)*
(D)	✓	**He wants his students to come for extra help.**	**= Il veut que ses élèves viennent le voir pour demander de l'aide.** ***PROFESSOR: Next time you find that you don't understand something, its best to come and see me during my office hours. STUDENT: Next time I won't hesitate*** ***(= « PROFESSEUR : La prochaine fois que vous ne comprenez pas quelque chose, le mieux est de venir me voir pendant mes heures de bureau. ÉTUDIANT : La prochaine fois, je n'hésiterai pas à venir vous voir. »)***

Conversion de votre résultat en score TOEFL iBT sur 30

Votre nombre de bonnes réponses	Estimation score TOEFL iBT
27-28	30
26	29
25	28
24	27
23	26
22	25
21	24
20	23
19	22
18	21
17	20
16	19
15	18
14	17
13	16
12	15
11	14
10	13
9	11
8	9
7	7
6	5
5	3
4	1
0-3	0

TOEFL iBT #2 - SPEAKING - Solutions

Utilisez la grille ci-dessous pour vous auto-évaluer sur chaque exercice. Additionnez vos scores et multipliez le résultat par 30/16 pour obtenir une note sur 30.

4 points	On retrouve toutes les caractéristiques suivantes : • débit rythmé et fluide, les fautes mineures d'intonation ou prononciation n'empêchent pas la compréhension • vocabulaire varié et maîtrise des structures complexes, les erreurs mineures n'empêchent pas la compréhension • utilisation de l'ensemble du temps imparti, les liens entre les idées sont clairs
3 points	On retrouve au moins 2 des caractéristiques suivantes : • débit assez fluide, les fautes d'intonation ou prononciation rendent plus difficile la compréhension mais le discours reste intelligible • les fautes de vocabulaire et de grammaire ne portent pas atteinte à l'intelligibilité du discours • utilisation de l'essentiel du temps imparti, le développement de la réponse est limité mais la réponse est globalement cohérente
2 points	On retrouve au moins 2 des caractéristiques suivantes : • rythme saccadé, mais le discours reste intelligible mais n'est pas clair par endroit • maîtrise limitée de la grammaire et du vocabulaire, seules les structures simples sont maîtrisées • la réponse correspond à la question mais n'est pas assez développée, le nombre des idées est limité avec des propos vagues et répétitifs
1 point	On retrouve au moins 2 des caractéristiques suivantes : • difficultés de prononciation et hésitations, rythme très saccadé. • les fautes de grammaire et de vocabulaire rendent difficile la compréhension • discours court et répétitions
0 point	Pas de réponse ou réponse hors-sujet

Nous avons pour projet de mettre en ligne un service de correction personnalisée pour les épreuves d'expression orale et écrite. Ce service fera appel à des correcteurs expérimentés qui vous attribueront une note en suivant les critères du TOEFL iBT. La correction détaillée incluera des conseils personnalisés pour vous améliorer. À l'heure où vous lirez ce manuel, le service sera peut-être déjà en ligne sur http://www.prepmyfuture.com/toefl

Réponses types

Reportez vos réponses pour analyser votre performance.

Entraînez-vous dans les conditions d'examen.

Écoutez les fichiers audio.

prepmyfuture.com/book/68/ex/1988

question 1	q. ouverte
question 2	q. ouverte
question 3	q. ouverte
question 4	q. ouverte

- **Question 1 - Solution**

DIRECTIONS: In this question, you will be asked to speak about a familiar topic. After you hear the question, you have 15 seconds to prepare your response and 45 seconds to speak.

QUESTION: Talk about an event in your life when you were successful in accomplishing a goal. Describe the experience and explain how it affected your life. Use specific details in your explanation.

Preparation Time: 15 seconds
Response Time: 45 seconds

FR :

DIRECTIONS : *Dans cette question, on vous demandera de donner votre opinion sur un sujet familier. Après avoir entendu la question, vous avez 15 secondes pour préparer votre réponse et 45 secondes pour parler.*

Parlez d'un événement de votre vie au cours duquel vous avez réussi à atteindre un objectif. Décrivez cette expérience et expliquez comment elle a marqué votre vie. Utilisez des détails spécifiques dans votre explication.

Temps de préparation : 15 secondes
Temps de réponse : 45 secondes

⇝ **explication**

Exemple de réponse

Back when I was a sophomore in college, I needed to do an internship in an international company. It was challenging because I had never lived by myself in a foreign country before, let alone work in such an international environment. The goal I set for myself was to be as independent as I could while living abroad.

As I arrived in Vietnam, where my internship was located, I struggled with the language barrier and the culture shock. Throughout my 6 months there, though, I managed to get accustomed to the local way of doing things and I even learned some words of their language. While on the job, I also had to use English as my main communication tool. It was challenging because I had never used this language outside of a classroom.

In the end, this experience was a success, both personally and professionally. I created bonds with some locals, whom I am still in touch with to this day, and I learned a lot about working in an intercultural environment. It has really had an impact on my life. Now, my career goal is to move abroad to live and work there permanently.

Évaluation de l'exemple de réponse

Remarques générales / niveau CECRL	Le candidat répond à la question présentée dans la consigne de manière bien structurée et complète, montrant ainsi une maîtrise avancée de la langue anglaise. Le niveau de compétence du candidat correspond approximativement au niveau C1 du CECRL et la qualité de la production orale serait égale à un 4/4 dans le système de score du TOEFL iBT.
Respect des consignes	Le candidat répond correctement à la question en se basant sur un exemple personnel et en prenant soin de respecter les différentes étapes de la consigne (décrire l'expérience et expliquer de quelle manière cette dernière a eu un impact sur sa vie).
Structure de la réponse	Le candidat commence par expliquer clairement et en une phrase de quoi il va être question dans sa réponse (ici, effectuer un stage à l'étranger dans le cadre de ses études). Il expose ensuite les différents problèmes auxquels il a dû faire face et enfin de quelle manière cette expérience a changé sa vie (dans ce cas précis, il s'agit principalement d'un impact sur sa carrière professionnelle et la façon dont ce stage lui a permis de gagner en autonomie).
Maîtrise de la langue	Le candidat fait preuve d'une maîtrise avancée de la langue anglaise tout au long de sa production orale. Il parvient à éviter les termes basiques pour un vocabulaire plus avancé (*sophomore in college, the local way of doing things, permanently*).
Pour aller plus loin	Le candidat a bien compris les exigences de l'exercice : la réponse est claire et répond à la question posée. De plus, les connecteurs logiques (*back when, while, in the end*) permettent à la production orale d'être bien structurée, et le temps imparti est respecté en gardant un débit de parole naturel.

▪ Question 2 - Solution

QUESTION: The man expresses his opinion about the new online seminar described in the article. Briefly summarize the announcement. Then state his opinion about the announcement and explain the reasons he gives for holding that opinion.

Preparation Time: 30 seconds
Response Time: 60 seconds

FR :

DIRECTIONS: *Donnez-vous 30 secondes pour préparer votre réponse à la question suivante. Puis enregistrez-vous en train de parler pendant 60 secondes.*

> ***L'homme exprime son opinion sur le nouveau séminaire en ligne décrit dans l'article. Résumez brièvement l'annonce. Puis exprimez son opinion sur l'annonce et expliquez les raisons qu'il donne pour justifier cette opinion.***

Temps de préparation : 30 secondes
Temps de réponse : 60 secondes

⇨ **explication**

Exemple de réponse

The announcement advertises a newly created online seminar that Pacific University is offering. This class is about science and takes a general approach to it. It does not target specific students. On the contrary, it is supposed to be for all people who are not majoring in a science field. Besides the wide array of topics covered by the class, the announcement also highlights that this class can be used to fulfill some of the university's core requirements.

The man expresses his interest in the class. An art major, he states that he isn't usually interested in science and had poor experience in prior science-related courses. However, the approach of the class seems to appeal to him. He believes he might be more engaged in the class because it covers many different scientific topics. What's more, he thinks the aspects related to the history of science and scientists might make it more interesting for him. Lastly, the main argument that convinced him to look into the class is that it is online. The freedom it gives him is a strong argument for him. He seems to dislike sitting in a classroom when he is not interested in its topic, the online feature hence becoming highly interesting.

Évaluation de l'exemple de réponse

Remarques générales / niveau CECRL	Le candidat répond à la question présentée dans la consigne de manière bien structurée et complète, montrant ainsi une maîtrise avancée de la langue anglaise. Le niveau de compétence du candidat correspond approximativement au niveau C1 du CECRL et la qualité de la production orale serait égale à un 4/4 dans le système de score du TOEFL iBT.
Respect des consignes	Le candidat répond correctement à la question de façon claire, n'oubliant aucun élément dans sa réponse. De plus, le temps de réponse est bien respecté.
Structure de la réponse	Le candidat commence par résumer de façon succincte le contenu de l'annonce (document écrit) puis rapporte les propos principaux de l'étudiant (document audio). La réponse est ainsi bien structurée, ce qui permet à l'examinateur de ne pas perdre le fil de la conversation.
Maîtrise de la langue	Le candidat fait preuve d'une maîtrise avancée de la langue anglaise tout au long de sa production orale. Il parvient à éviter les termes basiques pour un vocabulaire plus avancé (*wide array of topics, prior science-related courses, requirements*).
Pour aller plus loin	Le candidat a bien compris les exigences de l'exercice : la réponse est claire, structurée, et répond à la question posée. De plus, le temps imparti est respecté en gardant un débit de parole naturel.

▪ Question 3 - Solution

QUESTION: Describe Frank Lloyd Wright's style of architecture and how this style can be seen in the buildings described in the lecture.

Preparation Time: 30 seconds
Response Time: 60 seconds

FR :

DIRECTIONS: *Donnez-vous 30 secondes pour préparer votre réponse à la question suivante. Puis enregistrez-vous en train de parler pendant 60 secondes.*

Décrivez le style architectural de Frank Lloyd Wright et expliquez comment ce style se manifeste dans les bâtiments décrits dans le cours.

Temps de préparation : 30 secondes
Temps de réponse : 60 secondes

⇝ **explication**

Exemple de réponse

Frank Lloyd Wright's style of architecture is described as being "uniquely American." The central point of Wright's vision is that the proximity and the close relationship between humans and nature has to be reflected in buildings, both the commercial ones and the homes. The buildings he designed thus were a reflection, an echo, of their natural environment. Furthermore, their interior spaces were very open and featured horizontal layouts.

The professor mentions a couple of examples of Wright's work. Both underline the main features of Wright's style. The two houses she mentions share similar features. First, they are both composed of many windows that open the interior to the exterior, the manmade to nature. Second, they are both composed of long horizontal layers and terraces. Finally, Robie House and Fallingwater both are in harmony with nature, the former's walls being reminiscent of layers of soil, the latter's terraces blending in with the natural elements surrounding them, such as the waterfall and the trees.

Évaluation de l'exemple de réponse

Remarques générales / niveau CECRL	Le candidat répond à la question présentée dans la consigne de manière bien structurée et complète, montrant ainsi une maîtrise avancée de la langue anglaise. Le niveau de compétence du candidat correspond approximativement au niveau C1 du CECRL et la qualité de la production orale serait égale à un 4/4 dans le système de score du TOEFL iBT.
Respect des consignes	Le candidat répond correctement à la question de façon claire, n'oubliant aucun élément dans sa réponse. De plus, le temps de réponse est bien respecté.
Structure de la réponse	Le candidat commence par résumer de façon succincte le style architectural de Franck Lloyd Wright, avant d'illustrer son propos par des exemples tirés de la conférence, montrant ainsi sa bonne compréhension du document.
Maîtrise de la langue	Le candidat fait preuve d'une maîtrise avancée de la langue anglaise tout au long de sa production orale. Il parvient à éviter les termes basiques pour un vocabulaire plus avancé (*underline, manmade, the latter*).
Pour aller plus loin	Le candidat a bien compris les exigences de l'exercice : la réponse est claire, structurée, et répond à la question posée. De plus, le temps imparti est respecté en gardant un débit de parole naturel.

- **Question 4 - Solution**

QUESTION: Using points and examples from the lecture, explain the importance of Skylab.

Preparation Time: 20 seconds
Response Time: 60 seconds

FR :

DIRECTIONS: *Donnez-vous 20 secondes pour préparer votre réponse à la question suivante. Puis enregistrez-vous en train de parler pendant 60 secondes.*

En utilisant les arguments et les exemples du cours, expliquez l'importance de Skylab.

Temps de préparation : 30 secondes
Temps de réponse : 60 secondes

⇨ **explication**

Exemple de réponse

Skylab was America's first space station. It was in orbit for six years during the 70s. It was a continuation of the prior efforts in the space discovery, such as the Apollo missions that had sent humans in space. Men from the three expeditions to Skylab could spend up to three months in that station.

Skylab was of the utmost importance for NASA. First, it allowed to learn more about the Earth: its surface, its weather... Moreover, these men learned how to live and work in space over a longer period of time than prior expeditions, teaching us a lot about what could be done and what could not. Finally, Skylab's importance, though it wasn't as widely broadcast as the previous space missions, resides in the fact that it marked the switch from spectacular spaceflights to more businesslike space shuttles.

Évaluation de l'exemple de réponse

Remarques générales / niveau CECRL	Le candidat répond à la question présentée dans la consigne de manière bien structurée et complète, montrant ainsi une maîtrise avancée de la langue anglaise. Le niveau de compétence du candidat correspond approximativement au niveau C1 du CECRL et la qualité de la production orale serait égale à un 4/4 dans le système de score du TOEFL iBT.
Respect des consignes	Le candidat répond correctement à la question de façon claire, n'oubliant aucun élément dans sa réponse. De plus, le temps de réponse est bien respecté.
Structure de la réponse	Le candidat commence par expliquer ce qu'est *Skylab*, avant de donner des éléments montrant l'importance de ce projet, démontrant par là même sa bonne compréhension du document.
Maîtrise de la langue	Le candidat fait preuve d'une maîtrise avancée de la langue anglaise tout au long de sa production orale. Il parvient à éviter les termes basiques pour un vocabulaire plus avancé (*utmost importance, the switch, prior expeditions*).
Pour aller plus loin	Le candidat a bien compris les exigences de l'exercice : la réponse est claire, structurée, et répond à la question posée. De plus, le temps imparti est respecté en gardant un débit de parole naturel.

TOEFL iBT #2 - WRITING - Solutions

Utilisez la grille ci-dessous pour vous auto-évaluer sur chaque exercice. Additionnez vos scores et multipliez par 3 pour obtenir une note sur 30.

5 points	On retrouve toutes les caractéristiques suivantes : • réponse efficace à la question • bien organisés et développés, les arguments sont expliqués et soutenus par des détails/exemples • vocabulaire et grammaire variés. Bon niveau d'anglais même si le texte contient quelques erreurs mineures
4 points	On retrouve toutes les caractéristiques suivantes : • réponse efficace à la question même si certains points ne sont pas élaborés. Le texte peut être un peu redondant • bien organisés et développés, les arguments sont expliqués et soutenus par des détails/exemples • vocabulaire et grammaire variés. Le texte contient des erreurs mineures qui n'empèchent pas la compréhension
3 points	On retrouve au moins l'une des caractéristiques suivantes : • réponse à la question avec des explications développées et des détails/exemples • le texte est cohérent et organisé même si certaines idées ne sont pas bien liées entre elles • les mauvaises formations syntaxiques rendent certains passages difficiles à comprendre • la grammaire et le vocabulaire sont corrects mais avec peu de variété
2 points	On retrouve au moins l'une des faiblesses suivantes : • réponse courte et peu développée • texte mal organisé, mauvaises connexions entre les idées • arguments non développés, peu de détails/exemples. Trop de généralisations • vocabulaire inexacte ou inapproprié • nombreuses erreurs de grammaire
1 point	On retrouve au moins l'une des faiblesses suivantes : • texte complétement désorganisé • détails inexistants ou hors-sujets • erreurs grammaticales fréquentes et graves
0 point	• pas de réponse ou réponse hors-sujet • recopiage de quelques mots du sujet • écrit dans une autre langue que l'anglais

Nous avons pour projet de mettre en ligne un service de correction personnalisée pour les épreuves d'expression orale et écrite. Ce service fera appel à des correcteurs expérimentés qui vous attribueront une note en suivant les critères du TOEFL iBT. La correction détaillée incluera des conseils personnalisés pour vous améliorer. À l'heure où vous lirez ce manuel, le service sera peut-être déjà en ligne sur http://www.prepmyfuture.com/toefl

Réponses types

Reportez vos réponses pour analyser votre performance.

Entraînez-vous dans les conditions d'examen.

Écoutez les fichiers audio.

prepmyfuture.com/book/68/ex/1989

question 1	q. ouverte

question 2	q. ouverte

- **Question 1 - Solution**

DIRECTIONS: You have 20 minutes to plan and write your response. Your response will be evaluated on the quality of your writing on how well you present the points in the lecture and their relationship to the reading passage. Typically, an effective response will have 150 to 225 words.

Response Time: 20 minutes

QUESTION: Summarize the points made in the lecture, explaining how they contrast with points made in the reading.

FR :

CONSIGNES : *Donnez-vous 20 minutes pour planifier et rédiger votre réponse. Votre réponse sera jugée sur la qualité de l'écriture et sur la façon dont elle présente les points du cours et leur relation avec le passage lu. En général, une réponse efficace comptera entre 150 et 225 mots. Vous pouvez consulter le passage à lire pendant que vous répondez.*

Temps de réponse : 20 minutes

QUESTION : *Résumez les points soulevés dans la conférence, en veillant à expliquer comment ils remettent en question certains points spécifiques du passage lu.*

⇝ **explication**

Exemple de réponse

While the **reading** seems to indicate that the stone ruins located in the British Isles and Northern France demonstrate scientific knowledge and precision, the lecture tends to counter these arguments.

On the one hand, the **reading** highlights the precision of the **layout of the stones**. It expresses the idea that these sites were not just religious monuments but were more likely to have been constructed thoroughly in order to be used scientifically. On the other hand, the professor mentions that these alignments might have occurred out of pure coincidence and that they are not as precise as we **believed**.

Furthermore, the lecture emphasizes that there are too many discrepancies between the sites for them to have been mathematically constructed, as the **reading seemed** to imply.

The last debating point **that** is the existence of astronomer-priests who would have been science experts and who would have been involved in the creation of these megaliths. While the text presents them as an explanation of the uniformity of these sites, the lecturer underlines that this belief might **merely** be an extrapolation made by modern **researcher** in an attempt to find plausible explanations to these constructions.

To sum it up, it seems that the debate is far from over and that opposing views exist as regards the stone ruins that are studied in the **reading** and in the lecture.

Évaluation de l'exemple de réponse

Remarques générales / niveau CERCL	Le candidat rédige une analyse bien structurée, cohérente et convaincante des arguments avancés par le conférencier. En résumant de manière appropriée les points soulevés par le conférencier et en les comparant à ceux du passage lu, le candidat prouve qu'il a une maîtrise adéquate des principales compétences analytiques (lecture et écoute). Le niveau de compétence du candidat correspond approximativement au niveau C1 du CECRL et la qualité du texte écrit serait égale à un 5/5 dans le système de score du TOEFL iBT.
Forme	Le court essai est divisé de manière appropriée en cinq paragraphes (introduction ; 1er argument ; 2e argument ; 3e argument ; conclusion). Le candidat utilise un registre essentiellement standard avec quelques exceptions formelles qui confirment l'adéquation de la production écrite en fonction de son objectif et du sujet. La phrase d'introduction plante les bases de l'essai et démontre que le candidat a saisi les enjeux de l'exercice. De même, la dernière phrase vient conclure l'essai de façon simple mais efficace.
Variété et précision du vocabulaire	Le candidat utilise un éventail relativement large d'options qui témoignent d'un vocabulaire varié et approprié, sans copier des expressions ou des phrases entières du passage lu. Des expressions telles que *to counter arguments, discrepancies, plausible explanations* démontrent une maîtrise avancée de la langue anglaise.
Grammaire, cohésion et cohérence	Le candidat emploie une série de solutions pour relier chaque paragraphe au suivant (*While*, *On the one hand*, *On the other hand*, *Furthermore*, *To sum it up*). Pour cette raison, le texte est cohérent, puisque le candidat ne formule pas d'affirmations contradictoires qui entravent l'efficacité de l'argument principal de la dissertation. La seule véritable faute de grammaire est celle du candidat qui, dans le 4e paragraphe, ajoute le pronom relatif *that* qui fait perdre à la phrase sa cohérence. Les autres passages surlignés en rouge représentent des exemples de formulation qui pourraient être améliorés afin de rehausser le niveau de la production écrite du candidat.
Pour aller plus loin	Le candidat parvient à rapporter objectivement le contenu de la lecture et de l'exposé.

Réponse corrigée

While the reading passage seems to indicate that the stone ruins located in the British Isles and Northern France demonstrate scientific knowledge and precision, the lecture tends to counter these arguments.

On the one hand, the reading passage highlights the precision of the stones' layout. It expresses the idea that these sites were not just religious monuments but were more likely to have been constructed thoroughly in order to be used scientifically. On the other hand, the professor mentions that these alignments might have occurred out of pure coincidence and that they are not as precise as we may think.

Furthermore, the lecture emphasizes that there are too many discrepancies between the sites for them to have been mathematically constructed, as the reading passage seems to imply.

The last debating point is the existence of astronomer-priests who would have been science experts and who would have been involved in the creation of these megaliths. While the text presents them as an explanation of the uniformity of these sites, the lecturer underlines that this belief might be a mere extrapolation made by modern researchers in an attempt to find plausible explanations to these constructions.

To sum it up, it seems that the debate is far from over and that opposing views exist as regards the stone ruins that are studied in the reading passage and in the lecture.

■ **Question 2 - Solution**

DIRECTIONS: Read the question below. You have 30 minutes to plan, write, and revise your essay. Typically, an effective response will contain a minimum of 300 words.

Response Time: 30 minutes

QUESTION: Does the success and happiness someone experiences in life depend more on the choices they make rather than factors outside their control? Use specific reasons and examples to support your opinion.

FR :

DIRECTIONS : *Lisez la question ci-dessous. Vous avez 30 minutes pour planifier, rédiger et réviser votre essai. En général, une réponse efficace comprendra un minimum de 300 mots.*

Temps de réponse : 30 minutes

QUESTION : *Le succès et le bonheur d'une personne dans la vie dépendent-ils davantage des choix qu'elle fait que de facteurs indépendants de sa volonté ? Utilisez des raisons et des exemples spécifiques pour étayer votre opinion.*

⇝ **explication**

Exemple de réponse

Success and happiness are what most people yearn for. Their origins are very personal and the **reasons** one might become successful or happy can vary immensely from one person to another. In my opinion, personal choices play a major role in someone's fulfillment, even more so than outside factors.

To begin with, factors outside one's control do have an impact on one's happiness. Indeed, the events unfolding in the lives of **our** loved ones do influence one's happiness. For example, if a family member falls ill or goes through hard times, it will necessarily impact our own mental and physical well-being. Similarly, one might feel less **happy** if they are refused a job or a promotion while being convinced they **deserve** it.

However, these outside factors are not the only ones that need to be taken into account. Indeed, I believe that our own choices are even more crucial to our happiness. The central reason behind this is that if something goes wrong because of outside factors, it is easier for someone to move on with their **own lives**. For instance, if one does not get a job, one can keep looking for other opportunities and keep being motivated. On the contrary, if one misses a job opportunity because they **do** not apply for it on time, the responsibility of this failure falls on the person and it is then much harder to move forward.

The third point I would like to mention is that life is a succession of decisions, some **harder** than others, and that someone's path is determined by them. Consequently, I do believe these decisions are central to one's success and happiness to the extent that they determine our life journey.

To put it in a nutshell, the answer to this question cannot be fully black or white. Still, form my point of view, personal choices have more of an impact on one's happiness and success than outside factors.

Évaluation de l'exemple de réponse

Remarques générales / niveau CERCL	Le candidat rédige une réponse bien structurée, cohérente et convaincante. Le niveau de compétence du candidat correspond approximativement au niveau C1 du CECRL et la qualité du texte écrit serait égale à un 4/5 dans le système de score du TOEFL iBT.
Forme	Le court essai est divisé de manière appropriée en cinq paragraphes (introduction ; 1er argument ; 2e argument ; 3e argument ; conclusion). Le candidat utilise un registre essentiellement standard avec quelques exceptions formelles qui confirment l'adéquation de la production écrite en fonction de son objectif et du sujet. La phrase d'introduction plante les bases de l'essai et démontre que le candidat a saisi les enjeux de l'exercice. De même, la dernière phrase vient conclure l'essai de façon simple mais efficace. Cependant, l'essai aurait gagné en efficacité si le candidat s'était appuyé sur des exemples tirés de son expérience personnelle pour illustrer ses arguments.
Variété et précision du vocabulaire	Le candidat utilise un éventail relativement large d'options qui témoignent d'un vocabulaire varié et approprié. Des expressions telles que *to yearn for, fulfillment, unfolding* démontrent une bonne maîtrise de la langue anglaise.
Grammaire, cohésion et cohérence	Le candidat emploie une série de connecteurs logiques pour relier chaque paragraphe au suivant (*To begin with, however, On the contrary, Consequently, To put it in a nutshell*). Pour cette raison, le texte est cohérent, puisque le candidat ne formule pas d'affirmations contradictoires qui entravent l'efficacité de l'argument principal de la dissertation. Le candidat ne fait aucune faute majeure, seules quelques reformulations auraient pu rendre l'essai plus fluide.
Pour aller plus loin	Dans ce type de question, il n'est pas nécessaire de défendre les deux points de vue (par exemple, ici, les facteurs extérieurs influent plus sur notre bonheur, mais les choix faits par les individus y contribuent également). De fait, il est possible de ne défendre qu'un seul argument, et de n'en montrer les limites que dans la conclusion, par exemple.

Réponse corrigée

Success and happiness are what most people yearn for. Their origins are very personal and the reasons why one might become successful or happy can vary immensely from one person to another. In my opinion, personal choices play a major role in someone's fulfillment, even more so than outside factors.

To begin with, factors outside one's control do have an impact on one's happiness. Indeed, the events unfolding in the lives of their loved ones do influence one's happiness. For example, if a family member falls ill or goes through hard times, it will necessarily impact our own mental and physical well-being. Similarly, one might feel less content if they are refused a job or a promotion while being convinced they deserved it.

However, these outside factors are not the only ones that need to be taken into account. Indeed, I believe that our own choices are even more crucial to our happiness. The central reason behind this is that if something goes wrong because of outside factors, it is easier for someone to move on with their life. For instance, if one does not get a job, one can keep looking for other opportunities and keep being motivated. On the contrary, if one misses a job opportunity because they did not apply for it on time, the responsibility of this failure falls on the person and it is then much harder to move forward.

The third point I would like to mention is that life is a succession of decisions, some harder to make than others, and that someone's path is determined by them. Consequently, I do believe these decisions are central to one's success and happiness to the extent that they determine our life journey. To put it in a nutshell, the answer to this question cannot be fully black or white. Still, form my point of view, personal choices have more of an impact on one's happiness and success than outside factors.

Achevé d'imprimer en Juillet 2022
par IPS Imprimerie à Pacy-sur-Eure / France
Dépôt légal Juillet 2022